LIVING  LITURGY™

LIVING ✠ LITURGY™

Spirituality, Celebration, and Catechesis for Sundays and Solemnities

Year B • 2024

Jessie Bazan
Brenna Davis
Stephanie DePrez
Rachel Drotar
M. Roger Holland, II
Orin E. Johnson
Jessica Mannen Kimmet
Victoria McBride
Barbara E. Reid, OP
Janèt Sullivan Whitaker
Steven C. Warner
Kate Williams

LITURGICAL PRESS
Collegeville, Minnesota

www.litpress.org

Cover design by Monica Bokinskie. Art by Ruberval Monteiro da Silva, OSB.

Published with the approval of the Committee on Divine Worship, United States Conference of Catholic Bishops.

ISSN 1547-089X

ISBN 978-0-8146-6806-1

CONTENTS

CONTRIBUTORS

Jessie Bazan helps Christians explore their life callings in her work with the Collegeville Institute for Ecumenical and Cultural Research. She is editor and coauthor of *Dear Joan Chittister: Conversations with Women in the Church* (Twenty-Third Publications) and teaches a course on Benedictine spirituality at the College of Saint Benedict and Saint John's University.

Brenna Davis lives in Cleveland, Ohio, and currently serves as the director of integral ecology at the Ignatian Solidarity Network. She is a 2010 graduate of Boston College. An avid reader and spiritual director, she most easily feels God's presence when outside delighting in creation.

Stephanie DePrez is an award-winning writer, teacher, and musician. She holds a BA from the University of Notre Dame and an MM from UCLA. Stephanie taught music and theology in Jesuit classrooms for five years and worked as a parish music director for three. Her writing has appeared in the *National Catholic Reporter, Grotto Network, Notre Dame Magazine,* and *FemCatholic.*

Rachel Drotar lives in Cleveland, Ohio, and currently serves as a clinical therapist focusing on work with the LGBTQIA+ community and older adults. She is a co-facilitator of the Cleveland chapter of Nuns and Nones and a graduate of Xavier University in Cincinnati and Washington University in St. Louis. Rachel is a poet, musician, and theatre performer.

M. Roger Holland, II, is a teaching associate professor in music and religion and director of The Spirituals Project at the Lamont School of Music, University of Denver. A graduate of Union Theological Seminary in New York City where he received a master of divinity degree, Roger also served as artist-in-residence and director of the Union Gospel Choir for over thirteen years. Roger serves as liturgical music consultant for the Archdiocese of New York's Office of Black Ministry and music director for their special masses at St. Patrick's Cathedral.

Orin E. Johnson has held professional music and liturgy positions for twenty-five years, currently at St. Margaret of Scotland Catholic Church in St. Louis, Missouri. He holds degrees in music and theology from Harvard University, Radford University, and Aquinas Institute of Theology. His liturgical music is published with OCP and GIA, his writings are published by Liturgical Press, Liguori, and Twenty-Third Publications, and he is active nationally as a speaker, performer, catechist, and retreat and workshop leader.

Jessica Mannen Kimmet is a freelance writer and liturgical musician. Formerly a full-time college campus minister, she now spends her days overseeing a domestic church and the growth of her three young sons. She holds a BA in theology and music theory and a master of divinity, both from the University of Notre Dame.

Victoria (Vickey) McBride is the vice president of mission at Saint Martin de Porres High School in Cleveland. She has been a featured preacher twice for the publication and website *Catholic Women Preach*. She serves as a music minister for her parish and is passionate about creative expression, spirituality, and building loving communities.

Barbara E. Reid, OP, is a Dominican Sister of Grand Rapids, Michigan. She is the president of Catholic Theological Union in Chicago. She holds a PhD in biblical studies from The Catholic University of America in Washington, DC. She is the author of numerous books and is the general editor of the Wisdom Commentary series published by Liturgical Press.

Janèt Sullivan Whitaker is a composer of liturgical music, with works published by OCP, GIA, and WLP. She holds a BA in music and an MTS in liturgical theologies from the Jesuit School of Theology in Berkeley. A longtime veteran of pastoral music ministry in the Diocese of Oakland, California, she now works as a freelance presenter of concerts, workshops, missions, and retreats.

Steven C. Warner (BA in religious studies, St. Michael's College, Vermont; MA in liturgical studies, University of Notre Dame) is the founder and director emeritus of the Notre Dame Folk Choir and the principal composer for the *Songs of the Notre Dame Folk Choir* series. A longtime collegiate campus minister, Steve served as associate director of the Notre Dame-Newman Centre in Dublin, Ireland. Steve is published by both OCP and GIA.

Kate Williams is the vice president of sacred music at GIA Publications, Inc. She holds a bachelor of music composition from DePaul University in Chicago, as well as a master of arts in liturgical studies from Catholic Theological Union in the Hyde Park neighborhood of Chicago where it was her privilege to study as a distinguished Bernardin Scholar. She serves as a workshop leader, consultant, and musician in the Archdiocese of Chicago and abroad, following a passion to serve in multicultural, multigenerational communities, while mentoring young voices and building bridges through music ministry.

PREFACE

Introduction

As a premier Catholic publisher, Liturgical Press remains committed to offering liturgical, spiritual, and scriptural resources rooted in the Benedictine tradition. While these resources have changed and developed over the years, the commitment to sound theology and best pastoral practice remain hallmarks of our mission and ministry. *Living Liturgy*™ is one of our most loved and widely used incarnations of this commitment.

Living Liturgy™ will always help people prepare for liturgy and live a liturgical spirituality—a way of living that is rooted in liturgy. The paschal mystery is the central focus of liturgy, of the gospels, and of this volume. *Living Liturgy*™ is more than a title. Rather, "living liturgy" is a commitment to a relationship with Jesus Christ, embodied in our everyday actions and interactions.

We hope this edition of *Living Liturgy*™ will continue to facilitate this relationship, making liturgical spirituality a lived reality.

Authors

As always, we are extremely proud of our team of *Living Liturgy*™ authors. Many of the "Reflecting on the Gospel" sections for this year are taken from Barbara E. Reid's *Abiding Word: Sunday Reflections for Year B*. We are thrilled to share Sr. Barbara's excellent work in this capacity. Her exceptional biblical scholarship and seasoned pastoral proficiency are unmatched.

To offer even more ministerial expertise and diversity of experiences, we have expanded the number of contributors for each section of *Living Liturgy*™. We hope you appreciate the varied writing styles and enjoy hearing from additional expert practitioners in the field. Some aspects of each section look different from day to day, allowing the gifts of each individual author to shine as they share their own experiences of "living liturgy" in a multitude of communities and contexts. Jessie Bazan, Brenna Davis, Stephanie DePrez, Rachel Drotar, M. Roger Holland, II, Jessica Mannen Kimmet, Victoria (Vickey) McBride, Janèt Sullivan Whitaker, Steven C. Warner, and Kate Williams write at the intersection of theology and pastoral reality. As always, we know that you will find these contributions to be prayerful, practical, and relevant to our church and world today.

Finally, we heard your request for more "Prompts for Faith Sharing" and are excited to include additional questions from Orin E. Johnson in an appendix at the back of this edition. We hope they will serve as rich fodder for discussion and reflection.

Artwork

This edition features a stunning new series of original artwork from Ruberval Monteiro da Silva, OSB. Fr. Ruberval, a native of Brazil, resides in the Benedictine community of Sant'Anselmo in Rome. His colorful mosaics grace the walls of churches around the world, and we are excited to once again include his work in *Living Liturgy*™.

SEASON OF
ADVENT

SPIRITUALITY

GOSPEL ACCLAMATION
Ps 85:8

℟. Alleluia, alleluia.
Show us, Lord, your love;
and grant us your salvation.
℟. Alleluia, alleluia.

Gospel

Mark 13:33-37; L2B

**Jesus said to his disciples:
"Be watchful! Be alert!
You do not know when the
time will come.
It is like a man traveling
abroad.
He leaves home and places his
servants in charge, each
with his own work,
and orders the gatekeeper
to be on the watch.
Watch, therefore;
you do not know when the
lord of the house is coming,
whether in the evening, or at
midnight,
or at cockcrow, or in the morning.
May he not come suddenly and find you
sleeping.
What I say to you, I say to all:
'Watch!'"**

Reflecting on the Gospel

"Be watchful! Be alert!" Don't be caught unaware! Jesus warns his disciples in this Sunday's gospel. We begin another Advent season of watching and waiting. For some, it is a time of delight, waiting eagerly for Christmas, for anticipated gifts, for time off from work and school, and for happy gatherings of family and friends. For others, it is a dreaded time, as they approach their first holiday without a loved one or worry about how they will pay for the gifts and meals they want to provide. Whatever our situation, the Scripture readings today help us to adopt a stance of faithful watching and waiting.

Advent is not a time of waiting for the coming of the Christ Child—that already happened more than two thousand years ago. It is, rather, a time when we break our normal routine and move into heightened alert to perceive more intensely the ways of Emmanuel, "God-with-us." The watchfulness that Jesus speaks about in today's gospel is not waiting in dread, nor is the object of our vigilance unknown. Rather, it is attentive listening for the familiar footstep of the returning Beloved. We would not want to be found sleeping but ready with open arms.

Most of us find waiting very difficult. We try to eliminate it as much as possible with fast food, express lines, and ever speedier internet connections. Waiting for the end of a prolonged illness or at the unemployment office is another kind of torturous waiting. Waiting for the return of a long-expected loved one can seem impossibly long. It is this last kind of waiting of which today's gospel speaks: constant vigilance for the return of the Beloved who has entrusted everything to our care in the interim.

The time of waiting and watching is not idle biding of time or maintaining the status quo. Like parents anticipating the birth of a child, we have much work to do during the expectant months. In today's gospel Jesus talks about each one having his or her own work to do and having been given the power to accomplish it. Paul too encourages the Corinthians and us by reminding us that we lack no spiritual gift as we wait for the revelation of Christ.

We may wonder how we will recognize the coming One. In today's first reading, the exiles want God to manifest divine power in a way that will be absolutely unmistakable. They pray that God would "rend the heavens and come down, with the mountains quaking before [him]." Such a revelation would compel belief and good behavior. But in Advent we call to mind again that divine power is revealed not in pyrotechnic displays of fire and quaking mountains but in the immense love that comes in the form of a vulnerable child. God has ruptured the dividing line between divinity and humanity by taking on human flesh in Christ. Advent asks us, likewise, to both embody Christ and to watch for his presence in each one we meet, particularly those who are most needy.

Preparing to Proclaim

Key words and phrases: "You do not know when the time will come."

To the point: Few people understand the demands of watchful waiting like a woman in her last weeks of pregnancy. This waiting may look passive, but it is work. Both the extra weight her body carries and the extra vigilance her mind bears are exhausting. Labor, like Jesus's coming, arrives when it will; there are ways to generally prepare, but the moment of its onset remains a mystery until it is upon her. There is one major difference: the physical demands of late pregnancy are such that many expectant women report that they are never not watching for labor to begin. It is far easier to forget to watch for Christ, which is why he reminds us so fervently in today's gospel to do so. But since watchful alertness takes a great deal of energy and can wear us down over time, we need to also take care to make our spiritual practices sustainable.

Psalmist Preparation

This psalm asks God to let us see God's face; in ancient Israel, this was playing with fire. To encounter God in all of God's fullness was a dangerous thing; many believed that to see God's face would result in death. Even Moses is instructed to cover his face when he encounters God; when God does grant a glimpse it is of God's back (Exod 33:20-23). After Christ, though, the meaning changes: in Jesus, God takes on a literal human face that people *can* encounter. That face is again hidden, although we find Jesus in the sacraments and in each other. As you prepare the psalm this week, think of at least one place you find God revealed. Give thanks for that. Think of another place you struggle to see God, and pray and proclaim this psalm as an earnest plea that you will find God there too.

Making Connections

Between the readings: The gospel reminds us to be alert; the first reading reminds us that even such alertness is a gift from God. The demands of Christian life may seem tedious at times, but everything we have and everything we are is owed to God. This debt is not an exacting transaction though; it is a warm call from the God who loves us more than we can imagine. God made us with the same care and tenderness of a potter shaping clay, and God promises to keep us, as the second reading says, "firm to the end."

To experience: Those who claim to be spiritual masters often enjoin us to "live in the present." There is a wisdom to this advice; becoming too caught up in looking ahead to the future can cause undue anxiety. But the things we hope for and wait for reflect something about who we are, and Advent is a time to look forward. This does not exclude living in the present though—looking for Christ's coming is not just about looking to the future but also includes seeking and finding it here and now, in the realities of our lives as they are actually lived.

Homily Points

• Advent is a time for big, bold hope—the kind showcased in today's first reading. The Babylonians return from exile to a city in ruins. Conquerors destroyed their temple. Current residents shooed them away. They compare themselves to "polluted rags" and withering leaves. Such hardships left the returned exiles at their wits' end—and they let God know it. The people recognize God's anger and disappointment. But they never lose hope in the promise of God's redemption. With audacity, the people demand of God: "Oh, that you would rend the heavens and come down, with the mountains quaking before you." They long to see God's awesome deeds. In the face of such destruction, the people never stop hoping that God will make something new. We too are called to keep big, bold hope alive. Like our ancestors in faith, God calls us to trust in God's saving power even—especially—in our lowest moments.

• What does the image of God as a potter have to teach us about the divine? Like a potter, God continually shapes and molds God's people. Like a potter, God is ready to get messy for the sake of our formation. God carefully crafts God's people in the divine image. How might we recognize our callings to be vessels of the divine more fully this Advent season?

• Jesus offers the summons to "Be watchful! Be alert!" in the thirteenth chapter of Mark's Gospel, in the days before he is crucified. Birth, life, death, resurrection—these are all parts of one narrative. As we prepare for Christmas these next few weeks, let us always be mindful of great transformations still to come.

CELEBRATION

Model Penitential Act

Presider: In today's gospel, Jesus cautions his disciples to be watchful and be alert for the coming of the Son of Man. For the times we have overlooked the divine presence, let us ask for pardon and mercy . . . *[pause]*

Lord Jesus, you are mighty God and Prince of Peace: Lord, have mercy.

Christ Jesus, you are the Son of God and son of Mary: Christ, have mercy.

Lord Jesus, you are the Word made flesh and splendor of the Father: Lord, have mercy.

Model Universal Prayer (Prayer of the Faithful)

Presider: As the church begins a new liturgical year, let us give voice to our prayers and petitions.

Response: Lord, hear our prayer.

Animate the work of congregations and their efforts to address systemic racism . . .

Give peace and focus to students preparing for final exams and projects . . .

Settle the hearts of people overwhelmed with anxiety, restlessness, or uncertainty . . .

Inspire each of us to take time for prayer and reflection this Advent season . . .

Presider: Watchful God, you reveal the ways of love and mercy to all of creation through Jesus your Son. Receive our prayers that we might follow Jesus into the peace of everlasting life with you. We ask this through Christ, our coming Lord. **Amen.**

Liturgy and Music

In the deep, quiet beginnings of our new liturgical year, when days in the northern hemisphere are nearing their shortest and darkest with little natural light to illuminate our daily work, Isaiah does not mince words or speak with pleasant, cozy platitudes. Tear apart the heavens, God. Come down, now, O God in heaven, for we are mindful, watching, and waiting with powerful urgency and desire. Who cries out to us now, in these days, begging for us to be the ones through whom God's urgent love need be made manifest?

Is it not the appropriate response to our baptismal call that we hold this sense of urgent love in all that we do? Think of those in your choir, pouring even more time and talent into extra rehearsals to prepare for the coming days to celebrate the mystery of the incarnate God, who already dwells among us and who is still yet to come. Do we have the capacity to hold the space for all their lives too? All who show up, as regularly as able, putting aside the piles of laundry, leaving the warmth and peace of their homes to come together to learn to make something beautiful for God and God's people: are we offering them the urgent love that holds their joy and their sorrow too? Pray with them, even more so during these sacred days of waiting and watching. Their presence in this place is a gift, not a requirement. How urgently we need to convey that sense of awe.

How urgently, too, must we remember our place of privilege as God's children. Let our music choices reflect the alertness of the gospel, of the need to be awake to all of God's children who have been brutalized, abandoned, or neglected in our particular sociopolitical context. Who has been made welcome here, as shown in our hymn texts and musical styles? Who is most comfortable? Who is left out? Tear apart the heavens, God: Come down, now, and show us the still more beautiful songs of your kingdom. Squeeze and shape our hearts to know that the kindling of this season's light is blazing within the very people you are coming to save.

COLLECT

Let us pray.

Pause for silent prayer

Grant your faithful, we pray, almighty God,
the resolve to run forth to meet your Christ
with righteous deeds at his coming,
so that, gathered at his right hand,
they may be worthy to possess the heavenly Kingdom.
Through our Lord Jesus Christ, your Son,
who lives and reigns with you in the unity of the Holy Spirit,
God, for ever and ever. **Amen.**

FIRST READING
Isa 63:16b-17, 19b; 64:2-7

You, Lord, are our father,
    our redeemer you are named forever.
Why do you let us wander, O Lord, from your ways,
    and harden our hearts so that we fear you not?
Return for the sake of your servants,
    the tribes of your heritage.
Oh, that you would rend the heavens and come down,
    with the mountains quaking before you,
while you wrought awesome deeds we could not hope for,
    such as they had not heard of from of old.
No ear has ever heard, no eye ever seen,
    any God but you
    doing such deeds for those who wait for him.
Would that you might meet us doing right,
    that we were mindful of you in our ways!
Behold, you are angry, and we are sinful;
    all of us have become like unclean people,
    all our good deeds are like polluted rags;
we have all withered like leaves,
    and our guilt carries us away like the wind.
There is none who calls upon your name,
    who rouses himself to cling to you;
for you have hidden your face from us
    and have delivered us up to our guilt.
Yet, O Lord, you are our father;
    we are the clay and you the potter:
    we are all the work of your hands.

RESPONSORIAL PSALM
Ps 80:2-3, 15-16, 18-19

℞. (4) Lord, make us turn to you; let us see
　　your face and we shall be saved.

O shepherd of Israel, hearken,
　　from your throne upon the cherubim,
　　　　shine forth.
Rouse your power,
　　and come to save us.

℞. Lord, make us turn to you; let us see
　　your face and we shall be saved.

Once again, O LORD of hosts,
　　look down from heaven, and see;
take care of this vine,
　　and protect what your right hand has
　　　　planted,
　　the son of man whom you yourself
　　　　made strong.

℞. Lord, make us turn to you; let us see
　　your face and we shall be saved.

May your help be with the man of your
　　right hand,
　　with the son of man whom you yourself
　　　　made strong.
Then we will no more withdraw from you;
　　give us new life, and we will call upon
　　　　your name.

℞. Lord, make us turn to you; let us see
　　your face and we shall be saved.

SECOND READING
1 Cor 1:3-9

Brothers and sisters:
Grace to you and peace from God our
　　Father
　　and the Lord Jesus Christ.

I give thanks to my God always on your
　　account
　　for the grace of God bestowed on you in
　　　　Christ Jesus,
　　that in him you were enriched in every
　　　　way,
　　with all discourse and all knowledge,
　　as the testimony to Christ was
　　　　confirmed among you,
　　so that you are not lacking in any
　　　　spiritual gift
　　as you wait for the revelation of our
　　　　Lord Jesus Christ.
He will keep you firm to the end,
　　irreproachable on the day of our Lord
　　　　Jesus Christ.
God is faithful,
　　and by him you were called to
　　　　fellowship with his Son,
　　Jesus Christ our Lord.

Living Liturgy
Liturgy and Spirituality: In the gospel reading, we are asked to be watchful and alert for the coming of the Lord. We can often be anxious that we will miss the "right time." What a big responsibility!

God is present and ready to present Godself to us at any moment. Consider the watchfulness as a present state of awe and contemplation. How often are we able to see the tree for what it is, the grass as beautiful and green, the wind as refreshing? How often do we remain present in our daily lives, opening ourselves up to the presence of God acting in real time? What if being "watchful" and "alert" means to be present to all the ways God is always arriving at our doorstep, asking to be let in?

When we doubt ourselves and if what we are doing is "right" or "good," we see God there: trusted, consistent, and present in our lives no matter what state we are in. We can look to Scripture to see how God remains faithful to us. Are we feeling joyful for our lives, unable to keep it to ourselves? God is here to listen and to celebrate with us. Are we struggling, feeling isolated in grief, or confused as to where to turn in times of hardship? God is here to listen and to hold us in the grief we carry.

PROMPTS FOR FAITH-SHARING

• What are you waiting for? What hopes remain unfulfilled? What does that reveal to you about who you are and who God is?

• How do you practice watchfulness in your spiritual life?

• How can you make your practices of watchful alertness sustainable?

• Who and what reveals God's face to you as you wait for the fullness of Christ's return?

See Appendix B, p. 309, for additional prompts.

GOSPEL ACCLAMATION
cf. Luke 1:28

℟. Alleluia, alleluia.
Hail, Mary, full of grace, the Lord is with you;
blessed are you among women.
℟. Alleluia, alleluia.

Gospel

Luke 1:26-38; L689

The angel Gabriel was sent from God
  to a town of Galilee called Nazareth,
  to a virgin betrothed to a man named
    Joseph,
  of the house of David,
  and the virgin's name was Mary.
And coming to her, he said,
  "Hail, full of grace! The Lord is with
    you."
But she was greatly troubled at what
    was said
  and pondered what sort of greeting
    this might be.
Then the angel said to her,
  "Do not be afraid, Mary,
  for you have found favor with God.
Behold, you will conceive in your womb
    and bear a son,
  and you shall name him Jesus.

Continued in Appendix A, p. 261

See Appendix A, p. 261 for the other readings.

Reflecting on the Gospel

We believe that when Mary was conceived, she did not have original sin. Unlike every other person in human history, Mary entered the world without the "fallen"-ness that is part of our human experience. Put simply: she did not sin.

Fortunately for us, the communion of saints is made up of sinners who we believe are in heaven. This means that it is possible to be both a sinner and a saint, and move from a life of sin to a life of sanctity worthy of the kingdom of heaven. Mary models this call for us as someone who lived her life fully, with death and grief, interacting and having relationships with every sort of sinner, yet without sinning herself. She is our life, our sweetness, and our hope. There is a reason that we look to her for intercession.

She is also the Queen of Heaven. A human—one of us!—is *the Queen of Heaven*. Her existence confirms the possibility of heaven for every one of us. She is offered to us as a model of humanity that is not unattainable. In fact, it's the goal. And we know Mary is the goal because of the thousands of faithful who have reached that goal and joined her in heaven.

Today, as we celebrate the immaculate conception of our mother in heaven, we are given space to dream of our own salvation. It is not some distant thing. It is, in fact, what we are all called to do, every single one of us, from every point in time and on earth.

Mary led a remarkable life, perhaps the most remarkable of anyone in history. Today's gospel tells the story of the inciting moment when Mary's life changed forever. It is that moment that we are invited to contemplate in a special way today.

Preparing to Proclaim

Key words and phrases: "[T]he virgin's name was Mary."

To the point: The Christian tradition has bestowed many titles on Mary, including the "Immaculate Conception" that we celebrate today. This gospel names her as "virgin" and "betrothed to a man named Joseph" before revealing her given name. The angel greets her by naming her "full of grace." Mary responds to God's invitation by calling herself "handmaid of the Lord." These titles, and many others, are helpful—they reflect the manifold realities of who Mary is. Like all of us, she is a full, complex human with emotions and struggles and a history. But when Mary is troubled by what the angel says, it is her simple name that he uses in response. We return to the fact that before she was called blessed by all generations (Luke 1:48b), Mary was a real person with a name. There is a tenderness in the angel's use of her name. He responds to her fear with reassurance; he gives her not only the promise of God's presence but also the recognition of who she is, using the name her parents lovingly chose for her. When Jesus comes to adulthood, we will see him use names powerfully too. It is in calling Mary Magdalene by name that he will reveal himself as risen (John 20:16).

Model Penitential Act

Presider: Mary witnesses the way of discipleship by her boldness, bravery, and unwavering trust in God. Let us ask God to strengthen our discipleship by forgiving our sins . . . *[pause]*

  Lord Jesus, you are the Son of God: Lord, have mercy.
  Christ Jesus, you are the son of Mary: Christ, have mercy.
  Lord Jesus, you are guided by the Spirit: Lord, have mercy.

Model Universal Prayer (Prayer of the Faithful)

Presider: All-powerful God, you cast down the mighty and lift up the lowly. With Mary as our guide, let us pray.

Response: Lord, hear our prayer.

Raise up strong, faithful role models for young girls in the church . . .

Bless the vocations of mothers, godmothers, and mother figures . . .

Answer the prayers of couples struggling with infertility . . .

Guide our local community to work for peace and justice for all people . . .

Presider: Almighty God, receive our prayers and help us to grow in wisdom and courage so that, like Mary, we might say yes to your callings in our lives. We ask this through Christ, our coming Lord. **Amen.**

Living Liturgy

So many of the Marian hymns we sing this day seem to sing of a small, meek, submissive young girl. The truth, as we know from her own *Magnificat* song, is that this brave woman is the necessary foundation on which God propels a complete flipping of the tables of the world: by her co-creation with God, the world and all its disorder can come to know salvation through the Way, the Truth, and the Life.

Today's readings speak of not one but two women who have been uniquely interpreted throughout history, despite the fundamental message God conveys through these sacred stories. Though we understand this story to be part of the primeval myth of creation, Eve was a woman tricked into believing there was goodness being kept from her. She was not a temptress, not evil. She was tricked. Mary was a young woman who used her own agency to collaborate with God; she was not an unwilling slave. Both of these women show us the capacity of humanity: our capacity to collaborate with evil despite our best intentions, and our capacity to bear God to the world despite our marginalized status. After her error, Eve still showed awareness of her misstep. And contrary to previous threats, God still found her worthy of living.

How do your song selections characterize women, today and every day? Think especially of the children in your community: What does it teach them when we praise women to be "meek and mild?" What does it say when we tend to pit them against each other, as many often do when juxtaposing Mary and Eve, rather than describing them as two necessary pieces of our whole—two examples of the capacity of humankind? Let us be careful of the things we say: children will listen. May they hear that constant heartbeat of Mary's *Magnificat*, telling us that no matter what status quo may dominate today, God's table-turning way will continue to surprise and challenge.

COLLECT
Let us pray.

Pause for silent prayer

O God, who by the Immaculate Conception of
    the Blessed Virgin
prepared a worthy dwelling for your Son,
grant, we pray,
that, as you preserved her from every stain
by virtue of the Death of your Son, which you
    foresaw,
so, through her intercession,
we, too, may be cleansed and admitted to your
    presence.
Through our Lord Jesus Christ, your Son,
who lives and reigns with you in the unity of
    the Holy Spirit,
God, for ever and ever. **Amen.**

FOR REFLECTION

• What is your name? Do you know why it was chosen for you? Have you ever gone by any names or nicknames other than your full given name? What story do they tell?

• What people, places, pets, or things have you had the opportunity to name? How did you choose the names? What do they mean? What do they mean to you?

• Do you have a favorite title for Mary? Why is that one meaningful to you? Look up the Litany of Loreto if you need ideas.

See Appendix B, p. 309, for additional questions.

Homily Points

• Tradition tends to put Mary the Mother of God on a pedestal. Images of a young woman bent in constant prayer or glowing with a halo make Mary's reality seem far out of reach for your average Christian. Of course, Mary lived a unique life. She birthed the Savior and spent her life free from original sin. Still, in many ways Mary could relate to the plights of everyday people. She found herself an unwed pregnant teenager and surely felt the confusion, fear, and uncertainty that comes at such times. She was poor in a society that valued the rich. She was a woman in a world that gave men the power. Mary knew hardship. She also knew the power of God's redemption.

• Like Mary, we can and will know the freedom that comes from God's saving mercy. The same Spirit that filled Mary with grace will also give us the grace to follow Christ. The Spirit will empower us to say our own "yes" to God's callings in our life. What spiritual practices can you engage in this Advent season to listen more deeply to the Spirit?

• The Second Vatican Council leaned on Mary as the model of the church. She is the first and greatest disciple, the one whose commitment to Christ serves as inspiration for our own. Let us pray that the church may grow in its boldness and discernment so that like Mary, we can make Christ known to the world.

SPIRITUALITY

GOSPEL ACCLAMATION
Luke 3:4, 6

℟. Alleluia, alleluia.
Prepare the way of the Lord, make
   straight his paths:
all flesh shall see the salvation of God.
℟. Alleluia, alleluia.

Gospel

Mark 1:1-8; L5B

**The beginning of the gospel of
   Jesus Christ the Son of God.**

As it is written in Isaiah the
   prophet:
*Behold, I am sending my
   messenger ahead of you;
he will prepare your way.
A voice of one crying out in
   the desert:
"Prepare the way of the
   Lord,
make straight his paths."*
John the Baptist appeared in the desert
   proclaiming a baptism of repentance
      for the forgiveness of sins.
People of the whole Judean
   countryside
   and all the inhabitants of Jerusalem
   were going out to him
   and were being baptized by him in
      the Jordan River
   as they acknowledged their sins.
John was clothed in camel's hair,
   with a leather belt around his waist.
He fed on locusts and wild honey.
And this is what he proclaimed:
   "One mightier than I is coming after
      me.
I am not worthy to stoop and loosen the
      thongs of his sandals.
I have baptized you with water;
   he will baptize you with the Holy
      Spirit."

Reflecting on the Gospel

The new beginning John the Baptist announces has everyone abuzz. The gift of forgiveness awaits any who acknowledge their sins and let God's grace wash over them. This fresh start is brought to completion by the One coming after John, who will baptize with the Holy Spirit. The opening verse of the gospel, "The beginning of the gospel," reprises the first line of Genesis. Mark raises our expectations that God is doing something new with the coming of Jesus—a new creation that begins again in our own day, every time we turn to God and let our hearts be moved to follow the "straight way."

The second reading speaks of the newness that we long for in terms of "new heavens and a new earth." Other biblical authors speak of such a new creation (see Isa 65:17; 66:22; Rev 21:1; 2 Cor 5:17; Gal 6:15), but only in 2 Peter does the writer envision a fiery consummation and destruction of the whole of creation before the coming of the new. Such a notion originated in Persia, and then spread to the Greco-Roman world. There are times when we, too, may find ourselves wishing that God would do something dramatic to start over again.

The good news of the gospel is that God has done something dramatic and continues to make dramatic transformations, not with fiery conflagration, but with every hardened heart that lets itself be held to God's bosom and washed in Jesus's purifying love. It is by such ordinary yet extraordinary means that Holy Wisdom incarnate transforms our world and our hearts.

For some, it can take a very long time to open up to God's love. For others, it happens in a twinkling. It is not God's promise of newness that is delayed but we who sometimes dawdle. Today's second reading assures us that God is patient and does not use the same timetables we do. In the divine reality "one day is like a thousand years and a thousand years like one day." The delay, says 2 Peter, is so that all have time to accept the transforming love of God that enables them to reshape their lives.

In today's readings there is a dual dynamic: It is God who brings about the new beginnings, but it cannot happen without human response. We must acknowledge and let go of all that stands in the way of our openness to God's coming. The first and second readings invite us into the desert to do this. Desert space is always ambivalent: it is both a place of terror and emptiness and, at the same time, a hollowed-out space of grace. From the desert comes a voice of hope, bringing the good news that God's love never wavers, but when we fall short, with God's grace we can always begin again.

There are two other important feasts that celebrate God's extraordinary grace in the person of Mary, the patroness of the Americas: the Immaculate Conception (December 8) and Our Lady of Guadalupe (December 12). God's maternal care for us is palpably present in these graced symbols.

Preparing to Proclaim

Key words and phrases: "John the Baptist appeared in the desert."

To the point: At the beginning of Mark's Gospel, John the Baptist simply appears. He suddenly and out of nowhere is there in the desert proclaiming repentance and preparing the way for Jesus's coming. His childhood is completely invisible, but we who have also read Luke know what it took to get him here. We know the story of Elizabeth's unlikely pregnancy; we know her baby leapt in her womb, recognizing and revealing Christ's presence before he was even born. God does not suddenly start working through John; God gave him a special mission and a special connection to Christ from the moment of his conception. We do not know much about John's childhood, but we know he was raised by parents who were holy and faithful and also geriatric, likely unable to keep up with their boy, full as he was of the Spirit. Their labor, all that went into raising him, all they taught him, is overlooked here. Mark has him appear with nice dramatic effect. But John doesn't really appear out of nowhere.

Psalmist Preparation

When you proclaim this psalm, remember that it is really about what God proclaims. In music ministry, we focus a lot on making sound and on making that sound beautiful. But like John the Baptist, you are merely lending your voice so that others can hear what you have heard. These are not your words, and it is not about you. There is a humility needed, a humility that mimics John the Baptist's proclamation that one mightier than him is coming. In music ministry—in all music-making—there is an ongoing dance between silence and sound, between hearing and responding. In preparation for your proclamation of this psalm, spend some time in silence this week. Get out of the way and let God speak.

Making Connections

Between the readings: The many layers of meaning of the word "tender" make God's charge to Isaiah a complex one. "Tenderness" can be kindness, sympathy, affection; it can also be sensitivity and gentleness. To speak tenderly and to offer comfort implies the invisible work of mothering. But Isaiah is also charged with going to a high mountain, to cry at the top of his voice. There is need for both kinds of speaking, for both whispers and shouts. Ministry is made up of both public preaching and intimate conversation. God relates to us both as a community and as individuals.

To experience: Mark's Gospel does not give us John's background, and neither does it tell us much about those affected by his ministry. It would be nice to know some individual stories, how the real people who made up his audience were changed by him. In ministry we very often don't get to know these stories. We are rarely thanked. We scatter seeds in hopes something will take root. This reminds us that, like John, we are not the primary workers here; God is. We clear ways and create conditions in which God can work, but God is the real agent and actor here.

Homily Points

• For the next two Sundays, the gospels encourage us to encounter Christ through the ministry of John the Baptist. The great prophet, clothed in camel's hair and munching on locusts, prepares the way of the Lord with a singular focus. John does not worry about his appearance. He does not worry about upsetting those in power—as evidenced by his eventual beheading at the hands of Herod. As the son of a priest, John could have proclaimed his message from the ritzy steps of the temple. Instead, John humbly preaches from the banks of the Jordan River. He goes to the place where the Israelites made their journey into the Promised Land and made another promise: the Mighty One is coming. Prepare your hearts.

• John exemplifies humility. Mark notes that "people of the whole Judean countryside and all the inhabitants of Jerusalem were going out to him," yet John never loses his focus on Jesus. He knows God did not call him to preach the good news of John. Rather, the Baptist uses his popularity to point the way to Jesus the Christ, whose good news will bring salvation to the world.

• The prophet Isaiah assures the returning exiles of God's faithfulness in today's first reading. The people suffered greatly and even lost faith that God would rescue them. Hard times can do this to people. Difficulties can lead to doubt. Yet Isaiah promises that God will carry the people to safety and lead them with care like a shepherd who tends to their sheep.

CELEBRATION

Model Penitential Act

Presider: Today's reading from Second Peter reminds us of the Lord's patience. God recognizes the brokenness of creation and journeys with us toward healing. Let us lean into God's patient nature and ask for mercy . . . *[pause]*

Lord Jesus, you came to gather the nations into the peace of God's kingdom: Lord, have mercy.

Christ Jesus, you come in word and sacrament to strengthen us in holiness: Christ, have mercy.

Lord Jesus, you will come in glory with salvation for your people: Lord, have mercy.

Model Universal Prayer (Prayer of the Faithful)

Presider: Merciful God, you listen to the needs of your beloved people. In hope we pray.

Response: Lord, hear our prayer.

Bless the work of hospital chaplains, hospice chaplains, and all who bring comfort to people who are sick and dying . . .

Raise up prophetic voices in local and state leadership who advocate for the needs of people who are poor and vulnerable . . .

Draw into your loving embrace people whose families do not accept them . . .

Guide our thoughts and actions so that we may prepare the way of the Lord in our daily lives . . .

Presider: Look kindly upon your people, Lord, and hear our prayers that all of creation might be filled with the peace of your son. We ask this through Christ our Lord. **Amen.**

Liturgy and Music

Comfort and the way of the prophet seem so clearly incompatible for those who have dared to use a prophetic voice. Those who have spoken up on behalf of another resonate deeply with Scripture passages that speak of those who are without honor in their own country. Prophetic work is often lonely. It is an uphill climb, one that can feel endless, unsupported, full of doubt. Hardly the way we would describe comfort.

We're not there yet: we're not at the top of the mountain, we've only seen a glimpse of what is to come. Our divine comfort waits for us when we've completed the race—not this short sprint, but the ultimate marathon.

And yet, there are those glorious moments of comfort that are all around us: the joy of creating beautiful music together, the peace that comes when a congregation of full voices carries you even when you cannot carry yourself. A moment of perfect harmony. A song that transports you to another time and place.

Again, you are challenged: do not lean solely on those moments of material comfort through songs that avoid necessary truths. In the words of Bishop Ken Untener, "We are workers, not master builders; ministers, not messiahs. We are prophets of a future not our own" (https://www.usccb.org/prayer-and-worship/prayers-and-devotions/prayers/prophets-of-a-future-not-our-own). Our comfort will come. The foretastes of heaven will sustain us until then. For now, we take comfort in knowing that our hope is in God, the one who never changes, the one who has decided that we are worthy. Like John the Baptist, our mission in this life is to prepare the way for the greatness that comes next—the one that no eye has seen, no ear has heard. Take comfort that it is true; take comfort in knowing that the labor of prophetic work knows a reward that is great in heaven.

COLLECT

Let us pray.

Pause for silent prayer

Almighty and merciful God,
may no earthly undertaking hinder those
who set out in haste to meet your Son,
but may our learning of heavenly wisdom
gain us admittance to his company.
Who lives and reigns with you in the unity
    of the Holy Spirit,
God, for ever and ever. **Amen.**

FIRST READING

Isa 40:1-5, 9-11

Comfort, give comfort to my people,
    says your God.
Speak tenderly to Jerusalem, and proclaim
        to her
    that her service is at an end,
    her guilt is expiated;
indeed, she has received from the hand of
        the LORD
    double for all her sins.

    A voice cries out:
In the desert prepare the way of the LORD!
    Make straight in the wasteland a
        highway for our God!
Every valley shall be filled in,
    every mountain and hill shall be made
        low;
the rugged land shall be made a plain,
    the rough country, a broad valley.
Then the glory of the LORD shall be
        revealed,
    and all people shall see it together;
    for the mouth of the LORD has spoken.

Go up onto a high mountain,
    Zion, herald of glad tidings;
cry out at the top of your voice,
    Jerusalem, herald of good news!
Fear not to cry out
    and say to the cities of Judah:
    Here is your God!
Here comes with power
    the Lord GOD,
    who rules by his strong arm;
here is his reward with him,
    his recompense before him.
Like a shepherd he feeds his flock;
    in his arms he gathers the lambs,
carrying them in his bosom,
    and leading the ewes with care.

RESPONSORIAL PSALM

Ps 85:9-10, 11-12, 13-14

℟. (8) Lord, let us see your kindness, and
    grant us your salvation.

I will hear what God proclaims;
　the Lord—for he proclaims peace to his
　　people.
Near indeed is his salvation to those who
　　fear him,
　glory dwelling in our land.

R̥. Lord, let us see your kindness, and
　grant us your salvation.

Kindness and truth shall meet;
　justice and peace shall kiss.
Truth shall spring out of the earth,
　and justice shall look down from heaven.

R̥. Lord, let us see your kindness, and
　grant us your salvation.

The Lord himself will give his benefits;
　our land shall yield its increase.
Justice shall walk before him,
　and prepare the way of his steps.

R̥. Lord, let us see your kindness, and
　grant us your salvation.

SECOND READING
2 Pet 3:8-14

Do not ignore this one fact, beloved,
　that with the Lord one day is like a
　　thousand years
　and a thousand years like one day.
The Lord does not delay his promise, as
　　some regard "delay,"
　but he is patient with you,
　not wishing that any should perish
　but that all should come to repentance.
But the day of the Lord will come like a
　　thief,
　and then the heavens will pass away
　　with a mighty roar
　and the elements will be dissolved by
　　fire,
　and the earth and everything done on it
　　will be found out.

Since everything is to be dissolved in this
　　way,
　what sort of persons ought you to be,
　conducting yourselves in holiness and
　　devotion,
　waiting for and hastening the coming
　　of the day of God,
　because of which the heavens will be
　　dissolved in flames
　and the elements melted by fire.
But according to his promise
　we await new heavens and a new earth
　in which righteousness dwells.
Therefore, beloved, since you await these
　　things,
　be eager to be found without spot or
　　blemish before him, at peace.

CATECHESIS

Living Liturgy
Liturgy and Community: I was baptized when I was five years old, surrounded by community members, friends, godparents, and teachers. This highlights the communal aspect of the sacrament, as we are reminded that we are never alone on our spiritual journey. Even though I was only five years old when I received the sacrament, I still remember being surrounded and supported by so many people.

How much more intentional and loving can special moments be when celebrated in community? How might we recommit ourselves to community during these days of Advent?

PROMPTS FOR FAITH-SHARING

• Who in your life provides invisible work that makes yours possible? Whose work do you support in quiet, unacknowledged ways?

• Do you proclaim God mostly in whispers or in shouts? Do you feel called to speak of God in intimate settings or in public ones? Do you work best through personal relationship or in large-group settings?

• What makes it hard for you to hear God's voice? How could you make room for greater silence in your life?

See Appendix B, p. 309, for additional prompts.

DECEMBER 10, 2023
SECOND SUNDAY OF ADVENT

GOSPEL ACCLAMATION
cf. Luke 1:28

℟. Alleluia, alleluia.
Blessed are you, holy Virgin Mary, deserving of
all praise;
from you rose the sun of justice, Christ our God.
℟. Alleluia, alleluia.

Gospel   Luke 1:26-38; L690A

**The angel Gabriel was sent from God
 to a town of Galilee called Nazareth,
 to a virgin betrothed to a man named
 Joseph,
 of the house of David,
 and the virgin's name was Mary.
And coming to her, he said,
 "Hail, full of grace! The Lord is with
 you."
But she was greatly troubled at what was
 said
 and pondered what sort of greeting
 this might be.
Then the angel said to her,
 "Do not be afraid, Mary,
 for you have found favor with God.
Behold, you will conceive in your womb
 and bear a son,
 and you shall name him Jesus.**

Continued in Appendix A, p. 262.

See Appendix A, p. 262, for the other readings.

Reflecting on the Gospel

Mary's first act after discovering she is pregnant is to go and be present to her cousin. This shows us an impulse for self-gift, in which she places her cousin's needs above her own, traveling to assist the family member going through pregnancy at an advanced age and thus likely requiring help. But it also offers a meditation on the beauty of women ministering to women.

The visitation, as a decade of the Joyful Mysteries and as a gospel story, is often told within the context of Mary's selflessness. It's presented as an extension of her fiat, the yes that she says to God as she receives Jesus in her womb. Consider, for a moment, that Mary also chooses to visit Elizabeth because, in the face of a mystical act that will fulfill the covenant and reorder history, she just really wants to talk to another woman.

Mary's pregnancy naturally invokes shame. To be pregnant before marriage within the culture of the time was to subject oneself to extreme societal rejection and a total lack of support or resources. Mary, by saying yes to Gabriel, is playing a dangerous game. Thankfully, her fiancé does not exacerbate that shame by publicly renouncing her, which demonstrates Joseph's natural kindness, apparent even before Gabriel came to him in a dream.

Mary, knowing that she is on the precipice of a possible removal from society's good graces, prioritizes being with her cousin. Elizabeth plays many roles here: confidant, older sister/aunt, mentor, and friend. Mary's choice to visit Elizabeth is as much a sign of seeking comfort as it is a sign of support for the older pregnancy. In this way, Mary both ministers to Elizabeth and allows herself to be cared for. Rarely in the gospels do we hear about space created by women for women. The visitation is a moment when the experience of the pregnant body is centered and celebrated, and Mary and Elizabeth are free to be present to one another without any expectations or requirements. This gospel reminds us to protect and value spaces where people are free to express experiences that take place outside of what is traditionally prioritized.

Today we celebrate a moment when Mary created space for another group of people who were frequently left uncentered in church conversation. The feast of Our Lady of Guadalupe is a reminder that those society deems unimportant are those that the church is called to prioritize. Mary chose Juan Diego, a peasant, who had no money or title or position within the church. This reflects the choice of Mary as the mother of God—a young woman with no money or title, from an unimportant town in an occupied territory. Similarly, Mary did not appear to a bishop or a priest. She appeared to a parishioner who faced an uphill battle to get any member of the clergy to listen to him. She aligned herself with his experience.

Preparing to Proclaim

Key words and phrases: "Do not be afraid, Mary."

To the point: Despite all the serene depictions of her throughout Christian art history, Mary is not unfamiliar with fear. The annunciation follows the pattern we often see in biblical moments of calling: the heavenly messenger offers reassurance, reassurance needed because what is happening is scary. At Tepeyac, Mary will in turn offer reassurance to Juan Diego: "Let not your heart be disturbed." She, the best of mothers, offers consolation not because she does not know fear but precisely because she does. She who needed reassurance offers that same reassurance in turn to Juan Diego—and to us.

Model Penitential Act

Presider: Our Lady of Guadalupe appears to Juan Diego and helps him to deepen his trust in the divine presence. Calling to mind our need for God's merciful presence, let us ask for forgiveness . . . *[pause]*

Lord Jesus, you are the Son of God: Lord, have mercy.

Christ Jesus, you are the son of Mary: Christ, have mercy.

Lord Jesus, you reveal the way to eternal life: Lord, have mercy.

Model Universal Prayer (Prayer of the Faithful)

Presider: In company with Our Lady of Guadalupe, let us offer our prayers and petitions.

Response: Lord, hear our prayer.

Continue to cultivate the many gifts within the Latino Christian communities . . .

Raise up the wisdom and insights of Indigenous leaders in the public square . . .

Grant safety and justice to people seeking asylum at the border between the United States and Mexico . . .

Foster ever-growing devotion to Mary and the saints among our community . . .

Presider: Creative God, you reveal yourself to people of all cultures and creeds. Listen to our prayers and grace us with the openness to receive all people as Christ. We ask this through Jesus our Lord. **Amen.**

Living Liturgy

Good morning, Paloma Blanca. We greet you with sweet morning hymns, as we gently wake you from your slumber.

Too early, some might say, as they watch parents carry still-sleeping babes to the sanctuary before the sun comes up. But there's something so sacred about the community's instinct to be together for this celebration, something so extraordinary we would sacrifice our precious last hours of sleep to be present. We can't help but lean into the mystery of what compels an assembly of people to rise and greet the morning in honor of Our Lady of Guadalupe.

Central to this holy celebration of a Marian apparition is her physical appearance: she appears to Juan Diego clearly bearing the brown skin of the people of the land that we know today as Mexico. She speaks the language of the people, using words that Juan Diego can understand. She makes sense of the community's time and place, of their local traditions and customs and the context that is relevant and necessary to opening hearts to good news.

And what better model is that for our music ministry? Imagine encountering our liturgies, hearing music that resonates with your particular time and space. Perhaps many white, English-speaking Catholics have come to take this for granted, as the majority of music in many parishes has had that "home-grown Americana" flavor for most of their Catholic experience. But as the church in this country continues to grow, including even more immigrants and the need for relevant style and genre as effective models of sung prayer, how can we *not* lean into the idea that the divine is still showing up for us, that is looks and sounds like us, that it speaks in languages and through melodies that we can understand. Take a look through your music planning for this whole season: Whose voice is privileged? What sound takes up the most space? Who feels seen and heard through the language and genre resounding through each liturgy?

COLLECT

Let us pray.

Pause for silent prayer

O God, Father of mercies,
who placed your people under the singular protection
of your Son's most holy Mother,
grant that all who invoke the Blessed Virgin of Guadalupe,
may seek with ever more lively faith
the progress of peoples in the ways of justice and of peace.
Through our Lord Jesus Christ, your Son,
who lives and reigns with you in the unity of the Holy Spirit,
God, for ever and ever. **Amen.**

FOR REFLECTION

• Most of us don't receive clear messages as Mary did from Gabriel or as Juan Diego did from Mary. But many of us can point to moments of clear revelation or calling in our lives, when God's presence seemed clear and we felt in sync with God. What is one of yours?

• For both Mary and Juan Diego, God's reassurances are paired with a challenge; they are called to do seemingly impossible things. Where have you struggled with God's call? What reassurances has God given you?

See Appendix B, p. 309, for additional questions.

Homily Points

• The feast of Our Lady of Guadalupe calls for festive celebration. In the words of the prophet Zechariah, "Sing and rejoice . . . !" Legend says Mary appeared to the Indigenous Juan Diego dressed as an Aztec princess. She met Juan Diego as one of his people. She believed in him. Beautiful music rang out from the hilltop. Their story highlights the gifts of encounter and understanding.

• Our Lady of Guadalupe is the patron saint of Mexico. In honor of her feast day, let us give thanks for the gifts of the Mexican church and pray for justice for the Mexican people, particularly those facing hardships at the border. May Our Lady of Guadalupe guide them and keep them safe.

SPIRITUALITY

GOSPEL ACCLAMATION
Isa 61:1 (cited in Luke 4:18)

℞. Alleluia, alleluia.
The Spirit of the Lord is upon me,
because he has anointed me
to bring glad tidings to the poor.
℞. Alleluia, alleluia.

Gospel   John 1:6-8, 19-28; L8B

A man named John was sent from God.
He came for testimony, to testify to the
    light,
    so that all might believe through
        him.
He was not the light,
    but came to testify to the light.

And this is the testimony of John.
When the Jews from Jerusalem sent
        priests and Levites to him
    to ask him, "Who are you?"
    he admitted and did not deny it,
    but admitted, "I am not the Christ."
So they asked him,
    "What are you then? Are you
        Elijah?"
And he said, "I am not."
"Are you the Prophet?"
He answered, "No."
So they said to him,
    "Who are you, so we can give an answer
        to those who sent us?
What do you have to say for yourself?"
He said:
    "I am *the voice of one crying out in the
        desert,*
    'make straight the way of the Lord,'
    as Isaiah the prophet said."
Some Pharisees were also sent.
They asked him,
    "Why then do you baptize
    if you are not the Christ or Elijah or the
        Prophet?"
John answered them,
    "I baptize with water;
    but there is one among you whom you do
        not recognize,
    the one who is coming after me,
    whose sandal strap I am not worthy to
        untie."
This happened in Bethany across the Jordan,
    where John was baptizing.

Reflecting on the Gospel

On this Sunday, called Gaudete from the Latin for "rejoice," rejoicing is a thread that weaves through all of the readings, from the joy of the exiles returning to Jerusalem, to the rejoicing of Mary in the *Magnificat* (the responsorial psalm), to Paul's insistence that the Thessalonians rejoice at every moment. What is notable in each instance is that joy is not a vague sentiment or an abstract concept. It wells up in response to very concrete signs of God's providential care.

Isaiah's list of what makes for glad tidings is very familiar: healing of broken hearts, liberty for all who are captive, and release for those imprisoned. It is the same mission that Jesus claims for his own in Luke 4:18-19. These freeing acts are prescribed for the jubilee year in Leviticus 25. Every fifty years debts are to be erased, land returned to its original owners, and those held bound are to be released. We do not know whether the jubilee year was ever observed in the way it is described in Leviticus, but jubilee practices are always in season, especially in Advent. They cost nothing but an open and giving spirit. For example, extending forgiveness to someone I have held bound with resentment is the kind of gift that makes a springtime of new possibilities burst forth in the midst of winter.

In her *Magnificat*, Mary's rejoicing is caused not only by God's mysterious workings in her own life but by all the ways God's mercy has been manifest in every generation. Mary sings of a leveling: all who have been hungry are filled to satisfaction, and those who have gorged themselves to excess are emptied out. To accomplish this, those who have hoarded too much must relinquish some to the rightful owners—that is, those who have been made poor by others' greed and who have the right to eat and be satisfied too.

How are we to cultivate open and generous hearts that move us to give these kinds of gifts? Paul advises the Thessalonians and us to do three things constantly: rejoice, pray, and give thanks, no matter what the circumstances in which we find ourselves. If we stay centered on God, the Spirit is aflame in us, and we are able to discern truth and follow its demands.

In the gospel, we hear John the Baptist using Isaiah's words to present himself as "the voice of one crying out in the desert, 'Make straight the way of the Lord.'" John is simply the one pointing toward the expected One. He himself is not "the light"; he came to testify to the light and bring others to believe through his testimony. In a certain sense, though, John is a light to others. Just as effective lighting in a room does not call attention to itself but rather enables you to see what is in the room, so too John is not the focus but rather points to the One who is the Light. This expected One is already in their midst, and in our midst. Do you recognize him?

Preparing to Proclaim

Key words and phrases: "I am not the Christ."

To the point: John the Baptist gets so much of our Advent airtime—but why do we have him at all? He is not the main event; he is very clear about this from the beginning. What he offers is incomplete revelation, a promise yet to be fulfilled, a lesser baptism than the one who is to come. Why does God work in this way? Why not send us Christ directly and immediately and get right down to the work of salvation? We may not ever know why, but we can take a cue from John the Baptist in accepting the partial nature of what we see of God's work. John knows his place and accepts it in humility. He embodies the prayer by Bishop Ken Untener that reminds us: "We are . . . ministers, not messiahs. We are prophets of a future not our own." Like John, we each play some small but irreplaceable role in revealing and announcing Christ. The partial nature of this work can be frustrating, but God's ways are not our ways, and God's timing cannot be rushed.

Psalmist Preparation

This week you sing a New Testament canticle instead of an Old Testament psalm. There are three canticles in Luke's infancy narratives that have pride of place in the Liturgy of the Hours—Zechariah's *Benedictus* is always sung at Morning Prayer, Simeon's *Nunc Dimittis* at Night Prayer, and this one, Mary's great *Magnificat*, at Evening Prayer or Vespers. More rare are the occasions when we sing any of these at eucharistic liturgies. Unfortunately, Liturgy of the Hours is not often celebrated in parishes and can be hard for laypeople to participate in even when it is, so many of your congregation will not know of its liturgical import. There is no way to communicate all this information to a congregation assembled for Mass, but perhaps you can find ways to communicate the transformative nature of this prayer. Prayer and relationship with God is not about information but transformation. And this is, after all, a canticle about God upending the ways of the world and replacing them with true justice.

Making Connections

Between the readings: The first reading imagines God's work as plants, both wild and cultivated, which seem to spring into life out of nowhere. This passage jumps straight to the visible growth, but the image is evocative because growing plants requires a lot of waiting. Gardeners cannot force their plants to life; all they can do is set the conditions (water, light, nutrient-rich soil) and hope and wait. Our spiritual growth is similar; we can set conditions—silence, time in prayer, where we're turning our attention (and Advent is a good time to check on those)—but it is really up to God.

To experience: John the Baptist is at first identified by what he is not—he is not the light, not the Christ, not Elijah. The laity of the church is often described in similar ways; laypeople are not ordained, not priests, cannot preside or preach at Eucharist. But John's interlocutors push for a positive identification, and perhaps we should too. The laity is not just what it is not; it has a special call to bring the sacred in touch with the more mundane occupations of workplaces and friendships and childrearing. Every place where there is a layperson is a place the church is present.

Homily Points

• The prophet Isaiah announces a year of the Lord's favor in today's first reading—and it could not have come at a better time for the Israelites. Still reeling from their experience of exile, the Israelites longed for signs of the steadfast love promised by God. Isaiah declares that God's vindication will shine forth in a time of jubilee. The poor will receive glad tidings. The brokenhearted will be healed. Liberty will go to the captives and release to the prisoners. God's generosity blooms in the face of sorrow. God's justice grows before all the nations. Such is cause for great rejoicing—for the Israelites then and for us now.

• Imagine a jubilee happening today. How might God's blessings transform lives? What might God do to relieve the sorrow and suffering of creation? We need not wait passively for a jubilee to happen. The prophet Isaiah paves a way for dreaming of a year of favor from the Lord. We too can imagine the freedom of jubilee time—and work to make it happen. In ways big and small, we can be people of jubilee. We can tend to the needs of people who are vulnerable and hurting. Through our words and actions, we can bring about rejoicing in the name of God.

• Much of the northern hemisphere is in a time of extended darkness due to movements of the sun. Communities all over are also facing the darkness of injustice and sin. John comes to testify to the light. We too are called to reflect the light of Christ to the world. Where will you shine in these days leading up to Christmas?

CELEBRATION

Model Penitential Act

Presider: In today's second reading, Saint Paul calls on the Thessalonians to "pray without ceasing." Let us heed his call and ask God to look mercifully upon our sins and the sins of the world . . . *[pause]*

Lord Jesus, you are the Light of the World: Lord, have mercy.

Christ Jesus, you shine upon those who dwell in darkness: Christ, have mercy.

Lord Jesus, you will come again to guide your people into life everlasting: Lord, have mercy.

Model Universal Prayer (Prayer of the Faithful)

Presider: Reflecting on the many needs present in our world, let us offer our prayers and petitions to God.

Response: Lord, hear our prayer.

Bless the voices of our liturgical cantors, musicians, and all who lift their voices in song . . .

Bolster efforts to protect the environment and slow down the harmful effects of the climate crisis . . .

Give rest to overworked employees, new parents, and all who struggle to find respite in their days . . .

Foster a spirit of joy within our families, friends, and neighbors . . .

Presider: Grant peace to your people, O Lord, and stir in us the joy of the gospel so that we might be heralds of good news to the ends of the earth. We ask this through Christ our Lord. **Amen.**

Liturgy and Music

Gaudete! Indeed, it is our privilege to rejoice, as well as our responsibility. What a joy to be able to proclaim liberty to captives, to bring glad tidings to the poor, to heal the broken-hearted. We have been anointed, chosen by God, to do this sacred and crucial work of declaring goodness and thanksgiving that comes from the God in whose image and likeness each of us were made.

Remember in the midst of this ceaseless prayer of joy that there are many among you who are grieving. Does our song of rejoicing hold real space for those whose experience longs for that truth? Or are we inadvertently dismissing the realities of lived experience simply in favor of the ease and comfort associated with a joyful noise? Consider this tension, as you discern the best texts to sing, and the framework of prayer time within your choir rehearsals.

Think of our role as joy-announcers as one akin to that of John the Baptist. John's message of hope and light is always pointing to Jesus, clearly and with humility. For music ministers, our ongoing reflection on the power that comes from placing words and melodies on the lips of the faithful must always be at the forefront of our discernment about how to serve our communities, continuing that work of John the Baptist that beckons us to look for the divinity among us, the one that draws us toward the kingdom of peace and justice. Think of your ministry as a platform for this proclamation: Who's message is heard the loudest? How does this message point to Christ? And think, too, of the platforms beyond our worship spaces: social media, email communication, the simple way we choose to greet one another each day. How can we use these everyday platforms as tools to elevate the voices that most clearly help us to prepare the way?

COLLECT

Let us pray.

Pause for silent prayer

O God, who see how your people
faithfully await the feast of the Lord's
    Nativity,
enable us, we pray,
to attain the joys of so great a salvation
and to celebrate them always
with solemn worship and glad rejoicing.
Through our Lord Jesus Christ, your Son,
who lives and reigns with you in the unity
    of the Holy Spirit,
God, for ever and ever. **Amen.**

FIRST READING
Isa 61:1-2a, 10-11

The spirit of the Lord GOD is upon me,
    because the LORD has anointed me;
he has sent me to bring glad tidings to the
    poor,
    to heal the brokenhearted,
to proclaim liberty to the captives
    and release to the prisoners,
to announce a year of favor from the LORD
    and a day of vindication by our God.

I rejoice heartily in the LORD,
    in my God is the joy of my soul;
for he has clothed me with a robe of
    salvation
    and wrapped me in a mantle of justice,
like a bridegroom adorned with a diadem,
    like a bride bedecked with her jewels.
As the earth brings forth its plants,
    and a garden makes its growth spring
    up,
so will the Lord GOD make justice and
    praise
    spring up before all the nations.

RESPONSORIAL PSALM
Luke 1:46-48, 49-50, 53-54

R̸. (Isa 61:10b) My soul rejoices in my God.

My soul proclaims the greatness of the
    Lord;
    my spirit rejoices in God my Savior,
for he has looked upon his lowly servant.
    From this day all generations will call
        me blessed:

R̸. My soul rejoices in my God.

The Almighty has done great things for
    me,
    and holy is his Name.
He has mercy on those who fear him
    in every generation.

R̸. My soul rejoices in my God.

He has filled the hungry with good things,
    and the rich he has sent away empty.
He has come to the help of his servant
    Israel
    for he has remembered his promise of
        mercy.

R̸. My soul rejoices in my God.

SECOND READING
1 Thess 5:16-24

Brothers and sisters:
Rejoice always. Pray without ceasing.
In all circumstances give thanks,
    for this is the will of God for you in
        Christ Jesus.
Do not quench the Spirit.
Do not despise prophetic utterances.
Test everything; retain what is good.
Refrain from every kind of evil.

May the God of peace make you perfectly
    holy
    and may you entirely, spirit, soul, and
        body,
    be preserved blameless for the coming
        of our Lord Jesus Christ.
The one who calls you is faithful,
    and he will also accomplish it.

Living Liturgy

Liturgy and Community: During a night of studying in college, feeling full in my friendships and finally getting comfortable with the freedom of being away from home, I remember having an immense feeling that I loved everyone around me.

Unable to contain this feeling, I called my dad and started to cry. "Everything is just so beautiful!" I said, knowing he would understand. As people with the capacity to live in joy, we have the urge to share these feelings with people closest to us, whether to feel seen by another person or share in a universal feeling that connects all people.

In Louisville, Kentucky, at the corner of Fourth and Walnut Streets, there is a plaque explaining a similar experience by the spiritual master Thomas Merton:

> [In] the center of the shopping district, I was suddenly overwhelmed with the realization that I loved all these people, that they were mine and I theirs, that we could not be alien to one another even though we were total strangers. It was like waking from a dream of separateness, of spurious self-isolation in a special world. (*Conjectures of a Guilty Bystander*)

PROMPTS FOR FAITH-SHARING

• John the Baptist is not the Christ but plays a unique role in revealing and reflecting him to the world. How do you reveal and reflect Christ in the world?

• John shows true humility, knowing he is not Christ but not shying away from the role of leadership to which he has been called. What can you learn from his self-knowledge?

See Appendix B, p. 309, for additional prompts.

SPIRITUALITY

GOSPEL ACCLAMATION
Luke 1:38

℟. Alleluia, alleluia.
Behold, I am the handmaid of the Lord.
May it be done to me according to your word.
℟. Alleluia, alleluia.

Gospel   Luke 1:26-38; L11B

The angel Gabriel was sent from God
  to a town of Galilee called Nazareth,
  to a virgin betrothed to a man named
      Joseph,
  of the house of David,
  and the virgin's name was Mary.
And coming to her, he said,
  "Hail, full of grace! The Lord is with you."
But she was greatly troubled at what was
      said
  and pondered what sort of greeting this
      might be.
Then the angel said to her,
  "Do not be afraid, Mary,
  for you have found favor with God.

"Behold, you will conceive in your womb
      and bear a son,
  and you shall name him Jesus.
He will be great and will be called Son of
      the Most High,
  and the Lord God will give him the throne
      of David his father,
  and he will rule over the house of Jacob
      forever,
  and of his kingdom there will be no end."
But Mary said to the angel,
  "How can this be,
  since I have no relations with a man?"
And the angel said to her in reply,
  "The Holy Spirit will come upon you,
  and the power of the Most High will
      overshadow you.
Therefore the child to be born
  will be called holy, the Son of God.
And behold, Elizabeth, your relative,
  has also conceived a son in her old age,
  and this is the sixth month for her who
      was called barren;
  for nothing will be impossible for God."
Mary said, "Behold, I am the handmaid of
      the Lord.
May it be done to me according to your word."
Then the angel departed from her.

Reflecting on the Gospel

In today's gospel reading, Gabriel's message to Mary is that God now takes up residence in human flesh. While there is a place for magnificent temples and churches where we can gather as a people to glorify God, the Holy One would have us first recognize that divinity walks around in our midst in human skin.

The scene of the annunciation to Mary is the subject of much Christian art. Oftentimes Mary is portrayed as serenely praying, surrounded with light and joy. But in the Lukan annunciation story there is an undercurrent of distress,

incomprehension, and scandal. Henry Ossawa Tanner captures this sense in his painting *The Annunciation*, in which Mary sits at the edge of her disheveled bed, with a look of puzzlement and concern, while gazing toward a golden beam in the form of a cross. Megan Marlatt's fresco *The Annunciation* in St. Michael's Chapel at Rutgers University likewise depicts the topsy-turvy aspect of the event, as the angel appears upside down, uttering the word "Blessed" backward. Mary's life as she thought it would be is entirely upended, and this is greatly troubling.

What God is asking is incomprehensible. Mary questions how it can be. In addition, in her tiny village, where everyone knows everyone else and many people are related to one another, everyone knows that she and the man who is already her legal husband have not yet begun to live together. And all of them can count to nine. What will they say about her, what kinds of nasty looks will they cast her way when her precious child is born too soon?

While not spelling out how, Gabriel reassures Mary that in the midst of this messy situation, God will bring forth blessing, holiness, and salvation for all. Twice God's messenger assures her that she is grace-filled and is favored in God's sight, even if others will question this. He also reassures her that she is not alone. Her relative, Elizabeth, will help mentor and support her. Without knowing how God will accomplish all this, Mary opens a space for God to dwell within her, enabling the divine to make a new home within all humankind.

Mary makes a physical home for the Holy One in her womb; hers was a unique role. But we too are asked by God to make a dwelling place within ourselves and within our world for the Christ. The circumstances are always messy. It is not in glorious buildings beautifully adorned but in the humblest of persons, in the most difficult of circumstances, that God takes up residence. The irony is that in trying times we may feel abandoned by God, or question why it is that God is punishing us or why we have lost God's favor. It is precisely in such times that God dwells most intimately with us, assuring us that we are full of grace and favor, asking us to trust that God can and will bring forth blessing, even if we cannot see how.

Preparing to Proclaim

Key words and phrases: "[N]othing will be impossible for God."

To the point: We celebrate Christ's coming at Christmas, but it is so intimately tied to the moment of this gospel. Here, nearly at the end of our Advent waiting, we hear of Jesus's conception and the beginning of Mary's waiting. She has all the pain and discomfort and uncertainty of pregnancy ahead of her; as we join her in waiting for Christ we often carry pain and uncertainty too. Yet her discomfort—and ours—is wrapped up by the God who can take all things and make them work for good. We are not left with suffering that remains meaningless. We are not left alone. The same Holy Spirit that came upon Mary has been promised to us, and we are always overshadowed by the power of the Most High. God is with us even as we wait for God's return in glory. We are seen, we are known, we are loved.

Psalmist Preparation

This psalm has quotes within quotes that make it fulfill itself. God promises to God's chosen people such kindness and faithfulness that the chosen ones will sing out in gratitude—and here we are doing just that. God is fulfilling promises and has chosen to rely on us, unreliable as we are, to participate in their fulfillment. As you prepare to proclaim this psalm, spend some time praying with those quotes within quotes: "You are my father, my God, the rock, my savior." God has given us this prayer, and God promises to earn it from us. God promises goodness and fidelity that impel us to respond with such trust and love.

Making Connections

Between the readings: God's promise to David is fulfilled in our gospel. David was not destined to build the temple he wished to offer God; that work was left to his son. But God did promise David that he would dwell always with the people of Israel and particularly with David's descendants. The promise is fulfilled in our gospel—Jesus, descendant of David through his mother's marriage to Joseph, comes to dwell in a new sort of tabernacle, his mother's womb.

To experience: Mary receives her calling in a moment of solitude, stressing her utter uniqueness in salvation history. But Gabriel's message ends with a reference to Elizabeth. This serves not only to affirm God's power with another miraculous conception but also to place Mary back into the context of her community and her relationships. Like her, we do not receive our callings in isolation. We are always part of a larger story.

Homily Points

• Advent is a season of surprises. God's Spirit shows up in a myriad of unexpected places: in a raggedy man dressed in camel's hair, in the hope of the long-suffering Israelite people, in the blind who can now see, in the deaf who can now hear, in the dead who are now raised. There is perhaps no greater surprise in human history than when God's Spirit appears to a young, poor, unwed woman in Nazareth and asks her to carry God's Son. God finds Mary—Mary!—to be full of favor and grace. She holds none of the characteristics that society deems favorable, yet she is entirely worthy in God's eyes.

• Mary's story can inspire us to also see ourselves as worthy in God's eyes. It can be easy to doubt our worth, particularly during the holiday season. Perhaps you are struggling to find meaning after a divorce, a family dispute, or a layoff. Maybe you are deep in the throes of a mental health crisis, cannot afford the gifts you want to give, or are feeling lonely while everyone else looks merry and bright.

• Mary empathizes with our pain. She asked similar questions. And in the end, the young girl from Nazareth trusted in God's almighty power. She believed that indeed nothing is impossible for God. She believed God could lift up the lowly and bring the holiest of holies to life within her. On this last day of Advent, spend some time in prayer with Mary. We ask her to intercede for us so that we might come to see ourselves as worthy.

CELEBRATION

Model Penitential Act

Presider: Today's responsorial psalm summons us to "sing the goodness of the Lord." One way we can take up this call is to lean into God's mercy and ask for forgiveness for our sins . . . *[pause]*

Lord Jesus, you were conceived by the power of the Holy Spirit: Lord, have mercy.
Christ Jesus, you were carried in the womb of your mother, Mary: Christ, have mercy.
Lord Jesus, you are called holy, the Son of God: Lord, have mercy.

Model Universal Prayer (Prayer of the Faithful)

Presider: Almighty God, nothing is impossible with you. In joyful hope for the coming of the Savior, we pray . . .

Response: Lord, hear our prayer.

Embolden your church to recognize the divine presence in those people whom society casts aside . . .

Inspire civic leaders to prioritize safe housing for all people, particularly those facing harsh winter weather . . .

Grant strength and perseverance to mothers in the late stages of pregnancy . . .

Bless single parents in our community and surround them with loving support . . .

Presider: Favor us, gracious God, with your care so that we might have the grace to make the hope of your Son known in these final days of Advent. We ask this through Jesus, the Son of God, born of Mary. **Amen.**

Liturgy and Music

So many different perspectives and elevated emotions are coming into your worship spaces on these days. For some, the excitement of the season, that glimmering in the expectant eyes of children, and the pageantry of domestic and faith-based rituals brings a feeling of warmth and comfort. For others, the weight of expectation simply hovers like a dark cloud over every breath: the expectation to be joyful, the expectation to be surrounded by family, the expectation to fit into a commercialized or cookie-cutter design of what the holiday season "should" look like.

Remember, too, that we've passed the winter solstice. We've turned the corner after the longest night of the year and, for some, the metaphorical significance that nothing lasts forever—not even the darkest night—is a balm to an environment of extra stress and disappointment.

Nothing lasts forever—except the faithfulness of God in the caring of God's people. And for this everlasting God, *nothing* is impossible. The once-barren Elizabeth is with child, an unwed Jewish girl has been chosen to be the mother of Christ, and you, too, are children gifted with the opportunity to say "yes" to all the seemingly impossible ways that God is calling us to be co-creators of goodness.

Make space for all of this. In the bustling to prepare for the celebration of this wedding of heaven and earth, be careful not to gloss over the humanity that sits right before you, in your choir, your parish staff, your parishioners, and visitors. Hold and treasure each encounter with the same reverence and awe of a mother who holds new life in her womb, unsure of what comes next but recognizing that each stretch and pull and pain in her being is simply a sign of new and precious life. And this, too, will not last forever.

COLLECT

Let us pray.

Pause for silent prayer

Pour forth, we beseech you, O Lord,
your grace into our hearts,
that we, to whom the Incarnation of Christ
    your Son
was made known by the message of an
    Angel,
may by his Passion and Cross
be brought to the glory of his
    Resurrection.
Who lives and reigns with you in the unity
    of the Holy Spirit,
God, for ever and ever. **Amen.**

FIRST READING

2 Sam 7:1-5, 8b-12, 14a, 16

When King David was settled in his
    palace,
    and the LORD had given him rest from
        his enemies on every side,
    he said to Nathan the prophet,
    "Here I am living in a house of cedar,
        while the ark of God dwells in a tent!"
Nathan answered the king,
    "Go, do whatever you have in mind,
    for the LORD is with you."
But that night the LORD spoke to Nathan
    and said:
    "Go, tell my servant David, 'Thus says
        the LORD:
    Should you build me a house to dwell
        in?'

"'It was I who took you from the pasture
    and from the care of the flock
    to be commander of my people Israel.
I have been with you wherever you went,
    and I have destroyed all your enemies
        before you.
And I will make you famous like the great
    ones of the earth.
I will fix a place for my people Israel;
    I will plant them so that they may dwell
        in their place
    without further disturbance.
Neither shall the wicked continue to afflict
    them as they did of old,
    since the time I first appointed judges
        over my people Israel.
I will give you rest from all your enemies.
The LORD also reveals to you
    that he will establish a house for you.
And when your time comes and you rest
    with your ancestors,
    I will raise up your heir after you,
        sprung from your loins,
    and I will make his kingdom firm.

I will be a father to him,
  and he shall be a son to me.
Your house and your kingdom shall
    endure forever before me;
  your throne shall stand firm forever.'"

RESPONSORIAL PSALM
Ps 89:2-3, 4-5, 27, 29

℟. (2a) For ever I will sing the goodness of
    the Lord.

The promises of the LORD I will sing
    forever;
  through all generations my mouth shall
    proclaim your faithfulness.
For you have said, "My kindness is
    established forever";
  in heaven you have confirmed your
    faithfulness.

℟. For ever I will sing the goodness of the
    Lord.

"I have made a covenant with my chosen
    one,
  I have sworn to David my servant:
forever will I confirm your posterity
  and establish your throne for all
    generations."

℟. For ever I will sing the goodness of the
    Lord.

"He shall say of me, 'You are my father,
  my God, the Rock, my savior.'
Forever I will maintain my kindness
    toward him,
  and my covenant with him stands firm."

℟. For ever I will sing the goodness of the
    Lord.

SECOND READING
Rom 16:25-27

Brothers and sisters:
To him who can strengthen you,
  according to my gospel and the
      proclamation of Jesus Christ,
    according to the revelation of the
      mystery kept secret for long ages
  but now manifested through the
      prophetic writings and,
    according to the command of the
      eternal God,
  made known to all nations to bring
      about the obedience of faith,
to the only wise God, through Jesus
    Christ
  be glory forever and ever. Amen.

Living Liturgy

Liturgy and Spirituality: Long distance runners often make time to train for their next race. Whether it is two miles or ten miles, beginner distance runners sometimes get nervous that their training has not been enough to complete an upcoming race without stopping. To be successful they not only need to increase their mileage over time but also maintain the confidence and trust that they have done the necessary work to prepare for the race. In the same way, God has been laying the groundwork for the coming of Jesus in the teachings of Scripture and in fulfilling promises along the way.

On this Christmas Eve, let us trust in the ways we have been told of the coming of the kingdom of God in our everyday life. What clues have been laid that Christ is with us, here on earth? In what ways can we continue to form a long-lasting relationship with God based on faith and trust?

PROMPTS FOR FAITH-SHARING

• What discomforts and uncertainties has God asked you to sit with in this season of your life?

• What discomforts and uncertainties have you overcome? How might God be calling you to support others with similar trials?

• Advent, the season of liturgical waiting, is coming to an end, but most of us will still be waiting for God in some way as we move into the Christmas season. How are you still waiting for God? How do you hope God will appear in your life?

See Appendix B, p. 309, for additional prompts.

SEASON OF CHRISTMAS

The nativity offers the chance to look at the year anew, and to contemplate how we have built the kingdom, humbly, in our own lives. Professional grandeur and sweeping accomplishments have no place here in this manger. This is a place for the unremarkable things: cows and chickens and a good rest after a long journey. This is a place for the mundane to be made new. This is a place to contemplate how everyday moments from the past year have been filled with an unnoticed dignity: trips to the grocery store, family dinners, morning routines, the laundry, the coffee break, the video calls home.

✠ SPIRITUALITY

The Vigil Mass

GOSPEL ACCLAMATION
℟. Alleluia, alleluia.
Tomorrow the wickedness of the earth will be
    destroyed:
the Savior of the world will reign over us.
℟. Alleluia, alleluia.

Gospel

Matt 1:1-25; L13ABC

**The book of the genealogy of Jesus
    Christ,
    the son of David, the son of
    Abraham.**

**Abraham became the father of Isaac,
    Isaac the father of Jacob,
    Jacob the father of Judah and his
        brothers.
Judah became the father of Perez and
    Zerah,
    whose mother was Tamar.
Perez became the father of Hezron,
    Hezron the father of Ram,
    Ram the father of Amminadab.
Amminadab became the father of
    Nahshon,
    Nahshon the father of Salmon,
    Salmon the father of Boaz,
    whose mother was Rahab.
Boaz became the father of Obed,
    whose mother was Ruth.
Obed became the father of Jesse,
    Jesse the father of David the king.**

**David became the father of Solomon,
    whose mother had been the wife of
        Uriah.
Solomon became the father of
    Rehoboam,
    Rehoboam the father of Abijah,
    Abijah the father of Asaph.**

Continued in Appendix A, p. 263, or
Matt 1:18-25 *in Appendix A, p. 263.*

See Appendix A, p. 264, for the other readings.

Reflecting on the Gospel

The food is prepared. The presents are wrapped. The Christmas outfits are on. Now families sit eagerly in the pews on this holy night to hear . . . a laundry list of names?

The relevance of tonight's gospel is deceptive. At first glance, the gospel looks like a series of tongue-twisters for whichever priest or deacon is unlucky enough to be tasked with pronouncing the names of all of Jesus's male ancestors in his paternal line. But the act of reading these names out loud is a powerful reminder of what we wait for and witness tonight: Jesus's humanity.

We hear about Mary and Joseph, and sometimes about Anne and Joachim, Mary's parents. Tonight we hear the names of every one of Jesus's forebears, from Abraham to Joseph. This provides some context. Jesus is a direct descendent of Abraham, the man with whom God made the covenant. This genealogy gives us a tangible way of viewing the timeless devotion that God the Father has for his people, because we get to see just how long and enduring the relationship has been. The jump from Abraham to Jesus happens over more than a thousand years. That's more than a thousand years of God leading the Jewish people, the tribes of Israel, to this moment. Today, in the year 2023, we are about as far away from Jesus as Abraham was in the other direction. That is how long and consistent God's relationship with us has been.

The genealogy also offers us a moment to participate in ritual "pomp," that is, a moment of drawn-out ceremony to mark time differently. Tonight is supposed to be different than other nights, and the liturgy is built to reflect the elevated nature of the nativity. Like graduates parading by name to receive a diploma at a commencement ceremony, or a memorial of victims' names spoken publicly after a tragic accident, tonight offers us a moment to step out of how we normally experience time and instead be present to the names of Jesus's ancestors. It is precisely the drawn out nature of a list of names—the time, perhaps uncomfortable, it takes to hear them spoken aloud—that is the benefit of this gospel.

This gospel also bluntly states one of the most powerful beliefs we hold: Mary conceived of Jesus through the Holy Spirit. Whether Joseph's reaction was anger or shame, he chose not to make a spectacle of her lack of chastity but instead chose to break off the engagement quietly. That is, until Gabriel let Joseph in on the plan.

These are foundational beliefs for us, that Mary conceived Jesus through the Holy Spirit, and that Joseph decided to continue with the engagement because an angel of the Lord spoke to him. To go from the listicle nature of a genealogy to two of the most radical beliefs of our faith is a bit of a whiplash, and yet this is what we are offered in tonight's gospel. This pairing of the banal and the extraordinary is one of the hallmarks of Catholicism.

SPIRITUALITY

Mass during the Night

GOSPEL ACCLAMATION
Luke 2:10-11

℟. Alleluia, alleluia.
I proclaim to you good news of great
    joy:
today a Savior is born for us,
Christ the Lord.
℟. Alleluia, alleluia.

Gospel

Luke 2:1-14; L14ABC

In those days a decree went out
    from Caesar Augustus
    that the whole world should
        be enrolled.
This was the first enrollment,
    when Quirinius was governor
        of Syria.
So all went to be enrolled, each
    to his own town.
And Joseph too went up from
    Galilee from the town of
    Nazareth
    to Judea, to the city of David that is
        called Bethlehem,
    because he was of the house and
        family of David,
    to be enrolled with Mary, his be-
        trothed, who was with child.
While they were there,
    the time came for her to have her
        child,
    and she gave birth to her firstborn
        son.
She wrapped him in swaddling clothes
    and laid him in a manger,
    because there was no room for them
        in the inn.

Continued in Appendix A, p. 264.

See Appendix A, p. 265, for the other readings.

Reflecting on the Gospel

One of the great ironies of the Christian faith is that the situation of Jesus's birth was determined by a census law. Christ enters into the world in the midst of an administrative business trip that Joseph was required to take.

The humble surroundings in which the Son of God is born are an early glimpse into how God's relationship with us works. God does not elevate Mary to the status of an earthly queen when she says yes, but instead her words set in motion her journey to become Queen of Heaven. Jesus is not born into great riches and wealth; instead, his kingdom is built of loving relationships. The dichotomy of the nativity overturns expectations. The greatest human to walk the earth is born an ethnic minority in a backwater town in an occupied territory. This is the focal point of God's entrance into our world.

No matter how many times we've heard this story in Luke, we have to find ways to make it feel new. This is the story—shocking, really!—that's so often repeated it becomes rote, predictable, and boring. Generations of Catholics have watched the character of Linus read this gospel in the climax of the 1965 animated film *A Charlie Brown Christmas*. How do we allow the awe to slip back in?

One way to do this is to examine how we encounter the gospel this year. We return to this story every year, and that means every year we are given a chance to evaluate our values and expectations, measuring them against the humility and values expressed in the nativity.

Tonight we have the opportunity to take stock of the year that has passed since the last time we were invited into the manger. The nativity offers the chance to look at the year anew, and to contemplate how we have built the kingdom, humbly, in our own lives. Professional grandeur and sweeping accomplishments have no place here in this manger. This is a place for the unremarkable things: cows and chickens and a good rest after a long journey. This is a place for the mundane to be made new. This is a place to contemplate how everyday moments from the past year have been filled with an unnoticed dignity: trips to the grocery store, family dinners, morning routines, the laundry, the coffee break, the video calls home.

Like the King of Kings being born in a manger, the smallest places in our lives can hold remarkable holiness. Tonight's gospel is a chance to name those mundane moments in the past year that have been filled with beauty. Where are the mangers in your life? The experiences that arose as an afterthought? The side pockets of a career and home life? Perhaps what we are all invited to realize is just how much joy lines these pockets of our life, and how much holiness slips in, in unexpected places.

SPIRITUALITY

Mass at Dawn

GOSPEL ACCLAMATION
Luke 2:14

℟. Alleluia, alleluia.
Glory to God in the highest,
and on earth peace to those
on whom his favor rests.
℟. Alleluia, alleluia.

Gospel   Luke 2:15-20; L15ABC

When the angels went away from them
   to heaven,
  the shepherds said to one another,
  "Let us go, then, to Bethlehem
  to see this thing that has taken place,
  which the Lord has made known
   to us."
So they went in haste and found Mary
   and Joseph,
  and the infant lying in the manger.
When they saw this,
  they made known the message
  that had been told them about this
   child.
All who heard it were amazed
  by what had been told them by the
   shepherds.
And Mary kept all these things,
  reflecting on them in her heart.
Then the shepherds returned,
  glorifying and praising God
  for all they had heard and seen,
  just as it had been told to them.

See Appendix A, p. 265, for the other readings.

Reflecting on the Gospel

The main character of this morning's gospel isn't Jesus, or even Mary. It's the shepherds. Their evening has been totally disrupted. Angels appear to them in the middle of the night, when they've likely drawn the short stick to work the night shift. The first thing the angels do is tell them not to be afraid, and then the shepherds are informed of the arrival of the Messiah.

This makes no sense. Why shepherds? Why the lowliest night workers? Illiterate, poor, and probably mere employees, these shepherds have no business being the first humans on planet earth, besides Jesus's parents, to learn about his birth.

These shepherds continue the pattern in this unfolding story: minority parents in an occupied territory, giving birth in a barn without the help of a midwife, which is now announced to a group of uneducated day laborers. Every piece of this story contradicts expectation. And yet the shepherds don't just stand in the field, terrified and in awe. They exercise agency and go find this child, the King of Kings of whom the angels have just spoken. Their first act, once they've found out that the Messiah is on earth, is to get close to him. They want to be near him, to visit him, to pay homage to him.

Imagine those shepherds, living life as Jews under Roman rule, likely used to being second class citizens in most things, arriving to find out that their savior is, remarkably, just like them. Poor. Unhoused, in the middle of the night. The child of a carpenter.

Mary has just given birth to the most powerful and important human to ever walk the earth, and the retinue is a bunch of shepherds. This scene, retold for thousands of years on this very morning, offers a tableau that defies all logic. Painters and sculptors and artists across centuries have captured the nativity to invite us into this decidedly unremarkable scene. God chooses to enter into the world here, in this manger, with shepherds holding the prized position: the first to know. The angels didn't alert the innkeeper, or the town council, or the local rabbi. They appeared to the shepherds, the first invited to be so close to Jesus.

This gospel invites us to contemplate how we prioritize the "shepherds" in our lives: those whose labor we benefit from without seeing. These are people like the grocery bagger, or the receptionist at the doctor's office. Maybe it's the nail technician at the salon, or the hardware store employee. Our lives are filled with shepherds, people whose work we consider necessary but who receive little fanfare. Perhaps we are the shepherds, and tonight is the night when we are reminded that it is us who are chosen to be closest to Christ at his birth.

Jesus's arrival flips the world on its head. A baby born to a virgin. A king born in a manger. A heavenly announcement made to a group of shepherds. This is how God enters the world.

SPIRITUALITY

Mass during the Day

GOSPEL ACCLAMATION
℟. Alleluia, alleluia.
A holy day has dawned upon us.
Come, you nations, and adore the Lord.
For today a great light has come upon the earth.
℟. Alleluia, alleluia.

Gospel

John 1:1-18; L16ABC

In the beginning was the Word,
    and the Word was with God,
    and the Word was God.
He was in the beginning with God.
All things came to be through him,
    and without him nothing came to be.
What came to be through him was life,
    and this life was the light of the human
        race;
the light shines in the darkness,
    and the darkness has not overcome it.

A man named John was sent from God.
He came for testimony, to testify to the
        light,
    so that all might believe through him.
He was not the light,
    but came to testify to the light.
The true light, which enlightens everyone,
    was coming into the world.
    He was in the world,
    and the world came to be through him,
    but the world did not know him.
    He came to what was his own,
    but his own people did not accept him.

But to those who did accept him
    he gave power to become children of
        God,
    to those who believe in his name,
    who were born not by natural
        generation
    nor by human choice nor by a man's
        decision
    but of God.

Continued in Appendix A, p. 266, or
John 1:1-5, 9-14 *in Appendix A, p. 266.*

See Appendix A, p. 266, for the other readings.

Reflecting on the Gospel
In the gospel today, the climactic verse 14 of the prologue of John exultantly proclaims that God likes to camp with us! (The Greek verb *eskenosen* literally means "pitched his tent.") This is not a new message. During the wilderness wandering, Yhwh's presence was experienced in the tent of meeting (Exod 25:8; Num 35:34). Israel's God was not thought of as remaining stationary in a temple but rather as traveling with the people throughout their desert sojourn. What is new is when the Holy One tents in human flesh, journeying with us in the most intimate way possible.

The first part of the gospel describes a cozy at-homeness that existed from the beginning between *Theos* (God) and the *Logos* (Word). The two share a oneness and together take delight in giving birth to all that came to be. (The Greek word *ginomai*, usually translated here as "came to be," has this primary definition: "to come into being through process of birth or natural production, be born.") Their intimacy is fruitful; their love does not stay at home in a closed circle but gives birth to all that lives. The supreme act of self-emptying love is the pouring forth of God's love in the tent of human skin.

Just as leaving a sturdy home to camp in a nylon or canvas tent makes one vulnerable to the elements and to danger, so does Jesus's donning of human flesh. John's prologue already points toward his rejection and execution. There would be those who would not recognize the Creator's love masked in human flesh. They miss the truth that the divine impulse is to become one with the most fragile of humanity. Jesus seeks out and identifies with those who camp on the edge of poverty, not so much those who live in fine palaces or luxurious dwellings. There are, however, those who do receive him, who believe in his name.

The amazing thing is that, although the *Logos* has gone camping with humankind, he has not left the home he has with *Theos*. Even as he dwells with humanity, he is yet "at the Father's side" (*eis ton kolpon* is literally, "at the breast" or "bosom") (1:18). Here is another extraordinary image: not only are gender boundaries blurred as *Theos* and *Logos* are birthing children of God and all creation (vv. 3, 12-13), but the unique (*monogenes*, "one of a kind") Son is at the "breast" of the Father—an image of ongoing unbreakable intimacy (v. 18). It is the same intimacy that is shared between Jesus and all his disciples, symbolized in the figure of the nameless Beloved Disciple, who at the Last Supper (13:23) reclines at Jesus's side (literally, "in the bosom," *en to kolpo*, of Jesus).

In our celebration of Christmas, we not only rejoice in God tenting with us in human form but as followers of Christ we too are invited out of our comfortable abodes to pitch our tent with the most vulnerable and needy, while resting always in our one permanent home: the bosom of the Holy One.

Model Penitential Act
Presider: Saint Paul writes of "the kindness and generous love of God our savior" in today's second reading. Jesus pours out such kindness and generous love at the times we need it most. On this most sacred day, let us ask for mercy for our sins . . . *[pause]*

Lord Jesus, you are mighty God and Prince of Peace: Lord, have mercy.
Christ Jesus, you are the Son of God and son of Mary: Christ, have mercy.
Lord Jesus, you are the Word made flesh and splendor of the Father: Lord, have mercy.

Model Universal Prayer (Prayer of the Faithful)

Presider: Embraced by Emmanuel, God with us, let us offer our Christmas prayers and petitions.

Response: Lord, hear our prayer.

Lift up in joyful praise the ministry of church musicians, choir members, liturgists, environment teams, and all whose work benefits our Christmas celebrations . . .

Bring peace to war-torn parts of our world . . .

Bless the work of medical professionals, first responders, church ministers, and all who are providing essential services today . . .

Fill each of us with the joy of Christmas as we glory in the Savior's birth . . .

Presider: Generous God, you brought your Son into the world to be one with your beloved creation. Receive our prayers on this most holy day, that we might spread the hope of Christmas to everyone we meet. We ask this through Jesus, the Son of God, born of Mary. **Amen.**

Living Liturgy

The light will shine on us this day! A light dawns for the just. A light shines in the darkness, and the darkness will not overcome it. Jesus, the Light of the World. Candles, Christmas lights, stars; these images that dominate this season in Scripture and in symbols speak so clearly of the radiance of the divine child.

Remember to treat this metaphor responsibly. Ask yourself, how does it impact our understanding of race when "light" and "dark" are too easily cast as "good" and "bad"? Do we inadvertently weaponize or harm the children of God if our metaphor stops there, if it is exclusive in its interpretation? We have a tendency to privilege white over black through the symbols and rituals of our faith: white albs, white and gold fabrics on feast days, black ashes on Ash Wednesday, darkness that needs to be illuminated.

Perhaps one way we can imagine ourselves as the shepherds who decide to visit the infant Jesus is to have the pure curiosity and compulsion to see the truth with our own eyes, and then to tell that truth as far and wide as possible, using our whole lives to spread the good news. Certainly, our music is a beautiful vehicle for this mission; as we sing our community's beloved favorite hymns of the Christmas season, be mindful to remain open to the beloved hymns of our neighbor, as well. It will take all of us to tell this whole truth: no one song, no one community has the complete story themselves. Remember that this glorious light is dependent on the precious, necessary, safe, and dark world of the womb that has nurtured it into being. Remember the things we are still holding in that space, like Mary, who "kept all these things, reflecting on them in her heart."

FOR REFLECTION

• Where have you experienced Christ's coming this Advent season?

• Where do you still hope to find Christ dwelling with you?

• We are called in baptism to participate in Christ's mission as priest, prophet, and king. As we prepare for a new year, think about ways to live that would make Christ more present on earth.

See Appendix B, p. 309, for additional questions.

COLLECT

(from the Mass during the Day)

Let us pray.

Pause for silent prayer

O God, who wonderfully created the dignity
of human nature
and still more wonderfully restored it,
grant, we pray,
that we may share in the divinity of Christ,
who humbled himself to share in our humanity.
Who lives and reigns with you in the unity of
the Holy Spirit,
God, for ever and ever. **Amen.**

Homily Points

• Christmas tends to be a day of "bests." Many dress in their "Sunday best" for worship. People may dine on a fancy meal tonight and share thoughtful gifts with loved ones. It makes sense that today would be a day of festive celebration. The Savior has been born! Glory to God in the highest! Still, let us take careful note of the scene playing out in this morning's gospel. Luke tells of no decorations or expensive presents lying in the manger. No royalty make haste to visit. Instead, this Christmas scene takes place in a stable made for animals. It features people who are poor and marginalized: a young, unwed girl who just gave birth; a carpenter who stays by her side; a baby wrapped in swaddling clothes; and a group of shepherds.

• Shepherds are the first people invited to visit the newborn Jesus. Society considered shepherds to be on the lowest rung in first-century Palestine. They had little money. Their proximity to animals rendered them ritually unclean and, therefore, most treated them as outcasts. Yet the shepherds who kept watch of their sheep on the hillside were the first to bear witness to God incarnate, the Word made flesh.

• In the grand scheme of the gospels, this Christmas scene makes perfect sense. People who are poor and lowly are exactly the people Christ came to redeem. These are the ones sent to glorify and praise God. May their witnesses, then and now, be an inspiration and motivation to us all.

SPIRITUALITY

Heb 1:1-2

℟. Alleluia, alleluia.
In the past God spoke to our ancestors through
    the prophets;
in these last days, he has spoken to us
    through the Son.
℟. Alleluia, alleluia.

or:

Col 3:15a, 16a

℟. Alleluia, alleluia.
Let the peace of Christ control your
    hearts;
let the word of Christ dwell in you
    richly.
℟. Alleluia, alleluia.

Gospel

Luke 2:22-40; L17B

**When the days were completed
    for their purification
    according to the law of Moses,
    they took him up to Jerusalem
    to present him to the Lord,
    just as it is written in the law of the
        Lord,**
***Every male that opens the womb
        shall be consecrated to the Lord,***
and to offer the sacrifice of
***a pair of turtledoves or two young
        pigeons,***
**in accordance with the dictate in the
    law of the Lord.**

**Now there was a man in Jerusalem
    whose name was Simeon.
This man was righteous and devout,
    awaiting the consolation of Israel,
    and the Holy Spirit was upon him.
It had been revealed to him by the Holy
    Spirit
    that he should not see death
    before he had seen the Christ of the
        Lord.**

*Continued in Appendix A, p. 267, or
Luke 2:22, 39-40 in Appendix A, p. 267.*

Reflecting on the Gospel

During the holiday season much attention is placed on romanticizing the family. Christmas movies and advertisements portray happy reunions and joyous family gatherings. In reality, however, many families experience pain and loss that is all the more acute during the holidays. Perhaps a loved one has died during the past year. A family member may be fighting in a distant war. Old hurts may keep some from wanting to be with family. A failed marriage may have split apart parents, who struggle with how to share their love and time equitably with their children. Most families do not match the Norman Rockwell picture of everyone living happily as one. Today's readings may sound at first like an idealized portrait of family life, but a closer look reveals a very realistic understanding of what it takes to create a harmonious home.

But those who do good and who try to follow God's ways in everything often experience great pain and suffering. In the first reading, Sarah and Abraham yearn for a child, wondering desperately how the gifts from God could possibly last without an heir. Similarly, Mary and Joseph are completely devoted to God and follow all the prescriptions of the law, yet, as Simeon prophesies, they struggle, like all faithful people, to understand God's ways. At the annunciation Mary says yes, even as she questions, "How can this be?" (Luke 1:34). What God asks of her puts her in very difficult circumstances. Other people in Nazareth know that she and Joseph formally belong to each other but have not begun to live together. What kinds of things will they think and say about her when her blessed child is born too soon? Contemplation, faithfulness, and trust are three essential virtues that Mary exemplifies for weathering difficult times that challenge harmonious family life.

As we strive to live lives of contemplation, faithfulness, and trust, we can find hope in the words of the psalmist: "He remembers forever his covenant / which he made binding for a thousand generations / which he entered into with Abraham and by his oath to Isaac." Even amid the daily trials of family life, God was present with Sarah and Abraham, Mary and Joseph, and is just as much present in our lives today.

Take a few moments to pray with "A Weary Couple" (GIA Publications, Inc.), an evocative Holy Family hymn text by M. L. Adam Tice set to a traditional Irish tune by Tony Alonso.

Scan to listen to
"A Weary Couple."

Preparing to Proclaim

Key words and phrases: "The child grew and became strong."

To the point: The last sentence of this gospel hides a whole lot of life within it. "The child grew," yes, but it didn't just happen! He grew because Mary and Joseph worked tirelessly, as good parents do, to provide for his needs. They fed him and cleaned him; they taught him to sleep through the night and to walk and to feed himself. They cheered when the Word spoke his first word. But at the same time, they can't take full responsibility for the child's growth; it is wonderful and mysterious that children grow up. Parenthood is work undertaken in partnership with God. God was with Mary and Joseph in the painful parts of the job, both those unique to raising the Son of God and those sorrows that every parent feels. There is much pain in giving your heart over to someone who is constantly changing. "The child grew" and Mary and Joseph, like many of us, must have felt simultaneous delight at all he was learning and grief for the smaller versions of him that they loved so dearly and would never get back.

Psalmist Preparation

Today's psalm has us singing about how God fulfills God's promises, faithfully through generations. As you prepare this psalm, think of a time that God fulfilled a promise to you. When have you known God's mercy and care? Bring a prayer of gratitude into your proclamation of this psalm. God's promises also call us into partnership; Abraham is promised descendants and land and in return is called to great faith, faith that witnesses to God's goodness and makes it more present in the world. Think about how God calls you to faith, and bring a "yes" to this call into your proclamation of this psalm.

Making Connections

Between the readings: Like Mary and Joseph, Abraham and Sarah are blessed with a child that should not have happened. Mary's virginity and Sarah's old age meant that these women should have been excluded from motherhood, but God takes up special partnership with them and gives them and their children special roles in salvation history. The second reading reminds us that God asks families for their faith; the work of parenthood involves a lot of letting go.

To experience: In a church that affirms the goodness of children and the sacredness of the work of parenting, there can be a tendency to equate family size with holiness. But the Holy Family had only one child, and this group of three serves as a model for all our families, regardless of size. Large families are a beautiful gift to the church, a visible sign of God's life-giving creativity. And God calls us to a legitimate variety of family sizes and is no less present in smaller families too.

Homily Points

• The presentation of Jesus in the temple showcases the gift of intergenerational relationships. A righteous and devout elder man, Simeon, meets Mary, Joseph, and Jesus in the temple. He responds to the sight of baby Jesus, just forty days old, with awe and wonder. The wise prophet recognizes Jesus as the one who will bring salvation upon all the people. Simeon reflects this reality back to Mary who, as Jesus's mother, will feel the acceptance and rejection of her beloved son deep in her bones.

• Today's gospel also introduces us to the prophetess Anna. Advanced in age, Anna experienced various forms of family life throughout her years. Now widowed, Anna worships in the temple day and night. She believed in the Christ Child who would redeem Jerusalem and proclaimed his coming to all who would listen. Anna stands in the prophetic tradition of Old Testament greats like Deborah and Miriam, who prepared the way for God.

• With their resolute faith and years of wisdom, Simeon and Anna provide Mary and Joseph with perspective. They remind the new parents of their son's identity. They affirm Jesus's mission to be light for the world. Those of us who parent or care for children know the value of intergenerational perspectives. Families, whether by birth or by choice, thrive when members of all ages encourage each other and draw on their own experiences for the betterment of the whole. Like Jesus, each of us is part of a larger system of support.

CELEBRATION

Model Penitential Act

Presider: The Holy Family witnesses the way of discipleship. Let us ask God to strengthen our discipleship by forgiving our sins . . . *[pause]*

Lord Jesus, you are the light of revelation: Lord, have mercy.

Christ Jesus, you are glory for your people: Christ, have mercy.

Lord Jesus, you will bring salvation to all: Lord, have mercy.

Model Universal Prayer (Prayer of the Faithful)

Presider: In company with the Holy Family, let us voice aloud our prayers and the prayers of the world.

Response: Lord, hear our prayer.

Grace godparents with wisdom and insights to share with their godchildren . . .

Protect refugee families and keep them together in their times of trial . . .

Shower your mercy upon families who are grieving losses . . .

Help us to be open to the movements of the Holy Spirit in our lives . . .

Presider: Compassionate God, through your son Jesus the world came to know the power of divine love. Receive our prayers that as we continue in the Christmas season, we may spread joy in our homes and communities. We ask this through Christ our Lord. **Amen.**

Liturgy and Music

All families are holy—chosen families, adopted families, royal families, broken families. Whether your bloodline stands to inherit a fortune or a generational trauma, the story of your coming to be in this time and place is a sacred one. This can be a tough truth to cling to on this feast day when the language of family can be used to subordinate, to suppress, or to stoke the embers of guilt that never quite die away.

Remember that Jesus was adopted. Mary was an unwed mother. The Holy Family members were refugees, running for their lives, constantly living in the threat of danger. Imagine the denunciation of cultural norms that would have been a part of Joseph's fatherhood–there is no handbook for how to be married to the Queen of Heaven. The Holy Family we celebrate today would have been, by any measure of today's standards, a mess.

Think of the families who sit in your pews today. Statistics show that as many as 1 in 3 women and 1 in 4 men are victims of domestic violence. Many of the children of these families are in the midst of another stretch of prolonged exposure to abuse, as they continue a holiday break from school. Some grown children have made the tough decision to return home for the holidays, and others discern to be near chosen family instead.

Remember that it takes a village to raise a child. God does not want for our suffering, despite the way that many have misinterpreted the messages of today's Scripture passages. What might you prepare in your liturgies that makes this space and this feast a safe space that recognizes the dignity of each person, beloved children of God, above all? Who feels welcome by your definition of "family?" Do your prayer language and hymn texts offer the radical inclusivity of all the holy families among us?

COLLECT

Let us pray.

Pause for silent prayer

O God, who were pleased to give us
the shining example of the Holy Family,
graciously grant that we may imitate them
in practicing the virtues of family life and
    in the bonds of charity,
and so, in the joy of your house,
delight one day in eternal rewards.
Through our Lord Jesus Christ, your Son,
who lives and reigns with you in the unity
    of the Holy Spirit,
God, for ever and ever. **Amen.**

FIRST READING

Gen 15:1-6; 21:1-3

The word of the LORD came to Abram in a
    vision, saying:
  "Fear not, Abram!
    I am your shield;
    I will make your reward very great."
But Abram said,
  "O Lord GOD, what good will your gifts be,
    if I keep on being childless
    and have as my heir the steward of my
      house, Eliezer?"
Abram continued,
  "See, you have given me no offspring,
    and so one of my servants will be my heir."
Then the word of the LORD came to him:
  "No, that one shall not be your heir;
    your own issue shall be your heir."
The Lord took Abram outside and said,
  "Look up at the sky and count the stars,
    if you can.
Just so," he added, "shall your descendants be."
Abram put his faith in the LORD,
  who credited it to him as an act of
    righteousness.

The LORD took note of Sarah as he had
    said he would;
  he did for her as he had promised.
Sarah became pregnant and bore
    Abraham a son in his old age,
  at the set time that God had stated.
Abraham gave the name Isaac to this son
    of his
  whom Sarah bore him.

RESPONSORIAL PSALM

Ps 105:1-2, 3-4, 6-7, 8-9

℟. (7a, 8a) The Lord remembers his
    covenant for ever.

Give thanks to the LORD, invoke his name;
  make known among the nations his deeds.
Sing to him, sing his praise,
  proclaim all his wondrous deeds.

℟. The Lord remembers his covenant for ever.

Glory in his holy name;
　　rejoice, O hearts that seek the Lord!
Look to the Lord in his strength;
　　constantly seek his face.

℟. The Lord remembers his covenant for
　　ever.

You descendants of Abraham, his servants,
　　sons of Jacob, his chosen ones!
He, the Lord, is our God;
　　throughout the earth his judgments
　　　prevail.

℟. The Lord remembers his covenant for
　　ever.

He remembers forever his covenant
　　which he made binding for a thousand
　　　generations
which he entered into with Abraham
　　and by his oath to Isaac.

℟. The Lord remembers his covenant for
　　ever.

SECOND READING
Heb 11:8, 11-12, 17-19

Brothers and sisters:
By faith Abraham obeyed when he was
　　called to go out to a place
　　that he was to receive as an inheritance;
　　he went out, not knowing where he was
　　　to go.
By faith he received power to generate,
　　even though he was past the normal age
　　—and Sarah herself was sterile—
　　for he thought that the one who had
　　　made the promise was trustworthy.
So it was that there came forth from one
　　man,
　　himself as good as dead,
　　descendants as numerous as the stars
　　　in the sky
　　and as countless as the sands on the
　　　seashore.
By faith Abraham, when put to the test,
　　offered up Isaac,
　　and he who had received the promises
　　　was ready to offer
　　his only son,
　　of whom it was said,
　　"Through Isaac descendants shall bear
　　　your name."
He reasoned that God was able to raise
　　even from the dead,
　　and he received Isaac back as a symbol.

*See Appendix A, pp. 267–268, for optional
readings.*

Living Liturgy

Liturgy and Community: A year after college graduation, I lost my mother to breast cancer. During her treatments, I moved home to stay close by and told myself that recovery was possible, even if the prognosis didn't confirm this.

　　Although it may seem counterintuitive to talk about grief during the time we remember the Holy Family, Scripture reminds us that hope is found in the most unlikely of places. When we are grieving the loss of a loved one, we don't believe we will ever feel good again. It is only when we start to notice the many blessings in our lives, including the ways our loved ones are still with us, that we begin to see that even death does not limit the power of God. We are able to find new ways to connect with those who have passed on and notice opportunities to thank God for that blessing. It is often not the comfort we expect, but as we see with Abraham and Sarah, nothing is impossible with God.

PROMPTS FOR FAITH-SHARING

• What does family look like for you at this stage in life? How do your relationships with your parents, siblings, or children reveal God to you?

• Where do you struggle to see God in your family? Where might God be inviting you to grow in patience and love for them?

• How could you include God more fully in your familial relationships?

See Appendix B, p. 309, for additional prompts.

DECEMBER 31, 2023
THE HOLY FAMILY OF JESUS, MARY, AND JOSEPH

GOSPEL ACCLAMATION
Heb 1:1-2

R̸. Alleluia, alleluia.
In the past God spoke to our ancestors through the prophets;
in these last days, he has spoken to us through the Son.
R̸. Alleluia, alleluia.

Gospel

Luke 2:16-21; L18ABC

The shepherds went in haste to Bethlehem and found Mary and Joseph,
and the infant lying in the manger.
When they saw this,
they made known the message
that had been told them about this child.
All who heard it were amazed
by what had been told them by the shepherds.
And Mary kept all these things,
reflecting on them in her heart.
Then the shepherds returned,
glorifying and praising God
for all they had heard and seen,
just as it had been told to them.

When eight days were completed for his circumcision,
he was named Jesus, the name given him by the angel
before he was conceived in the womb.

See Appendix A, p. 269, for the other readings.

Reflecting on the Gospel

"Sometimes I sits and thinks and sometimes I just sits." This was one of the many maxims for which the legendary baseball player Satchel Paige (1906–82) was known. Luke's image of Mary in today's gospel offers a similar image of restful contemplation. Having just given birth to her child in a makeshift abode, and having been visited by shepherds who relay to her the angelic message they had received, Mary responds by treasuring all these things in her heart. She holds within both painful realities and delightful surprises. She savors her own encounter with God's angel, the joys of companionship with Elizabeth, and the delight of the new life she has just birthed. At the same time, she holds within her all the struggles that came from carrying this child before her marriage was consummated, the difficulties of the journey to Bethlehem, and the makeshift circumstances in which she gave birth.

In this contemplative space, Mary holds both joy and pain, anguish and delight, and receives all as blessing from God. As in the first reading, divine blessing and peace are given precisely in the midst of the most arduous of struggles. God instructs Aaron to have the priestly leaders bless the people, reminding them of God's protection and graciousness toward them just as they are about to depart from Sinai and embark on the next stage of the difficult desert crossing.

Mary carves out hollow space in the midst of tumultuous circumstances so that in contemplative oneness with the Holy One, she experiences the face of God shining upon her, transforming any troubled feelings into a calm radiance. She moves ever more deeply into divine mystery, not needing to understand all that has occurred nor to know what lies ahead, once again abandoning herself in trust to the One who always bestows blessing and graciousness. This is not something that Mary does only once; she habitually retreats into contemplative pondering. Luke tells us again at the end of the story of the finding of the twelve-year-old Jesus in the temple that Mary "kept all these things in her heart" (2:51).

It seems counterintuitive to just sit with God in trying times. Shouldn't we instead try to do something? Mary exemplifies for us the oft-repeated formula in Luke's gospel: discipleship consists in hearing and doing the word of God. It is a both/and injunction, not either/or. It is in the depths of contemplation that we experience oneness with God, the ability to see from the divine perspective, to accept the gift of blessedness offered us, and thus become empowered to act in ways that will bring about peace.

This feast day is also celebrated as the World Day of Peace. The reading from Numbers reminds us that peace is first of all a gift from God, for which we pray. Luke's Christmas story repeatedly emphasizes that Jesus is the bringer of peace (see 1:79, 2:14, and 2:29). This drumbeat of peace in the gospel brings home the message that true peace comes from Christ taking on human flesh, raising up all the lowly, and feeding the hungry, of which Mary dreams (1:52-53).

Preparing to Proclaim
Key words and phrases: "[H]e was named Jesus."

To the point: The act of naming a child only takes a moment, but it is one of the most sacred and privileged responsibilities of parents. Parents get to choose the name that the whole world will call a new person. Even God, who promises to call us each by name, will use the names we give our children. God partners with parents in bringing new human life into the world. In the case of Jesus, that partnership is even more evident and even more important. While we all become adopted children of God by virtue of our baptism, this is the literal Son of God. Even his name is given by God, revealed to Mary at the moment of the annunciation. Mary is a mother like all mothers, giving over her body and heart to make space for a new person in the world. At the same time, she is unlike any other, called to partner with God in a unique way to bring about salvation for the world.

Model Penitential Act

Presider: The Blessed Virgin Mary, the Mother of God, shows us the way of peace. In company with her, let us ask God to bring peace to our hearts through the forgiveness of our sins . . . *[pause]*

Lord Jesus, you shine light into the darkness: Lord, have mercy.

Christ Jesus, you bless all nations: Christ, have mercy.

Lord Jesus, you will bring us all into the peace of everlasting life: Lord, have mercy.

Model Universal Prayer (Prayer of the Faithful)

Presider: Guided by Mary the Mother of God, let us share our prayers and petitions.

Response: Lord, hear our prayer.

Bring joy to Christians and Christian vocations . . .

Bring peace to our homes, streets, and all places plagued with violence . . .

Bring rest to weary parents and caregivers . . .

Bring hope to all of us and our families as we enter a new year . . .

Presider: God of new beginnings, you create all life in your image and desire to see all of creation flourish. Hear our prayers at the start of this new year that we might glorify and praise you in all that we say and do. We ask this through Christ our Lord. **Amen.**

Living Liturgy

A new year is always a good time to take stock, to evaluate, to make goals and plans. Some people make an annual New Year's resolution: a personal commitment to make one's self or situation somehow better, instilling new, better habits or making room for something new, letting go of something old.

Why not then use this as a chance to reflect on the habits and commitment of our liturgies: Have we followed through on our plans to incorporate music from a diversity of style and compositional voice? Have we saved time in each rehearsal or gathering to pray with one another, leaving space for the lived experiences of one another? Have we centered only on what happens inside the walls of our church, or have we encouraged one another to pay attention to the way we live the gospel message in between our Sunday celebrations? What difference does it make?

God is still speaking to us today and every day. As adopted sons and daughters of God, it is simply not enough to read the Scriptures, to attend a weekly worship service. We are called to bring that message out into the world, as a blessing to one another and as a blessing from God's very self. Let us, on this first day of the year, recommit ourselves once again to that mission, to the ongoing discernment of that still small voice that resides in our hearts, like it did and will forever reside in the heart of our Mother, Mary. Remember, in this wrestling and recommitting and negotiating with self and community, the ultimate source of blessing, and may God's merciful blessing—resounding through the Scriptures today—continue to ring in our ears the whole year through.

COLLECT

Let us pray.

Pause for silent prayer

O God, who through the fruitful virginity of
 Blessed Mary
bestowed on the human race
the grace of eternal salvation,
grant, we pray,
that we may experience the intercession of her,
through whom we were found worthy
to receive the author of life,
our Lord Jesus Christ, your Son.
Who lives and reigns with you in the unity of
 the Holy Spirit,
God, for ever and ever. **Amen.**

FOR REFLECTION

• If you have had the opportunity to name a child, what name(s) did you choose and why? If you could name a child now, what name would you choose?

• What prophetic voices are you prone to dismiss because they come from people or places you do not expect?

See Appendix B, p. 309, for additional questions.

Homily Points

• Amid the commotion of the events following the birth of Jesus, the gospel writer directs us to Mary, the new mother who "kept all these things, reflecting on them in her heart." She is a beacon of stability, a model of contemplation. Mary listened to the shepherds' testimonies about her son. She experienced the wonder of his virgin birth. Now Mary quietly considers all that has been, all that is, and all that will be for her son, the destined savior of the world.

• We would do well to follow Mary's direction at the beginning of this new year. Let us take time today to quietly reflect in our hearts on the year that was and the year that is to come. Where did you experience God's presence last year? What struggles do you carry into this new year? How might you follow God's call more faithfully in the days ahead? May Mary the Mother of God and model of contemplation guide our prayers and action throughout the year.

SPIRITUALITY

GOSPEL ACCLAMATION
Matt 2:2

℟. Alleluia, alleluia.
We saw his star at its rising
and have come to do him homage.
℟. Alleluia, alleluia.

Gospel

Matt 2:1-12; L20ABC

When Jesus was born in
Bethlehem of Judea,
in the days of King Herod,
behold, magi from the east arrived in Jerusalem, saying,
"Where is the newborn king of the
Jews?
We saw his star at its rising
and have come to do him
homage."
When King Herod heard this,
he was greatly troubled,
and all Jerusalem with him.
Assembling all the chief priests and
the scribes of the people,
he inquired of them where the Christ
was to be born.
They said to him, "In Bethlehem of
Judea,
for thus it has been written through
the prophet:
And you, Bethlehem, land of
Judah,
are by no means least among
the rulers of Judah;
since from you shall come a ruler,
who is to shepherd my people
Israel."
Then Herod called the magi secretly
and ascertained from them the time
of the star's appearance.
He sent them to Bethlehem and said,
"Go and search diligently for the child.
When you have found him, bring me
word,
that I too may go and do him homage."

Continued in Appendix A, p. 269.

Reflecting on the Gospel

For those who live in the northern hemisphere, today's celebration of divine light, glory, and shining radiance comes in the darkest time of the year. Isaiah exults in God's brilliance, which bursts forth for the returning exiles, as Jerusalem rises up in splendor once again. The prophet envisions thick clouds covering all the other peoples. They are drawn to Israel, like a moth to a flame.

Jerusalem will light the way, not only for its own inhabitants, but it now provides a welcome refuge for all others. All people, from near and far, come to the holy city bearing their priceless gifts: riches from the sea, caravans of camels bulging with treasures, gold, frankincense, and wealth beyond measure.

The gospel tells of the fulfillment of this prophecy with a vivid story. The exotic visitors from the East, who come with their priceless gifts for the newborn Christ, signal the welcome of all peoples in God's embrace. The gift of the Christ is to all, Jew and Gentile alike, as the author of the letter to the Ephesians also insists. This author, who writes in Paul's name, continues to assert, as did Paul, that God's grace, made known first to the Jews, is now revealed to all. Moreover, there is no distinction between those who were the first stewards of this mystery and those who now enter in. "The Gentiles are coheirs, members of the same body, and copartners in the promise in Christ Jesus through the gospel." There is no special privilege for those who arrived first.

The readings today also help us to reflect on the kind of welcome we provide to the twelve million undocumented immigrants who live and work in the United States and the even greater number of refugees worldwide. Those who are settled face similar challenges in welcoming outsiders as did the early church, which struggled to accept Gentiles into the faith community. Like the foreign magi, these newcomers bear gifts of immeasurable value for the whole community.

Today is a good day for we who follow the immigrant Christ to ask ourselves: What gifts do immigrants bring to settled communities? What gifts do those who are settled offer to immigrants? It's also a good day to pray for the grace to let go of any sense of entitlement that regards a newcomer as less than "coheir" and "copartner."

Preparing to Proclaim

Key words and phrases: "They were overjoyed at seeing the star."

To the point: When the magi come to Jerusalem, they head for the palace; they came, after all, looking for a king. Their searching leads them ultimately to a much more ordinary abode. They trust that this is what they were seeking, and they respond with joy and praise. What extraordinary trust—the humble life of Mary and Joseph does not look like the king they were expecting. The magi and their extraordinary trust stand in sharp contrast with King Herod. They are open to the workings of God in places and people foreign to them. He, on the other hand, clings so tightly to his power and title that he cannot see God's hand even as God fulfills promises to the people Herod purports to represent. The magi ask questions earnestly, driven by curiosity and passion. Herod makes inquiries maliciously, intending to maintain his hold on what was never really his. The magi give us an example of the wonders that can happen when we drop our defenses and receive God's presence in each other even when it does not appear as we would have expected.

Psalmist Preparation

This psalm offers praise to both the king and to the God who gives him power, but it balances this praise with expectations for leadership. Justice and peace are the fruits of rightly-ordered power. The king receives praise not for his own glory but in honor of the justice he enacts. As you prepare this psalm, take some time to reflect on your own liturgical leadership. Do you sing as a performance or as a ministry? Do you think of the congregation as an audience or as fellow participants in the Body of Christ? Do you sing for your own glory or for the glory of God?

Making Connections

Between the readings: The magi's appearance in Jerusalem fulfills the first reading, but in a rather small and humble way. Yes, light guides foreigners to Jerusalem; yes, they bring some riches as gifts. But this is not the full gathering up of the nations that Isaiah predicts; this is three guys on camels asking directions to a newborn king that is news to everyone else. And Jerusalem does not respond with the throbbing, overflowing heart that Isaiah calls for; its political leader responds rather with a greedy clinging to power. The fullness of God's promises is yet to be seen.

To experience: In this life, we do not always see the splendor that God has promised. It can be hidden under all the pain and brokenness still present in our world. But God has fulfilled these promises and continues to fulfill them. Like the magi, we might need to look in places we don't expect. God is present not in wealth and worldly splendor, but in humble family homes.

Homily Points

• Life, death, resurrection—these crucial movements of the paschal mystery are evident throughout Christ's life. Just days after his birth, Jesus is already causing trouble for King Herod. The magi arrive in Jerusalem and ask, "Where is the newborn king of the Jews?" These holy people recognize the sacredness of the life that just came into the world. Herod, on the other hand, senses a threat to his power—a threat that eventually leads him to plot the death of Jesus. Still, we know what comes next. Jesus's suffering brings about salvation. His death ushers in new life. The magi were right to pay homage to the babe wrapped in swaddling clothes. Jesus's glory will shine forever.

• A star leads the magi to Jesus in today's Epiphany story. Throughout Scripture, God reveals the way to the divine through the natural world. For instance, God promises Abraham that his descendants will be "as numerous as the stars in the sky" (Gen 26:4). The father of many nations learns to trust God by gazing up at the night sky. Next week's gospel tells of Jesus emerging from water to God's Spirit descending upon him in baptism. How is God revealing Godself to you through the natural world?

• The magi must make a major decision in today's gospel: obey the powers of the established king, Herod, or risk following the newborn king, Jesus. Knowing the consequences that await, the magi still choose Jesus. They choose the new over the old, the helpless over the powerful. Jesus ushers in a new kingdom.

CELEBRATION

Model Penitential Act

Presider: Today's first reading from Isaiah describes a people whose "light has come," whose hearts shall "throb and overflow." Let us ask God to remove anything that impedes our hearts from overflowing and forgive our sins . . . *[pause]*

Lord Jesus, you are the one whom we follow: Lord, have mercy.

Christ Jesus, you are a beacon of light: Christ, have mercy.

Lord Jesus, you will bring everlasting hope to all the world: Lord, have mercy.

Model Universal Prayer (Prayer of the Faithful)

Presider: Guided by the light of Christ, let us place our prayers and petitions before the Lord . . .

Response: Lord, hear our prayer.

Guide young people who are discerning their callings . . .

Thwart the plans of powerful people seeking to harm others . . .

Keep safe people whose brave decisions put them in harm's way . . .

Inspire each of us to seek out the divine presence in the natural world . . .

Presider: Creator God, you draw people across time to the teachings of your Son. Hear our prayers that, like the magi, we might journey to meet Jesus in word, sacrament, and action. We ask this through Christ our Lord. **Amen.**

Liturgy and Music

All is preparation. Those who prepare the liturgy know this work well: the rehearsing, the planning, the early arrivals and pre-prayer set up. We wonder what type of divine foresight would have been possible for the wise men as they gathered their items before making the long journey to the manger. Such strange gifts to bring to a newborn babe—frankincense, gold, and myrrh—each one foreshadowing death. From the very beginning, each step of Jesus's life and the life of those within his inner circle was preparing for death and resurrection. Every step, every gift, every miracle, every table: preparation.

Not all of our planning is quite literally written in the stars as it was for these early travelers. How we long for such clarity or symbol confirming we are on the right path. Perhaps most days the best we can do is echo those deeply honest words of Thomas Merton's prayer: "My Lord God, I have no idea where I am going . . . and the fact that I think I am following your will does not mean that I am actually doing so. But I believe that the desire to please you does in fact please you. . . . And I know that if I do this you will lead me by the right road."

All the liturgical work we do is preparing for the beautiful kingdom that awaits us. Keep this always in mind: it is not about the most beautiful liturgy, or the most perfectly sung song. It is about the most sincere effort, despite all our reasons to give up. It's about showing up, even when it would be easier to sit it out. It's about all those little things we prepared just to get ourselves to the table each week, and all the ways we are changed because of our having broken bread and having shared it with friends and strangers.

And when we have journeyed, pay attention to the dreaming. Listen to the inner voice that leads us in another way. Leave lots of room to pray with your community, to discern: what dreams guide us now? Where will we go from here, and what should we bring?

COLLECT

Let us pray.

Pause for silent prayer

O God, who on this day
revealed your Only Begotten Son to the
     nations
by the guidance of a star,
grant in your mercy
that we, who know you already by faith,
may be brought to behold the beauty of
     your sublime glory.
Through our Lord Jesus Christ, your Son,
who lives and reigns with you in the unity
     of the Holy Spirit,
God, for ever and ever. **Amen.**

FIRST READING

Isa 60:1-6

Rise up in splendor, Jerusalem! Your light
     has come,
     the glory of the Lord shines upon you.
See, darkness covers the earth,
     and thick clouds cover the peoples;
but upon you the Lord shines,
     and over you appears his glory.
Nations shall walk by your light,
     and kings by your shining radiance.
Raise your eyes and look about;
     they all gather and come to you:
your sons come from afar,
     and your daughters in the arms of their
     nurses.

Then you shall be radiant at what you see,
     your heart shall throb and overflow,
for the riches of the sea shall be emptied
     out before you,
     the wealth of nations shall be brought
     to you.
Caravans of camels shall fill you,
     dromedaries from Midian and Ephah;
all from Sheba shall come
     bearing gold and frankincense,
     and proclaiming the praises of the Lord.

RESPONSORIAL PSALM
Ps 72:1-2, 7-8, 10-11, 12-13

℟. (cf. 11) Lord, every nation on earth will
adore you.

O God, with your judgment endow the
king,
and with your justice, the king's son;
he shall govern your people with justice
and your afflicted ones with judgment.

℟. Lord, every nation on earth will adore
you.

Justice shall flower in his days,
and profound peace, till the moon be no
more.
May he rule from sea to sea,
and from the River to the ends of the
earth.

℟. Lord, every nation on earth will adore
you.

The kings of Tarshish and the Isles shall
offer gifts;
the kings of Arabia and Seba shall
bring tribute.
All kings shall pay him homage,
all nations shall serve him.

℟. Lord, every nation on earth will adore
you.

For he shall rescue the poor when he cries
out,
and the afflicted when he has no one to
help him.
He shall have pity for the lowly and the
poor;
the lives of the poor he shall save.

℟. Lord, every nation on earth will adore
you.

SECOND READING
Eph 3:2-3a, 5-6

Brothers and sisters:
You have heard of the stewardship of
God's grace
that was given to me for your benefit,
namely, that the mystery was made
known to me by revelation.
It was not made known to people in other
generations
as it has now been revealed
to his holy apostles and prophets by the
Spirit:
that the Gentiles are coheirs, members
of the same body,
and copartners in the promise in Christ
Jesus through the gospel.

Living Liturgy

Liturgy and Stewardship: The narrative of the Epiphany centers on the treatment of those who are most vulnerable. Whether it is Jesus as a refugee, people in Pakistan devastated by deadly floods, or those who are incarcerated within a system of racism and bigotry, protecting the vulnerable is a critical component of our Christian faith.

Greta Thunberg, a young and globally renowned climate activist from Sweden, knows that large and decisive action is the only way to shift the tide. As a key player in beginning the modern-day youth climate strike movement, she challenges powerful people and institutions to protect the most vulnerable, often those most impacted by environmental degradation. We must do the same. What big, decisive actions are we willing to take to prevent further damage to our common home, and all people and creatures who live among it?

PROMPTS FOR FAITH-SHARING

• The magi come looking for Jesus, but they start by looking in the wrong place. Where might your expectations be keeping you from seeing the fullness of God's work?

• Herod's wickedness has him clinging fast to power. What is a place in your life where you might need to let go of some power or control?

• The magi finally encounter Jesus not in the palace they expected but just in a house. When have you encountered God in a surprising place?

See Appendix B, p. 309, for additional prompts.

ORDINARY
TIME I

SPIRITUALITY

GOSPEL ACCLAMATION
John 1:41, 17b

R̸. Alleluia, alleluia.
We have found the Messiah:
Jesus Christ, who brings us truth and
    grace.
R̸. Alleluia, alleluia.

Gospel

John 1:35-42; L65B

**John was standing with two of
    his disciples,
    and as he watched Jesus walk
        by, he said,
    "Behold, the Lamb of God."
The two disciples heard what he
    said and followed Jesus.
Jesus turned and saw them
    following him and said to
    them,
    "What are you looking for?"
They said to him, "Rabbi"—which
    translated means Teacher—,
    "where are you staying?"
He said to them, "Come, and you will
    see."
So they went and saw where Jesus was
    staying,
    and they stayed with him that day.
It was about four in the afternoon.
Andrew, the brother of Simon Peter,
    was one of the two who heard John
        and followed Jesus.
He first found his own brother Simon
    and told him,
    "We have found the Messiah"—which
        is translated Christ.
Then he brought him to Jesus.
Jesus looked at him and said,
    "You are Simon the son of John;
    you will be called Cephas"—which is
        translated Peter.**

Reflecting on the Gospel

Unlike the other three gospels, the Gospel of John does not depict Jesus calling the first disciples while walking along the shore of the Sea of Galilee. It is John the Baptist who points two of his disciples toward "the Lamb of God."

As in the other gospels, they take heed and follow Jesus. But there is a different dynamic in John's Gospel. Jesus has not called these two, and seeing them following, he turns and questions them, "What are you looking for?" Their reply might seem at first to be oddly out of place: "Where are you staying?"

Here the evangelist introduces one of the key theological emphases of this gospel: abiding, or staying, with Jesus. The Greek verb *menein*, "to abide," is repeated twice more, as the two went "and saw where Jesus was staying [*menei*], and they stayed [*emeinan*] with him." Later, in John 15, the image of the vine and branches helps us envision what it means to be intimately connected to and abide in Jesus and the One who sent him.

In the Fourth Gospel, the call to discipleship comes through the witness of someone else. John the Baptist brings Andrew and another unnamed disciple to Jesus. Andrew then brings his brother, Simon Peter, to Jesus (notice that Peter is not the first follower in John's Gospel). Later, Philip brings Nathanael to Jesus (1:45-51), and the Samaritan woman brings her townspeople to him (4:29-42). Today's readings show the diverse ways that the call to discipleship can come. Samuel has a direct experience of God, and, with the help of a more experienced companion, is able to understand what God is asking. In the gospel, the call comes through the mediation of another's witness.

In whatever way the call to discipleship comes, Paul reminds us that we do not encounter the Holy as disembodied spirits. Rather, our bodies are sacred, "temple[s] of the Holy Spirit." That Jesus took on human flesh and that God raised him bodily underscore the importance of the body. A corporeal spirituality helps us counter any exploitation of the body: in sex trade, or overexposure in the manner of dress, or the battering of bodies with abuse or torture, or the devaluing of aging bodies. It is through our bodies that we experience godliness and in them that we glorify God.

Reflecting on our own experience in the light of the gospel today, it's a good time to consider the person or people who have been most instrumental in bringing us to Jesus and to pray in thanksgiving for them. And the more challenging question: Who have we brought, or are we bringing, to Jesus?

Preparing to Proclaim

Key words and phrases: "Then he brought him to Jesus."

To the point: This gospel has a chain of witnessing: John the Baptist points Jesus out to John's own disciples; they leave John behind and follow Jesus. One of them in turn brings his brother to Jesus, and these brothers are Andrew and Simon Peter, who we now know as apostles and saints. This is also a fascinating moment in their story. We know how it turns out and how important these men will become to the Christian tradition. But they don't know that yet. They are just meeting Jesus and about all they know about him is that he's the kind of guy who gives you a nickname whether you asked for it or not. And yet this ordinary moment of meeting turns into an extraordinary moment of calling and of seekers saying yes in a way that will change their lives—and the lives of countless others to come. Saints are not made in a vacuum; God offers each of us not just a personal relationship but a community in which to grow and thrive. All of us are dependent on others to bring us closer to Christ and to know him more fully.

Psalmist Preparation

As we settle into Ordinary Time after the festivity of the Christmas season, we sing this psalm to demonstrate the listening posture with which we hope to respond to all God's callings. We sing it in direct response to the first reading, joining our voices to Samuel's as we strive to respond with his trust and obedience. It is also connected to the gospel, where a series of invitations—and a series of "yes" responses—brings Jesus and Peter into contact for the first time. As you prepare to proclaim this psalm, spend some time reflecting on all the ways God calls you and how you respond to those calls.

Making Connections

Between the readings: Like the gospel, the first reading has a calling that is not received without the help of another. Samuel is unable to understand God's call until Eli helps him hear with new ears. And the last sentence of that first reading is important—Samuel grows up and lives his whole life with his ears attuned to God. That one moment of calling, received in trust and love, changes everything going forward.

To experience: Biblical stories of calling can sometimes inspire envy among those of us who do not get to hear God's call so clearly. The fact of the matter is that such clear and immediate callings are rare. For most of us, our work of discernment, of learning to listen to God, is long and slow. With practice, we become more familiar with the ways God works in our hearts, learning to sit with apparent silence until we hear God's voice within it. We also learn to hear and see God at work in the people in our lives, in the needs present to us, and in our own giftedness.

Homily Points

• Has God ever spoken to you in a dream? Are you one of the few people who even remember your dreams? Today's first reading may feel like a foreign experience to most of us. God calls Samuel in his dreams. Three times, the Lord calls the sleeping Samuel to the point of waking him up. Only after the wise elder Eli helps interpret the happenings does Samuel understand and respond to God's call: "Speak, LORD, for your servant is listening."

• Samuel's experience shows it is not out of the realm of God's power to call to us through our dreams. However, dreams during sleep are not the only way in which God communicates God's desires for us. God also calls to us through our hopes and daydreams, in times of quiet prayer and in the presence of beloved community. Carve out space to let your mind wander this week. Pay attention to the people, experiences, and interactions that bring you joy. What are the dreams that rest in your heart? How might God be calling you through your desires?

• Jesus is perhaps more direct with his calling of the disciples than God was with Samuel. According to John's account, John and his disciples see the Lamb of God walking by and follow him. Jesus prompts the curious followers: "Come, and you will see." He calls the disciples into an experience of encounter. It is by entering into the experience that the followers come to realize their call to be disciples of Christ Jesus, the Son of God. We too can discern our callings by being open to new and unexpected encounters.

CELEBRATION

Model Penitential Act

Presider: In today's second reading, Saint Paul reminds the Corinthians that "your body is a temple of the Holy Spirit within you." For those times we have not honored our bodies or the bodies of others, let us ask God for mercy and forgiveness . . . *[pause]*

Lord Jesus, you are the Word made flesh: Lord, have mercy.

Christ Jesus, you came into this world to strengthen your people in holiness: Christ, have mercy.

Lord Jesus, you will come again bringing salvation to your people: Lord, have mercy.

Model Universal Prayer (Prayer of the Faithful)

Presider: Confident that God hears our prayers and provides for our needs, let us offer our petitions.

Response: Lord, hear our prayer.

Bring joy and strong community to people living the single vocation . . .

Bless the people who labor across the supply chain to bring necessary items to people and communities in need . . .

Give gentle rest to people suffering from insomnia, stress, and other disorders that make sleep difficult . . .

Deepen our practices of discernment as individuals and as a congregation striving to listen to God's callings . . .

Presider: Guide us, Lord, we pray, to respond to the needs of the world in ways that are true to our callings. Help us live as faithful stewards of the gospel. We offer our prayers through Christ our Lord. **Amen.**

Liturgy and Music

How many times have we asked ourselves how to engage young people in our liturgies? Often, we must caution ourselves from resorting to a "check the box" type of relationship: get a young person to lector, or cantor, or serve as an usher, acolyte, greeter. This active engagement in liturgical roles is of course important, but is only one way to experience the vitality of community life through the gifts of youth.

As was true for Samuel, God is speaking directly to young people today. God calls their name, as God has called yours. And they answer, "Here I am!" often greeted only by the invitation to "Wait your turn" or "We don't do that here."

What platforms are available for young people to speak, ask questions, present the challenges of Christian life—of life itself!—as a coming-of-age person in the world today? Is the community ready to change because of the conviction of these young voices, or does it treat the challenge as a threat?

One of the beautiful things about working with young people is that cynicism is learned—and, for the most part, they haven't learned it yet. But when their enthusiasm for a new idea is met with "We've always done it this way," or "We tried that before," or "We don't do that here," learning the way of cynicism and doubt is almost certain. What is communicated most clearly is that their ideas, their dreams, their presence is not essential, and is received as wrong, out of place, less-than.

Think deeply as you engage with young ministers. Meet each "Here I am" with an attitude of "Thank God!" Leave a softness of heart that is inspired and motivated by the endless possibilities that new eyes can see, new ears can hear. Lead with a willingness to change, and practice what it means to lead from the back, letting others take the reins when they're ready. Prove to them that they are vital to the collective work of communal prayer.

COLLECT

Let us pray.

Pause for silent prayer

Almighty ever-living God,
who govern all things,
both in heaven and on earth,
mercifully hear the pleading of your people
and bestow your peace on our times.
Through our Lord Jesus Christ, your Son,
who lives and reigns with you in the unity of the Holy Spirit,
God, for ever and ever. **Amen.**

FIRST READING
1 Sam 3:3b-10, 19

Samuel was sleeping in the temple of the LORD
  where the ark of God was.
The LORD called to Samuel, who answered, "Here I am."
Samuel ran to Eli and said, "Here I am. You called me."
"I did not call you," Eli said. "Go back to sleep."
So he went back to sleep.
Again the LORD called Samuel, who rose and went to Eli.
"Here I am," he said. "You called me."
But Eli answered, "I did not call you, my son. Go back to sleep."

At that time Samuel was not familiar with the LORD,
  because the LORD had not revealed anything to him as yet.
The LORD called Samuel again, for the third time.
Getting up and going to Eli, he said, "Here I am. You called me."
Then Eli understood that the LORD was calling the youth.
So he said to Samuel, "Go to sleep, and if you are called, reply,
  Speak, LORD, for your servant is listening."
When Samuel went to sleep in his place, the LORD came and revealed his presence,
  calling out as before, "Samuel, Samuel!"
Samuel answered, "Speak, for your servant is listening."

Samuel grew up, and the LORD was with him,
  not permitting any word of his to be without effect.

RESPONSORIAL PSALM

Ps 40:2, 4, 7-8, 8-9, 10

℟. (8a and 9a) Here am I, Lord; I come to
    do your will.

I have waited, waited for the LORD,
    and he stooped toward me and heard
        my cry.
And he put a new song into my mouth,
    a hymn to our God.

℟. Here am I, Lord; I come to do your will.

Sacrifice or offering you wished not,
    but ears open to obedience you gave me.
Holocausts or sin-offerings you sought not;
    then said I, "Behold I come."

℟. Here am I, Lord; I come to do your will.

"In the written scroll it is prescribed for me,
to do your will, O my God, is my delight,
    and your law is within my heart!"

℟. Here am I, Lord; I come to do your will.

I announced your justice in the vast
    assembly;
    I did not restrain my lips, as you, O
        LORD, know.

℟. Here am I, Lord; I come to do your will.

SECOND READING

1 Cor 6:13c-15a, 17-20

Brothers and sisters:
The body is not for immorality, but for the
    Lord,
    and the Lord is for the body;
    God raised the Lord and will also raise
        us by his power.

Do you not know that your bodies are
    members of Christ?
But whoever is joined to the Lord becomes
    one Spirit with him.
Avoid immorality.
Every other sin a person commits is
    outside the body,
    but the immoral person sins against his
        own body.
Do you not know that your body
    is a temple of the Holy Spirit within
        you,
    whom you have from God, and that you
        are not your own?
For you have been purchased at a price.
Therefore glorify God in your body.

Living Liturgy

Liturgy and Community: In the first reading, the Lord calls Samuel. Samuel, the son of Eli, was not familiar with God when being called and did not know what it meant at first. This story parallels the story of a religious sister who joined her congregation later in life. "Joan" joined a local community after she turned thirty, a unique story compared to her fellow community members who joined in their teens and twenties. Joan had lived her life as a teacher and musician, expecting that life would lead her to marriage, buying a home, and having children. She felt lost and confused when she was working full time and owned a home, but her vocational path had yet to be discovered. She was not considering the vocation to be a vowed religious, nor was even a Catholic at the time!

It was only when Joan stumbled upon a church that was looking for a musician, a pastime she knew, that a Catholic sister at the parish began to form a relationship with her, welcoming Joan into the community. From that moment forward, not only did Joan find community and purpose in filling a need, but it led her to respond to the Lord's call.

How are we called into deeper relationship with God? What pieces of our life get in the way of our calling?

PROMPTS FOR FAITH-SHARING

• John the Baptist points out Jesus to Andrew, and Andrew brings Simon to Jesus. Who has pointed the way to Christ for you? Who brings you closer to Jesus?

• What are some of the times you've heard God's call in your life? How have you responded?

• Where do you struggle to hear God's voice?

See Appendix B, p. 309, for additional prompts.

SPIRITUALITY

GOSPEL ACCLAMATION

Mark 1:15

R⁄. Alleluia, alleluia.
The kingdom of God is at hand.
Repent and believe in the Gospel.
R⁄. Alleluia, alleluia.

Gospel

Mark 1:14-20; L68B

After John had been arrested,
　Jesus came to Galilee
　　　proclaiming the gospel of
　　　God:
　"This is the time of
　　　fulfillment.
The kingdom of God is at hand.
Repent, and believe in the
　　　gospel."

As he passed by the Sea of
　　　Galilee,
　he saw Simon and his brother
　　　Andrew casting their nets
　　　into the sea;
　they were fishermen.
Jesus said to them,
　"Come after me, and I will make you
　　　fishers of men."
Then they abandoned their nets and
　　　followed him.
He walked along a little farther
　and saw James, the son of Zebedee,
　　　and his brother John.
They too were in a boat mending their
　　　nets.
Then he called them.
So they left their father Zebedee in the
　　　boat
　along with the hired men and
　　　followed him.

Reflecting on the Gospel

"Give me chastity, but not yet." This famous prayer of St. Augustine well captures the reluctance that most of us have to changing our ways. Yet we hear the exact opposite when the Ninevites instantly repent at Jonah's preaching and the fishermen immediately leave their nets to follow Jesus. There is an urgency with regard to the time, and a totality of response is needed. In Ordinary Time in the liturgical year, it may seem more natural to settle into the ordinary ways in which we have been living out our discipleship. Instead, these Scriptures urge us to recognize that a new time presses upon us, requiring different responses than before. There is nothing ordinary about the invitation to follow Jesus more radically in this urgent time.

Paul, thinking the Parousia was right over the horizon, insists that time is running out and that our usual way of doing things will no longer serve. Similarly, Jonah prophesizes to Nineveh that their destruction is imminent. When we think the end is near, we lose some of our inertia toward change. Today we hear this kind of urgency from those who study climate change or the causes of poverty, food shortages, war, and epidemics. To turn around these global ills requires profound turning around of our patterns of living. Still, we find ourselves reluctant, praying with Augustine, "yes, but not yet."

In Mark, the response of the fishermen is instant. These adroit fishermen immediately accept Jesus's invitation to use their skills to "fish for people." Abandoning their nets is a way of speaking of what must be left behind when one embraces radical discipleship. The fishermen do not leave their family, as the next episodes in the gospel show. Rather, Jesus becomes part of their family, making Capernaum his home (Mark 2:1), and the disciples become Jesus's new family, reorienting all relationships.

There are also many women, including Mary Magdalene, Mary the mother of James and Joses, Salome, and many others, who become part of Jesus's family of disciples. While the evangelists do not preserve the story of their call, all agree that these women had been following Jesus and ministering with him when he was in Galilee and continued to do so all the way to the cross (Mark 15:40). The cost of such a radical response to Jesus is already in view when Mark prefaces the call of the first disciples with the notice that John had been arrested. But like impulsive lovers who commit themselves to one another while still wrapped in their initial infatuation with each other, it is a compelling love that causes disciples to follow Jesus instantly. Just as a couple grows into love and learns the costly self-surrender it takes to make that love continue to flourish, so too disciples learn the deeper conversion demanded as they grow in their radical love affair with the Holy One. It is then not so much the threat of destruction that moves us to convert our ways but an irresistible love that turns our hearts.

Preparing to Proclaim

Key words and phrases: "Come after me, and I will make you fishers of men."

To the point: Last week's gospel gave us John's depiction of Simon and Andrew's calling; here we have the same moment as depicted by Mark. Here the brothers are together rather than called one by one, and since John is imprisoned he is not involved in pointing the way. The stories seem contradictory and cannot both be factually true, but their different emphases help to reveal more of the ever-unfolding truth about Jesus and what it means to follow him. In this story, the apostles-to-be are called when they are in the midst of their daily work. Jesus interrupts them, and rather than ignoring him and pressing on with their work, they stop. Something about him compels them to accept this disruption to their everyday lives. They respond with extraordinary trust to something that could have been received as mere inconvenience, and they encounter God there.

Psalmist Preparation

This psalm reminds us to take a posture of listening and humility with God. No matter how experienced we are in the life of faith, no matter how well-practiced we are at prayer, we are students, disciples, learners; God is the one who teaches. Our other readings show us that God is often present in interruption and inconvenience; perhaps these "ways" of God are something we always need to be learning. As you prepare to proclaim this psalm, reflect on times you have encountered God in interruption or inconvenience; think also about times you may have missed God by dismissing such a disruption. Bring these to prayer, and ask God to help you grow in gracious reception of people who might seem inconvenient to you.

Making Connections

Between the readings: In the first reading, an entire city responds with faith to the same sort of interruption that Simon and Andrew receive. No one in Nineveh wanted to hear that they were doing something wrong, and they could have responded to this prophet as if he were crazy. Instead, they embrace the interruption, realizing that they need it. They need to disrupt their evil ways and make a change. Not all interruptions are so dramatic, but God is often in them.

To experience: Most of the time, we won't perceive any great message in our interaction with the panhandler who asks us for change or the child who won't let us get anything done around the house. But if we practice responding to them with love and trust, we might just find in them a place of very real encounter with God. After all, the readings make clear that interruptions and inconveniences often hide opportunities for God to speak to us.

Homily Points

• The people of Nineveh turned from their evil ways. Together this "enormously large city" answered God's warning spoken through the prophet Jonah. God spared the people because of their faithfulness. What might it look like for a community today to repent from its shared sins and take seriously its need for reform? How might this group—whether it be a whole city, a small family, or something in between—commit to communal acts of repentance so that it might be a space of dignity and justice for all?

• Jesus calls Simon and Andrew from their work catching fish. He opens new possibilities for the disciples, saying, "Come after me, and I will make you fishers of people." Conversations about calling often center on what we are being called *to*—like a career change, budding relationship, or new way of being in the world. But being called *to* something almost always necessitates being called away *from* something else. God did not create humans with unlimited time and attention. We are constantly negotiating between giving up and taking on. There are times in life when God calls us *from* a particular situation or relationship. In today's gospel, Jesus calls Simon and Andrew from their job as fishermen so that they could be free to embrace a life of discipleship. What might God be calling you away from these days? What new calling may be emerging in its place?

• Today's gospel makes an intriguing statement on the priority of work. To a culture that values climbing the corporate ladder and giving your whole self to your job, Mark's Gospel says stop. There is a different way. We cannot make work into a god. Discipleship must take priority.

Model Penitential Act

Presider: As we come before God at the start of this Eucharist, let us pause to reflect on our sins and ask for God's mercy to strengthen us . . . *[pause]*

Lord Jesus, you call your people to repentance: Lord, have mercy.

Christ Jesus, you heal the wounds of sin and division: Christ, have mercy.

Lord Jesus, you empower your people to spread the good news: Lord, have mercy.

Model Universal Prayer (Prayer of the Faithful)

Presider: Guided by God who makes all things come into being, let us pray for the needs of the church and the needs of the world.

Response: Lord, hear our prayer.

Reconcile divisions and strengthen the unity between Christians of all traditions . . .

Animate the creativity of spiritual writers, artists, and poets . . .

Give comfort and support to people who are homebound . . .

Welcome our loved ones who have died into the peace of eternal life . . .

Presider: Almighty and ever-living God, we thank you for nourishing us in word and sacrament. In you all things are possible. Hear our prayers that the world might come to know the hope of Christ your Son, who lives and reigns with you in the unity of the Holy Spirit, God for ever and ever. **Amen.**

Liturgy and Music

All things are passing. Nothing is forever, except the faithful love of God. Scripture passages like the ones heard this weekend can evoke a sense of urgency about all that we hold dear and how fragile it all is. "Time is running out," as the second reading reminds us. It's normal to feel a knee-jerk reaction to hold on tighter, to cling to the familiar and beloved things of this current time and place.

Of course, the gospel invites us to leave it all behind, to quite literally drop what is in our hands in favor of the more excellent way of Christ. How do we know when it's worth letting go? How do we know when it's time?

We get just one life, but many opportunities to live it to the fullest. Think together with your ministry teams this week: What are we willing to do right now, in this singular precious life, as chosen followers of Christ? Can we leave our work? All that brings us comfort? Can we let go of what is predictable? Are we willing to take a risk, to chart a new way forward, to be bold?

Are we brave enough to leave our family, or our *familiar*? Think of all of the comforts that music brings to us—melodies of praise and joy and lament that have accompanied us along life's journey. Has this music caused harm to anyone? Has its creator used it for personal gain? Has its culture been appropriated to be more convenient or less threatening to us? Is it time to let go of what currently sustains us, in favor of something or someone greater?

COLLECT

Let us pray.

Pause for silent prayer

Almighty ever-living God,
direct our actions according to your good
     pleasure,
that in the name of your beloved Son
we may abound in good works.
Through our Lord Jesus Christ, your Son,
who lives and reigns with you in the unity
     of the Holy Spirit,
God, for ever and ever. **Amen.**

FIRST READING

Jonah 3:1-5, 10

The word of the LORD came to Jonah,
     saying:
     "Set out for the great city of Nineveh,
     and announce to it the message that I
         will tell you."
So Jonah made ready and went to Nineveh,
     according to the LORD's bidding.
Now Nineveh was an enormously large
     city;
     it took three days to go through it.
Jonah began his journey through the city,
     and had gone but a single day's walk
         announcing,
     "Forty days more and Nineveh shall be
         destroyed,"
     when the people of Nineveh believed
         God;
     they proclaimed a fast
     and all of them, great and small, put on
         sackcloth.

When God saw by their actions how they
     turned from their evil way,
     he repented of the evil that he had
         threatened to do to them;
     he did not carry it out.

RESPONSORIAL PSALM

Ps 25:4-5, 6-7, 8-9

℟. (4a) Teach me your ways, O Lord.

Your ways, O LORD, make known to me;
  teach me your paths,
guide me in your truth and teach me,
  for you are God my savior.

℟. Teach me your ways, O Lord.

Remember that your compassion, O LORD,
  and your love are from of old.
In your kindness remember me,
  because of your goodness, O LORD.

℟. Teach me your ways, O Lord.

Good and upright is the LORD;
  thus he shows sinners the way.
He guides the humble to justice
  and teaches the humble his way.

℟. Teach me your ways, O Lord.

SECOND READING

1 Cor 7:29-31

I tell you, brothers and sisters, the time is
  running out.
From now on, let those having wives act
  as not having them,
  those weeping as not weeping,
  those rejoicing as not rejoicing,
  those buying as not owning,
  those using the world as not using it
  fully.
For the world in its present form is
  passing away.

Living Liturgy

Liturgy and Community: Many communities of Catholic sisters are aging and seeing a drop in vocations. With this in mind, many communities in the United States are faced with the choice to continue recruiting members, merge with other communities, or "come to completion," meaning their religious community will end when the last member dies.

Catholic sisters are a group of people who model contemplation and active discernment in their daily lives. With this, discernment of the future of the order can be difficult. But their work is rooted in the reality of the resurrection. Seeming endings are invitations to transformation.

When faced with endings, whether the "death" of religious communities or loved ones, we have the power to view these endings as simply the ending of the world in its "present form" and not complete extinction.

PROMPTS FOR FAITH-SHARING

• How do you respond to disruptions to your plans?

• Have you ever encountered God in an interruption or inconvenience?

• Where might you have missed God by dismissing something (or someone!) as a disruption?

See Appendix B, p. 310, for additional prompts.

SPIRITUALITY

GOSPEL ACCLAMATION
Matt 4:16

℟. Alleluia, alleluia.
The people who sit in darkness have
    seen a great light;
on those dwelling in a land
    overshadowed by death,
light has arisen.
℟. Alleluia, alleluia.

Gospel

Mark 1:21-28; L71B

**Then they came to Capernaum,
    and on the sabbath Jesus
        entered the synagogue
        and taught.
The people were astonished at
    his teaching,
    for he taught them as one hav-
        ing authority and not as
        the scribes.
In their synagogue was a man
    with an unclean spirit;
    he cried out, "What have you to do
        with us, Jesus of Nazareth?
Have you come to destroy us?
I know who you are—the Holy One of
    God!"
Jesus rebuked him and said,
    "Quiet! Come out of him!"
The unclean spirit convulsed him and
    with a loud cry came out of him.
All were amazed and asked one
    another,
    "What is this?
A new teaching with authority.
He commands even the unclean spirits
    and they obey him."
His fame spread everywhere
    throughout the whole region of
    Galilee.**

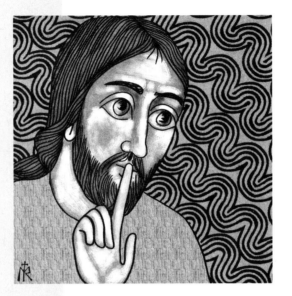

Reflecting on the Gospel

Prophets. You either love them or hate them. There is no lukewarm or neutral response to their incisive message. When a prophet's words challenge unjust systems and liberate folks who have been oppressed, those set free sing the praises of the prophet. But those whose power, privilege, and status are threatened by the prophet's words and actions will do all they can to silence them.

In today's first reading, the Israelites have prayed for a prophet like Moses, and God promises to raise up another such leader. They want one from among their midst who is deeply prayerful and close to God, who will know and convey God's desires, and who can lead the people out of their enslavements and their desert desolation. Moses assures them their prayer is heard. As Israel's history continues, many prophets arise. They are not confined to those whose words and deeds are recorded in the Scriptures.

In our own day, it is easy to identify prophets like Oscar Romero, Martin Luther King Jr., Dorothy Stang, Jean Donovan, Dorothy Kazel, Maura Clarke, Ita Ford, and Ignacio Ellacuría because they each died for their prophetic witness. There are also everyday prophets whose difficult and agitating work for justice never comes into the spotlight. They know that trouble is sure to come alongside any triumph of justice. The trouble can come not only from outside opponents, but even from within one's own community of faith. When Saint Mary MacKillop (1842–1909), founder of the Sisters of Saint Joseph in Australia, was building communities of sisters who would teach in schools and care for orphans, everyone lauded her. But once she turned a critical eye to an abusive situation in the church itself, she found herself excommunicated.

In the gospel, we see Jesus acclaimed as the promised "prophet like Moses," who teaches with authority and has power to cast out unclean spirits. While at first people respond with amazement and wonder, they will quickly turn on him as the gospel progresses, as his challenging message upsets the status quo. To ask for such a prophet is not only to ask for a leader who will confront unjust forces external to the faith community but also that we ourselves be confronted by the prophet's searing ability to speak truth.

We might think from today's second reading that such prophetic figures come only from the ranks of celibate believers. Paul depicts married people as being more anxious about pleasing their spouses and worldly affairs than godly concerns. To a certain extent, the notion that those who are vowed to celibacy are more single-hearted toward God has persisted through the ages. But the Second Vatican Council insists that all disciples are equally called to holiness and to mission. It is precisely through engagement with the concerns of the world, the council tells us, that Jesus's followers exercise their discipleship. In a sense, all followers of Jesus are called to exercise a prophetic ministry like Moses and Jesus. The readings today invite us not only to pray for prophetic leaders but also to exercise our own prophetic gifts both within and without our faith communities.

Preparing to Proclaim

Key words and phrases: "What is this? A new teaching with authority."

To the point: People are astonished at Jesus's teaching; his authority contrasts sharply with the way the scribes have been teaching. Parenting experts like to make a distinction between authoritarian and authoritative parenting. Authoritarian parents are strict and cold; they strive to control their children, expect obedience without question, and mete out punishment for noncompliance. Authoritative parents are also strict, but they set boundaries with warmth and compassion and involve their children in decision-making. Their work is slower—it takes longer to explain the rules than to simply set them—but putting in this time sets them up for a parental authority based on trust rather than on fear. At the beginning of Jesus's public ministry, we get a hint of which kind of authority Jesus will exert. He will set boundaries and declare difficult moral teachings, but he is able to do so because his authority is based on love.

Psalmist Preparation

This psalm calls us to keep our hearts soft so that we may be ready to hear God's voice and respond to it. It makes the claim that God's voice is there to be heard, although the "if" of the antiphon implies that we might not hear it all the time or every day. But there is no better preparation for this psalm than trying to hear God's voice yourself. Take some time this week to sit in silence. Bring your prayers before God, and be sure to give God time to answer. Keeping our ears and hearts open for God often means just making space in lives that are often too busy and too loud.

Making Connections

Between the readings: Moses reminds us that a prophet's authority comes not from the prophet's own merit but from their reliance on God. True prophets speak not their own words but God's. They are like a musical instrument, which is silent without a musician but which allows the musician to make beauty that would not exist without the instrument. Prophets lend their voice to someone else's music-making, but that does not mean there is no room for their own gifts.

To experience: Jesus's haste and clarity of mission might seem to contrast with most of our lives. After decades of prayer and discernment, he is confident in his mission when the right time comes for it. He is now in haste; Mark's gospel leaves no room for delay. In this passage, he arrives in Capernaum and sets straight to teaching. It is perhaps unusual for us to be called with such clarity; our missions usually unfold over a lifetime. But when we attend to God's callings, we can move with the same confidence that Jesus does.

Homily Points

• The scene that plays out in today's gospel is likely familiar to many of us. We are gathered for an important occasion—a church service, a keynote speaker, a business meeting—when suddenly someone begins to shout. Heads turn in horror. People begin to murmur: What's wrong with this person? Some may feel afraid or angry over the disruption. As Christians, how are we to respond in such a scenario?

• Jesus models the way. Early in his public ministry, Jesus is teaching in the synagogue when a man with an unclean spirit cries out. Presumably the authorities would have tried to remove the man as quickly as possible. But Jesus recognizes the troubled man's humanity. He does not send the man away. Rather, Jesus exorcises the demon out of the man's body. He moves to help. We too are called not to judge those who cry out but to address their needs with compassion.

• Jesus acts with authority over the unclean spirit. This is one of many instances where Jesus takes on the supposed power of demonic forces and emerges victorious. Those gathered in the synagogue witness Jesus's exorcism and wonder in amazement, "What is this?" Acceptance of Jesus's authority remains a challenge for the faithful today. Many of us benefit from demonic forces like racism, sexism, capitalism, or other unjust social structures. How might our lives change if we refused to be tempted by the perceived benefits of those demons and instead placed all our trust in Jesus's saving power?

Model Penitential Act

Presider: In today's second reading, Saint Paul tells the Corinthians of his wish for them to be free of anxieties. Let us call to mind the times we have sinned that are now causing anxiety in our hearts and ask for God's mercy . . . *[pause]*

Lord Jesus, you are the great teacher: Lord, have mercy.

Christ Jesus, you are the one who even the unclean spirits obey: Christ, have mercy.

Lord Jesus, you are the healer of all: Lord, have mercy.

Model Universal Prayer (Prayer of the Faithful)

Presider: In communion with the Body of Christ, let us offer our prayers and petitions before God.

Response: Lord, hear our prayer.

Grace the efforts of congregations to reach out to people who have stopped participating in their faith communities . . .

Awaken a greater and more urgent ecological awareness in government leaders . . .

Help people released from prison find housing, employment, and communal support during their time of transition . . .

Deepen our appreciation of cultural diversity in our local neighborhoods . . .

Presider: Prophetic God, you raise up leaders among your people to live out the compassionate, challenging word of Jesus Christ your Son. Receive our prayers that we too may answer your call to be agents of healing in the world. We ask this through Christ our Lord. **Amen.**

Liturgy and Music

Even the unclean spirits recognize the authority of Christ's voice. As Jesus commands the evil spirit to leave the man in Capernaum, believers are validated and empowered by the miracle before their eyes, and unbelievers surely found it difficult to argue with the mysterious inability for evil to ignore his voice.

Jesus becomes quite famous for healing physical disabilities or ailments in public, so that all might bear witness: the man born blind, the woman with a hemorrhage, people with mental illness, Lazarus. Whenever these physical or mental challenges are healed through the saving power of Jesus, take the opportunity to prayerfully discern what this means for your community. While the metaphorical language of physical transformation is certainly a way that we come to understand Christ's authority, and a way that we reflect on the spiritual transformation and personal conversion each of us needs in our own lives, there is great risk in placing too much emphasis on physical limitations. Think of the persons with disabilities in your congregation: Are they not already whole? Are they not already holy? How accessible have we made our spaces to allow access to those who use a wheelchair or other mobility aid?

Turn these readings on their heads a bit: How have *we* become the thing that disables? Think about the challenges of our physical spaces: too many stairs, too narrow of aisles, too small for comfort. Think of our sonic spaces: too cavernous for deciphering spoken word, too amplified for sensitive ears, too dependent solely on aural catechesis. Think of our hearts: too hardened to be molded, too comfortable to accommodate, too certain to be challenged. Think of our language and its limits: would we stigmatize or ostracize the risen Christ, who himself appears as a body wounded and disabled by the cruelty of the cross?

Let us pray.

Pause for silent prayer

Grant us, Lord our God,
that we may honor you with all our mind,
and love everyone in truth of heart.
Through our Lord Jesus Christ, your Son,
who lives and reigns with you in the unity
    of the Holy Spirit,
God, for ever and ever. **Amen.**

FIRST READING
Deut 18:15-20

Moses spoke to all the people, saying:
    "A prophet like me will the LORD, your
        God, raise up for you
    from among your own kin;
    to him you shall listen.
This is exactly what you requested of the
        LORD, your God, at Horeb
    on the day of the assembly, when you
        said,
    'Let us not again hear the voice of the
        LORD, our God,
    nor see this great fire any more, lest we
        die.'
And the LORD said to me, 'This was well
        said.
I will raise up for them a prophet like you
        from among their kin,
    and will put my words into his mouth;
    he shall tell them all that I command
        him.
Whoever will not listen to my words
        which he speaks in my name,
    I myself will make him answer for it.
But if a prophet presumes to speak in my
        name
    an oracle that I have not commanded
        him to speak,
    or speaks in the name of other gods, he
        shall die.'"

RESPONSORIAL PSALM

Ps 95:1-2, 6-7, 7-9

℟. (8) If today you hear his voice, harden
not your hearts.

Come, let us sing joyfully to the LORD;
let us acclaim the rock of our salvation.
Let us come into his presence with
thanksgiving;
let us joyfully sing psalms to him.

℟. If today you hear his voice, harden not
your hearts.

Come, let us bow down in worship;
let us kneel before the LORD who made
us.
For he is our God,
and we are the people he shepherds, the
flock he guides.

℟. If today you hear his voice, harden not
your hearts.

Oh, that today you would hear his voice:
"Harden not your hearts as at Meribah,
as in the day of Massah in the desert,
where your fathers tempted me;
they tested me though they had seen
my works."

℟. If today you hear his voice, harden not
your hearts.

SECOND READING

1 Cor 7:32-35

Brothers and sisters:
I should like you to be free of anxieties.
An unmarried man is anxious about the
things of the Lord,
how he may please the Lord.
But a married man is anxious about the
things of the world,
how he may please his wife, and he is
divided.
An unmarried woman or a virgin is
anxious about the things of the Lord,
so that she may be holy in both body
and spirit.
A married woman, on the other hand,
is anxious about the things of the
world,
how she may please her husband.
I am telling you this for your own benefit,
not to impose a restraint upon you,
but for the sake of propriety
and adherence to the Lord without
distraction.

Living Liturgy

Liturgy and Justice: Racism in the United States takes many forms and is at the heart of many other social oppressions, including economic inequality and health disparities. These disparities, set up by the housing, education, and healthcare systems, are only exacerbated by structural policies like "redlining." We are left with the stark reality that racism not only exists at the personal level, but on an institutional level as well.

When met with the harsh realities of racism and its effects, we do not want to acknowledge our role in oppression. But as community members helping to build the kingdom of God, we have a responsibility to open our hearts to the realities of the oppressed, specifically the most vulnerable. In doing so, we are able to hear the voice of God in its truest form. As a child born into poverty, Christ came to us hungry and lowly, and comes to us still in the form of the most vulnerable, impacted by the effects of racism, economic injustice, and health disparities. When we hear God's voice today, will we harden our hearts?

God's voice can look like the most vulnerable crying out for help. Are we listening? Will we recognize it? How do we stay focused on the harsh realities of the world without hardening our hearts to the voice of God?

PROMPTS FOR FAITH-SHARING

- How do you tend to respond to authority?

- Who have you experienced as a true prophet? Who has revealed God's voice to you?

- How do you lend your voice to Jesus's teachings?

See Appendix B, p. 310, for additional prompts.

SPIRITUALITY

GOSPEL ACCLAMATION
Matt 8:17

℟. Alleluia, alleluia.
Christ took away our infirmities
and bore our diseases.
℟. Alleluia, alleluia.

Gospel

Mark 1:29-39; L74B

On leaving the synagogue
  Jesus entered the house of
    Simon and Andrew with
    James and John.
Simon's mother-in-law lay sick
  with a fever.
They immediately told him
  about her.
He approached, grasped her
  hand, and helped her up.
Then the fever left her and she
  waited on them.

When it was evening, after
  sunset,
  they brought to him all who were ill
    or possessed by demons.
The whole town was gathered at the
  door.
He cured many who were sick with
  various diseases,
  and he drove out many demons,
  not permitting them to speak because
    they knew him.

Rising very early before dawn, he left
  and went off to a deserted place,
    where he prayed.
Simon and those who were with him
  pursued him
  and on finding him said, "Everyone is
    looking for you."
He told them, "Let us go on to the
  nearby villages
  that I may preach there also.
For this purpose have I come."
So he went into their synagogues,
  preaching and driving out demons
    throughout the whole of Galilee.

Reflecting on the Gospel

What often makes the difference between experiencing life as endless drudgery and utter misery and being alive with energy and joy is our state of health, be it physical, emotional, or spiritual. Illness and other profound losses color the whole of our perception. When an illness persists, whether one's own or that of a loved one, one can empathize with Job's feeling of utter weariness. One longs for relief, and there is sometimes no hope of happiness ever again.

From such a place of pain, we believers, like Job, pour out our hearts to God. Whether or not the healing we desire comes in the form we want, God is always with us, binding up our wounds and mending our broken hearts (Ps 147:3). In the gospels, it is Jesus who embodies this power to repair shattered minds, bodies, and spirits. Regardless of what stands in the way of our being able to receive and share the good news, Jesus binds up or casts out, thus releasing the power within us to experience and pass on God's love.

That is what happens with Simon's mother-in-law. Ablaze with fever, she lacks her usual energy for service to others. In much the same way that Jesus calls her son-in-law to be a disciple, Jesus approaches her and frees her from all that impedes her from responding to the good news. Just as Simon Peter leaves behind his net so he can "fish for people" (see Mark 1:17), so his mother-in-law, holding on to Jesus's hand as the fever leaves her, takes up her own ministry.

The verb *diekonoun*, usually translated as "served" or "waited on" (Mark 1:31), not only refers to serving dinner but also to a wide range of ministries, including ministries of the word and of the table (Acts 6:1-6), and service that is apostolic (Acts 1:25), financial (Luke 8:3), and administrative (Rom 16:1). Although this Scripture passage doesn't say what kind of service she engaged in, the early believers remembered how she ministered to and with them.

When Jesus heals people, he does not simply restore them to a former state of well-being. Rather, physical healings are outer signs of deeper transformation of body, mind, and spirit. As many people who have had a near-death experience attest, nothing is ever the same afterward. Similarly, Simon's mother-in-law experiences a "resurrection." The verb *egeiro*, "lifted up" (Mark 1:31), is the same word used for Jesus's resurrection. A new life has been given her, but not for her only. As with all disciples, it is a transformed life that is to be shared in service.

Jesus's purpose includes not only healing but also preaching (Mark 1:38-39). He frees people from whatever binds them so that they can join him in proclaiming the transforming power of God's love. Paul says that there is not really any choice in the matter. When one has experienced God's gracious healing love, one is obliged to tell it forth. In whatever circumstances we find ourselves, we are called to share God's love according to our own gifts and calling.

Preparing to Proclaim

Key words and phrases: "Everyone is looking for you."

To the point: Mark's depiction of Jesus is often noted for its frenetic pace, and that whirlwind is on full display in this passage. Jesus meets need after need, and he responds time and time again. He heals those with whom he has a connection, like Simon's mother-in-law, and he heals those who come to him as strangers. All who encounter him leave changed by the encounter, but at the speed he's working it's hard to see how he'd have time to interact personally, to see each person wholly as they are. Even at his frenetic pace, Jesus also prioritizes prayer—he rises early, before the crowds can catch him, and he finds a deserted place. There is perhaps a bit of tension here between his mission—"for this purpose have I come"—and his very human need to be alone, to regroup, to spend time with God.

Psalmist Preparation

Nearly all of us have experienced some sort of heartbreak. Unrequited love, unchosen singleness, infertility, miscarriage, bereavement, and on and on. Even the people of God are not exempt from the tragedies of this world broken by sin. But God promises to heal our heartbreaks. All of them, eventually. God's very self binds up our wounds, tending them with care and nursing us back to wholeness. As you prepare to proclaim this psalm, take some time to bring a heartbreak, past or present, into the presence of God. Thank God for whatever ways this pain has healed, and pray for further healing. Approach this psalm with empathy, knowing that every single person in your congregation has some heartbreak in need of God's healing care.

Making Connections

Between the readings: Job laments the pace of human life—it is too quick, it is too busy. Jesus shares in the quickness and the busyness, but he shows us that it is not in vain. When a human life makes God more present on earth, it is worth it. But we cannot do this alone; Jesus's retreat to prayer is key to making meaning out of what could have been seen as a drudgery, one long line of anonymous healings.

To experience: Whatever sort of work we do—manual labor, parenting, office work, scholarly work—can be sanctified to God. All of these can become part of bringing God's love and truth more fully into the world. But they can also run the risk of becoming tedious. Even Jesus retreats from his work, escaping the crowds for a deserted place in which to pray. God made us for rest too.

Homily Points

• The prophet Job speaks with brutal yet refreshing honesty in today's first reading. Job struggles to find purpose in the drudgery of everyday life. He bemoans how days and nights seem to go by with the mechanical movement of a weaver's shuttle until the thread runs out and death comes knocking. Do his laments sound familiar? Surely all of us have reasons to lament in our lives as individuals or as members of communities facing hardship. No human being is exempt from experiencing the spectrum of emotions, including anger, frustration, boredom, and other difficult emotions.

• Job demonstrates the value of bringing these emotions to prayer. God can handle lamentations—in fact, Scripture is filled with such prayers. How might we, as individuals and as a community, practice greater honesty in prayer? Where might we need to make space for honest lamentations?

• Jesus responds to prayers of lamentation, although not always in ways we hope. Today's gospel can be difficult to digest for people who prayed for healing, for themselves or for a loved one, and did not experience a cure like Simon's mother-in-law. Why did I or my loved one have to suffer? Why didn't Jesus answer our prayers for a complete cure? These are the sorts of difficult, honest questions Jesus wants us to bring to him. God's ways are deeply mysterious. Jesus is not Santa or a fairy godmother. He does not make all our wishes come true exactly as we imagine. Rather, Jesus remains close to us in our times of need. He listens to the longing of our hearts and promises healing will come in time.

CELEBRATION

Model Penitential Act

Presider: Jesus drives out demons in today's gospel, demonstrating God's power over the forces of evil that plague our world. Let us ask Jesus to rid our bodies of sin so that we might be better able to reflect God's love to the world . . . *[pause]*

    Lord Jesus, you heal the wounds of those who cry out to you: Lord, have mercy.

    Christ Jesus, you intercede for us at the right hand of the Father: Christ, have mercy.

    Lord Jesus, you preach the good news to all creation: Lord, have mercy.

Model Universal Prayer (Prayer of the Faithful)

Presider: Trusting in God's everlasting love for all of creation, let us lift in prayer the needs of our community and world.

Response: Lord, hear our prayer.

Bless the work of spiritual directors and all who listen to the stories of others . . .

Pour out your Spirit among survivors of sexual abuse and their support system . . .

Give relief to people plagued by mental illnesses . . .

Give us the courage to share our honest, difficult emotions in times of prayer . . .

Presider: Favor us, compassionate God, with your care so that we might grow in awareness of your hopes for the Body of Christ. We ask this through Jesus, our healing Lord who lives and reigns with you in the unity of the Holy Spirit, God for ever and ever. **Amen.**

Liturgy and Music

It's almost too easy for many of us to claim those words of Job. Are we working to live, or living to work? What is the right balance between work and the rest of life? What is the point of living if we are made miserable by the work demanded of us?

Think about all with whom you will minister this week. Whether you are a paid minister or a volunteer, this too is work. We hope that we can always approach this work acknowledging that it is pure gift and privilege that we are invited to this feast. And while we strive to hold joy and reverence for the invitation, we know, too, that the work it entails can seem overwhelming, never-ending, and thankless. If you are a leader of ministry, or a supervisor of labor in any vocation, take extra time to pray this week: Do we create a healthy workplace? Do we practice justice and compassion for the people we lead? Have we prioritized the labor over the laborer? Have we created an idol out of our worship while demeaning the very image and likeness of God before us?

Consider going an extra step in your preparation this week: check in with your priests and pastor. As resources continue to dwindle in many parishes across the country, more and more demands are made of our ordained leaders. We often expect clergy to be administrators, supervisors, preachers, coordinators, healers, counselors, and well-rounded humans—sometimes, all at once. If there's no way for you personally to relieve some of those duties, even a check-in might provide some much-needed recognition of their humanity in the midst of so much labor.

Remember that the gospel's mention of the "demons" that plague our communities includes that of mental illness. Some statistics show that twenty-five percent of our population struggles with this in some form, which means it is certainly present in our worshipping body. What a gift it would be to see this struggle recognized in our preaching, acknowledged in our hymn texts, and followed up by our outreach.

COLLECT

Let us pray.

Pause for silent prayer

Keep your family safe, O Lord, with
    unfailing care,
that, relying solely on the hope of
    heavenly grace,
they may be defended always by your
    protection.
Through our Lord Jesus Christ, your Son,
who lives and reigns with you in the unity
    of the Holy Spirit,
God, for ever and ever. **Amen.**

FIRST READING

Job 7:1-4, 6-7

Job spoke, saying:
    Is not man's life on earth a drudgery?
      Are not his days those of hirelings?
    He is a slave who longs for the shade,
      a hireling who waits for his wages.
    So I have been assigned months of
      misery,
      and troubled nights have been
      allotted to me.
    If in bed I say, "When shall I arise?"
      then the night drags on;
    I am filled with restlessness until the
      dawn.
    My days are swifter than a weaver's
      shuttle;
      they come to an end without hope.
    Remember that my life is like the wind;
      I shall not see happiness again.

RESPONSORIAL PSALM

Ps 147:1-2, 3-4, 5-6

℟. (cf. 3a) Praise the Lord, who heals the
    brokenhearted.
    or:
℟. Alleluia.

Praise the LORD, for he is good;
    sing praise to our God, for he is gracious;
    it is fitting to praise him.
The LORD rebuilds Jerusalem;
    the dispersed of Israel he gathers.

℟. Praise the Lord, who heals the
    brokenhearted.
    or:
℟. Alleluia.

He heals the brokenhearted
    and binds up their wounds.
He tells the number of the stars;
    he calls each by name.

℟. Praise the Lord, who heals the
    brokenhearted.
    or:
℟. Alleluia.

Great is our Lord and mighty in power;
    to his wisdom there is no limit.
The LORD sustains the lowly;
    the wicked he casts to the ground.

℟. Praise the Lord, who heals the
    brokenhearted.
    or:
℟. Alleluia.

SECOND READING

1 Cor 9:16-19, 22-23

Brothers and sisters:
If I preach the gospel, this is no reason for
    me to boast,
    for an obligation has been imposed on
    me,
    and woe to me if I do not preach it!
If I do so willingly, I have a recompense,
    but if unwillingly, then I have been
    entrusted with a stewardship.
What then is my recompense?
That, when I preach,
    I offer the gospel free of charge
    so as not to make full use of my right in
    the gospel.
Although I am free in regard to all,
    I have made myself a slave to all
    so as to win over as many as possible.
To the weak I became weak, to win over
    the weak.
I have become all things to all, to save at
    least some.
All this I do for the sake of the gospel,
    so that I too may have a share in it.

Living Liturgy

Liturgy and Justice: In the book of Job we find a man practiced in speaking about the happiness he will never find. We come to realize, however, Job is talking about life *on earth*. As builders of the kingdom of God, we are charged with staying focused on heaven. While we know we can actively create heaven on earth and experience the kingdom of God now, we get caught up in the realities we create for ourselves as earthly beings: the drudgery, the disappointment, the loneliness. We think things will never change and forget what God has planned for us.

When do we get caught up in the difficult realities of life and forget about what God has planned? How do we see ourselves reflected in Job's story? How are we called to build God's kingdom on earth, recognizing it is both "here" and "not yet"?

PROMPTS FOR FAITH-SHARING

• How does your work—at your job, at home, in your community—bring glory to God? Where might it present an opportunity to live your faith more fully?

• How do you carve out time for prayer in the midst of the busyness of your life?

• How do you respond to God's call to rest?

See Appendix B, p. 310, for additional prompts.

FEBRUARY 4, 2024
FIFTH SUNDAY IN ORDINARY TIME

SPIRITUALITY

GOSPEL ACCLAMATION
Luke 7:16

℟. Alleluia, alleluia.
A great prophet has arisen in our midst,
God has visited his people.
℟. Alleluia, alleluia.

Gospel

Mark 1:40-45; L77B

A leper came to Jesus and
    kneeling down begged him
    and said,
"If you wish, you can make
    me clean."
Moved with pity, he stretched
    out his hand,
    touched him, and said to him,
"I do will it. Be made clean."
The leprosy left him
    immediately, and he was
    made clean.
Then, warning him sternly, he
    dismissed him at once.

He said to him, "See that you tell no
    one anything,
    but go, show yourself to the priest
    and offer for your cleansing what
        Moses prescribed;
    that will be proof for them."

The man went away and began to
    publicize the whole matter.
He spread the report abroad
    so that it was impossible for Jesus to
        enter a town openly.
He remained outside in deserted
    places,
    and people kept coming to him from
        everywhere.

Reflecting on the Gospel

Those who suffer chronic illness may experience themselves as being outside all of the usual spheres of human activity. As the workplace carries on without them and their family goes about its business, they can feel isolated, out of the loop, helpless to contribute to the daily doings, and left alone with their own suffering. While Christianity does not have regulations concerning ritual uncleanness and separation from sick persons,

certain contagious conditions may require physical isolation. Even when this is not the case, many people avoid those with illness. It can seem to such a person that even God is keeping at a distance. The loneliness can be as bad as or worse than the illness itself.

In today's gospel, a person with leprosy leaves his prescribed separate space and reaches out for Jesus's help. He is tentative in his request: "If you wish, you can make me clean." Jesus responds with deep emotion. The verb *splanchnizomai*, usually translated "moved with compassion," literally means to "have a gut reaction"—that is, to be moved in the internal parts, the entrails. Ancient peoples considered the intestines as the seat of emotion. Mark's use of this strong verb emphasizes the depth of Jesus's feeling for the person with leprosy. Instead of recoiling from the man, Jesus reaches out his hand to him, touches him, and says how much he wants to be with the man and to see him "be made clean" and reintegrated into the heart of the life of the community. And so it happens.

Jesus's oneness with the person who had been ostracized because of his leprous condition is emphasized at the end of the episode, when Jesus experiences an outsider status similar to that of the man who had been ill. Jesus "remained outside in deserted places," perhaps not only because of the crowds who kept coming to him but also because he deliberately sought to be in solidarity with those who were relegated to isolated places, offering them the compassion of God who does want to be one with them.

This gospel offers encouragement to those who suffer illness or disability, so that they may reach out in prayer to Jesus and to the believing community, to ask not only for compassion but also for incorporation of them and their gifts into the community of faith. Likewise, it reminds those who are well not to avoid or to relegate to the sidelines those who are ill or who have disabilities but to stretch out their hands to them, recognizing the gifts that they bring for spreading the gospel. At the end of today's gospel, the man who had leprosy proclaims the story everywhere. Some translations render the expression *keryssein ton logon* as "publicize the whole matter," but it literally says "preach the word."

There is a powerful word to be preached both by those who are well and by those who have an illness or disability. How have you experienced God's compassion through illness or disability? How do persons with chronic illnesses or disabilities proclaim the gospel in your faith community?

Preparing to Proclaim

Key words and phrases: "I do will it. Be made clean."

To the point: Our reactions to the leper in this story may be understandably mixed. On the one hand, he rewards Jesus's generosity with immediate disobedience, making Jesus's life harder. On the other hand, who could blame him? He has been seen and received and loved in a way his disease made impossible. Jesus's willingness to stop and hear him healed an ailment that should have been incurable. He has been the recipient of such love and such a wondrous gift that he cannot help but overflow in gratitude. When he approached Jesus to ask for healing, he likely was hoping to return to the life he had before the leprosy set in. He had been cast out from family and friends, from religious observance and social participation. But Jesus's healing disrupts all that. Instead of going to the priest and restoring his ritual cleanliness, he *has* to go out and preach what he has seen.

Psalmist Preparation

The psalm reassures us that we are always able to bring our troubles to God. We can bring physical troubles, like the leper's illness; we can also bring spiritual troubles, acknowledging our sin. In both cases, God promises healing and to return us to a place of joy. As you prepare to proclaim this psalm, try to bring some of your own troubles before God. Do not hesitate to be honest with God in prayer; God is big enough to handle the worst of your disappointment or anger. Your troubles might not be resolved immediately just by bringing them to prayer, but try to rest in trust that God *wants* to heal them and bring you back to a place of wholeness and joy.

Making Connections

Between the readings: The first reading makes apparent why Jesus's healing is so important to the leper. Its last line reads almost like a sentence, but for a sickness rather than a crime: "He shall dwell apart, making his abode outside the camp." Leprosy was not only a terrible disease in itself; the fact that it separated its sufferers from their community gave it a social aspect as well. The leper Jesus encounters is not just sick in body; he is also, until he meets Jesus, extremely alone.

To experience: The COVID-19 pandemic changed how we think about sickness. In some ways this was good—we were reminded of how connected we are and that our actions have a meaningful effect on others. But one result has sometimes been an over-moralizing of getting sick. Instead of responding to illness with compassion, many of us now wonder what that person did wrong to get sick. As we continue to heal from the pandemic, consider how you and your community might return to a place of compassion for those who are ill.

Homily Points

• People with the leprosy skin condition —today known as Hansen's disease— described in today's first reading and gospel found themselves banished to the margins of society. Those in power deemed people with leprosy both physically and morally unclean. They believed the painful skin condition revealed some sort of sinful transgression made by the sick person and that anyone who encountered such a person would also become unclean. Sadly, similar ostracization continues to be practiced today. Time and again people with privilege cast fellow human beings aside because of differences in race, ethnicity, gender, sexual orientation, religion, income, and abilities. Who are the modern day "lepers" in our community? How can this congregation follow the model of Jesus and encounter those on the margins with mercy and compassion?

• Jesus would have been keenly aware of the stigmas against people with leprosy. He knew what it meant to be caught speaking—much less touching—someone with this disease. Yet Jesus did not back away. Rather, he moved closer. Jesus touched the scabbed, swollen flesh of the man kneeling in front of him and made him clean.

• Jesus's actions remind us of the healing qualities of appropriate touch. Human beings are made to be in communion with each other in physical, embodied ways. We hug, hold hands, offer a pat on the back, and touch in other ways as signs of support and affection. Who in our community is isolated and could use a visit? Who is experiencing grief and might find solace in a hug? After asking for and receiving consent, such actions can be sources of healing.

CELEBRATION

Model Penitential Act

Presider: In today's responsorial psalm we pray: "I turn to you, Lord, in time of trouble, and you fill me with the joy of salvation." Let us turn now to the Lord and ask for forgiveness for the times we have caused trouble for ourselves or others . . . *[pause]*

 Lord Jesus, you shine light on those who dwell in darkness: Lord, have mercy.

 Christ Jesus, you forgive our sins: Christ, have mercy.

 Lord Jesus, you nourish us with your body and blood: Lord, have mercy.

Model Universal Prayer (Prayer of the Faithful)

Presider: Almighty God, you listen to the needs of your beloved people. In hope we pray.

Response: Lord, hear our prayer.

Foster respect and dialogue between Christian and Jewish people . . .

Help us show appreciation for custodians, technicians, plumbers, and all whose labor keeps our buildings open . . .

Heal those who face bullying or find themselves the targets of harassment . . .

Raise up the callings of women in our parish community . . .

Presider: Strengthen us, God of all goodness, with the recognition and compassion to respond to the needs of the world. We ask this through Jesus Christ our Lord who lives and reigns with you in the unity of the Holy Spirit, God for ever and ever. **Amen.**

Liturgy and Music

Being an imitator of Christ requires our reaching out to the margins of the world. There is no way around the reality that our baptismal call insists that we claim this as our mission, no matter how uncomfortable or how inconvenient. Who is on the margins around us? Who is not yet at the table? Who is sitting right in front of us, begging to be seen?

We have an incredible opportunity as we gather around this table: when we do liturgy well, this can be perhaps one of the only safe places where people feel like they can truly belong, where they are safe and welcomed and loved. If we are careless, ill-prepared, or unwilling to be open to the new ways God calls us to recognize the Body of Christ in our midst, we can be the last place one might choose to be on a Sunday morning. Perhaps the lowest-hanging fruit that may help us to work toward better diversity, equity, and inclusion in our community is that of music. Consider this checklist: What language are we singing in? What style or styles of music are employed? What types of people are represented in our hymn texts or in the compositional voice we have elevated? Is there room for women's voices? Do we assume able-bodied participants? Have we done our homework about appropriately including music that is not born of the dominant culture? Whose voice is amplified? How is the congregation prepared to join in the song with full, conscious, and active voices?

Recall the actions of the one who is healed in the gospel. He felt seen and valued, maybe for the first time in a very long time. Imagine what that might mean for us to see and value the marginalized through our singing, through our outreach, through our full-voiced inclusion of each and every person, declaring their dignity and worthiness. What growth is possible by our attention to imitating this radical act of Christ's healing love?

COLLECT
Let us pray.

Pause for silent prayer

O God, who teach us that you abide
in hearts that are just and true,
grant that we may be so fashioned by
 your grace
as to become a dwelling pleasing to you.
Through our Lord Jesus Christ, your Son,
who lives and reigns with you in the unity
 of the Holy Spirit,
God, for ever and ever. **Amen.**

FIRST READING
Lev 13:1-2, 44-46

The LORD said to Moses and Aaron,
 "If someone has on his skin a scab or
  pustule or blotch
  which appears to be the sore of leprosy,
  he shall be brought to Aaron, the priest,
  or to one of the priests among his
   descendants.
If the man is leprous and unclean,
  the priest shall declare him unclean
  by reason of the sore on his head.

"The one who bears the sore of leprosy
  shall keep his garments rent and his
   head bare,
  and shall muffle his beard;
  he shall cry out, 'Unclean, unclean!'
As long as the sore is on him he shall
   declare himself unclean,
  since he is in fact unclean.
He shall dwell apart, making his abode
  outside the camp."

RESPONSORIAL PSALM
Ps 32:1-2, 5, 11

℟. (7) I turn to you, Lord, in time of
trouble, and you fill me with the joy
of salvation.

Blessed is he whose fault is taken away,
whose sin is covered.
Blessed the man to whom the LORD
imputes not guilt,
in whose spirit there is no guile.

℟. I turn to you, Lord, in time of trouble,
and you fill me with the joy of
salvation.

Then I acknowledged my sin to you,
my guilt I covered not.
I said, "I confess my faults to the LORD,"
and you took away the guilt of my sin.

℟. I turn to you, Lord, in time of trouble,
and you fill me with the joy of
salvation.

Be glad in the LORD and rejoice, you just;
exult, all you upright of heart.

℟. I turn to you, Lord, in time of trouble,
and you fill me with the joy of
salvation.

SECOND READING
1 Cor 10:31–11:1

Brothers and sisters,
whether you eat or drink, or whatever
you do,
do everything for the glory of God.
Avoid giving offense, whether to the Jews
or Greeks or the church of God,
just as I try to please everyone in every
way,
not seeking my own benefit but that of
the many,
that they may be saved.
Be imitators of me, as I am of Christ.

Living Liturgy

Liturgy and Community: In the second reading, we are instructed to do everything for the glory of God: "Brothers and sisters, whether you eat or drink, or whatever you do, do everything for the glory of God." This passage helps us consider what lens we use for our work in the world, no matter where or how we decide to be of service. In the same way, we are instructed to move through the world for the glory of God. Whether it's in work, relationships, play, or pleasure, having our mind on God helps focus our life to be one with a Spirit lens.

What does it mean to do everything for the glory of God? How can we lead a Spirit-filled life in even our most mundane endeavors?

PROMPTS FOR FAITH-SHARING

• When is a time you felt that your plans had been disrupted by Jesus? How did you respond?

• The leper's illness separated him from his community; what keeps you from living in full communion with yours? How might you ask Jesus to heal that?

• The psalm reassures us that God is with us in troubled times and wants to bring us through them to a place of joy. What troubles do you need to bring to God right now? How can your community help you endure them?

See Appendix B, p. 310, for additional prompts.

SEASON OF LENT

If today you hear his voice,
harden not your hearts.

Gospel   Matt 6:1-6, 16-18; L219

Jesus said to his disciples:
"Take care not to perform righ-
    teous deeds
  in order that people may see them;
  otherwise, you will have no
      recompense from your
      heavenly Father.
When you give alms,
  do not blow a trumpet before you,
  as the hypocrites do in the
      synagogues and in the streets
  to win the praise of others.
Amen, I say to you,
  they have received their reward.
But when you give alms,
  do not let your left hand know
      what your right is doing,
  so that your almsgiving may be
      secret.
And your Father who sees in secret
    will repay you.

"When you pray,
  do not be like the hypocrites,
  who love to stand and pray in the
      synagogues and on street corners
  so that others may see them.
Amen, I say to you,
  they have received their reward.
But when you pray, go to your inner room,
  close the door, and pray to your Father in
      secret.
And your Father who sees in secret will
    repay you.

"When you fast,
  do not look gloomy like the hypocrites.
They neglect their appearance,
  so that they may appear to others to be
      fasting.
Amen, I say to you, they have received their
    reward.
But when you fast,
  anoint your head and wash your face,
  so that you may not appear to be fasting,
  except to your Father who is hidden.
And your Father who sees what is hidden
    will repay you."

See Appendix A, p. 270, for the other readings.

Reflecting on the Gospel

We are deeply social creatures. Humans love to know what's going on with other humans. We are naturally inclined to learn as much about one another as we can, from watching other people at the grocery store to following the personal lives of celebrities. We even greet one another by asking, "How are you?" This penchant for knowledge means that we are also inclined to delight in the extremes, especially when others have successes or failures. Traffic accidents can cause backups not because lanes are blocked, but because everyone passing it is looking at what happened. Our curiosity bends in all directions.

That's why today's reading can be so hard for us. Do good things without being noticed? Do *anything* without being noticed? It's counterintuitive, especially for actions that we would be pleased to share with others. Today's gospel goes against our natural inclinations to know and be known, because it reminds us that our first and primary "known-ness" is through God.

This gospel is often presented as a critique of the desire for approval, or a reprimand for those who are boastful about good deeds. There's another way to view it, however: as an invitation to delight in the private relationship that we have with our Creator, and the fullness of being seen by God's eyes. Nothing we do goes unseen, even if we feel that way in our day-to-day life. No frustration or act of love occurs in a vacuum. Our Father sees everything we do, and shares it with us, whether our life is filled with frustration or delight.

Today is Ash Wednesday, when Catholics traditionally decide to begin an extra act of penance or to give up something indulgent. Perhaps this year, instead of announcing it and asking for accountability, the task you take up is less performative. Is it possible to focus, instead, on an intimate relationship with the Lord? What would a task directed at fostering time with Christ look like? The gospel offers an opportunity, instead of designing your Lenten journey to correspond with those around you, to take time aligning it with Christ, in a private exchange of devotion, to nourish that unique relationship.

It is not sinful to share successes and moments of joyful faith with community. It helps us be better Catholics and emphasizes shared social mores. However, this gospel is a reminder to us that our primary relationship is with God. When God knows what we do, it is fully and deeply known. God knows our innermost thoughts and desires, and God is equally present to our outward actions and choices. In this way, demonstrating our devotion or prayer practices for others is an additional gift that may inspire, but it is by no means necessary to impact ourselves and God. Your primary audience is, and always has been, the benevolent Creator who knit you in your mother's womb.

Preparing to Proclaim

Key words and phrases: "And your Father who sees what is hidden will repay you."

To the point: In a world where everyone has a platform and in which our lives are often performed for the sake of content creation, this gospel reminds us that Lent is not performative. The work of Lent is really God's work, and it is not visible in ways that can be posted on social media. The work of Lent is really work on our hearts, which need renewal and conversion and transformation. It is hidden, quiet, humble work, but God sees and knows it. God partners with our own efforts, small though they may be.

Model Penitential Act

Presider: Let us enter this season of Lent mindful of our sins so that we may come to know the greatness of God's mercy . . . *[pause]*

Confiteor: I confess . . .

Model Universal Prayer (Prayer of the Faithful)

Presider: Trusting in God's mercy and the greatness of God's compassion, let us offer our prayers and petitions.

Response: Lord, hear our prayer.

Inspire the prayers of the church to lead to acts of justice on behalf of people who are oppressed . . .

Further the reach of humanitarian aid organizations who provide food, clean water, and shelter to people in need . . .

Keep healthy and safe all communities who will receive our alms during the season of Lent . . .

Sustain your people gathered here and in churches across the world during our times of fasting . . .

Presider: Embolden us, Lord we pray, to begin this season of Lent with prayerful hearts so that we may answer your call to be ambassadors for Christ your Son, who lives and reigns with you and the Holy Spirit, God forever and ever. **Amen.**

Living Liturgy

Liturgy and Spirituality: We have all heard many versions about the "right" way to begin the season of Lent. As children, it can feel like a challenge or a game to see who will last the longest before giving in to their indulgences. As we grow older, we are challenged to add something to our lives, like more kindness or generosity toward others.

Although the messages may change throughout the years, the core meaning remains: What activities, indulgences, or ways of treating our neighbor keep us from growing in relationship with ourselves, others, and God?

COLLECT

Let us pray.

Pause for silent prayer

Grant, O Lord, that we may begin with holy fasting
this campaign of Christian service,
so that, as we take up battle against spiritual evils,
we may be armed with weapons of self-restraint.
Through our Lord Jesus Christ, your Son,
who lives and reigns with you in the unity of the Holy Spirit,
God, for ever and ever. **Amen.**

FOR REFLECTION

• What Lenten practices have been fruitful for you in the past? What disciplines are you taking up this year?

• How do your Lenten disciplines make room for God to work in your heart? What transformation are you hoping for?

• How can you seek out the hidden, quiet work of God? How can you trust in transformations that we may not always see?

See Appendix B, p. 310, for additional questions.

Homily Points

• Today's reading from the prophet Joel features several powerful verbs, among them: return, proclaim, call, gather, assemble, and spare. Consider selecting one of these or another verb to reflect on this Lenten season. See how one word can impact your spiritual practices over the next forty days.

• Saint Paul proclaims, "We are ambassadors for Christ." Ambassador is a serious title. People who are ambassadors are entrusted to represent a person or industry with great commitment and dignity. How will you be an ambassador for Christ this Lent? What practices of prayer, fasting, and almsgiving can our community take on in hopes of drawing others into Christ's everlasting love?

SPIRITUALITY

GOSPEL ACCLAMATION
Matt 4:4b

One does not live on bread alone,
but on every word that comes forth from the
mouth of God.

Gospel

Mark 1:12-15; L23B

**The Spirit drove Jesus out into the
desert,
and he remained in the desert for
forty days, tempted by Satan.
He was among wild beasts,
and the angels ministered to him.**

**After John had been arrested,
Jesus came to Galilee proclaiming
the gospel of God:
"This is the time of fulfillment.
The kingdom of God is at hand.
Repent, and believe in the gospel."**

Reflecting on the Gospel

In today's gospel, Jesus invites all to choose a change in lifestyle. It is not imposed, but failure to accept it will have disastrous consequences. "Repentance," *metanoia*, is a change of mind and heart, a lifelong process of transformation. Jesus is not asking for the temporary foregoing of something pleasurable, like giving up chocolate for Lent. The *metanoia* to which Jesus invites us is both a turning away from whatever inhibits the full flourishing of the divine intent for creation and a turning toward the source of divine love. There is no better time to begin turning than now. Good intentions to make better lifestyle choices in the future become empty rhetoric in light of Jesus's urgent invitation: "This is the time," the *kairos*. *Kairos* means the opportune time, the right time, as distinguished from *chronos*, simple chronological time.

This crucial time is marked by the presence of two simultaneous forces: the divine Spirit who empowers us to choose what is of God, and Satan, the adversary, pulling us in the opposite direction. In the gospel, the Spirit drives Jesus into the desert, where choices are clearer. In biblical tradition, the desert symbolizes the place where these two opposing forces meet. The desert can be a place of danger, where wild beasts dwell, or where revolutionaries hide out. It was a place of testing for Israel, where they turned on their leaders and murmured against God (Num 10:11–21:34). In prophetic tradition, the desert wandering became romanticized into a honeymoon time for Israel, where the people could be alone with their beloved God, with nothing to distract from their heart-to-heart sharing. So too, for Jesus, the Spirit is with him in the desert, but also the adversary—all those systems and forces that are opposed to God.

Unlike Matthew and Luke, Mark does not describe in detail the precise ways in which Jesus was tempted. What Mark emphasizes is that God's power is stronger than satanic forces. Using Greek verbs in the imperfect tense, which indicate ongoing action that began in the past, Mark says that the divine presence is always with Jesus, as angels "ministered to him" (*diekonoun auto*). Mark's entire Gospel is framed by this phrase. At the close of the gospel, Mary Magdalene and the other Galilean women who followed Jesus to Jerusalem and stood at the cross "ministered to him," *diekonoun auto* (Mark 15:41).

The good news that Jesus announces and embodies is that God's ministering, comforting, and empowering presence is at hand now, at this *kairos* time, and at every moment, especially in times of crisis. Jesus does not announce that God will rescue us from experiencing bleak times of trial, or of frightening chaos, as with the out-of-control flood waters in the story of Noah. The good news is that God never abandons the beloved creation and all the living beings with whom the covenant has been made.

To accept this good news is to accept the invitation to change—to conform our manner of living to God's ways. To what change in lifestyle is the Spirit leading you this Lent?

Preparing to Proclaim

Key words and phrases: "The kingdom of God is at hand."

To the point: One of the Luminous Mysteries of the Rosary, introduced in 2002 by John Paul II, is Jesus's proclamation of the kingdom of God. It is a different mystery from most of the others—rather than commemorating one moment from the life of Jesus or Mary, it gives us the heart of his work, an ongoing process throughout his public life. This gospel perhaps gives us the one moment that best represents this mystery: Jesus emerges from his desert pilgrimage and starts proclaiming. That this is a Mystery of Light is telling: light is emerging here, scattering darkness before it and illuminating what was once unclear. It is also a moment of light in Jesus's life as he emerges from the darkness of his desert temptation and into the light of public life and work.

Psalmist Preparation

This psalm affirms that God is our guide and companion on the journey of life. God shows us the way to go in order to end up in union with God. The image of "the way" can be a powerful one, reminding us that this life is a journey, a pilgrimage. It brings both challenges and joys. We can lose our way, too, stumbling for a while when we are not in tune with God. As you prepare to reflect on this psalm, spend some time reflecting on your faith journey thus far. Where have you come from? Where do you hope you are going? How has God been accompanying you as you go?

Making Connections

Between the readings: The first reading gives us the end of the Noah story, in which God establishes a covenant and promises never again to send such a devastating flood. In the second reading, Peter reads the Noah narrative as a prefiguration of baptism. The water of baptism cleanses not our bodies but the stain of original sin, leaving us with new hearts ready to hear and act on the word of God.

To experience: Jesus's public ministry starts from a moment of crisis. It is in response to John's arrest that Jesus begins his proclamation of the kingdom. For us, too, moments of crisis are often moments of clarity. They present us with an opportunity to take stock of our lives and our priorities and to reassess how we are spending our time and resources. They are a privileged moment for hearing God's call.

Homily Points

• Today's readings remind us of the divine presence in the created world. The first reading from Genesis tells of God's covenant with Noah and all living creatures. God promises to set a rainbow in the clouds to serve as a sign of the covenant with earth. Never again will flood waters be used to destroy humankind.

• The gospel situates Jesus in an opposite type of climate: the desert. Satan tempts Jesus on harsh, barren land and still, the Son of God comes out victorious. Let today's readings serve as an invitation to spend time in nature this Lent. Try to get out on those pristine days where the temperature feels just right, as well as days when the climate pushes you out of your comfort zone. Remember that the divine is present in all times and places.

• The second readings throughout Lent assert the importance of baptism as the entryway into the paschal mystery of Jesus. In the waters of baptism, God's mercy embraces us. We are clothed as a new creation and welcomed into the life of Christ. Lent is a time to recall our own baptismal promises, as well as journey with the catechumens who will be baptized at the Easter Vigil. The presence of catechumens is a great gift to the church. They remind us of our commitment to Christian discipleship and the power of saying "yes" to God's call. Let us keep all catechumens and their sponsors in prayer this Lent.

CELEBRATION

Model Penitential Act

Presider: Jesus faces forty days of temptation in the desert. Afterwards, he goes to Galilee and proclaims to the people: "Repent, and believe in the gospel." Let us answer Christ's call to repent as we begin this Eucharist . . . *[pause]*

   Confiteor: I confess . . .

Model Universal Prayer (Prayer of the Faithful)

Presider: Confident in God's presence among creation, let us offer our prayers and petitions.

Response: Lord, hear our prayer.

Envelope in your love all catechumens and candidates preparing to receive the sacraments of initiation this Easter . . .

Expand the hearts of judges, lawyers, and all who work in the criminal justice system . . .

Relieve the temptations of people addicted to pornography . . .

Bless the lands on which we live, work, and worship . . .

Presider: Creator God, you sustained Jesus through his time of temptation in the desert. Sustain us through our prayers and acts of service, that we may be signs of your love to the world. We offer this prayer through Christ our Lord. **Amen.**

Liturgy and Music

As musicians, we have a special relationship with the sacred space. When the sanctuary is filled with community, the space has its own nature. When empty, the same space is a different place.

In the days to come, I invite you to spend some time each week in reflection, and if possible, to do so alone within those empty spaces that are home to your ministry.

As Lent begins, we see Jesus driven alone into the desert, where he is tempted and tested. At the same time, John emerges from the wilderness to begin his ministry as herald of the coming Messiah, and the urgent need for all to repent. For both of these cousins, the wilderness is harsh, lonely and desolate, a place to prepare for the important work to come.

For most of the faithful, the Triduum is far away on the distant horizon. Meanwhile, many of you are already rehearsing music for those highest of holy days. For you, there is a kind of dispensation that attends your solitary duty to rehearse new Alleluias or Easter anthems in the cold, empty church during the late winter weeks of February.

And as we labor to learn the notes, rhythms, and dynamics that will be unleashed at the great Easter Vigil, we know that the walls of the sacred space themselves are rehearsing their work: to be a place that resonates and rings with the jubilant strains of new life when the time in the wilderness has ended.

COLLECT

Let us pray.

Pause for silent prayer

Grant, almighty God,
through the yearly observances of holy
    Lent,
that we may grow in understanding
of the riches hidden in Christ
and by worthy conduct pursue their
    effects.
Through our Lord Jesus Christ, your Son,
who lives and reigns with you in the unity
    of the Holy Spirit,
God, for ever and ever. **Amen.**

FIRST READING
Gen 9:8-15

God said to Noah and to his sons with
    him:
"See, I am now establishing my covenant
    with you
    and your descendants after you
    and with every living creature that was
      with you:
    all the birds, and the various tame and
      wild animals
    that were with you and came out of the
      ark.
I will establish my covenant with you,
    that never again shall all bodily
      creatures be destroyed
    by the waters of a flood;
    there shall not be another flood to
      devastate the earth."
God added:
"This is the sign that I am giving for all
    ages to come,
    of the covenant between me and you
    and every living creature with you:
    I set my bow in the clouds to serve as
      a sign
    of the covenant between me and the
      earth.
When I bring clouds over the earth,
    and the bow appears in the clouds,
    I will recall the covenant I have made
    between me and you and all living
      beings,
    so that the waters shall never again
      become a flood
    to destroy all mortal beings."

RESPONSORIAL PSALM

Ps 25:4-5, 6-7, 8-9

℟. (cf. 10) Your ways, O Lord, are love
  and truth to those who keep your
  covenant.

Your ways, O LORD, make known to me;
  teach me your paths,
guide me in your truth and teach me,
  for you are God my savior.

℟. Your ways, O Lord, are love and truth
  to those who keep your covenant.

Remember that your compassion, O LORD,
  and your love are from of old.
In your kindness remember me,
  because of your goodness, O LORD.

℟. Your ways, O Lord, are love and truth
  to those who keep your covenant.

Good and upright is the LORD,
  thus he shows sinners the way.
He guides the humble to justice,
  and he teaches the humble his way.

℟. Your ways, O Lord, are love and truth
  to those who keep your covenant.

SECOND READING

1 Pet 3:18-22

Beloved:
Christ suffered for sins once,
  the righteous for the sake of the
    unrighteous,
  that he might lead you to God.
Put to death in the flesh,
  he was brought to life in the Spirit.
In it he also went to preach to the spirits
    in prison,
  who had once been disobedient
  while God patiently waited in the days
    of Noah
  during the building of the ark,
  in which a few persons, eight in all,
  were saved through water.
This prefigured baptism, which saves you
    now.
It is not a removal of dirt from the body
  but an appeal to God for a clear
    conscience,
  through the resurrection of Jesus Christ,
  who has gone into heaven
  and is at the right hand of God,
  with angels, authorities, and powers
    subject to him.

Living Liturgy

Liturgy and Spirituality: In 1910, Helen Todd, an American women's suffrage activist and state factory inspector, gave a speech on the condition of working women. Along with a group of fellow activists, the words "Bread for all, and Roses too" rose up as an influential phrase in her speech, inspiring the writing of many poems and songs of similar names.

In today's verse before the gospel, we are reminded that we do not live by bread alone, but also by the word of God. This message parallels the words of Helen Todd, especially the ways we can live a fulfilling and Spirit-filled life. With our mind and hearts on God, we know that the "Roses" we seek in life, such as books, music, and other forms of leisure, can sustain our spirit when times are hard and food is not enough. Our life feels less purposeful when we are without that which animates us, including the word of God.

What animates our Spirit-filled lives? In what ways does the word of God inspire us, in ways food or other basic needs do not? What activist inspires you to live out the word of God?

PROMPTS FOR FAITH-SHARING

• How do you feel called to proclaim God's kingdom in your current season of life?

• What does your baptism mean to you and how do you try to live out your baptismal identity?

• The psalm uses the image of "the way" to represent our journey of faith. Reflect on your own faith journey—where you have been, where you are going, and how God accompanies you as you go.

See Appendix B, p. 310, for additional prompts.

SPIRITUALITY

GOSPEL ACCLAMATION
cf. Matt 17:5

From the shining cloud the Father's voice is
    heard:
This is my beloved Son, listen to him.

Gospel

Mark 9:2-10; L26B

**Jesus took Peter, James, and
    John
    and led them up a high
        mountain apart by
        themselves.
And he was transfigured before
    them,
    and his clothes became
        dazzling white,
    such as no fuller on earth
        could bleach them.
Then Elijah appeared to them
    along with Moses,
    and they were conversing with
        Jesus.
Then Peter said to Jesus in reply,
    "Rabbi, it is good that we are here!
Let us make three tents:
    one for you, one for Moses, and one
        for Elijah."
He hardly knew what to say, they were
    so terrified.
Then a cloud came, casting a shadow
    over them;
    from the cloud came a voice,
    "This is my beloved Son. Listen to
        him."
Suddenly, looking around, they no
    longer saw anyone
    but Jesus alone with them.**

**As they were coming down from the
    mountain,
    he charged them not to relate what
        they had seen to anyone,
    except when the Son of Man had
        risen from the dead.
So they kept the matter to themselves,
    questioning what rising from the
        dead meant.**

Reflecting on the Gospel

What kind of parents would meekly comply with an order to kill their only
child? What kind of God would ask such a thing? Disturbing questions arise
from today's first reading, which opens: "God put Abraham to the test." The
narrative that follows sounds a lot like what Scripture scholars have come to
call a "call story." God calls Abraham by name, and Abraham twice responds
with the same words Samuel used in his
own call story (in 1 Samuel 3) and that
Isaiah did in his: "Here I am!"

Call stories emphasize the eager willingness of a person to respond to God,
as well as the great sacrifices they are
asked to make for the sake of the mission that God offers them. Genesis 12,
prior to today's passage, recounts the
call of Abraham and his willingness,
even at the age of seventy-five, to leave
his home in Haran to journey into the
unknown. Abraham has shown himself
responsive to all that God asks; he has
committed himself fully to God in a
covenant (Gen 15:1-21). Unsettling questions arise as we ponder why God would
now demand that Abraham sacrifice his
precious son, an act that would seem to
make impossible the fulfillment of God's promise of numerous descendants.

Might it be that the biblical writer is relating how Abraham continued to
experience trials and tribulations, even as he tried his best to follow God's call?
Having the mindset that whatever happens is God's doing, the writer attributes
the "testing" of Abraham to God's intent. Did Abraham find, as we do, that
even when we try to be most faithful, tragic things still happen? Or does this
story in fact recall a time when Isaac's life was in jeopardy and Abraham felt
responsible, and helpless to protect him? What parent has not had such frightening experiences? Parents also know that loving their children demands that
they be willing to let them go. All love relationships flourish only when there
is freedom to let go of what is most precious, so as to receive it back as a gift.
Even if Abraham had lost Isaac, that would not have nullified God's covenant
of love.

The story of Abraham and Isaac invites us to reflect on times when, even
though we try to be faithful, we do not correctly hear what God is saying.
In rabbinic tradition, some sages have interpreted this text not as a test of
Abraham but of his misunderstanding. The author of one of the earliest
midrashic works, called Genesis Rabbah, puts these startling words into God's
mouth as he speaks to Abraham: "What, do you think I meant for you to
slay him? No! I said only to take him up . . . and now I say take him down."
Perhaps an important lesson to be drawn here, then, is that practices of communal discernment offer an alternative model to that of relying on the decisions of one person who might misunderstand what God has said. Often God
speaks through a community of believers more clearly than through a single
individual.

Preparing to Proclaim

Key words and phrases: "This is my beloved Son. Listen to him."

To the point: Like last week, this gospel tells the account of one of the Rosary's Luminous Mysteries. The Transfiguration is a mysterious episode. It seems hard to describe—Jesus's clothes became white, but whiter than you're thinking, Mark seems to say. The whiteness is bright enough to dazzle; there seems to be some kind of light here. There is also darkness; a cloud comes and casts a shadow over the disciples on the mountain. Not much is clear about what this is or what it means. But one thing is clear: the voice from the cloud that says "This is my beloved Son. Listen to him." Following Christ does not always make life easy or clarify our decisions, but when we rest in what the disciples heard on that mountain, we can be assured that it is the right thing to do.

Psalmist Preparation

This is a psalm of reciprocal faithfulness. The psalmist pledges to walk with God and to fulfill his vows; this is in response to God's lasting faithfulness, his love that endures beyond death. As you prepare to proclaim this psalm, think about the evidence from your own life of God's faithfulness. When have you had a promise fulfilled or a calling come to life? Think also about your response to God in your life. How do you walk with God? How do you fulfill the promises of a follower of God?

Making Connections

Between the readings: Like the gospel, the first reading has a mysterious encounter between humanity and God. The sacrifice of Isaac is a hard story to grapple with; the idea that God would call Abraham to something so obviously immoral is disquieting. But Abraham shows here that his faith is not dependent on God's gifts; he is ready to sacrifice even his cherished promise of descendants in order to keep following God.

To experience: Our own encounters with God are rarely as remarkable as the transfiguration. We are more likely to hear God's voice in a whisper than with the clarity the disciples heard on the mountain. But God's voice, whether whispering or thundering, always speaks love. God is always trying to get through to us that we are wildly, unreservedly loved. God looks on us, and God loves us, and God is well pleased in us.

Homily Points

• Today's readings focus on two beloved sons of adoring parents: Isaac, the child promised to Abraham and Sarah; and Jesus, the Son of God. In the first reading, Abraham faces an unimaginable call from God to offer his son Isaac, "your only one, whom you love," as a sacrifice. The same God who promised Abraham that his descendants would be "as countless as the stars of the sky" is now asking him to give up his only son? No doubt with an aching heart, Abraham responds to his Creator: "Here I am!"

• Abraham displays incredible trust in God and in God's ability to fulfil promises in new, mysterious ways. God rewards Abraham's trust by allowing a ram to take Isaac's place on the altar of sacrifice. God may never ask us to make such a dramatic sacrifice, but God does ask us for complete trust. Especially in times of destruction and death, God wants us to be assured of God's steadfast love for us. We will surely be tested, and as with Abraham, God will give us the strength to persevere.

• The gospel of the transfiguration also centers on a son who will be sacrificed. The cross is a scandalous and integral part of Jesus's narrative. We cannot jump to resurrection without journeying though the pain of the cross. From the cloud, God calls Peter, James, John, and all disciples in the future to listen to God's beloved Son. Listen to his passion. Listen to his death. Listen for his glory in the world to come.

Model Penitential Act

Presider: Saint Paul poses a profound question in today's second reading: "If God is for us, who can be against us?" Trusting in God's mercy and compassion for us, let us confess our sins and ask for healing . . . *[pause]*

 Confiteor: I confess . . .

Model Universal Prayer (Prayer of the Faithful)

Presider: Loving God, in you rests all our hope. With confidence, we offer our prayers and petitions.

Response: Lord, hear our prayer.

Bless the relationships between godparents, sponsors, and those people preparing for the sacraments of initiation . . .

Strengthen government assistance for families struggling to find adequate food, housing, healthcare, and education . . .

Grant comfort and safety to children living in abusive homes . . .

Inspire the spiritual directors, writers, and artists in our midst . . .

Presider: Strengthen us, gracious God, in our practices of prayer, fasting, and almsgiving this Lent. Help us to be attentive to the needs of our neighbors and the world, so that all may come to know your beloved Son. We ask this through Christ our Lord. **Amen.**

Liturgy and Music

Each year the gospel account of our Lord's transfiguration gleams like a shining jewel among the somber Scriptures appointed for the early weeks of Lent. The experiences of the startled and confused disciples were far from what they could have anticipated when they trudged up that hill with Jesus. Indeed, their amazement reminds us that, although we experience more than we can understand, the light of Jesus Christ shines around and within us, erasing our confusion.

The empty sacred space is transformed and brought to life when the community fills it. When we sing, our imperfect prayers are transformed and made more profound in the arms of sacred music. Any time our inmost thoughts and words move from silence into sound, they become more real, just as seeing was believing for the disciples who beheld the transfigured Son of God.

The climactic message from God at the moment of his Son's transfiguration is specific: "This is my beloved Son. Listen to him." Are we listening?

We use our ears to hear, tune, and correct the pitches sung by our choirs, to shape the roundest, vowel sounds and most perfect diction. But are we listening to the love song that is being sung? The Divine Singer wants to change our hearts. If we are not listening to his voice, how can we help those whose voices we are training? In our ministry as servant leaders, our work is to listen to him, but also to help God's beloved in their listening.

COLLECT

Let us pray.

Pause for silent prayer

O God, who have commanded us
to listen to your beloved Son,
be pleased, we pray,
to nourish us inwardly by your word,
that, with spiritual sight made pure,
we may rejoice to behold your glory.
Through our Lord Jesus Christ, your Son,
who lives and reigns with you in the unity
 of the Holy Spirit,
God, for ever and ever. **Amen.**

FIRST READING
Gen 22:1-2, 9a, 10-13, 15-18

God put Abraham to the test.
He called to him, "Abraham!"
"Here I am!" he replied.
Then God said:
 "Take your son Isaac, your only one,
  whom you love,
 and go to the land of Moriah.
There you shall offer him up as a
 holocaust
on a height that I will point out to you."

When they came to the place of which
 God had told him,
 Abraham built an altar there and
  arranged the wood on it.
Then he reached out and took the knife to
 slaughter his son.
But the LORD's messenger called to him
 from heaven,
 "Abraham, Abraham!"
"Here I am!" he answered.
"Do not lay your hand on the boy," said the
 messenger.
"Do not do the least thing to him.
I know now how devoted you are to God,
 since you did not withhold from me
  your own beloved son."
As Abraham looked about,
 he spied a ram caught by its horns in
  the thicket.
So he went and took the ram
 and offered it up as a holocaust in place
  of his son.

Again the LORD's messenger called to
 Abraham from heaven and said:
 "I swear by myself, declares the LORD,
that because you acted as you did
in not withholding from me your
 beloved son,
I will bless you abundantly
 and make your descendants as
  countless
as the stars of the sky and the sands of
 the seashore;

your descendants shall take possession
of the gates of their enemies,
and in your descendants all the nations
of the earth shall find blessing—
all this because you obeyed my
command."

RESPONSORIAL PSALM
Ps 116:10, 15, 16-17, 18-19

℟. (116:9) I will walk before the Lord, in
the land of the living.

I believed, even when I said,
"I am greatly afflicted."
Precious in the eyes of the LORD
is the death of his faithful ones.

℟. I will walk before the Lord, in the land
of the living.

O LORD, I am your servant;
I am your servant, the son of your
handmaid;
you have loosed my bonds.
To you will I offer sacrifice of
thanksgiving,
and I will call upon the name of the
LORD.

℟. I will walk before the Lord, in the land
of the living.

My vows to the LORD I will pay
in the presence of all his people,
in the courts of the house of the LORD,
in your midst, O Jerusalem.

℟. I will walk before the Lord, in the land
of the living.

SECOND READING
Rom 8:31b-34

Brothers and sisters:
If God is for us, who can be against us?
He who did not spare his own Son
but handed him over for us all,
how will he not also give us everything
else along with him?

Who will bring a charge against God's
chosen ones?
It is God who acquits us. Who will
condemn?
Christ Jesus it is who died—or, rather, was
raised—
who also is at the right hand of God,
who indeed intercedes for us.

Living Liturgy

Liturgy and Justice: When we connect the words of Scripture to the realities in our daily lives, for example, the changing face of a neighborhood as the result of gentrification, we start to see a model of holding space for peace within chaos. When higher income housing development begins to stake a claim on the street corners of our unhoused neighbors, there are fewer places for the unhoused to gather, pushing them out from services they need. Poverty is soothed by collaborative community relationships, but made more difficult when housing and commercial spaces are not accessible to all.

A diversity of individuals make up the most collaborative, loving, and generous communities. As neighborhoods become less diverse, it threatens communities where unhoused and housed individuals and families could exist, which creates a reality that feels more divisive, with an atmosphere of "us" and "them." We are reminded of the second reading: "If God is for us, who can be against us? He who did not spare his own Son but handed him over for us all, how will he not also give us everything else along with him?"

As we navigate through difficult relationships, we must dare to ask some significant questions: Can animosity survive if God is with us? How do we hold space for all people? What does radical welcome look like?

PROMPTS FOR FAITH-SHARING

• Where and how do you see God in your life? This could be an extraordinary moment of revelation or a series of ordinary occurrences; God is present in both.

• Where do you find God hard to see? How could this be an invitation to further seek God?

• Peter says "Rabbi, it is good that we are here!" When in your life might you say the same? Where do you encounter God in a way that makes you want to linger in God's presence?

See Appendix B, p. 310, for additional prompts.

SPIRITUALITY

GOSPEL ACCLAMATION
John 3:16

God so loved the world that he gave his
    only Son,
so that everyone who believes in him
    might have eternal life.

Gospel   John 2:13-25; L29B

Since the Passover of the Jews
    was near,
    Jesus went up to Jerusalem.
He found in the temple area
    those who sold oxen, sheep,
    and doves,
    as well as the money changers
    seated there.
He made a whip out of cords
    and drove them all out of the
    temple area, with the
    sheep and oxen,
    and spilled the coins of the
    money changers
    and overturned their tables,
    and to those who sold doves he said,
    "Take these out of here,
    and stop making my Father's house a
    marketplace."
His disciples recalled the words of
    Scripture,
    Zeal for your house will consume me.
At this the Jews answered and said to
    him,
    "What sign can you show us for doing
    this?"
Jesus answered and said to them,
    "Destroy this temple and in three
    days I will raise it up."
The Jews said,
    "This temple has been under
    construction for forty-six years,
    and you will raise it up in three
    days?"

Continued in Appendix A, p. 270.

*Year A readings may be used, see Appendix A,
pp. 271–273.*

Reflecting on the Gospel

Have you ever puzzled over what to give someone who has everything? We face a similar dilemma when we try to figure out what response we can make to the total, free self-gift of God to us. Sometimes friends and family members drop hints about what they would like, and sometimes they come right out and tell us. So does God in the Decalogue, or Ten Commandments. God has taken the initiative, leading Israel out of slavery in Egypt. How can Israel respond to such a gift of loving kindness?

The Decalogue spells out ten specific ways to be faithful. First and foremost is single-hearted devotion to God. No other being or thing is to be at the center of our attention. Second, the sacred name is to be held in reverence; it is not to be used in false oaths or in profanity, since the name carries the identity and power of the person. Third is observance of Sabbath. One day a week God wants to spend time with us to relish the joy of being together. The second half of the Decalogue gives examples of how love of God goes hand in hand with loving care of other people.

The God who asks this response from us offers ardent love. The Hebrew word *qanna* in Exodus 20:5, often translated as "jealous," can have the connotation "ardor" or "zeal." The way we choose to respond to this fervent offer of love carries consequences, and the effects ripple down to subsequent generations. It is not so much that God threatens punishment if we do not follow the divine commands, as that rejected love leads to unhappy consequences.

In addition to keeping the commandments, faithfulness to God was expressed through temple worship. All four gospels tell of an incident when Jesus performed a protest action in the temple. It is difficult to know the intent of the historical Jesus, and each evangelist gives a slightly different theological interpretation. In the Gospel of John, Jesus quotes the prophet Zechariah, who spoke of an ideal day when there would no longer be traders in the house of God (Zech 14:21). It may be that Jesus is challenging the attitudes of economic exchange that underlie sacrificial thinking: if we offer this sacrifice to God, then God will forgive our sins or bestow blessings.

Repeatedly the Scriptures counter this tit-for-tat notion telling how God's love and gifts are offered unconditionally. The Fourth Evangelist emphasizes that it is Jesus's very person that embodies God's ardent love. It is not in any building but in the person of Jesus that we encounter God. When Jesus's disciples recall Psalm 69:10, "Zeal for your house will consume me," there is a double meaning. *House* can refer both to the temple and to God's "household." The zealous love that Jesus enfleshes for members of God's household not only fills him but literally consumes, or destroys, his life. No sacrifice can be offered in exchange for this gift. The only response is to believe and act toward others with consummate love.

Preparing to Proclaim

Key words and phrases: "Zeal for your house will consume me."

To the point: The anger and suspicion Jesus displays in this gospel are hard to reconcile with the Jesus we usually see in the gospel. Jesus usually encounters sinners with patience, calling them to conversion by offering them an encounter with God's unfailing love. But this episode reminds us that he is fully human. He is not a one-dimensional character; he is not limited to whichever characteristics resonate for us. He experiences the full range of human emotion, including anger. While this emotion can lead many of us to sin, this gospel passage makes it clear that the anger itself is not a sin. Jesus himself experienced even forceful anger. But this was anger in the face of evil, and it is channeled productively to restore sanctity to the temple. Jesus gives us a model even for how to be angry, and is with us whenever our anger at sin drives us to make the world a better place.

Psalmist Preparation

In response to the first reading, in which God gives the law, we sing this psalm in praise of God's law. The commandments are not intended to be a burden. They are given as a gift, one that has the power to set us free from sin's hold on us. Following God's law brings us closer to God and closer to who we truly are. Our response in this psalm is one of gratitude. As you prepare to proclaim it, reflect on the role of God's commands in your life. Are there any moral teachings you struggle with? How might you receive them as a gift, an invitation to grow closer to God?

Making Connections

Between the readings: In the first reading, God gives Moses what we will come to know as the Ten Commandments. The basis for the entire Judeo-Christian moral system is here. It starts with the command to worship God above all; it is a violation of this commandment that elicits the angry response from Jesus that we see in today's gospel.

To experience: The merchants and money changers that Jesus drives from the temple probably did not think they were doing anything wrong. They were providing a service for those who came to worship, making the required materials available. But their work was becoming a distraction, taking over space that should have belonged only to God. This can remind us that many things in our life that are inherently harmless can become problematic when they are prioritized in an unhealthy way. Whenever something takes up space in our heart that ought to belong to God, it is time to work on detaching from it, perhaps even driving it out for a time so that we can reset our priorities.

Homily Points

• Today's first reading offers a chance to reflect on a primary goal of the Ten Commandments: freedom. Rather than viewing the Ten Commandments as a series of actions we ought not do, let us consider it as a list of liberation. By commanding us to refrain from such sins as worshipping false gods, distorting relationships, and harming others, God invites us to direct our energy to relationships and ways of being in the world that bring life. God longs to liberate God's people from the slavery of sin.

• The passage featured today from John's Gospel lifts up anger as a holy emotion. Upon finding the temple turned into a shopping center, an angry Jesus overturns the tables and drives out the money changers. One can imagine an exasperated, red-faced Jesus shouting, "stop making my Father's house a marketplace." The Son of God demonstrates a righteous anger in this scene that moves him to act for justice. Recall times when you felt or saw anger expressed at an injustice. Perhaps you were one of countless people to take to the streets in protests over the killings of Black people by police officers or the inhumane treatment of refugees. In light of this week's gospel, consider how individual and collective anger can be expressed for positive change.

• Lent is a season of cleansing out the sanctuaries of our bodies. We work to rid ourselves of the temptations that distract us from discipleship through times of prayer, fasting, and almsgiving.

Model Penitential Act

Presider: The season of Lent is a time to grow ever more aware of our need for God's mercy. Trusting that God will provide the healing we need, let us confess our sins . . . *[pause]*

Confiteor: I confess . . .

Model Universal Prayer (Prayer of the Faithful)

Presider: Jesus Christ is the Way, the Truth, and the Life. Trusting in his presence among creation, let us bring our needs before the Lord.

Response: Lord, hear our prayer.

Strengthen congregational ministries to people suffering from addiction to drugs and alcohol . . .

Prosper anti-bullying legislation and efforts within schools and greater communities . . .

Pour your grace upon survivors of sexual assault and all who have had the temples of their bodies harmed . . .

Lead us to true repentance and conversion of heart during this Lenten season . . .

Presider: Triune God, you sent your beloved Son and Spirit into the world for the salvation of all of creation. Hear our prayers that we might grow in our awareness of the divine presence in our world and reflect that presence to everyone we meet. We ask this through Christ our Lord. **Amen.**

Liturgy and Music

Did you ever have one of those nights? You didn't *mean* to upset someone in the choir, but you did. Maybe you pushed your singers a little too hard. Maybe tensions rose, just a bit. Did someone forget that the reason for all this is love? And when it was over, and everyone was gone, did you linger to sit and play the piano, or pray quietly before the Blessed Sacrament? In those moments, the empty space can be like a dear friend who is there to listen, or a wise, compassionate confessor.

Mistakes *should* be humbling. We all make them, especially if we have been overly ambitious in planning, say, Bruckner's *Christus Factus Est* for Good Friday. Even when our repertoire choices are safe, tried, and true, there can be potholes on that winding, wondrous road to the Triduum. Fret not. The sun will come up on Easter Sunday morning. The people of God will stand to sing praise to the risen One. And they will still be singing long after you and I have gone on to our reward. Breathe. Consider the lilies of the field. You've got this.

This weekend we hear the account of the Ten Commandments in the first reading. If you're having a rough time, go home, pop some popcorn, snuggle in a comfy blanket, and watch the movie *The Ten Commandments* with your cat. Celebrate this simple, ancient truth: The foolishness of God is wiser than all human wisdom combined, and the weakness of God is stronger than human strength—yours included.

COLLECT

Let us pray.

Pause for silent prayer

O God, author of every mercy and of all goodness,
who in fasting, prayer and almsgiving have shown us a remedy for sin,
look graciously on this confession of our lowliness,
that we, who are bowed down by our conscience,
may always be lifted up by your mercy.
Through our Lord Jesus Christ, your Son,
who lives and reigns with you in the unity of the Holy Spirit,
God, for ever and ever. **Amen.**

FIRST READING
Exod 20:1-17

In those days, God delivered all these commandments:
"I, the LORD, am your God,
who brought you out of the land of Egypt, that place of slavery.
You shall not have other gods besides me.
You shall not carve idols for yourselves
in the shape of anything in the sky above
or on the earth below or in the waters beneath the earth;
you shall not bow down before them or worship them.
For I, the LORD, your God, am a jealous God,
inflicting punishment for their fathers' wickedness
on the children of those who hate me,
down to the third and fourth generation;
but bestowing mercy down to the thousandth generation
on the children of those who love me and keep my commandments.

"You shall not take the name of the LORD, your God, in vain.
For the LORD will not leave unpunished
the one who takes his name in vain.

"Remember to keep holy the sabbath day.
Six days you may labor and do all your work,
but the seventh day is the sabbath of the LORD, your God.
No work may be done then either by you,
or your son or daughter,
or your male or female slave, or your beast,
or by the alien who lives with you.

In six days the LORD made the heavens and
      the earth,
   the sea and all that is in them;
   but on the seventh day he rested.
That is why the LORD has blessed the
      sabbath day and made it holy.

"Honor your father and your mother,
   that you may have a long life in the land
   which the LORD, your God, is giving you.
You shall not kill.
You shall not commit adultery.
You shall not steal.
You shall not bear false witness against
      your neighbor.
You shall not covet your neighbor's house.
You shall not covet your neighbor's wife,
   nor his male or female slave, nor his ox
      or ass,
   nor anything else that belongs to him."

or

Exod 20:1-3, 7-8, 12-17

In those days, God delivered all these
      commandments:
   "I, the LORD, am your God,
who brought you out of the land of
      Egypt, that place of slavery.
You shall not have other gods besides me.

"You shall not take the name of the LORD,
      your God, in vain.
For the LORD will not leave unpunished
   the one who takes his name in vain.

"Remember to keep holy the sabbath day.
Honor your father and your mother,
   that you may have a long life in the land
   which the LORD, your God, is giving you.
You shall not kill.
You shall not commit adultery.
You shall not steal.
You shall not bear false witness against
      your neighbor.
You shall not covet your neighbor's house.
You shall not covet your neighbor's wife,
   nor his male or female slave, nor his ox
      or ass,
   nor anything else that belongs to him."

RESPONSORIAL PSALM
Ps 19:8, 9, 10, 11

SECOND READING
1 Cor 1:22-25

See Appendix A, p. 271.

Living Liturgy

Liturgy and Spirituality: In the midst of commandments that demand we avoid murder and theft, the call "to keep holy the sabbath day" should give us pause. Rest and restoration are held in equal esteem to larceny and violent crime. While this might seem like an exaggeration, restoration of Sabbath as a path toward restoration of all of God's creation on earth is needed now more than ever.

Economy and ecology begin with the same prefix, *oikos*, which means home, family, or household, depending on the context. Jesus is angered that they were making his "Father's house a marketplace." The temple had been turned into a hub of economic activity instead of a house of worship.

Living in a society with an economy that often values profit above all other measures of success, intrinsic human dignity can be conflated with a human life being "worth" only how much a person can do or produce. Living in this reality, rest can be a radical act. In the book *How to Do Nothing: Resisting the Attention Economy*, the author Jenny Odell writes, "I think that 'doing nothing'—in the sense of refusing productivity and stopping to listen—entails an active process of listening that seeks out the effects of racial, environmental, and economic injustice and brings about real change. . . . There is a kind of nothing that's necessary for, at the end of the day, doing something."

Inherent in practicing Sabbath is making time to listen to God's deepest desires for your life to discern the most loving response. Sabbath provides space for restoration of right relationship with God, your neighbor, yourself, and the earth.

PROMPTS FOR FAITH-SHARING

• What makes you angry? How do you react to anger? How could you invite Jesus to accompany you in your anger?

• How does the angry Jesus of today's gospel make you feel? If there is any discomfort, how could that help you broaden your understanding of God?

• Which of the church's moral teachings are a struggle for you? How might you see them as an invitation to grow closer to God?

See Appendix B, p. 310, for additional prompts.

SPIRITUALITY

GOSPEL ACCLAMATION

John 3:16

God so loved the world that he gave his only Son,
so everyone who believes in him might
have eternal life.

Gospel

John 3:14-21; L32B

Jesus said to Nicodemus:
"Just as Moses lifted up the
serpent in the desert,
so must the Son of Man be
lifted up,
so that everyone who believes
in him may have eternal
life."
For God so loved the world that
he gave his only Son,
so that everyone who believes
in him might not perish
but might have eternal life.
For God did not send his Son into the
world to condemn the world,
but that the world might be saved
through him.
Whoever believes in him will not be
condemned,
but whoever does not believe has
already been condemned,
because he has not believed in the
name of the only Son of God.
And this is the verdict,
that the light came into the world,
but people preferred darkness to light,
because their works were evil.
For everyone who does wicked things
hates the light
and does not come toward the light,
so that his works might not be exposed.
But whoever lives the truth comes to
the light,
so that his works may be clearly seen
as done in God.

Year A readings may be used, see Appendix A,
pp. 273–275.

Reflecting on the Gospel

In today's gospel, the image of light and darkness is central to Jesus's teaching. Coming to the light is presented as a conscious choice, one that can be difficult to make. Some people "preferred darkness." Jesus contrasts those doing wicked things, who shun the light, with those who live the truth, who come to the light so that their works "may be clearly seen as done in God." The gospel paints the two in stark opposition, seeming to leave no space in between: we are either doing wicked things in the darkness or living the truth in the light. Yet our experience is that we all do wicked things that we want to hide, while at the same time we carry that spark of divine light that urges us toward truth.

Just as Earth gradually comes into full light between its turn at the spring equinox and the summer solstice, so our coming to the Light is a gradual process. That is how it is for Nicodemus. He first meets Jesus in the darkness, taking an initial, tentative step toward the Light. But by the end of John 3, he is still not ready to commit himself fully to Jesus. He reappears in John 7:50-51, where he tentatively defends Jesus before his fellow religious leaders who are looking to arrest Jesus. Finally, at the end of the gospel, he comes with Joseph of Arimathea, bringing a hundred pounds of spices for Jesus's burial (19:39)—a truly grandiose expression of his definitive choice to come to the Light.

Whatever fears keep us from coming to the Light can be allayed by the mercy and compassion to be found there. All of today's readings stress God's mercy and compassion, the great love, kindness, and grace extended to us in Christ. He lifts us up from whatever darkness holds us bound. To Nicodemus, Jesus recalls the time when the Israelites were bitten by poisonous snakes in the desert and Moses fashioned a bronze serpent on a pole; whenever people were bitten, they looked upon it and lived (Num 21:8-9). In the same way, whenever we look at the battered body of Jesus raised up on a cross, he helps us to overcome our fears of violence and death, or of anything that the darkness hides, as not only he but all of us are raised up with him (Eph 2:6) in God's light.

It is for life eternal, which we can already taste now, that the Light has come, not for condemnation. The famous verse, John 3:16, "For God so loved the world that he gave his only Son," stresses God's love, not God's wish to condemn anyone. The "world" is the special object of God's love and the arena in which we respond to the offer of divine love. The giving of the Son is not handing him over to death but rather the giving of him to us as Light incarnate. Refusal of the gift is choosing darkness that brings condemnation. Acceptance of the gift draws us into deepening faith as we choose again and again to live into the Light.

Preparing to Proclaim

Key words and phrases: "[T]he light came into the world, but people preferred darkness to light."

To the point: We may feel tempted to distance ourselves from the people to whom Jesus refers when he talks to Nicodemus. Surely we would choose light over darkness, given the choice. But think about the experience of emerging from darkness into light—when we are not accustomed to it, the light is painful and blinding. A more gradual approach might help, but Jesus does not promise to progress us to holiness only insofar as we are comfortable. Jesus only is what he is, and he is light—pure and radiant. This light can seem blinding at first, confusing us as we strive to turn more fully toward a life of faith. But as our eyes grow used to its brilliance, it enables us to travel farther and faster than we ever could without it.

Psalmist Preparation

This is a psalm of lament, sung by the Israelites as they live out their years of captivity in Babylon. It reveals that even the wickedness that earned them their exile did not stamp out the need for God in their hearts. When their luxuries and sins are stripped away, they are reminded of this need. As you prepare to proclaim this psalm, think about the ways you long for God. How do you hope God will work in your life? How can you make space for God to enter in more fully? Bring your petitions for God into the pleading proclamation of this psalm.

Making Connections

Between the readings: The first reading shows some of those to whom Jesus refers, those who prefer darkness to light. The people of Judah defy God's law and repeatedly scorn the prophets God sends to warn them of their wickedness. The result of their sin is the result of all sin: they are separated from God and from their homeland. But God's love is unrelenting even in this exile, and God restores them eventually to their land and their freedom.

To experience: We do not always seek God as we should; we sometimes choose darkness over light. But God never stops seeking us. God is always calling us with love, trying to get into our hearts in a way that will keep us close. Our Lenten practices of prayer, fasting, and almsgiving are intended to make room for God. With the clarity that comes from these practices, we can more readily choose to live in the light of God.

Homily Points

• Today's well-known gospel is set in the darkness of night. Nicodemus, a Jewish leader and Pharisee, visits Jesus after the sun goes down to avoid being seen with the man who makes the religious leaders of the day tremble. Professing belief in Jesus brings about real consequences. We may be judged or dismissed by others. Perhaps even more difficult, we may have our own sinfulness exposed as we strive to live in the light of Christ.

• Lent is a season of transition as we journey with Jesus from the darkness of death to the Easter light of new life. Consider spending time this week intentionally reflecting on your sins. Ask for God's healing mercy through the sacrament of reconciliation or in the quiet of your prayer time.

• The reading from the Second Book of Chronicles details the darkness that has befallen the Jewish people in the wake of the desecration of the temple and Babylonian exile. Their suffering is real and profound—and still, God shows up. God's love for the people remains steadfast and strong. God's mercy is at work in the actions of King Cyrus of Persia, who is not Jewish but recognizes the centrality of the temple for the Jewish people and allows them to return to rebuild it. God shines the divine light on the people in their darkest hour. This is the same light that came into the world for the salvation of all creation. It is the same light into which we are baptized. The light of Christ reveals the truth and draws people toward the truth.

CELEBRATION

Model Penitential Act

Presider: Saint Paul tells the Ephesians of their God, who is rich is mercy and filled with love for God's people. Confident in God's grace, let us confess our sins and ask for God's pardon . . . *[pause]*

    Confiteor: I confess . . .

Model Universal Prayer (Prayer of the Faithful)

Presider: Jesus Christ, the Light of the World, shines for all to see. Basking in his glow, let us bring our prayers before the Lord.

Response: Lord, hear our prayer.

Heal divisions among Christians of different traditions . . .

Inspire global efforts to lessen the spread of infectious diseases . . .

Keep safe migrants, refugees, and all who are relocating . . .

Open our minds and hearts to your sacred words proclaimed through Scripture . . .

Presider: Gracious God, you created humankind in your image to do good works in the world. Receive our prayers and strengthen our resolve to live as disciples of Christ in our communities. We offer this prayer through Christ our Lord. **Amen.**

Liturgy and Music

It is not often that Psalm 137 comes around in the Sunday lectionary. In this weekend's Scripture readings, this psalm follows an account from the Second Book of Chronicles that vividly describes an exiled people, imprisoned and far from home. This psalm must inevitably follow this account. It gets out attention because it embodies a human emotion that is rarely heard in church on Sundays: rage. The psalmist is bitter. Forced to entertain his captors, he refuses, and instead aches to repay their cruel abuse.

Imagine all that God has seen throughout the ages of human existence! Unimaginable acts inflicted upon the vulnerable, the destruction of beloved, holy places. God's creation and the earth's inhabitants defiled, debased, and brutalized. In our own time, the abuse of our fellow human beings continues, unabated. Where is God?

In our own darkest times, we have experienced painful trials. There will surely be more to come. They challenge our faith, and lead us to ask this same question: Where is God?

We may know someone in the midst of despair right now. How painful is it to stand by helplessly while someone we love is suffering!

Witnessing the suffering of others—or enduring it ourselves—binds us to the very suffering of Christ. When we profess the life, death, and resurrection of the Son of God, we accept this same path for ourselves. And just as it was for Jesus himself, our only way to eternal life is through his death.

COLLECT

Let us pray.

Pause for silent prayer

O God, who through your Word
reconcile the human race to yourself in a
    wonderful way,
grant, we pray,
that with prompt devotion and eager faith
the Christian people may hasten
toward the solemn celebrations to come.
Through our Lord Jesus Christ, your Son,
who lives and reigns with you in the unity
    of the Holy Spirit,
God, for ever and ever. **Amen.**

FIRST READING

2 Chr 36:14-16, 19-23

In those days, all the princes of Judah, the
    priests, and the people
  added infidelity to infidelity,
  practicing all the abominations of the
    nations
  and polluting the LORD's temple
  which he had consecrated in Jerusalem.

Early and often did the LORD, the God of
    their fathers,
  send his messengers to them,
  for he had compassion on his people
  and his dwelling place.
But they mocked the messengers of God,
  despised his warnings, and scoffed at
    his prophets,
  until the anger of the LORD against his
    people was so inflamed
  that there was no remedy.
Their enemies burnt the house of God,
  tore down the walls of Jerusalem,
  set all its palaces afire,
  and destroyed all its precious objects.
Those who escaped the sword were
    carried captive to Babylon,
  where they became servants of the king
    of the Chaldeans and his sons
  until the kingdom of the Persians came
    to power.
All this was to fulfill the word of the LORD
    spoken by Jeremiah:
  "Until the land has retrieved its lost
    sabbaths,
  during all the time it lies waste it shall
    have rest
  while seventy years are fulfilled."

In the first year of Cyrus, king of Persia,
in order to fulfill the word of the Lord
spoken by Jeremiah,
the Lord inspired King Cyrus of Persia
to issue this proclamation throughout
his kingdom,
both by word of mouth and in writing:
"Thus says Cyrus, king of Persia:
All the kingdoms of the earth
the Lord, the God of heaven, has given
to me,
and he has also charged me to build him
a house
in Jerusalem, which is in Judah.
Whoever, therefore, among you belongs to
any part of his people,
let him go up, and may his God be with
him!"

RESPONSORIAL PSALM
Ps 137:1-2, 3, 4-5, 6

℟. (6ab) Let my tongue be silenced, if I
ever forget you!

By the streams of Babylon
we sat and wept when we remembered
Zion.
On the aspens of that land
we hung up our harps.

℟. Let my tongue be silenced, if I ever
forget you!

For there our captors asked of us
the lyrics of our songs,
and our despoilers urged us to be joyous:
"Sing for us the songs of Zion!"

℟. Let my tongue be silenced, if I ever
forget you!

How could we sing a song of the Lord
in a foreign land?
If I forget you, Jerusalem,
may my right hand be forgotten!

℟. Let my tongue be silenced, if I ever
forget you!

May my tongue cleave to my palate
if I remember you not,
if I place not Jerusalem
ahead of my joy.

℟. Let my tongue be silenced, if I ever
forget you!

SECOND READING
Eph 2:4-10

See Appendix A, p. 273.

✚ CATECHESIS

Living Liturgy

Liturgy and Spirituality: Light and darkness are important themes of our faith. "But whoever lives the truth comes to the light, so that his works may be clearly seen as done in God."

Saint Ignatius is well known for writing *The Spiritual Exercises*, a series of prayers and meditations that are often given in the format of a retreat, and that invite retreatants to deepen their relationship with God and discern God's deepest desire for their lives. In *The Spiritual Exercises*, Saint Ignatius provides practical Rules for Discernment that help a person to better understand if their orientation is toward God, consolation, or away from God, desolation.

Margaret Silf, retreat leader and writer, has described these states as turning toward the light for consolation and turning away from the light as desolation. Sometimes our actions can look like they are oriented toward God, but upon reflection we might realize our intentions are not so holy. Saint Ignatius uses the images of "the good spirit" and "the enemy of our human nature" to demonstrate the importance of knowing which spirit is leading us as we choose a particular action.

For example, someone may volunteer for a task solely for the accolades and fame they will receive as a result. If fame is their central motivation, they will probably find themselves on a different path than that of God's deepest desire for their life.

Similarly, in today's gospel we read that although light came into the world, "people preferred darkness." The gospel goes on to say, "For everyone who does wicked things hates the light and does not come toward the light."

In Rule Thirteen in the *Exercises*, Saint Ignatius shares a similar piece of wisdom. He says that when "the enemy of human nature brings his wiles and persuasions to the just soul," he wants them to remain a secret. When we bring these issues that we might feel ashamed about "to the light" by sharing them with a spiritual friend, they begin to lose their power over us and we have more freedom to choose what brings about God's greater glory.

PROMPTS FOR FAITH-SHARING

• The gospel speaks of God's great enduring love, a love that gives God's only Son. How do you experience this love?

• Even though God is light, God does not abandon us to the darkness. What is a time you felt God's presence through a dark time?

• What do you need to detach from in your life in order to make more room for God to work?

See Appendix B, p. 310, for additional prompts.

SPIRITUALITY

GOSPEL ACCLAMATION
John 12:26

Whoever serves me must follow me, says
the Lord;
and where I am, there also will my
servant be.

Gospel

John 12:20-33; L35B

**Some Greeks who had come to
worship at the Passover Feast
came to Philip, who was from
Bethsaida in Galilee,
and asked him, "Sir, we would
like to see Jesus."
Philip went and told Andrew;
then Andrew and Philip went
and told Jesus.
Jesus answered them,
"The hour has come for the Son
of Man to be glorified.
Amen, amen, I say to you,
unless a grain of wheat falls to the
ground and dies,
it remains just a grain of wheat;
but if it dies, it produces much fruit.
Whoever loves his life loses it,
and whoever hates his life in this world
will preserve it for eternal life.
Whoever serves me must follow me,
and where I am, there also will my
servant be.
The Father will honor whoever serves me.**

**"I am troubled now. Yet what should I
say?
'Father, save me from this hour'?
But it was for this purpose that I came to
this hour.
Father, glorify your name."
Then a voice came from heaven,
"I have glorified it and will glorify it
again."**

Continued in Appendix A, p. 275.

*Year A readings may be used, see Appendix A,
pp. 275–277.*

Reflecting on the Gospel

There is a very troublesome assertion in today's second reading: "Son though
he was, he learned obedience from what he suffered." This verse conjures up an
image of God as a disgruntled parent, who inflicts punishment on a disobedient
child to teach the wayward one a lesson. Such an explanation for Jesus's passion is highly problematic, both theologically and pastorally.

It is important to understand the context of this passage from Hebrews, both
within the whole of the document and in
the broader biblical and liturgical context. Today's second reading is part of
an elaborate exposition on Jesus's high
priesthood. The author knows that the
earthly Jesus was not a priest (Heb 7:14);
he speaks metaphorically, arguing that
Jesus's suffering and death have the saving effects that the temple sacrifices had,
which were offered by the high priest.
The author asserts that Jesus's sacrifice put an end to all need for further
sacrifices (7:27). In the section we hear
in today's reading, the emphasis is that
in Jesus we have a "high priest" who can
sympathize with us in every way.

Jesus is not removed from humanity in some inaccessible sacred sphere; he
experienced everything that we do, except sin. The author of Hebrews is saying
that the earthly Jesus, like all human beings, grew in consciousness of what his
mission was and learned through his experience the full meaning of what it is
to be obedient to God. In verse 9, the verb *teleiotheis*, "made perfect," does not
refer to moral perfection but has at its root a sense of "completeness," "wholeness." Thus, it is Jesus's process of coming to full understanding of his mission
and its cost to him that the author speaks of Jesus becoming "perfected."

The whole purpose of this exposition in Hebrews is to exhort the hearers to
imitate Jesus's attitude toward God. As this Christian community experiences
suffering, its members are directed to do as Jesus did. First, they should pour
out their hearts to God, as Jesus was shown in the Synoptic Gospels to have
done in Gethsemane. Similarly, the psalms of lament, like today's responsorial
psalm, supply a pattern. No human being, including Jesus, wants to suffer and
die, and God hears such pleas. At the same time, Jesus approaches God with
"reverence" (Heb 5:7), that is, awe before the power of God. He knows that God
hears him, and at the same time, he hears God, and knows the cost of being
obedient to the divine mission of extending salvific love to all. This is what
the author of Hebrews wants us to emulate: obedience as faithfulness to God's
desire for life to the full for all, and willingness to embrace the suffering this
mission entails. We can learn this kind of obedience by imitating ("obeying")
Jesus (Heb 5:9).

God is not intent on teaching us obedience by imposing suffering but leads us
to follow Jesus, trusting that God accompanies us and strengthens us through
experiences of suffering and death, which bring the full flourishing of life.

Preparing to Proclaim

Key words and phrases: "[U]nless a grain of wheat falls to the ground and dies, it remains just a grain of wheat; but if it dies, it produces much fruit."

To the point: Jesus speaks in paradox here, reminding us that God is in the business of transcending boundaries and surpassing our expectations. He also reminds us that he is in the midst of transforming death. No more will it be a final end for humans. After Jesus completes the work of the crucifixion and resurrection, death is rather a moment of transition. It is a part of life rather than its end. Jesus himself is also a paradox here. He is, of course, troubled by the thought of dying. All humans are; it is not the fate for which God made us. But he accepts his impending death as the purpose for which he came to earth, and in his calm acknowledgment of this shows himself as something more than human as well. He is both fully human and fully divine.

Psalmist Preparation

In this psalm, we plead with God to create us anew. We trust that God has the power to do so; the one who made us can make us again. As you prepare to proclaim this psalm, spend some time reflecting on how you would like God to make you new. What hurts would you like healed? What tendencies do you need help resisting? Know and trust that God wants to make you new and to give you all the joy in the world. When you proclaim this psalm, strive to do so with trust that God is hearing the prayer it contains. God hears it and wants to answer it, and is already answering it, accompanying you in whatever ways you are being made new right now.

Making Connections

Between the readings: In the gospel, Jesus reminds his followers that they are to hold onto even their very lives with a loose grasp. It is encouraging to read this gospel with this first reading, which reminds us that we are not alone in the radical transformations God calls us to. Making ourselves new hearts is not really our work; it is the work of God. We need to create the conditions in which God can work (which is what our Lenten disciplines are for) but God never leaves us to do this work of renewal alone.

To experience: In today's world, few of us will be called to die a martyr's death. But this gospel reminds us that our lives are not really ours. We are called to give over our lives in service to others. These sacrifices unite us to Christ and his suffering and death, enabling us to share also in his resurrection and life with God.

Homily Points

• We come to know God through forgiveness. Today's first reading from Jeremiah tells of God's covenant with the house of Israel. God assures the people that they will no longer have to teach their friends and relatives how to know the Lord. That relationship, God says, is built through mercy: "All, from least to greatest, shall know me, says the Lord, for I will forgive their evildoing and remember their sin no more." In these waning days of Lent, we too are called to open our hearts to God's forgiveness.

• Jeremiah tells of God's decision to "place my law within [the people] and write it upon their hearts" during a time of deep despair. The prophet wrote at the beginning of the sixth century BCE, when the Israelites carried great anxiety over the looming fall of Jerusalem and Babylonian exile. It seemed their God was nowhere to be found in the face of such suffering. Yet Jeremiah insists "the days are coming" when God will breathe new life into the people. God will not just write the new covenant on stone, but rather on the very hearts of the people. Here God will make an intimate promise: "I will be their God, and they shall be my people."

• Now is the time to remember the new covenant etched in our hearts through the waters of baptism and affirmed in the Eucharist. Christ Jesus, through his suffering, death, and resurrection, draws us into the hope of eternal life.

CELEBRATION

Model Penitential Act

Presider: Jesus tells the disciples in today's gospel: "Whoever serves me must follow me . . ." Following in Christ's example of mercy, let us reflect on our sins and ask God for forgiveness . . . *[pause]*

   Confiteor: I confess . . .

Model Universal Prayer (Prayer of the Faithful)

Presider: Guided by the steady hand of God, let us humbly offer our needs before the Lord.

Response: Lord, hear our prayer.

Make your presence known to all those preparing to receive the sacraments of initiation this Easter . . .

Bring a swift end to all wars and the production of nuclear weapons . . .

Grant us wisdom to care for the earth and preserve natural resources for future generations . . .

Extend our circles of inclusion so that all may feel welcomed as Christ . . .

Presider: Almighty God, you sent your son into the world for the sake of your people. Through Christ we will be redeemed and brought into the fullness of life. Receive our prayers that we might reflect your generosity to everyone we meet. We ask this through Christ our Lord. **Amen.**

Liturgy and Music

The streets of my neighborhood are lined with seventy-five-year-old sycamore trees. Their tall branches form an arch over the street, providing dappled shade in the summer, and releasing mountains of dry leaves in the fall and winter. They are like old friends.

During my years of parish ministry, I would often miss the seasonal changes in these old trees. Springtime would sneak up on me while I had my head down, focused on Holy Week preparations. Many times it was not until I returned home after the last Easter Sunday liturgy that I would notice that the trees were covered in a flush of young, tender leaves.

Profound change can unfold so slowly that we unaware of it—until suddenly we are. This happens in trees, and in the hearts of people like you and me.

In this weekend's gospel, Jesus reminds us: "Unless a grain of wheat falls to the ground and dies, it remains just a grain of wheat; but if it dies, it produces much fruit."

Are we waiting for some kind of sudden, dramatic death-to-self that we will know when we experience it? It could happen this way. But death can also be slow, silent, and inevitable. As you sit alone in the silent solitude of the empty church space, I invite you to look up from your work. Be aware of the changes unfolding around and within you. Then be still and listen to what dying to self really means.

COLLECT

Let us pray.

Pause for silent prayer

By your help, we beseech you, Lord our
    God,
may we walk eagerly in that same charity
with which, out of love for the world,
your Son handed himself over to death.
Through our Lord Jesus Christ, your Son,
who lives and reigns with you in the unity
    of the Holy Spirit,
God, for ever and ever. **Amen.**

FIRST READING
Jer 31:31-34

The days are coming, says the LORD,
    when I will make a new covenant with
        the house of Israel
    and the house of Judah.
It will not be like the covenant I made with
    their fathers
    the day I took them by the hand
    to lead them forth from the land of
        Egypt;
    for they broke my covenant,
    and I had to show myself their master,
        says the LORD.
But this is the covenant that I will make
    with the house of Israel after those
        days, says the LORD.
I will place my law within them and write
    it upon their hearts;
    I will be their God, and they shall be my
        people.
No longer will they have need to teach
    their friends and relatives
    how to know the LORD.
All, from least to greatest, shall know me,
    says the LORD,
    for I will forgive their evildoing and
        remember their sin no more.

RESPONSORIAL PSALM

Ps 51:3-4, 12-13, 14-15

℟. (12a) Create a clean heart in me, O God.

Have mercy on me, O God, in your
goodness;
in the greatness of your compassion
wipe out my offense.
Thoroughly wash me from my guilt
and of my sin cleanse me.

℟. Create a clean heart in me, O God.

A clean heart create for me, O God,
and a steadfast spirit renew within me.
Cast me not out from your presence,
and your Holy Spirit take not from me.

℟. Create a clean heart in me, O God.

Give me back the joy of your salvation,
and a willing spirit sustain in me.
I will teach transgressors your ways,
and sinners shall return to you.

℟. Create a clean heart in me, O God.

SECOND READING

Heb 5:7-9

In the days when Christ Jesus was in the
flesh,
he offered prayers and supplications
with loud cries and tears
to the one who was able to save him
from death,
and he was heard because of his
reverence.
Son though he was, he learned obedience
from what he suffered;
and when he was made perfect,
he became the source of eternal
salvation for all who obey him.

Living Liturgy

Liturgy and Justice: On March 17, 1992, a referendum vote was held in South Africa that ended Apartheid. Almost 70 percent of White voters voted "yes" to end a violent system of institutionalized racial segregation that had existed since 1948. Systems of oppression fall due to the persistent work of people on the ground speaking truth to power and demanding that their society be better than the current reality. Prophetic voices help us to imagine that living in a world of justice and peace is possible.

Nelson Mandela was an internationally known "voice of one crying out in the desert" about the injustices and inhumanity experienced during Apartheid. At the Rivonia Trial where he was ultimately sentenced to life in prison instead of to the death penalty, Mandela made a speech that ended with these words: "During my lifetime I have dedicated myself to this struggle of the African people. I have fought against white domination, and I have fought against black domination. I have cherished the ideal of a democratic and free society in which all persons live together in harmony and with equal opportunities. It is an ideal which I hope to live for and to achieve. But if need be, it is an ideal for which I am prepared to die" (Pretoria, South Africa, April 20, 1964).

As he prepares for the coming walk to Calvary, Jesus shares a similar sentiment with the crowd, "I am troubled now. Yet what should I say? 'Father, save me from this hour'? But it was for this purpose that I came to this hour." Jesus has broken into the world in order to heal the brokenness of the world. He has come to create a world of peace in which the lion sleeps with the lamb, and he is ultimately willing to die to make that peace a reality. It was for this purpose that he came to this hour.

As you prepare to enter into Holy Week and follow in Jesus's footsteps, for what purpose have you come to this hour? What is being asked of you, and how is the Spirit moving you to respond?

PROMPTS FOR FAITH-SHARING

• How do you experience God's renewing work? How do you need God to make your heart new this Lent?

• How are you called to "lose your life" in order to follow Jesus? What sacrifices do you make and how do you find life within them?

• How might God be inviting you to take part in God's ongoing work of giving and sustaining life?

See Appendix B, p. 310, for additional prompts.

GOSPEL ACCLAMATION
Ps 84:5

Blessed are those who dwell in your house,
    O Lord;
they never cease to praise you.

Gospel

Matt 1:16, 18-21, 24a; L543

Jacob was the father of Joseph,
    the husband of Mary.
Of her was born Jesus who is
    called the Christ.

Now this is how the birth of Jesus
    Christ came about.
When his mother Mary was be-
    trothed to Joseph,
    but before they lived together,
    she was found with child
        through the Holy Spirit.
Joseph her husband, since he was
    a righteous man,
    yet unwilling to expose her to
        shame,
    decided to divorce her quietly.
Such was his intention when, behold,
    the angel of the Lord appeared to
        him in a dream and said,
"Joseph, son of David,
    do not be afraid to take Mary your
        wife into your home.
For it is through the Holy Spirit
    that this child has been conceived in
        her.
She will bear a son and you are to
    name him Jesus,
    because he will save his people from
        their sins."
When Joseph awoke,
    he did as the angel of the Lord had
        commanded him
    and took his wife into his home.

or Luke 2:41-51a *in Appendix A, p. 278.*

See Appendix A, pp. 278–279, for the other readings.

Reflecting on the Gospel

Today's gospel contains one line that tells us a great deal about Joseph: "Joseph her husband, since he was a righteous man, yet unwilling to expose her to shame, decided to divorce her quietly." Right off the bat, we know that Joseph values dignity over scrupulosity.

Joseph's fiancée is pregnant. Society grants him every right to not only end the relationship, but explain why he's calling off the betrothal. This means that he is granted the power to obliterate Mary's reputation, and by doing so maintain his social standing and good moral character. However, Joseph chooses not to do this. He decides to end things "quietly." He will not bring more shame to Mary than will be brought already by the mere fact that she's going to be an unwed mother. Joseph demonstrates his knowledge of her extreme circumstance and decides he won't add to it.

Before Joseph has any idea that he's going to be invited to raise the Son of God, he's acting with concern for someone who has wronged him. Joseph doesn't know the Holy Spirit has asked Mary to bear God's Son. All Joseph knows is that his fiancée slept with someone else. Instead of reacting with anger, he reacts with discretion. He owes Mary nothing. But he chooses to be kind to her.

Joseph models to us what it means to resolve a situation without a need to feel "righted." So often we want justice to come with public shaming. We want to *feel* the justice, bringing ourselves emotional retribution via community agreement. We want others to see how we were wronged and to agree with how awful it is. It is so tempting to feed the beast of social revenge. So often we think of restitution as not just about righting the wrong, but about feeling emotionally satisfied through some form of group shame. This permeates our entire society and feeds vicious division.

Joseph may have felt the same. What a deep betrayal, for his fiancée to reveal that she not only didn't share his commitment to chastity, but that she was with another man during their engagement. Social shame seems like the normal response. No one could fault Joseph for calling her out in the village. And yet, he chose to save her future opportunities and divorce her quietly. This was a good call, especially since Gabriel soon appears to let Joseph know what is *really* going on with Mary. His discretion was rewarded. By reacting not with revenge but with grace, he set himself up for a positive, life-giving relationship with his wife when the truth was revealed.

Preparing to Proclaim

Key words and phrases: "Joseph her husband, since he was a righteous man, yet unwilling to expose her to shame, decided to divorce her quietly."

To the point: Many historical women, despite being well-accomplished in their own right, are best known for the famous men to whom they were married. Saint Joseph is the rare man who reverses this pattern; he is known not for any worldly accomplishments but for playing a supporting role in the life of his family. Mary is often held up as a model for women, but Joseph reveals that all of us are called to receptivity before God and hospitality to children.

Model Penitential Act

Presider: In his gospel, Matthew describes Joseph as a righteous man. He listened closely to God and did as the Lord commanded. In the spirit of Saint Joseph, let us pause to listen to God and ask for forgiveness for our sins . . . *[pause]*
    Confiteor: I confess . . .

Model Universal Prayer (Prayer of the Faithful)

Presider: Spurred on by the intercession of Saint Joseph, let us bring our prayers and petitions before the Lord.

Response: Lord, hear our prayer.

Energize the hearts of fathers, godfathers, and all father figures who help to raise and mentor young people . . .

Encourage elected officials to pass legislation that protects the rights of workers and affirms their dignity . . .

Give safety and peace to people living in abusive situations . . .

Help each of us gathered here to carve out moments of quiet prayer in our days . . .

Presider: Mysterious God, you entrusted Mary and Joseph to raise your Son and teach him the ways of faith. Hear our prayers that, inspired by the witness of the Holy Family, we might grow in devotion to you. We ask this through Christ our Lord. **Amen.**

Living Liturgy

Liturgy and Witness: In his genealogy, Saint Joseph is connected with King David. Through his connection to this holy ancestor and Mary's first courageous "yes," Joseph also says "yes" to do his part to bring the King of Peace into the world.

Today, then, is an opportunity to celebrate our ancestors in the church who said "yes" to God's call and have been our guides in co-creating the reign of God on earth, a world characterized by justice and peace. In particular, I pray in thanksgiving for the "yes" of witnesses such as Sister Thea Bowman, Sister Antona Ebo, Saint Hildegard of Bingen, and Saint Alberto Hurtado.

Who are the ancestors that have modeled for you the courage needed to live a faith that does justice? Consider beloved family members, the communion of saints, and the cloud of witnesses that surrounds you. How can you be a good ancestor to future generations?

COLLECT
Let us pray.

Pause for silent prayer

Grant, we pray, almighty God,
that by Saint Joseph's intercession
your Church may constantly watch over
the unfolding of the mysteries of human salvation,
whose beginnings you entrusted to his faithful care.
Through our Lord Jesus Christ, your Son,
who lives and reigns with you in the unity of the Holy Spirit,
God, for ever and ever. **Amen.**

FOR REFLECTION
• Joseph is not the star of his own story, rather playing a supporting role to Mary and Jesus. How do you support others' callings and ministries?

• It is well known that Joseph does not speak in the gospels. He was not literally silent, of course—he lived a full life with loving relationships—but since we have no record of his words he is remembered as a silent figure in the life of Jesus. How might you be called to greater silence in your life?

See Appendix B, p. 310, for additional questions.

Homily Points
• Saint Joseph, the husband of Mary and adoptive father of Jesus, has no lines in any of the gospels. We can only imagine his conversations with pregnant Mary or the baby Jesus while lulling him to sleep. Surely Joseph spoke—yet his silence in Scripture offers a profound invitation to each of us to grow quiet and give our full attention to Christ in our midst.

• Today's celebration of Saint Joseph, the patron saint of workers, offers an opportunity to express gratitude to the essential workers who make our communities run. From medical professionals to grocery store clerks to firefighters, countless people take up the call to help others in their professional lives. May their services be respected and appreciated.

SPIRITUALITY

GOSPEL ACCLAMATION
Phil 2:8-9

Christ became obedient to the point of death,
even death on a cross.
Because of this, God greatly exalted
    him
and bestowed on him the name which is
    above every name.

Gospel at the procession with palms

Mark 11:1-10; L37B (John 12:12-16
may also be read.)

**When Jesus and his disciples
    drew near to Jerusalem,
    to Bethphage and Bethany at
        the Mount of Olives,
    he sent two of his disciples and
        said to them,
    "Go into the village opposite
        you,
    and immediately on entering it,
    you will find a colt tethered on
        which no one has ever sat.
Untie it and bring it here.
If anyone should say to you,
    'Why are you doing this?' reply,
    'The Master has need of it
    and will send it back here at once.'"
So they went off
    and found a colt tethered at a gate
        outside on the street,
    and they untied it.**

Continued in Appendix A, p. 279.

Gospel at Mass   Mark 14:1–15:47; L38B
or Mark 15:1–39; L38B *in Appendix A,
pp. 279–282.*

Reflecting on the Gospel

In this holiest of weeks, we could not have two more opposite portraits of Jesus than Mark's account of the passion, which we read today, and John's on Good Friday.

Mark's version is stark, depicting a very human Jesus. In Gethsemane, Jesus falls prostrate to the ground, in deep distress. Three times he begs God to let the cup pass him by; three times his pleas are met with silence. At earlier crucial turning points, Jesus had concrete signs of God's presence and affirmation: an overshadowing cloud and a heavenly voice, but in Gethsemane there is only terrifying silence. Before him, across the Kidron Valley, rises the temple, with its officials who want him dead. Behind him, over the Mount of Olives, is the Judean desert. He could yet slip away and avoid death for the time being. What was God's will? Jesus finds no discernible response; all he can do is rely on his previous experiences of God's faithful love. Not knowing how God will bring the divine will for life and love to fullness through his brutal execution, Jesus chooses to remain in trust.

As the Sanhedrin and Pilate interrogate Jesus, he remains silent, like the Servant in Isaiah 53:7. Throughout his ministry, Jesus was not silent in the face of injustice; he denounced it and acted to rectify it. Here, his refusal to engage with representatives of corrupt systems can be read as a silent protest against them.

The desolate portrait of a Jesus abandoned continues unrelieved as Mark recounts the mockery by the soldiers, the march to the place of execution, and the verbal and physical abuse at Golgotha. Jesus's final words are an anguished cry: "My God, my God, why have you forsaken me?" By invoking Psalm 22, Mark helps us to see that even when one cannot sense God's presence or understand how God's saving purposes are at work in excruciating suffering, the Holy One never abandons any beloved daughter or son.

A far different portrait of Jesus is offered to us by John. Jesus knows all that is to happen and even seems to direct the action. In the garden, Jesus does not fall prostrate or beg God to take away the cup. Rather, it is the soldiers who fall to the ground when Jesus speaks the revelatory words, "I AM." He is eager to move toward his "hour," saying, "Shall I not drink the cup that the Father gave me?" The disciples don't abandon Jesus but are ready to defend him. It is Jesus, however, who protects them, insisting that the arresting party take only him. At the trial before Pilate, Jesus does not remain silent. Rather, it is he who is conducting the proceedings, and the procurator is the one under scrutiny. In the end, it is Pilate who brings condemnation upon himself, because he cannot decide in favor of the one who is true king before him. In John's account of the crucifixion, Jesus appears to be reigning already from the cross.

Both gospels offer important portraits of Jesus during his last hours on earth, each depicting different facets of his personality and saving work.

Preparing to Proclaim

Key words and phrases: "The disciples then went off . . . and found it just as he had told them."

To the point: In both the gospel at the procession and the passion narrative, Jesus gives his disciples instructions that are striking in their specificity and which occur just as he says. They find a donkey where they are supposed to; the bystanders allow them to take it. They follow a man carrying water and find the Upper Room waiting for them. Jesus continues to make predictions as he moves through the passion, like the shaking of the disciples' faith and the approach of Judas. In all this, Jesus seems to be in control, accepting calmly the horrific things that await him. Even as he prays from a place of deep sorrow, even as he pleads with God to "take this cup away," he accepts with steadfast courage what he is about to suffer. Jesus knows that the death that awaits him is not the end of his story. His faith in the God who gives life enables him to face his unthinkable torment.

Psalmist Preparation

This psalm is brutally honest in its expression of pain. The psalmist is in dire straits, left wondering why God has left him alone in his anguish. But by the end of the psalm, he remembers that God does *not* leave him alone; God is with him even as he suffers. He gives praise by the end of the psalm for God's unfailing goodness. As you prepare to proclaim this psalm, think of a time when you felt abandoned by God (maybe you are going through such a time now). Bring your pain to prayer; feel free to express whatever anger and hurt you feel. God is big enough to handle it, and God will not leave you alone with whatever you are going through.

Making Connections

Between the readings: The second reading gives us the glorious Philippians hymn that reveals so much of the meaning of Jesus's suffering and death. Paul summarizes for us here all that Jesus has taught: the last will be made first, to lose one's life is to gain it. All of these paradoxical teachings are present in the passion. By humbling himself to take on the entire human experience—even unto death—Jesus became king and ruler of the universe.

To experience: All of our own sufferings are wrapped up in the passion of Christ. His suffering was not in vain but rather became the source of abundant life for us. So our suffering, too, can be joined to Christ's. Every loss, every heartbreak, every physical pain can be transformed by God into a source of life. This is not to say that our pain no longer hurts; it certainly does. But Christ promises to be with us in that pain, so we are never left alone.

Homily Points

• Where is your Calvary? No person is exempt from suffering. Until God's kingdom fully and finally comes, we live in a world mixed with joy and sorrow, suffering and hope, death and resurrection. We will all find ourselves at the foot of the cross at some point. Perhaps the death of a loved one or the end of an important relationship brought you there. Maybe it was a painful injustice or a tragic accident. Spend some time this week reflecting on the realities of your life that bring you to Calvary, to the foot of the cross.

• In today's second reading, Saint Paul puts forth the image of Jesus emptying himself. The Son of God took on the form of a slave, emptying himself of all divine privileges so that he might fully enter the sufferings of humanity. Jesus's act of emptying created space for him to be filled again with the glory of God. Emptying can be difficult work—and it can also be life-giving in the end. Consider how you might empty yourself this Holy Week so that you might have more space to receive the joys of resurrection at Easter.

• Over the coming days, the church invites us to accompany our brother Jesus on his journey to Jerusalem. The liturgies of Holy Week offer chances to feel with Jesus and his disciples—the palm branches waving in the streets, the water that washes over our feet, the bread and wine shared in memory of Christ, the wood of the cross.

Model Penitential Act

Presider: As we begin this most sacred week of the church year, let us pause to ask God for mercy and healing from our sins . . . *[pause]*

 Confiteor: I confess . . .

Model Universal Prayer (Prayer of the Faithful)

Presider: Jesus cries out to God in his time of need. With trust that God listens to our prayers, let us bring our needs before the Lord.

Response: Lord, hear our prayer.

Unite Christians in our common mission to care for people on the margins . . .

Bring an end to the death penalty and all forms of execution . . .

Rouse the weary, hurting, and hopeless among us . . .

Sustain the hearts of people preparing to be initiated in the Easter season . . .

Presider: God who hears the cries of the hurting, your Son gave himself up to death on the cross for the forgiveness of sins and the salvation of all. Hear our prayers that during Holy Week we might enter ever more deeply into the suffering, death, and resurrection of Jesus. We ask this through Christ our Lord. **Amen.**

Liturgy and Music

My April birthday has fallen on every possible day of Holy Week. My fortieth birthday fell on Passion Sunday. After one of the Masses, the presider told the community that "This woman will work harder this week than the entire staff combined." As a musician-turned-priest, he was speaking from experience. Still, to have this kind of attention focused on me on that day made me uneasy.

You will work hard in the coming days. You are about to begin one of the most exhausting weeks of the church year. The sacred space will be transformed by red banners and palms, and filled with lectors rehearsing. All hands will be on deck, making it happen.

And when all the work is done, a hush will descend upon the assembly. The Easter fire will be kindled anew, and the people will praise the Author of our salvation story. Deo Gratias! Light of Christ!

Today our sacred space is silent and dark, a witness to our pre-Holy Week meditations. Soon it will resonate with the Spirit-filled voices of God's beloved people. Will you be ready? I pray that you will be, and that everything on your to-do list is crossed off. If not, set it aside. Breathe. Then give yourself to the greatest love story of all time. And as we work together with all those whose music and non-music related ministries help our liturgies come to life, let us remember that all of us are uniquely beloved in the sight of God.

COLLECT

Let us pray.

Pause for silent prayer

Almighty ever-living God,
who as an example of humility for the
  human race to follow
caused our Savior to take flesh and submit
  to the Cross,
graciously grant that we may heed his
  lesson of patient suffering
and so merit a share in his Resurrection.
Who lives and reigns with you in the unity
  of the Holy Spirit,
God, for ever and ever. **Amen.**

FIRST READING
Isa 50:4-7

The Lord GOD has given me
 a well-trained tongue,
that I might know how to speak to the
  weary
 a word that will rouse them.
Morning after morning
 he opens my ear that I may hear;
and I have not rebelled,
 have not turned back.
I gave my back to those who beat me,
 my cheeks to those who plucked my
  beard;
my face I did not shield
 from buffets and spitting.

The Lord GOD is my help,
 therefore I am not disgraced;
I have set my face like flint,
 knowing that I shall not be put to
  shame.

RESPONSORIAL PSALM
Ps 22:8-9, 17-18, 19-20, 23-24

℟. (2a) My God, my God, why have you
 abandoned me?

All who see me scoff at me;
 they mock me with parted lips, they
  wag their heads:
"He relied on the LORD; let him deliver him,
 let him rescue him, if he loves him."

℟. My God, my God, why have you
 abandoned me?

Indeed, many dogs surround me,
   a pack of evildoers closes in upon me;
they have pierced my hands and my feet;
   I can count all my bones.

℟. My God, my God, why have you
   abandoned me?

They divide my garments among them,
   and for my vesture they cast lots.
But you, O LORD, be not far from me;
   O my help, hasten to aid me.

℟. My God, my God, why have you
   abandoned me?

I will proclaim your name to my brethren;
   in the midst of the assembly I will
      praise you:
"You who fear the LORD, praise him;
   all you descendants of Jacob, give glory
      to him;
   revere him, all you descendants of
      Israel!"

℟. My God, my God, why have you
   abandoned me?

SECOND READING
Phil 2:6-11

Christ Jesus, though he was in the form
      of God,
   did not regard equality with God
      something to be grasped.
Rather, he emptied himself,
   taking the form of a slave,
   coming in human likeness;
   and found human in appearance,
   he humbled himself,
   becoming obedient to the point of
      death,
      even death on a cross.
Because of this, God greatly exalted him
   and bestowed on him the name
   which is above every name,
   that at the name of Jesus
   every knee should bend,
   of those in heaven and on earth and
      under the earth,
   and every tongue confess that
   Jesus Christ is Lord,
   to the glory of God the Father.

Living Liturgy

Liturgy and Justice: On Palm Sunday we celebrate Jesus's triumphant entry into Jerusalem; however, we also read the passion narrative and remember that Jesus was ultimately crucified for the good news he proclaimed to the poor. He has been sent "to bring glad tidings to the poor. / He has sent me to proclaim liberty to captives / and recovery of sight to the blind, / to let the oppressed go free, / and to proclaim a year acceptable to the Lord" (Luke 4:18-19). This message of liberation and justice was a threat to the Roman Empire, and ultimately Jesus was crucified for it.

Today we also celebrate the feast of Saint Óscar Romero, a modern saint who was martyred in El Salvador on this day in 1980. Romero, like Jesus, spoke truth to power on behalf of the Salvadoran people who were suffering due to extreme economic inequality and military repression.

Romero was selected as the archbishop of El Salvador because people in power believed that he would not be outspoken. Less than three weeks after his installation, however, his friend and Jesuit priest, Father Rutilio Grande, was murdered with two companions on the way to celebrate Mass in the countryside. Grande worked closely with landless peasants and was outspoken about the injustices they experienced at the hands of wealthy landowners. The assassination of his friend was a turning point for Romero, and he followed in Grande's footsteps by speaking out against the injustices he saw the Salvadoran people experience, even though he knew his life would be in danger.

He is quoted saying, "I have often been threatened with death. I must tell you, as a Christian, I do not believe in a death without resurrection. If am killed, I shall arise again in the Salvadoran people . . . If they manage to carry out their threats, as of now, I offer my blood for the redemption and resurrection of El Salvador." Saint Romero was assassinated by a bullet to his heart the day after a homily in which he criticized the government by saying," I order you in the name of God: Stop the repression!"

PROMPTS FOR FAITH-SHARING

• What suffering have you gone through or are you going through? How can you unite that suffering to Christ's?

• How do you discern between suffering you are called to accept and suffering you are called to resist?

• Read the passion narrative with an eye out for all the unnamed side characters who help bring the story to life. If you were present at the passion, what role do you hope you would play?

See Appendix B, p. 310, for additional prompts.

EASTER
TRIDUUM

GOSPEL ACCLAMATION

John 13:34

I give you a new commandment, says the Lord:
love one another as I have loved you.

Gospel   John 13:1-15; L39ABC

Before the feast of Passover,
    Jesus knew that his hour had
    come
to pass from this world to the
    Father.
He loved his own in the world and
    he loved them to the end.
The devil had already induced
    Judas, son of Simon the
    Iscariot, to hand him over.
So, during supper,
    fully aware that the Father had
      put everything into his
      power
    and that he had come from God
      and was returning to God,
he rose from supper and took
    off his outer garments.
He took a towel and tied it around
    his waist.
Then he poured water into a basin
    and began to wash the disciples' feet
    and dry them with the towel around his
    waist.
He came to Simon Peter, who said to him,
    "Master, are you going to wash my
    feet?"
Jesus answered and said to him,
    "What I am doing, you do not
      understand now,
    but you will understand later."
Peter said to him, "You will never wash
    my feet."
Jesus answered him,
    "Unless I wash you, you will have no
      inheritance with me."
Simon Peter said to him,
    "Master, then not only my feet, but my
      hands and head as well."
Jesus said to him,
    "Whoever has bathed has no need
      except to have his feet washed,
    for he is clean all over;
    so you are clean, but not all."

Continued in Appendix A, p. 283.
See Appendix A, p. 283, for the other readings.

Reflecting on the Gospel

This gospel contains a microcosm of the entirety of salvation. God, as the person of Jesus, knowingly prepares for death, and in preparation teaches his friends how to care for one another by exemplifying care for them.

One of the early controversies of the church was whether Christ was God in a human suit, a human with "god-ness," or fully both at once. We believe the final assertion: Jesus was both fully human and fully divine, with neither part of his being compromised. Saint Gregory of Nazianzus first proposed, "That which is not assumed is not redeemed," meaning any aspect of humanity that was not shared by Jesus is not saved by Jesus's resurrection. Put plainly, everything that makes being a human tough and wonderful, Jesus also had.

"He loved his own in the world and he loved them to the end." This statement is intensely impactful in the light of the knowledge that Jesus was fully human, and as such fully present to the friendships and relationships around him. Jesus was not distant and removed from his friends. They shared inside jokes, laughed at stupid things, and picked on one another. They had favorite foods. They had wives and children. They had siblings and aunts and uncles. They had jobs and lives that existed before Jesus arrived to invite them on a journey to change the world. They, like Jesus, were fully human.

Jesus loved them, and he loved them to the end. And during their last party, their last meal together, a goodbye party that only Jesus knew meant goodbye, he taught them with blunt demonstration how to love one another. He didn't share a parable or an analogy. The time for words had passed, and in a prelude to the bodily demonstration of love Jesus would perform days later, he physically bent to their feet and washed the dirtiest part of their bodies in front of them. And then he asked them to continue to do that, for one another, forever.

Today we begin the Triduum, and the journey into the corporeal reality of God's death. Christianity makes a flagrant and scandalous claim: God became a human, and that human died. God died containing all the pieces of humanity: joys, sorrows, friendships, family, worry about things left undone, anticipation for the future, and the resolve to do what needs to be done to save one's friends. In doing so, all humans are saved.

Today, in many churches, members of the parish are invited to have their feet washed. This can often feel theatrical or contrived. Yet every year, as the nervous parishioners take off their shoes and those washing their feet begin to kneel, there is a sense of intimacy and closeness that almost feels inappropriate. To be so physically close to someone, in such a submissive capacity, is highly abnormal. The lack of anonymity adds to the elevated awareness. But this is exactly the kind of shocking form of physical servitude that Jesus offers to his disciples. It should feel strange. It should move us.

Preparing to Proclaim
Key words and phrases: "If I, therefore, the master and teacher, have washed your feet, you ought to wash one another's feet."

To the point: Poor Peter in this gospel just cannot seem to grasp the point. He resists Jesus's efforts to wash his feet, as he cannot reconcile the idea of his master doing the work of a servant. And when Jesus insists, Peter asks to be washed all over. He rushes to his own conclusions without letting Jesus do his slow and intentional work of teaching. We, too, would do well to take our time as we strive to absorb and live out the teachings of Jesus.

Model Penitential Act
Presider: In today's gospel, Jesus calls his disciples to follow his model of servant leadership and love. As we prepare to celebrate the Eucharist, let us ask for forgiveness for the times we have failed to love as Christ . . . *[pause]*

Lord Jesus, you give us your body, the bread of life: Lord, have mercy.
Christ Jesus, you give us your blood, the cup of salvation: Christ, have mercy.
Lord Jesus, you will come again in glory: Lord, have mercy.

Model Universal Prayer (Prayer of the Faithful)
Presider: With faith in Christ's generosity, let us offer our prayers and petitions.

Response: Lord, hear our prayer.

Grant all Christians the space to slow down and the openness to enter these sacred Triduum days . . .

Inspire government leaders to be models of servant leadership . . .

Thwart the plans of those who seek to harm or betray others this night . . .

Sustain the energy of liturgists, musicians, lay ministers, ordained ministers, and all others who lead worship . . .

Presider: Gracious God, your love for creation is on full display on this most sacred night. Hear our prayers that we might follow your example and serve all people with tender care. We ask this through Christ our Lord. **Amen.**

Living Liturgy
Liturgy and Discipleship: Holy Thursday reminds us that the Mass we celebrate is indeed a living liturgy! Jesus washes the disciples' feet and says, "I have given you a model to follow, / so that as I have done for you, you should also do." In this radical act of servant leadership, Jesus demonstrates that liturgy is not meant to be an event limited to an hour each Sunday inside a church, but rather a way of being in the world. It is an invitation to get our hands dirty in service of our neighbors and to bring more abundant life to the world. How do you practice a living liturgy in your own life?

COLLECT
Let us pray.

Pause for silent prayer

O God, who have called us to participate
in this most sacred Supper,
in which your Only Begotten Son,
when about to hand himself over to death,
entrusted to the Church a sacrifice new for all
    eternity,
the banquet of his love,
grant, we pray,
that we may draw from so great a mystery,
the fullness of charity and of life.
Through our Lord Jesus Christ, your Son,
who lives and reigns with you in the unity of
    the Holy Spirit,
God, for ever and ever. **Amen.**

FOR REFLECTION

• In this gospel, Jesus gives us a model of servant leadership, of teaching not by authoritarian methods but by loving example. Where have you experienced servant leadership? How can you strive to live it out in your own life?

• At the Last Supper, Jesus both establishes the Eucharist and washes his disciples' feet. How are these two acts connected for you? What do they reveal about each other?

See Appendix B, p. 311, for additional questions.

Homily Points
• On the night before his death, Jesus pours out his body and blood for the disciples. Then he washes their feet. Through this deeply human act of service, Jesus models the way forward for his followers. Jesus washes the feet of the one who betrayed him. He washes the feet of the one who denied him. He washes the feet of those who fell asleep in his greatest hour of need.

• Jesus knows his disciples are not perfect— and he washes their feet anyway. The Son of God includes all in his ministry. As disciples, we too are called to serve others without discrimination. We are called to take after Jesus and love others with our whole selves.

GOSPEL ACCLAMATION
Phil 2:8-9

Christ became obedient to the point of death,
even death on a cross.
Because of this, God greatly exalted him
and bestowed on him the name which is above
every other name.

Gospel John 18:1–19:42; L40ABC

Jesus went out with his disciples
across the Kidron valley
to where there was a garden,
into which he and his disciples
entered.
Judas his betrayer also knew the
place,
because Jesus had often met
there with his disciples.
So Judas got a band of soldiers
and guards
from the chief priests and the
Pharisees
and went there with lanterns,
torches, and weapons.
Jesus, knowing everything that
was going to happen to him,
went out and said to them, "Whom are
you looking for?"
They answered him, "Jesus the Nazorean."
He said to them, "I AM."
Judas his betrayer was also with them.
When he said to them, "I AM,"
they turned away and fell to the ground.
So he again asked them,
"Whom are you looking for?"
They said, "Jesus the Nazorean."
Jesus answered,
"I told you that I AM.
So if you are looking for me, let these
men go."
This was to fulfill what he had said,
"I have not lost any of those you gave me."
Then Simon Peter, who had a sword,
drew it,
struck the high priest's slave, and cut
off his right ear.
The slave's name was Malchus.

Continued in Appendix A, pp. 284–285.
See Appendix A, p. 286, for the other readings.

Reflecting on the Gospel

Out of the entire year, this is the reading that is the longest and contains the most drama. It's grisly and full of intrigue. And it's been told to us so many times that we've probably grown weary, dreading the long minutes we might be required to stay standing during the service since many of us already know all the players and their lines.

There is a reason the church is built to be experienced cyclically. Our liturgies follow the same basic format. The Mass has a beginning, a middle, and an end. The liturgical year begins with Advent and then moves through seasons. The readings follow a three-year cycle. This allows us to enter into the flow of the church. We participate in the rhythm of Catholicism, moving in a series of circles as small as the daily movements of the Liturgy of the Hours and as large as the annual liturgical calendar. Even the sacraments offer us touchstones in an arch from baptism (birth) to anointing of the sick (death). The church, in all her wisdom, knows our tendencies as a narrative people accustomed to moving through seasons.

The gospel for Good Friday tells us the story of Christ's death. It is the seed at the center of the entire year. The fast-paced movements of this story from the garden to the tomb take us through the arrest, trial, and execution of Jesus. It's such a long stretch of plot, with so many crucial moments packed in, that we will spend our entire lives working to make sense of what exactly is going on here. Jesus is arrested. Certain folks in places of authority want him gone. Peter pretends not to know him. Pilate can't be bothered and just really wants to keep the peace. Jesus is cryptic, as always. Suddenly he's bleeding to death as his lungs collapse and telling his best friend to take care of his mom and a secret disciple comes out of the woodwork and offers to bury the body. Phew!

This is the story that Christians have heard so many times it runs the risk of becoming "boring." Good Friday offers us a chance, every year, to allow this story to offend us. If we take it seriously, and listen as if we've never heard it before, today's gospel offers us the chance to feel moved. We can join Jesus in his frustration and understand the pithy irony of his responses. We can better understand the humanity of Pilate, weighing the death of an innocent man against revolution within his territory. We can feel the fear of Peter, lying about his friends while doing his best to stay alive. We can sympathize with the sorrow and horror Mary felt watching her son be executed. There are so many entry points into this story that allow us to be moved by it. The gift of the rhythmic nature of the church is that we are invited to participate in this story every year we are alive, and if we let it, every day as well.

Preparing to Proclaim

Key words and phrases: "So they laid Jesus there . . . for the tomb was close by."

To the point: Even the passion of Christ has the reversal of roles that Jesus has been preaching all along. Up until now, we have seen Peter as the confident leader of the disciples, the one who knows who Jesus is, the "rock" on which Christ will build his church. Here, though, when his faith is really tested, he cowers away and denies his association with Jesus. On the other hand, Joseph of Arimathea and Nicodemus have both been secret, nighttime disciples. But when it really matters, they step up, taking responsibility for Christ's burial and offering him a final act of care.

Living Liturgy

Liturgy and Justice: During the passion narrative, Pilate states to the crowd that he finds no guilt in Jesus; however, when he tries to release Jesus, the crowd shouts, "If you release him, you are not a Friend of Caesar. Everyone who makes himself a king opposes Caesar." Upon hearing these words, Pilate hands Jesus over to be crucified, remaining silent instead of using his access to power to save the life of an innocent man in fear for his own. When have I remained silent to injustice or oppression when I had the power or opportunity to speak out or take action?

Take some time for reflection with "Crux Fidelis" by Steven C. Warner (World Library Publications [WLP], a division of GIA).

Homily Points

• God calls Christians toward the cross with courage. The virtue of courage is like any muscle. It can only be strengthened through practice. Consider the three women who bore witness to Jesus's death at the foot of the cross: Mary, the mother of Jesus; Mary, the wife of Clopas; and Mary of Magdala. These women heard Jesus speak of his impending death many times along the road. They knew of the suffering that would befall their beloved friend. Still, when the hour came, the three women stood courageously by Christ's side.

• Like these brave women, we are called to move toward the suffering. We are called to stay in the shadow of the cross at its darkest moments. We are called to summon the courage of the three Mary's and bear witness to the holy cycle of life, death, and resurrection.

FOR REFLECTION

• Jesus's disciples and family appear throughout this passion narrative and their responses range from cowardly denial to courageous accompaniment. Where do you see yourself in this passion story? How would you accompany Jesus in his last moments before death?

• Jesus's suffering and death are heartbreaking for those who love him. And yet we call this "Good" Friday because we know that the pain is only temporary; God promises to recreate all that is broken by sin. What is a time when you have experienced pain being transformed and God accompanying you through it into joy?

See Appendix B, p. 311, for additional questions.

Scan to listen to "Crux Fidelis."

Gospel

Mark 16:1-7; L41B

When the sabbath was over,
  Mary Magdalene, Mary, the mother
      of James, and Salome
  bought spices so that they might go
      and anoint him.
Very early when the sun had risen,
  on the first day of the week,
      they came to the tomb.
They were saying to one
      another,
  "Who will roll back the stone
      for us
  from the entrance to the
      tomb?"
When they looked up,
  they saw that the stone had
      been rolled back;
  it was very large.
On entering the tomb they saw a
      young man
  sitting on the right side,
      clothed in a white robe,
  and they were utterly amazed.
He said to them, "Do not be
      amazed!
You seek Jesus of Nazareth, the
      crucified.
He has been raised; he is not here.
Behold the place where they laid him.
But go and tell his disciples and Peter,
  'He is going before you to Galilee;
      there you will see him, as he told
      you.'"

*See Appendix A, pp. 287–292, for the other
readings.*

Reflecting on the Gospel

This year the gospel is from Mark, the oldest of the four gospel narratives. This is the first written account we have in the Canon that tells us about the resurrection. These same words have been shared in hundreds of languages for thousands of years.

Three women go to anoint the body, in line with Jewish custom. They are participating in a tradition they've likely done a few times before. It's worth nothing that these are not direct family members of Jesus, but friends and the relatives of his friends. The community that Jesus created in life is not one bound by bloodlines, but one that expanded to include these women and other friends.

The first sentence of this gospel tells us that the people with immediate concern and responsibility for Jesus's body are what we might call "chosen" family. They are women who have become surrogate sisters and mothers, showing up to do a caretaking role that they are not obligated to perform, but feel it is their duty to complete. The act they arrive to do is one that will necessarily receive no thanks, for the person they are attending to is dead. This should tell us a great deal about the type of relationships Jesus cultivated, particularly with women, during his ministry.

The big twist in this story is, of course, that the body is not there. They showed up and "were utterly amazed." The first thought isn't resurrection—it's fear that someone has stolen the body. It's a trick, it's disrespectful, and it's humiliating. And yet, there's a man in a white robe telling them that everything is fine. What on earth!

The age and translation of these words do not reveal the nuance that we desire and expect in modern storytelling. We don't hear about Mary Magdalene's panic or Salome's gasps. We only read about what the (presumed) angel says to them. Yet in order for this story to make it into the Gospel of Mark, these women had to tell it to someone. Which means a part of the story we can safely imagine is the scene of these three women sharing it with the disciples.

In today's reading of Mark's Gospel, the person in the tomb says, "You seek Jesus of Nazareth, the crucified. He has been raised; he is not here." In Luke's Gospel (written after Mark, and having read the account in Mark), the person in the tomb connects the dots for the women: "Why do you seek the living one among the dead? He is not here, but he has been raised. Remember what he said to you while he was still in Galilee, that the Son of Man must be handed over to sinners and be crucified, and rise on the third day" (Luke 24:5-7). It's good for us to acknowledge the progression of storytelling here, from Mark to Luke. Both are writing from the point of view of knowing Jesus resurrected and will continue to appear. But Mark's Gospel is less direct, allowing for more narrative anticipation.

Preparing to Proclaim

Key words and phrases: "Do not be amazed!"

To the point: The young man who greets the myrrh-bearing women gives them an impossible charge. "Do not be amazed," he says, as he sits in a tomb that should not even be open and proclaims the resurrection of a man they saw die. Of course the women are amazed at this; of course we are, too. Perhaps we should not be; this is, after all, a God of consistency. God has always given life and second chances to the people God loves. This is far greater than anything God has done before, but it is the same God at work, persistently giving life where there was death.

Model Universal Prayer (Prayer of the Faithful)

Presider: Called to walk as children of the light, let us joyfully voice to God our prayers and petitions.

Response: Lord, hear our prayer.

Animate God's holy church to make the buildings shake with joy on this most sacred of nights . . .

Grace with faith, hope, and love all those who are being baptized, confirmed, and welcomed to the eucharistic table tonight . . .

Shine the paschal flame upon those who dwell in darkness . . .

Strengthen the baptismal call of all gathered here in celebration of Christ's resurrection . . .

Presider: God of hope, you sent your son Jesus into this world to live among creation. Through his resurrection, we are forever freed from the power of sin and death. Hear our prayers that our lives may reflect your great love. We ask this through Christ our Lord. **Amen.**

Living Liturgy

Liturgy and Media: The Easter Vigil readings share important moments in salvation history, from creation through the resurrection of Jesus Christ. Throughout this history, God continually renews a covenant with the people. Like the forgetful fish Dory from the movie *Finding Nemo*, we often don't remember the promises we've made to God, but we "just keep swimming" forward continuing this history, trusting that the currents around us are wrapped in God's love. These Scripture passages from salvation history, then, are like short clips from a movie with a final screen that says, "God's mercy endures forever." How are you being called to live out a covenant with God this Easter season?

FOR REFLECTION

• In this gospel, the women who come to the tomb do not actually see the risen Jesus. They have to trust the word of the man who greets them. Who proclaims God's power to you? How do you witness the life-giving work of God?

• The women are not given much time to rest in their awe of what happens at the tomb. They are sent out with a mission; they are to pass on this news to Peter and the disciples. What work does God give you as one who has witnessed the resurrection? How do you share its joy?

See Appendix B, p. 311, for additional questions.

Homily Points

• This is the night Christians all over the world make our holy buildings shake with joy in remembrance of our Savior's great victory over death. Like the women at the tomb, we remember who Jesus was during his time on earth—the preacher, the peacemaker, the listener.

• We also remember who Jesus is today, for Christ is still preaching, still making peace, and still listening through the hands and hearts of every baptized person called to remember Christ's promise by our lives. The Son of Man has been raised! Amen, Alleluia!

GOSPEL ACCLAMATION
cf. 1 Cor 5:7b-8a

℟. Alleluia, alleluia.
Christ, our paschal lamb, has been sacrificed;
let us then feast with joy in the Lord.
℟. Alleluia, alleluia.

Gospel   John 20:1-9; L42ABC

On the first day of the week,
  Mary of Magdala came
     to the tomb early in
     the morning,
  while it was still dark,
  and saw the stone
     removed from the
     tomb.
So she ran and went to
  Simon Peter
  and to the other disciple
     whom Jesus loved,
     and told them,
  "They have taken the
     Lord from the tomb,
  and we don't know
     where they put
     him."
So Peter and the other
  disciple went out and
  came to the tomb.
They both ran, but the other disciple ran
  faster than Peter
  and arrived at the tomb first;
  he bent down and saw the burial cloths
     there, but did not go in.
When Simon Peter arrived after him,
  he went into the tomb and saw the
     burial cloths there,
  and the cloth that had covered his head,
  not with the burial cloths but rolled up
     in a separate place.
Then the other disciple also went in,
  the one who had arrived at the tomb
     first,
  and he saw and believed.
For they did not yet understand the
  Scripture
  that he had to rise from the dead.

or Mark 16:1-7; L41B in Appendix A, p. 293,

or, at an afternoon or evening Mass,
Luke 24:13-35; L46 *in Appendix A, p. 293.*

See Appendix A, p. 294, for the other readings.

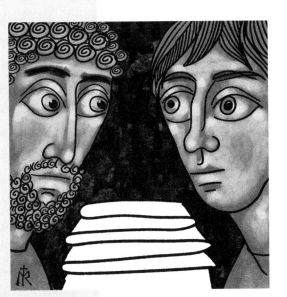

Reflecting on the Gospel

When a loved one dies, the world seems at first completely out of kilter. Daily rhythms are disrupted. Relationships shift. Things that seemed important before take a back seat, while other urgent concerns come to the fore. A whole reorientation to life without the physical presence of the loved one is necessary. In the gospel, we catch a glimpse of how the first disciples of Jesus navigated the difficult days in the aftermath of his death, how they had to construct their lives and meaning anew.

One of the key messages of the Gospel of John, from which the gospel of Easter Sunday morning comes, is that the resurrection is not simply a "happily-ever-after" ending or the fulfillment of our expectations. It turns the world on end, and defies explanation. It is God's final parable.

John's Gospel drives home the central question: Where is Jesus now? A single character, Mary Magdalene, represents the voice of the community, as she seeks her beloved, and laments, "We don't know where they put him" (20:2). Her search echoes that of the lover in the Song of Songs: "I sought him whom my soul loves; I sought him, but found him not" (Song 3:1). The question, "Where?" permeates the whole of John's Gospel. The first followers want to know, "Where are you staying?" (1:38). And in his final address to his disciples, Jesus speaks to them about an eternal dwelling place, which is not a geographical space but his very self (15:4-10).

In John 20 there are two parts to the answer of where Jesus is now. On Easter morning, we hear the first half: he has returned to the Father (20:1-9). Mary, Peter, and the Beloved Disciple all verify that he is not in the tomb. The latter two return home, not understanding, but Mary refuses to leave and continues her search.

In the gospel reading that will be proclaimed at the weekday Mass in just a couple of days, on Tuesday in the octave of Easter, we hear the second half of the answer. Jesus himself appears directly to Mary Magdalene and tells her not to cling to him as the earthly person she knew previously. He directs her to go to the gathered community of the brothers and sisters: it is there that he is to be found alive (20:17). In the resurrection appearance stories, the gospel focuses more on what happens to us than what happened to Jesus. A gospel that began by reflecting on how "the Word became flesh and made his dwelling among us" (1:14) concludes with the Word becoming enfleshed in each individual believer and in the whole body of the faith community. That is where he is to be found, as his transformation is completed in our own.

Where do you experience Christ most present today in your own life? And where in the life of our faith community?

Preparing to Proclaim

Key words and phrases: "For they did not yet understand the Scripture that he had to rise from the dead."

To the point: Even on Easter Sunday, the disciples do not quite get it. Jesus's resurrection is still hidden in mystery. There are hints here—an empty tomb and burial cloths. But Mary Magdalene misreads the empty tomb; she assumes that someone has taken Jesus's body. The fullness of what has happened has yet to be revealed. So it is for us, who live in the light of the resurrection and yet still experience pain and suffering and loss. Easter joy is not always accessible in its fullness, but we know there is more there than we can see.

Model Penitential Act

Presider: Christ is risen, alleluia! As we celebrate the Easter victory, let us be grateful for the unending love of our Savior . . . *[pause]*

Lord Jesus, you rose from the grave and conquered death: Lord, have mercy.
Christ Jesus, you sent Mary Magdalene to preach the good news:
    Christ, have mercy.
Lord Jesus, you will shine forever in the light of your glory: Lord, have mercy.

Model Universal Prayer (Prayer of the Faithful)

Presider: Christ our Savior rose from the dead and is now seated at the right hand of God. With praise and thanksgiving, let us offer our Easter prayers and petitions.

Response: Lord, hear our prayer.

Shower Easter joy upon the newly baptized, confirmed, and communed members of the Body of Christ . . .

Empower women in the church to preach the good news of Christ . . .

Envelop in divine hope those who grieve the death of a loved one . . .

Transform the lives of each of us gathered here to enter more deeply into the Easter spirit . . .

Presider: Redeeming God, you promise your people life in glory alongside your son Jesus. Hear our prayers, that through the paschal mystery we may grow in faith, hope, and love. We ask this through Christ our risen Lord. **Amen.**

Living Liturgy

The tomb is empty, and the empty church is full again. For all those who make music in the church, Easter Sunday can feel like the mountaintop after a long, up-hill hike. Having made it through the intense liturgies of the previous days, we are now showered, dressed in our nicest clothes, a little sleep deprived, and happily running on fumes. Joyful. Elated. Grateful. Eyeing the exits, perhaps: for in just a few hours, there will be respite. Maybe we are given a few days off, and a chance to reconnect with the ones who have been waiting patiently for us at home.

Throughout my decades of parish ministry, Easter Sunday meant capacity crowds, extra brass, and high-end solemnity. After church came the family gatherings. The next day I would drive to the little town of Calistoga, California where a vat of volcanic ash mud would receive me. Then a hot springs soak, then a massage. After four days of conducting, the treatment was pure mystagogia for my sore arms and shoulders. And as they did for Jesus when he was in the desert, angels ministered to me.

When that brief rest was over, it was back to the business of sustaining the progressive solemnity of the paschal feast. Fifty days of rejoicing, singing, and renewed enthusiasm for living our baptismal "yes."

Rest up, dear pastoral musicians. You deserve it. In a few short days you will be back at it again, keeping those Alleluias alive. Thanks be to God!

COLLECT

Let us pray.

Pause for silent prayer

O God, who on this day,
through your Only Begotten Son,
have conquered death
and unlocked for us the path to eternity,
grant, we pray, that we who keep
the solemnity of the Lord's Resurrection
may, through the renewal brought by your Spirit,
rise up in the light of life.
Through our Lord Jesus Christ, your Son,
who lives and reigns with you in the unity of
    the Holy Spirit,
God, for ever and ever. **Amen**

FOR REFLECTION

• The disciples of this gospel do not encounter the risen Jesus but rather see hints of what has happened. What hints and whispers of the resurrection do you see in your own life?

• Even faced with the empty tomb, Mary Magdalene and Peter and the other disciple need to grow in their understanding of Jesus's death-defying work. How do you still need to grow in your understanding of God's work in your life?

See Appendix B, p. 311, for additional questions.

Homily Points

• "We are witnesses of all that [Christ] did," proclaimed Peter to the Christian people shortly after Jesus's resurrection. Centuries have passed since the Son of God walked the earth, died on the cross, and rose to new life—yet we remain witnesses of Christ today. Christ's victory remains just as powerful in this moment in history.

• The story of Christ's sacrifice, the meaning of his mercy and compassion, lives on in all of us called to proclaim Jesus's promise with our lives. Empowered in the waters of baptism, we are called and commissioned to bear witness to the Easter victory. Amen, Alleluia!

SEASON OF EASTER

SPIRITUALITY

℟. Alleluia, alleluia.
You believe in me, Thomas, because you
    have seen me, says the Lord;
blessed are those who have not seen me,
    but still believe!
℟. Alleluia, alleluia.

Gospel   John 20:19-31; L44B

On the evening of that first day of
    the week,
when the doors were locked,
        where the disciples were,
for fear of the Jews,
    Jesus came and stood in their
        midst
and said to them, "Peace be
    with you."
When he had said this, he showed
    them his hands and his side.
The disciples rejoiced when they
    saw the Lord.
Jesus said to them again, "Peace be with
    you.
As the Father has sent me, so I send you."
And when he had said this, he breathed
    on them and said to them,
"Receive the Holy Spirit.
Whose sins you forgive are forgiven them,
    and whose sins you retain are retained."

Thomas, called Didymus, one of the
    Twelve,
    was not with them when Jesus came.
So the other disciples said to him, "We
    have seen the Lord."
But he said to them,
    "Unless I see the mark of the nails in
        his hands
    and put my finger into the nailmarks
    and put my hand into his side, I will
        not believe."

Continued in Appendix A, p. 294.

Reflecting on the Gospel

At a gathering, there's always someone who's willing to speak up when everybody else may be wondering the same thing but is afraid to ask. In today's gospel it's Thomas who voices the doubts and fears with which others are also struggling. The Fourth Evangelist frequently uses one character as a representative figure. In today's gospel, Thomas stands for everyone who is a follower of Jesus yet harbors doubts.

In the first scene, the disciples are together, locked in their fear, when Jesus stands in their midst. His double declaration, "Peace be with you," recalls his promise of peace that casts out fear (14:27). Jesus then shows the disciples his hands and side, the unerasable evidence of the brutality inflicted on him. Oddly enough, instead of increasing their terror, this gesture causes them to rejoice. The explanation is found in the Last Supper scene, where Jesus spoke to his disciples about his impending death, likening his pain and theirs to the labor pangs of a woman giving birth, whose agony turns to joy after the new life is brought forth. Jesus had assured them that when they would see him again, their hearts would rejoice with a joy no one could take from them (16:20-22).

Jesus then sends the disciples to continue the mission for which the Father sent him. In John's Gospel there is no calling or sending of the Twelve; the mission is entrusted to all disciples here, as they are empowered with the Spirit. As Jesus breathes on them, the new life brought forth through his death and resurrection vivifies them. The image is reminiscent of the creation of the first human being, into whose nostrils the Creator breathes the breath of life (Gen 2:7). It also calls to mind Ezekiel's vision of the valley of dry bones, over which he prophesies, "I will make breath enter you so you may come to life" (Ezek 37:5). Just as God restored hope to the disheartened Babylonian exiles, so the risen Christ breathes peace and joy into the fearful disciples.

The power that the disciples receive with this infusion of the Spirit is the ability to heal and forgive. When Jesus shows his wounds, we see that forgiveness does not erase them, nor does it dismiss them as unimportant. Telling the truth about them is essential for forgiveness and healing.

In the second scene, Thomas stands for all who were not present in the initial experience with the resurrected Christ. Just as Mary Magdalene did, so the disciples declare, "We have seen the Lord" (20:17, 25). But belief on the basis of another's word is not sufficient (see 4:42); one must have firsthand experience of Christ in order to participate in the mission. Jesus once again stands in their midst, bringing peace. He directs Thomas to probe the meaning of his wounds so that he too can become an agent of forgiveness and healing. When Thomas makes his acclamation of faith, Jesus affirms that there are two ways of blessedness: believing by having seen, and believing without having seen. The crucial thing is to believe, so as to have life.

Preparing to Proclaim

Key words and phrases: "Now, Jesus did many other signs in the presence of his disciples that are not written in this book."

To the point: The last paragraph of this gospel passage is a little frustrating. Why would John not write down all the signs that Jesus did? It seems like more preservation of this story would be better! But the incompleteness of John's retelling reveals an important thing: we need each other. None of us holds the complete story of Jesus, but we all see him in different ways according to our various places in life. When we come together to share what we have seen of Jesus, we may begin to realize that he far surpasses our hopes for him. Our images of Jesus are always too small. Thomas, too, would have understood more of Christ had he trusted those who had experienced him differently.

Psalmist Preparation

We complete the Easter octave with the same psalmody that started it, repeating this week the psalm of Easter Sunday. There is a unity to our rejoicing as it extends beyond the one day, and we join in heaven's never-ending song of praise that is the response to God's enduring love. As you prepare to proclaim this psalm, reflect on your Easter octave experience. Are you able to carry the joy of Easter Sunday throughout these eight days? How will you continue to celebrate the resurrection throughout the entire Easter season?

Making Connections

Between the readings: Thomas is a last holdout in the disciples' coming to believe in the resurrection. When he also encounters Christ, the disciples are finally unified in their experience and belief. This paves the way for the unity of heart and mind we see in the first reading's description of the early community of Christians. Because they have in common their belief in the risen Christ, they are able to share all else in common, too.

To experience: The first reading reveals what a community looks like when it has really encountered the risen Christ. It is hard to envision this today because we are so shaped by a society that values money above all else. Our capitalist and consumerist culture makes the early believers' common distribution of goods seem a wildly unattainable dream. But we are called to at least hold loosely to our possessions, being ready to distribute them to others when we encounter need in our neighbors.

Homily Points

• Fear grips the disciples as they huddle together on that first day of the week. Their leader and friend just died an excruciating death on the cross. A woman from Magdala claims Jesus still lives—but her story sounds like nonsense. Jesus died. The tomb is closed. The story is over, right? Doors are not the only things locked on that first day.

• Then Jesus appears. Jesus, the one who died, stands in their midst in all his glorified humanity—and with his scars. The resurrected Jesus still bears the marks of the cross on his hands and side when he offers the disciples the gift they so desperately needed: peace. The peace Jesus offers does not promise the absence of fear, violence, or suffering. Rather, it is a promise of wholeness and fulfillment, an assurance of the divine presence always and everywhere. Peace be with you wherever you go. Peace be with you in your darkest hours. Peace be with you when you feel most alone. Peace be with you in the face of death. Peace will be with you because I will be with you.

• Jesus returns to the disciples a week later when Thomas is with them. Knowing he missed the first appearance, Jesus gives Thomas exactly what he needs. He invites Thomas to touch the wounds on his resurrected body. Thomas often gets a bad rap for doubting—but what about his desire to draw close to his Savior? Thomas asks for what many of us need: the assurance that Jesus is truly present in our midst.

CELEBRATION

Model Rite for the Blessing and Sprinkling of Water

Presider: In the healing waters of baptism, we are freed from the powers of sin and death. May these waters draw us ever closer to Christ and his resurrection . . . *[pause]*
  [continue with The Roman Missal, *Appendix II]*

Model Universal Prayer (Prayer of the Faithful)

Presider: Drawn together as a community of believers, let us place our prayers and petitions before the risen Lord.

Response: Lord, hear our prayer.

Fortify the faith and community support of all people initiated into the church at Easter . . .

Make your promise of peace known to all people suffering from the tragedies of war . . .

Draw close to your tender care all people who grieve or suffer at the foot of the cross . . .

Give new life to all those who have died and grant them joy in your everlasting kingdom . . .

Presider: Compassionate God, your resurrected Son appeared to the disciples with his wounds from the cross on full display. Hear our prayers and embrace our wounds with your healing power so that we too might experience the joy of resurrection. We offer this prayer through Christ our risen Lord. **Amen.**

Liturgy and Music

In 2000, Pope John Paul II declared that the Second Sunday of Easter be called Divine Mercy Sunday. While the entire season of Lent has been about God's mercy and forgiveness, it reverberates for another week, forming a backdrop to Thomas's doubt.

Thomas was called "Didymus," a name that means "Twin." Who is Thomas's twin? It is each of us! Despite what we claim to believe, we still need to be convinced that the mercy of the risen One is with us and all around us, all the time.

One of the challenges we face as pastoral musicians is in crafting a musical arc that accompanies the contours of progressive solemnity. The paschal Triduum has its own arc, as do the seasons of Advent, Christmastide, and Lent. The added layers of ritual language and action are certainly a crucial part of the shaping of these arcs. But as we make our way through those familiar hills and valleys, is it not the music that most conspicuously adds dimensional fervor, emotion, emphasis, height and depth to our liturgies? A tympani roll starts out at pianissimo. With the gradual crescendo, our anticipation builds to the moment of climax when the cymbal crashes and the emotional wave breaks on the shore. With the music, there is no doubt that something extraordinary has happened, and a new day has dawned. Easter Sunday, with all its mountaintop splendor, is the easy part. The work of sustaining it throughout the great fifty days is just beginning.

COLLECT

Let us pray.

Pause for silent prayer

God of everlasting mercy,
who in the very recurrence of the paschal feast
kindle the faith of the people you have made your own,
increase, we pray, the grace you have bestowed,
that all may grasp and rightly understand
in what font they have been washed,
by whose Spirit they have been reborn,
by whose Blood they have been redeemed.
Through our Lord Jesus Christ, your Son,
who lives and reigns with you in the unity of the Holy Spirit,
God, for ever and ever. **Amen.**

FIRST READING
Acts 4:32-35

The community of believers was of one heart and mind,
  and no one claimed that any of his possessions was his own,
  but they had everything in common.
With great power the apostles bore witness
  to the resurrection of the Lord Jesus,
  and great favor was accorded them all.
There was no needy person among them,
  for those who owned property or houses would sell them,
  bring the proceeds of the sale,
  and put them at the feet of the apostles,
  and they were distributed to each according to need.

RESPONSORIAL PSALM
Ps 118:2-4, 13-15, 22-24

℟. (1) Give thanks to the Lord for he is good, his love is everlasting.
  or:
℟. Alleluia.

Let the house of Israel say,
  "His mercy endures forever."
Let the house of Aaron say,
  "His mercy endures forever."
Let those who fear the LORD say,
  "His mercy endures forever."

℟. Give thanks to the Lord for he is good, his love is everlasting.
  or:
℟. Alleluia.

I was hard pressed and was falling,
  but the LORD helped me.
My strength and my courage is the LORD,
  and he has been my savior.
The joyful shout of victory
  in the tents of the just.

℟. Give thanks to the Lord for he is good,
  his love is everlasting.
  or:
℟. Alleluia.

The stone which the builders rejected
  has become the cornerstone.
By the LORD has this been done;
  it is wonderful in our eyes.
This is the day the LORD has made;
  let us be glad and rejoice in it.

℟. Give thanks to the Lord for he is good,
  his love is everlasting.
  or:
℟. Alleluia.

SECOND READING
1 John 5:1-6

Beloved:
Everyone who believes that Jesus is the
    Christ is begotten by God,
  and everyone who loves the Father
  loves also the one begotten by him.
In this way we know that we love the
    children of God
  when we love God and obey his
    commandments.
For the love of God is this,
  that we keep his commandments.
And his commandments are not
    burdensome,
  for whoever is begotten by God
    conquers the world.
And the victory that conquers the world is
  our faith.
Who indeed is the victor over the world
  but the one who believes that Jesus is
    the Son of God?

This is the one who came through water
    and blood, Jesus Christ,
  not by water alone, but by water and
    blood.
The Spirit is the one that testifies,
  and the Spirit is truth.

Living Liturgy

Liturgy and Media: The Acts of the Apostles provides a vision of a world where everyone's needs are met through the community. "The community of believers was of one heart and mind, and no one claimed that any of his possessions was his own, but they had everything in common." We are called into this legacy of communal sharing and mutual aid by our early Church ancestors.

The song "Crowded Table" by the Highwomen imagines the world in a similar way. The chorus states, "I want a house with a crowded table / And a place by the fire for everyone / Let us take on the world while we're young and able / And bring us back together when the day is done."

I have been blessed quite a few times in my life to experience the beauty of community, particularly during the Catholic volunteer program I participated in after graduating from college. There was a large wooden table in the kitchen where the eight of us volunteers would gather each evening to eat meals and share about our days at our different justice-based work placements. We pooled our money to buy groceries and would take turns cooking in pairs throughout the week so that the other members of our community could simply come home to enjoy a home-cooked meal, especially after an intense day at work.

Since we were already cooking for eight people, we would often invite friends or neighbors to join us at these meals as well, and that table became a sacred space that connected us with past and future volunteer communities. I often left that table hours after dinner began with my stomach and heart full.

The last verse of "Crowded Table" is "The door is always open / Your picture's on my wall / Everyone's a little broken / And everyone belongs / Yeah, everyone belongs." Acts reminds us that as Christians we are called to share our lives with the people around us. We may not individually have enough to sustain ourselves, but when we all share what little we have, we experience an abundance that leaves no one outside.

PROMPTS FOR FAITH-SHARING

• How do you encounter the risen Christ? What evidence does Jesus give you of his presence and power?

• What might you learn about Jesus from people who are different from you? Think of differences in age, culture, and vocation. How might you seek out others' stories of Jesus so that you might appreciate him more fully?

• The first reading reveals an early church that holds all things in common. Shaped as we are by capitalism and consumerism, it is hard for us to envision living in such a way, but what is one way you could loosen your grasp of possessions and share with those who are in need?

See Appendix B, p. 311,
for additional prompts.

GOSPEL ACCLAMATION
John 1:14ab

℟. Alleluia, alleluia.
The Word of God became flesh and made his
    dwelling among us;
and we saw his glory.
℟. Alleluia, alleluia.

Gospel Luke 1:26-38; L545

The angel Gabriel was sent from God
    to a town of Galilee called Nazareth,
    to a virgin betrothed to a man
        named Joseph,
    of the house of David,
    and the virgin's name was Mary.
And coming to her, he said,
    "Hail, full of grace! The Lord is
        with you."
But she was greatly troubled at what
        was said
    and pondered what sort of greeting
        this might be.
Then the angel said to her,
    "Do not be afraid, Mary,
    for you have found favor with God.
Behold, you will conceive in your
        womb and bear a son,
    and you shall name him Jesus.
He will be great and will be called Son of
        the Most High,
    and the Lord God will give him the throne
        of David his father,
    and he will rule over the house of Jacob
        forever,
    and of his Kingdom there will be no end."
But Mary said to the angel,
    "How can this be,
    since I have no relations with a man?"
And the angel said to her in reply,
    "The Holy Spirit will come upon you,
    and the power of the Most High will
        overshadow you.
Therefore the child to be born
    will be called holy, the Son of God.
And behold, Elizabeth, your relative,
    has also conceived a son in her old age,
    and this is the sixth month for her who
        was called barren;
    for nothing will be impossible for God."
Mary said, "Behold, I am the handmaid of
        the Lord.
May it be done to me according to your word."
Then the angel departed from her.

See Appendix A, p. 295, for the other readings.

Reflecting on the Gospel

This gospel holds the moment that sets in motion our salvation: Mary's fiat to the Lord, and her openness to letting God disrupt her life in a radical way. The "yes" that Mary shares here is even more consequential given the time during which she lived. To have a child out of wedlock was to ensure poverty. Mary essentially recused herself from society by taking a leap of faith and saying "yes" to Gabriel.

With the hindsight of the birth of the Messiah, we can comfortably say Mary made the right choice. At that moment, however, the stakes involved her entire life. A mystical entity interrupts her life and asks her to become the one thing a single teenage girl has always been taught by society to be terrified of: becoming pregnant.

This gospel invites us to imagine how we might react in a similar situation. What if the angel Gabriel appeared to you and asked you to evaporate the entirety of your retirement account and investments? Or quit your job and become a full-time caretaker? Or go blind? What if, suddenly and without preparation, you were asked to enter a situation that most consider extremely compromising?

The truth is that people are asked to do this every day, all over the world. Fortunes are lost, careers are halted, family members become ill, and we ourselves experience the breakdown of our own bodies. Everyone will eventually experience a jarring and life-altering incident, whether it's the loss of a parent, or a miscarriage, or a marriage falling apart, or losing a job. This type of existential upheaval is what Gabriel asks of Mary. The angel asks her to say "yes" to a lifetime of extreme social and economic struggle. She doesn't know that Joseph will keep the engagement. She doesn't know that her son will grow up to be a carpenter who's able to care for her. She certainly doesn't know what his ministry and death will look like. She's a kid, saying yes to an impossible request, all because she trusts that the Lord is good.

When modern Catholic thought asks us to contemplate mirroring Mary's fiat in our own lives, we rarely elevate the question to similar stakes. And yet, there is always a possibility that we will face a decision or situation that shares the gravity of an unmarried teenager getting pregnant in the time of Roman occupation. So when we think about how Mary's fiat might look today, we must make space for that which seems impossible or overwhelmingly uncomfortable.

How can we become more intentional about saying "yes" to the Lord, in all parts of our life? "Yes" to the favor asked by a neighbor, "yes" to the need for a volunteer, "yes" to quality time with a friend or child, "yes" to intentional moments of silence and prayer? Looking to Mary's example and honoring her as the Mother of God are easy things to say. It is more impactful—and significantly harder—to act upon her example.

Preparing to Proclaim

Key words and phrases: "The Holy Spirit will come upon you, and the power of the Most High will overshadow you."

To the point: Decades before the Holy Spirit descends at Pentecost, the Holy Spirit descends on Mary. The Spirit's descent plus her consent enable Jesus to become present in a unique way; he takes on his humanity from her. Mary says a big yes here; pregnancy is a dangerous thing, and motherhood forever alters a woman's life. She takes on all the unknowns with faith in the God who promises to be with her.

Model Penitential Act

Presider: Mary's "yes" changed the course of human history. May these waters empower us to say our own "yes" to changing the world for the better . . . *[pause]*

Lord Jesus, you are the Son of God: Lord, have mercy.
Christ Jesus, you are the Son of Mary: Christ, have mercy.
Lord Jesus, your kingdom will rule forever: Lord, have mercy.

Model Universal Prayer (Prayer of the Faithful)

Presider: Through the intercession of Mary the Mother of God, let us bring our prayers and petitions before the Lord.

Response: Lord, hear our prayer.

Deepen the callings of mothers, godmothers, foster mothers, and all mother-figures . . .

Bless the work of OB/GYNs, nurses, and all medical personnel who care for pregnant people . . .

Hold in your loving embrace the hopes of couples struggling with infertility . . .

Strengthen our resolve to faithfully answer God's callings in our lives . . .

Presider: Generous God, you sent your Son into the world to be a light for all people. Hear our prayers that we may accept your callings with confidence and reflect Christ's light to communities everywhere. We ask this through Jesus our risen Lord. **Amen.**

Living Liturgy

Liturgy and the Arts: The feast of the Annunciation occurs during the Easter season this year, and the announcement of Jesus's birth so close to the passion reminds us of the truth of our faith: that death transforms into new life. In Henry Ossawa Tanner's painting "The Annunciation," as she listens to the angel Gabriel, Mary's face also holds the tension of death along with the promise of new life. "Do not be afraid, Mary . . . for nothing will be impossible for God." Although she may be fearful of the death that likely awaits her as an unwed pregnant woman, Mary says "yes" to God, thereby birthing abundant life for all generations. How is God inviting you to walk in Mary's footsteps and transform death into new life?

FOR REFLECTION

• God asks Mary to do something big; pregnancy and motherhood will forever alter the course of her life. How willing are you to let God interrupt your plans? How open are you to saying yes when God asks something big of you?

• Reflect on your relationship with Mary. Do you see her as a mother, model, or companion? Which of her many titles most appeals to you?

See Appendix B, p. 311, for additional questions.

Homily Points

• In today's first reading from Isaiah, the Lord tells Ahaz to ask for a sign—a big sign "deep as the netherworld, or high as the sky!" When is the last time you asked God for a sign? In times of discernment, we can be assured of God's presence and desire to help us move into fullness of life.

• God can and will offer signs that point the way. Divine signs often span beyond our wildest dreams, like a virgin conceiving the child Emmanuel. Divine signs can also be hidden in the ordinary, like a beautiful sunset or an unexpected call from an old friend. In honor of today's solemnity, consider how you can heighten your awareness of God's signs in the world so that, like Mary, you can say a bold "yes" when God calls.

SPIRITUALITY

GOSPEL ACCLAMATION
cf. Luke 24:32

℟. Alleluia, alleluia.
Lord Jesus, open the Scriptures to us;
make our hearts burn while you speak to us.
℟. Alleluia, alleluia.

Gospel   Luke 24:35-48; L47B

The two disciples recounted what had taken
    place on the way,
    and how Jesus was made known to them
    in the breaking of bread.

While they were still speaking about this,
    he stood in their midst and said to them,
    "Peace be with you."
But they were startled and terrified
    and thought that they were seeing a ghost.
Then he said to them, "Why are you troubled?
And why do questions arise in your hearts?
Look at my hands and my feet, that it is I
    myself.
Touch me and see, because a ghost does not
    have flesh and bones
    as you can see I have."
And as he said this,
    he showed them his hands and his feet.
While they were still incredulous for joy
    and were amazed,
    he asked them, "Have you anything here
    to eat?"
They gave him a piece of baked fish;
    he took it and ate it in front of them.

He said to them,
    "These are my words that I spoke to you
    while I was still with you,
    that everything written about me in the
    law of Moses
    and in the prophets and psalms must be
    fulfilled."
Then he opened their minds to understand
    the Scriptures.
And he said to them,
    "Thus it is written that the Christ would
    suffer
    and rise from the dead on the third day
    and that repentance, for the forgiveness
    of sins,
    would be preached in his name
    to all the nations, beginning from
    Jerusalem.
You are witnesses of these things."

Reflecting on the Gospel

The gospel for today has many resonances with the gospel for the Second Sunday of Easter (John 20:19-31). In both accounts, the risen Christ appears to the disciples and stands "in their midst." In both, his first words are "Peace be with you," and then he shows them his hands, feet, and side. In both accounts the disciples move from terror to joy. Both stories end with a sending of the disciples in mission.

Despite the many similarities, the theological emphases in the two accounts are quite different. Luke's focus is on the identity of the risen Christ and his reality and tangibility. Unlike the story of Thomas in John's Gospel, which focuses on believing, in the Gospel of Luke, the reason for the disciples seeing and touching Jesus's hands and feet is to convince them that the Risen One is the same Jesus who was crucified, and who still bears the marks of this on his body, though he is real and alive. Jesus is not just a memory that lives on, nor is he a haunting ghost; instead he is truly alive and tangible. Unlike the preceding Emmaus scene, where Jesus eating with the two disciples is revelatory and eucharistic, in today's gospel Jesus's eating serves as proof that he is truly alive and tangible in bodily form.

In the second half of Luke's Gospel, the focus shifts to the mission of the disciples to be witnesses to the suffering Messiah who is raised. Key to being a witness is understanding of the Scriptures, as well as repentance and forgiveness of sins. These same emphases are echoed in the first reading. Peter's speech is set in Solomon's portico in the temple; it follows his healing of a man who was crippled and who begged daily at the "Beautiful Gate." Peter harshly accuses his fellow Jews, placing on them all the blame for handing over Jesus and putting to death the "author of life." But the gospel writer's focus is not on fixing blame for the death of Jesus; rather, the focus is on God's power in raising Jesus.

Peter excuses all those who were complicit in Jesus's death, saying that they acted out of ignorance. This is similar to what the Lukan Jesus does as he prays from the cross, "Father, forgive them; they know not what they do" (23:34). Luke consistently portrays Jesus as a rejected prophet and explains his death as fulfillment of Scripture. The notion of a suffering Messiah, found in the first reading, and the gospel, is one that occurs only in Lukan writings (Luke 24:26, 46; Acts 3:18; 17:3; 26:23); it is not found in any Old Testament texts.

Immediately linked to the affirmation that the Messiah must suffer is the invitation to repentance and forgiveness. Repentance and acceptance of forgiveness are not guilt-induced; it is the only adequate response to God's gift of new life offered in restored relationship with the risen Christ. Witnessing to this love and power begins at home (Jerusalem), and then radiates out "to all the nations."

Preparing to Proclaim

Key words and phrases: "But they were startled and terrified and thought that they were seeing a ghost."

To the point: It is reassuring to note that the disciples do not react with immediate joy when they first encounter the risen Christ. Their response instead is to be "startled and terrified." We, too, do not always react with wholehearted joy when we encounter Jesus. He often comes to us in unexpected ways and asks us for sacrifices we don't want to make. But Jesus's response is to offer reassurance. He has the disciples look more closely, showing them the wounds he endured on the cross and eating in front of them to reassure them that he is not the ghost they fear he is. Jesus responds to our hesitation with the same reassurance. He always invites us to come closer, to see more fully who he is and what he is doing. And when we do, when we finally see him well enough, our response will echo the disciples' amazement and joy.

Psalmist Preparation

In this psalm, we ask God to reveal God's self to us as Jesus reveals himself to the disciples in the gospel. It is not always easy to encounter Christ; we do not always recognize the ways he comes to us, and when we do we might shy away from the hard things he sometimes asks of us. But to see God's face is to see light, and God "does wonders for his faithful one," never leaving us alone with the hard tasks of Christian life. As you prepare to proclaim this psalm, reflect on what you hesitate to bring to Christ. Ask him to shine his light in that area and reassure you with the promise of his presence.

Making Connections

Between the readings: In the gospel, Jesus tells the disciples that they are witnesses to his suffering, death, and resurrection. In the first reading, we see Peter getting to work, acting as the witness Jesus asks him to be. He shares what he has seen, reminding his listeners both of their guilt in the crucifixion and of the hope that still awaits them. He preaches the repentance to which Jesus calls us all.

To experience: We do not experience the resurrected Jesus in the same way the disciples did. We do not get to examine his wounds or have him reassure us by eating that he is human. But Jesus does continue to come to us, and we are invited to encounter him in other ways that are sometimes hard to see. He is present to us in the sacraments, in Scripture, in loving relationships, and in the people in need we encounter.

Homily Points

• Today's gospel passage follows the story of Cleopas and his companion encountering Christ on the road to Emmaus. The two disciples invite the man to dine with them, not realizing he was Jesus. At the blessing and breaking of the bread, the disciples' eyes were opened, and they recognized that the one sitting around the table was their risen Savior. Soon after, Jesus startles another group of disciples who also did not recognize him at first glance. Their reactions beg the question: what keeps us from recognizing Christ in our midst? How can our senses be opened—through prayer, sacred encounters, and acts of service—so that we are ready to greet Christ when he comes again?

• Jesus proves the reality of his glorified human presence to the disciples when he poses the common, carnal question: Have you anything here to eat? The image of the risen Christ chowing down on baked fish is both amusing and profound. Our God rose to new life and brought the fullness of the human experience with him. There is no part of our realities that Christ did not redeem.

• A core part of Jesus's ministry was opening minds and hearts to the Scriptures. The Hebrew Scriptures—specifically the law of Moses, the writings of the prophets, and the psalms—shaped Jesus during his life. The Christian Scriptures that would come later continue the wisdom put forth in these ancient texts. The Son of God continues to open minds and hearts to the revelations in Scripture. Consider spending time each day praying with Scripture. See what Jesus may reveal to you through the sacred stories.

CELEBRATION

Model Rite for the Blessing and Sprinkling of Water

Presider: In baptism, we begin a special relationship with Jesus who journeys alongside us forever. By the sprinkling of this water, may we be reminded of Christ's great love for us . . . *[pause]*

   [continue with The Roman Missal, *Appendix II]*

Model Universal Prayer (Prayer of the Faithful)

Presider: Accompanied by the glorified Christ, let us entrust our needs to God who hears all prayers.

Response: Lord, hear our prayer.

Make your church an effective advocate for affordable food and housing for all people . . .

Inspire religious communities to live out their mission in our ever-changing world . . .

Bring a swift end to anti-Semitism and all acts of violence toward our Jewish sisters and brothers . . .

Open our minds and hearts to the divine word proclaimed through Scripture . . .

Presider: Loving God, you call us to be people of peace who live out the lessons of Scripture in our words and actions. Receive our prayers that strengthened by Jesus we might be witnesses of his glory to all the nations. We ask this through Christ our risen Lord. **Amen.**

Liturgy and Music

Have you ever been complimented for making what you do look easy? For selecting that perfect song that miraculously goes with the gospel? We smile, and accept the compliment as a gift, which it is. But it takes far more than meets the eye to do what we do. It takes real human work. And like much of life in the faith, it is anything but magic.

In Luke's Gospel, Jesus says to his disciples: "Why are you troubled? And why do questions arise in your hearts? Look at my hands and my feet, that it is I myself. Touch me and see, because a ghost does not have flesh and bones as you can see I have."

As a child, I imagined Jesus as a kind of magician. As an adult, I came to see the flaw in this simplistic thinking. A magician fools and tricks his or her audience into seeing something that is fake, an illusion meant to deceive. The resurrected body of Jesus was absolutely real: living flesh and blood. He sat down to eat with his friends because he was hungry. He did these things so that the truth would be known. Alive in the flesh when he ascended, his living spirit remains within us forever. This is no illusion. And though he may have made it all look easy, it was his human sweat, blood, sorrow, and death that brought us the reality of who he is and always will be.

This is anything but magic.

COLLECT

Let us pray.

Pause for silent prayer

May your people exult for ever, O God,
in renewed youthfulness of spirit,
so that, rejoicing now in the restored glory
   of our adoption,
we may look forward in confident hope
to the rejoicing of the day of resurrection.
Through our Lord Jesus Christ, your Son,
who lives and reigns with you in the unity
   of the Holy Spirit,
God, for ever and ever. **Amen.**

FIRST READING
Acts 3:13-15, 17-19

Peter said to the people:
"The God of Abraham,
   the God of Isaac, and the God of Jacob,
   the God of our fathers, has glorified his
      servant Jesus,
   whom you handed over and denied in
      Pilate's presence
   when he had decided to release him.
You denied the Holy and Righteous One
   and asked that a murderer be released
      to you.
The author of life you put to death,
   but God raised him from the dead; of
      this we are witnesses.
Now I know, brothers,
   that you acted out of ignorance, just as
      your leaders did;
   but God has thus brought to fulfillment
   what he had announced beforehand
   through the mouth of all the prophets,
   that his Christ would suffer.
Repent, therefore, and be converted, that
   your sins may be wiped away."

RESPONSORIAL PSALM

Ps 4:2, 4, 7-8, 9

℟. (7a) Lord, let your face shine on us.
or:
℟. Alleluia.

When I call, answer me, O my just God,
 you who relieve me when I am in
  distress;
 have pity on me, and hear my prayer!

℟. Lord, let your face shine on us.
or:
℟. Alleluia.

Know that the LORD does wonders for
  his faithful one;
 the LORD will hear me when I call
  upon him.

℟. Lord, let your face shine on us.
or:
℟. Alleluia.

O LORD, let the light of your countenance
  shine upon us!
 You put gladness into my heart.

℟. Lord, let your face shine on us.
or:
℟. Alleluia.

As soon as I lie down, I fall peacefully
  asleep,
 for you alone, O LORD,
 bring security to my dwelling.

℟. Lord, let your face shine on us.
or:
℟. Alleluia.

SECOND READING

1 John 2:1-5a

My children, I am writing this to you
 so that you may not commit sin.
But if anyone does sin, we have an
  Advocate with the Father,
 Jesus Christ the righteous one.
He is expiation for our sins,
 and not for our sins only but for those
  of the whole world.
The way we may be sure that we know
  him is to keep
 his commandments.
Those who say, "I know him," but do not
  keep his commandments
 are liars, and the truth is not in them.
But whoever keeps his word,
 the love of God is truly perfected in
  him.

✠ CATECHESIS

Living Liturgy

Liturgy and Advocacy: The word *advocate* comes from a word in Roman law that literally described someone who would plead cases in court. The word *paraclete* is another word that means advocate and comes from the Greek *paráklētos.* A rough translation of this word is "to be called to walk alongside." God, then, is our Advocate who walks beside us to comfort and support us.

As we are made in the image of God, we are called to follow the Trinitarian example and be advocates for one another. Sometimes, however, the idea of being an advocate is conflated with being a "voice for the voiceless." While the intention in this statement is likely good, we know that all people, all of creation, have a voice. No one is voiceless, simply silenced or ignored.

Bryan Stevenson is a modern example of what it means to be an advocate. He started the Equal Justice Initiative to provide legal support to people on death row. He pleads cases in court to protect the lives of the innocent and guilty who have been sentenced to death row due to systemic injustice and institutionalized racism in the legal system.

In a documentary about his life, *True Justice: Bryan Stevenson's Fight for Equality,* Stevenson shares a story about the conversion he has experienced in his life as an advocate: "If you stand next to the condemned, if you fight for the poor, if you push against systems that are rooted and heavy . . . you are going to get broken . . . I am part of the broken community. When you realize that, you don't have a choice in standing up for the rights of the other broken." Stevenson discovered that walking alongside others in our brokenness paradoxically creates a more loving and compassionate world.

PROMPTS FOR FAITH-SHARING

• Imagine yourself amidst the disciples when Jesus appears. What would your reaction be to seeing the one you had seen die and be buried?

• What are your encounters with Christ like in your own life? Where is his presence clear? Where could you use help seeing him?

• Where are you encountering joy this Easter season?

See Appendix B, p. 311, for additional prompts.

SPIRITUALITY

GOSPEL ACCLAMATION
John 10:14

℟. Alleluia, alleluia.
I am the good shepherd, says the Lord;
I know my sheep, and mine know me.
℟. Alleluia, alleluia.

Gospel

John 10:11-18; L50B

Jesus said:
"I am the good shepherd.
A good shepherd lays down his
    life for the sheep.
A hired man, who is not a
    shepherd
    and whose sheep are not his
        own,
    sees a wolf coming and leaves
        the sheep and runs away,
    and the wolf catches and scat-
        ters them.
This is because he works for pay and
    has no concern for the sheep.
I am the good shepherd,
    and I know mine and mine know me,
    just as the Father knows me and I
        know the Father;
    and I will lay down my life for the
        sheep.
I have other sheep that do not belong to
    this fold.
These also I must lead, and they will
    hear my voice,
    and there will be one flock, one
        shepherd.
This is why the Father loves me,
    because I lay down my life in order to
        take it up again.
No one takes it from me, but I lay it
    down on my own.
I have power to lay it down, and power
    to take it up again.
This command I have received from my
    Father."

Reflecting on the Gospel

"I hate this gospel," said a friend of mine from New Zealand, as she broke open the word for the assembly on Good Shepherd Sunday (which this fourth Sunday of Easter is often called), some years ago. Coming from a country that at that time had sixty million sheep and three million people, my friend knew sheep.

One image that the gospel might subtly conjure up is that of a flock of dumb animals who mindlessly follow after whoever herds them. What my friend was (rightly) objecting to was the implication that the disciples of Jesus are basically dumb sheep, easily led by deception. But *is* the gospel implying this? The metaphor falters when we notice that it emphasizes the intimate knowledge the sheep have of the shepherd and vice versa (10:14). In the vocabulary of the Bible, "to know" another oftentimes refers to sexual intimacy. Moreover, the intimacy between Jesus and "his own" reflects the relationship he has with the Father (10:15). It is an intimacy that is expressed ultimately in loving self-surrender, even unto death.

There is a kind of domino effect in the Gospel of John. First, God pours out the divine self in love through the gift of the Word made flesh (1:14; 3:16), a self-surrender that is replicated in Jesus's gift of self for those who are his own (10:15). This same action is what is asked of his followers, most especially those in leadership (15:13). The image of shepherd is used a number of times in the Scriptures to characterize a leader of the people. God is depicted as the Shepherd of Israel (see Gen 49:24; Ps 23:1; 78:52-53). And it's surely not accidental or irrelevant that Moses and David were both actual shepherds before each was called to lead the people of Israel.

When Israel's leaders were not tending to the needs of the people, they were denounced for being absent and stupid shepherds, who scattered the flock (see 1 Kgs 22:17; Jer 10:21; 23:1-2; Ezek 34:5-6). By contrast, Jesus is the "model" (the Greek word here is *kalos*, meaning "good," "beautiful," "exemplary") shepherd, who gathers all together into one, giving his very life for his own. We replicate this kind of shepherding not by actively seeking suffering but by putting love at the center: God's love made visible in Jesus, Jesus's love made manifest in us. It is a love that is freely chosen by an empowered self, with a willingness to go to the depths of calamity if necessary. This requires not blind following but intimate knowledge of the model Shepherd and the free choice to continue his work of gathering all the disparate into one.

Today is a good day to ask ourselves: How does intimacy with Christ, the Good Shepherd empower me to replicate his loving self-surrender for those who are "his own"? What image in my own culture conveys what shepherds did in Jesus's culture? Spending some time in prayer with *that* image might be a creative and fruitful way of reflecting on this gospel reading.

Preparing to Proclaim

Key words and phrases: "I am the good shepherd, and I know mine and mine know me."

To the point: In this gospel, Jesus calls himself the good shepherd, and his descriptions of this role make clear that having a shepherd like Jesus is not like being a sheep raised for wool or meat. No matter how tenderly shepherds care for their flock, it is an inherently utilitarian relationship. But having a good shepherd like ours is about being known and being loved. We are so loved that there is one willing to lay down his very life for us. Having a good shepherd is also about knowing the shepherd in turn. We may not always feel like we know Jesus, who often moves in subtle and mysterious ways. But we are promised that we have a home in him, and whenever our hearts stir with the recognition that we are known and loved, we can be assured that Jesus is there.

Psalmist Preparation

This is the third time we sing this psalm in the four Sundays of the Easter season so far. It may be starting to feel a little tired as our Easter enthusiasm is often flagging by now. We are beginning to be caught back up in the normal busyness of our lives; much of our work lives and social obligations march forward regardless of what the liturgical season is. So this week, as part of your preparation to proclaim this psalm, try to carve out a little time for an Easter mini-retreat. Revisit the readings from Easter Sunday; stand again with Mary Magdalene and the disciples at the empty tomb. Ask God to refresh your Easter joy so that you may proclaim this psalm wholeheartedly.

Making Connections

Between the readings: In the second reading, John writes of the same love that joins us to our good shepherd, but he takes it even further. We are not just sheep in God's flock but in Christ have been adopted as children of God. God looks at us as beloved sons and daughters, brothers and sisters and co-heirs with Christ. We continue to grow into the love that God offers and are to become something beyond our greatest imaginings: "[W]hat we shall be has not yet been revealed."

To experience: Sheep are raised by shepherds either for wool or meat. They give of themselves (although unknowingly) to provide warmth and nourishment for others. We, the sheep of our Good Shepherd, are also called to give of ourselves in order to provide shelter and nourishment for others. We are asked to extend the love that Jesus offers to us and to care for others as our shepherd cares for us.

Homily Points

• The image of Jesus as the Good Shepherd has more depth than perhaps first considered. Those of us with little experience herding sheep may picture an idyllic scene: a happy shepherd surrounded by cute, playful lambs on a luscious green countryside. The reality of a shepherd's work is much less romantic. Sheep get to be heavy and dirty. They do not always follow directions and often face threats from predators.

• Shepherds, then, have the difficult but necessary task of protecting the sheep. The imagery from today's gospel invites us to picture Jesus defending his people from evil and getting into the messy realities of human life. The Good Shepherd lays down his life out of great love for his sheep. How might we live into the Good Shepherd's model of servant leadership in our communities today?

• Jesus tells the people, "there will be one flock, one shepherd." His vision can lead us to consider the important work that lays ahead for the Christian church so that one day we may indeed live as one flock. Strides toward greater Christian unity have certainly been made over the years. The Second Vatican Council put forth a decree on ecumenical relations and called for the restoration of unity among all Christians. Imagine what it could look like for Christians of all different traditions to come together in our shared beliefs. Imagine all we can learn from one another across our differences in worship styles, ecclesial structures, and advocacy practices.

CELEBRATION

Model Rite for the Blessing and Sprinkling of Water

Presider: Through the waters of baptism, the Good Shepherd welcomes us into the divine flock. By the sprinkling of this water, let us recall the community to which we belong, now and forever . . . *[pause]*
 [continue with The Roman Missal, *Appendix II*]

Model Universal Prayer (Prayer of the Faithful)

Presider: Christ the Good Shepherd provides for his sheep, leading and guiding us along the right path. With trust, we bring our prayers and petitions before him.

Response: Lord, hear our prayer.

Grace the work of theologians, pastors, lay ministers, and all who are working to advance ecumenical relations in the church . . .

Bring joy and strength to shepherds, farmers, and all who care for animals . . .

Grant release to prisoners and all people held captive . . .

Bless the ministries of our Christian sisters and brothers of other traditions . . .

Presider: Protector and creator of all, by the care of your Son we have come to know the fullness of life. Hear our prayers that your sheepfold may join together for the building up of your kingdom. We ask this through Christ our risen Lord. **Amen.**

Liturgy and Music

"I have other sheep that do not belong to this fold. These also I must lead, and they will hear my voice, and there will be one flock, one shepherd."

In this beautiful and beloved passage, Jesus reminds us that he is our shepherd. The safety to which his wayward lambs are led is eternal life in him. In our Catholic tradition, the life of the shepherd is generally associated with the priests, bishops, and the Holy Father himself.

When we ponder the path of our own lives, we know that the Good Shepherd's hand has reached for us through many different kinds of people, of varying vocations. Indeed, most of us have had at least one teacher whose guidance and example inspired us to serve God's family as pastoral musicians. We ourselves may have mentored, encouraging someone else to use their gifts for God's glory. Compassionate leadership is part of our life as baptized, priestly people, a unique gift that flows through us by the grace of the Holy Spirit. Who are the good shepherds that have guided you along your way?

In turn, what kind of shepherd do you want to be? As we reflect upon the Good Shepherd who gathers us tenderly with love and guidance, let us look for new ways to welcome him every day into our hearts. Let us pray that he will teach us to love, and direct us in our way of serving those with whom we share our ministry of music.

COLLECT
Let us pray.

Pause for silent prayer

Almighty ever-living God,
lead us to a share in the joys of heaven,
so that the humble flock may reach
where the brave Shepherd has gone before.
Who lives and reigns with you in the unity
 of the Holy Spirit,
God, for ever and ever. **Amen.**

FIRST READING
Acts 4:8-12

Peter, filled with the Holy Spirit, said:
 "Leaders of the people and elders:
 If we are being examined today
 about a good deed done to a cripple,
 namely, by what means he was saved,
 then all of you and all the people of
  Israel should know
 that it was in the name of Jesus Christ
  the Nazorean
 whom you crucified, whom God raised
  from the dead;
 in his name this man stands before you
  healed.
He is *the stone rejected by you, the
  builders,*
 which has become the cornerstone.
There is no salvation through anyone else,
 nor is there any other name under
  heaven
 given to the human race by which we
  are to be saved."

RESPONSORIAL PSALM
Ps 118:1, 8-9, 21-23, 26, 28, 29

℟. (22) The stone rejected by the builders
 has become the cornerstone.
 or:
℟. Alleluia.

Give thanks to the Lord, for he is good,
 for his mercy endures forever.
It is better to take refuge in the Lord
 than to trust in man.
It is better to take refuge in the Lord
 than to trust in princes.

℟. The stone rejected by the builders has
 become the cornerstone.
 or:
℟. Alleluia.

116

I will give thanks to you, for you have
    answered me
  and have been my savior.
The stone which the builders rejected
    has become the cornerstone.
By the LORD has this been done;
    it is wonderful in our eyes.

R̸. The stone rejected by the builders has
    become the cornerstone.
    or:
R̸. Alleluia.

Blessed is he who comes in the name of
    the LORD;
  we bless you from the house of the
    LORD.
I will give thanks to you, for you have
    answered me
  and have been my savior.
Give thanks to the LORD, for he is good;
  for his kindness endures forever.

R̸. The stone rejected by the builders has
    become the cornerstone.
    or:
R̸. Alleluia.

SECOND READING

1 John 3:1-2

Beloved:
See what love the Father has bestowed
    on us
  that we may be called the children of
    God.
Yet so we are.
The reason the world does not know us
  is that it did not know him.
Beloved, we are God's children now;
  what we shall be has not yet been
    revealed.
We do know that when it is revealed we
    shall be like him,
  for we shall see him as he is.

Living Liturgy

Liturgy and Creation: Jesus is the Good Shepherd, and in the gospel he says, "I lay down my life in order to take it up again. No one takes it from me, but I lay it down on my own." He is clear that he has chosen to lay his life down for his sheep out of a deep love.

Jesus shows us that sacrifice born of love is different from action taken out of a sense of obligation or requirement. Love that is not freely given is not true love, and as people of faith, we are invited to enter into this posture of love with Jesus as we prepare to celebrate Earth Day tomorrow.

In his encyclical *Laudato Si': On Care for Our Common Home*, Pope Francis reminds us that the call to love our neighbor is inextricably tied to the call to care for all of creation. He writes, "[A] true ecological approach *always* becomes a social approach; it must integrate questions of justice in debates on the environment, so as to hear *both the cry of the earth and the cry of the poor*" (49). The cry of the earth and the poor are deafening as we recall recent headlines in the news. Jesus models for us what it means to respond to the suffering of the world in love as we find ourselves in a historic moment in which we need to imagine new ways of being and living on earth so that all life can flourish.

Pope Francis writes, "A person who could afford to spend and consume more but regularly uses less heating and wears warmer clothes, shows the kind of convictions and attitudes which help to protect the environment. There is a nobility in the duty to care for creation through little daily actions . . ." (211). As we consider the ways that we can live more gently on the earth, Jesus's witness invites us to remember that making changes in our daily lives to live more gently on the earth does not need to be a burden when the desire to change comes from a place of deep love.

PROMPTS FOR FAITH-SHARING

• What does the image of Jesus as good shepherd mean to you?

• Where do you most clearly recognize Jesus in your life? What makes your heart stir with recognition that you are known and loved?

• How can you extend Jesus's loving care to others in your life?

See Appendix B, p. 311, for additional prompts.

SPIRITUALITY

GOSPEL ACCLAMATION
John 15:4a, 5b

℟. Alleluia, alleluia.
Remain in me as I remain in you, says the Lord.
Whoever remains in me will bear much fruit.
℟. Alleluia, alleluia.

Gospel

John 15:1-8; L53B

Jesus said to his disciples:
"I am the true vine, and my
Father is the vine grower.
He takes away every branch in
me that does not bear fruit,
and every one that does he
prunes so that it bears
more fruit.
You are already pruned because
of the word that I spoke to
you.
Remain in me, as I remain in
you.
Just as a branch cannot bear
fruit on its own
unless it remains on the vine,
so neither can you unless you remain
in me.
I am the vine, you are the branches.
Whoever remains in me and I in him
will bear much fruit,
because without me you can do
nothing.
Anyone who does not remain in me
will be thrown out like a branch and
wither;
people will gather them and throw
them into a fire
and they will be burned.
If you remain in me and my words
remain in you,
ask for whatever you want and it will
be done for you.
By this is my Father glorified,
that you bear much fruit and become
my disciples."

Reflecting on the Gospel

In today's gospel, Jesus speaks of the Father as a vintner who prunes branches that are bearing fruit so that they will produce even more. There is a strong emphasis on bearing fruit; the expression "bear fruit" occurs five times in the passage. It speaks not only of the fecundity in our relationship with God but also of missionary outreach and of interdependence with the other branches on the vine.

The image of God as a vine grower and Israel as the vineyard is a familiar one in the Scriptures (e.g., Isa 5:1-7; 27:2-5; Jer 2:21; Ps 80:8-18). Most often the metaphor is used to express God's disappointment in the lack of yield from the vine so tenderly planted and nurtured. In the Gospel of John, this is not the case. The disciples Jesus is addressing in this Last Supper scene (15:3) are "already pruned" so that they will bear more fruit. Branches that do not bear fruit are taken away.

Pruning is a Johannine metaphor for the passion. It is akin to the image in John 12:24, where Jesus speaks of the seed that must fall to the ground and die in order to bear much fruit. The emphasis is on the life that sprouts forth from the dying and the pruning. Expert gardeners know that the place to prune is, paradoxically, where the nodes are bursting with life.

From pruning, the stress in the gospel shifts to the importance of the branch remaining united to the vine in order to bear fruit. A branch cannot bear fruit on its own; cut off from the vine, it withers and dies, and then is good only for kindling. That remaining or abiding in Jesus is crucial for disciples is evident in that the verb *menein*, "to abide," occurs eight times in these eight verses. This mutual indwelling has been spoken of since the opening chapter of the gospel, where the first question asked by the initial two disciples is "where are you staying [*pou meneis*]?" (1:38). Another important moment is when the Samaritans ask Jesus to stay (*menein*) with them (4:40). In the Bread of Life discourse, Jesus tells his followers, "Whoever eats my flesh and drinks my blood remains [abides: *menei*] in me and I in him" (6:56). True disciples abide in Jesus's word (8:31) and Jesus's words remain in disciples (15:7). When Jesus tells his disciples he is going to prepare a dwelling place for them (14:2), it becomes clear that the "abiding place" is not a geographical locale but is Jesus himself (14:6), where also the Father makes his home (14:23), along with the Spirit (14:17).

How can we ensure that we are abiding in Christ and he in us? In the second reading, 1 John 3:24 gives a simple formula: "Those who keep his commandments remain in him, and he in them, and the way we know that he remains in us is from the Spirit that he gave us." The writer also spells out what it means to keep the commandments: "we should believe in the name of . . . Jesus Christ, and love one another just as he commanded us" (1 John 3:23).

Preparing to Proclaim

Key words and phrases: "I am the vine, you are the branches."

To the point: Jesus's image of himself as vine and us as branches is a lovely pastoral image, but it includes some hard truths. Jesus warns that those who do not bear fruit will be removed from the vine, and even those that remain will be subjected to pruning. Pruning is a fascinating practice; beginner gardeners are often hesitant to cut large portions off their carefully grown plants. But plants respond to losing limbs by putting more energy forth to regrow. Their production is increased by having segments of themselves detached. We, too, often need to prune away those things that keep us from fruitfulness. Our lives can become cluttered with possessions and attachments that do not truly serve God. When we detach from those things, it makes more space for God to work in our lives and makes more space to become more fully ourselves, bearing beautiful fruit for God.

Psalmist Preparation

In this psalm, we promise to praise God in the company of others, to proclaim the love we have known. In this we echo Saul in the first reading, whose encounter with Christ compels him to speak boldly on Christ's behalf. As you prepare to proclaim this psalm, think about how you might be called to proclaim Christ's love to others. Who in your life might need a word of peace or kindness? Bring this person to prayer this week and discern how God might be inviting you to reveal God's presence to them by either word of deed.

Making Connections

Between the readings: When Saul arrives in Jerusalem, the disciples understandably have a hard time believing he has truly become a follower of Christ. But by his fruit they know him. His encounter with Christ results in courageous preaching of what he has learned. Thus do the disciples know that he has been joined to Christ the Vine. And the church is at peace—another fruit of being united with Jesus.

To experience: Jesus says in the gospel that we can ask for whatever we want and have it done for us, but that is not usually our experience with prayer. God's answer to prayers can seem cryptic and often unfolds slowly over time. God refuses all our attempts to make God into a vending machine that dispenses all our desires. God rather wills our good always, using our vocations and commitments to draw us ever closer to holiness.

Homily Points

• Today's passage from John's Gospel recalls the wisdom Jesus shared during his last meal with the disciples. The Son of God uses images from creation to break open his hopes for how the disciples are to be in relationship with one another and with God. Such images would have been familiar to the people of God who prayed with Old Testament images of Israel as the great vine. Jesus tells the disciples: "I am the true vine, and my Father is the vine grower." Their followers, then and now, are the branches.

• What do these images say about the Christian community? The people of God are all of great value. Branches in a vine mix with each other such that it can be difficult to tell when one branch starts and another ends. So too are our lives interconnected with one another. We cannot be church alone. Further, the Christian community gains its energy from Christ the Vine. Like branches need a strong vine in order to bear fruit, so too does the Christian community need the spirit of Christ in order to bear fruits of service in the world.

• Finally, the image of God as the vine grower signals the importance of pruning within Christian communities. We are not perfect on our own. We need the mercy of God to prune away the sins that stunt our growth and harm others. God created humankind with the capacity to bear great fruit. In order to do so, we must humbly open our hearts to the tending of the vine grower.

CELEBRATION

Model Rite for the Blessing and Sprinkling of Water

Presider: Through the waters of baptism, we die and rise with the living Christ. May these waters purify our hearts and draw us ever closer to the dwelling place of God . . . *[pause]*

[continue with The Roman Missal, *Appendix II]*

Model Universal Prayer (Prayer of the Faithful)

Presider: Trusting in Christ the true Vine, let us offer our prayers and petitions before the Lord.

Response: Lord, hear our prayer.

Watch over the newly initiated members of the church and help them to continue growing in their faith . . .

Further the work of conservationists, environmental educators, and all who care for our planet . . .

Break the bonds of racism, both within individual hearts and structures of oppression . . .

Raise to new life all our beloved dead . . .

Presider: God the vine grower, you remain with your people and enable us to bear much fruit. Receive our prayers that through careful tending and pruning, we might grow each day in our discipleship. We ask this through Jesus our risen Lord. **Amen.**

Liturgy and Music

"Children, let us love not in word or speech, but in deed and truth."

Sometimes I find the commands of Christ to be so broad and abstract that I am confounded by his simple directness: "Love one another." "Pray constantly." And what am I doing? People who work in full-time pastoral ministry need to follow the laws of love just like everyone else. We are commanded to pray. At the end of a long day, have you ever stopped and thought "I've been so busy all day, I haven't had time to pray!" Or, despite all the ways you are present to others, have you ever questioned your love for your neighbor? Certainly we can always listen more attentively and respond with more compassion. But my brothers and sisters, the reality is that we *are* loving the people of God through our faithful service.

This weekend's second reading reminds us that real Christian love is active, lived out most fully in the generous giving of ourselves. It is in the active, day-to-day work of our vocation that Christ reveals his loving heart to us—and to others.

Be at peace with this life of service to which you have been called. Give yourself to this work of love. Our very labors are a means of love and prayer, a gift offered in thanksgiving and gratitude. When we offer everything we do, and all that we are, as prayer, we are lovers in deed and truth.

COLLECT

Let us pray.

Pause for silent prayer

Almighty ever-living God,
constantly accomplish the Paschal
    Mystery within us,
that those you were pleased to make new
    in Holy Baptism
may, under your protective care, bear
    much fruit
and come to the joys of life eternal.
Through our Lord Jesus Christ, your Son,
who lives and reigns with you in the unity
    of the Holy Spirit,
God, for ever and ever. **Amen.**

FIRST READING

Acts 9:26-31

When Saul arrived in Jerusalem he tried to
    join the disciples,
  but they were all afraid of him,
    not believing that he was a disciple.
Then Barnabas took charge of him and
    brought him to the apostles,
  and he reported to them how he had
    seen the Lord,
  and that he had spoken to him,
  and how in Damascus he had spoken
    out boldly in the name of Jesus.
He moved about freely with them in
    Jerusalem,
  and spoke out boldly in the name of the
    Lord.
He also spoke and debated with the
    Hellenists,
  but they tried to kill him.
And when the brothers learned of this,
  they took him down to Caesarea
  and sent him on his way to Tarsus.

The church throughout all Judea, Galilee,
    and Samaria was at peace.
It was being built up and walked in the
    fear of the Lord,
  and with the consolation of the Holy
    Spirit it grew in numbers.

RESPONSORIAL PSALM

Ps 22:26-27, 28, 30, 31-32

℞. (26a) I will praise you, Lord, in the
    assembly of your people.
  or:
℞. Alleluia.

I will fulfill my vows before those who fear
    the LORD.
  The lowly shall eat their fill;
they who seek the LORD shall praise him:
  "May your hearts live forever!"

℞. I will praise you, Lord, in the assembly
    of your people.
  or:
℞. Alleluia.

All the ends of the earth
    shall remember and turn to the LORD;
all the families of the nations
    shall bow down before him.

℟. I will praise you, Lord, in the assembly
    of your people.
    or:
℟. Alleluia.

To him alone shall bow down
    all who sleep in the earth;
before him shall bend
    all who go down into the dust.

℟. I will praise you, Lord, in the assembly
    of your people.
    or:
℟. Alleluia.

And to him my soul shall live;
    my descendants shall serve him.
Let the coming generation be told of the
    LORD
    that they may proclaim to a people yet
        to be born
    the justice he has shown.

℟. I will praise you, Lord, in the assembly
    of your people.
    or:
℟. Alleluia.

SECOND READING
1 John 3:18-24

Children, let us love not in word or speech
    but in deed and truth.
Now this is how we shall know that we
    belong to the truth
    and reassure our hearts before him
    in whatever our hearts condemn,
    for God is greater than our hearts and
        knows everything.
Beloved, if our hearts do not condemn us,
    we have confidence in God
    and receive from him whatever we ask,
    because we keep his commandments
        and do what pleases him.
And his commandment is this:
    we should believe in the name of his
        Son, Jesus Christ,
    and love one another just as he
        commanded us.
Those who keep his commandments
    remain in him, and he in them,
    and the way we know that he remains
        in us
    is from the Spirit he gave us.

Living Liturgy

Liturgy and Spirituality: Saint Hildegard of Bingen was born in 1098, and was a German Benedictine abbess, mystic, and composer, to name just a few of her possible titles. She is also one of only four women who have been named a Doctor of the Church.

One of the best known concepts from Hildegard is that of *viriditas*. While there is no exact translation of the word to English, the greening power of the divine, greenness, growth, freshness, life force, and vitality are words that point in the direction of its meaning. Saint Hildegard lived in the Rhineland and was surrounded by the lush greenness that likely influenced her understanding of the divine force in nature directed toward healing and wholeness. She wrote, "The Word is living, being, spirit, all verdant greening, all creativity. This Word manifests itself in every creature." *Viriditas*, then, is God's creative power made manifest in all of creation, as sap flowing throughout a tree sustains life.

Saint Hildegard saw the greening power of God inside of each human. She described the opposite of *viriditas* (or viridity), as aridity, a spiritual dryness that did not empower creative action, particularly in relation to justice. She wrote, "A person who lacks the verdancy of justice is dry, totally without tender goodness, totally without illuminating virtue."

Today's gospel also speaks of this divine force in nature through the imagery of vines that bear fruit. "Remain in me, as I remain in you. Just as a branch cannot bear fruit on its own unless it remains on the vine, so neither can you unless you remain in me Whoever remains in me and I in him will bear much fruit." Without a sustained connection to God and what God cares about—justice—we too will dry up like withered leaves.

Remaining connected to God , however, allows us to bear fruit beyond what we imagine possible. Saint Hildegard reminds us, "Humankind, full of all creative possibilities, is God's work. Humankind alone is called to assist God. Humankind is called to co-create. With nature's help, humankind can set into creation all that is necessary and life-sustaining."

PROMPTS FOR FAITH-SHARING

• What in your life might need pruning away? What could you detach from in order to bear more fruit for God?

• How have you experienced God answering your prayers? How have you come to understand God's presence in prayers that seem to go unanswered?

• To whom do you feel called to preach God's love and kindness? How could you extend God's love to them through both word and deed?

See Appendix B, p. 311, for additional prompts.

SPIRITUALITY

GOSPEL ACCLAMATION
John 14:23

℟. Alleluia, alleluia.
Whoever loves me will keep my word,
    says the Lord,
and my Father will love him and we will
    come to him.
℟. Alleluia, alleluia.

Gospel

John 15:9-17; L56B

Jesus said to his disciples:
"As the Father loves me, so I
    also love you.
Remain in my love.
If you keep my commandments,
    you will remain in my love,
    just as I have kept my Father's
        commandments
    and remain in his love.

"I have told you this so that my
    joy may be in you
    and your joy might be complete.
This is my commandment: love one
    another as I love you.
No one has greater love than this,
    to lay down one's life for one's
        friends.
You are my friends if you do what I
    command you.
I no longer call you slaves,
    because a slave does not know what
        his master is doing.
I have called you friends,
    because I have told you everything I
        have heard from my Father.
It was not you who chose me, but I who
    chose you
    and appointed you to go and bear
        fruit that will remain,
    so that whatever you ask the Father
        in my name he may give you.
This I command you: love one another."

Reflecting on the Gospel

Today's readings speak of how God befriends humanity and shows no partiality.

In the verses previous to today's reading from Acts, Peter struggles with this new insight. Three times God speaks to him in a vision, so that he is able to say to Cornelius, "In truth, I see that God shows no partiality." Even as Peter is speaking and still trying to grasp the implications of this, the Holy Spirit preempts any further attempts at explanation, and in the divine erratic, inexplicable way, falls upon all without distinction. As Peter rightly asserts, those who consider themselves already to be God's best friends must not put obstacles in the way of others upon whom the Spirit falls. Like a parent who loves each child differently yet equally, so is the divine embrace.

John's Gospel uses the term *disciple* more than seventy times to refer to all the women and men who believed in and followed Jesus. John includes no scene of choosing or sending the Twelve, nor do the Twelve figure in any prominent way in the narrative. They are mentioned only in passing at 6:67, 70; 20:24.

In today's gospel reading, Jesus speaks of having chosen and befriended all who have remained with him. The offer of friendship to disciples is part of a chain of love that begins with the Father, whose love is poured out in the self-gift that is Jesus, who offers friendship to all. Jesus then tells his friends how to keep that chain unbroken: pay the love forward to others, befriending them in the way that he has done for them. He speaks of this as a "commandment," which seems an odd term in this context. How can one be commanded to "love" another person? In biblical parlance, "love" signifies not so much the feelings one has toward another. Rather, it designates deeds of loving kindness toward another that communicate to that one that they are part of the community of chosen friends of God and Jesus. We are commanded to act this way toward others, no matter how we might feel about them and whether or not they reciprocate the love offered.

Jesus demonstrated what such love entails when he washed the feet of all "his own" (13:1), the many beloved friends gathered for their final meal with him. He did not skip Peter and Judas. He explains this as the greatest kind of love: the willingness to lay down one's life for one's friends. This is not an obligatory service, such as a slave is bound to render. Rather, the love of friendship is freely chosen self-surrender. The most challenging aspect of this kind of love is that the friends of Jesus are asked not only to embrace within the community of beloved disciples all those whom Jesus befriends, especially those to whom we are not naturally drawn, but even to be willing to risk our own lives for such people. When this seems a humanly impossible choice, Jesus assures disciples that when they ask God in his name, the necessary grace will be given.

Preparing to Proclaim

Key words and phrases: "I have called you friends, because I have told you everything I have heard from my Father."

To the point: This gospel is full of lovely and memorable lines that call our attention to them. Jesus affirms here what he has elsewhere revealed as the greatest commandment: love. God has loved his Son so he can love us, and we are likewise called to love because we are loved. We are so loved that Jesus gave his life for us. We are so loved that Jesus relinquishes his role as master that leaves us as slaves. He yet again tips the power scales that the secular world so treasures. We are rather his friends, elevated to a sharing in his life and his relationship with God the Father. Jesus shares everything he has with us; his love, his healing, his life are all now ours.

Psalmist Preparation

In this psalm, we proclaim that God has revealed God's saving power to all nations. No longer is God's redeeming work limited to the people of Israel; God calls people from all ends of the earth to see God's work of salvation and to respond with praise. This psalm emphasizes the message of the first reading, in which the Holy Spirit comes upon the Gentiles and makes clear that the waters of baptism are not to be restricted to those who have been circumcised. As you prepare to proclaim this psalm, think about limits you might be unknowingly setting for God. Know that God is always a boundary-breaker, bigger and wilder than anything we can imagine.

Making Connections

Between the readings: The second reading clearly echoes the gospel and takes it one step further. God not only loves us; God *is* love itself. Loving and being loved is how we know God and how we participate in God's life. And love is to sacrifice for the sake of another. As God sent us his Son, who loved us unto death, so are we called to give of ourselves out of love.

To experience: Most of us will not be called to be crucified for the sake of those we love. Our crosses are far more metaphorical, but their pain can be very real. Mothers live this out in a particular way as they sacrifice their very bodies and sometimes their well-being to bring life into the world. Making such sacrifices out of love does not take away the pain, but it does transform it. When our suffering is not in vain, when it in some way brings about life for another, it is far easier to endure.

Homily Points

• How do you most often relate to Jesus? Common responses might include Jesus as Lord, Savior, leader, or brother. But what about Jesus as a friend? In today's gospel, the Son of God invites the disciples to draw close to him through the sacred way of relating as friends. Consider how your relationship with Jesus might evolve through the framework of friendship. Friends are people with whom we can be completely ourselves. Friends encourage us to be open and honest about both the joys and the challenges of life. We can count on friends to show up in our times of need, to celebrate with us in times of success, and to listen with caring hearts. Consider spending some time in prayer this week connecting with Jesus as a friend.

• God loves us. In today's second reading, we hear God—the all-powerful, all-knowing creator of the universe—affirm the divine love showered upon all of creation. We remember especially during this season of Easter that God's greatest showing of love was sending Jesus into the world "so that we might have life through him."

• Love can be a complex experience in many relationships. In moments of loneliness or doubt, let us hold fast to the truth that God loves fully. We need not prove anything to gain God's love. God loves humankind unconditionally. How can we reflect the divine love to our neighbors? To strangers? To our enemies? God's love challenges our love to expand evermore.

Model Rite for the Blessing and Sprinkling of Water

Presider: God's Spirit of love came upon us in the waters of baptism and dwells with us always. May the Spirit of truth continue to transform our hearts and inspire our lives . . . *[pause]*

  [continue with The Roman Missal, *Appendix II]*

Model Universal Prayer (Prayer of the Faithful)

Presider: Clinging to the hope of the resurrected Christ, let us offer our prayers and petitions to God.

Response: Lord, hear our prayer.

Increase love and respect for LGBTQ+ people in the church and broader world . . .

Fix oppressive political and economic systems in our world that cause suffering . . .

Inspire the work of artists, writers, musicians, and other creatives who bring hope to the world . . .

Open our senses to the wonders of your creation and the joy of Christ alive in our world . . .

Presider: Loving God, you put forth the greatest commandment: love one another as I love you. Receive our prayers that our hearts might expand and love for the world might deepen. We ask this through Christ our risen Lord. **Amen.**

Liturgy and Music

We know that every human fingerprint is unique. Each of us was born with a specific nature, and a set of gifts unlike those of anyone else in the world. As a mother knows and loves her child, so our Creator knows and loves us.

But we are not in this love alone. We belong to a communal faith tradition. If you are reading these words, you are probably a pastoral musician whose job it is to create, prepare, and direct music for the liturgy. The power of our liturgy lies in the fact that we do the work of our worship together. Our oneness in the body of Christ does nothing to diminish the individual beauty, strength, and worth that each of us possesses. In fact, our uniqueness takes on even greater significance when we consider the words of our Lord when he says: "It was not you who chose me, but I who chose you."

For what have we been chosen? In this week's gospel, Jesus continues with the answer: "[I] appointed you to go and bear fruit that will remain, so that whatever you ask the Father in my name he may give you.

For the pastoral musician, the fruit that remains is the robust song of the assembly. Regardless of the detailed day-to-day work we do in any given community, our fruitfulness is the strength of the assembly's sung prayer. With God's help, the people will sing on, full-throated, long after your work is finished.

COLLECT
Let us pray.

Pause for silent prayer

Grant, almighty God,
that we may celebrate with heartfelt
    devotion these days of joy,
which we keep in honor of the risen Lord,
and that what we relive in remembrance
we may always hold to in what we do.
Through our Lord Jesus Christ, your Son,
who lives and reigns with you in the unity
    of the Holy Spirit,
God, for ever and ever. **Amen.**

FIRST READING
Acts 10:25-26, 34-35, 44-48

When Peter entered, Cornelius met him
    and, falling at his feet, paid him
        homage.
Peter, however, raised him up, saying,
    "Get up. I myself am also a human
        being."

Then Peter proceeded to speak and said,
    "In truth, I see that God shows no
        partiality.
Rather, in every nation whoever fears him
    and acts uprightly
    is acceptable to him."

While Peter was still speaking these
        things,
    the Holy Spirit fell upon all who were
        listening to the word.
The circumcised believers who had
        accompanied Peter
    were astounded that the gift of the Holy
        Spirit
    should have been poured out on the
        Gentiles also,
    for they could hear them speaking in
        tongues and glorifying God.
Then Peter responded,
    "Can anyone withhold the water for
        baptizing these people,
    who have received the Holy Spirit even
        as we have?"
He ordered them to be baptized in the
        name of Jesus Christ.

RESPONSORIAL PSALM

Ps 98:1, 2-3, 3-4

R̪. (cf. 2b) The Lord has revealed to the
nations his saving power.
or:
R̪. Alleluia.

Sing to the LORD a new song,
for he has done wondrous deeds;
his right hand has won victory for him,
his holy arm.

R̪. The Lord has revealed to the nations
his saving power.
or:
R̪. Alleluia.

The LORD has made his salvation known:
in the sight of the nations he has
revealed his justice.
He has remembered his kindness and his
faithfulness
toward the house of Israel.

R̪. The Lord has revealed to the nations
his saving power.
or:
R̪. Alleluia.

All the ends of the earth have seen
the salvation by our God.
Sing joyfully to the LORD, all you lands;
break into song; sing praise.

R̪. The Lord has revealed to the nations
his saving power.
or:
R̪. Alleluia.

SECOND READING

1 John 4:7-10

Beloved, let us love one another,
because love is of God;
everyone who loves is begotten by God
and knows God.
Whoever is without love does not know
God, for God is love.
In this way the love of God was revealed
to us:
God sent his only Son into the world
so that we might have life through him.
In this is love:
not that we have loved God, but that he
loved us
and sent his Son as expiation for our sins.

*Or, where the Ascension is celebrated on
Sunday, the second reading and gospel for
the Seventh Sunday of Easter may be used
on this Sunday.*

1 John 4:11-16, p. 133.

John 17:11b-19, p. 130.

Living Liturgy

Liturgy and Spirituality: Radical welcome and love are themes at the heart of today's readings. Peter says, "In truth, I see that God shows no partiality." God models and calls us to consider how we can radically welcome all members of the Body of Christ; however, as humans we experience the sin of exclusion here on earth.

In her book, *Subversive Habits: Black Catholic Nuns in the Long African American Freedom Struggle*, Dr. Shannen Dee Williams breaks open this history of racism in the Catholic church and particularly in women's religious communities. She shares stories and histories of prophetic Black women in the church whose voices have been erased in our history but who demonstrate strength and a lived commitment of what it means to remain in God's love.

Sister Thea Bowman spoke authentically about her experience as a Black Catholic nun in the church to the United States Conference of Catholic Bishops in the last year of her life. She shared the pain of exclusion as well as the many gifts that she and Black Catholics have offered and continue to offer the church.

She said, "What does it mean to be Black and Catholic? It means that I come to my church fully functioning. That doesn't frighten you, does it? I come to my church fully functioning. I bring myself; my Black self, all that I am, all that I have, all that I hope to become. I bring my whole history—my traditions, my experience, my culture, my African-American song and dance and gesture and movement and teaching and preaching and healing and responsibility—as gifts to the church."

As we reflect on the call to "love one another," Sister Thea's words encourage us to reflect on whose stories, voices, and culture gets uplifted in our church communities, and how we can make space to welcome and uplift the gifts and traditions of every member of the Body of Christ.

PROMPTS FOR FAITH-SHARING

• How have you experienced the love of God? How do you pass it on to others?

• What sacrifices have others made for you that let you know you are loved?

• How can you imitate Christ who loves us to the point of laying down his life for us?

See Appendix B, p. 311, for additional prompts.

SPIRITUALITY

GOSPEL ACCLAMATION
Matt 28:19a, 20b

℟. Alleluia, alleluia.
Go and teach all nations, says the Lord;
I am with you always, until the end of
   the world.
℟. Alleluia, alleluia.

Gospel   Mark 16:15-20; L58B

Jesus said to his disciples:
   "Go into the whole world
   and proclaim the gospel to every
      creature.
Whoever believes and is baptized
      will be saved;
   whoever does not believe will be
      condemned.
These signs will accompany those
      who believe:
   in my name they will drive out
      demons,
   they will speak new languages.
They will pick up serpents with
      their hands,
   and if they drink any deadly thing, it
      will not harm them.
They will lay hands on the sick, and they
      will recover."

So then the Lord Jesus, after he spoke to
      them,
   was taken up into heaven
   and took his seat at the right hand of God.
But they went forth and preached
      everywhere,
   while the Lord worked with them
   and confirmed the word through
      accompanying signs.

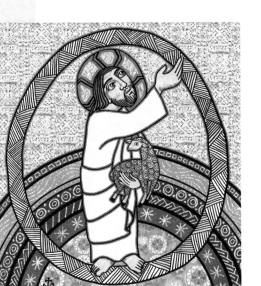

Reflecting on the Gospel

In a sense, it would be better to hear today's first reading, the opening verses of the Acts of the Apostles, proclaimed *after* rather than before today's gospel reading from Mark, since the former picks up the thread of the narrative where the latter leaves off. Luke, the author of Acts, addressed that book to Theophilus (Acts 1:1), whose name means "beloved of God" or "lover of God." The symbolic meaning allows every hearer of Luke's account to insert her- or himself into the role of the beloved to whom these words are addressed, and we can extend that dynamic today to our hearing of the gospel as well.

Mark concludes his account at the point where Jesus was "taken up into heaven" (16:19), before Acts picks it up from there. Like Elijah, who was taken up to heaven in a whirlwind by a fiery chariot (2 Kgs 2:11), and Moses, who was taken up in a cloud at the end of his earthly life (Josephus, *Antiquities of the Jews*, 4.326), so Jesus's earthly sojourn is ended in the manner of these great figures. In Mark's Gospel, the ascension takes place on Easter Sunday, while Acts speaks of a forty-day period of appearances between the resurrection and ascension. The number forty is symbolic: Moses spent forty days on Mount Sinai, and the Israelites wandered forty years in the desert. Luke uses "forty days" to link the time Jesus spent in preparation for his public ministry after his baptism (Luke 4:1-12) with the preparation that the disciples undergo before they are "baptized with the Holy Spirit" (Acts 1:5) and begin their public witnessing to the resurrected Christ.

In the Gospel of John—the only other gospel to mention the ascension (20:17)—the passion, resurrection, ascension, exaltation, and giving of the Spirit are all one moment, not separated in time and space (see John 19:30; 20:17, 22); in God's time, all these transformations are instantaneous. Human reality is bound by time and space, and so Luke narrates these mysteries as separate episodes. These time gaps allow us to reflect on how the mystery unfolds gradually for us, allowing us to be transformed step by step.

Acts 1 voices the questions that the early community needed answers to in this in-between time. They wanted to know when the Parousia and the end time would be. They struggled to shift their expectations from a nationalistic messiah who would restore the sovereign reign of Israel to one who would empower them to be witnesses of the gospel not only to their own people but throughout the known world.

Even though the disciples do not receive all the answers they seek and even though their transformation is incomplete, the ascension marks the point at which they must take up the mission begun by Jesus. There can be no idle looking up at the sky. Rather, as the two angelic messengers affirm, the time has come for them to go forth as witnesses "to the ends of the earth."

Today is a good day to consider: How does my witness spread in ever widening circles "to the ends of the earth"? How is it possible to proclaim the good news without having all the answers we seek?

Preparing to Proclaim

Key words and phrases: "Go into the whole world and proclaim the gospel to every creature."

To the point: When Jesus ascends into heaven, he completes the work of the resurrection. His conquest of death opens the gates of heaven and restores humanity's ability to be fully with God. Now Jesus enters into the fullness of that presence, the first human person to be so united with God. He waits for us to follow him there. And in the meantime, he leaves his disciples with a mission. They are to preach and to heal—that is, they are to continue the work that Christ did in his years of public ministry. They are to make him present and visible and accessible when the ascension makes him less so. But he does not leave them alone in this work—the last line of this gospel has him as the subject, working with the disciples and confirming their preaching by working signs through them.

Psalmist Preparation

At first glance, this psalm seems to fit this feast day perfectly. But the disciples do not really shout with joy when they witness Christ's ascension. They probably feel a moment of bewilderment before they get to work with the mission Christ has left to them. It is only in hindsight that we recognize the ascension for what it is—the fulfillment of Jesus's death-defying work and a preview of what the followers of Jesus can expect to participate in. As you prepare to proclaim this psalm, think about a time when hindsight gave you clearer insight into God's presence. Remind yourself that God is with you now, too, even when you can't see it.

Making Connections

Between the readings: The first reading has another depiction of the ascension. In the Acts version, Jesus gives a less detailed charge, reminding his apostles only that they are to be his witnesses. He leaves rather suddenly, disappearing into a cloud. And two men in white appear to finish the message. Jesus promises to send the Holy Spirit so they will not be left alone; these men make the promise that Jesus himself will return in the flesh.

To experience: Those of us who live in a post-ascension world can feel envious of the disciples who got to share this life and this world with Jesus. We might long to hear his voice and encounter his presence as they did. We rely on their witness and their testimony for our own faith. But Jesus is no less present to us; he comes in word and sacrament to be close to us always.

Homily Points

• Goodbyes can be emotional and challenging, especially if we care deeply about the person leaving. Goodbyes mark a transition in the relationship. Something ends while something new begins. The Ascension of the Lord marks the last time the disciples saw their beloved Jesus in his current state before God assumed him into heaven. Yet this was far from the final encounter with the risen Lord. Jesus continues to bridge the gap between heaven and earth. He lives on through the Christian community, the Eucharist, and in all of creation.

• The Ascension ushers us into a week of waiting. Jesus has ascended into heaven and the Holy Spirit has not yet come down. Pentecost is still days away. Times of waiting can often be uncomfortable, yet this unique time in the liturgical year affords us the space to step back with the original eleven disciples and ponder: What does Christ's resurrection mean for our lives? How can I carry the hope of Easter into the next season?

• Luke opens the Acts of the Apostles with an address to Theophilus, whose name means "Lover of God." The readings from today, last week—and throughout the Easter season—remind us of the mutual love we are called to share with God. In the waters of baptism, the Lord invites all of us to be "lovers of God." The invitation grows each day as God invites us into divine love through our relationships with other people, care for the natural world, celebration of the sacraments, and a myriad of small yet profound ways.

CELEBRATION

Model Rite for the Blessing and Sprinkling of Water

Presider: In the waters of baptism, we die and rise with Christ. By the sprinkling of this water, may we be empowered to "[g]o into the whole world and proclaim the gospel to every creature . . . *[pause]*
  [continue with The Roman Missal, *Appendix II]*

Model Universal Prayer (Prayer of the Faithful)

Presider: Strengthened by our Lord who ascended into heaven and now sits at the right hand of God, let us offer our prayers and petitions.

Response: Lord, hear our prayer.

Inspire the church to advocate for justice for migrants, refugees, and immigrants . . .

Deliver a good word to preachers everywhere, from the pulpits to the streets . . .

Hold in your gentle care all those who are grieving the transition or end of a relationship . . .

Accompany to their heavenly home all those who have died . . .

Presider: God of eternity, your son Jesus promised to be with us always until the end of the age. Hear our prayers that we might embrace his presence in our lives and encourage others to do the same. We ask this through Christ our resurrected Lord. **Amen.**

Liturgy and Music

"They said, 'Men of Galilee, why are you standing there looking at the sky? This Jesus who has been taken up from you into heaven will return in the same way as you have seen him going into heaven.'"

Sometimes, when consumed with getting our work done, we can't see anything else. This time of year, we may be juggling First Communions, graduations, ordinations, confirmation, weddings, funerals—along with preparations for Pentecost. At the end of a long day we might be grumpy and tired, having literally given all at the office. We don't feel we have much left.

But then, in the cracks between all these obligations, the real work of ministry finds us, whether we are ready or not. It's God's way of reminding us that music ministry, glorious as it can be, is not the only thing going on in the vineyard.

While I was out on my walk today, I came upon a stretch of downtown sidewalk that was covered over in scaffolding and orange tarps. I saw a sign that said "Pardon our dust. Walkway is open during construction." There was a lot of work going on beyond the barricades.

The mission of the risen Christ is at work, right here and right now. Like the reign of God itself, ever under construction, Christ is found in the inconvenient detours, in unexpected places. Rather than searching the heavens, we might look around us. In the face of someone looking right at us, we see him.

COLLECT

Let us pray.

Pause for silent prayer

Gladden us with holy joys, almighty God,
and make us rejoice with devout
    thanksgiving,
for the Ascension of Christ your Son
is our exaltation,
and, where the Head has gone before in
    glory,
the Body is called to follow in hope.
Through our Lord Jesus Christ, your Son,
who lives and reigns with you in the unity
    of the Holy Spirit,
God, for ever and ever. **Amen.**

or

Grant, we pray, almighty God,
that we, who believe that your Only
    Begotten Son, our Redeemer,
ascended this day to the heavens,
may in spirit dwell already in heavenly
    realms.
Who lives and reigns with you in the unity
    of the Holy Spirit,
God, for ever and ever. **Amen.**

FIRST READING

Acts 1:1-11

In the first book, Theophilus,
    I dealt with all that Jesus did and taught
    until the day he was taken up,
    after giving instructions through the
        Holy Spirit
    to the apostles whom he had chosen.
He presented himself alive to them
    by many proofs after he had suffered,
    appearing to them during forty days
    and speaking about the kingdom of God.
While meeting with them,
    he enjoined them not to depart from
        Jerusalem,
    but to wait for "the promise of the
        Father
    about which you have heard me speak;
    for John baptized with water,
    but in a few days you will be baptized
        with the Holy Spirit."

When they had gathered together they
        asked him,
    "Lord, are you at this time going to
        restore the kingdom to Israel?"
He answered them, "It is not for you to
        know the times or seasons
    that the Father has established by his
        own authority.
But you will receive power when the Holy
        Spirit comes upon you,
    and you will be my witnesses in
        Jerusalem,

throughout Judea and Samaria,
and to the ends of the earth."
When he had said this, as they were
looking on,
he was lifted up, and a cloud took him
from their sight.
While they were looking intently at the
sky as he was going,
suddenly two men dressed in white
garments stood beside them.
They said, "Men of Galilee,
why are you standing there looking at
the sky?
This Jesus who has been taken up from
you into heaven
will return in the same way as you have
seen him going into heaven."

RESPONSORIAL PSALM

Ps 47:2-3, 6-7, 8-9

℟. (6) God mounts his throne to shouts of
joy: a blare of trumpets for the Lord.
or:
℟. Alleluia.

All you peoples, clap your hands,
shout to God with cries of gladness,
for the Lord, the Most High, the awesome,
is the great king over all the earth.

℟. God mounts his throne to shouts of joy:
a blare of trumpets for the Lord.
or:
℟. Alleluia.

God mounts his throne amid shouts of joy;
the Lord, amid trumpet blasts.
Sing praise to God, sing praise;
sing praise to our king, sing praise.

℟. God mounts his throne to shouts of joy:
a blare of trumpets for the Lord.
or:
℟. Alleluia.

For king of all the earth is God;
sing hymns of praise.
God reigns over the nations,
God sits upon his holy throne.

℟. God mounts his throne to shouts of joy:
a blare of trumpets for the Lord.
or:
℟. Alleluia.

SECOND READING

Eph 1:17-23

or Eph 4:1-13

or Eph 4:1-7, 11-13

See Appendix A, p. 296.

Living Liturgy

Liturgy and the Arts: Before he is taken up into heaven, Jesus's last instruction to his disciples is "Go into the whole world and proclaim the gospel to every creature." The entire web of life is invited to hear the good news that has radically transformed the disciples' lives and the history of creation.

"Laudato si'" are the first words from the Canticle of Creation, Saint Francis of Assisi's song of thanksgiving to God for all of the gifts of creation. Pope Francis selected this phrase as the name of his encyclical on the environment. "Laudato si'" means "praise be to you," and the words summon an orientation of gratitude and awe for the goodness of creation.

Take some time today to pray with this stunning Canticle of Creation. There are many musical settings available for listening, including "Canticle of the Sun" by Marty Haugen and the traditional hymn "All Creatures of Our God and King."

Scan to listen to "Canticle of the Sun."

Scan to listen to "All Creatures of Our God and King."

PROMPTS FOR FAITH-SHARING

• Imagine yourself with the disciples at the ascension. What emotions does it evoke in you to see Jesus raised to heaven?

• We do not experience Jesus in body like the disciples did, but Jesus remains present with us. How do you most powerfully experience Jesus's ongoing presence on earth?

• How do you participate in the mission that Jesus left to the church? How do you preach the gospel and bring Jesus's healing to others?

See Appendix B, p. 311, for additional prompts.

MAY 9, 2024 (Thursday) or MAY 12, 2024
THE ASCENSION OF THE LORD

SPIRITUALITY

GOSPEL ACCLAMATION
cf. John 14:18

℟. Alleluia, alleluia.
I will not leave you orphans, says the Lord.
I will come back to you, and your hearts will
    rejoice.
℟. Alleluia, alleluia.

Gospel

John 17:11b-19; L60B

Lifting up his eyes to heaven,
    Jesus prayed, saying:
"Holy Father, keep them in
        your name that you have
        given me,
    so that they may be one just
        as we are one.
When I was with them I
        protected them in your
        name that you gave me,
    and I guarded them, and none
        of them was lost
    except the son of destruction,
    in order that the Scripture
        might be fulfilled.
But now I am coming to you.
I speak this in the world
    so that they may share my joy
        completely.
I gave them your word, and the world
        hated them,
    because they do not belong to the
        world
    any more than I belong to the world.
I do not ask that you take them out of
        the world
    but that you keep them from the evil
        one.
They do not belong to the world
    any more than I belong to the world.
Consecrate them in the truth. Your
        word is truth.
As you sent me into the world,
    so I sent them into the world.
And I consecrate myself for them,
    so that they also may be consecrated
        in truth."

Reflecting on the Gospel

The reading from Acts is set in the Upper Room, where the disciples are gathered between the ascension and Pentecost. About 120 persons are there (1:15), a symbol for the full number of disciples. In the preceding verse, Luke lists as present the Twelve along with the women, presumably Mary Magdalene, Joanna, Susanna, and the many others (Luke 8:1-3), who came up to Jerusalem and witnessed the crucifixion (Luke 23:49), saw Jesus laid in the tomb (Luke 23:55-56), and discovered it empty (Luke 24:1-9). Jesus's mother and his family are also there.

All are present except for Judas. We can hear the pain and disillusionment of the early community as they struggled to explain how it could be that one who was "numbered among us and was allotted to share in this ministry" could have ended as the guide for those who arrested Jesus. As always, the Scriptures provide the assurance that God is not absent even during these most horrific moments, even if they do not fully explain such tragic happenings.

In the first chapter of Acts, Peter emerges as spokesperson for the community. It is a turbulent time of transition, and they rely on the form of leadership with which they are familiar. This is the last time that the Twelve are reconstituted; a replacement is not chosen for James (the son of Zebedee) when he is killed by Herod (Acts 12:2). As the narrative progresses, the patterns of leadership shift. The Twelve disappear from the story after 6:2; Peter is not mentioned again after 15:7. James and the elders emerge as the leaders of the community in Jerusalem (12:17; 15:13; 21:18) and Paul takes center stage in the mission to the Gentiles.

In the gospel, we have the middle section of Jesus's prayer during the last discourse. We are meant to overhear this intimate conversation between Jesus and the Father so that we can be encouraged by the legacy bequeathed to us. Jesus addresses God as "Father," the one who, in a patriarchal culture, is responsible for protecting the whole household. Jesus has embodied this protective care of his disciples. His strong arms enwrapped them, like a father who fends off all threats to his children's well-being, or a mother who enfolds her little ones, shielding them from all harm.

Just as Jesus has been consecrated for mission, so he prays for the consecration of his followers. *Consecrated* means to be anointed and set apart for mission, not in the manner of kings whose anointing separates them from the realities of ordinary people, but in the truth, which immerses Jesus's disciples into the heart of the struggles of all their fellow creatures in "the world." While kings are anointed on the head to great acclaim, disciples of Jesus are "anointed" in foot washing, set apart for self-surrender in love to one another, particularly those who would seem most unlovable. This is the oil of truth that flows over the head of Jesus's disciples, consecrating them in the protective mantle of the "name" and the "word."

Preparing to Proclaim

Key words and phrases: "Holy Father, keep them in your name . . . so that they may be one just as we are one."

To the point: In this gospel, Jesus prays for his disciples prior to his arrest and death. He is preparing to be separated from them, and though he knows this first separation will be temporary, he also knows a more decisive one will come with the ascension. In his prayer, he speaks of "the world" as something the disciples do not belong to and something that hates them. Being his followers makes them different than they were before; they are no longer able to be fully at home in this life but are rather called to strive for heaven. At the same time, though, Jesus sends them into the world, consecrated and holy, so that they might make the world holy by being in it and bring it eventually to Jesus.

Psalmist Preparation

We often sing this psalm with the refrain "The Lord is kind and merciful." Here, though, we sing a new refrain that affirms Jesus is king of heaven, transcending all earthly power. We remind ourselves in this psalm to keep God's goodness and kindness in mind and to bless God with our praise and gratitude. As you prepare to proclaim it, spend some time recalling your Lenten and Easter journey this year. Where have you seen God's kindness? How has God called you away from sin and into freedom? How might you offer back praise with the way you live your life?

Making Connections

Between the readings: The second reading echoes the gospel, affirming that God remains in those who acknowledge Jesus as God's son. The theme of unity is strong, reassuring us that we are able to remain one with Jesus even beyond the apparent separation of the ascension. And of course, the way we achieve this unity is through love.

To experience: As he prepares to depart from his disciples, Jesus turns to God and prays for them. He gives us a powerful example for how to be apart from those we love. When we cannot see someone in person we can always ask God to be with them. When we cannot take care of their needs ourselves, entrusting them to God is a potent act of love.

Homily Points

• The week between the Ascension of the Lord and Pentecost invites us into a space of trust. Liturgically, we are living in the unknown. Jesus has ascended into heaven, and the Holy Spirit has not yet come down upon the church. How are we to act? Who are we to be during this tender in-between time? During this final week of Easter, the church calls us to trust God's abiding presence among us. The love of God is made known even in this transition time through the sprinkling of blessed water, reception of the Eucharist, and gathering in Christian community. Let us remember this truth during the in-between times of our own lives. God is with us always.

• Today's gospel gives us the special chance to listen to Jesus's prayer to God. He asks his Holy Father to make the people one, to protect us and allow us to share in the joy of the Good News. Jesus exclaims, "Consecrate them in the truth." Jesus prays for our good. He prays for our growth. In what ways might Jesus's prayer influence your own prayers during this last week of the Easter season?

• In today's first reading, Peter and his followers offer a specific prayer to the Lord: "Show which one of these two you have chosen to take the place in this apostolic ministry . . ." They demonstrate the power in offering a direct, specific intention to God. We may not always get a direct, specific response in return, but we can be assured that God listens closely to our prayers and will answer our needs.

CELEBRATION

Model Rite for the Blessing and Sprinkling of Water

Presider: Through the sacrament of baptism we come to share in the glory of God through Jesus Christ. By the sprinkling of this water may our hearts be united in the peace of Christ . . . *[pause]*

   [continue with The Roman Missal, *Appendix II]*

Model Universal Prayer (Prayer of the Faithful)

Presider: Drawn into the truth of Christ's love for creation, let us proclaim our prayers and petitions before the Lord.

Response: Lord, hear our prayer.

Sustain the joy of Easter in the Christian community as we sit on the cusp of a new liturgical season . . .

Support the work of therapists, counselors, chaplains, and others who serve in times of crisis . . .

Advance dialogue and respect between people of different religious traditions . . .

Give us the grace to forgive others with the generous spirit of Christ . . .

Presider: God of every truth and goodness, you sent your son into the world so that he might send your people out to proclaim the gospel message across generations. Hear our prayers that we might reflect your glory to the ends of the earth. We ask this through Christ our risen Lord. **Amen.**

Liturgy and Music

I have a friend, who, when praying the Lord's Prayer, always drops out when the community reaches the part that asks "Forgive us our trespasses, as we forgive those who trespass against us." When I asked him why he, a priest of forty years, would do that, he replied: "God help me if I am forgiven according to how I forgive." I was stunned, but also deeply moved by his honesty. This exchange still reminds me that honesty and truth are matters of personal integrity. And that I, too, am prone to falling short.

This Sunday we hear the beautiful, passionate prayer of Jesus to his Father in John 17. It is known by various names, among them the High Priestly Prayer, and the Farewell Prayer. It is the longest recorded prayer of Jesus to his Father in the gospels, and one that he intended to be heard by the disciples. In it, the Lord's begs for protection, unity, and fulfillment for his earthly family.

I am drawn to the final lines of this prayer: "I consecrate myself for them, so that they also may be consecrated in truth." Then I think of my friend's honesty regarding forgiveness.

Sacred liturgical music must always be honest and authentic. And when the truth rises, full-throated from the worshipping community, our song is consecrated by the one to whom we belong. It is up to each of us to *mean* what we sing. Likewise, this truth must live in every aspect of our lives.

COLLECT

Let us pray.

Pause for silent prayer

Graciously hear our supplications, O Lord,
so that we, who believe that the Savior of
    the human race
is with you in your glory,
may experience, as he promised,
until the end of the world,
his abiding presence among us.
Who lives and reigns with you in the unity
    of the Holy Spirit,
God, for ever and ever. **Amen.**

FIRST READING

Acts 1:15-17, 20a, 20c-26

Peter stood up in the midst of the brothers
    —there was a group of about one
        hundred and twenty persons
    in the one place—.
He said, "My brothers,
    the Scripture had to be fulfilled
    which the Holy Spirit spoke beforehand
    through the mouth of David,
        concerning Judas,
    who was the guide for those who
        arrested Jesus.
He was numbered among us
    and was allotted a share in this
        ministry.

"For it is written in the Book of Psalms:
    May another take his office.

"Therefore, it is necessary that one of the
    men
    who accompanied us the whole time
    the Lord Jesus came and went among
        us,
    beginning from the baptism of John
    until the day on which he was taken up
        from us,
    become with us a witness to his
        resurrection."
So they proposed two, Judas called
    Barsabbas,
    who was also known as Justus, and
    Matthias.
Then they prayed,
    "You, Lord, who know the hearts of all,
    show which one of these two you have
        chosen
    to take the place in this apostolic
        ministry
    from which Judas turned away to go to
        his own place."
Then they gave lots to them, and the lot
    fell upon Matthias,
    and he was counted with the eleven
        apostles.

RESPONSORIAL PSALM

Ps 103:1-2, 11-12, 19-20

℟. (19a) The Lord has set his throne in
    heaven.
    or:
℟. Alleluia.

Bless the LORD, O my soul;
    and all my being, bless his holy name.
Bless the LORD, O my soul,
    and forget not all his benefits.

℟. The Lord has set his throne in heaven.
    or:
℟. Alleluia.

For as the heavens are high above the
    earth,
    so surpassing is his kindness toward
        those who fear him.
As far as the east is from the west,
    so far has he put our transgressions
        from us.

℟. The Lord has set his throne in heaven.
    or:
℟. Alleluia.

The LORD has established his throne in
    heaven,
    and his kingdom rules over all.
Bless the LORD, all you his angels,
    you mighty in strength, who do his
        bidding.

℟. The Lord has set his throne in heaven.
    or:
℟. Alleluia.

SECOND READING

1 John 4:11-16

Beloved, if God so loved us,
    we also must love one another.
No one has ever seen God.
Yet, if we love one another, God remains
    in us,
    and his love is brought to perfection
        in us.

This is how we know that we remain in
    him and he in us,
    that he has given us of his Spirit.
Moreover, we have seen and testify
    that the Father sent his Son as savior of
        the world.
Whoever acknowledges that Jesus is the
    Son of God,
    God remains in him and he in God.
We have come to know and to believe in
    the love God has for us.

God is love, and whoever remains in love
    remains in God and God in him.

Living Liturgy

Liturgy and Spirituality: "God is love, and whoever remains in love / remains in God and God in him." The Christian mystics throughout history have provided various descriptions of how they strive to remain in God's love and to see the world through the eyes of Christ.

One contemplative practice that many Christians find fruitful is centering prayer. The "goal" of this prayer is to simply sit, resting and abiding in God's love. A sacred word or phrase is chosen before the prayer begins, and as distractions arise while sitting in silence, the word or phrase is used to gently shift our attention back to being present with God. The desire to rest in and be present to God is all that a person needs to engage in this prayer, even if they find themselves distracted.

Contemplative prayer can sometimes feel intimidating for people who have never experienced it before. An adapted version of this prayer that was once suggested to me by a spiritual director was a bit simpler. They told me to sit down for five minutes and to imagine God delighting in me just as I am. This type of prayer is a reminder that we do not need to "do" anything to be worthy of God's love and that if God remains and delights in us as we sit, we should also delight in ourselves and trust in our ability to live out our vocation in the world as we remain in God.

For anyone who is interested in learning more about the mystics, the *Turning to the Mystics* podcast with Dr. James Finley explores the wisdom of the Christian mystics in a modern context. Each season focuses on a different mystic, beginning with Thomas Merton, and it is a wonderful introduction to how mystics throughout history have attempted to live their lives fully immersed in the heart of God.

Saint Teresa of Avila, a sixteenth-century mystic, invites us all on this journey when she writes in *The Interior Castle* of prayer, "taking time frequently to be alone with Him who we know loves us. The important thing is not to think much but to love much; and so do that which best stirs you to love."

PROMPTS FOR FAITH-SHARING

• How do you deal with long-term departures and being far from the people you love? How does prayer help you maintain those relationships?

• How do you feel about "the world" that Jesus prays about? How do you move through the world while knowing it is not your final home?

• How do you live in love in order that you might remain in God?

See Appendix B, p. 311, for additional prompts.

SPIRITUALITY

GOSPEL ACCLAMATION
℟. Alleluia, alleluia.
Come, Holy Spirit, fill the hearts of your faithful
and kindle in them the fire of your love.
℟. Alleluia, alleluia.

Gospel   John 20:19-23; L63B

On the evening of that first day of the
    week,
    when the doors were locked, where the
        disciples were,
    for fear of the Jews,
    Jesus came and stood in their midst
    and said to them, "Peace be with you."
When he had said this, he showed them his
    hands and his side.
The disciples rejoiced when they saw the
    Lord.
Jesus said to them again, "Peace be with
    you.
As the Father has sent me, so I send you."
And when he had said this, he breathed on
    them and said to them,
    "Receive the Holy Spirit.
Whose sins you forgive are forgiven them,
    and whose sins you retain are retained."

or John 15:26-27; 16:12-15

Jesus said to his disciples:
    "When the Advocate comes whom I will
        send you from the Father,
    the Spirit of truth that proceeds from the
        Father,
    he will testify to me.
And you also testify,
    because you have been with me from the
        beginning.

"I have much more to tell you, but you
    cannot bear it now.
But when he comes, the Spirit of truth,
    he will guide you to all truth.
He will not speak on his own,
    but he will speak what he hears,
    and will declare to you the things that are
        coming.
He will glorify me,
    because he will take from what is mine
        and declare it to you.
Everything that the Father has is mine;
    for this reason I told you that he will take
        from what is mine
        and declare it to you."

Reflecting on the Gospel

Like a faceted gem whose brilliance takes different contours when examined from distinct angles, today's readings open up multiple dimensions of meaning for the feast of Pentecost. The gift of the Spirit to the disciples is one more facet of the ineffable mystery that encompasses Jesus's passion, death, resurrection, ascension, and glorification. For the Fourth Evangelist these all occur in one

instant. Luke, in contrast, narrates each of these as a separate event, with precise time markers. He tells of resurrection appearances that took place over forty days before the ascension (Acts 1:3). Now on Pentecost, literally, the fiftieth day after Passover, the gift of the Spirit comes with audible and visible signs.

In Luke's infancy narrative, all the characters are filled with the Spirit: John the Baptist (1:15, 17), Mary (1:35), Elizabeth (1:41), Zechariah (1:67), and Simeon (2:25-27). But once Jesus begins his ministry, only he is said to be empowered by the Holy Spirit. Now, on Pentecost, his followers receive this gift. Its first manifestation is facile communication across boundaries of difference. In Jerusalem there are Jewish residents (*katoikountes* means residents, not visitors for the feast) from every nation, and each understands in their native language. Luke gives us a powerful image of unity that is created when preachers, teachers, and catechists, gifted by the Spirit, adopt the culture and language of those with whom they share the good news.

In the Gospel of John, the Spirit is handed over at the moment of Jesus's death: Jesus declares, "It is finished," and simultaneously he "handed over the Spirit" (19:30). This expression is not a euphemism for death; it is nowhere used that way in Scripture or in secular Greek literature. Again at 20:22 Jesus breathes on the disciples on Easter evening, saying, "Receive the holy Spirit." He revivifies them, just as the Creator did in bringing to life the first human being by blowing the breath of life into the nostrils (Gen 2:7).

The risen Christ passes through locked doors and empowers the disciples with the Spirit to continue his mission of unlocking with the gift of forgiveness any hearts bound in fear. The offer of forgiveness does not erase or make light of the wounds that have been inflicted, but it surrounds the woundedness with a power that moves toward healing and peace. The Spirit also enables the community of believers to hold on to each member and not lose anyone. In the second half of verse 23 there is no word "sins" in the Greek text. It does not speak of retaining "sins" of others but of a Spirit-enabled power to retain every beloved one, just as Jesus did not let a single one be lost (6:37, 39; 10:27-29; 17:12; 18:9).

Today we can consider: What gifts has the Spirit given me for welcoming the stranger? How can I understand better their ways of hearing the gospel? We can also ask the Spirit to help us claim the gift of forgiveness and the wisdom not to let go of any of God's beloved.

Preparing to Proclaim

Key words and phrases: "But when he comes, the Spirit of truth, he will guide you to all truth."

To the point: The gift of the Spirit at Pentecost completes and concludes the Easter season. The resurrection of Christ affirmed that his love and presence endure beyond death; the sending of the Spirit affirms that they also endure beyond the visible, physical presence that his disciples enjoyed. This same Spirit has been present throughout Jesus's life. It is the same Spirit that came upon Mary at the annunciation; it is the same Spirit that drove Jesus into the desert to pray. It is a Spirit that accompanies and guides and sustains Jesus throughout his ministry; it is the same Spirit that accompanies and guides and sustains us as we strive to continue Jesus's ministry on earth. This is a Spirit that brings about unity, dissolving the many barriers that divide us.

Psalmist Preparation

In this psalm, we ask God to renew the face of the earth. All things that God has created have been damaged by the presence of sin in the world. All creatures—including us—are in need of re-creation. As you prepare to proclaim this psalm, identify one place in your life where you would like the Spirit to come in and do some work of renewal or re-creation. What brokenness could the Spirit heal? What hurt could the Spirit turn to joy? Trust that God wills this joy and this healing for you, and sing this psalm in praise of a God who never stops making all things new.

Making Connections

Between the readings: The first reading has the classic Pentecost story, the Acts account where the Spirit descends in driving wind and tongues of fire. In the gospel, Jesus promises "the Spirit of truth"; in this first reading, the disciples are empowered to speak that truth not only in their own language but in a way that is understandable to all the diverse groups present in Jerusalem.

To experience: We humans often have a hard time understanding how vast God's love really is. We are comfortable with the boundaries we draw between us, content to rest in our small worlds of people like us. But Jesus insists on greater unity than that. At Pentecost, the Holy Spirit transcends the very language barriers that would keep Jesus's gospel from being heard. Jesus's message and Jesus's saving work are for all, and it is not for us to exclude people from them.

Homily Points

• As we come to the end of the Easter season, let us reflect on the transformative journey undertaken by Jesus out of love for us. Eight weeks ago, we entered the church waving palm branches to mark Jesus's entry into Jerusalem. During that holiest of weeks, we remember how Jesus, on the night he was betrayed, shared bread and wine with his disciples. Then after an agonizing evening in the garden, Jesus takes up his cross. Nails pierce his skin as he cries out and soon, breathes his last. The story should have ended here with death—and yet, Jesus made sure that death did not have the final say.

• Throughout the last fifty days of Easter, we soaked in stories of the resurrected Lord who still had some teaching and revealing to do. Jesus was not ready to leave quite yet. Now, on this solemnity of Pentecost, Jesus turns the work over to his disciples. Jesus's journey continues, though now we are the ones to take on the preaching and praying, the forgiving and healing. Guided by the Holy Spirit, we—the disciples of today—are called to carry on Christ's saving work.

• How do we take on such a major mission? We do so by coming together like our ancestors did for that first Pentecost celebration—a diverse group of people bonded by their amazement at the mighty acts of God. We do so by remembering that we are part of one body with many parts, each part called to use its gifts for the betterment of the whole.

CELEBRATION

Model Rite for the Blessing and Sprinkling of Water

Presider: The Holy Spirit embraced us in the waters of baptism. Through the sprinkling of this water, may the Spirit animate us to live as sisters and brothers in Christ . . . *[pause]*
   [continue with The Roman Missal, *Appendix II]*

Model Universal Prayer (Prayer of the Faithful)

Presider: Guided by the Spirit of truth, let us offer our prayers and petitions to God.

Response: Lord, hear our prayer.

Unite all Christians in our common mission to spread Christ's love to the world . . .

Help our churches and community centers to become safe, inclusive places for people with disabilities . . .

Show mercy and compassion to Christians who have been hurt and no longer participate in a faith community . . .

Foster our abilities to listen to the promptings of the Holy Spirit in our prayer and in the world around us . . .

Presider: Creative God, you sent the Holy Spirit to fill the hearts of your faithful and kindle in them the fire of your love. On this Solemnity of Pentecost, we give thanks and praise for your Spirit's attention to our prayers and abiding presence in our lives. We offer this prayer through Christ our Lord. **Amen.**

Liturgy and Music

"And suddenly there came from the sky a noise like a strong driving wind, and it filled the entire house in which they were."

When the Holy Spirit rushed into that room where the disciples were hiding, they were already afraid for their lives. This powerful atmospheric event had to be terrifying. I wonder if they were at all reassured by Jesus's promise to send another Advocate. Nevertheless, by the power of the Holy Spirit, they were equipped with all the wisdom and courage they would need to do the important work that lay ahead. Can you imagine trying to commit to a ministry that could very well cost you your life? Many of the Twelve were martyred, the end of a dangerous mission that began with the Lord's words: "Peace be with you."

What are you afraid of in your ministry? Criticism? Change? Job security? Not being able to live up to your own lofty standards? As a public, professional minister in the church, you may occasionally find yourself holding back from what you feel called to do. Indeed, those who make music in the church will always be vulnerable to the estimation of the very people they serve.

The beautiful Pentecost Sequence is worth visiting throughout the year. Ponder it deeply, visit it when you are alone in the darkened, empty church. Find in it a litany of all the encouragement, strength, and assistance you need from the Holy Spirit.

Fear not. Rather, be at peace.

COLLECT
Let us pray.

Pause for silent prayer

O God, who by the mystery of today's
   great feast
sanctify your whole Church in every
   people and nation,
pour out, we pray, the gifts of the Holy Spirit
across the face of the earth
and, with the divine grace that was at work
when the Gospel was first proclaimed,
fill now once more the hearts of believers.
Through our Lord Jesus Christ, your Son,
who lives and reigns with you in the unity
   of the Holy Spirit,
God, for ever and ever. **Amen.**

FIRST READING
Acts 2:1-11

When the time for Pentecost was fulfilled,
   they were all in one place together.
And suddenly there came from the sky
   a noise like a strong driving wind,
   and it filled the entire house in which
      they were.
Then there appeared to them tongues as
   of fire,
   which parted and came to rest on each
      one of them.
And they were all filled with the Holy Spirit
   and began to speak in different tongues,
   as the Spirit enabled them to proclaim.

Now there were devout Jews from every
   nation under heaven staying in
      Jerusalem.
At this sound, they gathered in a large
      crowd,
   but they were confused
   because each one heard them speaking
      in his own language.
They were astounded, and in amazement
      they asked,
   "Are not all these people who are
      speaking Galileans?
Then how does each of us hear them in
   his native language?
We are Parthians, Medes, and Elamites,
   inhabitants of Mesopotamia, Judea and
      Cappadocia,
   Pontus and Asia, Phrygia and
      Pamphylia,
   Egypt and the districts of Libya near
      Cyrene,
   as well as travelers from Rome,
   both Jews and converts to Judaism,
      Cretans and Arabs,
   yet we hear them speaking in our own
      tongues
   of the mighty acts of God."

RESPONSORIAL PSALM

Ps 104:1, 24, 29-30, 31, 34

℟. (cf. 30) Lord, send out your Spirit, and
    renew the face of the earth.
    or:
℟. Alleluia.

Bless the Lord, O my soul!
    O Lord, my God, you are great indeed!
How manifold are your works, O Lord!
    The earth is full of your creatures.

℟. Lord, send out your Spirit, and renew
    the face of the earth.
    or:
℟. Alleluia.

If you take away their breath, they perish
    and return to their dust.
When you send forth your spirit, they are
    created,
    and you renew the face of the earth.

℟. Lord, send out your Spirit, and renew
    the face of the earth.
    or:
℟. Alleluia.

May the glory of the Lord endure forever;
    may the Lord be glad in his works!
Pleasing to him be my theme;
    I will be glad in the Lord.

℟. Lord, send out your Spirit, and renew
    the face of the earth.
    or:
℟. Alleluia.

SECOND READING

1 Cor 12:3b-7, 12-13

or

Gal 5:16-25

SEQUENCE

See Appendix A, p. 297.

Living Liturgy

Liturgy and Community: The Holy Spirit is present and active among us today. I have seen this through the liturgical music ministry in my parish. During the height of the COVID-19 pandemic when churches were closed, our liturgical music group gathered regularly on Zoom because we missed each other so much. By the time conditions became safer, however, many members had plugged into other ministries or found other avenues of worship. When we resumed in-person worship, some worried that the group would never return to its formerly robust size. Emails and invitations were sent. Meetings were held and concerns were voiced. As time went on, the tone of those outreaches gradually became a little more urgent, a little more tense. This liturgical music group had been a fixture for years, and gave many parishioners a sense of stability and comfort amidst many changes in the parish and the surrounding neighborhood. Pleas, handwringing, and bulletin announcements did not change the tide, though.

The thing that ultimately saved the group was the gentle faithfulness of a few individuals who continued to show up week after week without knowing if anybody else would come. Their courage to show up and sing (even those who didn't consider themselves to be vocalists) lifted the spirits of our community. Their willingness to adapt and simplify music made participating feel more approachable to some who had never considered joining the group before. An unexpected type of evangelization took place that feels similar to what we read happened to the disciples on Pentecost. Through the power of the Holy Spirit, people who had withdrawn out of fear were brought back into the light of day to tell of God's glory and call others into community.

Today's reading from Galatians gives us a litany of words to describe how the Spirit is made manifest among us. Let us celebrate that, while we may sometimes see the Holy Spirit appear in a fiery display, we can also feel the Spirit at work in more subtle ways—like the gentle faithfulness of those in our community who simply continue to show up.

PROMPTS FOR FAITH-SHARING

• How do you see the Holy Spirit present in the church and in the world today?

• What obstacles hinder unity in your community? How might you cooperate with the Holy Spirit to overcome these obstacles?

• The second reading names the fruit of the Spirit as "love, joy, peace, patience, kindness, generosity, faithfulness, gentleness, self-control." How have you experienced these this Easter season? How do they reveal the Spirit's presence to you?

*See Appendix B, p. 311,
for additional prompts.*

MAY 19, 2024
PENTECOST SUNDAY

ORDINARY
TIME II

SPIRITUALITY

℟. Alleluia, alleluia.
Glory to the Father, the Son, and the
Holy Spirit;
to God who is, who was, and who is to
come.
℟. Alleluia, alleluia.

Gospel

Matt 28:16-20; L165B

**The eleven disciples went to
Galilee,
to the mountain to which
Jesus had ordered them.
When they all saw him, they
worshiped, but they
doubted.
Then Jesus approached and said
to them,
"All power in heaven and on
earth has been given to me.
Go, therefore, and make disciples of all
nations,
baptizing them in the name of the
Father,
and of the Son, and of the Holy
Spirit,
teaching them to observe all that I
have commanded you.
And behold, I am with you always, until
the end of the age."**

Reflecting on the Gospel

Go only "to the lost sheep of the house of Israel"—this was Jesus's firm instruction to the disciples when he first sent them out on mission (Matt 10:6). Later, when a Canaanite woman pleaded with Jesus to heal her daughter, he again declared that he "was sent only to the lost sheep of the house of Israel" (Matt 15:24). His concern was to feed his own people (15:26) and he did not see her as one of them. It seems that her respectful and insistent response in word and gesture, however, helped trigger a profound change in Jesus's understanding of the scope of his mission. At the end of the gospel, he commissions his disciples to go everywhere, making disciples of all nations (28:19).

A similarly profound shift occurred in the life of the apostle Paul, who went from persecuting Christians who were reinterpreting the parameters of the family of God to being the most ardent proponent of inclusion of all. By the time Paul writes to the community in Rome in the late 60s, he is able to say that all people who are led by the Spirit are "children of God." This same expression had been used of the Israelites (Deut 14:1). Paul presses the metaphor further, insisting that all these varied children of God are not just appendages to the family but are full and true heirs. Being a full member of the family and an heir means inheriting the pattern of life set by Jesus: a life of loving service that is costly but that ends in glorious transformation.

The relationship between parents and children who are full heirs is only one metaphor by which to speak of the mysterious love of the Trinity. Saint Augustine liked to speak of the three persons as "Lover, Beloved, and Love." Saint Hildegard of Bingen favored "Fire, Burning, and Flashing Forth." One might name them "Eternal Giver, Receiver, and Outburst of Joy." There is no limit to the ways we can speak of the profound mystery of the Three-in-One. The three persons are a communion of love that interweave each other in endless patterns of saving activity.

The first reading today assures us the mystery of the divine love is not something that remains nebulous and intangible. Rather, the saving activity of God is concrete and visible both in great moments and in the routines of everyday life. Jesus's promise, "I am with you always" (Matt 28:20), assures all God's Spirit-led children in every race and nation that the divine presence continues to create, save, and vivify whenever we allow it free rein to draw us into the Trinity's ever-expanding circles of love.

On this feast of the Holy Trinity, talk with Jesus about the ways you see "outsiders." What could turn your heart to see them more truly as God's beloved children? Also consider what names capture best for you the ever-expanding communion of love that is the Trinity. Try out a new name for the Three-in-One in your prayer.

Preparing to Proclaim

Key words and phrases: "[I]n the name of the Father, and of the Son, and of the Holy Spirit."

To the point: We start many of our prayers in the threefold name of the Trinity; along with it, we make the sign of the cross so often that this gesture and these words become a nearly meaningless throwaway gesture. But we are making a great claim when we begin in the name of the Father, Son, and Spirit. To act or speak in someone's name is to be their agent, to take part in their work, to act on their behalf. This is exactly what God invites us to—participation in the ongoing work of God, in all work that moves this world a little closer to the goodness and justice that God intends for us. And the Trinity reveals this, too; to participate in God's life is to participate in the life of loving relationship that the three persons of the Trinity share.

Psalmist Preparation

This psalm proclaims the goodness of God, including God's presence throughout time. It affirms the past goodness of God in creation; it affirms the present goodness of God in delivering those who follow him. It even affirms the future, trustworthy goodness of God who will continue this creative and redeeming work unto the end of time. This God—Father, Son, and Spirit—remains with us, faithful to promises. As you prepare to proclaim this affirmation of God's enduring kindness, think of those times in your life that you struggle to believe in it for yourself. Spend time in prayer asking God to increase your awareness of God's promised presence in times it is not very evident to you.

Making Connections

Between the readings: Our God longs to be with us. Our God takes action to be with us. That is what we see in all three persons of the Trinity. God is present to Israel in fire, letting them hear his voice and the commandments that will lead them into life. God is present to the disciples in Jesus, in whom God's union with humanity takes on a new intensity. And God continues to be with us in the Holy Spirit, who accompanies and guides the church on earth.

To experience: The church continues the work of this gospel as we continue to baptize our children and adult converts. We continue to baptize in the name of the Father, and of the Son, and of the Holy Spirit; God continues to dispense grace. God's presence is an ongoing gift, flowing out of the love with which we are created and called.

Homily Points

• We can never know the fullness of our all-powerful, mysterious God. But today's readings point to a crucial aspect of the divine human relationship: our triune God—Father, Son, and Holy Spirit—dwells with us, always. Our God is not one to stay up in the clouds. Just the opposite—in today's first reading, Moses recalls hearing the voice of God coming forth from the fire of a burning bush. He recalls God's fidelity to God's people, as demonstrated when God took a nation from another nation for the Hebrew people. Many of us may wish the Lord would give us such clear, direct signs of the divine presence. Frustration can arise in prayer when we do not receive the clarity desired from God. Yet while our divine dialogue may look different than Moses's, God assures us that God will be with us always until the end of the ages.

• In today's gospel, we receive further assurance of God's presence. Out of great love for us, God sent God's only son to save the world. We spent the last few months of Lent and Easter hearing stories of Jesus's time on earth, both before and after his death on the cross. Even death cannot separate us from God!

• Then last week we celebrated the outpouring of the Holy Spirit, breathed upon the earliest disciples by Christ himself, who continues to be our advocate and guide. Our triune God dwells with us and invites us into the divine relationship. As Saint Paul writes in today's second reading: "The Spirit himself bears witness with our spirit that we are children of God, and if children, then heirs, heirs of God and joint heirs with Christ . . ."

CELEBRATION

Model Penitential Act

Presider: In today's first reading, Moses directs the people to keep God's statutes and commandments. For the times that we have fallen short of the way of life to which God calls us, let us ask for mercy . . . *[pause]*

> Lord Jesus, you are the Son of God: Lord, have mercy.
>
> Christ Jesus, you call us into glory with you: Christ, have mercy.
>
> Lord Jesus, you sent the Holy Spirit to bear witness to God's love of creation: Lord, have mercy.

Model Universal Prayer (Prayer of the Faithful)

Presider: With faith in the triune God, let us offer our prayers and petitions.

Response: Lord, hear our prayer.

Bless liturgical choirs and musicians who fill our worship with joyful noise . . .

Further efforts of scientists and public health experts to produce effective vaccines . . .

Ease tensions between countries at war . . .

Instill in this community a hospitality that extends to those who live with mental illness . . .

Presider: Eternal God, your son Jesus promises that he will be with us always until the end of the age. Hear our prayers and transform our hearts that we might make disciples of all nations through our witness to the gospel. We ask this through Christ our Lord. **Amen.**

Liturgy and Music

As children of God, heirs and joint heirs with Christ, we are connected to one another, relationally. As with any family, the children have different personalities and may even disagree from time to time, yet remain equal in the sight of the parent, equally loved, cherished, and recipients of the benefits and blessings that are available to every child in the family.

So it also should be within our parish communities. Each member is to be seen as a co-equal member of the family, granted the same rights and privileges, the same access, and the same dignity and respect as any other member. Each deserve our love, support, and attention. Just as God has three distinct persons and/or personalities, so do our brothers and sisters in Christ have distinctions that should be recognized and honored—equally.

Spend some time in prayer with "A Walking Prayer," a beautiful trinitarian hymn by Karen Schneider Kirner published by WLP/GIA. As you listen, reflect on how you might be more intentional about honoring the distinct persons and personalities of those in your choir and community.

Scan to listen to "A Walking Prayer."

COLLECT

Let us pray.

Pause for silent prayer

God our Father, who by sending into the world
the Word of truth and the Spirit of sanctification
made known to the human race your wondrous mystery,
grant us, we pray, that in professing the true faith,
we may acknowledge the Trinity of eternal glory
and adore your Unity, powerful in majesty.
Through our Lord Jesus Christ, your Son,
who lives and reigns with you in the unity of the Holy Spirit,
God, for ever and ever. **Amen.**

FIRST READING

Deut 4:32-34, 39-40

Moses said to the people:
"Ask now of the days of old, before your time,
ever since God created man upon the earth;
ask from one end of the sky to the other:
Did anything so great ever happen before?
Was it ever heard of?
Did a people ever hear the voice of God
speaking from the midst of fire, as you did, and live?
Or did any god venture to go and take a nation for himself
from the midst of another nation,
by testings, by signs and wonders, by war,
with strong hand and outstretched arm,
and by great terrors,
all of which the LORD, your God,
did for you in Egypt before your very eyes?
This is why you must now know,
and fix in your heart, that the LORD is God
in the heavens above and on earth below,
and that there is no other.
You must keep his statutes and commandments that I enjoin on you today,
that you and your children after you may prosper,
and that you may have long life on the land
which the LORD, your God, is giving you forever."

RESPONSORIAL PSALM

Ps 33:4-5, 6, 9, 18-19, 20, 22

℟. (12b) Blessed the people the Lord has
　　chosen to be his own.

Upright is the word of the LORD,
　　and all his works are trustworthy.
He loves justice and right;
　　of the kindness of the LORD the earth
　　　　is full.

℟. Blessed the people the Lord has chosen
　　to be his own.

By the word of the LORD the heavens were
　　made;
　　by the breath of his mouth all their
　　　　host.
For he spoke, and it was made;
　　he commanded, and it stood forth.

℟. Blessed the people the Lord has chosen
　　to be his own.

See, the eyes of the LORD are upon those
　　who fear him,
　　upon those who hope for his kindness,
to deliver them from death
　　and preserve them in spite of famine.

℟. Blessed the people the Lord has chosen
　　to be his own.

Our soul waits for the LORD,
　　who is our help and our shield.
May your kindness, O LORD, be upon us
　　who have put our hope in you.

℟. Blessed the people the Lord has chosen
　　to be his own.

SECOND READING

Rom 8:14-17

Brothers and sisters:
Those who are led by the Spirit of God are
　　sons of God.
For you did not receive a spirit of slavery
　　to fall back into fear,
　　but you received a Spirit of adoption,
　　through whom we cry, "Abba, Father!"
The Spirit himself bears witness with our
　　spirit
　　that we are children of God,
　　and if children, then heirs,
　　heirs of God and joint heirs with Christ,
　　if only we suffer with him
　　so that we may also be glorified with
　　　　him.

Living Liturgy

Liturgy and Spirituality: Theologians and other faithful believers have devoted countless hours of scholarship, reflection, and prayer to questions about the nature of the Holy Trinity and how God can exist as three persons in one divine entity. These questions are eternally incomprehensible—one could study forever and still have more to uncover about this mystery. In my own reflections, each person of the Trinity has revealed to me a unique truth about life and our seemingly improbable but serendipitous existence.

In meditating on God the Father, I have felt deeply reassured of the holiness of our mere existence—and that of all creatures. In his book *Time Management for Mortals*, Oliver Burkeman tries to shed new light on the sometimes vexing idea of mortality by noting that all of life is borrowed time and that any amount of time we have is miraculous. To ever feel joy, even briefly, is such a gift when we could very well never have existed at all. As the psalmist sings in Psalm 33, "Blessed the people the Lord has chosen to be his own." Blessed indeed are we to have been gifted by God with the spark of life. Through the miracle of the incarnation, Jesus Christ revealed the beauty of being enfleshed and embodied. Our existence as creatures is a reminder that we exist in relationship. We did not create ourselves, nor do we sustain ourselves. Living in right relationship with God our Creator, with the earth, and with our fellow creatures is essential to our existence. Finally, the Holy Spirit, the Advocate, teaches us that there is divinity in all that inspires and energizes us. When we feel emboldened and empowered to participate in co-creation with God, we are experiencing a taste of heaven here on earth.

Having a theology that understands God as being multidimensional enables us to see God in all things, including in the miracle of our multifaceted existence.

PROMPTS FOR FAITH-SHARING

• What does your baptism mean to you? How do you live out its promises in your everyday life?

• How do you feel Jesus's promised ongoing presence? How do you struggle to perceive it?

• Which person of the Trinity do you most often picture when you are praying? Why do you think that is?

See Appendix B, p. 312,
for additional prompts.

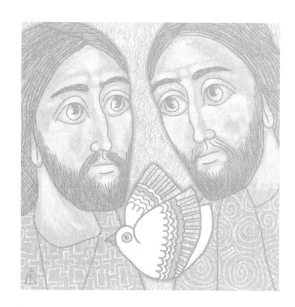

SPIRITUALITY

℟. Alleluia, alleluia.
I am the living bread that came down from
    heaven,
says the Lord; whoever eats this bread will live
    forever.
℟. Alleluia, alleluia.

Gospel   Mark 14:12-16, 22-26; L168B

On the first day of the Feast of Unleavened
    Bread,
  when they sacrificed the Passover lamb,
  Jesus' disciples said to him,
  "Where do you want us to go
  and prepare for you to eat the Passover?"
He sent two of his disciples and said to
    them,
  "Go into the city and a man will meet you,
  carrying a jar of water.
Follow him.
Wherever he enters, say to the master of
    the house,
  'The Teacher says, "Where is my guest
    room
  where I may eat the Passover with my
    disciples?"'
Then he will show you a large upper room
    furnished and ready.
Make the preparations for us there."
The disciples then went off, entered the
    city,
  and found it just as he had told them;
  and they prepared the Passover.

While they were eating,
  he took bread, said the blessing,
  broke it, gave it to them, and said,
  "Take it; this is my body."
Then he took a cup, gave thanks, and gave
    it to them,
  and they all drank from it.
He said to them,
  "This is my blood of the covenant,
  which will be shed for many.
Amen, I say to you,
  I shall not drink again the fruit of the
    vine
  until the day when I drink it new in the
    kingdom of God."
Then, after singing a hymn,
  they went out to the Mount of Olives.

Reflecting on the Gospel

As youngsters, we had ways of sealing the bond of friendship with our best friends. We girls would exchange friendship rings, pledging our undying loyalty to one another. Our brothers would make a small cut on their finger and then mingle their blood with their buddy's to signify the unbreakable bond between them as "blood brothers." Today's readings evoke this symbol of blood bonds that can never be broken.

In the first reading, Moses sprinkles half the blood of a sacrificed animal on the altar and the other half on the people. The blood signifies the life force that seals the commitment between the Holy One and Israel. Not only are God and the people bound together irrevocably but the people themselves are united to one another. The twelve pillars erected at the foot of the mountain represent the whole of the people. They acclaim with one voice their loyalty to all the words and ordinances of God.

In the same way, Jesus's blood shed for all reaffirms God's unbreakable bond with us. What Jesus says and does at the Last Supper is the culmination of an entire lifelong pouring out of himself in love. The words and gestures echo God's life-sustaining self-gift to Israel in the wilderness, symbolized in manna (Exod 16:12-35), and Jesus's feeding of the hungry multitudes during his Galilean ministry (Mark 6:30-44; 8:1-9). These continual manifestations of God's commitment to us reach their climax in Jesus's gift of self. In Mark's Gospel, the Last Supper is a Passover meal, recalling how the blood of lambs smeared on the doorposts kept the fleeing Israelites safe from the destroyer, and how the flesh of the lamb was consumed in haste for the journey to freedom.

So Jesus's flesh and blood sustains, protects, and frees us as a people who then embody for others his unbreakable commitment of love. His blood seals this covenant for all people. Four times in describing the preparation for the meal Mark uses the word *methetai*, "disciples," signifying all the women and men who have followed Jesus and who have ministered with him. In the words over the cup, Jesus says his blood "will be shed for many." This reflects a Hebrew idiom, where the contrast is between "one" and "the many." *Many* does not mean that some are left out; instead, it signifies the totality.

This blood bond is already a reality for us, yet it awaits perfect fulfillment, as Jesus's final words in today's gospel indicate. In our eucharistic gatherings we make present again Jesus's gift of self while we also celebrate a foretaste of the eternal feasting, where we will experience perfect oneness with the Holy One and with one another.

How have you experienced God's undying commitment to you through an unbreakable bond with a loved one? Today, meditate on how "the cup" symbolizes both suffering and the life force that empowers us to endure suffering for the sake of the gospel. Or reflect on how every time we say "Amen" in receiving Christ's body and blood, we recommit ourselves to the irrevocable blood bond with the Holy One.

Preparing to Proclaim

Key words and phrases: "While they were eating, he took bread, said the blessing, broke it, gave it to them, and said, 'Take it; this is my body.'"

To the point: This gospel gives us Mark's account of the institution of the Eucharist. The pattern established here continues at every Mass; we take bread, bless it, break it, and share it. We recall all of Jesus's incredible gifts—the Eucharist, the Holy Spirit, his very death and resurrection. Through him we are given abundant life that cannot be destroyed by death. In the light of all these plentiful gifts we do well to remember that the word Eucharist means "thanksgiving." Giving is the very nature of God; it is what God does and what God is. It is a response of gratitude that God asks of us, and we offer it in the celebration of the Eucharist.

Psalmist Preparation

This psalm summarizes beautifully the liturgical action we take part in at Mass. Our intention is to "make a return . . . for all the good [God] has done." Our prayers of gratitude are our response to all God's many gifts. We express this gratitude in ritual form, taking up the "cup of salvation" and offering "sacrifice of thanksgiving." As you prepare to proclaim this psalm, reflect on your current relationship with the Mass. Are you attending out of love or out of obligation? Are you participating with intention or by rote? Ask God in prayer how you could renew your commitment to your own liturgical worship.

Making Connections

Between the readings: The first reading gives us Moses making a covenant between God and Israel. Like the Eucharist, it involves a "blood of the covenant." In Exodus, it is bulls' blood from a peace offering to God, sprinkled on the people to ratify their covenant with God. In Mark, it is Christ's blood, shed for many and offered to us to drink. Jesus both fulfills the Mosaic covenant and transcends it, bringing us to new levels of intimacy with God.

To experience: Our weekly celebration of the Eucharist can sometimes become routine. It is worthwhile to try to renew our gratitude for this gift and to participate with full awareness of what is happening. At times, however, we may not be granted the gift of a renewed emotional response. In these times, it is important to just keep showing up. Going through the motions when we do not feel like it can be a great act of love; it is where love transcends emotion and becomes a choice and a virtue.

Homily Points

• On the night of the Last Supper, Jesus broke bread and proclaimed it his body. He took the cup filled with wine and declared it his blood. Jesus entrusted the promise of eternal life to two of the most essential—and enjoyable!—human actions: eating and drinking. Jesus reveals the hope of everlasting joy in heaven from the ordinary fruits of the earth. Jesus's gifts of the bread and wine, his very body and blood, make the heavenly kingdom accessible to all who believe.

• Our regular partaking of the body and blood in the Eucharist strengthens us for the journey to heaven and draws us around a common table with others who believe in the power of Christ. The body and blood of Christ is entirely gift—a grace-filled meal. We cannot earn our place at the eucharistic table, nor can we lose our seat. Jesus sat among saints and sinners at the Last Supper and throughout his earthly ministry. He welcomed all to join in the feast—and he continues that welcome to us today. We are invited to receive the bread of life and the cup of salvation each week.

• Christ's body and blood serve as fuel so that we might go out and live into our God-given callings with energy and spirit. The grace broken and poured at the altar extends out into the world. Strengthened by Christ's body and blood, we will enjoy the fullness of everlasting life with Christ.

Model Penitential Act

Presider: In today's first reading. Moses reads the covenant to the people who promise to heed and do all that the Lord says. For the times we have strayed from God's commandments, let us ask the Lord for mercy and pardon . . . *[pause]*

Lord Jesus, you are the living bread that came down from heaven: Lord, have mercy.
Christ Jesus, you shed your precious blood for our salvation: Christ, have mercy.
Lord Jesus, you intercede for us at the right hand of God: Lord, have mercy.

Model Universal Prayer (Prayer of the Faithful)

Presider: Nourished by Christ who sacrificed his body and blood for us, let us give voice to our prayers and petitions.

Response: Lord, hear our prayer.

Bring Christians together around a common table and a common mission to share the Good News of Christ . . .

Bless blood donors, organ donors, and all who give their bodies to help others . . .

Nurture the growing bodies of children and ensure that all children have access to nutritious food and drinks . . .

Bring hope to all gathered here so that, nourished by the body and blood of Christ, we may be beacons of light to our communities . . .

Presider: God of hope, your son Jesus came into the world to save us through the sacrifice of his body and blood. Receive our prayers that we too may work to feed others in word, sacrament, and service. We ask this through Christ our Lord. **Amen.**

Liturgy and Music

At its heart, the Eucharist is a meal—a meal shared *in* community and *by* community. The partaking of this holy meal unites us to Christ and to one another. It is also the "source and summit" of our faith. Eucharist comes from the Greek word *eucharistia*, meaning thanksgiving. To celebrate the Eucharist reminds and connects us to the sacrifice made on our behalf and the divinity of Christ, for which we give thanks.

We derive the English word "communion" from the Latin *communio*, meaning mutual participation, sharing, and fellowship. By participating in the Holy Eucharist, we engage in an act of thanksgiving, one where we give gratitude to God in the midst of community. There is a mutuality that therefore exists in the Eucharist, a mutuality with Christ and a mutuality with our community, one of sacrifice and one of gratitude and thanksgiving.

As we celebrate the solemnity of the Most Holy Body and Blood of Christ, may we strive to hold all of these aspects in our head and in our heart: mutuality, participation, fellowship, sacrifice, gratitude, and thanksgiving. Perhaps we can reflect on various aspects this day, while focusing on one and strive to embody at least one in our *communio*, our community.

Consider "Communion Song" for the Communion procession for today's liturgy. It is the setting of the communion antiphon for Corpus Christi found in *Honey from the Rock* (GIA).

COLLECT

Let us pray.

Pause for silent prayer

O God, who in this wonderful Sacrament
have left us a memorial of your Passion,
grant us, we pray,
so to revere the sacred mysteries of your
    Body and Blood
that we may always experience in
    ourselves
the fruits of your redemption.
Who live and reign with God the Father
in the unity of the Holy Spirit,
God, for ever and ever. **Amen.**

FIRST READING

Exod 24:3-8

When Moses came to the people
    and related all the words and
        ordinances of the LORD,
    they all answered with one voice,
    "We will do everything that the LORD
        has told us."
Moses then wrote down all the words of
    the LORD and,
    rising early the next day,
    he erected at the foot of the mountain
        an altar
    and twelve pillars for the twelve tribes
        of Israel.
Then, having sent certain young men of
    the Israelites
    to offer holocausts and sacrifice young
        bulls
    as peace offerings to the LORD,
    Moses took half of the blood and put it
        in large bowls;
    the other half he splashed on the altar.
Taking the book of the covenant, he read
    it aloud to the people,
    who answered, "All that the LORD has
        said, we will heed and do."
Then he took the blood and sprinkled it on
    the people, saying,
    "This is the blood of the covenant
    that the LORD has made with you
    in accordance with all these words of
        his."

RESPONSORIAL PSALM
Ps 116:12-13, 15-16, 17-18

℟. (13) I will take the cup of salvation, and
   call on the name of the Lord.
or:
℟. Alleluia.

How shall I make a return to the LORD
   for all the good he has done for me?
The cup of salvation I will take up,
   and I will call upon the name of the
      LORD.

℟. I will take the cup of salvation, and call
   on the name of the Lord.
or:
℟. Alleluia.

Precious in the eyes of the LORD
   is the death of his faithful ones.
I am your servant, the son of your
      handmaid;
   you have loosed my bonds.

℟. I will take the cup of salvation, and call
   on the name of the Lord.
or:
℟. Alleluia.

To you will I offer sacrifice of
      thanksgiving,
   and I will call upon the name of the
      LORD.
My vows to the LORD I will pay
   in the presence of all his people.

℟. I will take the cup of salvation, and call
   on the name of the Lord.
or:
℟. Alleluia.

SECOND READING
Heb 9:11-15

OPTIONAL SEQUENCE

See Appendix A, p. 298.

Living Liturgy

Liturgy and the Arts: From the foot of the mountain to the dining table, from the blood of livestock to the blood of Christ: today's readings take us on a journey to the heart of salvation by asking, "What is the sacrifice God requires?" "Come to the Table" is a worship song written by Mark Alan Schoolmeesters and recorded by Common Hymnal. Each verse and refrain names various groups of people who are invited to participate in the heavenly feast. The groups are disparate and, many would say, in conflict—wealthy and poor, proud and shamed, sinners and saints—but they are *all* invited to this feast. Imagine the scene if such a group were actually invited to dine together. It's hard to picture, and even if you can, it's hard to picture it going *well* because of the stories we tell ourselves about those who are different from us. What would it really take for people from different political spheres, different ethnicities, different socioeconomic classes to come together and break bread harmoniously?

A sacrifice. But as we hear in the letter to the Hebrews, Christ has transformed that sacrifice. We no longer offer goats and bulls; like Christ, we must offer our very selves—our prejudices, our preferences, our cynicism, our impulse to protect our pride or save face. It may seem like a difficult price to pay, even for willing hearts, but perhaps it would help to focus on what we stand to gain from this sacrifice. How wonderful it would be to rest at a table knowing that we are seen and loved just as we are. This is the redeeming paradox of the paschal mystery. Just as we must die in order to be raised to new life, we also must set aside our desires for sameness and embrace difference in order to confidently bring ourselves, wounded and imperfect as we are, to God's heavenly table.

PROMPTS FOR FAITH-SHARING

• What do you understand the word "covenant" to mean? What covenants are you part of? How do you live out your commitment to them?

• How is your relationship with the Eucharist these days? Are you excited to attend Mass or do you attend mostly out of a sense of obligation?

• The word "Eucharist" comes from a Greek word that means "thanksgiving." Which of God's gifts do you feel most gratitude for?

See Appendix B, p. 312, for additional prompts.

GOSPEL ACCLAMATION
Matt 11:29ab

℟. Alleluia, alleluia.
Take my yoke upon you, says the Lord;
and learn from me, for I am meek and humble
     of heart.
℟. Alleluia, alleluia.

or

1 John 4:10b

℟. Alleluia, alleluia.
God first loved us
and sent his Son as expiation for our sins.
℟. Alleluia, alleluia.

Gospel   John 19:31-37; L171B

Since it was preparation day,
   in order that the bodies might not
        remain on the cross on the
        sabbath,
   for the sabbath day of that week was
        a solemn one,
   the Jews asked Pilate that their legs
        be broken
   and they be taken down.
So the soldiers came and broke the legs
   of the first
   and then of the other one who was
        crucified with Jesus.

Continued in Appendix A, p. 299.

See Appendix A, p. 299, for the other readings.

Reflecting on the Gospel

Today's gospel reminds us of the blatant brutality of crucifixion. Christians have taken the image of the cross, a symbol of horrendous death, and turned it into a symbol of hope. But in order for us to appreciate the magnitude of that symbology, we must understand the full extent of the torture involved in crucifixion.

To be crucified during Roman occupation was to be made an example. It was a horrible, long death, drawn out in order to cause the greatest amount of pain, and thus act as a deterrent for anyone else who might cause problems. Crucifixion was public. The body was to be hoisted up above a crowd so that anyone entering the area would see the punishment that awaited them if they did not follow Roman laws. Crucifixion victims were often placed along the main road leading to a town, as a show of force and as a deterrent. In Jesus's case, he's crucified on top of a hill.

The reason the legs were broken upon removing a body from a cross was to ensure a victim of crucifixion could not run away. They needed to ensure this because someone hanging on a cross might still be alive a few hours after being tied up. It depended on how long it took the lungs to collapse. This is why the soldier stabs Jesus in the gut: to confirm he was definitely dead.

The magnitude of this torture is an integral part of our understanding of salvation. The passion of Christ's death is a necessary part of the resurrection story. We are not saved without this scene. We do not gloss over it. We do not downplay it. We magnify it so much that a crucifix is traditionally placed above the altar of a church, the focal point of the whole building. This is because the physicality of Jesus is what facilitates the salvation of our souls. Jesus did not wish his pain away. He lived it unto death. And when we receive the Eucharist, we are participating in the tangible reality of the resurrected Christ.

Our faith is inescapably visceral. The body matters. St. Gregory of Nazianzus tells us, "That which is not assumed is not saved." Jesus experienced the full force of humanity, with a human body, unto its own failing and his death. That is the length he was willing to go to in order to provide us the opportunity to enter into a new Jerusalem. That is the extent of Jesus's love for us. It is total. It is the magnitude of the Sacred Heart.

Today's feast is a celebration of the love Jesus has for us, as a church and individually. Our dogmatic understanding of the death and resurrection of Jesus Christ is that it offers everyone who has ever lived an opportunity to dwell in the kingdom of heaven. It is also the inheritance of our faith to believe that if it had only been for one person—for Adam or for you—Jesus would have still allowed for his crucifixion.

Preparing to Proclaim

Key words and phrases: "[A]nd immediately blood and water flowed out."

To the point: When Jesus's body is pierced by a lance, his heart is revealed. It is revealed in the blood that flows forth, blood that consisted of plasma and red blood cells and white blood cells and platelets. Human blood that was pumped through his human body by his human heart. More than revealing his humanity, though, this moment reveals Jesus's great unfathomable love. This blood was not spilled in vain—it was spilled for us. It was given on purpose and with purpose, to restore us to the life and love that God wills for us.

Model Penitential Act

Presider: In today's gospel we hear the testimony of one who saw the blood and water flow from Jesus' side. For the times we have not testified to Christ by our lives, we ask for pardon and peace . . . *[pause]*

Lord Jesus, you teach us *agapic* love: Lord, have mercy.
Christ Jesus, you are the Way, the Truth, and the Life: Christ, have mercy.
Lord Jesus, you are merciful and show us the way to life in you: Lord, have mercy.

Model Universal Prayer (Prayer of the Faithful)

Presider: Trusting in the infinite mercy of God, we raise our prayers and petitions through the intercession of the Sacred Heart of Jesus:

Response: Lord, hear our prayer.

That the pope, bishops, and all lay women and men may follow Christ's example of love and mercy, standing in solidarity with those who are excluded and marginalized . . .

That local, national, and world leaders may work for peace and justice that is rooted in humility and service . . .

That all who experience hurt and loneliness may know the presence of the compassionate Christ . . .

That Christians everywhere might seek opportunities to grow in authentic friendship . . .

Presider: God of every good gift, in your great love you opened wide the heart of your son, Jesus, so that all of us might enjoy life with you. Hear these our prayers that in the days ahead we might serve you with grateful hearts and willing spirits. We ask this through Christ our Lord. **Amen.**

Living Liturgy

God nurtures us as a parent does a child, meeting us in our neediness, sustaining us, protecting us, and teaching us to walk for ourselves. God is more perfect than any parent, though, never losing patience or growing in resentment of our needs. When God's love is not met with recognition or gratitude, God's response is not one of anger but one of *even more love.* This is the love that sends us Jesus to enter into the human experience and to live and die for the beloved. It is the same love that awaits us in the sacraments, inviting us to draw ever closer to the undying love of God. It is this same love that burns even now in the heart of Jesus.

At Jesus's baptism, the heavens open, the Spirit descends, and God's voice calls him God's beloved Son. At our own baptisms, it is less visible but no less real that the heavens open, the Spirit descends, and God is pleased to name us as beloved daughters and sons. At baptism we are adopted into God's family, recalling the images of the first reading in which God loves us as a parent cares for a child. These images of love and patience tell us something about how God is with us and how we ought to be with each other.

FOR REFLECTION

• How does Jesus reveal his love for you in your everyday life? Where do you struggle to see his love?

• How can you take on the heart of Jesus? How can you make his heart more visible in the world?

• Who do you struggle to love? How might God be calling you to grow in compassion for them?

See Appendix B, p. 312, for additional questions.

COLLECT

Let us pray.

Grant, we pray, almighty God,
that we, who glory in the Heart of your
    beloved Son
and recall the wonders of his love for us,
may be made worthy to receive
an overflowing measure of grace
from that fount of heavenly gifts.
Through our Lord Jesus Christ, your Son,
who lives and reigns with you in the unity of
    the Holy Spirit,
God, for ever and ever. **Amen.**

or:
O God, who in the Heart of your Son,
wounded by our sins,
bestow on us in mercy
the boundless treasures of your love,
grant, we pray,
that, in paying him the homage of our devotion,
we may also offer worthy reparation.
Through our Lord Jesus Christ, your Son,
who lives and reigns with you in the unity of
    the Holy Spirit,
God, for ever and ever. **Amen.**

Homily Points

• In the Sacred Heart of Jesus, we will find the rest longed for by our weary souls. What does it look like to dwell in Jesus's Sacred Heart? How can we take Christ's yoke upon us in the busyness of our daily lives? Rest is not a given in today's fast-paced culture. Like any relationship, drawing close to the heart of Jesus requires time and attention.

• In describing the events surrounding Jesus's death, John's Gospel includes an interesting note: "An eyewitness has testified, and his testimony is true; he knows that he is speaking the truth, so that you also may come to believe." What eyewitness accounts of Jesus's love and mercy have you experienced that you can share with the world? Just as importantly, what might others offer as eyewitness accounts of the love and mercy we have shown?

• Pope Francis reminds us that "a little bit of mercy makes the world less cold and more just." What does this look like in our families, our workplaces, our schools, and our church? How can we more fully enter the Sacred Heart of Jesus by embodying just a little bit of mercy?

SPIRITUALITY

GOSPEL ACCLAMATION
John 12:31b-32

℟. Alleluia, alleluia.
Now the ruler of this world will be
    driven out, says the Lord;
and when I am lifted up from the earth, I
    will draw everyone to myself.
℟. Alleluia, alleluia.

Gospel   Mark 3:20-35; L89B

Jesus came home with his
    disciples.
Again the crowd gathered,
    making it impossible for them
        even to eat.
When his relatives heard of this
    they set out to seize him,
    for they said, "He is out of his
        mind."
The scribes who had come from
    Jerusalem said,
    "He is possessed by Beelzebul,"
    and "By the prince of demons
        he drives out demons."

Summoning them, he began to speak to
    them in parables,
    "How can Satan drive out Satan?
If a kingdom is divided against itself,
    that kingdom cannot stand.
And if a house is divided against itself,
    that house will not be able to stand.
And if Satan has risen up against himself
    and is divided, he cannot stand;
    that is the end of him.
But no one can enter a strong man's
    house to plunder his property
    unless he first ties up the strong man.
Then he can plunder the house.
Amen, I say to you,
    all sins and all blasphemies that
        people utter will be forgiven them.
But whoever blasphemes against the
    Holy Spirit
    will never have forgiveness,
    but is guilty of an everlasting sin."
For they had said, "He has an unclean
    spirit."

Continued in Appendix A, p. 300.

Reflecting on the Gospel

They say that "you can't go home again." That seems to be the dynamic playing out in today's gospel. Jesus, having launched out on his public mission, "came home" with his disciples. It is not to his hometown of Nazareth (6:1) that he returns but to Capernaum, where he has made a new home (2:1) and a new family. His relatives, who think he has lost his mind, first try to force him to come home to his family of origin. When that fails, his mother and siblings try to persuade him, but he has cast his lot with a newly formed family of disciples and there is no going back.

A second conflict erupts. Scribes accuse Jesus of being possessed. If he had responded with similar name-calling, they would have dug in their heels and the conflict would have escalated. Instead, Jesus points out the scribes' distorted logic and their mistaken interpretation of his deeds by posing pointed questions, pronouncing true maxims, and inviting his opponents to accept the forgiving power of the Spirit. While the scribes may lose face in this public debate about power, Jesus opens a way for them to gain true honor by acceding to the power of the Spirit. Every sin, he insists, even their blasphemous accusation that he has an unclean spirit, can be forgiven.

The first reading from Genesis tells in mythical terms of the entry of sin into the world. The first human couple, having succumbed to sin, has left the idyllic home provided by the Creator. The consequences are manifest in ruptured relationships with Earth, creatures, and human beings. They can never go home to what was before. When coupled with the gospel, however, there is a hope-filled assurance of forgiveness offered to all and an invitation into a new home and a new family in Christ.

In the gospel, immediately after the assurance that all sins will be forgiven (v. 28), comes an exception: "whoever blasphemes against the Holy Spirit will never have forgiveness" (v. 29). The meaning of this verse has long been a puzzle. Some scholars understand verses 28 and 29 to represent two opposing sides of an early Christian debate. They propose that some people in Mark's community thought it impossible to welcome back a repentant member who, under duress, had foresworn Christ ("blasphemed") and betrayed the community. Would they ever be able to forgive and trust such a one again? Some said yes; some said no. For some scholars, verse 28 represents Jesus's response of unqualified forgiveness for any sin, while verse 29 is not from Jesus's lips but represents the voice of the Markan community.

It is important to note that Jesus does not say that God will not offer forgiveness for the sin of blasphemy, but that one who does not rightly acknowledge the power of the Spirit will never have forgiveness. That is, those who refuse to open themselves to the power of the Spirit cannot experience forgiveness by their own decision not to allow in the forgiveness and healing that is offered them. All sinners, if they choose, can go home into God's welcoming arms.

Preparing to Proclaim

Key words and phrases: "Here are my mother and my brothers. For whoever does the will of God is my brother and sister and mother."

To the point: Sometimes hearing this reading can make us feel pity for Mary. Jesus's response to her presence seems a bit callous, almost as if he is rejecting her in favor of his faithful listeners. But Jesus's message is one of radical inclusion. He does not just offer us citizenship in heaven; he offers us places in God's very family. When we are adopted as children of God in baptism, we become co-heirs with Christ. Mary is not being rejected; after all, she too is one who "does the will of God." Jesus's inclusion of all echoes her *Magnificat* with its call to upend the world's power structures. We are called to echo Mary in saying "yes" to God's call and in bringing Jesus ever more fully into the world.

Psalmist Preparation

This psalm is a relief in light of the first reading. We have just heard the story of Adam and Eve being caught in their sin. Its effects seem irrevocable; we all still suffer from the inheritance of original sin. But the psalm reassures us that this is not the end of the story. God promises mercy and redemption. God hears our cries for forgiveness, and we can trust in God's kindness. As you prepare to proclaim this psalm, reflect on a sin or pattern of sin that you have brought to confession in the past. How did you experience God's mercy in the sacrament? Even if it was not an overwhelming emotional experience, trust that God's mercy was present just the same.

Making Connections

Between the readings: In the first reading, we see Satan in an instance of momentary triumph. He has succeeded in tricking the woman and man; they have eaten the fruit, and sin has entered the world. But it has not entered in irrevocably. God sends Jesus to reverse its effects and to end Satan's sway over our hearts and our world. We see Jesus's power over Satan in the gospel, where he is casting out demons. Jesus points out that Satan would not rise up against himself because that would be the end of him, but in Jesus we see the end of Satan anyway.

To experience: We very often forget to embrace others in the church as our brothers and sisters in Christ. We are all too often divided by liturgical preference and political leanings. But the unity Christ wants for us, the unity that is made real in the Eucharist, is far greater and more real than anything that divides us.

Homily Points

• Sin causes real consequences—and God will never leave us to face those consequences alone. Today's first reading harkens back to the very beginning when the man and the woman eat from the forbidden tree. They disobey God. The scene depicts two people hungry for more and better. The first people want to become gods themselves. The serpent lures the man and the woman in by promising to give them what they think they want. The serpent tries to create distance between the people and God—yet God does not allow that to happen.

• The sins of the man and the woman hurt their relationship with God. They face severe consequences for what they have done. Still, God does not end the relationship with the man and woman. In one of the more powerful biblical scenes, God is described as walking around the garden in search of the couple. God values both justice and mercy. Sin is not without consequence—and the people who sin remain beloved children of God.

• In today's gospel, Jesus goes up against the religious authorities of the time: the Jerusalem scribes. Jesus recognizes that while the scribes hold great influence within the community, they are corrupt and are not leading the people in the ways God intends. In response Jesus offers two parables to the scribes that call for liberation from sin and division. He shows that even those claiming to be religious authorities can be corrupt. This continues to be true in our times, particularly in the wake of the clerical abuse and cover-up crisis in the Catholic Church.

CELEBRATION

Model Penitential Act

Presider: Saint Paul reminds the Corinthians—and each of us—that "our inner self is being renewed day by day." Grateful for God's mercy, let us call to mind our sins and ask for forgiveness . . . *[pause]*

Lord Jesus, you call God's people to greater unity in you: Lord, have mercy.

Christ Jesus, you promote peace among all of creation: Christ, have mercy.

Lord Jesus, you create for us an eternal dwelling place: Lord, have mercy.

Model Universal Prayer (Prayer of the Faithful)

Presider: As God's beloved children, let us bring our needs and the needs of the world before the Lord.

Response: Lord, hear our prayer.

Bless and keep safe the elders in our church community . . .

Inspire elected officials to enact legislation that ensures all people have access to quality healthcare . . .

Give relief to people facing temptations in mind, body, or spirit . . .

Shower your blessings upon parents, guardians, and all who care for children . . .

Presider: Prophetic God, you sent your Son into the world to speak truth to power. Hear our prayers that in the days ahead we might serve you with courageous spirits. We ask this through Christ our Lord. **Amen.**

Liturgy and Music

As music leaders, we have a lot of influence. For those who serve with us in music ministry, what we say and do can have a lot of impact, sometimes more than we know. As leaders, some of us may see ourselves beyond reproach, even incapable of making a mistake. Of course, this is far from the truth! It requires a certain level of humility not only to acknowledge when we are in error, but for the self-reflection to even realize our flawed humanness.

When we have made an error in rehearsal or performance, given a flawed instruction, perhaps spoken harshly to someone, it can be difficult to recognize our error, accept responsibility, and repent. Sometimes that means humbling ourselves and apologizing to those we have injured. It has been said that it takes a big person to admit their mistakes. In most cases, people will respond favorably to a person who apologizes for their mistake and is sincere in their repentance. So, too, is God quick to forgive us in our repentance, which means to turn *away* from sin and *toward* God and right living.

In our first reading, rather than accept responsibility for his sin, Adam blames "[t]he woman whom [God] put here with me." Yet, when we accept responsibility for our sin and repent, the psalmist reminds us that "[w]ith the Lord there is mercy, and fullness of redemption." In our ministry let us strive to walk humbly with our God and those with whom we serve.

COLLECT

Let us pray.

Pause for silent prayer

O God, from whom all good things come,
grant that we, who call on you in our need,
may at your prompting discern what is
    right,
and by your guidance do it.
Through our Lord Jesus Christ, your Son,
who lives and reigns with you in the unity
    of the Holy Spirit,
God, for ever and ever.

FIRST READING Gen 3:9-15

After the man, Adam, had eaten of the tree,
    the LORD God called to the man and
        asked him, "Where are you?"
He answered, "I heard you in the garden;
    but I was afraid, because I was naked,
    so I hid myself."
Then he asked, "Who told you that you
        were naked?
You have eaten, then,
    from the tree of which I had forbidden
        you to eat!"
The man replied, "The woman whom you
    put here with me—
    she gave me fruit from the tree, and so
        I ate it."
The LORD God then asked the woman,
    "Why did you do such a thing?"
The woman answered, "The serpent
    tricked me into it, so I ate it."

Then the LORD God said to the serpent:
    "Because you have done this, you shall
        be banned
    from all the animals
    and from all the wild creatures;
    on your belly shall you crawl,
    and dirt shall you eat
    all the days of your life.
I will put enmity between you and the
        woman,
    and between your offspring and hers;
he will strike at your head,
    while you strike at his heel."

RESPONSORIAL PSALM
Ps 130:1-2, 3-4, 5-6, 7-8

℟. (7bc) With the Lord there is mercy, and
    fullness of redemption.

Out of the depths I cry to you, O LORD;
    Lord, hear my voice!
Let your ears be attentive
    to my voice in supplication.

℟. With the Lord there is mercy, and
    fullness of redemption.

If you, O LORD, mark iniquities,
   LORD, who can stand?
But with you is forgiveness,
   that you may be revered.

℟. With the Lord there is mercy, and
   fullness of redemption.

I trust in the LORD;
   my soul trusts in his word.
More than sentinels wait for the dawn,
   let Israel wait for the LORD.

℟. With the Lord there is mercy, and
   fullness of redemption.

For with the LORD is kindness
   and with him is plenteous redemption;
and he will redeem Israel
   from all their iniquities.

℟. With the Lord there is mercy, and
   fullness of redemption.

SECOND READING
2 Cor 4:13–5:1

Brothers and sisters:
Since we have the same spirit of faith,
   according to what is written, *I believed,*
      therefore I spoke,
   we too believe and therefore we speak,
   knowing that the one who raised the
      Lord Jesus
   will raise us also with Jesus
   and place us with you in his presence.
Everything indeed is for you,
   so that the grace bestowed in
      abundance on more and more
      people
   may cause the thanksgiving to overflow
      for the glory of God.
Therefore, we are not discouraged;
   rather, although our outer self is
      wasting away,
   our inner self is being renewed day by
      day.
For this momentary light affliction
   is producing for us an eternal weight
      of glory
      beyond all comparison,
   as we look not to what is seen but to
      what is unseen;
   for what is seen is transitory, but what
      is unseen is eternal.
For we know that if our earthly dwelling,
      a tent,
   should be destroyed,
   we have a building from God,
   a dwelling not made with hands, eternal
      in heaven.

Living Liturgy

Liturgy and the Arts: Today's readings remind us how shocking and radical God's mercy can be. The first reading from Genesis recounts the fall of Adam and Eve. Although they were banished from the garden, God continued (and continues) to extend grace and mercy to humanity time and time again. I remember hearing the story of Adam and Eve as a child and assuming the role of the Monday morning quarterback: how stupid could they be! God only asked for one simple thing. It wouldn't be long before I found myself in Adam and Eve's shoes, unable to do the one simple thing that was asked of me.

I started taking piano lessons in elementary school. I loved my teacher and I loved going to my lessons. What I didn't love was practicing. It's not that I *never* practiced, it's just that I often did the bare minimum. Each week my teacher would ask if I had practiced my scales and my assigned piece, and each week I lied even though I knew she'd find out the truth as soon as I started to play. Her patience was extraordinary. Instead of shaming me or kicking me out of lessons, she concocted different practice plans to help my wandering mind focus on and commit to the exercises that would help me learn to play piano. (She also told my mother because sometimes mercy must bow to justice—my mom deserved to know that her hard-earned money was not well-spent.)

I think about my piano teacher and the mercy she showed me often, especially now that I have my own students who occasionally neglect to do their homework. By not giving up on me, she gave me a gift that constantly adds joy to my life. I believe in mercy because of her. I like to think that I speak of that mercy (as we are instructed to do by Saint Paul in Corinthians) when I accompany the choir at my church or at my school. We must talk about our experiences of mercy. Whether these experiences be commonplace or extraordinary, our stories of mercy can sharpen others' vision of how God's mercy is at work in our world.

PROMPTS FOR FAITH-SHARING

• How do you discern the will of God in your own life? How do you respond to God's callings?

• How can you more fully embrace others in the church as your brothers and sisters in Christ?

• The psalm promises God's mercy and redemption in the face of sin. How have you experienced God's mercy in your own life?

See Appendix B, p. 312, for additional prompts.

SPIRITUALITY

GOSPEL ACCLAMATION
℟. Alleluia, alleluia.
The seed is the word of God, Christ is the sower.
All who come to him will live forever.
℟. Alleluia, alleluia.

Gospel

Mark 4:26-34; L92B

Jesus said to the crowds:
   "This is how it is with the
      kingdom of God;
   it is as if a man were to scat-
      ter seed on the land
   and would sleep and rise night
      and day
   and through it all the seed
      would sprout and grow,
   he knows not how.
Of its own accord the land
      yields fruit,
   first the blade, then the ear,
      then the full grain in the
      ear.
And when the grain is ripe, he wields
      the sickle at once,
   for the harvest has come."

He said,
   "To what shall we compare the
      kingdom of God,
   or what parable can we use for it?
It is like a mustard seed that, when it is
      sown in the ground,
   is the smallest of all the seeds on the
      earth.
But once it is sown, it springs up and
      becomes the largest of plants
   and puts forth large branches,
   so that the birds of the sky can dwell
      in its shade."
With many such parables
   he spoke the word to them as they
      were able to understand it.
Without parables he did not speak to
      them,
   but to his own disciples he explained
      everything in private.

Reflecting on the Gospel

Ordinarily, a woman taking a seat on a bus is totally inconsequential. But in December of 1955, when Rosa Parks refused to give up her seat to make room for a white passenger, it sparked the Montgomery bus boycott and launched the nation into the civil rights movement. One small action by one previously unknown woman set in motion the whole struggle to begin to dismantle racism in the United States.

In today's gospel Jesus tells a parable that uses the image of sowing a tiny seed to speak about the way radical change begins. Mustard seed is barely visible, and at first may escape notice when it settles into the soil. When it sprouts, however, it shoots up into a large, vigorous plant that spreads uncontrollably. It cannot be contained in defined plots but crosses over into fields where it is unwanted. And once it takes root, it is nearly impossible to eradicate. In Jesus's parable this weed that was the bane of many farmers' existence did not get into the field accidentally; it is deliberately sown.

In Mark's Gospel, the mustard seed parable is coupled with another parable that describes the way in which the reign of God comes about over time, seemingly imperceptibly. Once the seeds of God's reign are sown, the one who scatters them goes about his daily work, sleeping and rising, night and day, while the seeds germinate and poke forth their first sprouts. The seeds keep growing and developing until the propitious moment arrives to take action for reaping the full harvest.

God's reign does not come with military might, nor is it brought from the exterior or imposed on a subjugated people. Rather, it comes through the ordinary, everyday actions of seemingly insignificant people, whose seeds of faith and passion for justice have the power to make hope blossom forth for a transformed world. To plant such seeds takes the kind of courage that Paul urges upon the Corinthians in today's second reading. He speaks of courage to "walk by faith, not by sight," for those who sow the seeds of God's reign do not at the time see the end result. Rosa Parks's courageous action resulted in arrest, loss of her job, and personal hardship before she had the satisfaction of knowing that she had played a large role in turning the tide for civil rights.

Sowing tiny seeds of hope has unforeseen effects that go far and wide. At the end of the mustard seed parable, Jesus says that all the birds of the sky will dwell in the shade of the mustard plant's large branches. The image is the same as in the first reading, where Ezekiel speaks of the hoped-for messianic time when all nations would be drawn to Israel. They would be like birds of all varieties flocking to the sheltering boughs of a cedar tree. These readings give us courage that no action is too small for sowing God's reign. They bolster our hope that faithful, everyday choices to scatter the seeds of Christ's love unleashes a power that can transform the world.

Preparing to Proclaim

Key words and phrases: "Of its own accord the land yields fruit."

To the point: Jesus often uses farming metaphors in his parables. The imagery is strong: seeds are mysterious little things. They are often small and easy to overlook; if we didn't know what they were we'd assume they were of little value. They are not living things on their own. But in the right conditions they grow into so much more. They blossom forth with life, providing food and shade and homes for wildlife. Those who grow plants from seed can only do so much. They can provide the right conditions with water and light. But in the end the growth is not up to them. In much the same way, God calls us to partnership. We have a role to play in bringing about God's kingdom. But in the end it's not really up to us; it is God who does the work.

Psalmist Preparation

This psalm echoes the plant imagery of the other readings. "The just one" is assured that she will grow like a mighty plant, her vigor and fruitfulness evidence of God's goodness. The word "flourish" is repeated twice in this psalm, so spend some time sitting with that word in prayer as you prepare to proclaim this psalm. What does flourishing look like to you? Do you feel that you are flourishing? If not, what is keeping you from it? What do you need from God in order to grow like a sturdy tree? Bring your reflections to God in prayer.

Making Connections

Between the readings: The first reading echoes the planting imagery of the gospel. God takes something small and makes it majestic. It becomes a home for birds, offering shelter and shade to those creatures that take refuge in its branches. It stands as a symbol of God's power, as it is God who gives the growth.

To experience: To plant a garden is to witness God's creative work. There are endless delights to discover in the growth of seedlings, the visits of pollinators, the complex interactions in the mini-ecosystems we construct. We can spend endless time planning a garden, but there is always mystery involved. We never have full control over how plants grow or where weeds take root or what pests choose to consume. All we can do is cooperate with nature's processes, setting conditions that might favor the outcome we desire. So it is with God—our spiritual journey is not one of control and accomplishment but one of cooperation and participation.

Homily Points

• The Son of God is a master storyteller. Jesus knows how to hook his audience with vivid imagery and profound lessons. He is especially fond of using images and metaphors from creation. Unlike some lofty teaching or theological discourse, the gifts of creation are accessible to everyone. Seeds and sickle make sense to us. So Jesus draws on the wisdom of the natural world to help us reflect on our lives and our responsibilities to the kingdom of God.

• Through today's first parable, Jesus reflects on the importance of healthy, faithful rhythms. The kingdom of God is like seeds scattered by the farmer who then embraces the rhythms of day and night. The farmer need not do anything spectacular to further the growth of the seeds—or to bring about the kingdom of God. He must only practice patience. There is great mystery soaked into the growth of everything from a tiny seed to God's whole kingdom. We do not know the time or the season—the logistics are not ours to control. Rather, God calls us to listen faithfully and respond with courage to the divine invitation to grow.

• Such growth may happen in the smallest or least likely places, such as when the miniscule mustard seed develops into the largest of plants. Christian growth tends to happen on the margins, among people immersed in the struggle and creation crying out for help. Among such suffering is often where our mysterious God plants seeds of growth. We are called to be present, in mind, body, and spirit, to God's creative process.

CELEBRATION

Model Penitential Act

Presider: In today's second reading, Saint Paul speaks of the courage of the Christian people who put their faith in the Lord. Drawing from our own well of courage, let us recall our sins and ask God for mercy . . . *[pause]*

Lord Jesus, you teach your disciples the way of everlasting life: Lord, have mercy.

Christ Jesus, you sit at the right hand of God the creator of the universe: Christ, have mercy.

Lord Jesus, you welcome all people into the peace of God's kingdom: Lord, have mercy.

Model Universal Prayer (Prayer of the Faithful)

Presider: With faith in God's desire to hear our prayers, let us offer our petitions.

Response: Lord, hear our prayer.

Bless the listening ministries of spiritual directors, counselors, and confessors . . .

Grant success and good weather to all farmers whose labor feeds and sustains us . . .

Drive out the evils of racism, sexism, homophobia, and all other systems of oppression . . .

Unite your people in works of service and justice . . .

Presider: God of abundance, you make yourself known in the gifts of creation. Hear our prayers that we might be good stewards of the gifts you give us as individuals and as communities. We ask this through Christ our Lord. **Amen.**

Liturgy and Music

Have you ever considered that our music ministry is a conveyance of God's word? We sing the liturgy, and we sing the word. As a homily can communicate God's word to people and plant a seed of salvation and deliverance that is literally life changing, so, too, when we sing God's word our ministry has the power to transform lives and implant God's word within the hearts and minds of people.

"It is good to give thanks to the LORD, to sing praise to your name, Most High." When we proclaim God's word through song, when we praise God in the sanctuary, when we praise God with singing, we lift the hearts of God's people. But not only that. Especially when we sing Scripture, we are planting a seed, in much the same way as preaching. How often have you heard yourself or has someone told you they left a service humming or singing a song they heard during the liturgy? Whether you know it or not, you have planted a seed. Just as the apostle Paul said, "I planted, Apollos watered, but God caused the growth" (1 Cor 3:6), so it is with us when we sing God's praises. Praising God and singing God's praises bears fruit (Ps 92:15) that we may never see or taste.

Our ministry matters. It has the power to transform lives. Not because we're so great, but because we sing and proclaim a word that is great and mighty.

COLLECT
Let us pray.

Pause for silent prayer

O God, strength of those who hope in you,
graciously hear our pleas,
and, since without you mortal frailty can
do nothing,
grant us always the help of your grace,
that in following your commands
we may please you by our resolve and our
deeds.
Through our Lord Jesus Christ, your Son,
who lives and reigns with you in the unity
of the Holy Spirit,
God, for ever and ever. **Amen.**

FIRST READING
Ezek 17:22-24

Thus says the Lord GOD:
I, too, will take from the crest of the
cedar,
from its topmost branches tear off a
tender shoot,
and plant it on a high and lofty
mountain;
on the mountain heights of Israel I
will plant it.
It shall put forth branches and bear
fruit,
and become a majestic cedar.
Birds of every kind shall dwell beneath it,
every winged thing in the shade of
its boughs.
And all the trees of the field shall know
that I, the LORD,
bring low the high tree,
lift high the lowly tree,
wither up the green tree,
and make the withered tree bloom.
As I, the LORD, have spoken, so will I do.

RESPONSORIAL PSALM

Ps 92:2-3, 13-14, 15-16

℟. (cf. 2a) Lord, it is good to give thanks
to you.

It is good to give thanks to the LORD,
to sing praise to your name, Most High,
to proclaim your kindness at dawn
and your faithfulness throughout the
night.

℟. Lord, it is good to give thanks to you.

The just one shall flourish like the palm
tree,
like a cedar of Lebanon shall he grow.
They that are planted in the house of the
LORD
shall flourish in the courts of our God.

℟. Lord, it is good to give thanks to you.

They shall bear fruit even in old age;
vigorous and sturdy shall they be,
declaring how just is the LORD,
my rock, in whom there is no wrong.

℟. Lord, it is good to give thanks to you.

SECOND READING

2 Cor 5:6-10

Brothers and sisters:
We are always courageous,
although we know that while we are at
home in the body
we are away from the Lord,
for we walk by faith, not by sight.
Yet we are courageous,
and we would rather leave the body and
go home to the Lord.
Therefore, we aspire to please him,
whether we are at home or away.
For we must all appear before the
judgment seat of Christ,
so that each may receive recompense,
according to what he did in the body,
whether good or evil.

Living Liturgy

Liturgy and Creation: When I was growing up, my mother had a garden in our small backyard. I loved watching her go through the rituals of tending a garden—preparing the beds, planting seeds, weeding and watering consistently, and of course, harvesting. I helped with these gardening tasks as a child, but once I grew up and moved into my own home, I fell out of the habit. After accidentally killing a few houseplants, I even started to believe that I hadn't inherited her green thumb. Recently I was inspired to try again. My home is not exactly overflowing with beautiful, lush greenery (yet!), but my skills as a plant caretaker have improved.

One of the most important things I had to relearn was how to commit to small, consistent acts of care. I didn't know initially whether I was watering too much or too little, but I learned and adjusted when I took time each day to notice the changes in my plants. God cares for us in much the same way, offering us nourishment through the sacraments and turning a merciful, attentive eye to us when we pray. This doesn't even include all of the ordinary blessings made available to us in the course of simply living our lives. When we are receptive to God's small consistent acts of care, we are able to thrive and reach our highest potential.

As I think back on seeds I planted, unsure if I had waited too late in the season to plant them, I'm reminded of what we are told in today's second reading, "we walk by faith, not by sight." Sometimes we are called to act without knowing if those actions will yield fruit. In those moments, we ought to trust in God's bold imagination. No one would guess that the mustard seed could become such a large and robust plant and yet, with the care of a diligent gardener it is able to thrive. The same is true of our ambitions, especially our longings for justice and peace. This life offers us the chance to be both seed and gardener. Let us be open to God's imagination for our lives and hold on to hope in the small seeds we want to see grow.

PROMPTS FOR FAITH-SHARING

• Name a "seed" in your life, something that seemed small but grew in ways you didn't expect.

• Waiting for plants to blossom is slow work. Where do you struggle to have patience with God?

• We might occupy any number of places in the botanical imagery of today's readings. We are seeds, planted and tended to by God. We are also farmers, planting seeds in hope but unable to control the outcome. Which of these images resonates most with you? Why do you think that is?

See Appendix B, p. 312, for additional prompts.

SPIRITUALITY

℟. Alleluia, alleluia.
A great prophet has risen in our midst,
God has visited his people.
℟. Alleluia, alleluia.

Gospel

Mark 4:35-41; L95B

On that day, as evening drew on,
    Jesus said to his disciples:
    "Let us cross to the other
        side."
Leaving the crowd, they took
    Jesus with them in the boat
    just as he was.
And other boats were with him.
A violent squall came up and
    waves were breaking over
    the boat,
so that it was already filling
    up.
Jesus was in the stern, asleep
    on a cushion.
They woke him and said to him,
    "Teacher, do you not care that we are
        perishing?"
He woke up,
    rebuked the wind, and said to the
    sea, "Quiet! Be still!"
The wind ceased and there was great
    calm.
Then he asked them, "Why are you
    terrified?
Do you not yet have faith?"
They were filled with great awe and
    said to one another,
    "Who then is this whom even wind
        and sea obey?"

Reflecting on the Gospel

In our most fearful moments, several things can quell our terror. An imagined threat passes; the light of day reveals that the forms that seemed so scary in the night were only shadows; a real and well-founded terror is dissipated when loved ones bear it with us. In today's gospel the disciples are terrified that the sea will swallow them up. On the Sea of Galilee, especially late in the afternoon, strong wind squalls often surge suddenly. The lake is ringed by hills that funnel the wind, which whips up the waves. The disciples' fear is well-founded as their boat begins to be swamped. Meanwhile, Jesus is peacefully asleep, like

those the psalmist describes who rest undisturbed, having placed their trust entirely in God (Ps 3:6; 4:9).

When the disciples rouse Jesus, he rebukes the wind in the same way that he rebukes demons and unclean spirits (Mark 1:25; 3:12; 9:25), and it immediately obeys. Jesus's questions to the disciples, "Why are you terrified? Do you not yet have faith?" are not so much a rebuke to them, as they are a way of teaching them how to cross over from fear to faith. The disciples have addressed him as "Teacher" when they cry out to him (v. 38), and Mark portrays this as a teachable moment.

As frequently happens in the books of Wisdom, instruction is given through probing questions that lead the learner into deeper insight. This is the technique God uses with Job in the first reading for this Sunday. It is not with an accusatory tone that God asks Job about the primordial days. Job is in terrible anguish and has cried out in misery to God.

God's answer in the midst of the storm is to point Job to the awesomeness of creation. The Creator speaks of having birthed the sea as it "burst forth from the womb," and then of having put boundaries around it. Just as a mother wraps a newborn with "swaddling bands," giving the child a sense of security as it enters a new and frightening phase of existence, so God did with the sea at its creation.

God does not explain or take away Job's suffering as uncontrollable waves of loss threaten to swallow him up. Rather, the Holy One redirects Job to the awe and beauty of the created world and the divine power that recreates it in ever new and magnificent patterns of generativity. Turning from his own misery toward the inscrutable designs of the Creator, Job allows himself to be transformed through the pain.

So too in the gospel, Jesus's questions point the disciples toward deeper understanding of the power of the Creator at work in himself and in them. It is a power that creates and recreates through patterns of death and rebirth. As God does with Job, Jesus does not explain away the disciples' terror but redirects them toward the One who is the creative power at the center of the universe. He leads them through their fear, enabling them to cross over into awe at the One whose recreative power is manifest in Jesus's stilling of every storm.

Preparing to Proclaim

Key words and phrases: "They were filled with great awe and said to one another, 'Who then is this whom even wind and sea obey?'"

To the point: Storms can be a source of awe. Their thundering might can evoke in us an appreciation for the God who created the natural world. But we are only able to have this reaction when we are safe from them. The disciples are not observing this storm from a cozy cabin window; they are in its midst and at its mercy. So their awe comes not from this power of the natural world but from the peace to which it gives way in response to Jesus's power. They are filled with awe at the control he displays, at the commands the sea obeys, and at the peace he brings. Much of our appreciation for God comes from what God does for us—stilling storms or providing us shelter, watering the earth and allowing it to dry in due season.

Psalmist Preparation

The psalm affirms that God is there in the tossing of the storm and is there in the stilling of its threat. God is all-powerful and always wills our good, but God is not a puppet whose power we can harness for ourselves. God is not tame, not a vending machine that dispenses answered prayers. God is rather wonderfully wild, always operating far beyond what we can imagine or understand. As you prepare to proclaim this psalm, think of a time when you knew God through the peace God gives. Think also of a time when you knew God by God's invitation to an adventure. Bring an appreciation for both these sides of God into your proclamation of this psalm.

Making Connections

Between the readings: In the first reading, God speaks to Job from a storm. He claims power over the sea but does not demonstrate it here; he rather asks Job to trust on the strength of word alone. Jesus shows power by stilling a storm; God here shows power by being in the storm. Both things are true. God is able to calm our suffering, and when God doesn't God remains with us as we pass through it.

To experience: Jesus takes control of the storm in this gospel, but we know that God does not always interfere in the natural rhythms of the world, even when they are destructive. In a world with increasingly extreme weather patterns, it is important to remember that God calls us to partnership in caring for creation. God cares for the natural world with and through us, and we can and should take action to preserve God's great gift of creation.

Homily Points

• The disciples took Jesus in the boat "just as he was." The Son of God had just come off a full day of teaching crowds of people on the shore. It seems safe to assume that Jesus gave his whole self to those teaching sessions—and so was probably quite tired by the time evening rolled around. In the same day, the Son of God can be both energized and exhausted. He is fully human, after all. We can imagine—and relate to—Jesus moving more slowly as the day drew on. Maybe his eyelids got heavy. Maybe he let out more than a few yawns. The gospel writer includes for a reason the detail that the disciples took Jesus with them on the boat "just as he was." Our holiest book affirms that it is okay to be just as we are. We need not put on a show for God. Like Jesus, we can be tired when we are tired. We can rest when we need to rest.

• By calming the storm, Jesus shows his power over creation. The Son of God can calm the chaos. The question facing the disciples is: will they trust Jesus to do so? Their fear seems stronger than their faith in various gospel stories, including this one. What might it take for disciples of today to truly trust in God's power to save?

• Today's gospel can be summed up in one profound line: Jesus is present in the storm. From the literal storm on the sea to the storms in our lives, Jesus never leaves us to face our perils alone.

CELEBRATION

Model Penitential Act

Presider: In today's second reading, Saint Paul reminds us that whoever is in Christ is a new creation. We need not be held back by the old ways of sin and death. Let us ask for forgiveness and mercy so that we too may enter into the new things to come . . . *[pause]*

Lord Jesus, you are one with the Creator and the Spirit: Lord, have mercy.

Christ Jesus, you are a beacon of calm amid our storms: Christ, have mercy.

Lord Jesus, you will raise us up to new life in God's kingdom: Lord, have mercy.

Model Universal Prayer (Prayer of the Faithful)

Presider: With faith that God hears our prayers, let us give voice to our needs and the needs of the world.

Response: Lord, hear our prayer.

Safeguard all children in our churches, schools, and communities . . .

Further the work of environmental stewards, scientists, and activists working to combat the climate crisis . . .

Bring safety and hope to people impacted by hurricanes, fires, droughts, tornados, and other major weather events . . .

Deepen our trust in the divine presence during times of turbulence in our lives . . .

Presider: Compassionate God, your love is everlasting. Through your son Jesus we come to know the delight of life with you. Receive our prayers that we might grow in faith and trust in you. We ask this through Christ our Lord. **Amen.**

Liturgy and Music

What a mighty and awesome God we serve! All creation obeys his will. There's a hymn that says: "What a mighty God we serve. / Angels bow before him. / Heaven and earth adore him. / What a mighty God we serve" ("What a Mighty God We Serve," traditional).

Simple, yet profound. Another hymn writer conveys the sense of awe he must have felt when he penned these familiar words: "O Lord my God, when I in awesome wonder / consider all the works thy hand hath made, / I see the stars, I hear the mighty thunder, / thy pow'r throughout the universe displayed" ("How Great Thou Art," Stuart K. Hine).

God created the world and everything that exists within it. It should then come as no surprise that all of God's creation bends to his will. Jesus, God's Son and equally God, shares the ability to command the forces of nature. In fact, all that came into being did so through the Word of God, who is Jesus.

We should not be surprised, as were the disciples, that the violent waves out on the sea would obey Jesus when he spoke but the words, "Quiet! Be still!" The winds and the waves did indeed obey his will, as sung in the song "Peace, Be Still" by Mary A. Baker and Horatio R. Palmer and recorded by the legendary gospel artist James Cleveland. What a wonderful way to exalt the majesty of God! Consider sharing this timeless classic in the liturgy today.

COLLECT

Let us pray

Pause for silent prayer

Grant, O Lord,
that we may always revere and love your
holy name,
for you never deprive of your guidance
those you set firm on the foundation of
your love.
Through our Lord Jesus Christ, your Son,
who lives and reigns with you in the unity
of the Holy Spirit,
God, for ever and ever. **Amen.**

FIRST READING

Job 38:1, 8-11

The Lord addressed Job out of the storm
and said:
Who shut within doors the sea,
when it burst forth from the womb;
when I made the clouds its garment
and thick darkness its swaddling bands?
When I set limits for it
and fastened the bar of its door,
and said: Thus far shall you come but no
farther,
and here shall your proud waves be
stilled!

RESPONSORIAL PSALM

Ps 107:23-24, 25-26, 28-29, 30-31

℟. (1b) Give thanks to the Lord, his love is
everlasting.
or:
℟. Alleluia.

They who sailed the sea in ships,
trading on the deep waters,
these saw the works of the Lord
and his wonders in the abyss.

℟. Give thanks to the Lord, his love is
everlasting.
or:
℟. Alleluia.

His command raised up a storm wind
which tossed its waves on high.
They mounted up to heaven; they sank to
the depths;
their hearts melted away in their plight.

℟. Give thanks to the Lord, his love is
everlasting.
or:
℟. Alleluia.

They cried to the LORD in their distress;
  from their straits he rescued them,
he hushed the storm to a gentle breeze,
  and the billows of the sea were stilled.

℟. Give thanks to the Lord, his love is
    everlasting.
  or:
℟. Alleluia.

They rejoiced that they were calmed,
  and he brought them to their desired
    haven.
Let them give thanks to the LORD for his
  kindness
  and his wondrous deeds to the children
    of men.

℟. Give thanks to the Lord, his love is
    everlasting.
  or:
℟. Alleluia.

SECOND READING
2 Cor 5:14-17

Brothers and sisters:
The love of Christ impels us,
  once we have come to the conviction
    that one died for all;
  therefore, all have died.
He indeed died for all,
  so that those who live might no longer
    live for themselves
  but for him who for their sake died and
    was raised.

Consequently, from now on we regard no
    one according to the flesh;
  even if we once knew Christ according
    to the flesh,
  yet now we know him so no longer.
So whoever is in Christ is a new creation:
  the old things have passed away;
  behold, new things have come.

Living Liturgy

Liturgy and Spirituality: In today's first reading, God reminds Job (who is in the midst of a storm) that he has the power to calm the "proud waves." Psalm 107 encourages us to remember that we proclaim a God of rescue, a God who sees people in distress and listens to their pleas. And the story we hear in Mark's Gospel is a familiar one. While Jesus and his disciples are crossing the sea, Jesus lays down to rest just as a violent storm begins. The disciples panic and wake Jesus who calms the storm and asks the disciples, "Do you not yet have faith?" The characters in each of these readings are facing actual storms, but the lessons in their stories can be applied to the figurative storms we face today—the existential threat posed by climate change, the increasing gap between the rich and the poor, our continued struggles for racial justice, the lack of civility in political discourse, and more. Do we have faith that God will accompany us and bring us safely through these storms?

When I find myself despairing about the state of things, it helps to remember that the course of human history seems to move in a cycle, or perhaps a spiral. Although it can feel like we face the same struggles and make the same mistakes over and over again, when we look with a wider view we can see that the arc of history is indeed bending, however slowly, toward justice. Life spans are longer. The rate of abject poverty around the world is lower. The increase in technology gives more people access to resources and information. These are all reasons to have hope. The struggles we face today are quite serious, but we have so much evidence from the Scriptures and from our own lives that God will not leave us alone. Let us remember that if God did it before, God will do it again.

PROMPTS FOR FAITH-SHARING

• What in the natural world evokes awe in you? Where do you find God present in creation?

• How do you cling to God in the storms of life? What storms has God accompanied you safely through?

• How can you take action to care for creation in order to preserve the great gifts of God present there?

*See Appendix B, p. 312,
for additional prompts.*

JUNE 23, 2024
TWELFTH SUNDAY
IN ORDINARY TIME

GOSPEL ACCLAMATION
cf. Luke 1:76

℞. Alleluia, alleluia.
You, child, will be called prophet of the Most
    High,
for you will go before the Lord to prepare his
    way.
℞. Alleluia, alleluia.

Gospel   Luke 1:57-66, 80; L587

When the time arrived for Elizabeth to
    have her child
  she gave birth to a son.
Her neighbors and relatives
    heard
  that the Lord had shown his
    great mercy toward her,
  and they rejoiced with her.
When they came on the eighth
    day to circumcise the child,
  they were going to call him
    Zechariah after his father,
but his mother said in reply,
"No. He will be called John."
But they answered her,
  "There is no one among your
    relatives who has this
    name."
So they made signs, asking his
    father what he wished him
    to be called.
He asked for a tablet and wrote, "John
    is his name,"
  and all were amazed.
Immediately his mouth was opened, his
    tongue freed,
  and he spoke blessing God.
Then fear came upon all their
    neighbors,
  and all these matters were discussed
    throughout the hill country of Judea.
All who heard these things took them
    to heart, saying,
  "What, then, will this child be?"
For surely the hand of the Lord was
    with him.

The child grew and became strong in
    spirit,
  and he was in the desert until the day
    of his manifestation to Israel.

See Appendix A, p. 300, for the other readings.

Reflecting on the Gospel

Mary and Elizabeth are cousins whose experiences mirror each other. They share impossible births. Mary is a virgin and Elizabeth is barren. Both of their husbands receive divine information about the births of their sons. Joseph accepts it, while Zechariah cannot believe it. Their sons reveal something similar. John lives in the desert, eating locusts and publicly proclaiming his role. Jesus ministers by going town to town, staying and sharing meals with various friends and those he meets along the way. He keeps his true identity to himself.

These two families offer us two examples of how to love, fulfill vocation, and achieve salvation. All six of these people are in heaven: five saints and one Son of God.

In many ways, John is the black sheep of this family. His father works in the temple and has such devotion within the working context of his experience of faith and religion that when a literal angel appears to him, Zechariah's understanding of how things work cannot accommodate this new information. He doubts. And because of this doubt, because of the rigidity of his expectations for how to experience God, Zechariah loses the ability to speak.

John offers a sharp contrast to his father. Instead of working within the set religious hierarchy, John chooses the antithesis: he rejects society as a whole and instead lives outside of most of the conventions of his birth. He's probably received an extremely thorough religious education through his parents, and his determination for how to live a holy life is to radically reject the comforts of his world and instead stand as witness to the future. The way John chooses to live his faith radically challenges the status quo, and yet it is he who is the first person to out Jesus by recognizing him for who he is: the Son of God.

John's faith is so full and remarkable that it is John who is chosen to baptize God himself! The outsider, the crazy man, the spectacle that was likely considered an embarrassment by more than a few Jews, baptized Jesus.

Today's feast is an opportunity for us to remember that the way to live out one's faith and live a holy life can look extremely different from one person to the next. John the Baptist's shunning of his society and instead eating bugs and wearing skins is a testament to the variety of ways that are available. That's part of the comfort of the saints. As C. S. Lewis wrote in *Mere Christianity*, "How monotonously alike all the great tyrants and conquerors have been; how gloriously different are the saints."

Preparing to Proclaim

Key words and phrases: "No. He will be called John."

To the point: In this gospel we see the relative powerlessness of women in the ancient world. Elizabeth, who has just borne a miracle baby in her old age, is not entrusted with the act of naming her child. Because her husband is unable to speak, some unspecified "neighbors and relatives" take this important parental duty upon themselves. When she resists, they criticize her choice, finding it unacceptable. It is only when his father affirms the choice that the name is bestowed. But note that Elizabeth's choice *is* affirmed in the end. John the Baptist's birth is part of God's work of overturning the world's broken power structures and uplifting the lowly ones.

Model Penitential Act

Presider: In today's first reading, the prophet Isaiah cries out, "The Lord called me from birth, from my mother's womb he gave me my name." God names and claims each of us from birth. For the times we have not taken God's call seriously enough, let us ask for mercy . . . *[pause]*

Lord Jesus, you sought wisdom from John the Baptist: Lord, have mercy.
Christ Jesus, you bring peace to the world: Christ, have mercy.
Lord Jesus, in you we find everlasting life: Lord, have mercy.

Model Universal Prayer (Prayer of the Faithful)

Presider: Through the intercession of John the Baptist, let us offer prayers for ourselves and the world.

Response: Lord, hear our prayer.

Energize ministers of your church to follow the radical calls of Christ . . .

Protect people experiencing homelessness and all who will sleep on the streets this night . . .

Comfort and renew hope in couples struggling with infertility . . .

Equip this congregation to share the prophetic message of Jesus to the ends of the earth . . .

Presider: Eternal God, you make all things possible through your love and mercy. Raise up in your church prophets like John the Baptist who prepare the way of the Lord and empower others to serve you in everyone we meet. We ask this through Christ our Lord. **Amen.**

Living Liturgy

Liturgy and Vocation: Theodore Roosevelt said, "Comparison is the thief of joy." Comparison can also be the thief of authentic purpose. We can be tempted to judge our worth based on how well we measure up against someone else's yardstick. John the Baptist knew precisely who he was and was not. He was exalted, not because he himself was the messiah but because of how he dedicated his life to pointing others toward the Messiah, Jesus Christ. In what areas of our lives can we let go of harmful comparison? How do we lead others to Christ simply by being who we are?

FOR REFLECTION

• The act of naming is a sacred responsibility, one that signifies humanity's partnership with God in the ongoing work of creation. Tell the story of your own name. What does it mean? Why was it chosen for you?

• Elizabeth's pregnancy was a cause for great joy, but her age would have made it a dangerous time as well. How do you show support for mothers whose pregnancies are scary or challenging?

See Appendix B, p. 312, for additional questions.

Homily Points

• Neighbors gather to rejoice with Elizabeth and Zechariah over the most improbable birth of their son. The words of the angel came true: Nothing shall be impossible with God. Our prayers are not always answered exactly as we want. God is not a magician, after all! But there are precious moments in life where our hopes become reality. We ought to take time to come together as a community to celebrate and give thanks to God for such marvelous gifts.

• Earlier in Luke's gospel, Zechariah questioned God at the announcement of his wife's miraculous pregnancy. Immediately, the angel Gabriel struck Zechariah silent. As the baby grew in Elizabeth's belly, Zechariah undoubtably reflects on his relationship with God and trust in God's almighty power. God strengthens Zechariah's faith through months of silence.

GOSPEL ACCLAMATION
Matt 16:18

℟. Alleluia, alleluia.
You are Peter and upon this rock I will build my
    Church,
and the gates of the netherworld shall not
    prevail against it.
℟. Alleluia, alleluia.

Gospel

Matt 16:13-19; L591

When Jesus went into the region
    of Caesarea Philippi
he asked his disciples,
    "Who do people say that the
        Son of Man is?"
They replied, "Some say John
    the Baptist, others Elijah,
still others Jeremiah or one of
    the prophets."
He said to them, "But who do
    you say that I am?"
Simon Peter said in reply,
    "You are the Christ, the Son
        of the living God."
Jesus said to him in reply,
    "Blessed are you, Simon son of
        Jonah.
For flesh and blood has not revealed
    this to you, but my heavenly
        Father.
And so I say to you, you are Peter,
    and upon this rock I will build my
        Church,
    and the gates of the netherworld
        shall not prevail against it.
I will give you the keys to the Kingdom
    of heaven.
Whatever you bind on earth shall be
    bound in heaven;
    and whatever you loose on earth
        shall be loosed in heaven."

See Appendix A, p. 301, for the other readings.

Reflecting on the Gospel

Today's account comes from the Gospel of Matthew, which, like Luke, was written after the Gospel of Mark and uses Mark as a source. Matthew's rendition includes a full commissioning: "And so I say to you, you are Peter, and upon this rock I will build my Church, and the gates of the netherworld shall not prevail against it. I will give you the keys to the Kingdom of heaven. Whatever you bind on earth shall be bound in heaven; and whatever you loose on earth shall be loosed in heaven." Peter may have been a bit overwhelmed hearing Jesus say these things to him. Such power!

But this account is not what we hear in Mark. In Mark, it's much shorter: "Then he warned them not to tell anyone about him" (8:30). That's it. No grand statements about Peter the rock, or the power that Peter shall wield. The accounts of Peter's commissioning come from later sources and were included in the Gospels of Matthew and Luke by their respective authors due to information other than Mark, their main source text. Mark, the shortest gospel, was written a few decades after the death of Jesus.

The curious thing about the Gospel of Mark, and thus our first account of this interaction, is that the author's life likely overlapped with Peter's, and it's possible they knew each other. (Biblical scholarship offers multiple theories.) Whether or not they spoke, or Mark was Peter's "interpreter," as has been suggested, they did at least share the same time period in the decades right after Jesus's death and resurrection. Because Peter was busy building the church and being arrested by the Romans while Mark was writing this gospel, Peter hadn't yet garnered the legendary mystique seen in today's Gospel of Matthew. The stories about Peter's relationship with Jesus and his role as "the rock" were still circulating, probably as firsthand accounts. Luke and Matthew include more information in their accounts of Jesus's life because the oral tradition in the wake of his ministry had traveled further.

That makes today's gospel no less *true*. The church regards Scripture as holding spiritual truths. Matthew is telling the story of Jesus, and there is truth in this rendition of Peter's commissioning. Peter is the rock upon which the church is built. Peter does indeed hold the keys to the kingdom of heaven—for he builds the institution that helps us get there!

Preparing to Proclaim

Key words and phrases: "I will give you the keys to the Kingdom of heaven."

To the point: The keys we carry say something about us. They connect us to where we live, where we work, our daily transportation. They carry with them a sense of responsibility and stewardship; we might not own the things to which we have keys, but they have been entrusted to us. In today's gospel, Jesus gives Peter his role as key-keeper. Peter, with all his faults and follies, is to be responsible for the kingdom of heaven. He does not, of course, own heaven or the church he will come to lead. But they are entrusted to him so that he can open them and share them with others.

Model Penitential Act

Presider: In today's gospel, Jesus asks his disciples, "Who do you say that I am?" Peter replies, "You are the Christ, the Son of the living God." Trusting in God's living presence among us, let us ask for pardon and mercy . . . *[pause]*

Lord Jesus, you rescue us from every evil: Lord, have mercy.
Christ Jesus, you promise safety in the heavenly kingdom: Christ, have mercy.
Lord Jesus, to you be glory forever and ever: Lord, have mercy.

Model Universal Prayer (Prayer of the Faithful)

Presider: Through the intercession of Saints Peter and Paul, let us put forth our prayers and petitions to God.

Response: Lord, hear our prayer.

Raise up leaders within the church, particularly those to help guide our liturgical ministries, outreach ministries, and faith formation . . .

Guide leaders of nations to uphold the common good and take special care of the most vulnerable . . .

Eradicate the sin of racism from all social systems and human hearts . . .

Grace the lives of all gathered here with strength and resolve to live the Christian life . . .

Presider: God of power and might, you call leaders like Saints Peter and Paul to guide your church. Receive our prayers that we too might contribute to the building up of your kingdom on earth. We ask this through Christ our Lord. **Amen.**

Living Liturgy

Liturgy and Community: "Feed my sheep." Jesus tells Simon Peter the way to show his love of God with this simple instruction. The same is true for us: if we love God, we must give what we have, generously and lovingly, to God's people. Our minds might go instinctively to money, but often the harder and more valuable things one can give are not financial—companionship, mentorship, space to express difficult emotions, a seat at the table where decisions are made. Perhaps these too are the ways we are being called to show love and feed God's sheep.

FOR REFLECTION

• What keys do you carry? What do they reveal about you? What responsibility do you feel for the things they can open and close?

• Peter, like all church leaders who would come after him, was very human. He had moments of greatness and moments of failure. How have you experienced the leadership of the church? How do those experiences impact your relationship with Christ?

See Appendix B, p. 312, for additional questions.

COLLECT
Let us pray.

Pause for silent prayer

O God, who on the Solemnity of the Apostles Peter and Paul
give us the noble and holy joy of this day,
grant, we pray, that your Church
may in all things follow the teaching
of those through whom she received
the beginnings of right religion.
Through our Lord Jesus Christ, your Son,
who lives and reigns with you in the unity of the Holy Spirit,
God, for ever and ever. **Amen.**

Homily Points

• Every saint faced their share of hardships. Living a life committed to Christ takes risks. It can be easy to imagine saints sitting dutifully in church, hands clasped together in quiet prayer. Or one might imagine saints arriving to town with great fanfare, hurling miracles left and right. Yet take up most books about the saints and you will quickly notice that the Christian life is no walk in the park.

• Today's Scripture readings tell of Saint Peter chained up in a prison cell after the execution of James, his fellow apostle. Paul writes of being rescued from every evil threat. Following Christ does not ensure security. Rather, such a life ensures stability through the ongoing presence of Christ in good times and bad, on earth and in heaven. Saints like Peter and Paul serve as witnesses to the strength that comes from aligning with Christ.

• "But who do you say that I am?" Jesus poses this intimate question to Peter—and to each of us. Throughout history, Jesus has accumulated many titles: Word made flesh, Redeemer, Light of the World, and Prince of Peace just to name a few. These titles point to particular characteristics or realties of Jesus. They help us come to know Jesus. They help us to name our relationships with him. Who is Jesus to you? Who is Jesus for our church community? For our neighborhood and world? Inspired by Peter, may we share what we know to be true about Jesus.

SPIRITUALITY

GOSPEL ACCLAMATION
cf. 2 Tim 1:10

℟. Alleluia, alleluia.
Our Savior Jesus Christ destroyed death
and brought life to light through the Gospel.
℟. Alleluia, alleluia.

Gospel   Mark 5:21-43; L98B

When Jesus had crossed again in the
	boat
	to the other side,
	a large crowd gathered around him,
		and he stayed close to the sea.
One of the synagogue officials, named
	Jairus, came forward.
Seeing him he fell at his feet and
	pleaded earnestly with him,
	saying,
"My daughter is at the point of
	death.
Please, come lay your hands on her
	that she may get well and live."
He went off with him,
	and a large crowd followed him and
		pressed upon him.

There was a woman afflicted with
		hemorrhages for twelve years.
She had suffered greatly at the hands
	of many doctors
	and had spent all that she had.
Yet she was not helped but only grew
	worse.
She had heard about Jesus and came
	up behind him in the crowd
	and touched his cloak.
She said, "If I but touch his clothes, I
	shall be cured."
Immediately her flow of blood dried up.
She felt in her body that she was
	healed of her affliction.
Jesus, aware at once that power had
	gone out from him,
	turned around in the crowd and
		asked, "Who has touched my
		clothes?"

*Continued in Appendix A, p. 302, or
Mark 5:21-24, 35b-43 in Appendix A, p. 302.*

Reflecting on the Gospel

In today's gospel, a synagogue official named Jairus pleads with Jesus for his dying daughter. Ordinarily he would not humble himself at the feet of an itinerant healer, but his daughter's life hangs by a thread and he will try anything. Mark intertwines with this the story of another person whose interminable suffering causes her to step out of her normal behavior too. For twelve long years

a woman afflicted with hemorrhages (in modern medical terms, the meaning of this is unclear) has been seeking a cure. Having exhausted her money and her dignity, she forsakes the professional doctors, approaches a popular healer in the midst of a crowd, and grabs his cloak from behind. She too will try anything.

In both cases, people with status and resources take the unusual step of leaving their accustomed social circles and reaching out to an itinerant preacher and healer. Both beg for his healing touch, and they are not disappointed.

God's power to heal flows freely through Jesus into the bodies of these hurting women. Both are restored as beloved daughters. The gospel healings are dramatic enactments of God's will for life to the full for all, as the first reading asserts.

The gospel story leads us to grapple with a mystery: why does God not prevent other deaths? With his choice of words in describing the hemorrhaging woman, Mark paints her in parallel lines with Jesus, pointing toward the mystery of his suffering and death. He uses the same verb (*paschein*) in verse 25 to describe her suffering that Jesus uses to speak of his own passion (8:31; 9:12). In the third passion prediction Jesus says he will be scourged (10:34); she is healed of her "scourge" (*mastix*, vv. 29, 34; translated in NAB as "affliction," in NRSV as "suffering"). Finally, she tells the "whole truth" (v. 33) to Jesus, the truthful teacher (12:14, 32). Just as her faith both saves and heals her (the verb *sozein* in v. 34 has both connotations), so Jesus's faithfulness to God brings salvation and healing even through and beyond death.

This gospel does not focus on the boundaries Jesus crossed by letting an unclean woman touch him. Leviticus 15:19-30 forbids touching a woman "who has a flow of blood from her body." Yet the account in Mark does not say where on her body the woman's hemorrhage was, nor is ritual purity made an issue in the text. In fact, as a healer, Jesus was always touching and being touched by people who were ritually impure. Most Jews would have been ritually impure most of the time. The only time when it was necessary to be in a state of ritual purity was when one was going to the temple. Then, ritual washing and waiting until sundown would remove most kinds of impurities. Instead, the focus in the gospel is on faith in the divine power to heal and save that flows through Jesus, which is sometimes manifest in physical healing and that is mysteriously at work even when beloved daughters and sons pass through death.

Preparing to Proclaim

Key words and phrases: "Little girl, I say to you, arise!"

To the point: The stories of healing in this gospel reveal that Jesus sees and loves each of us as individuals. It seems contradictory, that Jesus can love all of us with such wholehearted devotion. But his love is not diminished or fractured by the fact that there are so many of us to love. Here, surrounded as he is by a crowd, he notices and extends kindness to the suffering ones around him. The woman with hemorrhages would have gone unnoticed by anyone else, but Jesus takes note of her and restores her dignity as well as her health. And there is utter tenderness in Jesus's approach to Jairus's daughter. He takes her hand, he calls her "little girl." He loves her back to life. Mark tells us of this girl and this woman, but Jesus looks at every member of the crowd—and at every one of us—with the same healing and life-giving love.

Psalmist Preparation

This psalm praises God for some act of rescue akin to the healings Jesus works in the gospels. God's work is transformative, turning weeping to rejoicing and mourning to dancing. Such healing is evidence of God's presence. At the same time, though, God remains with us when we are in mourning. We are never left alone with our suffering. As you prepare to proclaim this psalm, pray for those in your congregation who are suffering, whether from grief or illness or whatever other pain is in their lives right now. Pray that God will be with them as they suffer, and pray that God will take their pain and transform it into goodness.

Making Connections

Between the readings: The first reading affirms that "God did not make death." Our God is a God of life, who shares his own life with us and longs to give it with more and more abundance. This is what Jesus does in the gospels, restoring health and life to the suffering ones he encounters. The second reading reminds us that we are called to imitate the self-giving work of Jesus, fulfilling the needs of those we encounter.

To experience: The clinical word "hemorrhage" can blur the suffering of the woman who reached out to Jesus for healing. She was likely suffering from irregular menstrual cycles, the unpredictability of which meant she was unable to obtain the ritual cleanliness necessary for participation in temple worship. Female health issues are still often considered taboo, and their personal nature can make them hard to talk about. Those who suffer from them often feel alone, especially when they might affect fertility. But Jesus is with them; he sees their secret suffering and does not shy away. He invites all women—single or married, childless or mothers of many, hyperfertile or infertile—to reach out to him for healing.

Homily Points

• Suffering separates. It leaves those like the woman in today's gospel anguishing in physical and emotional pain. Her community excluded this woman because of her hemorrhaging, deeming her ritually unclean. By the time she got to Jesus, the woman must have been exhausted. She must have tried countless doctors and remedies. Nothing was working. The woman knew she was not supposed to be out in the crowd. She knew the judgments people would pass as she sought healing. Nevertheless, she persisted.

• This woman believed in Jesus's power to heal, and nothing—no pain, no social norms, nothing—was going to stop her from his help. The woman elbowed her way through the masses to get close enough to Jesus to touch the fringe of his garment. Her hemorrhaging stops. After being cast out for a dozen years, the woman bravely declares her faith for all to hear. She shared her story, which was part of the healing, too.

• In today's second reading, Saint Paul addresses the practice of generosity. It is not enough, he says, to excel in faith, discourse, knowledge, earnestness, and love. You must also excel in being gracious. Saint Paul puts forth a vision of community where people with abundance provide for the needs of those who have less. Jesus provides the model for exceling in generosity. The Son of God gave up his very life so that humankind may be raised up. In this spirit, we too are asked to use our time, talents, and treasures in service of others. We are called to care for the most vulnerable among us through tangible actions. Who might God be calling you to excel in generosity toward these days?

CELEBRATION

Model Penitential Act

Presider: Today's first reading from the book of Wisdom reminds us that we are made in the image of God—yet sometimes our words and actions do not live up to the divine standard. For those moments, let us ask God for mercy and forgiveness . . . *[pause]*

Lord Jesus, you are our help and salvation: Lord, have mercy.

Christ Jesus, you intercede for us before God the Creator: Christ, have mercy.

Lord Jesus, you will come again in glory to break the bonds of death: Lord, have mercy.

Model Universal Prayer (Prayer of the Faithful)

Presider: With faith that God listens to our prayers, let us voice aloud the needs of our community and world.

Response: Lord, hear our prayer.

Protect the dignity of all women and girls in the church . . .

Inspire congressional leaders to pass legislation that shows care and respect for migrants and refugees . . .

Bring swift peace and support to people considering ending their lives . . .

Quiet our hearts and give us space for Sabbath rest during these summer days . . .

Presider: Loving God, you call your people to arise out of the darkness of death and into the promise of eternal life. Hear our prayers that we might be people of peace and justice in the world. We ask this through Christ our Lord. **Amen.**

Liturgy and Music

We may never know the mental, physical, or emotional state of those who attend our services. People's outward appearance does not necessarily convey their inward struggle. This is one reason why our music should be as diverse as possible. The apostle Paul, in his letter to the Corinthians, speaks of the diversity of approach in his ministry that he might reach some. We would do well to adapt this approach in our musical choices that we, too, might reach some.

Though there is sickness in the world, Scripture tell us that this was not God's design for the world. In our first reading from the book of Wisdom, we are told that "God formed man to be imperishable." Jesus cares for us so much that he will heal us when we ask. The gospel reading from Mark tells us of the synagogue official who asked Jesus to lay hands on his daughter. In response, Jesus went to his home and healed her. In a similar fashion, the woman afflicted for twelve years with hemorrhages had the faith to believe that if she could but touch Jesus's clothes, she would be made whole. Consider ministering Andraé Crouch's song "Oh, It Is Jesus" in your service this Sunday (found in *Lead Me, Guide Me—Second Edition*, #352). Someone's faith may be activated just enough to invite the healing power of Jesus into their situation.

COLLECT

Let us pray.

Pause for silent prayer

O God, who through the grace of adoption
chose us to be children of light,
grant, we pray,
that we may not be wrapped in the
       darkness of error
but always be seen to stand in the bright
       light of truth.
Through our Lord Jesus Christ, your Son,
who lives and reigns with you in the unity
       of the Holy Spirit,
God, for ever and ever. **Amen.**

FIRST READING
Wis 1:13-15; 2:23-24

God did not make death,
       nor does he rejoice in the destruction of
          the living.
For he fashioned all things that they might
          have being;
       and the creatures of the world are
          wholesome,
and there is not a destructive drug among
          them
       nor any domain of the netherworld on
          earth,
       for justice is undying.
For God formed man to be imperishable;
       the image of his own nature he made
          him.
But by the envy of the devil, death entered
          the world,
       and they who belong to his company
          experience it.

RESPONSORIAL PSALM

Ps 30:2, 4, 5-6, 11, 12, 13

℟. (2a) I will praise you, Lord, for you have rescued me.

I will extol you, O LORD, for you drew me clear
 and did not let my enemies rejoice over me.
O LORD, you brought me up from the netherworld;
 you preserved me from among those going down into the pit.

℟. I will praise you, Lord, for you have rescued me.

Sing praise to the LORD, you his faithful ones,
 and give thanks to his holy name.
For his anger lasts but a moment;
 a lifetime, his good will.
At nightfall, weeping enters in,
 but with the dawn, rejoicing.

℟. I will praise you, Lord, for you have rescued me.

Hear, O LORD, and have pity on me;
 O LORD, be my helper.
You changed my mourning into dancing;
 O LORD, my God, forever will I give you thanks.

℟. I will praise you, Lord, for you have rescued me.

SECOND READING

2 Cor 8:7, 9, 13-15

Brothers and sisters:
As you excel in every respect, in faith, discourse,
 knowledge, all earnestness, and in the love we have for you,
 may you excel in this gracious act also.

For you know the gracious act of our Lord Jesus Christ,
 that though he was rich, for your sake he became poor,
 so that by his poverty you might become rich.
Not that others should have relief while you are burdened,
 but that as a matter of equality
 your abundance at the present time should supply their needs,
 so that their abundance may also supply your needs,
 that there may be equality.
As it is written:
 Whoever had much did not have more,
 and whoever had little did not have less.

Living Liturgy

Liturgy and Community: A few years ago, I got the opportunity to participate in a work of devised theatre. Devised theatre is a method in which the piece is created collaboratively by the performing ensemble. Our performing ensemble consisted of six women who were longtime musicians and performers. The creation and rehearsal process was exhilarating, challenging, and extremely humbling. We would often reach a point in our rehearsal where no one had a clear idea of what should happen next. At those moments our leader would usually pause and say, "The answer is in the circle," meaning that eventually, one of us would stumble upon an answer. Each member of the ensemble had a different expertise—blocking or choreographing, creating vocal harmonies, identifying narrative through lines—so between the six of us, the next right action was never too far away.

Today's gospel reading tell the stories of Jesus healing the hemorrhaging woman and raising a young girl from the dead. While Jesus is certainly depicted as the initiator of these miracles, he notes that they did not occur solely by his power but also due to the faith of the ones who requested the miracle. The hemorrhaging women believed enough to seek after Jesus and touch his cloak. Jairus, the father of the young girl, fell at Jesus's feet and begged him to come see the child even though others believed all hope was lost.

It takes a lot of courage to ask for help and perhaps even more to trust that help will come, especially when it's not clear where that help will come from. This is where our second reading comes in. Paul instructs the Corinthians to be gracious and that their abundance should supply the needs of the poor. So it is too with us. Where there is scarcity, we are called to draw upon our abundance to help meet our neighbors' needs. The answer, indeed, is in the circle. A strong community in which people can humbly voice their needs and tap into their diversity, talents, and insights will always find the next right action.

PROMPTS FOR FAITH-SHARING

• How have you experienced Jesus's healing in your life? What in your life do you still wish Jesus would heal?

• How do you show your faith in Jesus? How do you ask him to heal your suffering?

• How do you participate in the healing and life-giving work of God? How can you better partner with God in transforming the world's suffering?

See Appendix B, p. 312, for additional prompts.

SPIRITUALITY

℟. Alleluia, alleluia.
The Spirit of the Lord is upon me,
for he sent me to bring glad tidings to
    the poor.
℟. Alleluia, alleluia.

Gospel

Mark 6:1-6a; L101B

**Jesus departed from there
    and came to his native
    place, accompanied by his
    disciples.
When the sabbath came he
    began to teach in the
    synagogue,
and many who heard him
    were astonished.
They said, "Where did this
    man get all this?
What kind of wisdom has been
    given him?
What mighty deeds are wrought by his
    hands!
Is he not the carpenter, the son of
    Mary,
    and the brother of James and Joses
    and Judas and Simon?
And are not his sisters here with us?"
And they took offense at him.
Jesus said to them,
    "A prophet is not without honor
        except in his native place
    and among his own kin and in his
        own house."
So he was not able to perform any
    mighty deed there,
    apart from curing a few sick people
        by laying his hands on them.
He was amazed at their lack of faith.**

Reflecting on the Gospel

Have you ever done something you never thought you could do, but could because someone else has believed in you and urged you forward? On the contrary, have you found yourself hampered by others' preconceived notions and lack of confidence in you? In a certain sense, these are the experiences of Paul in the second reading and of Jesus in today's gospel.

Paul has had extraordinary revelations and has accomplished incredible things in his apostolic ministry. Yet he has a sense of true humility concerning these unusual gifts. They are not due to any power or qualifications of his own. Rather, he knows that they are pure grace.

He writes of "a thorn in the flesh" given to him. Biblical scholars have long puzzled over the nature of this "thorn." An ancient interpretation understands it as "the thorn of the flesh," that is, physical desires, or concupiscence, that plague Paul. Others have thought it to be a physical malady or a kind of suffering that is related to his ministry. When we look at the context of this passage, the latter is a real likelihood.

The phrase comes within the "fool's speech" that begins in 11:1 and goes through 12:10. Paul is refuting the charges of his opponents who accuse him of being weak (10:1-2), having no credentials (3:1-3), and being unimpressive in words, deeds, and physical presence (10:1-12). Paul counters with a surprising twist: instead of defending himself by taking a position of strength, he turns the tables and argues that his weaknesses are the very mark of his authenticity as an apostle. His own powerlessness makes evident that it is God's grace and power that work through him.

That the "superapostles" (11:5; 12:11) who oppose Paul are the "thorn" in his flesh sent by Satan is likely when we see that in 11:12-15 he compares them to Satan. Unlike these false apostles, Paul boasts of weakness that allows God's power to work through him.

Paul, with the grace of God, was enabled to do far more than he ever thought possible by his own abilities. Jesus, by contrast, was prevented from doing any mighty deeds in his hometown because of the limited expectations of his own people. Thinking they knew Jesus inside and out, they hindered his ability to let God's power work through him for their benefit. Sometimes this is referred to as the "tall poppy syndrome." Group dynamics often prevent anyone from rising above the rest. "Who do they think they are?" others will say about an emergent local leader. If an "expert" had come from outside the community and taught the same things as their native son, they would have been far more disposed to accept such teaching.

In both readings there is a recognition that the perceptions of others can strongly influence the exercise of prophetic and apostolic gifts within a faith community. Opposition and close-mindedness can squelch the flow of the Spirit, while expressed belief in the untapped abilities of another can cause him or her to flourish in extraordinary ways with the power of God.

Preparing to Proclaim

Key words and phrases: "A prophet is not without honor except in his native place and among his own kin and in his own house."

To the point: The whirlwind pace of Mark's Gospel includes lots of admiring crowds pressing around Jesus; it often seems he cannot get away from those who want to be near him and have access to his healing and preaching. In this gospel, though, he is met with skepticism. He returns to his hometown—a place where many of us hope to be embraced and have our accomplishments celebrated. But those who knew him as a child cannot accept who he has grown into. Their presuppositions prevent them from encountering what others have found in him. We, too, can make assumptions about what we think we know. It is all too easy to miss God's work, which often breaks into the mundane in surprising ways.

Psalmist Preparation

This psalm includes an unusual feminine image for God. God is compared to the mistress of a household wealthy enough to have a maid, a maid who watches and waits in order to respond properly. While masculine imagery for God is more common, such female images are sprinkled throughout Scripture and the Christian tradition. As you prepare to proclaim this psalm, reflect on your own working image of God. Do you imagine God as a father, mother, friend? How might this image, and others to which you're less accustomed, augment what you know of God?

Making Connections

Between the readings: Like Jesus, Ezekiel is sent to stubborn, obstinate people. His calling is to speak God's word to people who are not going to be able to hear it. God prepares him for the potential of rejection, but assures him that his mission is based on truth. Ezekiel is assured he will have an impact, even if it is not the full conversion to which he calls the Israelites. Sometimes God does not work all at once but in increments.

To experience: Our baptisms unite us to Christ as priest, prophet, and king. It is sometimes odd to claim these titles for ourselves; they seem like they should be reserved for just a few special chosen ones. But each of us *is* chosen, unique and unrepeatable and called by God to put our unique set of gifts into the service of others. We are all called to sanctify the world and to share God's word.

Homily Points

• We are made to do hard things. All three of today's readings feature people called by God to be prophetic in difficult situations. God sends Ezekiel to preach to the rebellious Israelites who want nothing to do with him. The scene begins with Ezekiel, who was a priest, laying prostrate before the Lord. He is keenly aware of his mortal stature as a "son of man." The odds of success are stacked against Ezekiel given the obstinance of the people. It is only through the power of the Spirit that Ezekiel can rise up and go out to do God's work.

• The prophet's responsibility is to God's call. He need not—and cannot—force people to receive God's word. God gave humankind free will. People are bound to fall short. Yet God calls Ezekiel to persist, to preach and teach anyway. We are called to embrace this same mentality.

• Jesus himself returns to his hometown of Nazareth to a faithless people eager to question his authority. We do not know exactly what Jesus said to the crowds in the synagogue, but they took offense to his teachings. Perhaps Jesus jarred them out of their comfortable ways of thinking about family, work, or religion. The message God calls Jesus to preach is a radical one. Perhaps it is no surprise that most people could not handle it. Their lack of faith made Jesus's job more difficult. Nevertheless, he persisted. Jesus continued to preach and teach, heal and bless. He did the hard thing time and time again. The world is forever changed because of it.

Model Penitential Act

Presider: In today's second reading, the Lord assures Paul: "My grace is sufficient for you, for power is made perfect in weakness." Aware of our need for God's grace and mercy, let us call to mind our sins and ask the Lord for forgiveness . . . *[pause]*

Lord Jesus, you are the Son of God and son of Mary: Lord, have mercy.

Christ Jesus, you teach the lost and forsaken: Christ, have mercy.

Lord Jesus, you are a prophet of the good news: Lord, have mercy.

Model Universal Prayer (Prayer of the Faithful)

Presider: Sustained by God's mercy and compassion, let us bring forward our petitions for the needs of the church and the world.

Response: Lord, hear our prayer.

Foster curious questions and a sense of generosity among the faithful . . .

Inspire legislators to work together to enact gun laws that will keep our schools and communities safe . . .

Grace with connection people who are lonely, anxious, or depressed . . .

Increase our sense of awe and respect for the natural world . . .

Presider: Merciful Creator, you sent your son into the world to embody divine love in the world. Receive our prayers that we too may be agents of your love to people and communities everywhere. We ask this through Christ our Lord. **Amen.**

Liturgy and Music

Most of us in our ministry have experienced a Sunday when the music just didn't go as planned. We practiced and prepared, but a wrong note or chord was played, a flat note was sung, we turned too many pages in the score or missed the page turn altogether. These moments can be devastating, or disappointing, to say the least. What we must remember is that we are human, and mistakes are part of the human condition. We are not diminished by a wrong note.

We should take comfort knowing that God does not expect perfection from us, but rather, that we strive toward godliness and holiness. What God desires for us is "to do justice and to love goodness, / and to walk humbly with [our] God" (Mic 6:8). In this, we may find consolation. God can take our imperfection and make it beautiful, using it in God's service. The apostle Paul came to this realization. Though we may never know what Paul's "thorn in the flesh" was, we do know that Paul found solace in the fact that his imperfections, his weakness allowed God's power to be made all the more evident.

Like Paul, we can learn to be content in our insufficiency, for it is then that God's grace can abound, and the power of the Holy Spirit can flow freely in our ministry.

COLLECT

Let us pray.

Pause for silent prayer

O God, who in the abasement of your Son
have raised up a fallen world,
fill your faithful with holy joy,
for on those you have rescued from slavery
    to sin
you bestow eternal gladness.
Through our Lord Jesus Christ, your Son,
who lives and reigns with you in the unity
    of the Holy Spirit,
God, for ever and ever. **Amen.**

FIRST READING

Ezek 2:2-5

As the LORD spoke to me, the spirit entered
    into me
    and set me on my feet,
    and I heard the one who was speaking
        say to me:
    Son of man, I am sending you to the
        Israelites,
    rebels who have rebelled against me;
    they and their ancestors have revolted
        against me to this very day.
Hard of face and obstinate of heart
    are they to whom I am sending you.
But you shall say to them: Thus says the
    Lord GOD!
And whether they heed or resist—for they
    are a rebellious house—
    they shall know that a prophet has been
        among them.

RESPONSORIAL PSALM

Ps 123:1-2, 2, 3-4

℟. (2cd) Our eyes are fixed on the Lord,
    pleading for his mercy.

To you I lift up my eyes
    who are enthroned in heaven—
as the eyes of servants
    are on the hands of their masters.

℟. Our eyes are fixed on the Lord,
    pleading for his mercy.

As the eyes of a maid
    are on the hands of her mistress,
so are our eyes on the LORD, our God,
    till he have pity on us.

℟. Our eyes are fixed on the Lord,
    pleading for his mercy.

Have pity on us, O LORD, have pity on us,
    for we are more than sated with
        contempt;
our souls are more than sated
    with the mockery of the arrogant,
    with the contempt of the proud.

℟. Our eyes are fixed on the Lord,
    pleading for his mercy.

SECOND READING

2 Cor 12:7-10

Brothers and sisters:
That I, Paul, might not become too elated,
    because of the abundance of the
        revelations,
    a thorn in the flesh was given to me, an
        angel of Satan,
    to beat me, to keep me from being too
        elated.
Three times I begged the Lord about this,
    that it might leave me,
    but he said to me, "My grace is
        sufficient for you,
    for power is made perfect in weakness."
I will rather boast most gladly of my
        weaknesses,
    in order that the power of Christ may
        dwell with me.
Therefore, I am content with weaknesses,
        insults,
    hardships, persecutions, and
        constraints,
    for the sake of Christ;
    for when I am weak, then I am strong.

Living Liturgy

Liturgy and the Arts: Heather Christian is a composer and performer best known for her works *Animal Wisdom* (2017) and *Oratorio on Living Things* (2022). In 2020, at the height of the COVID-19 pandemic, she also wrote a piece called *Prime: A Practical Breviary* that explored the sometimes difficult task of waking up and facing the day. In one song from that production, Christian sings a prayer to God asking for contentment in her smallness. "Lowly make me small / Shrink my needing to a tiny acorn / Dry my wishes up in new morn / I will not suffer when the dewdrop is my Adriatic Sea." There are parallels between Christian's "hymn" and Paul's letter to the Corinthians. In the face of suffering, whether from persecution as in Paul's case or from the feeling of being overwhelmed by isolation as in Christian's, solace can be found in the barefaced acceptance of what is or in humbly asking God to help us accept what is. Even Jesus found himself limited in the face of resistance as we see in today's gospel. His preaching in his hometown on the sabbath was met with skeptical, ungenerous amazement: Isn't this the carpenter's son? Who does he think he is to preach and perform miracles? Jesus performed few miracles in that place. No one, it seems, is immune to the vitriol of doubters and detractors.

These moments of struggle are not failures. They are reminders that we need the grace of God in all that we undertake. Miracles of justice and mercy do not occur from our own hands, but through the very power of God alive and working in us. Later in the same song, Christian sings, "If I am small, Lord / Let it be." Maybe it is okay that we don't always wake up feeling strong and capable. Maybe it will be okay when we face criticism from the people who profess to know us best. Maybe these are grace-filled moments that can remind us of how closely we walk with God and how blessed that walk is.

PROMPTS FOR FAITH-SHARING

• When do you make assumptions about people that might keep you from encountering Christ in others?

• When have you been surprised by the presence or action of God? How can you stay open to God's appearances in unexpected places?

• What do you understand a prophet to be? How do you participate in Jesus's office of prophet?

See Appendix B, p. 312, for additional prompts.

SPIRITUALITY

GOSPEL ACCLAMATION
cf. Eph 1:17-18

℟. Alleluia, alleluia.
May the Father of our Lord Jesus Christ
enlighten the eyes of our hearts,
that we may know what is the hope that
belongs to our call.
℟. Alleluia, alleluia.

Gospel

Mark 6:7-13; L104B

Jesus summoned the Twelve and
    began to send them out two
    by two
    and gave them authority over
      unclean spirits.
He instructed them to take noth-
    ing for the journey
    but a walking stick—
    no food, no sack, no money in
      their belts.
They were, however, to wear
    sandals
    but not a second tunic.
He said to them,
    "Wherever you enter a house, stay
      there until you leave.
Whatever place does not welcome you
    or listen to you,
    leave there and shake the dust off
      your feet
    in testimony against them."
So they went off and preached
    repentance.
The Twelve drove out many demons,
    and they anointed with oil many who
      were sick and cured them.

Reflecting on the Gospel

I'll never forget leading a group pilgrimage to the Holy Land when my luggage never arrived. Each day, pilgrims in the group loaned me clothes. It was humbling for me to rely so totally on others' generosity. Yet their acts of unselfishness created an instant bond; I was not the only one sharing from my "expertise."

In today's gospel, Jesus's disciples are sent out on their first foray in mission. Missionary journeying is never solitary; it is necessarily a communal endeavor. Jesus imparts to them his authority over unclean spirits and sends

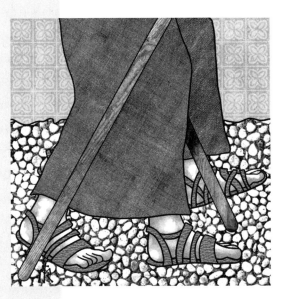

them out in pairs. He then gives them very specific instructions about what they are to pack—nothing! He does not say to travel lightly. He insists they take nothing with them, except a walking stick and sandals on their feet, just as the fleeing Israelites did at the exodus (Exod 12:11). As they proclaim liberation, they are to take no food, no bag, no money, and no change of clothing. They are to go completely empty-handed.

This is a totally different model of mission than one in which the persons sent consider themselves to have a whole cache of "goods" to share with people who have nothing. It's just the reverse. A Christian missionary is to go out needy and vulnerable, so that there can be a mutual exchange of gifts between missionaries and the people to whom they are sent. Missionaries are to put on the clothes of others and eat whatever the local people share, thus becoming one with those with whom they share the good news.

Sharing the gospel is always a two-way street. The message preached in such an exchange is that of a crucified and risen Christ, who makes it apparent that God's power works through vulnerability and mutuality. These kinds of exchanges do not take place in an instant. Jesus instructs his disciples to stay in one home so that the relationships can deepen and grow. It is also a warning not to look around for the best accommodations. A missionary is content to share whatever is offered.

Jesus warns his disciples that not all will accept the gospel message. Wherever there is sustained hostility toward them, the disciples are to "shake the dust" from their feet and move on. Christian missionaries are ready to experience tribulation, but they do not go looking for it.

A thread runs through all three readings today: the call to participate in the mission comes from divine initiative. Amos protests that he never belonged to a guild of prophets, nor ever wanted to be a prophet. He was a simple shepherd tending his flocks and his sycamore trees when God called him forth to prophesy. The reading from Ephesians highlights that it is by God's choice that believers, both Jews and Gentiles, belong to God and share the good news. In the gospel, it is Jesus who summons the Twelve, and sends them on mission. Christian missionaries are not self-appointed. The call to mission is part and parcel of every Christian's baptismal call.

Preparing to Proclaim

Key words and phrases: "Jesus summoned the Twelve and began to send them out two by two."

To the point: In this gospel Jesus begins to delegate. He sends his apostles to extend his work of preaching and healing. His instructions are hard. They are to go with no supplies and are to rely on the hospitality of others. They are to expect rejection and are to settle nowhere. Yet they do not go alone. Jesus sends them in pairs. And he goes with them too, in a way, giving them his own authority over unclean spirits and his own power to heal those who are sick. In the same way, Jesus goes with us, remaining with the church in the sacraments. God also gives us each other as companions on the long journey of Christian life, and is present to us in any relationship where love reigns.

Psalmist Preparation

In the midst of readings that promise rejection to those who speak for God, this psalm promises that this is a God of peace. God wants peace for all of us and wills that we all come ultimately to rest in peace with God. As you prepare to proclaim this psalm, reflect on where you find peace in the midst of your busy life. Is there a way you could carve out more room for silence and rest? Could you allow God to make peace in your heart even when you are overwhelmed by your commitments?

Making Connections

Between the readings: Like the disciples, Amos recounts his story of being plucked from his ordinary occupation and sent by God to prophesy and preach. Like the disciples, he is rejected, told to move on to others more willing to listen. He accepts his rejection with the humble confidence that comes from knowing his mission comes from God.

To experience: We might occupy any number of roles from the readings this week. We might be as the disciples, called and sent to minister to others, spreading Jesus's healing presence. We might also be as those who reject them, unwilling or unable to see God's presence in an unexpected prophet. Prophets often call our attention to inconvenient truths, and it is easier to ignore them than to accept the disruptions they cause. But God works through those disruptions, using them to shake off our apathy and call our attention to places that need conversion and healing.

Homily Points

• Jesus sent the disciples out in pairs. This decision highlights the deeply communal nature of discipleship. We are not made to share the good news alone. To a world that values a "me first" mentality, Jesus says go out together. Lean on one another. Learn from each other. The Son of God continues to call Christians to team up with each other in ministry. Who are your disciple partners? Who else from our congregation or neighborhood might be a valued partner for doing Christ's work?

• Jesus instructs the disciples on how to exit a difficult situation with dignity. If a place does not welcome them, the disciples are to leave by simply shaking the dust off their feet on the way out. This traditional Jewish gesture is a gentle yet pointed way to depart. The hostile household receives dirt rather than the word of God. Jesus wants the disciples to be prepared for rejection. Not every person is ready to receive the good news. That does not mean we stop preaching it, but it does require disciples to be discerning about when it is time to pack up and move on.

• God calls people to discipleship in the midst of everyday life. In today's first reading, a shepherd named Amos finds himself pulled from the fields and sent out to prophesy in the name of God. Amos claimed he was no prophet—but God had other plans in mind. We may not be sent to northern Israel, but like Amos, God calls each of us for the work of discipleship exactly where we are. In our homes, workplaces, schools, and communities, we are called to spread God's message of love to the world.

CELEBRATION

Model Penitential Act

Presider: In today's second reading, Saint Paul reminds the Ephesians that through Christ we receive forgiveness of transgressions. Grateful for Christ's eagerness to forgive our sins, let us call to mind the times we have fallen short of doing what is right and ask God for mercy . . . *[pause]*

> Lord Jesus, you answer those who cry for help: Lord, have mercy.
> Christ Jesus, you send your generous spirit upon the disciples: Christ, have mercy.
> Lord Jesus, you will come again to heal every one of our ills: Lord, have mercy.

Model Universal Prayer (Prayer of the Faithful)

Presider: Accompanied by Jesus our eternal guide, let us entrust our needs to the Lord.

Response: Lord, hear our prayer.

Grant safety to justice activists and other prophets of our time . . .

Further the work of soup kitchens, food pantries, and other organizations dedicated to feeding the hungry . . .

Safeguard partners and children fleeing from abusive situations . . .

Foster community among the disciples gathered here . . .

Presider: God of hope, through the breaking of the bread we come to know the love of your son Jesus. Hear our prayers that strengthened by his constant presence we might live with the flames of faith alive in our hearts. We ask this through Christ our resurrected Lord. **Amen.**

Liturgy and Music

Every community is unique and has its own personality. They are a family. There are all kinds of people that comprise that family, and it is the responsibility of pastoral leadership to make them feel welcome. Further, those individuals who don't quite fit the mold of what we may expect add to the personality of the community and can keep things lively!

Every community deserves a minister who will minister to them. This includes the music ministry and its leadership. As music leaders, it is our responsibility to facilitate the sung prayer of the people. We need to help them find their voice. Recall that the General Instruction of the Roman Missal (GIRM) says that the entrance song is meant to "foster the unity of those who have been gathered" (47). *Sing to the Lord: Music in Divine Worship* echoes this sentiment (142).

To that end, the selection of music should always reflect the culture and personality of the community gathered. Our selection of music should always take into consideration the gathered community, being careful that our selections are "sensitive to the spiritual and cultural milieu" of that community (*Sing to the Lord* 73).

Recognize that your presence in a parish is not by accident, but that you have been sent by God, just as the prophets of old and the disciples of Jesus were sent to minister to various communities. Go and minister faithfully, with all your heart, soul, mind, and strength.

COLLECT
Let us pray.

Pause for silent prayer

O God, who show the light of your truth
to those who go astray,
so that they may return to the right path,
give all who for the faith they profess
are accounted Christians
the grace to reject whatever is contrary to
    the name of Christ
and to strive after all that does it honor.
Through our Lord Jesus Christ, your Son,
who lives and reigns with you in the unity
    of the Holy Spirit,
God, for ever and ever. **Amen.**

FIRST READING
Amos 7:12-15

Amaziah, priest of Bethel, said to Amos,
    "Off with you, visionary, flee to the land
        of Judah!
There earn your bread by prophesying,
    but never again prophesy in Bethel;
        for it is the king's sanctuary and a royal
        temple."
Amos answered Amaziah, "I was no
    prophet,
    nor have I belonged to a company of
        prophets;
    I was a shepherd and a dresser of
        sycamores.
The LORD took me from following the
    flock, and said to me,
    Go, prophesy to my people Israel."

RESPONSORIAL PSALM
Ps 85:9-10, 11-12, 13-14

℟. (8) Lord, let us see your kindness, and
    grant us your salvation.

I will hear what God proclaims;
    the LORD—for he proclaims peace.
Near indeed is his salvation to those who
    fear him,
    glory dwelling in our land.

℟. Lord, let us see your kindness, and
    grant us your salvation.

Kindness and truth shall meet;
    justice and peace shall kiss.
Truth shall spring out of the earth,
    and justice shall look down from
        heaven.

℟. Lord, let us see your kindness, and
    grant us your salvation.

The LORD himself will give his benefits;
  our land shall yield its increase.
Justice shall walk before him,
  and prepare the way of his steps.

℟. Lord, let us see your kindness, and
  grant us your salvation.

SECOND READING

Eph 1:3-14

Blessed be the God and Father of our Lord
    Jesus Christ,
  who has blessed us in Christ
  with every spiritual blessing in the
    heavens,
  as he chose us in him, before the
    foundation of the world,
  to be holy and without blemish before
    him.
In love he destined us for adoption to
    himself through Jesus Christ,
  in accord with the favor of his will,
  for the praise of the glory of his grace
  that he granted us in the beloved.

In him we have redemption by his blood,
  the forgiveness of transgressions,
  in accord with the riches of his grace
    that he lavished upon us.
In all wisdom and insight, he has made
    known to us
  the mystery of his will in accord with
    his favor
  that he set forth in him as a plan for the
    fullness of times,
  to sum up all things in Christ, in heaven
    and on earth.

In him we were also chosen,
  destined in accord with the purpose of
    the One
  who accomplishes all things according
    to the intention of his will,
  so that we might exist for the praise of
    his glory,
  we who first hoped in Christ.
In him you also, who have heard the word
    of truth,
  the gospel of your salvation, and have
    believed in him,
  were sealed with the promised Holy
    Spirit,
  which is the first installment of our
    inheritance
  toward redemption as God's possession,
    to the praise of his glory.

or Eph 1:3-10

See Appendix A, p. 302.

Living Liturgy

Liturgy and Community: One of the things I appreciate most about working in a school is how much I've learned about what interdependence really means. Growing up, the messages I received glorified individualism and promised (threatened?) me that meritocracy was the rule; achievement would come primarily through my own power and perseverance. Working at school is a constant reminder that partnership and collaboration are the real engines of any community.

I understand why Jesus sent the disciples out two by two when he commissioned them. Everybody needs a spotter—someone who will look out for you and help you carry the load. We don't just need help with our day-to-day tasks either. Having a "spiritual spotter" is an invaluable gift. This person might hold you accountable to your values and principles in challenging moments. Perhaps they simply inspire you through their example.

I have many "spiritual spotters" that I look to in my school community when I need support. Most recently, the art teacher unknowingly offered me some much-needed inspiration when she installed new student artwork in our chapel. The students each picked a saint to learn about. They then designed stained glass windows for their chosen saint using symbols and imagery from their research. Many students took self-portraits or used peers as models for their saints, and this is the part that moved me to tears. To see saints of old reimagined and resembling the students in my school brought me back to the *real* mission of my and every Catholic school: to show young people their innate holiness and activate them to be people of faith, purpose, and service. The art teacher is doing a kind of work that I certainly cannot do, but when I observe her doing it with skill, with fidelity, and with love I am inspired to embrace my work with equal vigor.

We need community, and we need *diverse* communities because no one person or type of person can meet all of a community's need. It will take many different types of tools to build the kingdom of God.

PROMPTS FOR FAITH-SHARING

• Jesus sends the Twelve out to minister in groups of two. What companions do you have in your ministry? How do they support you?

• Have you experienced rejection for the sake of your faith? How did you respond?

• When the disciples arrived in a town, they would have interrupted the normal way of doing things. How have you found God in interruptions to the comfortable things in your life?

See Appendix B, p. 312, for additional prompts.

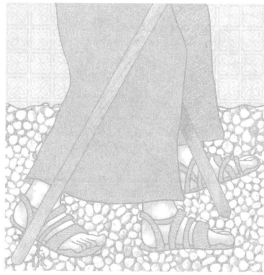

JULY 14, 2024
FIFTEENTH SUNDAY
IN ORDINARY TIME

SPIRITUALITY

℟. Alleluia, alleluia.
My sheep hear my voice, says the Lord;
I know them, and they follow me.
℟. Alleluia, alleluia.

Gospel

Mark 6:30-34; L107B

The apostles gathered together
  with Jesus
  and reported all they had
    done and taught.
He said to them,
  "Come away by yourselves to
    a deserted place and rest
    a while."
People were coming and going in
  great numbers,
  and they had no opportunity
    even to eat.
So they went off in the boat by
  themselves to a deserted
  place.
People saw them leaving and
  many came to know about it.
They hastened there on foot from all
  the towns
  and arrived at the place before them.

When he disembarked and saw the vast
  crowd,
  his heart was moved with pity for
    them,
  for they were like sheep without a
    shepherd;
  and he began to teach them many
    things.

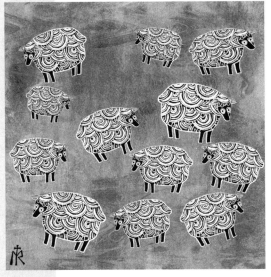

Reflecting on the Gospel

In ecumenical dialogues, today's second reading is often used to set forth the ideal of the visible oneness for which we long. How do peoples who are separated become united? Today's readings emphasize the role of compassionate leaders in the work of reconciliation. In the New Testament texts, the focus is on the person of Christ as the one who accomplishes oneness.

The first reading is an indictment of Israel's leaders who allowed the people to be "scattered" and "driven away" into exile. The contrast is great between their lack of care for the "flock" and God's complete provision for the people expressed in Psalm 23. The Divine Shepherd leads the "flock" with overflowing goodness and kindness to plentiful pasture, abundant food, rest from worry, and accompaniment in frightening times. In the gospel we see this same tender care embodied in Jesus. He attends to the disciples' need to be replenished after their first missionary journey and also to the needs of the vast crowd for whom he has heartfelt compassion.

To us who live in a context where many in church ministry fall prey to the pressure of responding constantly to nonstop demands, it may seem that the returning apostles in today's gospel are longing for an overdue rest. The gospel context offers another possible interpretation.

The apostles have just returned from their first attempts at teaching and expelling evil spirits, and their report to Jesus is probably an enthusiastic retelling of all the marvels they accomplished. Jesus invites them to a deserted place, the kind of place where he would customarily go apart to pray (Mark 1:35). Perhaps the disciples were in danger of becoming a bit too enamored of their own abilities to perform wonders. The deserted place will help them experience more deeply the divine compassion that calls them into mission and that is the source of all that they are able to do. From their ability to receive divine compassion in their own neediness, they become able to be the compassion of God toward others. Just so, in any work of reconciliation, the ability to experience compassion, that is, to "feel with" the other from the other's point of view, is crucial to moving toward oneness.

The author of Ephesians elaborates how "the dividing wall of enmity" between Jewish Christians ("those who were near") and Gentile Christians (those "who were far off") is broken down. Christ himself is that peace that brings unity (v. 14). He makes peace by the costly giving of himself that put enmity to death (v. 15), and finally, he preached peace (v. 16).

For creating unity in our own day, we can emulate this same pattern. We start with contemplative dwelling with the Source of our peace, allowing ourselves to be transformed into the very peace we desire. Second, making peace is costly; it demands crossing over dividing walls to listen deeply and with empathy to the "other," and being willing to engage in long processes of dialogue, clarifying where we have common ground and where we yet differ, and praying for the guidance of the Spirit to find the way through the impasses.

Preparing to Proclaim

Key words and phrases: "[H]is heart was moved with pity for them, for they were like sheep without a shepherd."

To the point: We might feel some pity for Jesus here—after a busy stretch of ministry he attempts to retreat with the apostles only to find that the crowds have walked to meet them. But his response is not one of annoyance or impatience, justified as those reactions would be. He rather sees the need of those who are seeking him, and he responds to that need with compassion. He is able to do so in part because he does not operate from a scarcity mindset. It seems there is not enough time for both ministry and rest, but Jesus operates from a place of trust. In God his needs and ours will be abundantly met, and Jesus is able to share that generosity with those who are seeking him.

Psalmist Preparation

This well-loved psalm can sometimes feel repetitious or dry. Many of us who cantor have sung it so many times that we now do so on autopilot. We assume we have gained what we can and that there is nothing to be added from one more repetition. As you prepare to proclaim this psalm yet again, strive to shake off the autopilot stupor. Spend some time with the words of the psalm, imagine yourself in the scene, and ask God to give you some new insight or renewed sense of peace. This prayer may or may not be granted in an obvious way, and that's okay; sometimes showing up and going through the motions when we don't particularly feel like it is a great act of love.

Making Connections

Between the readings: Jesus's compassion was stirred when the people seemed to be as sheep without a shepherd. The first reading emphasizes the importance of good shepherds. Without them, sheep scatter and are unsafe. With them, there is safety and security. In Jeremiah, God promises to take up the shepherding role that his people need. This is fulfilled in Jesus, who calls and shepherds people back into life with God.

To experience: It is common to be frustrated at the lack of rest available to those who work in ministry. The liturgical calendar never sleeps, and people are in continuous need of pastoral care. This episode where the crowds thwart Jesus's attempt to take a rest is almost comical. But it is notable that Jesus does *try* to step away. He acknowledges here that we cannot keep going without time to recharge and renew our commitment. Our attempts to rest might be imperfect and interrupted, but it is important to keep trying.

Homily Points

• Today's gospel highlights the importance of Sabbath practice. Jesus tells the apostles: "Come away by yourselves to a deserted place and rest a while." The Son of God recognizes that daily life demands a lot from disciples then and now. To-do lists never stop growing. Our callings may pull us in many directions—a reality that makes the practice of Sabbath even more necessary. To pause from work and worry, if even for an afternoon, can renew energy for the day-to-day grind. To worship, withdraw, wonder, walk, and welcome others draws us closer to God.

• Rabbi Abraham Joshua Heschel argued that the practice of Sabbath is not just a nice idea. It is a necessity, a command from God. Heschel wrote, "Unless one learns how to relish the taste of Sabbath . . . one will be unable to enjoy the taste of eternity in the world to come." Practicing Sabbath enables us to live into the fullness of our callings by restoring our bodies and minds. Whether practiced for a day or an hour, Sabbath invites us to listen to the song of God's Spirit. How might you answer Jesus's invitation to rest awhile this week?

• Jesus's heart is moved with "pity" for the crowds. This is perhaps better translated as compassion or mercy. Jesus sees in the crowds a deep hunger for a shepherd, someone to lead them into the promise of a better tomorrow. The Son of God allows himself to be interrupted by the needs of the crowd.

CELEBRATION

Model Penitential Act

Presider: Jesus's heart was moved with mercy for the crowds in today's gospel. Divine mercy continues to extend to all corners of the world, including right here. Let us take a moment to pause, call to mind our sins, and trust in the mercy of God . . . *[pause]*

Lord Jesus, you are our help and salvation: Lord, have mercy.

Christ Jesus, you intercede for us before God the Father: Christ, have mercy.

Lord Jesus, you will come again to break the bonds of death: Lord, have mercy.

Model Universal Prayer (Prayer of the Faithful)

Presider: Let us place our prayers and petitions before God with courage.

Response: Lord, hear our prayer.

Advance deepening respect and dialogue among Christians, Jews, and Muslims . . .

Foster the efforts of scientists, medical researchers, and all who are working to combat the spread of infectious diseases . . .

Give aid to people facing unemployment or underemployment . . .

Fill with hope those in our community who are near death . . .

Presider: God of abundant peace, through your son Jesus you assure us of a home in the kingdom of heaven. Receive our prayers that by following his example we might spread love and hope to all we meet. We ask this through Christ our Lord. **Amen.**

Liturgy and Music

The role of leadership in ministry is a serious thing. It carries with it a responsibility to care for others. It is therefore a responsibility that should never be taken lightly. Hence, the warning from the prophet Jeremiah: "Woe to the shepherds who mislead and scatter the flock of my pasture, says the LORD." This can be applied to more than simply misleading or scattering. We can substitute such actions as mistreat, neglect, abuse, starve.

The first reading, the responsorial psalm, and the gospel use the imagery of a shepherd in conveying their meaning. Throughout Scripture, authors use metaphors and analogies that speak to the experiences of their audience. That's why especially in the gospel Jesus uses the imagery of fishing and farming in his parables because these were images to which the people of his day could relate. Today, Jesus might use images of the internet, pop culture, and social media.

A shepherd was responsible for the livestock in his care. Of these, sheep were the most vulnerable and needed the most attention. Who in your care needs the most attention? Who in our ministry needs our loving attention so that they do not come to spiritual neglect or harm? It is especially these that God has called us to minister. We are called to love God's people and to minister to them, as servants of the Good Shepherd.

COLLECT
Let us pray.

Pause for silent prayer

Show favor, O Lord, to your servants
and mercifully increase the gifts of your grace,
that, made fervent in hope, faith, and charity,
they may be ever watchful in keeping your commands.
Through our Lord Jesus Christ, your Son,
who lives and reigns with you in the unity of the Holy Spirit,
God, for ever and ever. **Amen.**

FIRST READING
Jer 23:1-6

Woe to the shepherds
    who mislead and scatter the flock of my pasture,
    says the LORD.
Therefore, thus says the LORD, the God of Israel,
    against the shepherds who shepherd my people:
    You have scattered my sheep and driven them away.
You have not cared for them,
    but I will take care to punish your evil deeds.
I myself will gather the remnant of my flock
    from all the lands to which I have driven them
    and bring them back to their meadow;
    there they shall increase and multiply.
I will appoint shepherds for them who will shepherd them
    so that they need no longer fear and tremble;
    and none shall be missing, says the LORD.

Behold, the days are coming, says the LORD,
    when I will raise up a righteous shoot to David;
    as king he shall reign and govern wisely,
    he shall do what is just and right in the land.
In his days Judah shall be saved,
    Israel shall dwell in security.
    This is the name they give him:
    "The LORD our justice."

RESPONSORIAL PSALM

Ps 23:1-3, 3-4, 5, 6

℟. (1) The Lord is my shepherd; there is
   nothing I shall want.

The LORD is my shepherd; I shall not want.
   In verdant pastures he gives me repose;
beside restful waters he leads me;
   he refreshes my soul.

℟. The Lord is my shepherd; there is
   nothing I shall want.

He guides me in right paths
   for his name's sake.
Even though I walk in the dark valley
   I fear no evil; for you are at my side
with your rod and your staff
   that give me courage.

℟. The Lord is my shepherd; there is
   nothing I shall want.

You spread the table before me
   in the sight of my foes;
you anoint my head with oil;
   my cup overflows.

℟. The Lord is my shepherd; there is
   nothing I shall want.

Only goodness and kindness follow me
   all the days of my life;
and I shall dwell in the house of the LORD
   for years to come.

℟. The Lord is my shepherd; there is
   nothing I shall want.

SECOND READING

Eph 2:13-18

Brothers and sisters:
In Christ Jesus you who once were far off
   have become near by the blood of
      Christ.

For he is our peace, he who made both one
   and broke down the dividing wall of
      enmity, through his flesh,
   abolishing the law with its
      commandments and legal claims,
   that he might create in himself one new
      person in place of the two,
   thus establishing peace,
   and might reconcile both with God,
   in one body, through the cross,
   putting that enmity to death by it.
He came and preached peace to you who
      were far off
   and peace to those who were near,
   for through him we both have access in
      one Spirit to the Father.

Living Liturgy

Liturgy and Community: In today's readings, we hear a stern message against divisiveness and discord. We also hear a promise that the God of unity is constantly working to gather all people back together as one. In a time of political polarization, social media comment wars, and cancel culture, these readings can be a source of hope for us. Whatever divisiveness we feel in these times is not God's plan for us and it is not the final story. To change the story in our hearts and minds, we need to look for examples of authentic unity in our communities.

One encouraging example I've witnessed is a neighborhood group near me that meets regularly to address the needs of residents and business owners. There are two striking characteristics of this group. First, the composition of the group is truly representative of the make-up of the community. There are longtime and more recent neighborhood residents, business owners, representatives from the neighborhood development corporation, and people who simply work in the area. Members of the group vary in age, income level, gender, and education level. Each person brings a unique perspective and has a different strength to offer the group. The second striking aspect of the group is that in recent months they have made an enhanced push to simply *be present* for each other's events rather than trying to establish new initiatives and activities. There is greater proximity, consistency, and collaboration on shared tasks between members and because of this, deeper relationships are being forged. These may seem like very simple things, but it has been inspiring to see their powerful impact.

It has filled me with such hope to see this group start and flourish in my own backyard. This is how Christ who is our peace makes us one—through the small, ordinary acts of care performed by normal people every day in our neighborhoods. It may not make it onto the news, but the more we all look for it and take part in it, the more we will notice it. In this small, simple way, we can reacquaint ourselves with the peace and unity God wishes for us.

PROMPTS FOR FAITH-SHARING

• In this gospel, people hasten to be in Jesus's presence. How do you approach Jesus in prayer? Is it with urgency, hesitancy, eagerness, fear?

• How do you make room for rest in the midst of your ministry? How could you see Jesus's example as an invitation to balance both of these needs?

• How has God been generous with you? How do you extend that generosity to others?

See Appendix B, p. 312, for additional prompts.

SEVENTEENTH SUNDAY IN ORDINARY TIME

SPIRITUALITY

GOSPEL ACCLAMATION
Luke 7:16

℟. Alleluia, alleluia.
A great prophet has risen in our midst.
God has visited his people.
℟. Alleluia, alleluia.

Gospel

John 6:1-15; L110B

Jesus went across the Sea of
    Galilee.
A large crowd followed him,
    because they saw the signs he
        was performing on the sick.
Jesus went up on the mountain,
    and there he sat down with his
        disciples.
The Jewish feast of Passover was
    near.
When Jesus raised his eyes
    and saw that a large crowd was
        coming to him,
he said to Philip,
"Where can we buy enough food
    for them to eat?"
He said this to test him,
    because he himself knew what he was
        going to do.
Philip answered him,
"Two hundred days' wages worth of
    food would not be enough
    for each of them to have a little."
One of his disciples,
    Andrew, the brother of Simon Peter,
        said to him,
"There is a boy here who has five
    barley loaves and two fish;
but what good are these for so many?"
Jesus said, "Have the people recline."
Now there was a great deal of grass in
    that place.
So the men reclined, about five thousand
    in number.

Continued in Appendix A, p. 303.

Reflecting on the Gospel

One-sixth of the planet's population suffers from severe hunger. Not surprisingly, the hardest hit are those who live in the developing world: hundreds of millions of people are starving in some countries in Asia and Africa. But, developed countries are not immune; millions more go wanting in the richest countries of the world. Today's readings are both challenging and comforting in light of this food crisis.

The readings tell of two extraordinary acts of feeding hungry crowds: one by Elisha and one by Jesus. In the first, a man brings twenty loaves of barley bread as "firstfruits" to Elisha. The setting is most likely a shrine, and the bread is intended to be offered to God or placed as showbread, to be eaten later by the temple functionaries. The offer of firstfruits, the best of the harvest, was a way to express gratitude to God, and asks God's blessing on the remainder. It is surprising when Elisha tells the man offering the bread to give it to the people to eat instead. Only an extraordinary situation of hunger would demand such an action. Elisha's servant does not object but worries that there will still not be enough to feed one hundred people. Quoting an unknown saying, Elisha insists there will be enough and even some left over. And there is.

Jesus faces five thousand hungry people. He and the disciples explore possible solutions. They could buy food, but where would they find a sufficient stock? Even if they could find it, they do not have enough money to purchase the amount needed. There is a boy with five loaves and two fish, but the disciples reason, "What good are these for so many?" They are fixated on the enormity of need and the scarcity of resources.

At Jesus's urging, they entrust the boy's loaves and fishes to him. He instructs them to invite the people into a position of trust and receptivity to God's gracious care. Reclining on the grass is evocative of Psalm 23, which expresses trust in God, who leads the people to green pastures and provides for all their needs. Taking the loaves and giving thanks, Jesus rejoices in the abundance that God has given and distributes the bread to all until they are satisfied. He then directs the disciples to gather the leftovers, which fill twelve baskets.

Both readings urge us to take extraordinary actions to meet an urgent need. Global efforts to eradicate hunger can begin with one courageous boy who is willing to relinquish his few loaves and fishes, or one man making an offering to God, willing to let his gift be redirected to the people and to trust that in God's hands, there will be enough for all. Jesus reorients his disciples away from the inscrutable problem of scarcity and instead gives thanks for the abundance of God's provision. The resources to feed all, and for all to be satisfied, lie within the community. Jesus's careful attention to the fragments left over also directs us to prevent wastefulness. Through such extraordinary responses to divine abundance, God is able to "satisfy the desire of every living thing" (Ps 145:16).

Preparing to Proclaim

Key words and phrases: "Then Jesus took the loaves, gave thanks, and distributed them to those who were reclining."

To the point: This is a story that obviously foreshadows the Eucharist, and it is also a story about finding abundance where scarcity seems to reign. A common take on this story is that the food was there all along, but the crowd refused to share out of fear it would not be enough. Only when they saw the boy's generosity were others inspired to share what they had, too, and as loaves were passed more pockets were opened until there was more than enough. This read of the story does not mean to diminish this as a miracle but rather to point out that God often works miracles through us. Our generosity and our gifts are how God changes the world. Jesus feeds us through each other. When Jesus is present, abundance is there. When Jesus is with us, we will find we have everything we need.

Psalmist Preparation

In this psalm, we sing in gratitude for how God answers our prayers and provides for our needs. Of course, there are times when we're not so sure that God does this; prayers go unanswered and needs are not always met. Keep in mind that many in your congregation may not feel confident that God does provide for our needs. You yourself may be in a place of longing for an answer to a prayer that goes unanswered. But the final lines of the psalm give us the real answer to our prayers and the real way that God feeds us: "The Lord is near to all who call upon him." Even when we feel that our needs are unmet, God remains with us, sharing our hungers and heartbreaks and feeding us with God's very self.

Making Connections

Between the readings: The first reading foreshadows the gospel in obvious ways. Food is brought and shared with more people than it should feed, and it somehow feeds them. Even the food is the same—barley loaves, cheaper than wheat bread, a staple for peasant diets. In both stories, there is more than enough. The leftover bread shows that God is providing with reckless abundance. The stories follow the same trajectory but they differ in scope. Where Elisha feeds one hundred people, Jesus will feed five thousand. Jesus mimics the Old Testament prophets—this is the same God at work. At the same time, he far outpaces them—in Jesus, God is doing something completely new.

To experience: The abundance God promises is not always easy to see. We are often weighed down by a lack of resources—there is never enough time or energy or money to accomplish all we feel we should. But when God is with us, we most often find we have enough, whether that means creatively revisioning how we use existing resources or stripping away excess so that our resources are well-dedicated to our mission.

Homily Points

• Today's readings remind us that we are part of one Body and one Spirit. Humankind shares a common call. Thus, we are to care for one another just as we would care for our most cherished loved one. Particularly, biblical stories like today's first reading and gospel emphasize the need to care for people living in poverty. The hungry must be fed. It is the responsibility of those who have enough food to ensure that everyone else has their fill too. Bearing responsibility for each other is a foundational aspect of faith expressed in the Old and New Testaments.

• The story of the feeding of the five thousand is the only miracle account to be written about in all four gospels. John's framing helps readers know a deeper truth about Jesus: that he is the Son of the living God who has come to nourish our every need. The physical feeding of the crowds with five loaves and two fish is significant for sure. But what matters most to John is that people come to know and believe in the miracle-worker.

• The people deem Jesus a prophet upon benefiting from his miraculous feeding, but their understanding of Jesus is still limited to earthly frameworks of leadership. They want to make him a political king, which is not the type of kingship Jesus came to take on. So, the Son of God withdraws to the mountain alone. He takes time for silence and solitude with God to discern his next steps.

CELEBRATION

Model Penitential Act

Presider: In today's second reading, Saint Paul urges the Ephesians to "live in a manner worthy of the call you have received." For those times we have fallen short of this mark, let us ask God for mercy and forgiveness . . . *[pause]*

    Lord Jesus, you are the bread of life: Lord, have mercy.

    Christ Jesus, you feed the hungry with your very self: Christ, have mercy.

    Lord Jesus, you will come again to bring eternal life to your people: Lord, have mercy.

Model Universal Prayer (Prayer of the Faithful)

Presider: United under one Lord, one faith, and one baptism, let us express our prayers and petitions.

Response: Lord, hear our prayer.

Grant all Christians the awareness and courage to claim their baptismal authority for the strengthening of the church . . .

Bless all people in the food and agriculture industries who help food get from the ground to our tables . . .

Shine the light of your love on people who are incarcerated and their families . . .

Open our hearts to Christ's generous spirit of forgiveness . . .

Presider: Loving God, you empower each of us to proclaim the good news of your son, Jesus Christ. Receive our prayers that with faith and courage we might follow in the way of Jesus to everlasting life. We ask this through Christ our Lord. **Amen.**

Liturgy and Music

Where is your heart?

    There is a lyric that appears in the second verse of the hymn "Lift Him Up" that begins, "Oh! The world is hungry for the Living Bread, lift the Savior up for them to see" (*Lead Me, Guide Me—Second Edition*, #633). The people that come to our churches are hungry for relief, relief from the pressures of the world. They are hungry for what the church offers: the paschal mystery, revealed in the Eucharist. As baptized Christians we join Christ in his death and rising. As co-heirs with Christ we share in the inheritance of eternal life.

    This is what we offer to those who attend the liturgy of the Eucharist, Christ present in the word and in the gifts of bread and wine. This spiritual food of bread and wine is made available secondarily in the music we offer, for we, too, as music ministers offer Jesus through our music.

    In our ministry, we are called, like Peter, to love, which follows that we will serve God's people. To serve means to meet a need. We ought not serve God's people that which "does not satisfy" (Isa 55:2) or does not meet their need. Jesus was moved to pity when he encountered people hungry for the Living Word. He fed them. So must we.

COLLECT

Let us pray.

Pause for silent prayer

O God, protector of those who hope in
    you,
without whom nothing has firm
    foundation, nothing is holy,
bestow in abundance your mercy upon us
and grant that, with you as our ruler and
    guide,
we may use the good things that pass
in such a way as to hold fast even now
to those that ever endure.
Through our Lord Jesus Christ, your Son,
who lives and reigns with you in the unity
    of the Holy Spirit,
God, for ever and ever. **Amen.**

FIRST READING

2 Kgs 4:42-44

A man came from Baal-shalishah bringing
    to Elisha, the man of God,
    twenty barley loaves made from the
      firstfruits,
    and fresh grain in the ear.
Elisha said, "Give it to the people to eat."
But his servant objected,
    "How can I set this before a hundred
      people?"
Elisha insisted, "Give it to the people to
    eat.
For thus says the LORD,
    'They shall eat and there shall be some
      left over.'"
And when they had eaten, there was some
    left over,
    as the LORD had said.

RESPONSORIAL PSALM
Ps 145:10-11, 15-16, 17-18

℟. (cf. 16) The hand of the Lord feeds us;
 he answers all our needs.

Let all your works give you thanks, O
 LORD,
 and let your faithful ones bless you.
Let them discourse of the glory of your
 kingdom
 and speak of your might.

℟. The hand of the Lord feeds us; he
 answers all our needs.

The eyes of all look hopefully to you,
 and you give them their food in due
 season;
you open your hand
 and satisfy the desire of every living
 thing.

℟. The hand of the Lord feeds us; he
 answers all our needs.

The LORD is just in all his ways
 and holy in all his works.
The LORD is near to all who call upon him,
 to all who call upon him in truth.

℟. The hand of the Lord feeds us; he
 answers all our needs.

SECOND READING
Eph 4:1-6

Brothers and sisters:
I, a prisoner for the Lord,
 urge you to live in a manner worthy of
 the call you have received,
 with all humility and gentleness, with
 patience,
 bearing with one another through love,
 striving to preserve the unity of the
 spirit through the bond of peace:
 one body and one Spirit,
 as you were also called to the one hope
 of your call;
 one Lord, one faith, one baptism;
 one God and Father of all,
 who is over all and through all and in
 all.

Living Liturgy

Liturgy and Justice: Today's reading from the second book of Kings and our gospel reading from John tell important stories about perceived scarcity versus the abundance and generosity of God. These stories can also inspire us to look at the resources we have with fresh perspective. It's almost second nature to converse with each other about how nobody seems to have enough time, enough funding, or enough support but maybe we have more than we think. If nothing else, we probably have enough of the resources we need to *begin* the lifelong task of attempting to do God's will. These stories assure us that if we are willing to step out on faith, God can and will offer heavenly grace as a supplement to our efforts—sometimes through our own brothers and sisters in Christ.

At school when students arrive without the required uniform pieces, the dean of students will escort them to our wellness center where they can find extra shirts, ties, and belts to borrow for the day. Students are often shocked to discover that our school has so many extra uniform pieces on hand and ask how much the school paid to stock up. They're even more shocked to learn that the school has paid close to nothing and that almost all of the uniform pieces come from recent alumni who chose to donate their uniforms after graduation. This is just one ordinary example of how a perceived scarcity can be transformed to reveal the seemingly miraculous abundance of a community.

Maybe this is true of other settings and situations too. Maybe our neighborhoods do actually have enough safe, affordable housing to go around. Maybe we do have money to ensure that all people who want to can earn a college degree without being crushed by debt for decades. Maybe we do have enough technology and resources that everyone can receive adequate medical treatment when they need it (because at some point, everyone *will* need it).

Many will still question (like the servant in our first reading) whether or not we actually have enough to supply all of these societal needs. But today let us dare to entertain the idea that if we are willing to cooperate with God, we just might find that we do have enough.

PROMPTS FOR FAITH-SHARING

• Where do you find abundance in your life? Where do you feel lack?

• Have you had an experience of God making abundance from scarcity?

• How might you be called to share what you have, no matter how scarce it may seem?

See Appendix B, p. 313, for additional prompts.

SPIRITUALITY

GOSPEL ACCLAMATION
Matt 4:4b

R̸. Alleluia, alleluia.
One does not live on bread alone, but by every
word that comes forth from the mouth of God.
R̸. Alleluia, alleluia.

Gospel

John 6:24-35; L113B

**When the crowd saw that
neither Jesus nor his
disciples were there,
they themselves got into boats
and came to Capernaum
looking for Jesus.
And when they found him across
the sea they said to him,
"Rabbi, when did you get
here?"
Jesus answered them and said,
"Amen, amen, I say to you,
you are looking for me not because
you saw signs
but because you ate the loaves and
were filled.
Do not work for food that perishes
but for the food that endures for
eternal life,
which the Son of Man will give you.
For on him the Father, God, has set his
seal."
So they said to him,
"What can we do to accomplish the
works of God?"
Jesus answered and said to them,
"This is the work of God, that you
believe in the one he sent."
So they said to him,
"What sign can you do, that we may
see and believe in you?
What can you do?
Our ancestors ate manna in the desert,
as it is written:
*He gave them bread from heaven to
eat.*"**

Continued in Appendix A, p. 303.

Reflecting on the Gospel

"Better the devil you know than the one you don't know." Such popular wisdom reflects the reluctance of most people to change, even when the current situation is difficult. It is easier to hang on to what is, using familiar coping mechanisms, than it is to risk something new that might result in greater difficulties. Such is the complaint of the Israelites to Moses in the first reading. They would rather have stayed enslaved in Egypt with all the suffering that entailed, than to risk the freedom into which God was leading them, a freedom that brought a whole new set of challenges.

One challenge concerned food. For those who migrate from one land to another, one of the hardest changes is to eat the food of those of another culture. One longs for the familiarity of "comfort food" from home.

God is not indifferent to the plight of the Israelites. Morning and evening, God provides plenty of manna and quail. But the manna is completely unfamiliar to the Israelites. "What is this?" they ask. Moses has to tell them: "This is the bread which the LORD has given you to eat." It may have filled them physically, but it does not seem to have satisfied them on other levels. God's providence never fails, but it does not always come in the way we want or expect.

In the gospel, Jesus invites the crowd to shift their expectations from outward signs to inner transformation. He has just fed a hungry crowd of five thousand with five barley loaves and two fish, yet they ask him for a sign so that they may see and believe. They are looking right at the One who is the very bread of life, but they do not see him as such. He tells them that the same God who provided for their ancestors in the desert is also the One who fed the crowd, and who gives life to the world. To come to Jesus and believe in him requires letting go of familiar habits like filling up on "food that perishes," and allowing him to give "food that endures for eternal life."

Grazing on junk food or trying to satisfy our spiritual hungers with constant noise and busyness are the "devils" we know. What would happen if we carved out an inner emptiness to let the bread of life satisfy our deepest hungers and thirsts?

Risking an unknown future, the Israelites crossed the desert and entered the land of freedom into which God led them through Moses. The crowd in the gospel crossed over the Sea of Galilee, opening themselves to the possibility of being filled forever by the One who would also entrust to them the "works of God" to feed others and give "life to the world." This mission can take us into strange territory, where we risk letting go of the familiar and tasting the "bread" or rice or tortillas of others. Step by step, we turn from looking for the external "signs" toward seeking to become one with the very bread of life, who fills us to the full.

Preparing to Proclaim

Key words and phrases: "I am the bread of life."

To the point: Last Sunday's story of feeding the crowd began the Year B series of eucharistic gospels from John. Jesus is here making wild, radical claims. We, living with two thousand years of Christian history and a well-developed sacramental theology behind us, are accustomed to this. Of course Jesus is bread, of course he feeds us with his body. But for those hearing it, this is a new, weird, horrifying concept. It is so hard for them to grasp that our gospel in a few more weeks will see many of them forsake Jesus and return to their ordinary lives. In addition to the claim that cannibalism is suddenly okay, Jesus's "I am" statement is blasphemous; he is claiming for himself the name of God revealed to Moses. Jesus is shocking his audience here. His truths are not easy to wrap our minds around.

Psalmist Preparation

This psalm sings in gratitude for God's providence. Just as God provided manna for the Israelites in the desert, God continues to provide for us—most especially in the Eucharist. As you prepare to proclaim this psalm, rehearse this text in two ways. Sing it about the past, recalling the wonder of God feeding the Israelites in the desert. Place yourself imaginatively into the text of the first reading, sharing in the Israelites' surprised gratitude at finding food where there had been none. Sing this psalm about the present, recalling the wonder of God feeding us still.

Making Connections

Between the readings: The first reading gives us the sign to which the crowds will compare Jesus. This is one of the miracles that proves God's love to the Israelites, one they point back to again and again with wonder and gratitude. God transforms their desert experience of hunger to one of abundance. God sees their needs, hears their pleas, and provides for them. God continues to do so for us.

To experience: These readings affirm that God hears our prayers and provides for what we need, but the truth of the matter is that we often do *not* feel satisfied. Prayers go unanswered all the time. People who long for marriage and children remain inexplicably unmarried or infertile. Sicknesses are not cured. None of us is spared from death. And yet even when we don't feel it, God transforms these desert experiences, being abundance by refusing to desert us.

Homily Points

• Today's readings highlight the patient, generous characteristics of God. In the first reading from Exodus, we encounter Israelites who are "hangry" (hungry and angry). The community grumbles about Moses and Aaron, whom they accuse of leading them toward death in the desert. The Israelites even seem to regret their status as God's chosen people—an extreme example of how perspectives can shift when bodily needs are not met! God listens patiently to the people and then responds to their needs by filling the land with bread. God's acts show care for the Israelites and to test their obedience. Will they trust in God's ability to satisfy their hunger? Will they look out for their neighbors and ensure that the bread is shared equitably?

• The hungry crowds went in search of Jesus in today's gospel, hoping that he would fill their stomachs once more. Jesus took their pleas as an opportunity to teach about a different kind of food that will leave the people satisfied for eternity. Rather than gratefully accept Jesus's gift, the people want to know what they can do to earn such food. They do not understand that their work is to believe in God's Son. They need not do or say anything special to receive God's love. They need only to believe in the Bread of Life.

• The same is true for us today. We are called to believe in the one Lord, Jesus Christ. There is nothing we can say or do to earn God's love. In God's generosity, God gives of the divine love freely. We need only to open our hearts to receive it.

CELEBRATION

Model Penitential Act

Presider: The Lord is eager to nourish us for the journey ahead. With trust in God's everlasting mercy, let us call to mind our sins and ask for forgiveness . . . *[pause]*

Lord Jesus, you are the Bread of Life: Lord, have mercy.

Christ Jesus, you are the Son of God: Christ, have mercy.

Lord Jesus, you are the Prince of Peace: Lord, have mercy.

Model Universal Prayer (Prayer of the Faithful)

Presider: With minds and hearts open to God, let us offer our prayers and petitions.

Response: Lord, hear our prayer.

Enkindle the fire of your love in those who serve with Catholic Relief Services, Catholic Charities, and other charitable organizations . . .

Bless the work of therapists, spiritual directors, counselors, and coaches . . .

Hold in your tender care families suffering from miscarriage or infant loss . . .

Grant unending joy in your kingdom to our loved ones who have died . . .

Presider: Generous God, you sustain your people with the bread of life and the cup of salvation. Hear our prayers that we might answer your call to discipleship each day. We ask this through Christ our Lord. **Amen.**

Liturgy and Music

Bread is a staple in many diets across the globe. It may take many forms, such as injera bread served in Ethiopia or *la rosca de reyes*, a sweet bread served on El Día de Los Reyes (Three Kings' Day) in many Latin traditions. Bread is a food that sustains us and can be a source of sustenance for many.

When the Israelites were in the desert after being delivered out of bondage in Egypt, the Lord sent them bread from heaven, manna, to sustain them in the mornings. The crowd that followed Jesus to Capernaum also desired food, after seeing the miracle of the fishes and loaves. Jesus admonishes the people, telling them that their focus should not be on food that perishes, but on that which is eternal. It is here in John's Gospel that we read one of the great "I Am" statements of Jesus: "I am the bread of life."

Consider ministering the following songs today:

"I Am the Bread of Life" (Sr. Suzanne Toolan, RSM; GIA)

"Not By Bread Alone" (M. Roger Holland, II; GIA)

"You Are the Living Word" (Fred Hammond; *Capitol Christian Music Group*)

COLLECT

Let us pray.

Pause for silent prayer

Draw near to your servants, O Lord,
and answer their prayers with unceasing kindness,
that, for those who glory in you as their Creator and guide,
you may restore what you have created
and keep safe what you have restored.
Through our Lord Jesus Christ, your Son,
who lives and reigns with you in the unity of the Holy Spirit,
God, for ever and ever. **Amen.**

FIRST READING
Exod 16:2-4, 12-15

The whole Israelite community grumbled against Moses and Aaron.
The Israelites said to them,
"Would that we had died at the LORD's hand in the land of Egypt,
as we sat by our fleshpots and ate our fill of bread!
But you had to lead us into this desert
to make the whole community die of famine!"

Then the LORD said to Moses,
"I will now rain down bread from heaven for you.
Each day the people are to go out and gather their daily portion;
thus will I test them,
to see whether they follow my instructions or not.

"I have heard the grumbling of the Israelites.
Tell them: In the evening twilight you shall eat flesh,
and in the morning you shall have your fill of bread,
so that you may know that I, the LORD, am your God."

In the evening quail came up and covered the camp.
In the morning a dew lay all about the camp,
and when the dew evaporated, there on the surface of the desert
were fine flakes like hoarfrost on the ground.
On seeing it, the Israelites asked one another, "What is this?"
for they did not know what it was.
But Moses told them,
"This is the bread that the LORD has given you to eat."

RESPONSORIAL PSALM
Ps 78:3-4, 23-24, 25, 54

℟. (24b) The Lord gave them bread from
heaven.

What we have heard and know,
and what our fathers have declared
to us,
we will declare to the generation to come
the glorious deeds of the LORD and his
strength
and the wonders that he wrought.

℟. The Lord gave them bread from
heaven.

He commanded the skies above
and opened the doors of heaven;
he rained manna upon them for food
and gave them heavenly bread.

℟. The Lord gave them bread from
heaven.

Man ate the bread of angels,
food he sent them in abundance.
And he brought them to his holy land,
to the mountains his right hand had
won.

℟. The Lord gave them bread from
heaven.

SECOND READING
Eph 4:17, 20-24

Brothers and sisters:
I declare and testify in the Lord
that you must no longer live as the
Gentiles do,
in the futility of their minds;
that is not how you learned Christ,
assuming that you have heard of him
and were taught in him,
as truth is in Jesus,
that you should put away the old self of
your former way of life,
corrupted through deceitful desires,
and be renewed in the spirit of your
minds,
and put on the new self,
created in God's way in righteousness
and holiness of truth.

Living Liturgy

Liturgy and Spirituality: When I read today's gospel story, I find the crowds who follow Jesus to Capernaum in their boats very relatable. They have seen the wonders Jesus can do, they have heard his wisdom and they are hungry for more. They seek after him with eager hearts, hoping to feel more of what they've felt before: the deep spiritual joy that comes from hearing authentic, life-affirming truth. It feels like an almost universal human foible; after experiencing something transformational, we chase after things we believe will give us that same feeling again rather than looking inside to create new patterns of acting, thinking, and being. When they find him, Jesus tells the crowds, just as he tells us, to embrace newness with all of its challenges lest we turn blessings into burdens.

Today's reading from Exodus opens to the Israelites traveling through the desert, bemoaning their lot. They are a people liberated and freed from bondage, but the miracle of that freedom has dimmed. Now all they can see is the struggles they face in the desert. How many of us can remember a time when we felt at one moment like God answered our prayer only to feel stranded in a desert the next? These readings seem to be gently guiding us to see that answered prayers are not a finish line. Rather, they are preparation for a new stage of faithfulness and relationship with God.

What happens to the suffering Israelites in the desert? God answers their cries by giving them manna from heaven, nourishment to sustain them as they journey through the desert. And just as Jesus offers the crowds in Capernaum the promise of new life in him, we can be assured that God will meet us wherever we are in our spiritual journey to give us the sustenance we need to push on and continue to grow in faith, purpose, and service. May we gracefully receive the manna God offers us, the new challenges *and* blessings that will sustain us on our journeys.

PROMPTS FOR FAITH-SHARING

• Reflect on the oddness of Jesus's claim that he is bread that feeds our hunger. What would it be like to hear this statement in the first century, without the centuries of Christian tradition that make it so familiar?

• The Israelites do not receive manna as individuals but as a community; we, likewise, do not receive the Eucharist in isolation from each other. What role does your community play in your participation in the Eucharist?

• How is your relationship with the Eucharist right now? What might help renew your sense of wonder and gratitude as you approach the sacrament?

*See Appendix B, p. 313,
for additional prompts.*

SPIRITUALITY

GOSPEL ACCLAMATION
John 6:51

℟. Alleluia, alleluia.
I am the living bread that came down
    from heaven, says the Lord;
whoever eats this bread will live forever.
℟. Alleluia, alleluia.

Gospel

John 6:41-51; L116B

The Jews murmured about
    Jesus because he said,
"I am the bread that came
    down from heaven,"
and they said,
"Is this not Jesus, the son of
    Joseph?
Do we not know his father and
    mother?
Then how can he say,
'I have come down from
    heaven'?"
Jesus answered and said to them,
"Stop murmuring among yourselves.
No one can come to me unless the
    Father who sent me draw him,
    and I will raise him on the last day.
It is written in the prophets:
    They shall all be taught by God.
Everyone who listens to my Father and
    learns from him comes to me.
Not that anyone has seen the Father
    except the one who is from God;
    he has seen the Father.
Amen, amen, I say to you,
    whoever believes has eternal life.
I am the bread of life.
Your ancestors ate the manna in the
    desert, but they died;
    this is the bread that comes down
        from heaven
    so that one may eat it and not die.
I am the living bread that came down
    from heaven;
    whoever eats this bread will live
        forever;
    and the bread that I will give is my
        flesh for the life of the world."

Reflecting on the Gospel

Sometimes things are so horrible, we say we just want to die. Most of the time we intend that metaphorically. Elijah, in today's first reading, seems to mean it literally. He is fleeing for his life, as Jezebel is determined to kill him because he vanquished the prophets of Baal and put them to death. Parking himself under a broom tree a day's journey into the desert, he prays, "This is enough, O LORD! Take my life, for I am no better than my fathers." It is not clear whether Elijah is fed up with the difficulty of his ministry or he is lamenting his own actions, having just killed the prophets of Baal. Perhaps it is both. In any case, the frailty of God's fiery prophet is most visible.

When Elijah is at his lowest, God's messenger comes with food and water, urging him to continue onward. Obediently, he gets up and takes nourishment, continuing his sojourn in the desert for forty more days, a trek that is reminiscent of the Israelite desert wandering of forty years. Elijah's quest will culminate at Mount Horeb (also called Sinai in the J and P strands of the Pentateuchal narrative). There, like Moses, he encounters God.

But the Holy One is not in the fierce wind or the earthquake or the fire but in the voice that emerges out of sheer silence. In the desert Elijah learns of God's nonviolent ways. He does not find the Holy One in the violent wind or the earthquake or the fire but in the silence that instructs him to anoint others: an act of consecration and also of healing.

In the gospel, there is murmuring in the desert by the people surrounding Jesus, just as the Israelites did with Moses. In the latter instance, the complaint was about not having food, to which God responded by sending manna and quail. In the gospel, the problem is with the source of the spiritual nourishment being offered. Jesus claims to be the "bread that came down from heaven," echoing God's promise in Isaiah 55:10-11 of the nourishing and effective word that comes "down from heaven." In this first part of the bread of life discourse, the emphasis is on bread as a nourishing word. In the second half, which we will hear next Sunday, the emphasis is on eucharistic nourishment.

The source of this nourishing word is a point of contention. The people think they know Jesus's origins and family; is he not one just like them? Another stumbling block is his unusual manner of teaching. He does not preach in Elijah's fiery way, but he waits for God to draw open hearts to himself, letting themselves be taught through listening, learning while not seeing entirely, and finally, responding with belief. This is "living bread," a nourishing word that leads one to cherish all life, to choose life, and ultimately, to relinquish one's own life for the life of the world, believing that this is the way to life eternal.

Preparing to Proclaim

Key words and phrases: "[W]hoever eats this bread will live forever."

To the point: Jesus continues this week in likening himself to the manna given by God. He, too, is bread sent down from heaven. He gives life where death was before a certainty. He sustains us through this pilgrimage of earthly life until we can enter the fullness of God's promises. He fulfills the work of God in the Old Testament, while also surpassing it by far. While those who ate manna still died, eating this living bread will give life eternal. This was utterly mysterious for Jesus's hearers, for whom the concept of the Eucharist did not yet exist. It remains mysterious for us now. Partaking in the Eucharist is a radical act of trust in the God who made us and loves us and wants abundant life for us.

Psalmist Preparation

Psalm 34 is the eucharistic psalm *par excellence*. Its invitation to both taste and see God's goodness points our attention to the gift of Christ's presence in the eucharistic species, which we do in fact experience with both our taste and our sight. We will repeat this psalm at liturgy for two more weeks after this one, with slightly different verses each time if you're using settings that follow the lectionary precisely. As you prepare to proclaim it this week, try to really hear it as an invitation. Remember that God's loving presence is waiting for us always. Pray for those in your congregation who might especially need to hear this invitation, and sing this psalm with compassion for them.

Making Connections

Between the readings: The first reading is another story of God feeding God's people. Much like the Israelites were given manna in the desert, Elijah receives bread and water for his desert journey. Like the Israelites, he was prepared to die, but God sent food because he still had a mission to fulfill. He is strengthened by this food and goes on to meet God at Horeb. This, too, is a foreshadowing of the Eucharist, in which God feeds us to nourish and sustain us for the long pilgrimage of Christian life.

To experience: The meals we see God providing in these stories are rather sparse—the Israelites' manna, Elijah's hearth cake, the bread and fish for the five thousand. This is not the stuff of a great feast but is rather the bare minimum of a sustenance meal. These stories do not tell us everything, though; think of Psalm 23 with its prepared banquet and overflowing cup. God wants to provide us not just with the bare minimum but with abundance.

Homily Points

• The prophet Elijah finds himself in a dark place in today's first reading. So Elijah does what countless others have done during desperate times: he escapes into the wilderness. After a day of walking, the prophet sits beneath a broom tree—a fragile yet persistent plant that can survive in the desert. Overwhelmed and exhausted, Elijah "prayed for death." He cannot see a way forward. The only thing Elijah seems sure of is that God is present and will perhaps listen to his prayer for a merciful end. But God has other plans. First, the Lord takes care of Elijah's physical needs for sleep, food, and water. An angel of the Lord touches Elijah and offers him encouragement for the journey.

• The odds are strong that some of us have been in this type of dark situation before or are even there now. Let Elijah's story be a source of hope. We can get through difficult times. God is with us even in our darkest moments. So are other "angels of the Lord" in our midst who touch the suffering with a homemade meal, letter of encouragement, or other offer of support. Who are the angels in your life who accompany you during hard times? Who are you an angel for?

• The religious leaders in today's gospel claim to know all about Jesus. In their closed-mindedness, they miss the deeper truths of Jesus. He is the Bread of Life, the Son of God born into this world to set creation free.

CELEBRATION

Model Penitential Act

Presider: In today's second reading, Saint Paul talks about removing "all bitterness, fury, anger, shouting, and reviling" within us. Let us pause to consider how these or other harmful practices have taken root in our hearts and ask God for forgiveness . . . *[pause]*

Lord Jesus, you are the living bread that came down from heaven: Lord, have mercy.
Christ Jesus, you give of your flesh for the life of the world: Christ, have mercy.
Lord Jesus, you will come again in glory to save your people: Lord, have mercy.

Model Universal Prayer (Prayer of the Faithful)

Presider: With faith in our listening God, let us offer our prayers for the church and the world.

Response: Lord, hear our prayer.

Transform our church into a place and a people who welcome all as Christ . . .

Give rest to single parents, new parents, caretakers, and all who tend to the needs of others . . .

Bring into the light people suffering from depression and suicidal thoughts . . .

Further the work of our local communities to provide adequate housing and employment to people in need . . .

Presider: God of peace, through the gift of your son Jesus Christ you promise to bring all things into the light. Hear our prayers that with boldness we might proclaim your good news. We ask this through Christ our Lord. **Amen.**

Liturgy and Music

Rest is underrated. Self-care is a necessity. We need to take time to rest and care for ourselves in order to minister effectively. Most healthcare professionals recommend a minimum of eight hours of sleep nightly in order for the human body to function. It is also true that every body, every individual, is different. Some require more than eight hours, some are perfectly fine with less. Regardless, it is paramount that we allow ourselves time to rest, recover, and rejuvenate.

Elijah took time to rest from his labor. Actually, he took time to rest from being pursued by his enemies, as Jezebel sought to kill him because he did as God instructed him to do. Not everyone will be pleased with how you serve the Lord, nor may they agree with your methods. They may not like your music selections and have no compunction about telling you!

Ministry can often be difficult, even hard. And there are times that God's people can be challenging! We need to be fully rested so that we can call on all of our resources to serve well. When we are rested, we are less likely to respond to people in anger or be short-tempered. Paul told the Ephesians that they are to remove "all bitterness, fury, anger, shouting, and reviling." Rather, we are to be "kind to one another, compassionate, forgiving one another as God has forgiven you." Let us be patient with one another, or as my sister says, "practice the pause!"

COLLECT

Let us pray.

Pause for silent prayer

Almighty ever-living God,
whom, taught by the Holy Spirit,
we dare to call our Father,
bring, we pray, to perfection in our hearts
the spirit of adoption as your sons and
    daughters,
that we may merit to enter into the
    inheritance
which you have promised.
Through our Lord Jesus Christ, your Son,
who lives and reigns with you in the unity
    of the Holy Spirit,
God, for ever and ever. **Amen.**

FIRST READING

1 Kgs 19:4-8

Elijah went a day's journey into the desert,
    until he came to a broom tree and sat
        beneath it.
He prayed for death, saying:
    "This is enough, O LORD!
Take my life, for I am no better than my
    fathers."
He lay down and fell asleep under the
    broom tree,
    but then an angel touched him and
        ordered him to get up and eat.
Elijah looked and there at his head was a
    hearth cake
    and a jug of water.
After he ate and drank, he lay down again,
    but the angel of the LORD came back a
        second time,
    touched him, and ordered,
    "Get up and eat, else the journey will be
        too long for you!"
He got up, ate, and drank;
    then strengthened by that food,
    he walked forty days and forty nights
        to the mountain of God, Horeb.

RESPONSORIAL PSALM
Ps 34:2-3, 4-5, 6-7, 8-9

℟. (9a) Taste and see the goodness of the Lord.

I will bless the LORD at all times;
    his praise shall be ever in my mouth.
Let my soul glory in the LORD;
    the lowly will hear me and be glad.

℟. Taste and see the goodness of the Lord.

Glorify the LORD with me,
    let us together extol his name.
I sought the LORD, and he answered me
    and delivered me from all my fears.

℟. Taste and see the goodness of the Lord.

Look to him that you may be radiant with
    joy,
    and your faces may not blush with
      shame.
When the afflicted man called out, the
    LORD heard,
    and from all his distress he saved him.

℟. Taste and see the goodness of the Lord.

The angel of the LORD encamps
    around those who fear him and delivers
      them.
Taste and see how good the LORD is;
    blessed the man who takes refuge in
      him.

℟. Taste and see the goodness of the Lord.

SECOND READING
Eph 4:30–5:2

Brothers and sisters:
Do not grieve the Holy Spirit of God,
    with which you were sealed for the day
      of redemption.
All bitterness, fury, anger, shouting, and
    reviling
    must be removed from you, along with
      all malice.
And be kind to one another,
    compassionate,
    forgiving one another as God has
      forgiven you in Christ.

So be imitators of God, as beloved
    children, and live in love,
    as Christ loved us and handed himself
      over for us
    as a sacrificial offering to God for a
      fragrant aroma.

Living Liturgy

Liturgy and Spirituality: The life of a prophet certainly was not easy, and yet it is still jarring to hear Elijah pray for death in today's first reading. Depleted and discouraged, Elijah asks for the Lord to take his life because he sees himself as no better than his predecessors. What is it that ultimately rejuvenates Elijah? The magical combination of a nap, a hearth cake, and a jug of water. When we find ourselves utterly worn down by the many pressures of everyday life, what is it that fortifies us?

The women in the faith sharing group that I attend once talked about self-care activities, specifically how we can distinguish which self-care activities are lifegiving and which are neutral or even detrimental. For some people, the phrase "self-care" might evoke images of bubble baths, massages, and glasses of wine. Several women in our group, however, shared that those experiences, while enjoyable, did not ultimately have a lasting positive impact. The self-care that actually did offer significant comfort were much less glamorous: regular exercise, spending time in nature, attending therapy, and checking in with the friends and family who lovingly hold us accountable.

When we feel spiritually weary, it may be tempting to reach for the things that will bring us instant comfort. But in those moments, maybe we don't need comfort as much as we need nourishment.

PROMPTS FOR FAITH-SHARING

• What have been some desert journeys in your life? How has God sustained you through them?

• Name a time that God has fed your hunger—physical, emotional, or spiritual. Name a hunger that remains; how do you wish God would feed it?

• The Eucharist is our most powerful encounter with Christ, the place where we taste and see God's goodness in a concentrated way. Where else do you experience God's providence? How might you wrap up gratitude for this into your eucharistic participation?

See Appendix B, p. 313, for additional prompts.

AUGUST 11, 2024
NINETEENTH SUNDAY IN ORDINARY TIME

GOSPEL ACCLAMATION
℟. Alleluia, alleluia.
Mary is taken up to heaven;
a chorus of angels exults.
℟. Alleluia, alleluia.

Gospel Luke 1:39-56; L622

Mary set out
    and traveled to the hill country in haste
    to a town of Judah,
    where she entered the house of
        Zechariah
    and greeted Elizabeth.
When Elizabeth heard Mary's greeting,
    the infant leaped in her womb,
    and Elizabeth, filled with the Holy
        Spirit,
    cried out in a loud voice and said,
    "Blessed are you among women,
    and blessed is the fruit of your womb.
And how does this happen to me,
    that the mother of my Lord should
        come to me?
For at the moment the sound of your
        greeting reached my ears,
    the infant in my womb leaped for joy.
Blessed are you who believed
    that what was spoken to you by the
        Lord
    would be fulfilled."

Continued in Appendix A, p. 304.

See Appendix A., p. 304, for the other readings.

Reflecting on the Gospel

Today's gospel contains one of the greatest pieces of poetry in the Catholic imagination. The *Magnificat* has been set to music countless times, rewritten in new ways and expressed in paintings. It's one of the cornerstone prayers given to us in the gospel, alongside the Lord's Prayer and the Beatitudes.

It's unlikely that someone was sitting with Elizabeth and Mary, taking down her dictation. Instead, the *Magnificat* was included by the gospel writer at this moment to illuminate the person of Mary, and to place her within Jewish history. It's possible Mary did have an extraordinary moment of prayer upon greeting Elizabeth, which became part of family history, and then a piece of oral history, shared with the apostles. It is in Luke's Gospel for a reason, and it offers us an insight into Mary's disposition, and her relationship with Elizabeth.

Mary has done a profoundly irresponsible thing, by society's measure. She's agreed to become pregnant before being married. This is not a prudent decision. But she says yes, and takes one of the biggest leaps of faith in human history with that yes.

Why on earth would someone who's just agreed to torpedo her social standing and ability to get married react with such joy? Because Mary's faith is complete, and her trust all encompassing. When she arrives at Elizabeth's home and finds her cousin is indeed in the middle of a geriatric pregnancy, she begins to understand the "long game," and is overwhelmed. Mary now sees what she is a part of. "[F]or he has looked with favor on his lowly servant. / From this day all generations will call me blessed."

This is the moment when Mary realizes her role in salvation history. It's not a conclusion she reaches on her own, but in community with another woman who is sharing her journey of pregnancy. Elizabeth greets her and identifies her: "And how does this happen to me, that the mother of my Lord should come to me?" Mary hears these words, and suddenly the work of God is not a personal act, but one that is being noticed by someone outside of herself. In other words, Elizabeth's greeting makes it *real*.

The Assumption is a day of anticipation for the church. We are given space to wonder at the role of Mary in the story of our salvation, and to join in her *Magnificat*. The Lord is merciful. He disperses the arrogant. He lifts the lowly. He feeds the hungry and sends the wealthy away. Christ turns the world on its head, and Mary is the first person to say it out loud.

Preparing to Proclaim

Key words and phrases: "Blessed are you among women."

To the point: Mary is, of course, unique. The particular way she is called to bring God to the world is unprecedented and unrepeatable. But her story parallels Elizabeth's, and those of many Old Testament barren wives, even as it exceeds them. Mary does not exist in a vacuum, and her uniqueness does not mean she is meant to be alone. All of us are called to bear God to the world in some particular way. All of us are invited to listen to God's invitations and to give our own *fiats*. All of us are intended for the glory in heaven in which Mary now partakes.

Model Penitential Act

Presider: Today's first reading points out great signs that appeared in the sky from God. For the times we have not been attentive to the signs of God's presence and love in our lives, let us ask the Lord for mercy and forgiveness . . . *[pause]*

Lord Jesus, you are the Son of God and son of Mary: Lord, have mercy.
Christ Jesus, you fill the hungry with good things: Christ, have mercy.
Lord Jesus, you send the rich away empty: Lord, have mercy.

Model Universal Prayer (Prayer of the Faithful)

Presider: Through the intercession of Mary the Mother of God, let us voice aloud our prayers and petitions.

Response: Lord, hear our prayer.

Further the ministries of women in the church to proclaim the greatness of the Lord . . .

Bless the Elizabeths in our lives who support and celebrate us . . .

Grant comfort and healing to couples who are struggling to conceive or who have experienced miscarriage . . .

Inspire our community to stand by the poor and the oppressed with the vigor of Mary . . .

Presider: God, source of joy and anticipation, you gifted Mary with the courage to carry your son and embrace his call to justice. Receive our prayers that through Mary's intercession we might give praise to God by our lives. We ask this through Christ our Lord. **Amen.**

Living Liturgy

Women have not always enjoyed a place of dignity and respect in US culture. They are the victims of many social and political injustices and economic inequities. Our society, and unfortunately even our church, subjects them to patriarchy. Yet a great honor is bestowed upon a woman that no man can claim: God chose to enter the world in the form of a human being, through a woman. It is an honor of which no man can boast. The Son of God, in full humanity and full divinity, dwelt among us because of the willingness of a woman.

In the book of Revelation, the woman caught up to heaven ("God and his throne") amid a battle between good and evil is ascribed to the Virgin Mary in Catholic doctrine, thus also ascribing to her a victory not only for women, but for all of humanity. It is through the image of a woman that this victory is presented in Scripture.

In Mary's song of praise, her *Magnificat*, we are told that the lowly will be lifted up, the hungry will be filled with good things, and the rich will be sent away empty. Justice and equity come into the world because of the faithfulness of a woman who told God, "Yes." Because of the faithfulness and obedience of a woman, all humanity has access to salvation. Perhaps one day, full honor will be visited upon all women.

Consider singing a new setting of the *Magnificat* today:
"Jina La Bwana: The Name of the Lord Is Holy" (Steven C. Warner; WLP/GIA)
"Magnificat" (M. Roger Holland, II; GIA)
"Magnificat" (Marie-Jo Thum; WLP/GIA)
"My Soul Proclaims (Magnificat)" (Bernadette Farrell; Oregon Catholic Press [OCP])

COLLECT
Let us pray.

Pause for silent prayer

Almighty ever-living God,
who assumed the Immaculate Virgin Mary,
    the Mother of your Son,
body and soul into heavenly glory,
grant, we pray,
that, always attentive to the things that are
    above,
we may merit to be sharers of her glory.
Through our Lord Jesus Christ, your Son,
who lives and reigns with you in the unity
    of the Holy Spirit,
God, for ever and ever. **Amen.**

FOR REFLECTION

• Who is the Elizabeth to your Mary? To whom do you turn when your world has been turned completely upside down? To whom to you go with big news—both good and scary and overwhelming?

• Mary responds to God's work in her life with the *Magnificat*, singing praise and correctly predicting that we will still call her blessed all these centuries later. How do you respond to God's callings? How joyfully are you able to make sacrifices for God?

See Appendix B, p. •••, for additional questions.

Homily Points

• The Solemnity of the Assumption of the Blessed Virgin Mary invites us to give thanks and praise for our bodies. We are not just brains sitting across from each other at dinner or souls floating past each other at the grocery store. We are embodied people, called to glorify God with our full selves.

• We await the day when, like Mary, we will encounter our Creator in the halls of heaven. Until then, let us consider the people and places in which we meet God in our daily lives. What makes your heart leap for joy? When are you prompted to proclaim the greatness of the Lord?

SPIRITUALITY

GOSPEL ACCLAMATION
John 6:56

℟. Alleluia, alleluia.
Whoever eats my flesh and drinks my
    blood
remains in me and I in him, says the
    Lord.
℟. Alleluia, alleluia.

Gospel

John 6:51-58; L119B

Jesus said to the crowds:
    "I am the living bread that
        came down from heaven;
    whoever eats this bread will
        live forever;
    and the bread that I will give
    is my flesh for the life of the
        world."
The Jews quarreled among
    themselves, saying,
    "How can this man give us his
        flesh to eat?"
Jesus said to them,
    "Amen, amen, I say to you,
    unless you eat the flesh of the Son of
        Man and drink his blood,
    you do not have life within you.
Whoever eats my flesh and drinks my
    blood
    has eternal life,
    and I will raise him on the last day.
For my flesh is true food,
    and my blood is true drink.
Whoever eats my flesh and drinks my
    blood
    remains in me and I in him.
Just as the living Father sent me
    and I have life because of the Father,
    so also the one who feeds on me
    will have life because of me.
This is the bread that came down from
    heaven.
Unlike your ancestors who ate and still
    died,
    whoever eats this bread will live
        forever."

Reflecting on the Gospel

"How can this man give us [his] flesh to eat?" One's sympathies easily go with the people who ask this question in today's gospel, struggling to understand what Jesus meant by offering as "bread" his "flesh for the life of the world." Elsewhere in Scripture, eating flesh carries a very negative connotation. "Devouring flesh" is the action of evildoers from which the psalmist prays to be delivered (Ps 27:2). Drinking blood is forbidden because the life is in the blood, over which only God has power (Gen 9:4; Deut 12:23; Acts 15:20).

Coupled with the first reading, we can see in John's Gospel clear parallels between Jesus and Woman Wisdom. She prepares her meat and wine and sets her table and calls out to all to come and partake. She offers instruction to the simple and understanding that leads to life. Likewise, in the prologue (John 1:1-18) there are other unmistakable parallels between the Logos and Wisdom, who existed with God from the beginning (Prov 8:27; Wis 9:9 // John 1:1), "pitched her tent" among humankind (see Sir 24:4, 8 // John 1:14), lights the path for them (Bar 4:2 // John 1:4-5), and yet suffers rejection (Prov 1:25, 29-31 // John 1:11).

It is in this likeness to a woman that we may find one way to understand Jesus's words in John 6:51-58. Just as a mother gives her very flesh and blood to nurture a new life carried within her and then continues to feed the child from her own body after it is born, so Jesus nourishes with his very self all who are birthed to new life through him (John 3:3). Evoking at least subtly the union of mother and child while the latter dwells in the womb, Jesus promises, "Whoever eats my flesh and drinks my blood remains in me and I in him" (John 6:56). The life that results is eternal (6:54, 58) and for the whole world (6:51). The mystery of how this life will last forever is also expressed by the Fourth Evangelist in a birthing metaphor when at the Last Supper Jesus likens his coming passion to the pangs of a woman in labor (John 16:21). The death of his earthly body is the birth to new life for all.

Some of the medieval mystics also found the image of motherhood a help for understanding the mystery of Jesus giving us his flesh to eat and his blood to drink. Julian of Norwich spoke of "God-all wisdom" as "our natural mother" and elaborated on how "a mother can give her child milk to suck, but our precious mother, Jesus, can feed us with himself. He does so most courteously and most tenderly, with the Blessed Sacrament, which is the precious food of true life."

Our response to the One who gives his flesh and blood for our life and that of the world is not only intellectual assent. Jesus gives his "flesh and blood," an expression that connotes the whole person. So we entrust our whole selves to him, body, mind, and spirit, expressed in our physical partaking of the eucharistic body and blood.

Preparing to Proclaim

Key words and phrases: "For my flesh is true food, and my blood is true drink."

To the point: Here the hard part is made clear: Jesus's listeners start to quarrel at the tension introduced by all this talk of eating his body and drinking his blood. This is not normal, not what they expected from this preacher. But Jesus's insistence makes one thing clear: this God-made-flesh loves us wildly. He wants to be so close to us that he offers himself up with radical humility to be *eaten*. In eating the body of Christ we transcend the barriers of our bodies and are able to take him up into ourselves. We become more like Jesus as we are unified to him and we carry him to the world in an astonishingly real and concentrated way. We become "living tabernacles," holy places for Jesus to repose—and for Jesus to go to work. We, in receiving the body of Christ, become the body of Christ, called to continue his mission on earth.

Psalmist Preparation

This week you will again sing the great eucharistic Psalm 34, reiterating the continued discourses on the Eucharist we hear in the gospels. As you prepare to proclaim this psalm, spend some time reflecting on your relationship with the Eucharist. How did it start? Were you a child receiving your first Communion? Were you an adult convert partaking at the Easter Vigil? Think about what the Eucharist meant to you then, what it means to you now, and the journey you have taken in between. Have you had any particularly powerful moments with the Eucharist, where Christ's presence felt plain? Have you had times where participation felt rote and you received out of obedience and trust without really feeling much of anything? Bring gratitude for your eucharistic story—the highs and the lows—into your proclamation of the psalm this week.

Making Connections

Between the readings: The first reading gives us the ancient feminine characterization of Wisdom preparing a banquet and spreading her invitation far and wide. The eucharistic overtones are clear, especially when we remember that "Wisdom of God" is one of the church's ancient titles for Jesus. When we partake in Wisdom's feast we are granted participation in wisdom, growing in understanding and forsaking foolishness. When we partake in the feast that Jesus offers we have life through him, growing in his virtue and forsaking the sin that keeps us from him.

To experience: That Jesus gives himself to us as food speaks to our utter need for him. We can tend to think of our spiritual needs as optional, nice to have, not really needs at all. But food is not an optional add-on to our lives; it is one of the very basic needs that keep us running. Participation in liturgy is not one extracurricular among many; it is the very basic fulfillment of our spiritual needs.

Homily Points

• Receiving the Eucharist draws us closer together as a community of faith—in this life and in the next. Jesus calls us to eternal life with God through two of the most basic and satisfying human actions: eating and drinking. Jesus did not put everlasting hope out of human reach. The Son of God wants us to dwell with him at the right hand of God for the rest of time. The bread and wine that we receive in the Eucharist—the body and blood of Christ—nourish us for the ultimate journey. As we continue to make our way through the Bread of Life discourse, let us be grateful for Jesus Christ the living bread that came down from heaven and gave of his very self for the life of the world.

• Today's first reading presents a feminine image of the wisdom of God. While limited, images of the divine help us relate to God individually and as communities. The image of God as Father is the dominant image in a lot of church; however, "Father" is not the only acceptable image of God. One could argue it is problematic if a masculine image is one of the only ways people encounter God in church or prayer. It could be too easy to start to think that only men can reflect the image of God. We know this is not true.

• The language and images we use for God should reflect the expansiveness of the divine—which includes the fullness of femaleness. It is important that we experience feminine images of God. These images further expand our engagement with the mystery of God and deepen a theology that affirms God created males and females equally.

CELEBRATION

Model Penitential Act

Presider: In today's first reading, Lady Wisdom calls on the people to forsake foolishness in order to advance in the way of understanding. For the times we have acted foolishly and caused harm to ourselves or others, let us ask God for mercy . . . *[pause]*

Lord Jesus, you are the living bread that came down from heaven: Lord, have mercy.

Christ Jesus, you were sent by God to save your people: Christ, have mercy.

Lord Jesus, you promise eternal life to those who eat the bread you offer: Lord, have mercy.

Model Universal Prayer (Prayer of the Faithful)

Presider: Jesus calls us to be a church that listens to and prays for the needs of the world. Let us place our petitions before the Lord.

Response: Lord, hear our prayer.

Imbue lay and ordained leaders of the church with your spirit of wisdom . . .

Grant persistence and a listening spirit to journalists seeking to uncover truths about the world . . .

Give safety and peace to victims of sex trafficking . . .

Fill with joy those who seek you in the single vocation in our community . . .

Presider: God of Wisdom, you empower each of us to proclaim the good news of Christ Jesus your Son. Hear our prayers that with faith and hope we might follow in the way of Jesus to everlasting life. We ask this through Christ our Lord. **Amen.**

Liturgy and Music

You are what you eat. Another way of putting that is, "what you put in is what comes out." Our bodies depend on the food we eat to extract the essential nutrients in order to function. Deficiencies or too much of the wrong food can lead to malnutrition, disease, and maybe even death. Likewise, what we feed our mind, our soul, our spirit, will impact and influence how we think, feel, and behave. If we expose ourselves and ingest godly things, then we are more likely to develop a godly character. The reverse is also true.

We have a responsibility as music ministers to serve "healthy" music at our liturgies, music that meets the three judgments: that it be liturgical, pastoral, and musical, as stated in the church document *Sing to the Lord*. Especially in this era of multiculturalism, an additional consideration should be added, a cultural judgment. We ought to consider the community in which we find ourselves, and what music will resonate with them most. *Sing to the Lord* also states that pastoral musicians should be "sensitive to the cultural and spiritual milieu of their [community]" (73).

We need to be mindful what it is that we offer musically to the communities that we serve. After all, you are what you eat.

Consider using "Communion Song," a communion antiphon from the collection *Honey from the Rock* (GIA). Its text is from John 6, today's gospel: "Whoever eats my flesh and drinks my blood . . ."

Scan to listen to "Communion Song."

COLLECT

Let us pray.

Pause for silent prayer

O God, who have prepared for those who love you
good things which no eye can see,
fill our hearts, we pray, with the warmth of your love,
so that, loving you in all things and above all things,
we may attain your promises,
which surpass every human desire.
Through our Lord Jesus Christ, your Son,
who lives and reigns with you in the unity of the Holy Spirit,
God, for ever and ever. **Amen.**

FIRST READING

Prov 9:1-6

Wisdom has built her house,
    she has set up her seven columns;
she has dressed her meat, mixed her wine,
    yes, she has spread her table.
She has sent out her maidens; she calls
    from the heights out over the city:
"Let whoever is simple turn in here;
    To the one who lacks understanding,
        she says,
Come, eat of my food,
    and drink of the wine I have mixed!
Forsake foolishness that you may live;
    advance in the way of understanding."

RESPONSORIAL PSALM

Ps 34:2-3, 4-5, 6-7

℟. (9a) Taste and see the goodness of the
Lord.

I will bless the Lord at all times;
  his praise shall be ever in my mouth.
Let my soul glory in the Lord;
  the lowly will hear me and be glad.

℟. Taste and see the goodness of the Lord.

Glorify the Lord with me,
  let us together extol his name.
I sought the Lord, and he answered me
  and delivered me from all my fears.

℟. Taste and see the goodness of the Lord.

Look to him that you may be radiant with
  joy,
  and your faces may not blush with
    shame.
When the poor one called out, the Lord
  heard,
  and from all his distress he saved him.

℟. Taste and see the goodness of the Lord.

SECOND READING

Eph 5:15-20

Brothers and sisters:
Watch carefully how you live,
  not as foolish persons but as wise,
  making the most of the opportunity,
  because the days are evil.
Therefore, do not continue in ignorance,
  but try to understand what is the will
    of the Lord.
And do not get drunk on wine, in which
  lies debauchery,
  but be filled with the Spirit,
  addressing one another in psalms and
    hymns and spiritual songs,
  singing and playing to the Lord in your
    hearts,
  giving thanks always and for
    everything
in the name of our Lord Jesus Christ to
  God the Father.

Living Liturgy

Liturgy and Spirituality: In the readings for this week, we hear a call to live wisely. But what does it mean to be wise? If knowledge is the accumulation of information, wisdom can be thought of as information powered by intention. When a person is wise, they see a forest where others see only individual trees. The wise person is discerning. They are open to continuous learning, but hold in a special way the information that pushes them toward a larger goal.

In the first reading, we are given the image of Wisdom building a house, preparing a feast, sending out servants, and issuing a grand invitation: Come to me, all who are searching! Wisdom offers us sustenance and direction. The second reading from Ephesians provides more concrete direction on what it means to live wisely. Here, wisdom lived out looks like seeking to understand the will of God and not being wasteful or not engaging in "debauchery," but uplifting and glorifying God. In the gospel reading, Jesus tells the many followers gathered around him that in order to live forever, they must partake of the bread of life. With all of this spiritual context, then, what is wisdom?

Wisdom, it seems, requires us to be receptive. We must tap into a source that is larger than ourselves. We need to be humble enough to show up to the places where we can receive the sustenance we need. Is that church? Is it the forest? Is that therapy? Is that a simple dinner table with our family members present? The source of wisdom will likely look different for each person, and we owe it to ourselves and to God to seek it out. Once we find the wisdom God intends for us, we must use it to satisfy a greater end than our own indulgence. True wisdom will empower us to build up God's kingdom and God's people, not our own egos or agendas.

PROMPTS FOR FAITH-SHARING

• The Eucharist is a gift from a God who loves us wildly and wants to be close to us. How do you experience that love both within and outside of liturgy?

• When we receive the Eucharist we carry Jesus within us and are called to continue his mission on earth. How can your actions beyond the liturgy make Jesus's presence more visible in the world?

• Have you had any particularly poignant moments of eucharistic participation, where Christ's presence felt clear and obvious and joyful? Talk about them here.

*See Appendix B, p. 313,
for additional prompts.*

SPIRITUALITY

GOSPEL ACCLAMATION
John 6:63c, 68c

℟. Alleluia, alleluia.
Your words, Lord, are Spirit and life;
you have the words of everlasting life.
℟. Alleluia, alleluia.

Gospel

John 6:60-69; L122B

Many of Jesus' disciples who
    were listening said,
  "This saying is hard; who can
      accept it?"
Since Jesus knew that his
    disciples were murmuring
    about this,
  he said to them, "Does this
      shock you?
What if you were to see the Son
    of Man ascending
  to where he was before?
It is the spirit that gives life,
  while the flesh is of no avail.
The words I have spoken to you are
    Spirit and life.
But there are some of you who do not
    believe."
Jesus knew from the beginning the
    ones who would not believe
  and the one who would betray him.
And he said,
  "For this reason I have told you that
      no one can come to me
  unless it is granted him by my
      Father."

As a result of this,
  many of his disciples returned to
      their former way of life
  and no longer accompanied him.
Jesus then said to the Twelve, "Do you
    also want to leave?"
Simon Peter answered him, "Master, to
    whom shall we go?
You have the words of eternal life.
We have come to believe
  and are convinced that you are the
      Holy One of God."

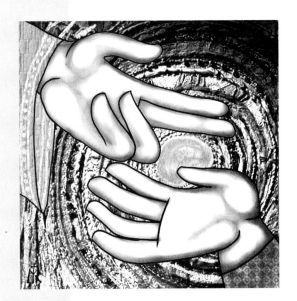

Reflecting on the Gospel

The commitment to be bound to another person for life is never made once and for all; it must be renewed again and again. This is true not only of our interpersonal commitments, like marriage, but also in our commitment to God. At certain moments, we must recommit ourselves rather than simply drift along.

In the first reading, Joshua calls together all the tribes of Israel and their leaders. Joshua puts the choice before them: either to serve the Lord who brought them out of slavery in Egypt, who performed great miracles before their eyes, and who protected them all along the journey; or serve the other gods of the land in which they dwelled. It seems impossible and illogical to make any other choice than to respond wholeheartedly to God, who had begun the relationship with such extraordinary saving acts. Joshua leads the way by declaring that he and his household will serve God alone.

A similar choice is set before the disciples of Jesus in today's gospel. The decision is whether to believe in the One whose words are "Spirit and life." The setting is the aftermath of Jesus's feeding of the multitude and Jesus's invitation to eat his flesh and drink his blood. Unlike the first reading, the choice here is not so evident and logical. The disciples say, "This saying is hard; who can accept it?" What Jesus asks of them is shocking, as he himself recognizes. It includes a mysterious element of gift that is inexplicable, like the fact that we can never fully or logically explain why we would choose to spend our whole life with another when such a commitment is bound to entail great difficulties. Love and the gracious gift of God are often all we can offer to explain such a choice.

Hard choices must also be made when we face changed circumstances. Sometimes commitments once made have to be reevaluated. One such example was when former president Jimmy Carter made the painful decision in 2000 to break his ties with the Southern Baptist Convention because they insisted on the subservience of women to men and barred women from serving as deacons, pastors, and chaplains in the military service. After belonging to this denomination for six decades, this was no easy choice.

The second reading today invites us to reexamine patterns of relationship that can cause harm rather than fostering greater love. This segment of Ephesians begins by exhorting the mutual subordination of husbands and wives to one another out of reverence for Christ, but then elaborates only one direction of the relationship: the responsibilities of husbands and the subservience of wives to them. It is often used to reinforce male domination over women. Yet the model presented to husbands is that of Christ's complete self-sacrificing love for the church. If husbands exercised such self-surrender in love toward their wives, it would result in the dismantling of structures of male domination and would initiate a whole new pattern of mutual respect and self-giving love.

Preparing to Proclaim

Key words and phrases: "[M]any of his disciples . . . no longer accompanied him."

To the point: In this gospel, Jesus's followers make a choice. Faced with teachings they find difficult, many who have followed him turn back, resuming the ordinary lives they lived before they were inspired to follow him. This can be a little disheartening; these are people who were lucky enough to live at the time of Jesus, hear his preaching, and witness his miracles. Surely his earthly presence with all its compassion and wisdom and power would have stirred a great deal of loyalty. But many heard his words, followed for a while, and turned back when they encountered something they could not understand. What hope is there for us, who do not have the same privilege of witnessing Jesus's human life? If nothing else, this reading can reassure us that following Jesus is *hard* sometimes. Its rewards are not always immediate or obvious. It takes a choice—in fact, a series of ongoing choices—to stay committed to this life.

Psalmist Preparation

This psalm comes in response to the first reading, where the Israelites have recounted the wonders God has wrought on their behalf. It is a psalm of gratitude and awe, an affirmation that God is deeply and abundantly good. It is also an invitation; the refrain invites two of our bodily senses to partake in God's gifts. God is not something to be passively observed but someone with whom relationship calls for a fully immersive experience. This culminates, of course, in the Eucharist, where we do literally taste and see God. As you prepare to proclaim this psalm, name some of the wonders God has wrought in your own life. Immerse yourself in memories of times you have known God's goodness fully. Bring gratitude for these times into your proclamation.

Making Connections

Between the readings: The first reading foreshadows the gospel; the people of Israel are given the choice to abandon God. But like Peter, they have experienced something true and good and beautiful in following this God, so they choose to recommit. In both cases, this is a response not of mere obedience but of wonder and gratitude at all that God has done for them.

To experience: There are only a few moments when we officially choose to follow Christ; most of the time, the life of discipleship is made up of smaller choices. Every day brings countless opportunities to recommit our hearts and actions to Jesus. This can seem overwhelming at times, but it is also hopeful—it is never too late to change course, to make new choices, and to turn toward the God who gives us all things.

Homily Points

• Can you accept the hard truths of Jesus's teachings? Do you want to leave? Or will you stick it out with faith that Jesus is indeed the Holy One of God and trust that his words of eternal life will bear fruit? These are the difficult questions facing the disciples in today's gospel—and continue to prompt disciples of the present day. Jesus's teachings are not for the faint of heart. Resurrection does not happen without suffering and death. The way of the cross is totally countercultural. It requires leaving behind the comforts of daily life and putting the needs of others first.

• Jesus recognizes how bizarre his teachings may seem from a purely human perspective—but he refuses to sugarcoat the gospel. The Son of God came into the world to preach the words of Spirit and life. He leaves it up to the people to make a choice: stay or leave.

• Today's second reading from the Letter to the Ephesians can be off-putting to hear in our current day. The traditional patriarchal marriage about which Paul writes stands in contrast to today's efforts for gender equality. Let us try to put aside the problematic gender issues for a moment and consider what wisdom we can glean from this reading. Paul compares the mystery of love expressed in marriage with the love Jesus has for his church. Both kinds of love are called to be sacrificial and self-giving. This type of love can transform individuals and the communities of which they are a part.

Model Penitential Act

Presider: Let us pause to reflect on the many ways we encounter the Son of God in the world today. Let us also call to mind the times we have failed to honor the divine presence and ask for mercy . . . *[pause]*

Lord Jesus, you came into this world out of love for creation: Lord, have mercy.

Christ Jesus, you come into our lives to show us the way: Christ, have mercy.

Lord Jesus: you will come again to bring peace to all: Lord, have mercy.

Model Universal Prayer (Prayer of the Faithful)

Presider: Let us place our petitions before the Lord with faith that God listens to our prayers and cares for our needs.

Response: Lord, hear our prayer.

Grant all Christians the awareness and courage to claim their baptismal authority for the strengthening of the church . . .

Deliver our communities from the sins of the patriarchy . . .

Grant safety and communal support to people in abusive relationships . . .

Bless with good health and happiness the many households in our communities who serve the Lord . . .

Presider: Creator God, you breathed new life into the world through the sending of your Son and Spirit. Receive our prayers that we might be drawn out into the world to share your love with everyone we meet. We ask this through Christ our Lord. **Amen.**

Liturgy and Music

Life is full of choices. Once we become adults, we find there are even more decisions that we are required to make. What to have for breakfast or dinner, what job to take, what time to get up in the morning, where to go for vacation, and even who to date or to marry. These kinds of decisions can be either very mundane or extremely consequential.

In the blues tradition, decisions such as these are referred to as "the crossroads." The term refers to a choice legendary blues guitarist Robert Johnson was faced with when he found himself at the crossroads of Route 49 and 61. It is there, legend has it, that Johnson made a deal with the devil, selling his soul in exchange for the ability to play the guitar exceptionally well.

In the first reading Joshua puts forth to the people the decision to follow the Egyptian gods, the gods of the Amorites, or the Lord. In the gospel, Jesus gives the crowd of followers (including his twelve disciples) the opportunity to follow him. Many chose to return to their former lives instead. We, too, face choices in our ministry—what music to select, whose advice to follow in difficult situations, and what authoritative voice to follow in church. As we endeavor to choose, when deciding, let us be sure that the voice we follow is the voice of the Lord.

COLLECT

Let us pray.

Pause for silent prayer

O God, who cause the minds of the faithful
to unite in a single purpose,
grant your people to love what you
  command
and to desire what you promise,
that, amid the uncertainties of this world,
our hearts may be fixed on that place
where true gladness is found.
Through our Lord Jesus Christ, your Son,
who lives and reigns with you in the unity
  of the Holy Spirit,
God, for ever and ever. **Amen.**

FIRST READING

Josh 24:1-2a, 15-17, 18b

Joshua gathered together all the tribes of
  Israel at Shechem,
 summoning their elders, their leaders,
  their judges, and their officers.
When they stood in ranks before God,
 Joshua addressed all the people:
  "If it does not please you to serve the
   Lord,
  decide today whom you will serve,
  the gods your fathers served beyond the
   River
  or the gods of the Amorites in whose
   country you are now dwelling.
As for me and my household, we will
  serve the Lord."

But the people answered,
 "Far be it from us to forsake the Lord
  for the service of other gods.
For it was the Lord, our God,
 who brought us and our fathers up out
  of the land of Egypt,
 out of a state of slavery.
He performed those great miracles before
  our very eyes
 and protected us along our entire
  journey
 and among the peoples through whom
  we passed.
Therefore we also will serve the Lord, for
  he is our God."

RESPONSORIAL PSALM

Ps 34:2-3, 16-17, 18-19, 20-21

℟. (9a) Taste and see the goodness of the
  Lord.

I will bless the Lord at all times;
 his praise shall be ever in my mouth.
Let my soul glory in the Lord;
 the lowly will hear me and be glad.

℟. Taste and see the goodness of the Lord.

The LORD has eyes for the just,
and ears for their cry.
The LORD confronts the evildoers,
to destroy remembrance of them from
the earth.

℟. Taste and see the goodness of the Lord.

When the just cry out, the LORD hears them,
and from all their distress he rescues
them.
The LORD is close to the brokenhearted;
and those who are crushed in spirit he
saves.

℟. Taste and see the goodness of the Lord.

Many are the troubles of the just one,
but out of them all the LORD delivers him;
he watches over all his bones;
not one of them shall be broken.

℟. Taste and see the goodness of the Lord.

SECOND READING
Eph 5:21-32

Brothers and sisters:
Be subordinate to one another out of
reverence for Christ.
Wives should be subordinate to their
husbands as to the Lord.
For the husband is head of his wife
just as Christ is head of the church,
he himself the savior of the body.
As the church is subordinate to Christ,
so wives should be subordinate to their
husbands in everything.
Husbands, love your wives,
even as Christ loved the church
and handed himself over for her to
sanctify her,
cleansing her by the bath of water with
the word,
that he might present to himself the
church in splendor,
without spot or wrinkle or any such thing,
that she might be holy and without
blemish.
So also husbands should love their wives
as their own bodies.
He who loves his wife loves himself.
For no one hates his own flesh
but rather nourishes and cherishes it,
even as Christ does the church,
because we are members of his body.
*For this reason a man shall leave his father
and his mother
and be joined to his wife,
and the two shall become one flesh.*
This is a great mystery,
but I speak in reference to Christ and
the church.

or Eph 5:2a, 25-32 in Appendix A, p. 305.

✝ CATECHESIS

Living Liturgy

Liturgy and Spirituality: The bread of life discourse Jesus addresses to the disciples is met with many challenging feelings, so much so that a number of people choose to walk away. They cannot understand or abide these teachings. The ones who walk away do not understand who Jesus is to be able to offer such confounding teachings to them, teachings that seem to buck against Jewish tradition. How do we, as a church, respond when faced with ideas that confound or confuse us?

The temptation to disengage, to cancel, to walk away is strong and understandable, but does not satisfy the dreams of true communion that God wishes for us. If one feels that another has misguided beliefs, there is a tendency to want to vote them off the island—to revoke endorsements, to terminate contracts, to deny participation in church life. Feeling called to protect and defend truth can make that impulse seem justifiable. If one feels wronged or ignored in interactions with the church and her members, there is a tendency to walk away and never look back. Nina Simone's words certainly ring true: "You've got to learn to leave the table / When love's no longer being served." Removing oneself from harmful environments to protect personal peace and mental health is wise and courageous. For most of us, though, just because the "eject" button is closest and easiest does not necessarily mean it is best.

When Peter is asked if he too will walk away from Jesus, he asks, "To whom shall we go?" Let us ask ourselves and each other: Where will we go if we walk away from this community? Where will others go if we dismiss them? If we believe that Jesus's words are in fact the way to eternal life, we ought to look for ways to keep all people close to Christ. Jesus invited all people to come together and break bread—not because of their perfection, but because we must come together in order to know, to teach, and to learn from each other. And to love each other. There are times when it is wise to love from a distance, but those times are not as frequent as we think. Let us keep one another close. Let us commit to approaching each other with humility and listening to each other with grace so that we can break bread together in loving harmony, as Jesus intended.

PROMPTS FOR FAITH-SHARING

• Talk about a decisive moment in your life when you committed or recommitted to following Jesus.

• How do you choose a Christian life in the midst of your everyday busyness?

• What wonders has God done for you? What inspires your gratitude to God and encourages you to stay committed when following Jesus is difficult?

See Appendix B, p. 313, for additional prompts.

SPIRITUALITY

GOSPEL ACCLAMATION
James 1:18

℟. Alleluia, alleluia.
The Father willed to give us birth by the
    word of truth
that we may be a kind of firstfruits of
    his creatures.
℟. Alleluia, alleluia.

Gospel   Mark 7:1-8, 14-15, 21-23;
L125B

When the Pharisees with some
        scribes who had come from
        Jerusalem
    gathered around Jesus,
    they observed that some of his
        disciples ate their meals
    with unclean, that is, unwashed,
        hands.
—For the Pharisees and, in fact,
    all Jews,
    do not eat without carefully
        washing their hands,
    keeping the tradition of the elders.
And on coming from the marketplace
    they do not eat without purifying
        themselves.
And there are many other things that
    they have traditionally observed,
    the purification of cups and jugs and
        kettles and beds.—
So the Pharisees and scribes questioned
    him,
    "Why do your disciples not follow the
        tradition of the elders
    but instead eat a meal with unclean
        hands?"
He responded,
    "Well did Isaiah prophesy about you
        hypocrites, as it is written:
    *This people honors me with their
        lips,*
        but their hearts are far from me;
    in vain do they worship me,
        *teaching as doctrines human
            precepts.*
You disregard God's commandment but
    cling to human tradition."

Continued in Appendix A, p. 305.

Reflecting on the Gospel

In today's gospel the Pharisees and scribes challenge Jesus, asking why his disciples don't follow the practices that have been handed on regarding ritual washing. The roots of these practices are found in Exodus 30:19; 40:12. They concern the custom of priests to wash their hands and feet before entering the tent of meeting. By the second century BCE, some Jews who were not priests had voluntarily assumed the practice of ritual washing of hands before Morning Prayer and before eating. In the gospel reading the washing extends also to the utensils for preparing the meal and to the purification of the dining couch. The Pharisees seem to presume these should be universal practices. But such observances would have been nearly impossible for peasant farmers, fishermen, and itinerants such as Jesus, given the scarcity of water and contact with dead fish and other pollutants. This "tradition of the elders" (v. 3) would have been largely defined and maintained by urban elites.

In response to the Pharisees, Jesus quotes the prophet Isaiah, exposing the disconnection between lip service and motivations of the heart. It is not only that Jesus's opponents have forgotten the true motivation for their religious practices; they have substituted humanly contrived practices for God's commandments. Jesus points toward examination of our inner motives. Our practices must flow from and reflect our profound experience of God's love and care.

It can happen, however, that originally good practices deteriorate over time into meaningless customs or, worse yet, into showy external observance. It is good to periodically examine our religious practices, assessing how well they embody God's love and how they impel us toward greater love of one another.

It is important to recognize the ways in which the heart can stray, as the ending of today's gospel emphasizes. The enumeration of vices is a typical teaching device used by Hellenistic philosophers (see also Rom 1:29-31; Gal 5:9-21). Jesus warns that it is not external observance or lack of it that determines one's relationship with God but a heart that is ever being transformed by divine love, which then becomes visible in concrete acts.

The letter of James elaborates on how our care for the most vulnerable serves as the measuring rod for how well we are putting into action the saving word that we hear. It is not enough to experience love within our hearts; love must find expression in outward deeds. And it is not only an individual recipient of a kind act who benefits from heart-motivated devotion to God; the faithful keeping of God's commandments gives far-reaching witness to others. In the reading from Deuteronomy, Moses tells the people that their observance of God's commands is not only for their benefit, but it will also cause the other nations to marvel at God's graciousness and justice.

Preparing to Proclaim

Key words and phrases: "Nothing that enters one from outside can defile that person; but the things that come out from within are what defile."

To the point: Jesus is not saying not to wash our hands before we eat—that is, in fact, a good idea. He is saying, though, that the ritual cleanliness practiced by the Pharisees and scribes is not the same as moral behavior. These things can, and often do, exist in the same person; they are not in opposition to each other. But ritual observance is not necessarily the same as a life lived with the goodness God wants for and from each of us. It is all too possible to have one without the other. We should participate in liturgy and ritual, but we cannot stop there. We need to let God accompany us not just on Sunday but throughout our everyday lives as well.

Psalmist Preparation

This psalm reiterates the gospel's message. Ritual observance is important, but by itself it does not grant access to God. God rather promises to walk with those who live their entire lives with justice, whose hearts are aligned with God's word. As you prepare this psalm, reflect on how your liturgical life is balanced with a life of service and goodness. This doesn't mean you need to spend all waking hours doing works of mercy, but it does mean they should be solidly represented in how you spend your time. Give thanks to God for the opportunities you have had to encounter him in service, or resolve to include more of these opportunities in your life.

Making Connections

Between the readings: The first reading reminds us that Jesus's rebuke to the Pharisees and scribes is not because they were following the law. The law is a good thing; it is a gift from God intended to make us more whole. But the Pharisees and scribes observed the law in a way that did not give evidence of their wisdom; they used it not to grow closer to God but to grow more self-assured. When their inward dispositions did not match their actions, their observance was no longer what God willed for them.

To experience: There are times for all of us when our inward disposition does not match what we are professing and doing at liturgy. This gospel is not meant to make us feel guilty for that; many of our emotional states are beyond our full control, and God can work with them all. The important thing is to let God work; it is when the Pharisees and scribes settle into their self-assurance that they grow stagnant and stop doing a good thing with their ritual observances.

Homily Points

• Jesus is not a fan of hypocrites. The Pharisees in today's gospel question Jesus over the actions of his disciples that appear impure and outside of religious tradition. Honoring such traditions is not in and of itself a bad thing. On the contrary, when rightly ordered, religious rituals can help draw people into their faith tradition and remind them of their responsibilities as people of God. But the Pharisees took the practices too far. They acted more like police officers than pastors in their enforcement of the practices. In their concern over unclean hands, the Pharisees decide to nitpick public action rather than examine areas in their own lives that may be unclean. So Jesus returns to the message from the prophet Isaiah who calls out people who honor God with their lips but not their hearts.

• Jesus is concerned about the inner lives of his followers. In today's gospel reading, Jesus makes clear that their internal obedience to religious law matters most. If matters of the heart are in good order, then faithful actions out in the world will follow. Discipleship is not a surface-level commitment. Those who follow in the way of Christ must be willing to open their hearts to true transformation in the Spirit.

• Today's second reading from James offers a stunning image of God's word planted in the depths of the heart. The metaphor evokes many questions for reflection: How can we tend the soil of our hearts? What needs to get weeded out so that God's word can grow deeper within us? Who in our communities can help cultivate the word alive within us?

Model Penitential Act

Presider: Our God is full of mercy and compassion. Let us pause now to call to mind our sins and ask for God's forgiveness . . . *[pause]*

Lord Jesus, you are the way to holiness: Lord, have mercy.

Christ Jesus, you are the truth that sets us free: Christ, have mercy.

Lord Jesus, you are the giver of life: Lord, have mercy.

Model Universal Prayer (Prayer of the Faithful)

Presider: With gratitude for God's presence among us, let us place before the Lord our prayers and petitions.

Response: Lord, hear our prayer.

Foster reconciliation and healing among Christians of different traditions . . .

Bless the work of teachers, school aides, and administrators, and all who educate our children . . .

Bring a swift end to the wars happening across the world and all acts of violence . . .

Be with those in our community who are grieving . . .

Presider: Generous God, you inspire disciples across generations to be people of integrity. Receive our prayers that we might be emboldened to proclaim your word to all those we meet, today and always. We ask this through Christ our Lord. **Amen.**

Liturgy and Music

It is said that those who work and preach in the fields of liturgy should have Scripture in one hand and a newspaper in the other. We are asked to both look back on tradition and forward to how tradition works itself out in contemporary life.

This weekend we sanctify the gift of labor, and we read of Jesus's radical redefinition of what contributes to the cleanliness or uncleanliness of a human being (and in doing so, throw Mosaic Law upside down).

Given that it is Labor Day weekend, let's recall Geoffrey Dearmer's text from the hymn "Those Who Love and Those Who Labor": "Lo, the Prince of common welfare dwells within the market strife! / Lo, the bread of heaven is broken in the sacrament of life" (Oxford University Press).

This beautiful intermingling of sacrament and sweat could well be a strong compass point as we prepare this liturgy, aware of all the incredibly hard (and most times unnoticed) work of farmers, union and blue-collar workers, and those in the service industry.

Jesus, in Mark's Gospel, moves to the heart of the matter, not satisfied with salvation by going through the motions. Love of God is all that matters. "Love Is His Word" by Luke Connaughton (McCrimmon Publishing) illustrates this perfectly.

Richer than gold is this wealth: wealth that sanctifies our work and holds holy, as our first commandment, the encouragement to love.

COLLECT

Let us pray.

Pause for silent prayer

God of might, giver of every good gift,
put into our hearts the love of your name,
so that, by deepening our sense of
reverence,
you may nurture in us what is good
and, by your watchful care,
keep safe what you have nurtured.
Through our Lord Jesus Christ, your Son,
who lives and reigns with you in the unity
of the Holy Spirit,
God, for ever and ever. **Amen.**

FIRST READING
Deut 4:1-2, 6-8

Moses said to the people:
"Now, Israel, hear the statutes and
decrees
which I am teaching you to observe,
that you may live, and may enter in and
take possession of the land
which the LORD, the God of your
fathers, is giving you.
In your observance of the commandments
of the LORD, your God,
which I enjoin upon you,
you shall not add to what I command
you nor subtract from it.
Observe them carefully,
for thus will you give evidence
of your wisdom and intelligence to the
nations,
who will hear of all these statutes and
say,
'This great nation is truly a wise and
intelligent people.'
For what great nation is there
that has gods so close to it as the LORD,
our God, is to us
whenever we call upon him?
Or what great nation has statutes and
decrees
that are as just as this whole law
which I am setting before you today?"

RESPONSORIAL PSALM

Ps 15:2-3, 3-4, 4-5

℟. (1a) The one who does justice will live in the presence of the Lord.

Whoever walks blamelessly and does justice;
  who thinks the truth in his heart
  and slanders not with his tongue.

℟. The one who does justice will live in the presence of the Lord.

Who harms not his fellow man,
  nor takes up a reproach against his neighbor;
by whom the reprobate is despised,
  while he honors those who fear the Lord.

℟. The one who does justice will live in the presence of the Lord.

Who lends not his money at usury
  and accepts no bribe against the innocent.
Whoever does these things
  shall never be disturbed.

℟. The one who does justice will live in the presence of the Lord.

SECOND READING

Jas 1:17-18, 21b-22, 27

Dearest brothers and sisters:
All good giving and every perfect gift is from above,
  coming down from the Father of lights,
  with whom there is no alteration or shadow caused by change.
He willed to give us birth by the word of truth
  that we may be a kind of firstfruits of his creatures.

Humbly welcome the word that has been planted in you
  and is able to save your souls.

Be doers of the word and not hearers only, deluding yourselves.

Religion that is pure and undefiled before God and the Father is this:
  to care for orphans and widows in their affliction
  and to keep oneself unstained by the world.

Living Liturgy

Liturgy and Ecumenism: There are many beautiful rituals and traditions in the Catholic faith. Our ways of worship have a way of engaging all five of the human senses, directing our attention to the glory of God. However, our ability to experience God is not limited to those gestures, expressions, and rituals. Let us remember that another beauty of our faith is our sense of universal sacramentality, the ability to see God in all things. God wants to meet us where we are, as we are—even as our traditions and expressions of reverence grow and change. If we remain open to these changes, we might also invite others to experience God in deeply profound ways.

Planning liturgies in a high school setting has shown me how beautiful it can be to listen to and collaborate with the Holy Spirit moving through the students, inspiring new traditions. Many of the students at my school are not Catholic, but they experience God's love in real and lasting ways at Mass when they see a praise dance offered prayerfully by their peers. The music we use during liturgies might not be considered "traditional" in some circles, but more students participate with full heart and voice in the liturgy when they hear music from Black gospel artists. This matters because the gospel story we hear today indicates that our faith is not meant to be static if that means closing the door on potential seekers of God.

PROMPTS FOR FAITH-SHARING

- What in your heart could you invite God to cleanse?

- What holds you back from full and wholehearted participation in liturgy?

- How is your Sunday-church-self congruent (or not) with who you are the rest of the week?

See Appendix B, p. 313, for additional prompts.

SPIRITUALITY

GOSPEL ACCLAMATION
cf. Matt 4:23

R℣. Alleluia, alleluia.
Jesus proclaimed the Gospel of the
    kingdom
and cured every disease among the
    people.
R℣. Alleluia, alleluia.

Gospel

Mark 7:31-37; L128B

Again Jesus left the district of
    Tyre
    and went by way of Sidon to
        the Sea of Galilee,
    into the district of the
        Decapolis.
And people brought to him a
    deaf man who had a speech
    impediment
    and begged him to lay his
        hand on him.
He took him off by himself away from
    the crowd.
He put his finger into the man's ears
    and, spitting, touched his tongue;
    then he looked up to heaven and
        groaned, and said to him,
    "Ephphatha!"—that is, "Be
        opened!"—
And immediately the man's ears were
    opened,
    his speech impediment was removed,
    and he spoke plainly.
He ordered them not to tell anyone.
But the more he ordered them not to,
    the more they proclaimed it.
They were exceedingly astonished and
    they said,
    "He has done all things well.
He makes the deaf hear and the mute
    speak."

Reflecting on the Gospel

Even without a hearing impairment, hearing someone speaking to us in the midst of a noisy crowd can be a challenge. In today's gospel, people bring to Jesus a man with a hearing and speech impediment and beg him to lay his hand on him. The first thing Jesus does is take the man away from the crowd. When the man's hearing is restored, the first voice he will hear is that of Jesus,

inviting him to greater openness. Jesus draws close to the man and then touches him. Using the same techniques as other healers, he touches the man's ears and tongue, and pronounces a word that Mark preserves in Aramaic: "'Ephphatha!'—that is, 'Be opened!'" We follow the pattern today with our sacraments, using not only words but also physical touch, and the tangible signs of oil, water, bread, and wine, which have power to transform. Jesus uses spittle on the man's tongue. In antiquity, spitting was thought to ward off evil spirits. But Jesus's power is not magical. Rather, he looks up to heaven to acknowledge the divine origin of his power and directs the onlookers to God as well. Through Jesus's power the man's ears are opened and his speech becomes clear. What the man says Mark does not tell us.

The crowd, meanwhile, becomes even more vociferous, proclaiming with astonishment the marvels Jesus is doing. Jesus orders them to be silent, but they do not heed him. It is a bit ironic that as Jesus enables a man with garbled speech to speak plainly, at the same time he enjoins silence on the babbling crowd. The crowd is focused on the flashy signs of the inbreaking of God's reign, such as Isaiah foretells in the first reading for this Sunday. But the crowd misses the deeper meaning of what the signs signify. Jesus is not a showy miracle worker. Unless one becomes open to a deeper encounter with Jesus as the crucified and risen One, and to being transformed into his image, one cannot fully proclaim the mystery of the good news he brings.

The physical ability to hear is not necessary for such an encounter with Christ; nor is the physical ability to speak necessary to proclaim the word of God. It is openness of mind, heart, and spirit to the breath of God within and without, and the willingness to respond wholeheartedly that are essential. In the second reading, it is clear that openness to God also results in our openness to others, especially those who are poor. James insists that all should be given the same welcome. There should be no partiality (prosopolempsia, literally, "lifting up of the face"), because when we display favoritism, it is generally toward the rich. When God, however, "shows no partiality" (Acts 10:34; Rom 2:11), it concerns God's graciousness that extends to all—Jew and Greek alike. When it comes to those who are poor, all through the Scriptures God is shown to be like a mother who loves all her children equally but shows partiality to the one who is most needy.

Preparing to Proclaim

Key words and phrases: " '*Ephphatha!*'—that is, 'Be opened!' "

To the point: Jesus's healing work often involves opening what is closed. Here it is ears and tongue—ears that are closed to the sounds of music and laughter and conversation, tongue that closes its owner off from communicating clearly. Jesus opens these, enabling the deaf man to hear and to speak, entering more fully into the dialogues that surround him. Elsewhere it is eyes; in curing blindness, Jesus opens eyes that once were closed. Jesus opens many other closures, too. Sometimes it is spiritual blindness, opening the eyes of our hearts through his teaching and preaching. Doors can be closed, and Jesus opens them, offering a way where there was none before. Hearts can be closed, unable to change or grow or connect, and Jesus can open them, willing us into life that is deeper and fuller and more vibrant and more joyful.

Psalmist Preparation

This psalm's antiphon commands our souls to offer praise to the God who offers us everything. The verses recount all the healing work that God has done and continues to do. As you prepare to proclaim this psalm, try to recount times that God has offered healing in your own life. When has God fed your hunger or freed you from some sort of captivity? When has God opened your eyes or been as a loving parent to you? Offer gratitude and praise for these times, and bring this to your proclamation of the psalm this week.

Making Connections

Between the readings: In the first reading we have Isaiah giving us the vision that Jesus is fulfilling in the gospel. When the gospel's deaf man encounters Christ, he becomes a fulfillment of this prophecy. The pairing of these readings reminds us that each of Jesus's miracles is part of a bigger project, the project of restoring creation to the wholeness God intended for it. But this big sweeping project, a work still in progress, is also made up of individuals like the deaf man—people whose stories and lives are changed by their encounter with Christ.

To experience: The Rite of Baptism includes an *Ephphatha* rite; the celebrant blesses the ears and mouth of the newly baptized and prays that their ears and mouth be open and able to receive and preach God's word. Baptism is the sacrament of salvation, opening the way once closed by sin. Jesus's healing work is for all of us, even those untouched by physical disability.

Homily Points

• Let us cling to the hope of the prophet Isaiah, who is utterly convinced that God will save God's beloved people. The prophet preaches a truth that frankly can be difficult to believe at times: that God will transform our hurting, broken world. There is so much suffering and sin around us. Racism, sexism, homophobia, ableism, classism, the climate crisis, and too many other harmful realities plague our communities. At times it can feel like healing will never come. Still, Isaiah encourages the faithful then and now to keep going. Keep persisting. Keep believing that God will make all things whole again someday.

• In today's gospel, the crowds bring to Jesus a man who is deaf and has a speech impediment. Let us consider for a moment this man's predicament. Being unable to hear or speak properly put this man at an extreme disadvantage in first-century society where people primarily communicated through spoken word. Some in the crowd brought this man to Jesus and begged him for a cure. Jesus heals the man in an unusual way—by touching his tongue, sticking his finger in the man's ear, and crying out "*Ephphatha!* . . . Be opened!" This message is meant for the deaf man and for all of us. Jesus tells us to be open to God's calling, to the work of healing, to caring for our neighbors in need.

• Where might Jesus be calling you to open your heart this week? What areas of your life need Christ's healing touch?

Model Penitential Act

Presider: The Lord longs to forgive our sins. Let us call to mind the times we have done harm to ourselves or others and ask God for mercy . . . *[pause]*

Lord Jesus, you shine brightly for all to see: Lord, have mercy.

Christ Jesus, you open the ears of the man who was deaf: Christ, have mercy.

Lord Jesus, you raise up all who have died to everlasting life in heaven: Lord, have mercy.

Model Universal Prayer (Prayer of the Faithful)

Presider: With faith in Christ's unending presence in our lives, let us offer our prayers and petitions to the Lord.

Response: Lord, hear our prayer.

Make our churches into accessible spaces of belonging for people with disabilities . . .

Inspire legislators to enact laws that ensure adequate housing and healthcare for all . . .

Lay your healing touch upon people recovering in hospitals and care facilities . . .

Give our community courage to preach the prophetic word of Christ . . .

Presider: Faithful God, you sent your Son into the world to heal the sick and teach the sinful. Hear our prayers that we might listen to the living word of Jesus and allow our hearts to be transformed by his saving power. We ask this through Christ our Lord. **Amen.**

Liturgy and Music

For a sense as fundamental as is vision, you'd think it would have a straightforward definition. But that very foundation allows it to be used in so many ways: "see an object," "see what the point is," "see with new eyes." Even the psalmist offers a challenge, to use our sense of taste to see (Ps 34). So too with blindness: it is not mere visual encounters that we might be missing, whether our eyes work correctly or not.

Over the past few months, our parish sponsored a course designed to open eyes and hearts to the aftermath of systems of slavery, class oppression, cultural genocide, and racism. What we found was a different vision, a dropping of scales from our eyes. As Shirley Erena Murray wrote: "For everyone born, a place at the table, for everyone born, clean water and bread, a shelter, a space, a safe place for growing, for everyone born, a star overhead, . . . yes, God will delight when we are creators of justice, justice and joy!" ("For Everyone Born," words © 1998 Hope Publishing Company, www.hopepublishing .com. All rights reserved. Used by permission.).

Today's readings are about how we see things: how our eyes need to be opened, how we should not fear this opening, how we allow justice to speak to our hearts, and how we allow our Savior, through the Eucharist, to affect our worldly vision, too. From my own take on Psalm 34: "Taste, that your eyes may be opened! Drink that your heart may be healed! / Joyful the feast that beckons you in love—the body and the blood of the Lord!" (Steven C. Warner, copyright © 2020 GIA Publications, Inc.).

COLLECT

Let us pray.

Pause for silent prayer

O God, by whom we are redeemed and
	receive adoption,
look graciously upon your beloved sons
	and daughters,
that those who believe in Christ
may receive true freedom
and an everlasting inheritance.
Through our Lord Jesus Christ, your Son,
who lives and reigns with you in the unity
	of the Holy Spirit,
God, for ever and ever. **Amen.**

FIRST READING

Isa 35:4-7a

Thus says the LORD:
	Say to those whose hearts are
		frightened:
		Be strong, fear not!
	Here is your God,
		he comes with vindication;
	with divine recompense
		he comes to save you.
	Then will the eyes of the blind be
		opened,
		the ears of the deaf be cleared;
	then will the lame leap like a stag,
		then the tongue of the mute will sing.
	Streams will burst forth in the desert,
		and rivers in the steppe.
	The burning sands will become pools,
		and the thirsty ground, springs of
			water.

RESPONSORIAL PSALM
Ps 146:6-7, 8-9a, 9bc-10

℟. (1b) Praise the Lord, my soul!
or:
℟. Alleluia.

The God of Jacob keeps faith forever,
    secures justice for the oppressed,
    gives food to the hungry.
The LORD sets captives free.

℟. Praise the Lord, my soul!
or:
℟. Alleluia.

The LORD gives sight to the blind;
    the LORD raises up those who were
        bowed down.
The LORD loves the just;
    the LORD protects strangers.

℟. Praise the Lord, my soul!
or:
℟. Alleluia.

The fatherless and the widow the LORD
        sustains,
    but the way of the wicked he thwarts.
The LORD shall reign forever;
    your God, O Zion, through all
        generations.
Alleluia.

℟. Praise the Lord, my soul!
or:
℟. Alleluia.

SECOND READING
Jas 2:1-5

My brothers and sisters, show no
        partiality
    as you adhere to the faith in our
        glorious Lord Jesus Christ.
For if a man with gold rings and fine
        clothes
    comes into your assembly,
    and a poor person in shabby clothes
        also comes in,
    and you pay attention to the one
        wearing the fine clothes
    and say, "Sit here, please,"
    while you say to the poor one, "Stand
        there," or "Sit at my feet,"
    have you not made distinctions among
        yourselves
    and become judges with evil designs?

Listen, my beloved brothers and sisters.
Did not God choose those who are poor in
        the world
    to be rich in faith and heirs of the
        kingdom
    that he promised to those who love him?

Living Liturgy

Liturgy and Justice: In today's gospel reading, Jesus performs a miracle. He touches a deaf and mute man and restores his ability to hear and speak plainly. The crowds are stunned and Jesus tells them not to tell anyone. This seems puzzling—why wouldn't Jesus want the good news of this miracle to spread? Throughout the gospels, Jesus repeatedly asks for discretion or practices humility in ways that range from merely curious to downright self-damaging. We do not receive clarification on this point, but it does remind me of what happens when one individual does a charitable deed for another. Who tells the story of that exchange and for what purpose?

We live in a time when social media specialists are sought after by corporations and nonprofits. People hired for these positions are tasked with telling an engaging story about organizations and their work. This is a valuable job. It helps community members who might not be involved in the day-to-day work of these organizations stay abreast of their goings on. My favorite form of social media sharing is the *takeover*, in which someone on the inside gets to create content for the social media page. Viewers get a more candid, less staged peek into what's going on.

It is important that stories of collaboration, compassion, and charity are told without airs and by the people experiencing them. If the purpose of justice work is right relationship, then receivers of aid deserve the chance to tell their stories in their own words. Justice work is not merely giving voice to the voiceless, it's having the grace and humility to let them speak for themselves. Jesus and his disciples did not need to tell the story of the deaf and mute man because the true miracle was restoring the man's power to speak for himself. As we work for justice, let us strive to honor and bring to light that same power in those we accompany.

PROMPTS FOR FAITH-SHARING

• How has an encounter with Christ changed your life and your story?

• How have you experienced Jesus's healing presence? How do you still hope to receive it?

• Where in your life could Jesus open what is closed?

See Appendix B, p. 313, for additional prompts.

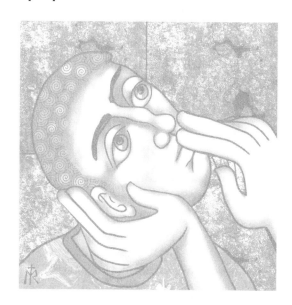

SEPTEMBER 8, 2024
TWENTY-THIRD SUNDAY IN ORDINARY TIME

SPIRITUALITY

GOSPEL ACCLAMATION
Gal 6:14

℟. Alleluia, alleluia.
May I never boast except in the cross of
    our Lord
through which the world has been
    crucified to me and I to the world.
℟. Alleluia, alleluia.

Gospel

Mark 8:27-35; L131B

**Jesus and his disciples set out
    for the villages of Caesarea
        Philippi.
Along the way he asked his
    disciples,
    "Who do people say that I am?"
They said in reply,
    "John the Baptist, others Elijah,
    still others one of the prophets."
And he asked them,
    "But who do you say that I am?"
Peter said to him in reply,
    "You are the Christ."
Then he warned them not to tell anyone
    about him.**

**He began to teach them
    that the Son of Man must suffer greatly
    and be rejected by the elders, the chief
        priests, and the scribes,
    and be killed, and rise after three days.
He spoke this openly.
Then Peter took him aside and began to
    rebuke him.
At this he turned around and, looking at
    his disciples,
    rebuked Peter and said, "Get behind
        me, Satan.
You are thinking not as God does, but as
    human beings do."**

**He summoned the crowd with his
    disciples and said to them,
    "Whoever wishes to come after me
        must deny himself,
    take up his cross, and follow me.
For whoever wishes to save his life will
    lose it,
    but whoever loses his life for my sake
    and that of the gospel will save it."**

Reflecting on the Gospel

The text of today's gospel has been sometimes understood in unhealthy and even dangerous ways by believers. Some women, for example, have endured every kind of suffering, including physical and verbal abuse from their batterers, all the while thinking that they were faithfully carrying their cross with Jesus. It's a tragic and appalling misunderstanding of the meaning of "taking up the cross." But it has been replicated and sometimes even preached in similar ways in most every corner of the globe.

While such a spirituality of the cross has enabled many people to endure great suffering and to give meaning to it, Jesus's invitation to take up one's cross actually refers to a very different kind of suffering. He is speaking to his disciples about the suffering that is likely to befall a person for being his follower. Illness or disease is not "the cross" in the sense in which Jesus speaks of it in today's gospel. There is nothing particularly Christian about this kind of suffering; it can happen to anyone. Nor is suffering that comes from abuse or injustice something that one should "take up." Jesus confronted and tried to stop that kind of suffering whenever he encountered it. The cross consists rather in the negative consequences to which Jesus's followers willingly expose themselves as the cost of being his disciples.

Hand in hand with taking up the cross is denial of self. This does not refer to ascetic acts, like giving up something you enjoy during Lent. Such practices can feed a spirituality of denial of self; but when Jesus enjoins denial of self, he speaks of a spirituality by which one chooses daily to place the common good and Christ at the center, not one's own desires. It is a free choice to live a life of ever-deepening self-surrender to love.

Just as people who commit themselves to one another for life must constantly give of themselves out of love for the other, so the love into which Jesus invites disciples is a costly one that asks more and more of us. It is a freely chosen self-surrender in love, which implies that only those who have a healthy sense of self and the freedom to choose to surrender themselves can authentically deny themselves and take up their cross. The cross of which Jesus speaks is not a suffering imposed on persons who are downtrodden.

The second reading today gives some concrete examples of this kind of costly love. If one encounters a brother or sister without adequate clothing or food or shelter, to deny oneself and take up the cross demands letting go of time and resources in self-surrender to the neediest ones. Simply talking about faith but not making it visible in concrete deeds of self-surrender is not authentic discipleship. Trying to skirt the cost of such love, as Peter did when he insisted to Jesus that the cross was not necessary, is an all-too-human way of thinking. To think as God does results in godly action, a lifelong surrender to a free and costly love.

Preparing to Proclaim
Key words and phrases: "Who do people say that I am?"

To the point: This gospel passage captures Peter in a moment of tension. He has come to understand Jesus as the Christ, as one anointed to redeem God's people. He cannot reconcile this understanding with what Jesus says about the suffering he will undergo. He does not seem to hear that Jesus gives him the end of the story; the suffering is something only to be passed through. We are often like Peter. We do everything in our power to relieve suffering, and we would rather not confront the truth that suffering is an inevitable part of every life. Relieving suffering is good—it is often the work that Christ calls us to—but it is not the end of the story. The end of every Christian's story is our sharing in the resurrection after passing through suffering like Jesus did.

Psalmist Preparation
This psalm counterbalances the first reading's predictions of Jesus's suffering. It does acknowledge his (and our) distress. The suffering is real and there's no way to go around it; we can only go through it. But it is not the end of the story, even when it seems to encompass us. God promises to take our suffering and make it life-giving. When we go with God, God can transform the struggles along the way. We are ultimately called to walk with God in the land of the living. As you prepare to proclaim this psalm, reflect on a time of suffering from your own life. If it is one that is firmly in the past, give thanks to God for bringing you through it. If it is one that is still hurting, ask God to accompany you as you journey to the other side.

Making Connections
Between the readings: The first reading is part of Isaiah's Suffering Servant passages; it foreshadows the suffering that Christ will endure in his passion. This passage highlights his acceptance of his suffering; he is able to accept it because he rests ultimately in God. We see this acceptance in the gospel; Jesus describes to his disciples the suffering that he will undergo and rebukes Peter for his inability to accept this.

To experience: Jesus's acceptance of his suffering in this gospel seems almost too easy. Mark does not reveal any emotion on his part as he speaks of his fate. But this is the same Jesus who will pray in Gethsemane for this cup to be taken away. When we are called upon to deny ourselves and take up our own crosses, it is normal to have feelings about that. Acceptance does not mean we do not struggle with the sacrifice. Jesus accompanies us in that struggle.

Homily Points
• The servant in today's first reading from Isaiah embraces God's word with his whole self. The servant proclaims that the Lord God opened his ear. He is now willing to undertake whatever God asks. In the face of suffering and persecution, the servant affirms his faith in the Lord's ability to protect and guide. No doubt his witness brought comfort to fellow exiles. The servant reminds them and us that God draws near in times of hardship. In God's presence, there is nothing we cannot do.

• Like the first reading, today's gospel recognizes the divine presence in difficult times. Jesus takes the disciples to Caesarea Philippi, where Herod the Great had erected a temple for Caesar Augustus and built shrines to pagan gods. Jesus chooses this space, with its tributes to earthly kingdoms, to teach his followers the true movements of discipleship: suffering, death, and resurrection. The disciples are understandably uncomfortable. This is not the first time Jesus talks about the cross in Mark's Gospel, but here Jesus makes clear that to follow him is to move closer to death. Resurrection is born of suffering.

• It can be difficult to believe that there is space for suffering in the coming of God's kingdom. It would of course be easier if the Son of God got rid of all pain and turmoil the first time around. Yet, God's way is not the easy way. We can hold fast to the belief that death will be defeated. Resurrection will have the final say—and in the meantime, we can draw near to God who knows both suffering and healing.

Model Penitential Act

Presider: Our God is compassionate and merciful, slow to anger and abounding in love for all of creation. Let us lean into the Lord's mercy and ask for forgiveness for our sins . . . *[pause]*

Lord Jesus, you are the Christ: Lord, have mercy.

Christ Jesus, you are the Son of the living God: Christ, have mercy.

Lord Jesus, you are the source of salvation: Lord, have mercy.

Model Universal Prayer (Prayer of the Faithful)

Presider: With faith in God's desire to heal and make whole, let us offer our prayers and petitions.

Response: Lord, hear our prayer.

Animate Christian congregations everywhere with the joy of the gospel . . .

Invigorate the work of teachers, administrators, and ministers during this new school year . . .

Keep safe all those who are in the path of severe weather and experiencing the effects of the climate crisis . . .

Prosper the hospitality and outreach efforts of our congregation . . .

Presider: Almighty God, by your generous spirit you let us see your kindness and grant us your salvation. Receive our prayers and the prayers of all the world that together we might find peace. We ask this through Christ our Lord. **Amen.**

Liturgy and Music

What abundant treasures are found in the readings for this day! We encounter Isaiah's text (one of the Suffering Servant passages)—except it's not Holy Week. The psalm instructs us, from the Hebrew הֲלָכָה, of our *halakha*—our walking with God. James's letter confronts our disposition toward faith versus good works. And then, to top it all, comes Peter's blunt (as always) confession of Jesus's identity. Where to start?

We do well to understand that our faith does not shield us from the torments and challenges of this world. We live, as the *Salve Regina* describes, in a "vale of tears." How we make this journey—how we walk through pain, how we choose to act, both in word and in deed—could well be summed up in Peter's exclamation: "You are the Christ!"

The wonderful Scotsman, Jesuit poet, and church musician James Quinn put Christ at the center of everything, weaving together the "Lorica (Breastplate) of Saint Patrick" with the beautiful Scots tune *Bunessan* in "Christ Be Beside Me" (OCP).

Our Anointed One, our Christ, is meant to be our compass point. By his own embrace of suffering he provided a road map, a *halakha*, for our day-to-day life.

COLLECT

Let us pray.

Pause for silent prayer

Look upon us, O God,
Creator and ruler of all things,
and, that we may feel the working of your mercy,
grant that we may serve you with all our heart.
Through our Lord Jesus Christ, your Son,
who lives and reigns with you in the unity of the Holy Spirit,
God, for ever and ever. **Amen.**

FIRST READING
Isa 50:4c-9a

The Lord GOD opens my ear that I may hear;
and I have not rebelled,
have not turned back.
I gave my back to those who beat me,
my cheeks to those who plucked my beard;
my face I did not shield
from buffets and spitting.

The Lord GOD is my help,
therefore I am not disgraced;
I have set my face like flint,
knowing that I shall not be put to shame.
He is near who upholds my right;
if anyone wishes to oppose me,
let us appear together.
Who disputes my right?
Let that man confront me.
See, the Lord GOD is my help;
who will prove me wrong?

RESPONSORIAL PSALM
Ps 116:1-2, 3-4, 5-6, 8-9

℟. (9) I will walk before the Lord, in the land of the living.
or:
℟. Alleluia.

I love the LORD because he has heard my voice in supplication,
because he has inclined his ear to me the day I called.

℟. I will walk before the Lord, in the land of the living.
or:
℟. Alleluia.

The cords of death encompassed me;
    the snares of the netherworld seized
        upon me;
    I fell into distress and sorrow,
and I called upon the name of the Lord,
    "O Lord, save my life!"

℟. I will walk before the Lord, in the land
    of the living.
    or:
℟. Alleluia.

Gracious is the Lord and just;
    yes, our God is merciful.
The Lord keeps the little ones;
    I was brought low, and he saved me.

℟. I will walk before the Lord, in the land
    of the living.
    or:
℟. Alleluia.

For he has freed my soul from death,
    my eyes from tears, my feet from
        stumbling.
I shall walk before the Lord
    in the land of the living.

℟. I will walk before the Lord, in the land
    of the living.
    or:
℟. Alleluia.

SECOND READING

Jas 2:14-18

What good is it, my brothers and sisters,
    if someone says he has faith but does
        not have works?
Can that faith save him?
If a brother or sister has nothing to wear
    and has no food for the day,
    and one of you says to them,
    "Go in peace, keep warm, and eat well,"
    but you do not give them the necessities
        of the body,
    what good is it?
So also faith of itself,
    if it does not have works, is dead.

Indeed someone might say,
    "You have faith and I have works."
Demonstrate your faith to me without
    works,
    and I will demonstrate my faith to you
        from my works.

Living Liturgy

Liturgy and Justice: Jesus's teaching in today's gospel reading is quite alarming. He says the Son of Man, the one set apart by God, would have to suffer many blows and indignities. Understandably, the disciples are troubled and Peter tries to convince Jesus to walk back this teaching. It just doesn't follow. Jesus has performed many miracles, has delivered people from pain, isolation, demonic possession. He has welcomed the outcast and restored dignity to those cast aside by the world. Why should all of this give way to suffering, abuse, and gruesome execution? What Jesus says to the disciples, and to us, is that striving to do justice will always have a cost. If we claim to be true followers of Christ, we cannot sit complacently and talk of that identity. It must be evident in our day-to-day actions, in the way we live our lives. We must be willing to pay the personal and societal cost, to take up our cross and truly follow Christ's footsteps.

This reading is a warning and lesson to those among us who have achieved a certain level of power and privilege. Our society rewards achievement with comfort, power with protection. In a world with so much suffering and insecurity, it is tempting to want to hold onto those things. Sometimes we even tell ourselves that the moral compromises we make are justifiable, that wanting to hold onto power and its privileges is the right thing to do because in doing so, we will have more influence and be able to enact bigger change. Christ is notably stern in addressing the disciples' fears and reservations though. He says to Peter, "Get behind me, Satan. You are thinking not as God does, but as human beings do." Can we push ourselves to see more clearly with the eyes of Christ? Can we challenge ourselves to sacrifice more than feels safe or necessary when moral questions present themselves? Can we courageously set down whatever amount of power and privilege we possess in order to take up the cross and follow Christ?

PROMPTS FOR FAITH-SHARING

• Who do you say that Jesus is? What role does Christ play in your life?

• The Christian tradition has many titles for Jesus: he is King, Savior, the Good Shepherd, the Way, the Bread of Life, and on and on. Of his many titles, which feels most relevant to your life right now?

• What sacrifices have you made in order to follow Christ? How easy is it for you to accept them?

*See Appendix B, p. 313,
for additional prompts.*

SPIRITUALITY

GOSPEL ACCLAMATION
cf. 2 Thess 2:14

R̸. Alleluia, alleluia.
God has called us through the Gospel
to possess the glory of our Lord Jesus
    Christ.
R̸. Alleluia, alleluia.

Gospel

Mark 9:30-37; L134B

Jesus and his disciples left from
    there and began a journey
    through Galilee,
but he did not wish anyone to
    know about it.
He was teaching his disciples and
    telling them,
"The Son of Man is to be
    handed over to men
and they will kill him,
and three days after his death
    the Son of Man will rise."
But they did not understand the saying,
    and they were afraid to question him.

They came to Capernaum and, once
    inside the house,
he began to ask them,
"What were you arguing about on the
    way?"
But they remained silent.
They had been discussing among
    themselves on the way
who was the greatest.
Then he sat down, called the Twelve,
    and said to them,
"If anyone wishes to be first,
he shall be the last of all and the
    servant of all."
Taking a child, he placed it in their midst,
    and putting his arms around it, he
    said to them,
"Whoever receives one child such as
    this in my name, receives me;
and whoever receives me,
receives not me but the One who sent
    me."

Reflecting on the Gospel

In some faith communities, the same people are called upon time after time to serve on the most influential committees and make all the important decisions. Certain other people are always passed over. They themselves may not recognize the gifts they have to offer until someone calls them forth and helps them develop their talents. This is what Jesus does in today's gospel.

While his disciples are wrangling over who is the greatest among them, Jesus turns to those who are left out and pulls him or her into the very center of the circle. He teaches his disciples that the one who appears most vulnerable and seems to need the greatest amount of care can also be the one who has the most to teach us about what it is to be Christlike and Godlike.

For most disciples, the temptation is not to seek honor and glory and high positions. Having interiorized Jesus's mandate to be "servant of all," we may find ourselves instead falling prey to the subtle desire to want to be the greatest of servants—the one who sits on the most committees, spends the most hours in prayer, teaches the greatest number of students, preaches the best homilies. Jesus redirects his disciples' attention to those who are most vulnerable and whose gifts are undervalued and least developed. Those who would be good leaders in the pattern of Jesus must turn to those of lowest status, embrace them, and bring them into the midst of the circle.

In this gospel passage Jesus is addressing disciples who have some measure of power, privilege, and status; he invites them to a leadership style based on relinquishment and service to all, especially the most needy. By contrast, Jesus's leadership empowers those who are forced into positions of servitude in society and places them at the center.

This manner of acting diffuses the jealousy and selfish ambition that James decries in the second reading. James chronicles all kinds of undesirable results that come from choices based on self-interest. The first reading, by contrast, like the gospel, speaks about a manner of leadership by persons devoted to justice and peacebuilding and warns of the negative consequences that befall them. It exposes the thinking of wicked ones who resent an upright person who speaks the truth to them about the need to mend their ways. They would sooner kill than heed such a messenger. They plot to torture and kill the upright one, testing not only the genuineness of the just one but even putting God's faithfulness on trial. They mistakenly think that the proof of intimacy with God is preservation from any kind of harm.

Saint Teresa of Avila remarked on this paradox, complaining to God about the trials and tribulations she had to endure on account of her closeness to God "If this is how you treat your friends, no wonder you have so few!" That God upholds the faithful, even if the manner of doing so is inscrutable to us, is affirmed in today's responsorial psalm.

Preparing to Proclaim

Key words and phrases: "Whoever receives one child such as this in my name, receives me."

To the point: This gospel has Jesus reiterating over and over that he is here to overturn our expectations. Three times he reminds us that God does not think or work as we do and that all our hoarding of power and honor and security is ultimately for naught. First, Jesus reminds the disciples of what we heard last week: he is going to suffer and die. This is not what they expect of the Christ, but God does not think or work as we do. Second, he responds to their bickering for status by redefining that status entirely. The one whom God will consider greatest is the one who will appear to our human eyes to be least. God does not think or work as we do. And finally, Jesus identifies with a child, one with no political power or social voice, one who would have likely been overlooked by those going about their adult business. Again (and again and again), God does not think or work as we do.

Psalmist Preparation

The psalm reiterates the humility called for in all of the other readings. We do not uphold our own lives; we are instead dependent on God, often in ways we do not see. Our culture prizes self-reliance and self-sufficiency; the myth of meritocracy has many of us believing that we have made ourselves and deserve the good things that come to us. As you prepare to proclaim this psalm, try to take some time to see how your life and your ministry is all ultimately dependent on God. Think about the gifts God has given you and give thanks for them.

Making Connections

Between the readings: The second reading from James echoes Jesus's gentle rebuke to the disciples in the gospel. "Jealousy and selfish ambition" are not of God, but bring about "disorder and every foul practice." Peace, though, comes from gentle and compliant dispositions. Both Jesus and James commend humility to their followers as a way of growing closer to God and, ultimately, happier.

To experience: Sometimes, those of us in ministry can be motivated by a desire for recognition or a public voice. We may enjoy the visibility of our roles and the compliments we receive for them. These things are not bad in themselves, but they are not motivations that can carry us for long. True ministry involves a constant reorientation of our hearts toward God. It means turning over ourselves to be servants for others. It means lending our time and hands and voices to do work that is ultimately God's, not our own.

Homily Points

• The disciples seemingly struggled to digest last week's message, as Jesus returns in today's gospel with more passion predictions. Suffering, death, resurrection. Suffering, death, resurrection. Jesus repeats the cycle to his curious followers. He once again refers to himself as the "Son of Man" and describes how he will be "handed over to men" to be killed. The disciples grow silent. They are afraid to ask questions, afraid to learn more about the fate that awaits them if they continue to follow Jesus. We too may tend to shut down in difficult moments and just hope that the issue will resolve itself. Yet Jesus is determined to keep his disciples together on the way.

• When they get to the house in Capernaum, Jesus presses the disciples to share their arguments out loud. They could not seem to find the words when Jesus talked about the cross, but when it came to bickering about who is the greatest, the disciples had plenty to say! They are still concerned about worldly ways, ways that say the powerful win and the lowly lose, the rich get rewarded while the poor suffer. Not so, Jesus says. In God's kingdom, "If anyone wishes to be first, he shall be the last of all and the servant of all." God's is not a kingdom of competition.

• To further his point, Jesus wraps his arms around a child—who had little if any social standing—and tells the disciples to receive the child as if receiving God's very self. The least and littlest are the ones who draw us closer to the divine.

Model Penitential Act

Presider: Time and again, Jesus invites us into a space of repentance so that we might grow ever closer to our Creator. Let us pause for a moment and embrace the mercy God longs to offer us . . . *[pause]*

Lord Jesus, you are the Son of Man: Lord, have mercy.

Christ Jesus, you journey with disciples then and now: Christ, have mercy.

Lord Jesus, you will lead us into eternal life: Lord, have mercy.

Model Universal Prayer (Prayer of the Faithful)

Presider: With faith in Jesus's constant presence in our lives, let us offer our prayers and petitions to the Lord.

Response: Lord, hear our prayer.

Fan the flames of our baptismal light within all members of the church . . .

Inspire leaders of nations to share bread with the hungry and clothe the naked . . .

Relieve the burdens of people who are oppressed or homeless . . .

Call forth peacemakers within our local communities . . .

Presider: God of all blessings, you teach us the way to eternal life. Hear our prayers that we might come to embody your lessons in the world today. We ask this through Christ our Lord. **Amen.**

Liturgy and Music

I sometimes think that one of the greatest tests of patience, love, and forbearance is for a parent to bring an antsy child to church. Crayons? Cheerios? Forget it! Somehow, they always want the car keys, with the pew serving as the head of a drum. Yet our Lord and Savior tells us that to enter into the kingdom, we must become like these little ones.

The psalm exhorts us to uphold life. This is not always an easy feat. The second reading challenges us beyond our own wants and ambitions—and the most effective way to cleanse a person of ego is tending to the thousand needs of a young child. Ask any parent.

It is not for nothing that Jesus takes one of these precious ones in his lap. They are the ones who still know how to laugh without reservation, look with wonder at the world, enter into the gift of eternity through playtime, look deep into your eyes and blow the universe apart with an innocent question. They are the perfect receivers of the word of God.

Kathleen Thomerson illustrates this childlike demeanor very well in her lovely hymn "I Want to Walk as a Child of the Light" (Celebration).

Please, God, may we rid ourselves of obnoxiousness, jealousy, and selfishness, such that we can be children in the presence of our Savior.

COLLECT

Let us pray.

Pause for silent prayer

O God, who founded all the commands of
    your sacred Law
upon love of you and of our neighbor,
grant that, by keeping your precepts,
we may merit to attain eternal life.
Through our Lord Jesus Christ, your Son,
who lives and reigns with you in the unity
    of the Holy Spirit,
God, for ever and ever. **Amen.**

FIRST READING

Wis 2:12, 17-20

The wicked say:
    Let us beset the just one, because he is
        obnoxious to us;
      he sets himself against our doings,
    reproaches us for transgressions of the
        law
      and charges us with violations of our
        training.
    Let us see whether his words be true;
      let us find out what will happen to
        him.
    For if the just one be the son of God,
        God will defend him
      and deliver him from the hand of his
        foes.
    With revilement and torture let us put
        the just one to the test
      that we may have proof of his
        gentleness
      and try his patience.
    Let us condemn him to a shameful
        death;
      for according to his own words, God
        will take care of him.

CATECHESIS

RESPONSORIAL PSALM

Ps 54:3-4, 5, 6-8

℟. (6b) The Lord upholds my life.

O God, by your name save me,
 and by your might defend my cause.
O God, hear my prayer;
 hearken to the words of my mouth.

℟. The Lord upholds my life.

For the haughty have risen up against me,
 the ruthless seek my life;
 they set not God before their eyes.

℟. The Lord upholds my life.

Behold, God is my helper;
 the Lord sustains my life.
Freely will I offer you sacrifice;
 I will praise your name, O LORD, for its
 goodness.

℟. The Lord upholds my life.

SECOND READING

Jas 3:16—4:3

Beloved:
Where jealousy and selfish ambition exist,
 there is disorder and every foul practice.
But the wisdom from above is first of all
 pure,
 then peaceable, gentle, compliant,
 full of mercy and good fruits,
 without inconstancy or insincerity.
And the fruit of righteousness is sown in
 peace
 for those who cultivate peace.

Where do the wars
 and where do the conflicts among you
 come from?
Is it not from your passions
 that make war within your members?
You covet but do not possess.
You kill and envy but you cannot obtain;
 you fight and wage war.
You do not possess because you do not
 ask.
You ask but do not receive,
 because you ask wrongly, to spend it on
 your passions.

Living Liturgy

Liturgy and the Arts: Today's readings all touch on the theme of how wisdom, peacefulness, and humility can overcome discord, confusion, and conflict. Music has a lot to teach us about how to live in diverse, cooperative, and harmonious community with one another. Be it an orchestra, a choir, a rock band, or a drum circle, there is an inherent need for all players to understand when to lead, when to follow, and how to support all of the other players in each moment of the performance.

In the first reading, wicked enemies threaten to abuse and bring suffering to the just one. They mockingly reason that if God truly cares for the wise and the just, then God will deliver them from the torture inflicted by the wicked ones' hands. The second reading from James delves deeper into the characteristics that lead to the violence of the first reading. Ego, jealousy, selfishness, and not being able to put one's passions in proper perspective are the ingredients that lead to disunity and conflict. We could all name at least one successful, beloved musical group that came to an end after one member fell out of step with the others. Maybe one of the members developed self-destructive habits or became more enamored with the fame and popularity than their craft. Either way, it leads to the same conclusion—the music comes to a screeching, sometimes tragic halt.

If you listen to a good musical performance of any genre, you will notice cycles of give and take. These moments of ebb and flow make the music complex and interesting to listen to. Each part or voice is important because it supports and enhances the beauty of all other parts. This is true in our spiritual lives as well. May we listen to the voice of Jesus who tells us to serve one another, to be mindful of when we are being called to lead and when we are called to follow. Let us make our spiritual communities into multifaceted and harmonious orchestras that sing God's praises and reveal the beauty of the world.

PROMPTS FOR FAITH-SHARING

• How can you become more of a servant to those with whom you share this life?

• How does your congregation receive the children in its midst? Is it with understanding for their developmentally appropriate behavior (and compassion for the parents who are shepherding them through it)? How could you improve your community's outreach to young children and their parents?

• What are the motivations for your ministry? How can you strive to more closely align them with Jesus's instruction to become the "last of all and the servant of all"?

See Appendix B, p. 313, for additional prompts.

SEPTEMBER 22, 2024
TWENTY-FIFTH SUNDAY
IN ORDINARY TIME

SPIRITUALITY

GOSPEL ACCLAMATION
cf. John 17:17b, 17a

℟. Alleluia, alleluia.
Your word, O Lord, is truth;
consecrate us in the truth.
℟. Alleluia, alleluia.

Gospel

Mark 9:38-43, 45, 47-48; L137B

At that time, John said to Jesus,
  "Teacher, we saw someone driv-
    ing out demons in your name,
  and we tried to prevent him be-
    cause he does not follow us."
Jesus replied, "Do not prevent him.
There is no one who performs a
    mighty deed in my name
who can at the same time speak
    ill of me.
For whoever is not against us is
    for us.
Anyone who gives you a cup of
    water to drink
  because you belong to Christ,
  amen, I say to you, will surely not lose his
    reward.

"Whoever causes one of these little ones
    who believe in me to sin,
  it would be better for him if a great
    millstone
  were put around his neck
  and he were thrown into the sea.
If your hand causes you to sin, cut it off.
It is better for you to enter into life maimed
    than with two hands to go into Gehenna,
    into the unquenchable fire.
And if your foot causes you to sin, cut it off.
It is better for you to enter into life crippled
    than with two feet to be thrown into
      Gehenna.
And if your eye causes you to sin, pluck it
    out.
Better for you to enter into the kingdom of
    God with one eye
  than with two eyes to be thrown into
    Gehenna,
  where 'their worm does not die, and the
    fire is not quenched.'"

Reflecting on the Gospel

In both the first reading and in the gospel, individuals who are not authorized by Moses and by Jesus, respectively, exercise a ministry akin to that of these leaders. Eldad and Medad had not gone out to the tent of meeting along with the other seventy, upon whom God bestowed a share of the Spirit that was upon Moses. Nonetheless, the Spirit came to rest upon them too; like the others, they began to speak prophetically in the camp.

Distressed by this, Joshua insisted that they be stopped. Was he resentful because he had trained at Moses's side from his youth and followed carefully all the directives, whereas these two appeared suddenly and began to minister with the others? Moses assures Joshua that the prophesying of Eldad and Medad in no way diminishes Moses's own authority as prophet.

In fact, it was Moses's own complaint to God about his too heavy burden of leadership that prompted God to bestow the Spirit on others who could lighten the load. Moses exclaims his wish that all the people would prophesy in God's Spirit. He recognizes that while not all are authorized to prophesy officially, all do have a measure of the prophetic gift to be shared.

A similar scene is played out in the gospel, where Jesus's disciples are upset about an exorcist who is claiming Jesus's authority as he casts out demons. Jesus insists that the disciples stop trying to prevent the exorcist from exercising his ministry, even though he is not an official follower of Jesus.

It is curious that in both instances, those who want to be officially recognized ministers are sadly focused on a perceived threat to their own authority, rather than on the recipients of the ministry. Joshua might have asked, What is the effect of the prophetic word spoken by the two who were not authorized? Is it unleashing God's freeing love in the hearers? Likewise, the disciples might have asked, Was the other exorcist freeing people from tormenting forces that blocked their ability to love and be loved? A word of approval from the wise leaders, Moses and Jesus, serves to reorient their followers toward the important matter of ensuring that the pressing needs of their people be addressed by whomever the Spirit empowered to do so.

One way for leaders and ministers to learn to see from this kind of perspective is to reflect on the ministry they receive from others. Jesus holds up to his disciples the example of one who offers them a cup of water to drink. With this simple act the giver recognizes in the thirsty one a shared humanity and a common thirst, as a member of Christ's body. Jesus also directs his disciples to reflect on the ministry they receive from others. When they know themselves as needy, they can learn, by accepting the gift of a cup of water, to shift their attention away from the prerogatives of credentialed ministry toward the neediness of those to whom the service is rendered.

Preparing to Proclaim

Key words and phrases: "If your hand causes you to sin, cut it off."

To the point: This gospel contains some hard words; it seems to suggest that the life of a Christian is a black-and-white, all-or-nothing proposition. We know, of course, that Jesus does not really want us to remove parts of our body that cause sin. Rather, our goal is to become whole in our pursuit of holiness. We are called to tend to the hand or the eye or the thoughts that cause us to sin, but we are called to transform and convert them. Every part of us can be put into service of bringing us closer to Christ. Every thought, every word, every deed is an opportunity to grow in our life as a Christian. It is integrity Christ wants from us—integrated lives of wholeness where every part contributes to the whole project of following Christ more closely.

Psalmist Preparation

This psalm is a love song to God's law. It might seem odd to sing with such joy over commandments God has given, which sometimes seem to limit our fun and freedom. But the psalmist knows and trusts wholeheartedly that God does not make rules for the sake of making rules. These are boundaries drawn in love and with our best interests in mind. To receive these directives from God is to receive a roadmap for life, one that guides us on our path to heaven. This is, in fact, a great gift. As you prepare to proclaim this psalm, reflect on your relationship with God's laws. Where are they a struggle? How could you receive them as a gift?

Making Connections

Between the readings: The first reading foreshadows Jesus's reaction to the person who prophesies in his name without following him. Both Jesus and Moses hold loosely to their power and position. While they know God has given them unique positions in their communities, they do not believe that God is therefore limited to speaking and acting only through them.

To experience: Humans are often quick to draw boundaries; we want to know who's in and who's out. There is a good impulse at the heart of this: we want to be able to focus our attention on what is real and true. But all too often, we miss the mark. Our human-made boundaries often cause us to over-focus, to the point of missing something about the bigger picture. God is always so much bigger than our human limits suggest. God always has more goodness in store than we can imagine.

Homily Points

• Jesus prioritizes the good deeds done by his expansive group of followers. He welcomes those who take action in his name without stopping to ask for their credentials. One could imagine Jesus echoing the words of Moses in today's first reading: "Would that all the people of the Lord were prophets! Would that the Lord might bestow his spirit on them all!" The work of discipleship is not to draw hard-and-fast boxes around who is "in" and who is "out" based on preconceived ideas. Discipleship is more dynamic than that. It operates from an ever-widening circle. Christian discipleship forms followers to see people in need of healing and to respond, period. All who take up this call—this cross—are "in." And let's be clear: being "in" is no easy task.

• Christian discipleship demands one's very life. Expectations are as high as the circle is wide for those who live in Christ's light. Along with prioritizing good deeds, Jesus denounces harmful deeds without mincing any words. "Cut if off," "pluck it out," Jesus demands of body parts used to sin. He asserts drowning is the *better* option for those who cause little ones to sin.

• Jesus does not take sin lightly—and neither should we. Sin persists in human beings after the Fall. Every person who walks this earth, besides Jesus and his mother Mary, commits sins. We lie and pass judgment. We lust and hoard wealth. We neglect neighbors in need, harm the earth, and do a whole host of other actions that break relationship with God and other living beings. And we all do it again and again. But we do not walk as people without hope.

Model Penitential Act

Presider: Our God is rich in mercy and compassion, slow to anger and abounding in love. With trust in God's power to forgive, let us call to mind our sins and ask for God's help to transform our hearts . . . *[pause]*

Lord Jesus, you defend the poor and vulnerable: Lord, have mercy.

Christ Jesus, you forgive sinners: Christ, have mercy.

Lord Jesus, you call humankind into everlasting life with God: Lord, have mercy.

Model Universal Prayer (Prayer of the Faithful)

Presider: United as one body in Christ, let us offer our prayers for the needs of the church and the world.

Response: Lord, hear our prayer.

Bring a swift end to clerical abuse and cover-up within the church . . .

Bless the ministries and communal lives of women and men religious . . .

Bring aid to people living in extreme poverty across the globe . . .

Help us use our gifts and talents to build up God's kingdom on earth . . .

Presider: Good and gracious God, through the example of your son Jesus, disciples of every age learned how to live with integrity and hope. Hear our prayers that we might grow closer to you and to our neighbors. We ask this through Christ our Lord. **Amen.**

Liturgy and Music

At first glance, the readings today are filled with cautionary, extreme language, even out-right violence; as a guitarist, I've always shuddered when encountering the exhortation, "If your hand causes you to sin, cut it off."

No one should water down Jesus's words, his zeal for leading a life of moral integrity. It's often a good thing to be disturbed by the good news. But looking at these readings as a whole, there is an overarching, universal call to unity—interior unity and collective unity, along with a moral humility and just action that can be found.

There is a motto long held as a compass point for citizens of the United States: *E Pluribus Unum*, which means "from the many comes one." This is not a political slogan; it is an expansive, mighty exhortation to embrace the common good, standing together through adversity. It is a deserving phrase for the aspirations of a republic.

God calls us to an even loftier sense of unity, a unity grounded in simple compassion, humility, servitude, good judgment, and moral accountability. Hear the words of the lyricist Joseph Brackett: "When true simplicity is gained, to bow and to bend we shan't be ashamed, / To turn, turn will be our delight, till by turning, turning we come 'round right" ("Simple Gifts").

Unity of heart and spirit—of "coming 'round right"—is not a cheap commodity, nor is it easily purchased. It takes place both personally and communally, unfolding over a life-time of spiritual work. As the psalmist exhorts, let the precepts of the Lord give wisdom to us, who hope to be simple.

COLLECT

Let us pray.

Pause for silent prayer

O God, who manifest your almighty power
above all by pardoning and showing
    mercy,
bestow, we pray, your grace abundantly
    upon us
and make those hastening to attain your
    promises
heirs to the treasures of heaven.
Through our Lord Jesus Christ, your Son,
who lives and reigns with you in the unity
    of the Holy Spirit,
God, for ever and ever. **Amen.**

FIRST READING

Num 11:25-29

The LORD came down in the cloud and
    spoke to Moses.
Taking some of the spirit that was on
    Moses,
    the LORD bestowed it on the seventy
      elders;
    and as the spirit came to rest on them,
      they prophesied.

Now two men, one named Eldad and the
    other Medad,
    were not in the gathering but had been
      left in the camp.
They too had been on the list, but had not
    gone out to the tent;
    yet the spirit came to rest on them also,
    and they prophesied in the camp.
So, when a young man quickly told Moses,
    "Eldad and Medad are prophesying in
      the camp,"
    Joshua, son of Nun, who from his youth
      had been Moses' aide, said,
    "Moses, my lord, stop them."
But Moses answered him,
    "Are you jealous for my sake?
Would that all the people of the LORD were
    prophets!
Would that the LORD might bestow his
    spirit on them all!"

RESPONSORIAL PSALM

Ps 19:8, 10, 12-13, 14

℞. (9a) The precepts of the Lord give joy
    to the heart.

The law of the LORD is perfect,
    refreshing the soul;
the decree of the LORD is trustworthy,
    giving wisdom to the simple.

℞. The precepts of the Lord give joy to
    the heart.

The fear of the L<small>ORD</small> is pure,
  enduring forever;
the ordinances of the L<small>ORD</small> are true,
  all of them just.

R̸. The precepts of the Lord give joy to
  the heart.

Though your servant is careful of them,
  very diligent in keeping them,
yet who can detect failings?
  Cleanse me from my unknown faults!

R̸. The precepts of the Lord give joy to
  the heart.

From wanton sin especially, restrain your
  servant;
  let it not rule over me.
Then shall I be blameless and innocent
  of serious sin.

R̸. The precepts of the Lord give joy to
  the heart.

SECOND READING

Jas 5:1-6

Come now, you rich, weep and wail over
  your impending miseries.
Your wealth has rotted away, your clothes
  have become moth-eaten,
  your gold and silver have corroded,
  and that corrosion will be a testimony
    against you;
  it will devour your flesh like a fire.
You have stored up treasure for the last
  days.
Behold, the wages you withheld from the
  workers
  who harvested your fields are crying
    aloud;
  and the cries of the harvesters
  have reached the ears of the Lord of
    hosts.
You have lived on earth in luxury and
  pleasure;
  you have fattened your hearts for the
    day of slaughter.
You have condemned;
  you have murdered the righteous one;
  he offers you no resistance.

Living Liturgy

Liturgy and Media: Do you remember the talent-based competitive reality shows of the early 2000s? Watching ordinary people reveal powerful singing voices, dance prowess, or other creative talents was breathtaking and exciting. Sometimes, contestants fit the mold of what we expect talented superstars to look and act like—young, physically attractive, charming, and personable. Sometimes, they did not. It is disappointing to go back and watch clips in which people who were not conventionally attractive were openly mocked or dismissed before they even got a chance to show their talents. Why is it so hard to be receptive to the message when we do not immediately connect to the messenger?

In the first reading, Eldad and Medad take the brunt of Joshua's disapproval. Because they were not present when the spirit came to rest on the other elders, it's immediately assumed that they are not fit to prophesy like the others. In the gospel reading from Mark, John tells Jesus how he tried to silence a person driving out demons in Jesus's name because this particular individual was not one of the core disciples. Moses and Jesus respond to their respective situations in similar ways. Both Moses and Jesus tell their followers not to silence the ones who are preaching even though they seem like outsiders. We in the church should also heed this instruction. Very likely, there are people in our communities who are preaching the good news but are being dismissed, ignored, or shut down because they don't look like the prophets we have come to expect.

God shows the desire to dwell among us and have a relationship with us by reaching out in innumerable, surprising ways. Jesus modeled for us what it means to revere and reimagine traditions and conventions. May we not miss God's lifegiving call to us simply because we are not willing or able to perceive it when it comes from unconventional places and faces.

PROMPTS FOR FAITH-SHARING

• Where in your life have you seen God at work in unexpected ways?

• What parts of your life need conversion or transformation so that they might be part of your integrated, whole self that is striving toward God?

• Have you ever missed God at work because you were maintaining an artificial boundary? How can you stay open to God's unanticipated work?

*See Appendix B, p. 313,
for additional prompts.*

SPIRITUALITY

GOSPEL ACCLAMATION
1 John 4:12

℟. Alleluia, alleluia.
If we love one another, God remains
     in us
and his love is brought to perfection
     in us.
℟. Alleluia, alleluia.

Gospel

Mark 10:2-16; L140B

The Pharisees approached
     Jesus and asked,
"Is it lawful for a husband to
          divorce his wife?"
They were testing him.
He said to them in reply, "What
          did Moses command you?"
They replied,
     "Moses permitted a husband to
          write a bill of divorce
     and dismiss her."
But Jesus told them,
     "Because of the hardness of your hearts
          he wrote you this commandment.
But from the beginning of creation, *God*
     made them male and female.
For this reason a man shall leave his father
     and mother
     and be joined to his wife,
     and the two shall become one flesh.
So they are no longer two but one flesh.
Therefore what God has joined together,
     no human being must separate."
In the house the disciples again questioned
          Jesus about this.
He said to them,
     "Whoever divorces his wife and marries
          another
     commits adultery against her;
     and if she divorces her husband and
          marries another,
     she commits adultery."

Continued in Appendix A, p. 305, or
Mark 10:2-12 in Appendix A, p. 305.

Reflecting on the Gospel
While no statistics are available for first-century Palestine, divorce was not uncommon. But marriage practices and attitudes toward marriage were considerably different from our own. In their patriarchal social system, marriages were arranged between families, to strengthen the social cohesion of the two clans. The terms were negotiated between the groom and his father and the father of the bride. Divorce would mean a messy separation of the two families and would bring shame on the family of the bride, since in Jewish tradition, only a man could initiate divorce.

It is in this context that the Pharisees "test" Jesus about the law concerning divorce. The only text in the Torah that deals with divorce is Deuteronomy 24:1-4, where Moses declares that a man who becomes displeased with his wife because he finds in her "something objectionable" may write her a bill of divorce and hand it to her and dismiss her from his house. The meaning of the Hebrew term used here had long been debated by the rabbis. In the time of Jesus, some important teachers interpreted it strictly, as meaning only sexual misconduct, whereas others thought it allowed even for spoiling a meal. Jesus's response is startling. He interprets Deuteronomy 24 as a concession on the part of Moses to the peoples' hardness of heart and redirects them to the ideal put forth in Genesis 2. He underscores the divine intent for oneness and harmonious relations among all creatures, most especially human beings, male and female created in God's image and likeness.

The creation of woman in Genesis 2:18-24 has often been misinterpreted in misogynistic ways: that the creation of woman as second, and from the man's side, makes her subordinate to and derivative from him. Moreover, the Hebrew phrase in verse 18 has been poorly rendered in some translations as "helpmate," making the sole purpose of woman's creation to be an aid in man's work. Most recent translations have rightly rendered it as "suitable partner" (NABRE, as we hear in today's reading) or "a helper as his partner" (NRSV). These capture the nuances of the Hebrew words for "strength, indispensable aid," often used of God's saving help, and for "corresponding to." As a myth of origins, Genesis 2 tells of how human beings came to be and how male and female relate to one another with mutuality and partnership. Having been created from man's side, woman is to stand alongside him as his equal. As the man's exclamation in verse 22 affirms, she corresponds to him exactly. She is strong just like him ("bone of my bones"), and weak like him ("flesh of my flesh"). Jesus quotes this text to his opponents, changing the focus from divorce to God's original intent for oneness and mutual correspondence. Just as later Christians would come to understand God as Three-in-One, so the unity of man and woman in marriage reflects this sacred unbreakable oneness.

The reasons not all marriages reflect this sacred unity are many. When the ideal cannot be realized, it is equally important to remember Jesus's insistence on compassion, forgiveness, and unconditional love.

Preparing to Proclaim

Key words and phrases: "Therefore what God has joined together, no human being must separate.'"

To the point: When marriage is good, it's really, really good. When marriage is hard, it's really, really hard. Both these truths come from the reality that Jesus preaches here—the oneness of spouses means that they are uniquely capable of hurting each other. That is why marriage is an ongoing commitment; husbands and wives need to commit daily to treating each other with care. They make the choice to marry not just once but every day, choosing each other again and again. The newlywed feeling of being "in love" often mellows over time, leaving in its stead love as a virtue, love that chooses the other's good even when the emotional payoff is lessened. Good marriages do not just happen; they take continuous work and tireless communication. Jesus reminds us that this work is worth it.

Psalmist Preparation

This psalm names marriage and children as one sign of God's blessing and favor. As you prepare to proclaim this psalm, spend some time praying for the married couples in your community. Pray for those who might be struggling in their marriage as well as for those for whom marriage is a joy. Pray for newlyweds learning how to live together. Pray for new parents as they take on the huge challenges of parenting together. Pray for those who long for children and have not received this blessing. Pray for older couples rediscovering each other as their children leave home. Pray for spouses supporting each other through illness or grief or job loss or any of the many other stresses this life brings.

Making Connections

Between the readings: The first reading gives the narrative to which Jesus refers in the gospel. This passage from Genesis reveals marriage as a gift, one intended to make partners out of spouses. They join in the shared project of bringing God to the world by making God's love more visible. And the importance of marriage is such that spouses leave behind their families of origin in order to commit fully to their new family.

To experience: Jesus's teachings about marriage are sometimes hard to hear in a world that is still broken by sin. In this complicated life, separation or divorce are sometimes necessary for the safety or well-being of a spouse or children. We who are church need to offer support to marriages *and* to those who, perhaps for reasons beyond our knowledge, need to live outside their marriage.

Homily Points

• Today's gospel can be a difficult reading to digest especially for the many of us who have experienced divorce firsthand—either within our own marriage or that of a loved one. Too many preachers over the years have used this gospel passage to judge and condemn. Today, let us instead approach the text with the greatest sensitivity and care for each other. It can be easy to chalk up Jesus's teaching on divorce and remarriage as legalistic without taking a deeper look. Phrases like "What God has joined together, no human being must separate" and "commits adultery" may seem harsh at first glance. But this is exactly the opposite of what Jesus intends.

• Upon further reflection, we encounter a Jesus in today's gospel who subverts patriarchal norms and sides with the oppressed. His radical actions give a glimpse of the kingdom of God still to come—a kingdom of possibility and grace. Jesus preached this message at a time when women held even less rights than they do today. Men held the power to initiate divorce, as we see in the Pharisees' question to Jesus: "Is it lawful for a husband to divorce his wife?" They pay no attention, legally or socially, to the needs of the wives despite the great threat of divorce to their livelihoods. The women Jesus encountered who experienced divorce could easily end up with nothing—no money, no shelter, no protections—regardless of the reason for the divorce.

• So Jesus, ever concerned for the lowly and least, expands the norms for divorce. In verse 12, he makes note of the woman's ability to divorce her husband. Both parties hold responsibility for proceeding with respect and reverence. Jesus's empowerment of women in the divorce proceedings reflects his push toward greater justice for the marginalized.

225

CELEBRATION

Model Penitential Act

Presider: God created humankind to be in communion with each other—yet we know that building community takes hard work and compromise. For the times we have hurt or ignored others, let us ask God for mercy . . . *[pause]*

Lord Jesus, you are brother to us all: Lord, have mercy.

Christ Jesus, you tasted death for the salvation of everyone: Lord, have mercy.

Lord Jesus, you will bring all people into the glory of life everlasting: Lord, have mercy.

Model Universal Prayer (Prayer of the Faithful)

Presider: Let us place our prayers for the church and the world before Christ with confidence.

Response: Lord, hear our prayer.

Grace the work of sanctuary churches and social services who provide aid to undocumented immigrants . . .

Foster greater respect for the lives and lands of Indigenous people . . .

Bring comfort and communal support to people experiencing divorce . . .

Bless the elders, teachers, and other storytellers of our community and all who receive their wisdom . . .

Presider: Liberating God, you sent your son Jesus to be our savior and guide. Hear our prayers that by his example, we live lives of service and justice. We ask this through Christ our Lord. **Amen.**

Liturgy and Music

I have preacher friends who hold their breath, hoping not to draw the straw and have to deliver a homily on this day. For once again, we come before the uncompromising words of Jesus, with a fair dose of searing judgment.

But looking closely at both the reading from Genesis and Mark's Gospel, I wonder if we don't miss the forest for the tree; that is, we focus on the magnitude of Jesus's statement about divorce, but neglect the intimacy of creation described in Genesis, as well as the conclusion of the gospel reading, which once again has the Son of God surrounded by little ones. (Hint: please consider choosing the long form of the gospel, which is worth taking the time for the few extra sentences!)

And from that, here is a clue, again on the lips of Jesus: "Because of the hardness of your heart [Moses] wrote you this commandment."

In an era when hardheartedness seems to reign supreme, when stubbornness and obstinacy rule the day, we are once again told that it is the childlike, the tenderhearted, who will enter God's kingdom. Consider Brian Wren's hymn text "When Love Is Found" (Hope Publishing).

The readings set before us this day are about far more than marriage. They are about a sense of wonder before created humanity, about an attitude of vulnerability, and about respect. To simply focus on divorce would deny the readings of their expansiveness.

COLLECT
Let us pray.

Pause for silent prayer

Almighty ever-living God,
who in the abundance of your kindness
surpass the merits and the desires of
    those who entreat you,
pour out your mercy upon us
to pardon what conscience dreads
and to give what prayer does not dare to
    ask.
Through our Lord Jesus Christ, your Son,
who lives and reigns with you in the unity
    of the Holy Spirit,
God, for ever and ever. **Amen.**

FIRST READING
Gen 2:18-24

The Lord God said: "It is not good for the
    man to be alone.
I will make a suitable partner for him."
So the Lord God formed out of the ground
    various wild animals and various birds
        of the air,
    and he brought them to the man to see
        what he would call them;
    whatever the man called each of them
        would be its name.
The man gave names to all the cattle,
    all the birds of the air, and all wild
        animals;
    but none proved to be the suitable
        partner for the man.

So the Lord God cast a deep sleep on the
    man,
    and while he was asleep,
    he took out one of his ribs and closed
        up its place with flesh.
The Lord God then built up into a woman
    the rib
    that he had taken from the man.
When he brought her to the man, the man
    said:
    "This one, at last, is bone of my bones
        and flesh of my flesh;
    this one shall be called 'woman,' for
        out of 'her man' this one has been
            taken."
That is why a man leaves his father and
    mother
    and clings to his wife,
    and the two of them become one flesh.

RESPONSORIAL PSALM
Ps 128:1-2, 3, 4-5, 6

℟. (cf. 5) May the Lord bless us all the
    days of our lives.

Blessed are you who fear the LORD,
    who walk in his ways!
For you shall eat the fruit of your
    handiwork;
    blessed shall you be, and favored.

℟. May the Lord bless us all the days of
    our lives.

Your wife shall be like a fruitful vine
    in the recesses of your home;
your children like olive plants
    around your table.

℟. May the Lord bless us all the days of
    our lives.

Behold, thus is the man blessed
    who fears the LORD.
The LORD bless you from Zion:
    may you see the prosperity of
      Jerusalem
all the days of your life.

℟. May the Lord bless us all the days of
    our lives.

May you see your children's children.
    Peace be upon Israel!

℟. May the Lord bless us all the days of
    our lives.

SECOND READING
Heb 2:9-11

Brothers and sisters:
He "for a little while" was made "lower
    than the angels,"
    that by the grace of God he might taste
      death for everyone.

For it was fitting that he,
    for whom and through whom all things
      exist,
    in bringing many children to glory,
    should make the leader to their
      salvation perfect through suffering.
He who consecrates and those who are
      being consecrated
all have one origin.
Therefore, he is not ashamed to call them
    "brothers."

Living Liturgy

Liturgy and Family: Each of today's readings draw attention to the sanctity of the bonds that create family, specifically the bonds between married people. As we reflect on these readings, let us consider the beautiful fruits of those bonds and how to protect and strengthen them. The first reading from Genesis talks about partnership and how life can be even more beautiful when it is not lived alone. (Notably, God first creates the animals of the land and sky to accompany Adam. We should remember that we have a sacred bond too with all of creation.) After a deep sleep, Adam awakes to find his new partner, Eve, with whom he will populate the earth and learn how to tend the land. All of life's relationships are a gift from God, and all of them—including marriage—invite us to co-create with God, to bring about beauty we could not have achieved alone.

In the gospel reading from Mark, we see Jesus being challenged yet again by the Pharisees who ask whether or not it is lawful for a husband to divorce his wife. They cite the teachings of Moses, but Jesus responds that "what God has joined together, no human being must separate." This teaching can shed wisdom and light on more situations than just divorce. Anything that severs our bond to the people we have promised ourselves to should be avoided. It doesn't just apply to sexual or emotional infidelity either. Perhaps we tend to put work or hobbies before nurturing our family life. Perhaps as a society, we have become too complacent and accepting of institutions that erode family life like harsh immigration policies that separate families or criminal justice policies that do not rehabilitate so much as remove people from their communities for decades or even lifetimes.

In giving us family and relationships, God gave us a great gift. With it we can do so much to glorify God and live full and enriching lives. Let us safeguard that gift in our personal lives and protect that gift for others in our communities.

PROMPTS FOR FAITH-SHARING

• Do you know a married couple whose relationship is inspiring to you? How do they reveal God's love in this world?

• Scripture often assigns the image of bridegroom to God. What can we learn about God's love from marriage? What can we learn about marriage from the way God loves us?

• Marriage opens us up to countless heartaches; how can your community best support those who are struggling with this vocation?

See Appendix B, p. 314, for additional prompts.

SPIRITUALITY

GOSPEL ACCLAMATION
Matt 5:3

℟. Alleluia, alleluia.
Blessed are the poor in spirit,
for theirs is the kingdom of heaven.
℟. Alleluia, alleluia.

Gospel

Mark 10:17-30; L143B

As Jesus was setting out on a
    journey, a man ran up,
knelt down before him, and
    asked him,
"Good teacher, what must I do
    to inherit eternal life?"
Jesus answered him, "Why do you
    call me good?
No one is good but God alone.
You know the commandments:
    You shall not kill;
    you shall not commit adultery;
    you shall not steal;
    you shall not bear false witness;
    you shall not defraud;
    honor your father and your
        mother."
He replied and said to him,
    "Teacher, all of these I have observed
        from my youth."
Jesus, looking at him, loved him and said
    to him,
"You are lacking in one thing.
Go, sell what you have, and give to the
    poor
    and you will have treasure in heaven;
        then come, follow me."
At that statement his face fell,
    and he went away sad, for he had many
        possessions.

Jesus looked around and said to his
    disciples,
"How hard it is for those who have
    wealth
to enter the kingdom of God!"
The disciples were amazed at his words.

Continued in Appendix A, p. 306, or
Mark 10:17-27 in Appendix A, p. 306.

Reflecting on the Gospel

In the popular 1990s film *City Slickers*, a crusty old cowboy named Curly asks city boy Mitch, "Do you know what the secret of life is?" Curly holds up one finger and continues, "One thing. Just one thing." When Mitch presses him for the "one thing," Curly says, "That's what you've got to figure out."

In today's gospel, a rich young man asks Jesus a similar question: "What must I do to inherit eternal life?" He seems to be looking for a formula. Though he has kept all the commandments since his youth, the young man lacks something. He looks to Jesus as the "good teacher" to tell him what it is. Jesus's answer seems strange at first. He doesn't tell him right away what he must do to inherit eternal life but focuses instead on the man's use of the word "good." In this way Jesus points the young man toward God's unique goodness, which is the "one thing" at the center of all.

Jesus invites the rich man to step across a threshold, to leave behind the spirituality of his youth, and to take on another spirituality that abandons all for the sake of love. It is the gaze of love that Jesus casts on each of us that enables us to abandon everything else. This love cannot be earned with actions but is sheer gift of the good God, who embodies the "one thing" that surpasses all else. The only condition for attaining the one thing is this: a person must be willing to let go of everything else.

Of course, that's easy to say. The young man's many possessions seem an insurmountable obstacle. For a rich person to enter the realm of God is like a heavily laden camel struggling to wriggle through a tiny opening with all its cargo intact. To hold on to the power, control, and security that abundant possessions bring is antithetical to the vulnerability, receptivity, and risk that abandoning oneself to the One Love requires. It is not impossible for people with riches to do so, but it is exceedingly difficult. As other gospel passages illustrate, it is not having riches that poses an obstacle; rather, it is what one does with one's possessions that is determinative. Total self-surrender to the Divine is the one thing that brings abundance of life to all.

There is a similar theme in the first reading, where Wisdom is the one thing sought. The king prays for and is granted the grace to choose Wisdom alone, over scepter and throne, riches and gems. Ironically, just as the disciples gained back a hundredfold all the family relations and land they relinquished, so the king's choice of Wisdom over all else brought him all good things and countless riches. The idea is not to guess the one thing that will bring abundant riches. Rather, the choice of the One Love, Wisdom incarnate in Christ, prompts one to let go of all else, only to receive in return all that the Beloved lavishes on us without reserve.

Preparing to Proclaim

Key words and phrases: "All things are possible for God."

To the point: This can be a disheartening reading. All of us have things we don't strictly need and most of us would struggle to let go of certain comforts. The idea of selling everything to follow Christ seems foolish—where would we find food and shelter? And without our most basic needs tended to, how would we possibly grow in the virtue and love that Christ calls us to? But in the end, this is not a reading about what we do (or don't do). Jesus acknowledges that this is impossible for human beings. This is instead a reading about what God does. God can loosen the grasp of these things on our heart; God can move those attachments that are getting between us and God. We need to offer willing cooperation with God, but this is ultimately not our work.

Psalmist Preparation

This psalm's antiphon asks God to fill us with God's love. In order to be so filled, we need to make room within ourselves. The rich man of today's gospel is unable to do so because he identifies too strongly with his possessions and wealth. As you prepare to proclaim this psalm, think about what in your life takes time and attention away from God and from who you truly are. What could you detach from or let go of in order to give God more space in your heart and in your life? Consider making a resolution to let one of these things go for the week in order to make space for God.

Making Connections

Between the readings: The author of the book of Wisdom here reveals a set of priorities in line with what God wants for us. Unlike the rich man of the gospel, this author chooses God's gift of wisdom over power, riches, and even bodily health. His preference is rewarded greatly, bringing more good things than those he gave up.

To experience: Our possessions are often a source of security; we feel taken care of and prepared for emergencies by owning certain things. This can create an illusion that we are in control and can lead us to forget our dependence on God. This is not to say that we cannot have any things, but it is good to intentionally practice detachment. We can try to envision our lives without some of our things; we can think about how others might need them more than we do.

Homily Points

• The rich man in today's gospel has a hard time saying goodbye to his possessions. Not only did individual items hold meaning for him, but in those days, society viewed material wealth as a sign of spiritual virtue. The rich man was living what he thought to be a good, holy life—so Jesus's ask to "Go, sell what you have, and give to the poor" floored him. Christians often criticize the man for feeling sad about this call, as if a major life move was not supposed to have any effect on him. But that's not how the human heart works.

• Jesus's ask is radical. Answering his call to "come, follow me" means giving up much—and gaining even more. Even so, the transition into deeper discipleship leads us toward holy indifference, a practice that may feel strange at first. Saint Ignatius of Loyola describes holy indifference as the freedom to love God above all else. People who practice holy indifference still care about the things of this world—people, places, objects, experiences—but they are detached enough that they can leave behind the things that pull them away from God and invest in the things that bring them closer to God. Growing in relationship with God is the end goal to which all things point. Such detachment often requires saying goodbye. The rich man's sadness makes sense.

• Luckily, Jesus promises his presence every step of the way. Neither the rich man nor any of us will ever have to say a hard goodbye to the Son of God. Jesus assures all of us that *together* with God and our neighbors, we will enter the heavenly kingdom. *Together* we will experience the glory of God's kingdom overflowing with grace and promises of salvation.

CELEBRATION

Model Penitential Act

Presider: In today's second reading, Saint Paul speaks of the "living and effective" word of God that is "able to discern reflections and thoughts of the heart." Let us turn to the living word to ask for mercy . . . *[pause]*

Lord Jesus, you are the great teacher of God's commandments: Lord, have mercy.

Christ Jesus, you came so that all might have eternal life: Christ, have mercy.

Lord Jesus, in you all things are possible: Lord, have mercy.

Model Universal Prayer (Prayer of the Faithful)

Presider: Let us bring our prayers and petitions before the Lord who listens to our every need.

Response: Lord, hear our prayer.

Grace the work of sanctuary churches and social services who provide aid to undocumented immigrants . . .

Foster the efforts of scientists, medical researchers, and all who are working to combat the spread of infectious diseases . . .

Energize young people struggling to find meaning and purpose in life . . .

Strengthen the spirit of forgiveness and reconciliation within this community . . .

Presider: Spirit of Wisdom, by your grace we will one day come to see good triumph over evil. Hear our prayers that as we move toward such a time, our hearts might expand in love of you and neighbor. We ask this through Christ our Lord. **Amen.**

Liturgy and Music

Being a disciple of wisdom doesn't mean that one is shielded from the difficulties of this world. What wisdom brings, though, is depth and meaning in the midst of suffering. The gift of wisdom looks at the world with different eyes, with deeper eyes.

Once again, Jesus moves outside the trajectory of conventional wisdom, a worldview that equates material wealth with blessings from above. It is a logic that persists even to this day, when we see images of the rich and powerful and think that all these things somehow reflect our nearness to God. The Teacher notes just the opposite: it's not what we have that saves us; it's what we're willing to let go of. Perhaps this is why Saint Francis, himself a lifelong disciple of wisdom, spoke so eloquently about the pursuit of Lady Poverty.

In the Hebrew Scriptures, wisdom is always portrayed in the feminine, enhancing the richness of our tradition. That journey is described here in the hymn "Wisdom, My Road":

Long before my journey's start, When in my youth I searched in my heart,
I would pray for her, wait for her, Wisdom, my road, my goal, and my star.

From the blossom to the seed, Long has she filled my cup in need,
May I cling to her vine, taste of her wine, Wisdom, my life, my perfect design.

When I stretched my hands to the sky, When in despair my soul raised a cry,
I was saved by her gaze, led in her ways, Wisdom, my love, the light of my days.

(Steven C. Warner, based on Ecclesiasticus 51; copyright © 1993 World Library Publications, a div. of GIA Publications, Inc.)

Jesus envisions a profound, wisdom-infused journey. It seeks to shed us of the possessions, the earthly goods that confuse our true spiritual compass.

COLLECT

Let us pray.

Pause for silent prayer

May your grace, O Lord, we pray,
at all times go before us and follow after
and make us always determined
to carry out good works.
Through our Lord Jesus Christ, your Son,
who lives and reigns with you in the unity
    of the Holy Spirit,
God, for ever and ever. **Amen.**

FIRST READING

Wis 7:7-11

I prayed, and prudence was given me;
    I pleaded, and the spirit of wisdom
        came to me.
I preferred her to scepter and throne,
and deemed riches nothing in comparison
    with her,
    nor did I liken any priceless gem to her;
because all gold, in view of her, is a little
    sand,
    and before her, silver is to be accounted
        mire.
Beyond health and comeliness I loved her,
and I chose to have her rather than the
    light,
    because the splendor of her never yields
        to sleep.
Yet all good things together came to me in
    her company,
    and countless riches at her hands.

RESPONSORIAL PSALM
Ps 90:12-13, 14-15, 16-17

℞. (14) Fill us with your love, O Lord, and
    we will sing for joy!

Teach us to number our days aright,
    that we may gain wisdom of heart.
Return, O Lord! How long?
    Have pity on your servants!

℞. Fill us with your love, O Lord, and we
    will sing for joy!

Fill us at daybreak with your kindness,
    that we may shout for joy and gladness
        all our days.
Make us glad, for the days when you
        afflicted us,
    for the years when we saw evil.

℞. Fill us with your love, O Lord, and we
    will sing for joy!

Let your work be seen by your servants
    and your glory by their children;
and may the gracious care of the Lord our
    God be ours;
    prosper the work of our hands for us!
    Prosper the work of our hands!

℞. Fill us with your love, O Lord, and we
    will sing for joy!

SECOND READING
Heb 4:12-13

Brothers and sisters:
Indeed the word of God is living and
    effective,
    sharper than any two-edged sword,
    penetrating even between soul and
        spirit, joints and marrow,
    and able to discern reflections and
        thoughts of the heart.
No creature is concealed from him,
    but everything is naked and exposed to
        the eyes of him
    to whom we must render an account.

Living Liturgy

Liturgy and Creation: God's word is indeed living and effective. When we look at the Scriptures, we see many examples of promises kept, prophesies fulfilled. We are encouraged to heed God's instruction, especially as it is laid out in the Ten Commandments, the Beatitudes, and other teachings in the Old and New Testaments. God also speaks to us through the richness and rhythms of creation. In today's second reading we hear that the word of God is sharp, incisive, and that in its light, everything is revealed and made clear. This truth is evident when we look at the state of our natural world which is suffering from the effects of climate change, human consumption, and pollution. Human actions have long-lasting consequences that cannot be ignored or concealed. If we continue to act wastefully, we will lay waste to our planet.

One remedy, which we hear in today's readings, is to let go of the habit of gathering and hoarding resources and wealth. In Mark's gospel, Jesus tells the inquisitive young man that following the commandments as he has done is not enough, he must also give away his possessions to the poor. The young man is understandably discouraged and apprehensive. This seems like a radical ask from Jesus. When we are asked to consider new energy sources or sustainable practices to offset the effects of climate change, we may balk because of the expense or the inconvenience of changing our practices. This is understandable, but let us be open and trusting of God's promise to us if we are faithful to these demanding teachings. In the book of Wisdom, the writer notes that by giving up the search for riches and focusing instead on the spirit of wisdom, "all good things together came." Maybe we too will realize even greater riches than what we think we've lost if we shift our focus from economic growth and expansion to greater stewardship of the earth.

PROMPTS FOR FAITH-SHARING

• What things in your life might you be too attached to? What would it take for you to give them up?

• How can you make room in your life to take better care of those who are poor?

• How can you grow in your awareness of your reliance on God?

See Appendix B, p. 314,
for additional prompts.

SPIRITUALITY

GOSPEL ACCLAMATION
Mark 10:45

℟. Alleluia, alleluia.
The Son of Man came to serve
and to give his life as a ransom for many.
℟. Alleluia, alleluia.

Gospel   Mark 10:35-45; L146B

James and John, the sons of Zebedee,
    came to Jesus and said to him,
"Teacher, we want you to do for us
    whatever we ask of you."
He replied, "What do you wish me to
    do for you?"
They answered him, "Grant that in
    your glory
we may sit one at your right and the
    other at your left."
Jesus said to them, "You do not know
    what you are asking.
Can you drink the cup that I drink
    or be baptized with the baptism with
        which I am baptized?"
They said to him, "We can."
Jesus said to them, "The cup that I drink,
    you will drink,
    and with the baptism with which I am
        baptized, you will be baptized;
    but to sit at my right or at my left is not
        mine to give
    but is for those for whom it has been
        prepared."
When the ten heard this, they became
    indignant at James and John.
Jesus summoned them and said to them,
"You know that those who are recognized
    as rulers over the Gentiles
    lord it over them,
    and their great ones make their authority
        over them felt.
But it shall not be so among you.
Rather, whoever wishes to be great among
    you will be your servant;
    whoever wishes to be first among you will
        be the slave of all.
For the Son of Man did not come to be
    served
    but to serve and to give his life as a
        ransom for many."

or Mark 10:42-45 in Appendix A, p. 306.

Reflecting on the Gospel

In today's gospel, James and John have just heard Jesus speak for the third time about being handed over, mocked, scourged, and condemned to death. The brothers focus their attention on what reward they will gain if they endure such abuse. They envision Jesus enthroned in glory after his ordeal and themselves seated in the places of honor at his right and left. The other disciples are indignant with the two brothers, probably not because James and John have missed Jesus's message but because they beat the others in requesting the honorable spots!

In response Jesus uses two powerful symbols. He asks if James and John can drink the cup that he will drink and whether they can be baptized with the baptism he will undergo. In the Scriptures, "cup" is frequently used as a metaphor for suffering. That meaning is clear in the Gethsemane scene where Jesus begs God to let the cup pass him by if possible. Likewise, baptism here signifies being plunged into suffering and going through the throes of death, to emerge into new life.

The self-confidence James and John exude is astounding. They quickly assert that they can drink this cup and undergo this baptism. But do they really know what they are saying? Their eagerness leads us to reflect on our own ability to answer Jesus's questions. Perhaps there have been times when we eagerly said "I do" or "We can" without fully knowing to what we were committing ourselves. Or we may know full well the demands of dedicating ourselves to Jesus's way of costly love, but the thought of a reward seems to make it worth the price.

Jesus takes the disciples another step deeper. The reward for which they hope beyond this life is not within Jesus's control to give, and it must not be their motivation. Jesus speaks disapprovingly about any who seek displays of greatness and authority over others—apparently even in the next life. The hope of reversal, of the servant becoming enthroned, is not what motivates Jesus, nor should it motivate his disciples.

The only "throne" that he shares with his disciples is the "throne of grace" (Heb 4:16). Here, one receives not places of honor alongside him but mercy, grace, and timely help. The wellspring for this mercy is that Jesus has himself endured all that we endure and is thus able to suffer with all those who suffer.

Jesus speaks about his life given as a "ransom for many." The term *ransom* here refers literally to the buying back of the freedom of a slave. It too is a metaphor that expresses in a limited way the freeing effects of Jesus's costly love. But this metaphor can lead us to slip again into a tit-for-tat mentality, in which a reward can be purchased or earned. Today's responsorial psalm captures the core of what Jesus attempts to teach his disciples: the only adequate response to suffering is to turn toward the Merciful One, in whom we place all our trust.

Preparing to Proclaim

Key words and phrases: "[W]hoever wishes to be great among you will be your servant."

To the point: This gospel passage repeats themes from several weeks ago. Jesus repeats that the disciples who wish to be great need to live lives of service to others. Those who appear "great" in worldly terms are not the ones who God rewards most richly. This seems repetitive, but it needs to be, because the disciples still do not get it. They are still vying for places of honor within their group, bickering over the glory they assume they will attain by their association with Jesus. We are often like the disciples; we hear these lessons again and again but we struggle to live them out fully. As he does with the disciples, Jesus offers endless patience for our slow learning. He offers repetition with love and with trust that we are capable of achieving what he asks of us.

Psalmist Preparation

In this psalm we proclaim the goodness of God and affirm our trust in that goodness. It reminds us that God is trustworthy, even when life brings us struggles and suffering. As you prepare to proclaim this psalm, reflect on the last line in which we affirm that we "have put our hope in [God]." Think about the role of hope in your life—what do you hope for both in the short- and long-term? Some of your hopes might be small and specific; some might be grander and more general. Spend time in prayer inviting God into all of these hopes, trusting that God sees them and sees you and responds with unfailing love and kindness.

Making Connections

Between the readings: The second reading reminds us that Jesus's loving patience for the disciples' repetitive follies comes from his unity with humanity. Because he has taken on flesh, he is able to sympathize with the weaknesses of our human condition. We find in him a God both utterly above us and unspeakably close to us. We are invited to approach him with confidence in his love; he wants to hear our needs and grant us the grace we need.

To experience: The disciples are attached to the all-too-human tendency to compare themselves with one another. They desire to be special and to stand out. Their desire is based on a false sense of scarcity; they believe there is only so much glory to go around and want to ensure they get their fair share of it. But such scarcity is not an issue with God. This is a God of abundance. When we enter into God's glory, comparison with each other will become meaningless as we are wrapped in God's loving embrace.

Homily Points

• "Follow me" to the cross is a frightening summons to a life of sacrifice and suffering. James and John saw the trials firsthand. It tried their trust. Who would not relish a guarantee that after a lifetime of hard work, a special seat sits waiting on the other side? Yet once again, Jesus invites his disciples—and all of us—to break free from our worldly wants. He promises the way of the cross, while challenging, will be the way of connection, growth, and ultimately, eternal life.

• Jesus's sacramental references remind us that the way of the cross is a communal way. We share in the waters of baptism. We drink from the same sacred cup. The ritual celebrations we engage in as a church are meant to draw us closer to one another and to Jesus himself, who promises his full presence when two or three are gathered in his name. Signed, sealed, and nourished by the sacraments, we are sent out into the world to be people of service. We are called to take up the cross in our homes and workplaces, across our neighborhoods and beyond. Each encounter with another person or the earth, each call answered, each forgiveness granted, each injustice challenged offers opportunities for growth. Our bodies—and hearts—know growth never comes without aches and pains.

• Yet we keep going, together. We keep taking up the cross of daily demands time and time again, trusting that this is the path to eternal life. Through affliction, we trust that we will "see the light in fullness of days" as the prophet Isaiah says in today's first reading. Jesus promises that the darkness of the cross leads to the light of resurrection. May we find strength in his promise.

CELEBRATION

Model Penitential Act

Presider: In today's second reading, Saint Paul reminds us that we can confidently approach God's "throne of grace to receive mercy and to find grace for timely help." Let us pause for a moment to do just that . . . *[pause]*

Lord Jesus, you are love incarnate: Lord, have mercy.

Christ Jesus, you came to show us the way to salvation: Christ, have mercy.

Lord Jesus, you are present when we gather in your name: Lord, have mercy.

Model Universal Prayer (Prayer of the Faithful)

Presider: Following in the way of Jesus, let us offer our prayers and petitions to God.

Response: Lord, hear our prayer.

Raise up leaders within the church, particularly those to help guide our liturgical ministries, outreach ministries, and faith formation . . .

Stop the harmful effects of the climate crisis and help all people to deepen their care for the natural world . . .

Support people on hospice and their caregivers . . .

Fill with love and community all widows and widowers in our community . . .

Presider: Loving God, in the waters of baptism you empower each of us to proclaim the good news of your son Jesus Christ. Hear our prayers that with hope we might follow in the way of Jesus to everlasting life. We ask this through Christ our Lord. **Amen.**

Liturgy and Music

From the outset of today's readings we again find ourselves in the midst of Isaiah's prophetic vision, the foretelling of Jesus's death. In this instance, we are in the midst of the fourth Suffering Servant song.

For years, spiritual leaders have spoken of the unitive vision between Christianity and Buddhism. Both acknowledge the presence of suffering in this world, rightly and with great wisdom. Both ascertain that suffering cannot be sidestepped. Today's readings confront us with an equally powerful message—to be a leader means to be a servant, and to be a servant means to suffer. These are sobering words, and in some ways a challenge to the notion of "good news." Yet sometimes good news needs to be honest news.

Once again, the very human, bumbling disciples illustrate for us how easy it is to allow ego to derail the best of intentions. Through James and John, the awkward question of power becomes a teaching moment for Jesus, an opportunity to show—through his own witness—what the cost of true glory really is. Hear these words from the lyricist Susan Wente: "Lord, make us prophets to cry out the way, / Telling the nations of mercy's new day. / Let us break barriers of hatred and scorn, / Speaking of hope to all people forlorn" ("Make Us True Servants," copyright © 1978 WLP).

History shows how peaceable leaders have suffered greatly so that others might be ransomed from a dehumanizing fate. They were willing to offer themselves in sacrifice. And many lost their lives so that others might live. They did so, armed not with weaponry, but with the armor of mercy and an unassailable trust in God.

COLLECT

Let us pray.

Pause for silent prayer

Almighty ever-living God,
grant that we may always conform our
    will to yours
and serve your majesty in sincerity of
    heart.
Through our Lord Jesus Christ, your Son,
who lives and reigns with you in the unity
    of the Holy Spirit,
God, for ever and ever. **Amen.**

FIRST READING
Isa 53:10-11

The LORD was pleased
    to crush him in infirmity.

If he gives his life as an offering for sin,
    he shall see his descendants in a long
        life,
    and the will of the LORD shall be
        accomplished through him.

Because of his affliction
    he shall see the light in fullness of days;
through his suffering, my servant shall
        justify many,
    and their guilt he shall bear.

RESPONSORIAL PSALM
Ps 33:4-5, 18-19, 20, 22

℟. (22) Lord, let your mercy be on us, as
    we place our trust in you.

Upright is the word of the LORD,
    and all his works are trustworthy.
He loves justice and right;
    of the kindness of the LORD the earth
        is full.

℟. Lord, let your mercy be on us, as we
    place our trust in you.

See, the eyes of the LORD are upon those
    who fear him,
    upon those who hope for his kindness,
to deliver them from death
    and preserve them in spite of famine.

℟. Lord, let your mercy be on us, as we
    place our trust in you.

Our soul waits for the LORD,
    who is our help and our shield.
May your kindness, O LORD, be upon us
    who have put our hope in you.

℟. Lord, let your mercy be on us, as we
    place our trust in you.

SECOND READING
Heb 4:14-16

Brothers and sisters:
Since we have a great high priest who has
        passed through the heavens,
    Jesus, the Son of God,
    let us hold fast to our confession.
For we do not have a high priest
    who is unable to sympathize with our
        weaknesses,
    but one who has similarly been tested in
        every way,
    yet without sin.
So let us confidently approach the throne
        of grace
    to receive mercy and to find grace for
        timely help.

Living Liturgy

Liturgy and Spirituality: In today's gospel, James and John approach Jesus and ask to be seated at his right and left hands. The disciples had walked with Jesus for quite some time by this point. They have witnessed the miracles he's performed and performed miraculous works in his name. They too have endured the scrutiny and judgment of religious authorities and the skepticism of their own people. The disciples have a very human response to all of this when they ask for recognition for all they have done alongside Jesus. However, Jesus continues to invert their ideas and expectations of what leadership and greatness truly mean.

"Can you drink the cup that I drink or be baptized with the baptism with which I am baptized?" Jesus asks the disciples (and us) if we can accept the life that is offered to us as believers and followers of God. Although we see Jesus perform many miraculous works, we cannot lose sight of the fact that his incarnation was a major act of humility and solidarity. In taking on our flesh, Jesus also took on our hunger, weariness, pains, and other perils of being human. He accepted God's will that he should sacrifice himself in order to bring all people back to God. Christ's greatness is matched only by his willingness to endure the many slings and arrows required of him in God's service.

When Jesus tells the disciples that the privilege of sitting at his right and left is not his to give, it suggests that he is leaving the choice up to us. Every day of our lives, in small and large ways, we get to choose where to position ourselves in relation to Christ. Are we truly willing to make ourselves small, to suffer and sacrifice in service to God? Are we willing to let go of our ideas of greatness in order to be truly great in the eyes of God?

PROMPTS FOR FAITH-SHARING

• What do you most want Jesus to do for you? What are the hopes you are harboring in your life with Christ?

• Who in your life has served you in a way you find inspirational? How could you emulate their acts of service?

• How could you take up a servant's posture toward those in your closest relationships?

See Appendix B, p. 314,
for additional prompts.

SPIRITUALITY

GOSPEL ACCLAMATION
cf. 2 Tim 1:10

℟. Alleluia, alleluia.
Our Savior Jesus Christ destroyed death
and brought life to light through the Gospel.
℟. Alleluia, alleluia.

Gospel

Mark 10:46-52; L149B

As Jesus was leaving Jericho
    with his disciples and a siz-
    able crowd,
    Bartimaeus, a blind man, the
    son of Timaeus,
    sat by the roadside begging.
On hearing that it was Jesus of
    Nazareth,
    he began to cry out and say,
    "Jesus, son of David, have
    pity on me."
And many rebuked him, telling
    him to be silent.
But he kept calling out all the
    more,
    "Son of David, have pity on me."
Jesus stopped and said, "Call him."
So they called the blind man, saying to
    him,
    "Take courage; get up, Jesus is
    calling you."
He threw aside his cloak, sprang up,
    and came to Jesus.
Jesus said to him in reply, "What do
    you want me to do for you?"
The blind man replied to him, "Master,
    I want to see."
Jesus told him, "Go your way; your
    faith has saved you."
Immediately he received his sight
    and followed him on the way.

Reflecting on the Gospel

In today's gospel passage about Jesus's encounter with the beggar Bartimaeus, there is a masterful interplay of sight and sound. Having told us that Bartimaeus is unable to see, Mark shifts the emphasis to auditory and vocal exchanges. Bartimaeus hears that Jesus is passing by, so the beggar starts shouting out his request for mercy. The others tried to silence Bartimaeus, but he calls out all the more. Jesus hears him and says, "Call him." They summon Bartimaeus, telling him that Jesus is calling him.

With the repetition of the verb *call*, Jesus now becomes the insistent one calling out to Bartimaeus. Jesus's attention is turned completely to this person in need. This is not a curt "What do you want?" but a deeply interpersonal exchange between Jesus and Bartimaeus as Jesus asks, "What do you want me to do for you?" It is not clear whether Bartimaeus is asking to see for the first time or to see again (the Greek verb has both senses). As with the woman healed of hemorrhages (5:34), Jesus tells Bartimaeus to go, assuring him that his faith has saved/healed him (the Greek verb used here also can have both senses). And like the fishermen at the shore of the Sea of Galilee (1:16-20), Bartimaeus does not go away but follows Jesus on the way.

In its original literary context in the Gospel of Mark, today's passage is the second in a pair of bookends. The first is the story at the beginning of the central section of teaching on discipleship, in which Jesus cures another blind man in Bethsaida (8:22-26).

The two healing stories enclose a section in which Jesus's followers are struggling mightily to understand and follow him. Yet they misunderstand and even oppose him, especially as Jesus begins to teach them about his coming passion. The story of Bartimaeus gives assurance that the disciples can be healed of their inner blindness and thus be enabled to follow Jesus on the way. Like Bartimaeus, who threw aside his cloak to come to Jesus, they may need to cast off whatever shields them from the demands of Jesus's way. Whatever keeps them from being vulnerable to the costly love of Jesus will need to be tossed away.

If the disciples were among those who were blinded to the needs of the beggar and who tried to muffle his cries for mercy, they will need to learn to attune their ears to such cries, and call such persons to Jesus, rather than stand in their way. The disciples must want to see as Jesus sees. And whenever they cannot see or understand what God is doing, as when their beloved teacher cries out in anguish from the cross, seemingly unheard by God (15:34), they will need to learn to follow blindly on the way, trusting their inner vision that assures them of divine love that is stronger than any suffering, and even than death.

Preparing to Proclaim

Key words and phrases: "He threw aside his cloak, sprang up, and came to Jesus."

To the point: It is a small detail, but perhaps significant, that Bartimaeus throws aside his cloak when Jesus calls him. His cloak is not a bad thing; it provides warmth and comfort and even a bit of privacy from prying eyes. But when he needs to move hastily to Jesus, it will trip him up and get in the way, so he simply casts it aside. It might be one of very few possessions for this man whose blindness prevents him from working, but he holds it loosely. He does not let attachment to worldly things—even good ones—keep him from responding wholeheartedly to his encounter with Christ. Many of us pray for Jesus's presence and healing, much like Bartimaeus did. But we are not always ready to drop what we need to in order to be present to the ways he's already working in our lives.

Psalmist Preparation

The psalm has a sense of the cyclical nature of our spiritual lives. There are times for going out weeping and times for coming back rejoicing. There are times of abundance and lack, of ease and struggle, of joy and suffering. But the overarching trajectory is one that brings us to the joy and healing that God promises; that's where the cycle promises to land us. As you prepare to proclaim this psalm, reflect on a time that in your life when you've been brought through suffering to greater joy. Give thanks to God for the strength granted to you, and bring this gratitude into your proclamation.

Making Connections

Between the readings: Jesus heals Bartimaeus of both his physical blindness and his social exclusion. When he receives his sight, Bartimaeus is able to follow Jesus, rejoining a community in which he'd been unable to take part. In the first reading, Jeremiah envisions a world in which those who are blind and lame are brought to God *in the midst* of God's beloved people. They are no longer excluded from community but rather are embraced even in the midst of their disability.

To experience: We might not be able to heal disability as Jesus did, but we can work to heal broken structures and societies that do not allow for full participation from people who are disabled. Rather than making exceptions for those who need accommodations, the disabled community invites us to re-vision our buildings and activities in ways that will not exclude people in the first place.

Homily Points

• Today's gospel is one of many passages that focus on Jesus's power to heal or cure. It is important to name up front that such passages have been used by preachers to further marginalize people with disabilities. Let us approach the story of Bartimaeus with a great respect for his dignity and autonomy. Jesus certainly shows Bartimaeus this respect. It can be easy to assume that someone who is blind would most certainly want to receive the gift of sight. However, disability advocates make clear that not everyone wants to be "cured" of their disability. People find meaning and purpose while living with all sorts of conditions. It matters that Jesus asks Bartimaeus what he wants. Jesus does not just assume and then act on Bartimaeus. He respects that Bartimaeus knows what is best for his body—and in this case, it is a desire to see.

• Healing narratives like today's gospel are meant to reveal something about Jesus as the Son of God. They are not meant to argue that people with disabilities need to be cured. Rather, such narratives show the listening, responsive presence of Jesus and the ways in which Christ's healing impacts the community.

• Notice how the crowds chastise Bartimaeus for crying out to Jesus at first. They tell him to be silent. But once Jesus responds, the crowd changes their tune. They begin encouraging Bartimaeus, "Take courage; get up, Jesus is calling you." The encounter between Jesus and Bartimaeus heals the crowd of their dismissive ways.

CELEBRATION

Model Penitential Act

Presider: Mindful of our need for God's mercy, let us call to mind our sins and ask the Lord for forgiveness . . . *[pause]*

Lord Jesus, you are the source of healing and wholeness: Lord, have mercy.

Christ Jesus, you are the font of every blessing: Christ, have mercy.

Lord Jesus, you are the Savior of the world: Lord, have mercy.

Model Universal Prayer (Prayer of the Faithful)

Presider: Trusting that the spirit of the Lord is always with us, we bring our needs before the Lord.

Response: Lord, hear our prayer.

Make congregations accessible to people of all abilities . . .

Further the work of disability advocates who lobby for more inclusive professional and social environments . . .

Free peoples oppressed by colonization . . .

Deepen the prayer and devotional lives of this community . . .

Presider: God of heaven and earth, you sent your Spirit to dwell with us and guide us in the ways of justice and faithfulness. Hear our prayers that we might stay rooted in your way. We ask this through Christ our Lord. **Amen.**

Liturgy and Music

Sometimes a rock and roll song hits the nail right on the head. I'm thinking of Bruce Springsteen's anthem, "Everybody's Got a Hungry Heart."

We all yearn. We yearn for clear vision, for healing, for a sense of purpose, for "happiness" (although I think a better word might be "contentment"). And what a gift it is when the tears we shed are transformed into cries of rejoicing: when, through God's grace, we move beyond impairment, whether it be physical or emotional; when we see healing take place in our divided world; when we put behind us the sorrow of yesterday and move forward with a sense of purpose, dedication, and exuberance. Such landmarks of a journey are beyond price.

Today's gospel from Mark is not Jesus's only encounter with the blind. But so often it was the physically blind, the infirm, who were the ones most alert to the Savior's presence. The religious experts, the ones who "saw," were those tagged as "blind fools." Bartimaeus yearned to see. And when given the chance, he called out to the One he knew could help him. Though impaired, the vision of his heart told him who to trust.

Some words from Taizé can help us focus on this journey toward light and healing. Consider "Jésus le Christ," "All My Heart Lies Open to You," or "Criste lux mundi" (GIA).

We pray for new vision, a vision that leads us from tear-stained faces to ones of exuberant joy. We need only ask, straightforwardly, as did Bartimaeus, the son of Timaeus, centuries ago.

Scan to listen to "Criste lux mundi."

COLLECT

Let us pray.

Pause for silent prayer

Almighty ever-living God,
increase our faith, hope, and charity,
and make us love what you command,
so that we may merit what you promise.
Through our Lord Jesus Christ, your Son,
who lives and reigns with you in the unity
    of the Holy Spirit,
God, for ever and ever. **Amen.**

FIRST READING
Jer 31:7-9

Thus says the LORD:
Shout with joy for Jacob,
    exult at the head of the nations;
    proclaim your praise and say:
The LORD has delivered his people,
    the remnant of Israel.
Behold, I will bring them back
    from the land of the north;
I will gather them from the ends of the
    world,
    with the blind and the lame in their
      midst,
the mothers and those with child;
    they shall return as an immense throng.
They departed in tears,
    but I will console them and guide them;
I will lead them to brooks of water,
    on a level road, so that none shall
      stumble.
For I am a father to Israel,
    Ephraim is my first-born.

RESPONSORIAL PSALM

Ps 126:1-2, 2-3, 4-5, 6

℟. (3) The Lord has done great things for
us; we are filled with joy.

When the LORD brought back the captives
of Zion,
we were like men dreaming.
Then our mouth was filled with laughter,
and our tongue with rejoicing.

℟. The Lord has done great things for us;
we are filled with joy.

Then they said among the nations,
"The LORD has done great things for
them."
The LORD has done great things for us;
we are glad indeed.

℟. The Lord has done great things for us;
we are filled with joy.

Restore our fortunes, O LORD,
like the torrents in the southern desert.
Those that sow in tears
shall reap rejoicing.

℟. The Lord has done great things for us;
we are filled with joy.

Although they go forth weeping,
carrying the seed to be sown,
they shall come back rejoicing,
carrying their sheaves.

℟. The Lord has done great things for us;
we are filled with joy.

SECOND READING

Heb 5:1-6

Brothers and sisters:
Every high priest is taken from among men
and made their representative before
God,
to offer gifts and sacrifices for sins.
He is able to deal patiently with the
ignorant and erring,
for he himself is beset by weakness
and so, for this reason, must make sin
offerings for himself
as well as for the people.
No one takes this honor upon himself
but only when called by God,
just as Aaron was.
In the same way,
it was not Christ who glorified himself
in becoming high priest,
but rather the one who said to him:
You are my son:
this day I have begotten you;
just as he says in another place:
You are a priest forever
according to the order of
Melchizedek.

Living Liturgy

Liturgy and Vocation: The last few years have shown us just how important the "helping professions" are to the well-being of society. People who work as nurses, social workers, and educators have been on the front lines, providing care and support with or without greater institutional support. In particular, we have seen that educators do so much more than simply teach content related to their area of expertise. They attempt to engage and connect with students on an individual level. They connect students to resources in the community to help meet basic needs or supplement classroom learning. Sometimes they even put themselves at great physical risk to protect students. If all baptized people are invited to step into the role of priest, prophet, and leader, then those who choose to be educators can be special role models to us about how to embody the kind of priesthood discussed in today's reading from the letter to the Hebrews.

Paul describes high priests as humble and patient. Aware of their own human frailty and weakness, they offer sacrifices to God for the people as well as for themselves. The life of an educator is one of constant learning and selfless partnership. They commit to continuous learning in their content area and in methods of pedagogy, and they reach out to the broader community—parents, community leaders, and fellow teachers—to support that work. Amid the challenges, they believe their efforts will have positive impacts that will outlive the challenges they endure.

This interpretation of priesthood is unique, but it can call us to hold in prayer in a special way all of the people who have made caregiving their life's work. Theirs are the hands and feet through which God gives comfort to the scattered, despairing masses and helps the blinded to see. Their humble and persistent efforts give hope to all of God's people.

PROMPTS FOR FAITH-SHARING

• Where do you still need Jesus's healing work in your life? He already knows and shares your suffering; how can you increase your awareness of his promised presence?

• How can your community revision its spaces and programming to be more inclusive of people with disabilities?

• Do you have attachments that might be holding you back from following Jesus as readily and wholeheartedly as Bartimaeus does?

See Appendix B, p. 314,
for additional prompts.

GOSPEL ACCLAMATION
Matt 11:28

℟. Alleluia, alleluia.
Come to me, all you who labor and are burdened,
and I will give you rest, says the Lord.
℟. Alleluia, alleluia.

Gospel

Matt 5:1-12a; L667

When Jesus saw the crowds, he went
   up the mountain,
   and after he had sat down, his
      disciples came to him.
He began to teach them, saying:

"Blessed are the poor in spirit,
   for theirs is the Kingdom of
      heaven.
Blessed are they who mourn,
   for they will be comforted.
Blessed are the meek,
   for they will inherit the land.
Blessed are they who hunger and
      thirst for righteousness,
   for they will be satisfied.
Blessed are the merciful,
   for they will be shown mercy.
Blessed are the clean of heart,
   for they will see God.

Continued in Appendix A, p. 340,

See Appendix A., p. 307, for the other readings.

Reflecting on the Gospel

Today's gospel is a recipe for happiness. The Beatitudes are a prescription for what we can do to achieve heaven, which is an appropriate reminder for today's feast. The original Latin, *beatus*, can be translated as either "blessed" or "happy." So another way of looking at the Beatitudes is that they are steps we can take to grow in more authentic happiness.

This makes very little sense. Meek? Mourning? Thirsting? These do not sound like the predispositions for happiness. Happiness, in the modern sense, indicates success, stability, or pleasure. To be happy is to have all of one's wants met. It is to be carefree, fulfilled, or financially successful. It is to be free from disruption.

Yet the Beatitudes are telling us that happiness will come to those who are striving for that which is not currently present. Happiness exists for those who look beyond what exists and what is considered possible. Happiness comes to those of us who can see beyond what is available and into a world that does not yet exist. In a way, the Beatitudes remind us that happiness is for those who see the world both as it is and what it can be. It is for those who mourn, but also look toward the universal comfort of all peoples.

The Beatitudes also give us a map for the long game. Blessed are those who mourn, for they shall be comforted. They aren't comforted immediately. It's a comfort—a happiness—that will come in the future. Those who thirst for justice are not satisfied right now. They may not be satisfied in their whole lifetime. But they will be satisfied one day, when the kingdom of heaven is here, and justice has come for everyone.

We celebrate the saints all year long, with feast days and private devotions. Today is a day when we have the opportunity as the church on earth to celebrate our shared salvation with the church in heaven. During the penitential act, we invoke the community of the kingdom of heaven: "all the Angels and Saints, and you, my brothers and sisters." We are counted among the saints in our attendance at Mass. At the celebration of the Eucharist we are uniquely present not only with the universal church on earth, but with the full host in heaven, including all of the saints. We are both in the grind of the fallen world and participating in the kingdom of heaven at the end of time. We are those who mourn, but at Mass, we can glimpse what it means to be comforted. It is during the liturgy that those who hunger and thirst for justice know a moment of satisfaction. As humans, we come from Love and return to Love, and today we celebrate the full thrust of that journey, through the experience of the Beatitudes.

Preparing to Proclaim
Key words and phrases: "[T]heirs is the Kingdom of heaven."

To the point: On this Solemnity of All Saints, we remember all those who have preceded us in death and who now live with God in heaven. This gospel reminds us of the promises of God: comfort, land, satisfaction, mercy—and, repeated most often, getting to see God and be with God in heaven. The saints in all their diversity suffered through all the pain we experience in this life; they remind us now that this is not the whole story. All of our suffering, all of our attempts at goodness, are seen and known and loved by God.

Model Rite for the Blessing and Sprinkling of Water
Presider: Today's second reading reminds us that we are God's children, beloved by the one who creates and calls us. Let us lean into God's mercy as we ask for forgiveness for our sins . . . *[pause]*
   [continue with The Roman Missal, *Appendix II]*

Model Universal Prayer (Prayer of the Faithful)

Presider: Guided by our ancestors in faith, let us bring our needs and the needs of the world before the Lord.

Response: Lord, hear our prayer.

Raise up in the church young people dedicated to service and justice . . .

Grant strength and perseverance to the mentors and teachers who show us how to embody the Christian faith . . .

Fulfill the desires of people seeking safe, affordable housing . . .

Welcome into the halls of heaven all those who have died . . .

Presider: Gracious God, you inspire people across time to live lives of holiness and to sacrifice for the good of the gospel. Receive our prayers that we might grow in holiness and readiness to serve you in word and deed. We ask this through Christ our Lord. **Amen.**

Living Liturgy

If we look across the vast horizon of personalities who make up the company of saints, it is, quite frankly, a breathtaking thing to ponder. Here are women who spoke their mind to popes and led armies; men who rejected armies and gave themselves over to peace (some became popes as well!); and men and women who turned conventional thought upside down in the name of another One who did the same thing.

Jesus gives us the Beatitudes as a new way to see the world, a vision that does not run away from suffering and challenge but rather sees purpose and blessing in it. That humble preacher from Galilee, the Son of God made man, also turned conventional thought upside down—and the saints followed suit.

Everything about our readings today involves a transformation of vision: truly, as Revelation says, the triumphant ones survived times of great distress—and because of that, they are now set apart from the world as "children of God." Note that with this appellation comes the recognition in John's first letter that "the world does not know us." We choose a different path, one not recognized by the world. We choose the path of the saints.

COLLECT
Let us pray.

Pause for silent prayer

Almighty ever-living God,
by whose gift we venerate in one celebration
the merits of all the Saints,
bestow on us, we pray,
through the prayers of so many intercessors,
an abundance of the reconciliation with you
for which we earnestly long.
Through our Lord Jesus Christ, your Son,
who lives and reigns with you in the unity of
   the Holy Spirit,
God, for ever and ever. **Amen.**

FOR REFLECTION

• God calls all of us to holiness and sainthood; God wants all of us to end up in heaven. How do you hear God's call to sainthood? How do you strive for holiness?

• Most of the canonized saints achieved great and visible works of holiness, but there are countless uncanonized saints who are in heaven after living lives of quieter and smaller holiness. How might you find ways to live out God's call to holiness in the midst of whatever else is going on in your life?

See Appendix B, p. 314, for additional questions.

Homily Points

• In today's gospel, Jesus offers a litany of blessings to those whom society often casts aside. Jesus does not say "Blessed are the rich, the powerful, and the successful." Instead, Jesus bestows blessings amid suffering. Consider Saint Josephine of Bakhita, who after years of enslavement experienced the grace to forgive her former owners. Jesus bestows blessings amid heartache. Consider Saint Monica, who after years of prayer saw her wayward son Augustine become an influential father of the church.

• Jesus bestows blessings amid injustice. Consider Saint Martin de Porres, who after initially being denied admission into a religious order because of his race went on to make vows and found a children's hospital. Jesus bestows blessing amid persecution. Consider Saint Oscar Romero, who served the people of El Salvador for years in dangerous conditions before his assassination while cele-

brating Mass. Saints across time trusted that Jesus meant what he said when he deemed people blessed in their darkest hours. Their lives bore witness to the inbreaking of the kingdom of heaven here on earth. In the moments that feel least blessed, Jesus asks his followers to trust him, trust that the Son of God is working to redeem what feels most broken.

• The vision of God's kingdom put forth in today's first reading from Revelation imagines a time when all people come together before the Lord. Their differences remain. The author recognizes in the multitude those from "every nation, race, people, and tongue." This insight lets us know that the kingdom of God is not a homogenous place. Rather, it is the dividing lines drawn so often between differences that wash away in God's kingdom. All join in their uniqueness to worship before the Lamb.

GOSPEL ACCLAMATION
See John 6:40

R̸. Alleluia, alleluia.
This is the will of my Father, says the Lord,
that everyone who sees the Son and believes
    in him
may have eternal life.
R̸. Alleluia, alleluia.

Gospel   John 6:37-40; L668

Jesus said to the crowds:
"Everything that the Father gives me
    will come to me,
    and I will not reject anyone who
        comes to me,
    because I came down from heaven
        not to do my own will
    but the will of the one who sent me.
And this is the will of the one who
    sent me,
    that I should not lose anything of
        what he gave me,
    but that I should raise it on the
        last day.
For this is the will of my Father,
    that everyone who sees the Son and
        believes in him
    may have eternal life,
    and I shall raise him on the last day."

See Appendix A, p. 308, for the other readings.

*or any other readings from L668 or any readings
from the Masses for the Dead (L1011–1016)*

Reflecting on the Gospel
"I will not reject anyone who comes to me."

Jesus is in a constant state of invitation. He invites John and James to travel with him. He invites children to sit with him. He invites Martha to abandon the cooking and chat. He invites the sick to be healed. The one group he doesn't seem particularly inclined to speak with are the Pharisees, and yet he still responds to them when they seek him out.

This position of invitation means that Jesus must also deal with rejection. There are those in Nazareth who don't want anything to do with Jesus, and those who threaten him and his disciples physically. Peter rejects their friendship three times. In the most crucial moment, Jesus is rejected by a crowd in favor of Barabbas, with deadly consequences. Jesus, we know, is well acquainted with rejection.

He tells us, "I will not reject anyone who comes to me." This is easy for someone to say, but difficult to live out. Yet Jesus tells us in the Gospel of John that his invitation exists for everyone. There is no amount of sin, shame, or personal despair that will cause Jesus to reject someone.

Modern life is rife with rejection. Many students are rejected from colleges. In professional life, the rejection of a job application is inevitable. In personal life, rejection is a natural part of the journey to finding one's spouse. People reject invitations to birthday parties and weddings, declining with great apology. Banks reject requests for a loan. When an invitation to friends is rejected, it can sting, even if it isn't very high stakes. We know what rejection feels like, whether it's large or small, consequential or minute. That means we should know how jarring it is for Jesus to say that he will not reject *anyone* who comes to him. His invitation is eternal and his rejection is unthinkable. The only way we separate ourselves from Jesus is if we choose it.

Today we celebrate all those who have gone before us in the hope of salvation, knowing that Jesus will not reject anyone who seeks him. We remember our family members and friends who have died, and we pray for the repose of their souls in heaven. But we do this with immense hope, because we know that those who seek Jesus, and the love he offers us, are never rejected. "And this is the will of the one who sent me, that I should not lose anything of what he gave me, but that I should raise it on the last day." Today we look toward that last day, alongside those whose physical presence we have lost, but whose spiritual hope we share.

Preparing to Proclaim
Key words and phrases: "[T]his is the will of my Father, that everyone who sees the Son and believes in him may have eternal life."

To the point: Where Christ goes, there is life. This theme resounds through all of the many options for today's gospel reading. It is through Christ that we come to share in the abundance of life he promises. On this day when we commemorate all the faithful departed, we remember that death is not the end of Christ's story. He has participated in it fully and has come through it and triumphed over it. And out of pure overflowing love, he shares that victory wit[us; death is not the end of our story, either.

Model Penitential Act
Presider: Jesus Christ, the resurrected Lord, intercedes for us at the right han[of God. With faith and hope in his mercy, let us call to mind our sins . . . [*paus[*
    Lord Jesus, you suffered out of love for your people: Lord, have mercy.

Christ Jesus, you died a painful death on the cross: Christ, have mercy.

Lord Jesus, you rose to new life and make way for us to do the same: Lord, have mercy.

Model Universal Prayer (Prayer of the Faithful)

Presider: As we await the coming of God's kingdom, let us lift up the needs of our community and the needs of the world.

Response: Lord, hear our prayer.

Bless those who minister to the dying with a compassionate spirit and listening heart . . .

Strengthen medical personnel, hospice workers, and all who care for the dying . . .

Make your loving presence known to all those who are near death . . .

Bring peace and consolation to everyone in this community who is grieving the death of a loved one . . .

Presider: Merciful God, you sent your Son to comfort those who mourn and bring all people into the peace of everlasting life. Hear our prayers that we might be attentive to your presence and live out our days to the fullest in praise of you. We ask this through Christ our Lord. **Amen.**

Living Liturgy

One of the greatest burdens the world bore through the recent global pandemic was the inability to grieve the loss of loved ones through funeral celebrations. Part of that grieving is placing before us (and within us, in our hearts) the hope that those who we lost are now at peace. Cultures all over the world cultivate this hope, from Mexico to Ireland to the Philippines. Oddly, it is America, that most modern of cultures, that seems to turn its back on death, ignoring the legacy of powerful memories and the advocacy of those who we have lost.

Scratch the surface among the living, though, and the stories will spill forth: a son who lost a father knows that his dad was present through a crisis; a young woman intuitively senses that her departed grandparent walked with her through a dark time. We all have such stories.

COLLECT (from the first Mass)
Let us pray.

Pause for silent prayer

Listen kindly to our prayers, O Lord,
and, as our faith in your Son,
raised from the dead, is deepened,
so may our hope of resurrection for your
    departed servants
also find new strength.
Through our Lord Jesus Christ, your Son,
who lives and reigns with you in the unity of
    the Holy Spirit,
God, for ever and ever. **Amen.**

FOR REFLECTION

• For whom specifically do you pray on this commemoration of all the faithful departed? What did you learn from them about faith or life? Share a memory of them here.

• Liturgical language tells us that "life is changed, not ended" by death. Spend some time envisioning life after death. What do you hope it looks like and feels like? What changes do you hope for in the life that is to come?

See Appendix B, p. 314, for additional questions.

Homily Points

• Guided by profound wisdom from today's Scripture and liturgical texts, we dare to wonder: What might life after death be like? How does God connect with those who have gone before us? The first reading from Wisdom imagines life after death as peaceful. The dying process can be painful for many. Perhaps your loved one experienced physical pain at the end of their life from a terminal illness or emotional pain that can come from reflecting on dreams unfulfilled. Regardless, we can take solace in the belief that our loved ones are being held "in the hand of God . . ." God cradles our beloved dead. The author of Wisdom assures us, "they are in peace."

• Today's second reading from Saint Paul's letter to the Romans imagines life after death as free from sin. No one dies perfect. Still,

Saint Paul describes the "newness of life" to come for those who have died. He exclaims: "We know that our old self was crucified with him, so that our sinful body might be done away with, that we might no longer be in slavery to sin." Sin and death do not have the final say. God shows mercy to our beloved dead. Saint Paul assures us that "a dead person has been absolved from sin."

• Finally, the gospel from John imagines life after death as eternity united with Christ. Death can be a time of reexamining faith. No matter where they landed on the faith spectrum during their time on earth, Jesus asserts: "that everyone who sees the Son and believes in him may have eternal life . . ." God desires to be in relationship with our beloved dead. No one will be lost or left behind.

SPIRITUALITY

GOSPEL ACCLAMATION
John 14:23

℟. Alleluia, alleluia.
Whoever loves me will keep my word,
says the Lord; and my Father will love
    him
and we will come to him.
℟. Alleluia, alleluia.

Gospel

Mark 12:28b-34; L152B

**One of the scribes came to
    Jesus and asked him,
"Which is the first of all the
    commandments?"
Jesus replied, "The first is this:**
Hear, O Israel!
The Lord our God is Lord
    alone!
You shall love the Lord your
    God with all your heart,
with all your soul,
with all your mind,
and with all your strength.
The second is this:
You shall love your neighbor as
    yourself.
**There is no other commandment
    greater than these."
The scribe said to him, "Well said,
    teacher.
You are right in saying,
    'He is One and there is no other than
    he.'
And 'to love him with all your heart,
    with all your understanding,
    with all your strength,
    and to love your neighbor as
    yourself'
is worth more than all burnt offerings
    and sacrifices."
And when Jesus saw that he answered
    with understanding,
he said to him,
"You are not far from the kingdom of
    God."
And no one dared to ask him any more
    questions.**

Reflecting on the Gospel

There's a famous scene in the play *Fiddler on the Roof*, where Tevye, the protagonist, tells his wife Golde that he has decided to give his permission for their daughter Hodel to marry Perchik, a student and Bolshevik revolutionary. Golde protests that he has absolutely nothing, but Tevye replies that it's a new world, that now people marry for love, and what can they do? Tevye then turns

to Golde and asks her if she loves him. She doesn't know how to respond; she skirts the question and when Tevye keeps pressing her for an answer, she recites all that she has been doing for him for twenty-five years: washing his clothes, cooking his meals, cleaning his house, giving him children, milking the cow. Still not satisfied, Tevye asks her again if she loves him. She observes, "For twenty-five years I've lived with him, fought with him, starved with him, twenty-five years my bed is his; if that's not love, what is?"

In the play, Golde gives all the evidence of love in action and then concludes that these constitute love. In today's gospel a scribe asks a question that comes at the issue of love from another direction. He wants to know which is the first of all the commandments, that is, what actions must take priority if one wants to respond correctly to God's love. Jesus doesn't help him out with the particulars. He simply advises him to love God back with his entire being: heart, soul, mind, and strength. And then a bit more concretely, he adds that loving one's neighbor as oneself puts flesh and bones on this loving response to divine love.

The dialogue between the scribe and Jesus, like that of Tevye and Golde, emphasizes that love does not consist so much in feelings, as in concrete loving deeds toward the other. This is how Jesus can speak about love as something that is commanded. One cannot be commanded to feel warmly toward another, but one can be mandated to treat another with loving kindness. Knowing oneself as the recipient of gratuitous divine acts of loving kindness enables one to respond in kind. A concrete way by which human beings can express love toward God is by extending that love toward fellow human beings.

The two-pronged formulation of the love command does not give hard-and-fast answers about how to make difficult choices for prioritizing loving deeds in daily circumstances. Jesus, for example, was faced with hard choices several times when the command to love seemed to clash with the command to observe the Sabbath. Which took priority? In a number of instances, he healed people on the Sabbath, choosing to raise up a woman bent double (Luke 13:10-17), to restore a man's withered hand (Mark 3:1-6), and a blind man's sight (John 9:16). When challenged, he interprets these actions as giving proper expression to the intent of Sabbath, fulfilling the prime commands to love God and neighbor. When one's whole self is centered on love, that's all that's needed to know how to make the day-to-day choices.

Preparing to Proclaim

Key words and phrases: "There is no other commandment greater than these."

To the point: The scribe who asks Jesus about the greatest commandment is an interesting character. It is hard to get a read on him: this kind of question, from a scribe, is usually intended as a trick for Jesus. His response, though, is one of sincere acceptance, showing an understanding that earns Jesus's approval. Perhaps his question, then, was not a trick but one of an earnest seeker striving after God in love. Jesus's response gives two commandments rooted in love; perhaps the scribe's recognition of the truth in Jesus's answer came from a heart already shaped by genuine love for God and neighbor. In any event, this gospel reminds us that many of our human boundaries fall apart in the face of the God who calls us to love. Jesus and the scribe—usually adversaries—here understand each other and are able to engage in honest dialogue.

Psalmist Preparation

This psalm includes a litany of titles for God that remind us of all the things that God is for us. It is this God, who creates and sustains and protects us, that deserves the response of love that is commanded by both the first reading and the gospel. As you prepare to proclaim this psalm, make your own litany of titles for God. Who has God been for you and what has God done for you? Bring wholehearted gratitude for these into your proclamation of this little love song for God.

Making Connections

Between the readings: The first reading gives the Mosaic command that Jesus will cite as the greatest. The wholehearted love for God that it enjoins upon Israel is the basis for all other commandments. God makes commandments out of loving desire for our well-being, not a desire to control. We are called to obedience but not thoughtless obeisance. We are called to respond to God's commands with the same love from which God makes them.

To experience: Love for neighbor and love for God are two sides of the same coin. Where one is truly found, so is found the other. Those of us who are interested and involved in ministry cannot engage in churchy affairs as one hobby among many. We, like all believers, are called to let ourselves be transformed by our encounter with Christ. Our love for God is evidenced by the way we treat those around us.

Homily Points

• Employee handbooks feature plenty of rules—but after a few weeks on the job, it becomes clear that not all rules are created equal. For instance, the dress code policy may mandate collared shirts and close-toed shoes. But if our church got a dollar for every time an employee got away with wearing sandals or a collar-less blouse, we could stop passing out the collection basket!

• On the flipside, a good handbook will also instruct employees to treat everyone with respect—and any action to the contrary should result in disciplinary action. It isn't that the dress code does not matter at all, but respect for persons matters more. This rule is what enables a healthy workplace culture, so it receives more attention.

• Similarly, the commandments that guide our faith life vary in weight. In terms of church teachings, a comment Pope Francis makes on an airplane is significant, but a decree put forth at a church council holds even more sway. Then we have today's gospel. Jesus says clearly—no commandment is greater than these: you shall love the Lord with all your heart, soul, mind, and strength. And you shall love your neighbor as yourself. Love God. Love your neighbor. Love yourself. Everything else stems from these ancient calls. As followers of Christ, baptized in the Holy Spirit, we are sent into the world to make God's steadfast love known to all of creation. We are also called to recognize the ways creation reflects God's love back to us.

Model Penitential Act

Presider: In today's first reading, Moses tells the people to fear the Lord and to keep God's commands. For the times we have fallen short of God's hopes for us, let us ask for mercy . . . *[pause]*

> Lord Jesus, you fulfill what the prophets foretold: Lord, have mercy.
> Christ Jesus, you bring communities together in love: Christ, have mercy.
> Lord Jesus, you draw people into the kingdom of God: Lord, have mercy.

Model Universal Prayer (Prayer of the Faithful)

Presider: With hearts open to the merciful love of God, let us offer our prayers and petitions.

Response: Lord, hear our prayer.

Enlighten all ministers who are preaching the good news of Jesus Christ today . . .

Foster a spirit of repentance among all people in need of healing . . .

Deepen the bonds of unity and respect among Christians of all traditions . . .

Awaken the call to discipleship in the ordinary lives of each of us gathered here . . .

Presider: God of blessing, you promised a great light for the people who sit in darkness. Receive our prayers that we too might be beacons of light for the church and the world. We ask this through Christ our Lord. **Amen.**

Liturgy and Music

If there were ever a set of readings that cut to the core of both Judaism and Christianity, this is the week. For today we encounter the pivotal admonition found in Deuteronomy 6: *"Shema, Yisrael!"* יִשְׂרָאֵל שְׁמַע. It lies at the very heart of the spiritual teachings of both faiths, as is recounted in the conversation between Jesus and the scribe.

But—and here is where we might go wrong, take a detour—it is not the law itself that is important. What counts is love. Read carefully the dialogue in Mark's Gospel and it's clear to see: it is not prescriptive actions ("burnt offerings and sacrifices") that matter most; it is, rather, holding a spirit of love—love of God and love of neighbor—that is at the heart of all we are called to be. To put law before love is to go astray. And that is why, at the end of the encounter, Jesus says to the scribe, "You are not far from the kingdom of God."

Love, then, is relational—between us and God, between us and our neighbor, and between us and our very selves. Consider Feargal King's "Love One Another" (WLP/GIA). Laws are important! But only insofar as they continue to challenge us to love with more intention.

COLLECT
Let us pray.

Pause for silent prayer

Almighty and merciful God,
by whose gift your faithful offer you
right and praiseworthy service,
grant, we pray,
that we may hasten without stumbling
to receive the things you have promised.
Through our Lord Jesus Christ, your Son,
who lives and reigns with you in the unity
  of the Holy Spirit,
God, for ever and ever. **Amen.**

FIRST READING
Deut 6:2-6

Moses spoke to the people, saying:
  "Fear the LORD, your God,
  and keep, throughout the days of your
    lives,
  all his statutes and commandments
    which I enjoin on you,
  and thus have long life.
Hear then, Israel, and be careful to observe
    them,
  that you may grow and prosper the
    more,
  in keeping with the promise of the
    LORD, the God of your fathers,
  to give you a land flowing with milk
    and honey.

"Hear, O Israel! The LORD is our God, the
    LORD alone!
Therefore, you shall love the LORD, your
    God,
  with all your heart,
  and with all your soul,
  and with all your strength.
Take to heart these words which I enjoin
    on you today."

RESPONSORIAL PSALM

Ps 18:2-3, 3-4, 47, 51

℟. (2) I love you, Lord, my strength.

I love you, O Lord, my strength,
 O Lord, my rock, my fortress, my
  deliverer.

℟. I love you, Lord, my strength.

My God, my rock of refuge,
 my shield, the horn of my salvation, my
  stronghold!
Praised be the Lord, I exclaim,
 and I am safe from my enemies.

℟. I love you, Lord, my strength.

The Lord lives! And blessed be my rock!
 Extolled be God my savior,
you who gave great victories to your king
 and showed kindness to your anointed.

℟. I love you, Lord, my strength.

SECOND READING

Heb 7:23-28

Brothers and sisters:
The levitical priests were many
 because they were prevented by death
  from remaining in office,
 but Jesus, because he remains forever,
 has a priesthood that does not pass
  away.
Therefore, he is always able to save those
 who approach God through him,
 since he lives forever to make
  intercession for them.

It was fitting that we should have such a
  high priest:
 holy, innocent, undefiled, separated
  from sinners,
 higher than the heavens.
He has no need, as did the high priests,
 to offer sacrifice day after day,
 first for his own sins and then for those
  of the people;
 he did that once for all when he offered
  himself.
For the law appoints men subject to
  weakness to be high priests,
 but the word of the oath, which was
  taken after the law,
 appoints a son,
who has been made perfect forever.

✝ CATECHESIS

Living Liturgy

Liturgy and Community: When Jesus became human and began his ministry of teaching and healing, he showed us more than how to understand death and how to achieve everlasting life. He also taught us how to live in right relationship with God and each other. At the time of Jesus, faithful people believed that God needed to be appeased through strict adherence to rituals and gestures. What we learn from Jesus in today's readings and throughout the gospels is that God is primarily concerned with our relationships. It is through loving, generous relationships that wounds are healed and reconciliation is achieved.

Consider the religious communities who showed great compassion and love to people affected by HIV and AIDS in the 1980s and 1990s. Ministries like the House of Ruth in Louisville, Mission Dolores Parish in San Francisco, and Bonaventure House in Chicago provided care to many men and women who had been cut off from family and community because of the fear and stigma associated with the disease. The clergy, religious, and laypeople who ministered to these communities did so without pausing to determine if the individuals needing care were upright or worthy. They simply saw people who deserved compassionate care because they were human beings, every one, blessed and beloved by God.

God's commandments and teachings are strong guideposts that we should pay attention to. They are a roadmap that helps us see if we are on the right path to finding and understanding God's will. However, the ministry of Christ throughout the gospels tells us that approaching our faith as a checklist is not the ultimate goal. God's commandments and decrees are meant to lead us deeper into the compassionate, relational, and merciful heart of God. If we are confused about which way to turn, Jesus tells us that we need to go in the direction of love—real and embodied.

PROMPTS FOR FAITH-SHARING

• If you had the opportunity to ask Jesus a question like the scribe does, what would you ask him?

• How do you most powerfully experience the love of God? Where do you need help in cultivating an awareness of God's presence?

• How do you show your love for God in how you live your daily life?

See Appendix B, p. 314, for additional prompts.

SPIRITUALITY

GOSPEL ACCLAMATION
Matt 5:3

℟. Alleluia, alleluia.
Blessed are the poor in spirit,
for theirs is the kingdom of heaven.
℟. Alleluia, alleluia.

Gospel

Mark 12:38-44; L155B

In the course of his teaching
    Jesus said to the crowds,
  "Beware of the scribes, who
      like to go around in long
      robes
  and accept greetings in the
      marketplaces,
  seats of honor in synagogues,
  and places of honor at
      banquets.
They devour the houses of
    widows and, as a pretext,
  recite lengthy prayers.
They will receive a very severe
    condemnation."

He sat down opposite the treasury
  and observed how the crowd put
      money into the treasury.
Many rich people put in large sums.
A poor widow also came and put in two
    small coins worth a few cents.
Calling his disciples to himself, he said
    to them,
  "Amen, I say to you, this poor widow
      put in more
  than all the other contributors to the
      treasury.
For they have all contributed from their
    surplus wealth,
  but she, from her poverty, has
      contributed all she had,
  her whole livelihood."

or Mark 12:41-44 in Appendix A, p. 308.

Reflecting on the Gospel

The first reading today offers the story of a widow who is down to her last handful of flour and a tiny bit of oil. She is just about to try to eke out something for her son and herself to eat, certain it would be their last meal. While gathering sticks at the entrance of the city, the widow encounters Elijah, who asks her first for a cup of water and then for a bit of bread. She explains her situation, and Elijah's response seems initially to be incredibly insensitive. He asks her to bring him a little cake first even before she prepares something for herself and her son. What the biblical author does not recount is what kind of conflict such a request must have produced for the widow. Should she trust Elijah's God, whom the prophet insists will ensure that her jar of flour will not go empty nor the jug of oil run dry? Or should she follow her motherly instincts to feed her child first? The obligations of hospitality win out; like the widow in the gospel, she gives all she had to live on. Miraculously, the prophet's promise of a never-ending supply of flour and oil comes true.

In the gospel, we see a similar vignette of a widow who puts her last two coins, a paltry sum, into the temple treasury. Jesus comments that in contrast to those who gave from their surplus, her contribution was "all she had, her whole livelihood." Literally, the Greek says she "gave her whole life." On the one hand, we see in this woman one who embodies Jesus' gift of his whole self. As this episode is positioned just before the passion narrative, it appears that Jesus's words are laudatory of the widow's total self-gift from her position of want, held out as a model to Jesus's disciples.

Another way to understand the gospel is to see that the widow's action comes on the heels of Jesus's critique of scribes who thrive on their privileges and seek out honor. Worst of all, they "devour the houses of widows." It is not clear to what practices this phrase refers, but the scribes may be the ancient equivalent of televangelists who bilk unsuspecting widows of their last dollars. In Mark's Gospel, Jesus is very critical of the temple institution, and he warns his disciples not to ever be the kind of leader who would prey on those who are most vulnerable.

In these readings there is a particular warning to religious leaders not to exploit those who are poorest. There is also an invitation to all the faithful to emulate the hospitality of God, whose total gift of self is replicated in Jesus's self-surrender in love. In no way does such a stance glorify poverty, for throughout the gospel we see Jesus's intense efforts to raise up those who are poorest. Rather, these readings provoke reflection on and analysis of the causes of hunger and poverty, urging us to do all in our power to eradicate them. Such work takes everything we have.

Preparing to Proclaim

Key words and phrases: "[S]he, from her poverty, has contributed all she had."

To the point: This poignant passage reiterates, as so much of the gospel does, that God's ways are not our ways. Without the protection and status of husband or sons, widows were left vulnerable to poverty and social exclusion. This widow faces those conditions bravely, enters the temple to offer what she can, and is commended by Jesus for her generosity. She makes a gift that seems small to those around her. She herself probably perceived this as a small gift, even though she alone knew how hard it would make her life. And yet this brief moment has been noticed and memorialized, celebrated all these thousands of years later. We, likewise, do not know what impact our sacrifices and generosity have. Things that might seem small or meaningless are noticed by God and taken up into the bigger project of bringing about God's vision of justice and love.

Psalmist Preparation

This psalm affirms God's care for those who are seen as less-than by society. Those who are oppressed, hungry, imprisoned, blind, foreign, orphaned, widowed—all these receive God's special care. We participate in this both as receivers of God's care and as agents of God's care. As you prepare to proclaim this psalm, reflect on both sides of this. Think about how you have received God's care when you've been in need; think also about how you have brought God's loving care to others in need. Remember that it is only through God's gifts and goodness that you are able to serve, and bring gratitude into your proclamation of this psalm.

Making Connections

Between the readings: The first reading also gives us a story of a widow whose generosity was noticed and amplified by God. She has only enough food for one more meal, and she expects that she and her son will starve when that meal is over. Even from this state of desperate poverty, though, she responds to Elijah with hospitality, tending to his needs in addition to her own. And God sees her and responds to her generosity with more generosity: her small supply of food miraculously stretches from one meal's worth to a full year's worth of meals.

To experience: The widow's agency in this story reminds us that "the poor" are not some passive group of people awaiting our generosity and care. People who are poor are *people*. They have families and friends. They have stories and dreams. They have callings and gifts; they are called to and capable of generosity. An awareness of their personhood and agency should permeate all our attempts to serve them.

Homily Points

• In today's first reading, Elijah follows through on a command from the word of God to visit a widow in Sidon. Everyone in the area at the time is facing a life-threatening drought and famine, so the bread and water that Elijah asks the widow for is especially precious. Elijah meets the widow as she is preparing the last supper for her and her son. Their bodies are ready to give out from lack of nutrition. Still, the widow receives her prophetic guest and shares what little she has.

• By sending Elijah to the widow, God created an opportunity for an Israelite and a non-Israelite to break bread with one another. God showed that the boundaries humans erect between people of different customs and nationalities are no match for the unifying power of God, whose hospitality knows no bounds. Both Elijah and the widow trust in God's word that "the jar of flour shall not go empty, nor the jug of oil run dry . . ."

• Today's familiar gospel story of the widow who donated two small coins to the treasury should not be read as an endorsement of poverty. The woman got to such a poor state because she fell victim to sins of fraud and prejudice. Many women today find themselves in similar unjust situations. Rather than glorify her economic situation, we would do well to celebrate her motivation for giving the coins in the first place. She loves her faith community. She believes in the holiness of the temple and wants to see it maintained.

Model Penitential Act

Presider: In today's second reading, Saint Paul writes of Christ's call to take away sin by his sacrifice. Grateful for Jesus's gift of self, let us ask the Lord for mercy and understanding . . . *[pause]*

Lord Jesus, you give life to those who trust in you: Lord, have mercy.

Christ Jesus, you call us to reconcile with our sisters and brothers: Christ, have mercy.

Lord Jesus, you came to fulfill the law for the good of your people: Lord, have mercy.

Model Universal Prayer (Prayer of the Faithful)

Presider: With hearts full of awe at the mysteries of God, let us bring our needs before the Lord.

Response: Lord, hear our prayer.

Foster an ever-growing spirit of generosity among people of faith . . .

Inspire politicians to enact legislation that ends cycles of poverty and oppression . . .

Draw out hope for new life in those people experiencing divorce and their families . . .

Inspire all of us gathered here to work toward healing of hurting relationships . . .

Presider: God whose love stretches beyond all telling, you sent your Son to show us the way to eternal life. Hear our prayers that we might follow his way in both word and deed. We ask this through Christ our Lord. **Amen.**

Liturgy and Music

Few of us can approach today's readings with a sense of lived experience. For who among us can say that we were a loaf of bread away from death, as is the widow and her son in the first reading? We live, rather, in the realm of wearing lovely clothes (paying extra money for them to be ripped), and of actually being able to choose what we eat. We deal with First World problems: the purchase of cars, the decision of where to be educated, the percentage point of a mortgage. Yet we fear poverty: we take out insurance policies to avoid it, and we build up defenses to buttress ourselves against such calamities. But the readings today challenge us to see that poverty often goes hand in hand with generosity and gratitude.

Once again, it comes down to a matter of the heart: prayerfulness is not about strutting but embracing an attitude that is "poor in spirit," as today's gospel acclamation proclaims. Generosity is not about flagrant philanthropy; rather, it is at its best when rooted in an attitude of humble stewardship.

And underlining it all is the quiet admonition of Elijah, "Do not be afraid." Fear not if our pantry is not well stocked, because God is feeding us in magnificent ways. Fear not emptiness, for God showers us with fulfillment beyond our understanding. Fear not poverty itself, for the joy of our Maker dwells in the hearts of the poor, the stranger, the heartbroken, the oppressed.

Rather than fear, we should put our trust in the source of all consolation, as we do when we sing Horatio Bonar's comforting text "I Heard the Voice of Jesus Say."

COLLECT

Let us pray.

Pause for silent prayer

Almighty and merciful God,
graciously keep from us all adversity,
so that, unhindered in mind and body
     alike,
we may pursue in freedom of heart
the things that are yours.
Through our Lord Jesus Christ, your Son,
who lives and reigns with you in the unity
     of the Holy Spirit,
God, for ever and ever. **Amen.**

FIRST READING

1 Kgs 17:10-16

In those days, Elijah the prophet went to
     Zarephath.
As he arrived at the entrance of the city,
     a widow was gathering sticks there; he
          called out to her,
     "Please bring me a small cupful of
          water to drink."
She left to get it, and he called out after
     her,
     "Please bring along a bit of bread."
She answered, "As the LORD, your God,
     lives,
     I have nothing baked; there is only a
          handful of flour in my jar
     and a little oil in my jug.
Just now I was collecting a couple of
     sticks,
     to go in and prepare something for
          myself and my son;
     when we have eaten it, we shall die."
Elijah said to her, "Do not be afraid.
Go and do as you propose.
But first make me a little cake and bring
     it to me.
Then you can prepare something for
     yourself and your son.
For the LORD, the God of Israel, says,
     'The jar of flour shall not go empty,
     nor the jug of oil run dry,
     until the day when the LORD sends rain
          upon the earth.'"
She left and did as Elijah had said.
She was able to eat for a year, and he and
     her son as well;
     the jar of flour did not go empty,
     nor the jug of oil run dry,
     as the LORD had foretold through Elijah.

RESPONSORIAL PSALM

Ps 146:7, 8-9, 9-10

℟. (1b) Praise the Lord, my soul!
or:
℟. Alleluia.

The LORD keeps faith forever,
  secures justice for the oppressed,
  gives food to the hungry.
The LORD sets captives free.

℟. Praise the Lord, my soul!
or:
℟. Alleluia.

The LORD gives sight to the blind;
  the LORD raises up those who were
    bowed down.
The LORD loves the just;
  the LORD protects strangers.

℟. Praise the Lord, my soul!
or:
℟. Alleluia.

The fatherless and the widow he sustains,
  but the way of the wicked he thwarts.
The LORD shall reign forever;
  your God, O Zion, through all
    generations. Alleluia.

℟. Praise the Lord, my soul!
or:
℟. Alleluia.

SECOND READING

Heb 9:24-28

Christ did not enter into a sanctuary made
    by hands,
  a copy of the true one, but heaven itself,
  that he might now appear before God
    on our behalf.
Not that he might offer himself repeatedly,
  as the high priest enters each year into
    the sanctuary
  with blood that is not his own;
  if that were so, he would have had to
    suffer repeatedly
  from the foundation of the world.
But now once for all he has appeared at
    the end of the ages
  to take away sin by his sacrifice.
Just as it is appointed that human beings
    die once,
  and after this the judgment, so also
    Christ,
  offered once to take away the sins of
    many,
  will appear a second time, not to take
    away sin
  but to bring salvation to those who
    eagerly await him.

Living Liturgy

Liturgy and Scripture: The stories in this week's readings are about faithful people giving what they can as an offering to God. In the first reading from the first book of Kings, the prophet Elijah encounters a widow who prepares a cake for him even though she knows that it will take the last of her supply, putting her son and herself in jeopardy. In the gospel reading, Jesus contrasts the scribes who move grandly throughout society and give from their largess with a poor widow who gives only two small coins. In these two stories, we are reminded that the greatest gift we can give is that which is most precious to us.

When you think about giving back to your community, what are you most inclined to give—your money, your time, your professional expertise, your possessions? What are you afraid to give and why? A common fear is probably fear of waste or futility. Giving that which is precious to us can feel like a great risk. What if we give and the gift is wasted? What if after sacrificing so much, it is still not enough to meet the need? These stories also remind and encourage us to put our faith in God. In the first book of Kings, Elijah reassures the widow that if she shares what she has with him, her supply will not run dry, and indeed, she and her son were delivered. For an entire year, they were able to eat well. The widow from the gospel was exalted by Christ because she gave even more generously than the wealthy scribes.

It is difficult to risk making a sacrifice when resources are scarce, but as in so many other stories throughout Scripture, our belief in God is what makes it possible for God to come to our aid. When we open our hands and our hearts wide enough, we make a channel through which God can enter in. May we faithfully put our trust in these stories of God's deliverance and believe that when we give generously of ourselves, God will not leave us to starve.

PROMPTS FOR FAITH-SHARING

• Jesus points out the difference between giving from one's surplus wealth and making a sacrificial gift. Where might you be able to make a sacrifice in order to support someone struggling with poverty?

• In the first reading, God miraculously provides for a woman living in poverty. More often, God provides through the work of God's people. How might you participate in God's care for those in need?

• Service and generosity to agencies that work with people in poverty is important; so, too, is more direct service in which we interact with people as people and form relationships of care. Which of these do you feel most comfortable with? How might God be calling you to expand your work in the other?

See Appendix B, p. 314, for additional prompts.

NOVEMBER 10, 2024
THIRTY-SECOND SUNDAY
IN ORDINARY TIME

SPIRITUALITY

℟. Alleluia, alleluia.
Be vigilant at all times
and pray that you have the strength to
    stand before the Son of Man.
℟. Alleluia, alleluia.

Gospel

Mark 13:24-32; L158B

Jesus said to his disciples:
"In those days after that
    tribulation
  the sun will be darkened,
  and the moon will not give its
    light,
  and the stars will be falling
    from the sky,
  and the powers in the heavens
    will be shaken.

"And then they will see 'the
    Son of Man coming in the
    clouds'
  with great power and glory,
  and then he will send out the angels
  and gather his elect from the four
    winds,
  from the end of the earth to the end
    of the sky.

"Learn a lesson from the fig tree.
When its branch becomes tender and
    sprouts leaves,
  you know that summer is near.
In the same way, when you see these
    things happening,
  know that he is near, at the gates.
Amen, I say to you,
  this generation will not pass away
  until all these things have taken
    place.
Heaven and earth will pass away,
  but my words will not pass away.

"But of that day or hour, no one knows,
  neither the angels in heaven, nor the
    Son, but only the Father."

Reflecting on the Gospel

In the first reading and the gospel, two different biblical writers reflect on the end times. Both are writing for a people under duress, a people who may feel that the trials and tribulations they are undergoing are the signs of the apocalyptic end time. Will there be something beyond this earthly life? The ancient Israelites thought not.

Some believed they would merely live on in the memories of their descendants. Some spoke of Sheol, the shadowy underworld in which a shade of the former self survived, but that is hardly an afterlife at all. It was only in the second century BCE that the belief in resurrection and an eternal reward for the righteous began to emerge. Daniel also mentions "everlasting horror and disgrace" for the wicked, but he focuses his attention on what happens to those who have lived wisely and who have led others to seek and do justice. He envisions these people as shining brightly, "like the splendor of the firmament . . . [they] shall be like the stars forever."

Cosmologists tell us that our bodies are literally stardust made flesh; they are made of particles that were present in the primeval fireball at the beginning of the universe. So Daniel's image of righteous people becoming stars, in a sense, invites us to be true to what we actually are. His words give hope that those who endure tribulation not only tend the divine light within but also radiate goodness to others, increasing the brilliance of the divine radiance.

In the gospel, Jesus speaks to his disciples about the days of final tribulation. They are a terrible undoing of creation, an extinguishing of the light of the sun and moon, with the stars falling from the sky. Against the backdrop of this cataclysm, Jesus interjects the assurance that he will come again in power and glory, gathering his elect from "the end of the earth to the end of the sky." He then offers the image of a tender green shoot at springtime, one that insistently bursts forth from the fig tree. Stripped of its leaves, and giving every appearance of having died, its life tenaciously sprouts forth anew. And so Jesus assures his disciples that no matter what horrendous suffering they endure, life will rise again in them through his power.

The question of when all this will take place hangs unanswered. There is a tension in the gospel. Jesus first says that it will happen in the lifetime of "this generation," but then he asserts that no one knows the day or the hour—not even he—but only the Father. In between the two sayings is the solid affirmation that Jesus's words are trustworthy.

Speculation about the end time may not be foremost in believers' minds these days. But when we are experiencing tribulation, the question of how long it will go on and what will happen afterward is front and center. The readings today give hope that everlasting radiance and tender new beginnings come after refinement in the fiery furnace of suffering.

Preparing to Proclaim

Key words and phrases: "[W]hen you see these things happening, know that he is near."

To the point: Jesus's description of the end times is a scary one, but also one of hope for those who strive to follow him. In its midst is an important reminder to *pay attention.* It is hard to imagine a scenario in which we would miss the signs Jesus describes—surely we would notice the sun being darkened and the stars falling from the sky. But Jesus's reminder implies that we *could* miss it. And in our ordinary lives, we often do miss all the manifold and subtle ways Jesus comes to us. Only those who are in the habit of noticing the fig tree will note its clues of an impending change of seasons. Only those who practice cultivating their attention will notice Jesus entering into their lives here and now.

Psalmist Preparation

In this psalm we sing of our trust in God even in the face of things as distressing as the end-times described by Jesus and Daniel in the other readings. These predictions are troubling, but we can hear them with hope because of God, who holds us fast. This God promises never to abandon us—neither everyday heartache nor world-ending catastrophe can keep God from us. As you prepare to proclaim this psalm, think about past or present areas of suffering in your own life. Spend time in prayer inviting God into even the darker and messier parts of you that you might prefer to keep hidden. Trust that God does not leave you alone in any of your struggles.

Making Connections

Between the readings: In the first reading, Daniel describes the end-times with imagery that will foreshadow Jesus's words in the gospel. In both, there is a distressing image of the world ending, but also a word of hope. Jesus says the angels will "gather his elect from the four winds;" Daniel has the wise "shin[ing] brightly like the splendor of the firmament." The destruction foretold is not for the sake of destruction; it is to make room for God's love to take in those God has chosen.

To experience: In the busyness of our lives on earth, it can feel burdensome to think about the end-times. Who has time for that kind of interruption? We're very often engaged in good work; how can we prepare for this, too? But Jesus gives us an important clue about what is needed to prepare. We need to *pay attention,* to look for the ways God is already present to us. We can do this in the midst of whatever else it is that occupies our time.

Homily Points

• Artists have tried for centuries to depict scenes from the end of the world. Through their creativity, painters, poets, writers, and thinkers have tried to help people imagine the unimaginable. How will life on earth end? What will it feel like? Who will be left when God's kingdom finally comes? God is the only one who can answer such questions, but Jesus gives the disciples an idea of what is to come: darkened sun, falling stars, the Son of Man emerging from the clouds with angels by his side.

• Jesus paints an image of glory and power, not death and destruction. The end of the world will be unlike anything ever experienced before in the history of the universe—that much is obvious. But the belief that such a time will be ultimately good and healing can feel like more of a stretch. Such profound change can be scary. Yet Jesus assures his followers that he will draw creation from all corners of the world into the peace of God's everlasting kingdom. Only peace and joy will remain.

• Jesus offers a lesson from the fig tree to the disciples, one of many agrarian images Jesus calls upon in his teachings. He compares the chaos of the end times to the sap rising from the roots of the fig tree, which ultimately enables the tree to bear fruit in the new season. We cannot know the time or place of the arrival of kingdom of God, but we can be assured that God's mercy and love will endure in this new season for creation.

Model Penitential Act

Presider: As we prepare to encounter God in Scripture and in sacrament, let us call to mind our sins and ask for God's forgiveness . . . *[pause]*

   Lord Jesus, you are the Son of God and Son of Man: Lord, have mercy.

   Christ Jesus, you gather your people into the peace of God's kingdom: Christ, have mercy.

   Lord Jesus, you will come again power and glory to save your people: Lord, have mercy.

Model Universal Prayer (Prayer of the Faithful)

Presider: With hearts filled with compassion for the needs of the world, let us voice aloud our prayers and petitions to God.

Response: Lord, hear our prayer.

Strengthen the integrity of the church and animate its members so that we may practice what we preach . . .

Guide our civil and religious discourse to greater respect, honesty, and openness . . .

Grant relief and healing to people suffering from addiction to drugs or alcohol . . .

Channel our energies toward the work of the gospel, particularly the care for people who are poor and marginalized . . .

Presider: Merciful God, you sent your Son to comfort those who mourn and bring all people into the peace of everlasting life. Hear our prayers that we might be attentive to your presence and live out our days to the fullest in praise of you. We ask this through Christ our Lord. **Amen.**

Liturgy and Music

"It shall be a time unsurpassed in distress since the nation began until that time" (Dan 12:1).

   November finds us in end-time, when much of what we think permanent is toppled over like sandcastles in an advancing tide. Nature herself seems to participate in this self-inflicting dance of seeming despair, abandoning her leaves, her greening power, and even the light of day to the advance of darkness.

   History provides plenty of examples of unsurpassed distress: the millions upon millions lost in the Black Death, the Spanish influenza, the "War to end all wars" (World War I), and the war that followed it, World War II, involving nearly the whole globe. Imagine living in times such as these: Would it not seem as if heaven and earth were, indeed, passing away?

   Yet despite the real horror of what humanity has experienced, the readings today do not jettison hope. Rather, they point to the stars, where the wise are firmly affixed; they speak of inheritance—not of worldly goods, but of our very Creator. They assert that the world as we know it will pass but that the word of God is everlasting. As we mark our celebrations, we do well to embrace this hope. We could do so with the hymn "Tesoros Ocultos/Treasures Out of Darkness" (Alan Revering, WLP/GIA).

COLLECT

Let us pray.

Pause for silent prayer

Grant us, we pray, O Lord our God,
the constant gladness of being devoted
   to you,
for it is full and lasting happiness
to serve with constancy
the author of all that is good.
Through our Lord Jesus Christ, your Son,
who lives and reigns with you in the unity
   of the Holy Spirit,
God, for ever and ever. **Amen.**

FIRST READING

Dan 12:1-3

In those days, I, Daniel,
   heard this word of the Lord:
"At that time there shall arise
   Michael, the great prince,
   guardian of your people;
it shall be a time unsurpassed in distress
   since nations began until that time.
At that time your people shall escape,
   everyone who is found written in the
   book.

"Many of those who sleep in the dust of
   the earth shall awake;
   some shall live forever,
others shall be an everlasting horror
   and disgrace.

"But the wise shall shine brightly
   like the splendor of the firmament,
and those who lead the many to justice
   shall be like the stars forever."

RESPONSORIAL PSALM
Ps 16:5, 8, 9-10, 11

℟. (1) You are my inheritance, O Lord!

O LORD, my allotted portion and my cup,
  you it is who hold fast my lot.
I set the LORD ever before me;
  with him at my right hand I shall not be
    disturbed.

℟. You are my inheritance, O Lord!

Therefore my heart is glad and my soul
    rejoices,
  my body, too, abides in confidence;
because you will not abandon my soul to
    the netherworld,
  nor will you suffer your faithful one to
    undergo corruption.

℟. You are my inheritance, O Lord!

You will show me the path to life,
  fullness of joys in your presence,
  the delights at your right hand forever.

℟. You are my inheritance, O Lord!

SECOND READING
Heb 10:11-14, 18

Brothers and sisters:
Every priest stands daily at his ministry,
  offering frequently those same sacrifices
    that can never take away sins.
But this one offered one sacrifice for sins,
  and took his seat forever at the right
    hand of God;
  now he waits until his enemies are made
    his footstool.
For by one offering
  he has made perfect forever those who
    are being consecrated.

Where there is forgiveness of these,
  there is no longer offering for sin.

✠ CATECHESIS

Living Liturgy

Liturgy and Spirituality: Today's readings speak about times "unsurpassed in distress," when nature's regular rhythms will be disrupted, the stars will stray from their course, and the Son of Man will descend from the clouds. Reading apocalyptic literature is challenging. The images are disturbing and full of complex symbolism. It is also just hard to contemplate the end of the world as we know it. Although the challenges are certainly great, there is a lot of beauty in the world as well and it is just scary to imagine all of that being consumed in the destruction of the end times.

This is a good time to remember what event we call to mind every time we attend Mass and celebrate the Eucharist. The paschal mystery—the suffering, death, and resurrection of Jesus Christ—is the central mystery of our faith. Each time we step into a church, we see a crucifix reminding us that the way to God requires sacrifice and sometimes great suffering. When we receive the body and blood of Christ, the Holy Eucharist, we are participating in a grand ritual of thanksgiving. Thanks be to God who saw fit to walk among us and share in the joys and sorrows of life. Thanks be to God who endured great pain and gloriously transformed that pain so that we might believe in the promise of everlasting life. Thanks be to God who reminds us constantly that suffering is neither the point nor the end of the story.

At the end of today's gospel from Mark Jesus says, "Heaven and earth will pass away, but my words will not pass away." In the reading from Daniel, we hear that "the wise shall shine brightly . . . and those who lead the many to justice shall be like the stars forever." Moments that seem destructive and catastrophic may be making way for goodness and truth to shine more brightly. As we approach the end of this liturgical year, may we look ahead and trust that God is forever bringing us into new beginnings, even when we must first pass through difficult endings.

PROMPTS FOR FAITH-SHARING

• How prepared do you feel for Jesus's final coming? What might you need to detach from in order to be more ready to greet him in whatever ways he comes?

• The liturgical year is nearly at its end; what have been some times of spiritual growth for you this year?

• These readings speak of the end-times and give us a hint of the themes of the upcoming Advent season. How might you begin to prepare for a fruitful Advent?

See Appendix B, p. 314, for additional prompts.

SPIRITUALITY

GOSPEL ACCLAMATION
Mark 11:9, 10

℟. Alleluia, alleluia.
Blessed is he who comes in the name of the
    Lord!
Blessed is the kingdom of our father David that
    is to come!
℟. Alleluia, alleluia.

Gospel

John 18:33b-37; L161B

Pilate said to Jesus,
    "Are you the King of the
        Jews?"
Jesus answered, "Do you say
    this on your own
    or have others told you about
        me?"
Pilate answered, "I am not a
    Jew, am I?
Your own nation and the chief
    priests handed you over to
    me.
What have you done?"
Jesus answered, "My kingdom
    does not belong to this
    world.
If my kingdom did belong to this world,
    my attendants would be fighting
    to keep me from being handed over
        to the Jews.
But as it is, my kingdom is not here."
So Pilate said to him, "Then you are a
    king?"
Jesus answered, "You say I am a king.
For this I was born and for this I came
    into the world,
    to testify to the truth.
Everyone who belongs to the truth
    listens to my voice."

Reflecting on the Gospel

There's something about royalty that fascinates us. Peasants in biblical times were no different. When one's life is a constant struggle, to believe in a powerful king who could, with a wave of his hand, make everything go well for the little ones fuels hope and gives a reason to keep plodding on.

It is not surprising, then, that Christians would think of Jesus in royal terms. Today's feast has a double edge to it, as is brought out in the readings. Jesus is "king" but in a most anti-imperial way. In the gospel we see Jesus on trial before Pilate, who is the extension of the imperial arm in Palestine.

Unlike the Synoptic Gospels, in John Jesus does not remain silent before the 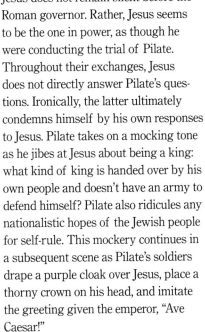 Roman governor. Rather, Jesus seems to be the one in power, as though he were conducting the trial of Pilate. Throughout their exchanges, Jesus does not directly answer Pilate's questions. Ironically, the latter ultimately condemns himself by his own responses to Jesus. Pilate takes on a mocking tone as he jibes at Jesus about being a king: what kind of king is handed over by his own people and doesn't have an army to defend himself? Pilate also ridicules any nationalistic hopes of the Jewish people for self-rule. This mockery continues in a subsequent scene as Pilate's soldiers drape a purple cloak over Jesus, place a thorny crown on his head, and imitate the greeting given the emperor, "Ave Caesar!"

When Pilate queries, "Are you the King of the Jews?" Jesus shifts the discussion away from himself as king and speaks instead about his "kingdom." By using imperial language to speak of God's realm where love and fullness of life reign supreme, Jesus subverts kingly expressions of power that exploit and abuse others. By his actions and words, he has undermined monarchical systems of authority and obedience. He calls his followers "friends" and invites them into a community of beloved disciples, in which the leaders are the first to wash the feet of those who are least regarded.

Later in his interrogation of Jesus, Pilate boasts of his power to release Jesus or to crucify him, but Jesus reminds the Roman ruler that he would have no power over him unless it was given to him from above (19:10-11). Moreover, Jesus has already declared to his disciples that no one has power over his life; he himself lays it down freely (10:18). Pilate has no desire to hear about this kind of "kingdom," and does not understand the anti-kingdom message of Jesus. Pilate is fixated on forcing Jesus to admit his claims to being a "king" so that he has ground on which to eliminate this supposed rival with pretensions to his own throne. Jesus will not give him that satisfaction and simply points out that it is Pilate who is using that kind of language, not Jesus. Jesus speaks of his mission not in terms of a conquering king but as one who testifies to the truth. All it takes to belong to this "kingdom" where truth reigns is to listen to his voice.

Preparing to Proclaim
Key words and phrases: "My kingdom does not belong to this world."

To the point: Jesus's cryptic dialogue with Pilate does not make much clear. One thing that is clear though—that has been clear throughout Jesus's teachings—is that his idea of kingship is very different from ours. His idea of power is different from ours. It does not look like what we expect. He carries on this very dialogue from a position of vulnerability, where he is held captive and his life threatened by those with worldly power. We who are baptized into Jesus's missions as priest, prophet, and king are called to challenge the notion of kingship that clings to power and sees some humans as more dignified and deserving than others. We have the ongoing challenge of wrapping our minds around a leadership that really does operate from a place of humility.

Psalmist Preparation
The gospel will remind us that Jesus's power does not look like that of earthly kings, but this psalm proclaims that power in all its splendor and fullness. As you prepare to proclaim it, reflect on the places in your life you *do* experience God's power. Perhaps it's in creation—a mighty mountain, the undeterred movement of the seasons, the intricate unfolding of petals blooming. Perhaps it's in a relationship where you feel loved without reserve. Sit with this evidence of God's power (and love) in prayer this week. Bring gratitude for it into your proclamation of this psalm.

Making Connections
Between the readings: Daniel's vision in the first reading contrasts sharply with the image of Jesus we have in the gospel. Jesus is not (yet) coming on a cloud to receive dominion over "all peoples, nations, and languages." He is rather a bound prisoner, subject to the political machinations of earthly powers. Even still, though, they are one and the same; Jesus's power is real even if it does not look like what we would expect.

To experience: In baptism we are anointed to share Jesus's office as king. As such, we are called to enact service and justice to others. Each of our relationships presents an opportunity to live Jesus's mind-bending leadership based not on power but on self-gift. Relationships where we hold some sort of power or authority are all the more an opportunity to hold that power in a way that serves those it affects.

Homily Points
• Are we too quick to discount our dreams these days? Throughout the Scriptures, we encounter prophets who received callings and visions from God in their sleep. These "visions during the night," as Daniel writes about in today's first reading, offered hope to a Jewish people suffering great hardships. Long before Mary gives birth to Jesus, Daniel dreams of "a Son of man coming, on the clouds of heaven." This being carries "dominion, glory, and kingship" that will be everlasting. At a time when earthly kingdoms brought about terror and destruction, this vision of a new reign gave the people strength to move forward.

• Jesus confronts Pilate about the meaning of kingship in today's gospel. As the governor of Rome, Pilate understands kingship in a strictly political sense and does not want anyone to challenge his reign. Jesus confronts Pilate with a new vision of kingship, one that is not *of* this world but very much *in* this world. Jesus came to usher in a kingdom of truth and justice, of peace and prosperity. We are called to help bring about this kingdom in our small corners of the world. In our homes and communities, we are called to make the love of God known.

• We have come to the end of another liturgical year. Before we jump too far into the freshness of Advent, let us pause and take stock of this past year of Christian living. Where did we encounter Christ? When did we act as Christ for another? In what ways did we succeed—and fall short—in answering the Christian call?

CELEBRATION

Model Penitential Act

Presider: Jesus Christ, king of the universe, intercedes for us at the right hand of God. Grateful for his mercy, let us call to mind our sins and ask for forgiveness . . . *[pause]*

Lord Jesus, you are the Son of God and Son of Man: Lord, have mercy.

Christ Jesus, you strengthen your people to spread the good news: Christ, have mercy.

Lord Jesus, you will come again in glory: Lord, have mercy.

Model Universal Prayer (Prayer of the Faithful)

Presider: As we celebrate the feast of Jesus Christ, King of the Universe, let us entrust the Lord with our prayers and petitions.

Response: Lord, hear our prayer.

Bless all catechists, ministers, priests, parish staff members, and volunteers who served the church over the past year . . .

Cultivate attention and care for the most vulnerable in elected and appointed government officials . . .

Reconcile friendships and family ties that are strained by hurt or misunderstanding . . .

Inspire all the baptized to live more deeply into our Christian calling to love God and neighbor in the new year ahead . . .

Presider: God of glory, in you we live and move and have our being. Hear our prayers that as we honor the kingship of Christ, we might contribute to the building up of your kingdom on earth. We ask this through Christ our Lord. **Amen.**

Liturgy and Music

If there is one consistent message that is woven throughout all the readings this week, it is this: do *not* look to earthly kingdoms for a model of what Jesus intended as his domain. Daniel sees the Son of Man as the possessor of dominion and glory, with all peoples serving him. For the psalmist, the king does not wear earthly garb, but majesty itself. The author of Revelation doesn't even *assign* the word "king" to our Creator, but instead uses words that point beyond time itself: beginning and end, Alpha and Omega.

And then, there is that dialogue between a country preacher and the representative of the Roman Empire, Pontius Pilate. We all know how that turned out, and whose words have endured.

Has there ever been a worldly kingdom whose aim was simply to "testify to the truth"? Has any country ever had the courage to name that as their goal, affix it to their currency, or hold it up as the holiest of ideals in setting forth their national charters? There can be no doubt—that simple answer given to Pilate illustrates just how radical a kingdom Jesus had in mind.

And that he would give his life for such a kingdom.

Consider Bryn Rees's hymn "The Kingdom of God Is Justice and Joy" (Alexander Scott).

COLLECT

Let us pray.

Pause for silent prayer

Almighty ever-living God,
whose will is to restore all things
in your beloved Son, the King of the
　　universe,
grant, we pray,
that the whole creation, set free from
　　slavery,
may render your majesty service
and ceaselessly proclaim your praise.
Through our Lord Jesus Christ, your Son,
who lives and reigns with you in the unity
　　of the Holy Spirit,
God, for ever and ever. **Amen.**

FIRST READING
Dan 7:13-14

As the visions during the night continued,
　　I saw
　　one like a Son of man coming,
　　　on the clouds of heaven;
　　when he reached the Ancient One
　　　and was presented before him,
　　the one like a Son of man received
　　　dominion, glory, and kingship;
　　　all peoples, nations, and languages
　　　　serve him.
His dominion is an everlasting dominion
　　that shall not be taken away,
　　his kingship shall not be destroyed.

RESPONSORIAL PSALM
Ps 93:1, 1-2, 5

℟. (1a) The Lord is king; he is robed in majesty.

The LORD is king, in splendor robed;
   robed is the LORD and girt about with
      strength.

℟. The Lord is king; he is robed in
   majesty.

And he has made the world firm,
   not to be moved.
Your throne stands firm from of old;
   from everlasting you are, O LORD.

℟. The Lord is king; he is robed in
   majesty.

Your decrees are worthy of trust indeed;
   holiness befits your house,
   O LORD, for length of days.

℟. The Lord is king; he is robed in
   majesty.

SECOND READING
Rev 1:5-8

Jesus Christ is the faithful witness,
   the firstborn of the dead and ruler of
      the kings of the earth.
To him who loves us and has freed us
      from our sins by his blood,
   who has made us into a kingdom,
      priests for his God and Father,
   to him be glory and power forever and
      ever. Amen.

Behold, he is coming amid the clouds,
   and every eye will see him,
      even those who pierced him.
All the peoples of the earth will lament
      him.
   Yes. Amen.

"I am the Alpha and the Omega," says the
      Lord God,
   "the one who is and who was and who
      is to come, the almighty."

Living Liturgy

Liturgy and the Arts: Throughout this liturgical year, we have heard the teachings of Christ as presented in the Gospel of Mark. We read and saw Christ assume the role of teacher, sharing wise and complicated truths with the disciples. We saw Christ as healer, banishing demons from the possessed and healing the maladies of the downtrodden. Now on this solemnity of Christ the King, we recall that Jesus's words and actions are sovereign and true. He is indeed the king who will restore proper order to the world and bring all people to God under himself.

"Ride On, King Jesus" is an African-American spiritual that dates back to the mid-1800s. One of the earliest published versions of the spiritual is from 1867, but it was shared through oral tradition earlier than that, and as the years passed it has been added onto, edited, and republished. The song has a triumphant, powerful, and defiant tone. Eileen Guenther, professor emeritus of church music from Wesley Seminary, cites a slave narrative in which White patrollers tried to prevent enslaved Black people from singing the song because of its subversive messaging: "No man can a-hinder me." This image of Jesus as a mighty and powerful king might seem like a departure from the Jesus we saw earlier in Mark's Gospel, who instructed his disciples not to tell others about the miracles he performed. But Christ the King is not a contradiction to our other depictions of Christ; Christ the King is consistent and unrelenting in wanting to upend social norms that keep certain classes of people enslaved, marginalized, and ignored. Christ the King is on the way and his message of justice and liberation will not be hindered by any person.

This image of Christ gave courage and strength to enslaved and newly freed Black people in the late nineteenth and early twentieth centuries, carrying them through the horrors of American White supremacy. As we celebrate this solemnity today may we embrace Christ, our defiant and powerful king, who will not rest until justice is achieved.

PROMPTS FOR FAITH-SHARING

• What work do you have to do to make this world a place that can more readily accept Jesus as king? What work does your own heart need to do the same?

• In what relationships do you hold some sort of power or authority? How can you bring Jesus's power, rooted in self-gift, into those relationships?

• The psalm proclaims Jesus's unfettered glory and majesty, which are often not obvious in the way earthly power is exercised. Where *do* you see God's power on display in your life?

*See Appendix B, p. 314,
for additional prompts.*

NOVEMBER 24, 2024
OUR LORD JESUS CHRIST, KING OF THE UNIVERSE

Readings *(continued)*

The Immaculate Conception of the Blessed Virgin Mary, *December 8, 2023*

Gospel (cont.)
Luke 1:26-38; L689

He will be great and will be called Son of the Most High,
  and the Lord God will give him the throne of David his father,
  and he will rule over the house of Jacob forever,
  and of his Kingdom there will be no end."
But Mary said to the angel,
  "How can this be,
  since I have no relations with a man?"
And the angel said to her in reply,
  "The Holy Spirit will come upon you,
  and the power of the Most High will overshadow you.
Therefore the child to be born
  will be called holy, the Son of God.

And behold, Elizabeth, your relative,
  has also conceived a son in her old age,
  and this is the sixth month for her who was called barren;
  for nothing will be impossible for God."
Mary said, "Behold, I am the handmaid of the Lord.
May it be done to me according to your word."
Then the angel departed from her.

FIRST READING
Gen 3:9-15, 20

After the man, Adam, had eaten of the tree,
  the LORD God called to the man and asked
  him, "Where are you?"
He answered, "I heard you in the garden;
  but I was afraid, because I was naked,
  so I hid myself."
Then he asked, "Who told you that you were
  naked?
You have eaten, then,
  from the tree of which I had forbidden you
  to eat!"
The man replied, "The woman whom you put
  here with me—
  she gave me fruit from the tree, and so I
  ate it."
The LORD God then asked the woman,
  "Why did you do such a thing?"
The woman answered, "The serpent tricked
  me into it, so I ate it."

Then the LORD God said to the serpent:
  "Because you have done this, you shall be
  banned
  from all the animals
  and from all the wild creatures;
on your belly shall you crawl,
  and dirt shall you eat
  all the days of your life.
I will put enmity between you and the
  woman,
  and between your offspring and hers;
he will strike at your head,
  while you strike at his heel."

The man called his wife Eve,
  because she became the mother of all the
  living.

RESPONSORIAL PSALM
Ps 98:1, 2-3ab, 3cd-4

℟. (1a) Sing to the Lord a new song, for he has
  done marvelous deeds.

Sing to the LORD a new song,
  for he has done wondrous deeds;
His right hand has won victory for him,
  his holy arm.

℟. Sing to the Lord a new song, for he has
  done marvelous deeds.

The LORD has made his salvation known:
  in the sight of the nations he has revealed
  his justice.
He has remembered his kindness and his
  faithfulness
  toward the house of Israel.

℟. Sing to the Lord a new song, for he has
  done marvelous deeds.

All the ends of the earth have seen
  the salvation by our God.
Sing joyfully to the LORD, all you lands;
  break into song; sing praise.

℟. Sing to the Lord a new song, for he has
  done marvelous deeds.

SECOND READING
Eph 1:3-6, 11-12

Brothers and sisters:
Blessed be the God and Father of our Lord
  Jesus Christ,
  who has blessed us in Christ
  with every spiritual blessing in the heavens,
  as he chose us in him, before the foundation
  of the world,
  to be holy and without blemish before him.
In love he destined us for adoption to himself
  through Jesus Christ,
  in accord with the favor of his will,
  for the praise of the glory of his grace
  that he granted us in the beloved.

In him we were also chosen,
  destined in accord with the purpose of the
  One
  who accomplishes all things according to
  the intention of his will,
  so that we might exist for the praise of his
  glory,
  we who first hoped in Christ.

Gospel (cont.)
Luke 1:26-38; L690A

He will be great and will be called Son of the Most High,
  and the Lord God will give him the throne of David his father,
  and he will rule over the house of Jacob forever,
  and of his Kingdom there will be no end."
But Mary said to the angel,
  "How can this be,
  since I have no relations with a man?"
And the angel said to her in reply,
  "The Holy Spirit will come upon you,
  and the power of the Most High will overshadow you.
Therefore the child to be born
  will be called holy, the Son of God.
And behold, Elizabeth, your relative,
  has also conceived a son in her old age,
  and this is the sixth month for her who was called barren;
  for nothing will be impossible for God."
Mary said, "Behold, I am the handmaid of the Lord.
May it be done to me according to your word."
Then the angel departed from her.

or Luke 1:39-47

Mary set out
  and traveled to the hill country in haste
  to a town of Judah,
  where she entered the house of Zechariah
  and greeted Elizabeth.
When Elizabeth heard Mary's greeting,
  the infant leaped in her womb,
  and Elizabeth, filled with the Holy Spirit,
  cried out in a loud voice and said,
  "Most blessed are you among women,
  and blessed is the fruit of your womb.
And how does this happen to me,
  that the mother of my Lord should come to me?
For at the moment the sound of your greeting reached my ears,
  the infant in my womb leaped for joy.
Blessed are you who believed
  that what was spoken to you by the Lord
  would be fulfilled."

And Mary said:

  "My soul proclaims the greatness of the Lord;
  my spirit rejoices in God my savior."

FIRST READING
Rev 11:19a; 12:1-6a, 10ab

God's temple in heaven was opened,
  and the ark of his covenant could be seen
    in the temple.

A great sign appeared in the sky, a woman
    clothed with the sun,
  with the moon under her feet,
  and on her head a crown of twelve stars.
She was with child and wailed aloud in pain
    as she labored to give birth.
Then another sign appeared in the sky;
  it was a huge red dragon, with seven heads
    and ten horns,
  and on its heads were seven diadems.
Its tail swept away a third of the stars in the
    sky
  and hurled them down to the earth.
Then the dragon stood before the woman
    about to give birth,
  to devour her child when she gave birth.
She gave birth to a son, a male child,
  destined to rule all the nations with an iron
    rod.
Her child was caught up to God and his
    throne.
The woman herself fled into the desert
  where she had a place prepared by God.

Then I heard a loud voice in heaven say:
  "Now have salvation and power come,
  and the Kingdom of our God
  and the authority of his Anointed."

or Zech 2:14-17

Sing and rejoice, O daughter Zion!
See, I am coming to dwell among you, says
    the Lord.
Many nations shall join themselves to the
    Lord on that day,
  and they shall be his people,
  and he will dwell among you,
  and you shall know that the Lord of hosts
    has sent me to you.
The Lord will possess Judah as his portion in
    the holy land,
  and he will again choose Jerusalem.
Silence, all mankind, in the presence of the
    Lord!
  For he stirs forth from his holy dwelling.

RESPONSORIAL PSALM
Jdt 13:18bcde, 19

R̷. (15:9d) You are the highest honor of our
    race.

Blessed are you, daughter, by the Most High
    God,
  above all the women on earth;
  and blessed be the Lord God,
  the creator of heaven and earth.

R̷. You are the highest honor of our race.

Your deed of hope will never be forgotten
  by those who tell of the might of God.

R̷. You are the highest honor of our race.

Gospel (cont.)
Matt 1:1-25; L13ABC

Asaph became the father of Jehoshaphat,
  Jehoshaphat the father of Joram,
  Joram the father of Uzziah.
Uzziah became the father of Jotham,
  Jotham the father of Ahaz,
  Ahaz the father of Hezekiah.
Hezekiah became the father of Manasseh,
  Manasseh the father of Amos,
  Amos the father of Josiah.
Josiah became the father of Jechoniah and his brothers
  at the time of the Babylonian exile.

After the Babylonian exile,
  Jechoniah became the father of Shealtiel,
  Shealtiel the father of Zerubbabel,
  Zerubbabel the father of Abiud.
Abiud became the father of Eliakim,
  Eliakim the father of Azor,
  Azor the father of Zadok.
Zadok became the father of Achim,
  Achim the father of Eliud,
  Eliud the father of Eleazar.
Eleazar became the father of Matthan,
  Matthan the father of Jacob,
  Jacob the father of Joseph, the husband of Mary.
Of her was born Jesus who is called the Christ.

Thus the total number of generations
  from Abraham to David
  is fourteen generations;
  from David to the Babylonian exile,
  fourteen generations;
  from the Babylonian exile to the Christ,
  fourteen generations.

Now this is how the birth of Jesus Christ came about.
When his mother Mary was betrothed to Joseph,
  but before they lived together,
  she was found with child through the Holy Spirit.
Joseph her husband, since he was a righteous man,
  yet unwilling to expose her to shame,
  decided to divorce her quietly.
Such was his intention when, behold,
  the angel of the Lord appeared to him in a dream and said,
  "Joseph, son of David,
  do not be afraid to take Mary your wife into your home.
For it is through the Holy Spirit
  that this child has been conceived in her.
She will bear a son and you are to name him Jesus,
  because he will save his people from their sins."
All this took place to fulfill
  what the Lord had said through the prophet:
    Behold, the virgin shall conceive and bear a son,
      and they shall name him Emmanuel,
  which means "God is with us."
When Joseph awoke,
  he did as the angel of the Lord had commanded him
  and took his wife into his home.
He had no relations with her until she bore a son,
  and he named him Jesus.

or Matt 1:18-25

This is how the birth of Jesus Christ came about.
When his mother Mary was betrothed to Joseph,
  but before they lived together,
  she was found with child through the Holy Spirit.
Joseph her husband, since he was a righteous man,
  yet unwilling to expose her to shame,
  decided to divorce her quietly.
Such was his intention when, behold,
  the angel of the Lord appeared to him in a dream and said,
  "Joseph, son of David,
  do not be afraid to take Mary your wife into your home.
For it is through the Holy Spirit
  that this child has been conceived in her.
She will bear a son and you are to name him Jesus,
  because he will save his people from their sins."
All this took place to fulfill
  what the Lord had said through the prophet:
    Behold, the virgin shall conceive and bear a son,
      and they shall name him Emmanuel,
  which means "God is with us."
When Joseph awoke,
  he did as the angel of the Lord had commanded him
  and took his wife into his home.
He had no relations with her until she bore a son,
  and he named him Jesus.

The Nativity of the Lord, *December 25, 2023 (Vigil Mass)*

FIRST READING
Isa 62:1-5

For Zion's sake I will not be silent,
    for Jerusalem's sake I will not be quiet,
until her vindication shines forth like the
        dawn
    and her victory like a burning torch.

Nations shall behold your vindication,
    and all the kings your glory;
you shall be called by a new name
    pronounced by the mouth of the Lord.
You shall be a glorious crown in the hand of
        the Lord,
    a royal diadem held by your God.
No more shall people call you "Forsaken,"
    or your land "Desolate,"
but you shall be called "My Delight,"
    and your land "Espoused."
For the Lord delights in you
    and makes your land his spouse.
As a young man marries a virgin,
    your Builder shall marry you;
and as a bridegroom rejoices in his bride
    so shall your God rejoice in you.

RESPONSORIAL PSALM
Ps 89:4-5, 16-17, 27, 29

℞. (2a) For ever I will sing the goodness of the
Lord.

I have made a covenant with my chosen one,
    I have sworn to David my servant:
forever will I confirm your posterity
    and establish your throne for all
        generations.

℞. For ever I will sing the goodness of the
Lord.

Blessed the people who know the joyful shout;
    in the light of your countenance, O Lord,
        they walk.
At your name they rejoice all the day,
    and through your justice they are exalted.

℞. For ever I will sing the goodness of the
Lord.

He shall say of me, "You are my father,
    my God, the rock, my savior."
Forever I will maintain my kindness toward
        him,
    and my covenant with him stands firm.

℞. For ever I will sing the goodness of the
Lord.

SECOND READING
Acts 13:16-17, 22-25

When Paul reached Antioch in Pisidia and
        entered the synagogue,
    he stood up, motioned with his hand, and
        said,
    "Fellow Israelites and you others who are
        God-fearing, listen.
The God of this people Israel chose our
        ancestors
    and exalted the people during their sojourn
        in the land of Egypt.
With uplifted arm he led them out of it.
Then he removed Saul and raised up David
        as king;
    of him he testified,
    'I have found David, son of Jesse, a man
        after my own heart;
    he will carry out my every wish.'
From this man's descendants God, according
        to his promise,
    has brought to Israel a savior, Jesus.
John heralded his coming by proclaiming a
        baptism of repentance
    to all the people of Israel;
    and as John was completing his course, he
        would say,
    'What do you suppose that I am? I am not
        he.
Behold, one is coming after me;
    I am not worthy to unfasten the sandals of
        his feet.'"

The Nativity of the Lord, *December 25, 2023 (Mass during the Night)*

Gospel (cont.)
Luke 2:1-14; L14ABC

Now there were shepherds in that region living in the fields
    and keeping the night watch over their flock.
The angel of the Lord appeared to them
    and the glory of the Lord shone around them,
    and they were struck with great fear.
The angel said to them,
    "Do not be afraid;
    for behold, I proclaim to you good news of great joy
    that will be for all the people.
For today in the city of David
    a savior has been born for you who is Christ and Lord.

And this will be a sign for you:
    you will find an infant wrapped in swaddling clothes
    and lying in a manger."
And suddenly there was a multitude of the heavenly host with the
        angel,
    praising God and saying:
    "Glory to God in the highest
        and on earth peace to those on whom his favor rests."

The Nativity of the Lord, December 25, 2023 (Mass during the Night)

FIRST READING
Isa 9:1-6

The people who walked in darkness
    have seen a great light;
upon those who dwelt in the land of gloom
    a light has shone.
You have brought them abundant joy
    and great rejoicing,
as they rejoice before you as at the harvest,
    as people make merry when dividing spoils.
For the yoke that burdened them,
    the pole on their shoulder,
and the rod of their taskmaster
    you have smashed, as on the day of Midian.
For every boot that tramped in battle,
    every cloak rolled in blood,
    will be burned as fuel for flames.
For a child is born to us, a son is given us;
    upon his shoulder dominion rests.
They name him Wonder-Counselor, God-Hero,
    Father-Forever, Prince of Peace.
His dominion is vast
    and forever peaceful,
from David's throne, and over his kingdom,
    which he confirms and sustains
by judgment and justice,
    both now and forever.
The zeal of the Lord of hosts will do this!

RESPONSORIAL PSALM
Ps 96:1-2, 2-3, 11-12, 13

℟. (Luke 2:11) Today is born our Savior,
    Christ the Lord.

Sing to the Lord a new song;
    sing to the Lord, all you lands.
Sing to the Lord; bless his name.

℟. Today is born our Savior, Christ the Lord.

Announce his salvation, day after day.
    Tell his glory among the nations;
    among all peoples, his wondrous deeds.

℟. Today is born our Savior, Christ the Lord.

Let the heavens be glad and the earth rejoice;
    let the sea and what fills it resound;
    let the plains be joyful and all that is in
        them!
Then shall all the trees of the forest exult.

℟. Today is born our Savior, Christ the Lord.

They shall exult before the Lord, for he
        comes;
    for he comes to rule the earth.
He shall rule the world with justice
    and the peoples with his constancy.

℟. Today is born our Savior, Christ the Lord.

SECOND READING
Titus 2:11-14

Beloved:
The grace of God has appeared, saving all
    and training us to reject godless ways and
        worldly desires
    and to live temperately, justly, and devoutly
        in this age,
    as we await the blessed hope,
    the appearance of the glory of our great
        God
    and savior Jesus Christ,
    who gave himself for us to deliver us from
        all lawlessness
    and to cleanse for himself a people as his
        own,
    eager to do what is good.

The Nativity of the Lord, December 25, 2023 (Mass at Dawn)

FIRST READING
Isa 62:11-12

See, the Lord proclaims
    to the ends of the earth:
say to daughter Zion,
    your savior comes!
Here is his reward with him,
    his recompense before him.
They shall be called the holy people,
    the redeemed of the Lord,
and you shall be called "Frequented,"
    a city that is not forsaken.

RESPONSORIAL PSALM
Ps 97:1, 6, 11-12

℟. A light will shine on us this day: the Lord
    is born for us.

The Lord is king; let the earth rejoice;
    let the many isles be glad.
The heavens proclaim his justice,
    and all peoples see his glory.

℟. A light will shine on us this day: the Lord
    is born for us.

Light dawns for the just;
    and gladness, for the upright of heart.
Be glad in the Lord, you just,
    and give thanks to his holy name.

℟. A light will shine on us this day: the Lord
    is born for us.

SECOND READING
Titus 3:4-7

Beloved:
When the kindness and generous love
    of God our savior appeared,
not because of any righteous deeds we had
        done
    but because of his mercy,
he saved us through the bath of rebirth
    and renewal by the Holy Spirit,
whom he richly poured out on us
    through Jesus Christ our savior,
so that we might be justified by his grace
    and become heirs in hope of eternal life.

Gospel (cont.)

John 1:1-18; L16ABC

And the Word became flesh
  and made his dwelling among us,
  and we saw his glory,
  the glory as of the Father's only Son,
  full of grace and truth.

John testified to him and cried out, saying,
  "This was he of whom I said,
  'The one who is coming after me ranks ahead of me
  because he existed before me.'"
From his fullness we have all received,
  grace in place of grace,
  because while the law was given through Moses,
  grace and truth came through Jesus Christ.
No one has ever seen God.
The only Son, God, who is at the Father's side,
  has revealed him.

or John 1:1-5, 9-14

In the beginning was the Word,
  and the Word was with God,
  and the Word was God.
He was in the beginning with God.

All things came to be through him,
  and without him nothing came to be.
What came to be through him was life,
  and this life was the light of the human race;
the light shines in the darkness,
  and the darkness has not overcome it.
The true light, which enlightens everyone, was coming into the world.

He was in the world,
  and the world came to be through him,
  but the world did not know him.
He came to what was his own,
  but his own people did not accept him.

But to those who did accept him
  he gave power to become children of God,
  to those who believe in his name,
  who were born not by natural generation
  nor by human choice nor by a man's decision
  but of God.

And the Word became flesh
  and made his dwelling among us,
  and we saw his glory,
  the glory as of the Father's only Son,
  full of grace and truth.

FIRST READING

Isa 52:7-10

How beautiful upon the mountains
  are the feet of him who brings glad tidings,
announcing peace, bearing good news,
  announcing salvation, and saying to Zion,
  "Your God is King!"

Hark! Your sentinels raise a cry,
  together they shout for joy,
for they see directly, before their eyes,
  the LORD restoring Zion.
Break out together in song,
  O ruins of Jerusalem!
For the LORD comforts his people,
  he redeems Jerusalem.
The LORD has bared his holy arm
  in the sight of all the nations;
all the ends of the earth will behold
  the salvation of our God.

RESPONSORIAL PSALM

Ps 98:1, 2-3, 3-4, 5-6

℞. (3c) All the ends of the earth have seen the
  saving power of God.

Sing to the LORD a new song,
  for he has done wondrous deeds;
his right hand has won victory for him,
  his holy arm.

℞. All the ends of the earth have seen the
  saving power of God.

The LORD has made his salvation known:
  in the sight of the nations he has revealed
  his justice.
He has remembered his kindness and his
  faithfulness
  toward the house of Israel.

℞. All the ends of the earth have seen the
  saving power of God.

All the ends of the earth have seen
  the salvation by our God.
Sing joyfully to the LORD, all you lands;
  break into song; sing praise.

℞. All the ends of the earth have seen the
  saving power of God.

Sing praise to the LORD with the harp,
  with the harp and melodious song.
With trumpets and the sound of the horn
  sing joyfully before the King, the LORD.

℞. All the ends of the earth have seen the
  saving power of God.

SECOND READING

Heb 1:1-6

Brothers and sisters:
In times past, God spoke in partial and
  various ways
  to our ancestors through the prophets;
in these last days, he has spoken to us
  through the Son,
  whom he made heir of all things
  and through whom he created the universe,
  who is the refulgence of his glory,
  the very imprint of his being,
  and who sustains all things by his mighty
  word.
When he had accomplished purification
  from sins,
he took his seat at the right hand of the
  Majesty on high,
as far superior to the angels
as the name he has inherited is more
  excellent than theirs.

For to which of the angels did God ever say:
  You are my son; this day I have begotten
  you?
Or again:
  I will be a father to him, and he shall be a
  son to me?
And again, when he leads the firstborn into
  the world, he says:
  Let all the angels of God worship him.

Gospel (cont.)

Luke 2:22-40; L17B

He came in the Spirit into the temple;
  and when the parents brought in the child Jesus
  to perform the custom of the law in regard to him,
  he took him into his arms and blessed God, saying:
    "Now, Master, you may let your servant go
      in peace, according to your word,
      for my eyes have seen your salvation,
        which you prepared in sight of all the peoples,
      a light for revelation to the Gentiles,
        and glory for your people Israel."
The child's father and mother were amazed at what was said about
    him;
  and Simeon blessed them and said to Mary his mother,
  "Behold, this child is destined
  for the fall and rise of many in Israel,
  and to be a sign that will be contradicted
  —and you yourself a sword will pierce—
  so that the thoughts of many hearts may be revealed."
There was also a prophetess, Anna,
  the daughter of Phanuel, of the tribe of Asher.
She was advanced in years,
  having lived seven years with her husband after her marriage,
  and then as a widow until she was eighty-four.

She never left the temple,
  but worshiped night and day with fasting and prayer.
And coming forward at that very time,
  she gave thanks to God and spoke about the child
  to all who were awaiting the redemption of Jerusalem.

When they had fulfilled all the prescriptions
  of the law of the Lord,
  they returned to Galilee,
  to their own town of Nazareth.
The child grew and became strong, filled with wisdom;
  and the favor of God was upon him.

or Luke 2:22, 39-40

When the days were completed for their purification
  according to the law of Moses,
  the parents of Jesus took him up to Jerusalem
  to present him to the Lord.

When they had fulfilled all the prescriptions
  of the law of the Lord,
  they returned to Galilee,
  to their own town of Nazareth.
The child grew and became strong, filled with wisdom;
  and the favor of God was upon him.

FIRST READING

Sir 3:2-6, 12-14

God sets a father in honor over his children;
  a mother's authority he confirms over her
    sons.
Whoever honors his father atones for sins,
  and preserves himself from them.
When he prays, he is heard;
  he stores up riches who reveres his mother.
Whoever honors his father is gladdened by
    children,
  and, when he prays, is heard.
Whoever reveres his father will live a long life;
  he who obeys his father brings comfort to
    his mother.

My son, take care of your father when he is
    old;
  grieve him not as long as he lives.
Even if his mind fail, be considerate of him;
  revile him not all the days of his life;
kindness to a father will not be forgotten,
  firmly planted against the debt of your sins
  —a house raised in justice to you.

RESPONSORIAL PSALM

Ps 128:1-2, 3, 4-5

℟. (cf. 1) Blessed are those who fear the Lord
    and walk in his ways.

Blessed is everyone who fears the Lord,
    who walks in his ways!
For you shall eat the fruit of your handiwork;
    blessed shall you be, and favored.

℟. Blessed are those who fear the Lord and
    walk in his ways.

Your wife shall be like a fruitful vine
    in the recesses of your home;
your children like olive plants
    around your table.

℟. Blessed are those who fear the Lord and
    walk in his ways.

Behold, thus is the man blessed
    who fears the Lord.
The Lord bless you from Zion:
    may you see the prosperity of Jerusalem
    all the days of your life.

℟. Blessed are those who fear the Lord and
    walk in his ways.

SECOND READING
Col 3:12-21

Brothers and sisters:
Put on, as God's chosen ones, holy and
    beloved,
    heartfelt compassion, kindness, humility,
        gentleness, and patience,
    bearing with one another and forgiving one
        another,
    if one has a grievance against another;
    as the Lord has forgiven you, so must you
        also do.
And over all these put on love,
    that is, the bond of perfection.
And let the peace of Christ control your hearts,
    the peace into which you were also called in
        one body.
And be thankful.
Let the word of Christ dwell in you richly,
    as in all wisdom you teach and admonish
        one another,
    singing psalms, hymns, and spiritual songs
    with gratitude in your hearts to God.
And whatever you do, in word or in deed,
    do everything in the name of the Lord Jesus,
    giving thanks to God the Father through
        him.

Wives, be subordinate to your husbands,
    as is proper in the Lord.
Husbands, love your wives,
    and avoid any bitterness toward them.
Children, obey your parents in everything,
    for this is pleasing to the Lord.
Fathers, do not provoke your children,
    so they may not become discouraged.

or Col 3:12-17

Brothers and sisters:
Put on, as God's chosen ones, holy and beloved,
    heartfelt compassion, kindness, humility,
        gentleness, and patience,
    bearing with one another and forgiving one
        another,
    if one has a grievance against another;
    as the Lord has forgiven you, so must you
        also do.
And over all these put on love,
    that is, the bond of perfection.
And let the peace of Christ control your
        hearts,
    the peace into which you were also called in
        one body.
And be thankful.
Let the word of Christ dwell in you richly,
    as in all wisdom you teach and admonish
        one another,
    singing psalms, hymns, and spiritual songs
    with gratitude in your hearts to God.
And whatever you do, in word or in deed,
    do everything in the name of the Lord
        Jesus,
    giving thanks to God the Father through
        him.

Solemnity of Mary, the Holy Mother of God, *January 1, 2024*

FIRST READING
Num 6:22-27

The LORD said to Moses:
  "Speak to Aaron and his sons and tell them:
  This is how you shall bless the Israelites.
Say to them:
  The LORD bless you and keep you!
  The LORD let his face shine upon
    you, and be gracious to you!
  The LORD look upon you kindly and
    give you peace!
So shall they invoke my name upon the
    Israelites,
  and I will bless them."

RESPONSORIAL PSALM
Ps 67:2-3, 5, 6, 8

℟. (2a) May God bless us in his mercy.

May God have pity on us and bless us;
  may he let his face shine upon us.
So may your way be known upon earth;
  among all nations, your salvation.

℟. May God bless us in his mercy.

May the nations be glad and exult
  because you rule the peoples in equity;
  the nations on the earth you guide.

℟. May God bless us in his mercy.

May the peoples praise you, O God;
  may all the peoples praise you!
May God bless us,
  and may all the ends of the earth fear him!

℟. May God bless us in his mercy.

SECOND READING
Gal 4:4-7

Brothers and sisters:
When the fullness of time had come, God sent
    his Son,
  born of a woman, born under the law,
  to ransom those under the law,
  so that we might receive adoption as sons.
As proof that you are sons,
  God sent the Spirit of his Son into our
    hearts,
  crying out, "Abba, Father!"
So you are no longer a slave but a son,
  and if a son then also an heir, through God.

The Epiphany of the Lord, *January 7, 2024*

Gospel (cont.)
Matt 2:1-12; L20ABC

After their audience with the king they set out.
And behold, the star that they had seen at its rising preceded them,
  until it came and stopped over the place where the child was.
They were overjoyed at seeing the star,
  and on entering the house
  they saw the child with Mary his mother.
They prostrated themselves and did him homage.
Then they opened their treasures
  and offered him gifts of gold, frankincense, and myrrh.
And having been warned in a dream not to return to Herod,
  they departed for their country by another way.

Ash Wednesday, *February 14, 2024*

FIRST READING
Joel 2:12-18

Even now, says the LORD,
    return to me with your whole heart,
    with fasting, and weeping, and mourning;
Rend your hearts, not your garments,
    and return to the LORD, your God.
For gracious and merciful is he,
    slow to anger, rich in kindness,
    and relenting in punishment.
Perhaps he will again relent
    and leave behind him a blessing,
Offerings and libations
    for the LORD, your God.

Blow the trumpet in Zion!
    proclaim a fast,
    call an assembly;
Gather the people,
    notify the congregation;
Assemble the elders,
    gather the children
    and the infants at the breast;
Let the bridegroom quit his room
    and the bride her chamber.
Between the porch and the altar
    let the priests, the ministers of the LORD,
      weep,
And say, "Spare, O LORD, your people,
    and make not your heritage a reproach,
    with the nations ruling over them!
Why should they say among the peoples,
    'Where is their God?'"

Then the LORD was stirred to concern for his
    land
    and took pity on his people.

RESPONSORIAL PSALM
Ps 51:3-4, 5-6ab, 12-13, 14, and 17

℟. (see 3a) Be merciful, O Lord, for we have
    sinned.

Have mercy on me, O God, in your goodness;
    in the greatness of your compassion wipe
      out my offense.
Thoroughly wash me from my guilt
    and of my sin cleanse me.

℟. Be merciful, O Lord, for we have sinned.

For I acknowledge my offense,
    and my sin is before me always:
"Against you only have I sinned,
    and done what is evil in your sight."

℟. Be merciful, O Lord, for we have sinned.

A clean heart create for me, O God,
    and a steadfast spirit renew within me.
Cast me not out from your presence,
    and your Holy Spirit take not from me.

℟. Be merciful, O Lord, for we have sinned.

Give me back the joy of your salvation,
    and a willing spirit sustain in me.
O Lord, open my lips,
    and my mouth shall proclaim your praise.

℟. Be merciful, O Lord, for we have sinned.

SECOND READING
2 Cor 5:20—6:2

Brothers and sisters:
We are ambassadors for Christ,
    as if God were appealing through us.
We implore you on behalf of Christ,
    be reconciled to God.
For our sake he made him to be sin who did
      not know sin,
    so that we might become the righteousness
      of God in him.

Working together, then,
    we appeal to you not to receive the grace of
      God in vain.
For he says:

In an acceptable time I heard you,
    and on the day of salvation I helped you.

Behold, now is a very acceptable time;
    behold, now is the day of salvation.

Third Sunday of Lent, *March 3, 2024*

Gospel (cont.)
John 2:13-25; L29B

But he was speaking about the temple of his body.
Therefore, when he was raised from the dead,
    his disciples remembered that he had said this,
    and they came to believe the Scripture
    and the word Jesus had spoken.

While he was in Jerusalem for the feast of Passover,
    many began to believe in his name
    when they saw the signs he was doing.
But Jesus would not trust himself to them because he knew them all,
    and did not need anyone to testify about human nature.
He himself understood it well.

RESPONSORIAL PSALM

Ps 19:8, 9, 10, 11

℟. (John 6:68c) Lord, you have the words of
    everlasting life.

The law of the LORD is perfect,
    refreshing the soul;
the decree of the LORD is trustworthy,
    giving wisdom to the simple.

℟. Lord, you have the words of everlasting life.

The precepts of the LORD are right,
    rejoicing the heart;
the command of the LORD is clear,
    enlightening the eye.

℟. Lord, you have the words of everlasting life.

The fear of the LORD is pure,
    enduring forever;
the ordinances of the LORD are true,
    all of them just.

℟. Lord, you have the words of everlasting life.

They are more precious than gold,
    than a heap of purest gold;
sweeter also than syrup
    or honey from the comb.

℟. Lord, you have the words of everlasting life.

SECOND READING

1 Cor 1:22-25

Brothers and sisters:
Jews demand signs and Greeks look for
    wisdom,
    but we proclaim Christ crucified,
    a stumbling block to Jews and foolishness
        to Gentiles,
    but to those who are called, Jews and
        Greeks alike,
    Christ the power of God and the wisdom
        of God.
For the foolishness of God is wiser than
    human wisdom,
and the weakness of God is stronger than
    human strength.

FIRST READING

Exod 17:3-7

In those days, in their thirst for water,
    the people grumbled against Moses,
    saying, "Why did you ever make us leave
        Egypt?
Was it just to have us die here of thirst
    with our children and our livestock?"
So Moses cried out to the LORD,
    "What shall I do with this people?
A little more and they will stone me!"
The LORD answered Moses,
    "Go over there in front of the people,
    along with some of the elders of Israel,
    holding in your hand, as you go,
    the staff with which you struck the river.
I will be standing there in front of you on the
    rock in Horeb.
Strike the rock, and the water will flow from it
    for the people to drink."
This Moses did, in the presence of the elders
    of Israel.
The place was called Massah and Meribah,
    because the Israelites quarreled there
    and tested the LORD, saying,
    "Is the LORD in our midst or not?"

RESPONSORIAL PSALM

Ps 95:1-2, 6-7, 8-9

℟. (8) If today you hear his voice, harden not
    your hearts.

Come, let us sing joyfully to the LORD;
    let us acclaim the Rock of our salvation.
Let us come into his presence with
    thanksgiving;
    let us joyfully sing psalms to him.

℟. If today you hear his voice, harden not
    your hearts.

Come, let us bow down in worship;
    let us kneel before the LORD who made us.
For he is our God,
    and we are the people he shepherds, the
        flock he guides.

℟. If today you hear his voice, harden not
    your hearts.

Oh, that today you would hear his voice:
    "Harden not your hearts as at Meribah,
    as in the day of Massah in the desert,
Where your fathers tempted me;
    they tested me though they had seen my
        works."

℟. If today you hear his voice, harden not
    your hearts.

SECOND READING

Rom 5:1-2, 5-8

Brothers and sisters:
Since we have been justified by faith,
    we have peace with God through our Lord
        Jesus Christ,
    through whom we have gained access by
        faith
    to this grace in which we stand,
    and we boast in hope of the glory of God.

And hope does not disappoint,
    because the love of God has been poured
        out into our hearts
    through the Holy Spirit who has been given
        to us.
For Christ, while we were still helpless,
    died at the appointed time for the ungodly.
Indeed, only with difficulty does one die for a
    just person,
    though perhaps for a good person one
        might even find courage to die.
But God proves his love for us
    in that while we were still sinners Christ
        died for us.

Gospel

John 4:5-42; L28A

Jesus came to a town of Samaria called Sychar,
    near the plot of land that Jacob had given to his son Joseph.
Jacob's well was there.
Jesus, tired from his journey, sat down there at the well.
It was about noon.

A woman of Samaria came to draw water.
Jesus said to her,
    "Give me a drink."
His disciples had gone into the town to buy food.
The Samaritan woman said to him,
    "How can you, a Jew, ask me, a Samaritan woman, for a drink?"
—For Jews use nothing in common with Samaritans.—
Jesus answered and said to her,

"If you knew the gift of God
and who is saying to you, 'Give me a drink,'
you would have asked him
and he would have given you living water."
The woman said to him,
    "Sir, you do not even have a bucket and the cistern is deep;
    where then can you get this living water?
Are you greater than our father Jacob,
    who gave us this cistern and drank from it himself
    with his children and his flocks?"
Jesus answered and said to her,
    "Everyone who drinks this water will be thirsty again;
    but whoever drinks the water I shall give will never thirst;

the water I shall give will become in him
a spring of water welling up to eternal life."
The woman said to him,
"Sir, give me this water, so that I may not be thirsty
or have to keep coming here to draw water."

Jesus said to her,
"Go call your husband and come back."
The woman answered and said to him,
"I do not have a husband."
Jesus answered her,
"You are right in saying, 'I do not have a husband.'
For you have had five husbands,
and the one you have now is not your husband.
What you have said is true."
The woman said to him,
"Sir, I can see that you are a prophet.
Our ancestors worshiped on this mountain;
but you people say that the place to worship is in Jerusalem."
Jesus said to her,
"Believe me, woman, the hour is coming
when you will worship the Father
neither on this mountain nor in Jerusalem.
You people worship what you do not understand;
we worship what we understand,
because salvation is from the Jews.
But the hour is coming, and is now here,
when true worshipers will worship the Father in Spirit and truth;
and indeed the Father seeks such people to worship him.
God is Spirit, and those who worship him
must worship in Spirit and truth."
The woman said to him,
"I know that the Messiah is coming, the one called the Christ;
when he comes, he will tell us everything."
Jesus said to her,
"I am he, the one speaking with you."

At that moment his disciples returned,
and were amazed that he was talking with a woman,
but still no one said, "What are you looking for?"
or "Why are you talking with her?"
The woman left her water jar
and went into the town and said to the people,
"Come see a man who told me everything I have done.
Could he possibly be the Christ?"
They went out of the town and came to him.
Meanwhile, the disciples urged him, "Rabbi, eat."
But he said to them,
"I have food to eat of which you do not know."
So the disciples said to one another,
"Could someone have brought him something to eat?"
Jesus said to them,
"My food is to do the will of the one who sent me
and to finish his work.
Do you not say, 'In four months the harvest will be here'?
I tell you, look up and see the fields ripe for the harvest.
The reaper is already receiving payment
and gathering crops for eternal life,
so that the sower and reaper can rejoice together.
For here the saying is verified that 'One sows and another reaps.'
I sent you to reap what you have not worked for;
others have done the work,

and you are sharing the fruits of their work."

Many of the Samaritans of that town began to believe in him
because of the word of the woman who testified,
"He told me everything I have done."
When the Samaritans came to him,
they invited him to stay with them;
and he stayed there two days.
Many more began to believe in him because of his word,
and they said to the woman,
"We no longer believe because of your word;
for we have heard for ourselves,
and we know that this is truly the savior of the world."

or
John 4:5-15, 19b-26, 39a, 40-42; L28A

Jesus came to a town of Samaria called Sychar,
near the plot of land that Jacob had given to his son Joseph.
Jacob's well was there.
Jesus, tired from his journey, sat down there at the well.
It was about noon.

A woman of Samaria came to draw water.
Jesus said to her,
"Give me a drink."
His disciples had gone into the town to buy food.
The Samaritan woman said to him,
"How can you, a Jew, ask me, a Samaritan woman, for a drink?"
—For Jews use nothing in common with Samaritans.—
Jesus answered and said to her,
"If you knew the gift of God
and who is saying to you, 'Give me a drink,'
you would have asked him
and he would have given you living water."
The woman said to him,
"Sir, you do not even have a bucket and the cistern is deep;
where then can you get this living water?
Are you greater than our father Jacob,
who gave us this cistern and drank from it himself
with his children and his flocks?"
Jesus answered and said to her,
"Everyone who drinks this water will be thirsty again;
but whoever drinks the water I shall give will never thirst;
the water I shall give will become in him
a spring of water welling up to eternal life."
The woman said to him,
"Sir, give me this water, so that I may not be thirsty
or have to keep coming here to draw water.

"I can see that you are a prophet.
Our ancestors worshiped on this mountain;
but you people say that the place to worship is in Jerusalem."
Jesus said to her,
"Believe me, woman, the hour is coming
when you will worship the Father
neither on this mountain nor in Jerusalem.
You people worship what you do not understand;
we worship what we understand,
because salvation is from the Jews.
But the hour is coming, and is now here,
when true worshipers will worship the Father in Spirit and truth;
and indeed the Father seeks such people to worship him.

Gospel (cont.)
John 4:5-15, 19b-26, 39a, 40-42; L28A

God is Spirit, and those who worship him
  must worship in Spirit and truth."
The woman said to him,
  "I know that the Messiah is coming, the one called the Christ;
  when he comes, he will tell us everything."
Jesus said to her,
  "I am he, the one who is speaking with you."

Many of the Samaritans of that town began to believe in him.
When the Samaritans came to him,
  they invited him to stay with them;
  and he stayed there two days.
Many more began to believe in him because of his word,
  and they said to the woman,
  "We no longer believe because of your word;
  for we have heard for ourselves,
  and we know that this is truly the savior of the world."

Fourth Sunday of Lent, *March 10, 2024*

SECOND READING
Eph 2:4-10

Brothers and sisters:
God, who is rich in mercy,
  because of the great love he had for us,
  even when we were dead in our
    transgressions,
  brought us to life with Christ—by grace
    you have been saved—,
  raised us up with him,
  and seated us with him in the heavens in
    Christ Jesus,
  that in the ages to come
  he might show the immeasurable riches of
    his grace
  in his kindness to us in Christ Jesus.
For by grace you have been saved through
    faith,
  and this is not from you; it is the gift of
    God;
  it is not from works, so no one may boast.
For we are his handiwork, created in Christ
    Jesus for the good works
  that God has prepared in advance,
  that we should live in them.

FIRST READING
1 Sam 16:1b, 6-7, 10-13a

The LORD said to Samuel:
  "Fill your horn with oil, and be on your
    way.
  I am sending you to Jesse of Bethlehem,
  for I have chosen my king from among his
    sons."

As Jesse and his sons came to the sacrifice,
  Samuel looked at Eliab and thought,
  "Surely the LORD's anointed is here before
    him."
But the LORD said to Samuel:
  "Do not judge from his appearance or from
    his lofty stature,
  because I have rejected him.

Not as man sees does God see,
  because man sees the appearance
  but the LORD looks into the heart."
In the same way Jesse presented seven sons
    before Samuel,
  but Samuel said to Jesse,
  "The LORD has not chosen any one of
    these."
Then Samuel asked Jesse,
  "Are these all the sons you have?"
Jesse replied,
  "There is still the youngest, who is tending
    the sheep."
Samuel said to Jesse,
  "Send for him;
  we will not begin the sacrificial banquet
    until he arrives here."
Jesse sent and had the young man brought to
    them.
He was ruddy, a youth handsome to behold
  and making a splendid appearance.
The LORD said,
  "There—anoint him, for this is the one!"
Then Samuel, with the horn of oil in hand,
  anointed David in the presence of his
    brothers;
  and from that day on, the spirit of the LORD
    rushed upon David.

RESPONSORIAL PSALM
Ps 23:1-3a, 3b-4, 5, 6

℟. (1) The Lord is my shepherd; there is
  nothing I shall want.

The LORD is my shepherd; I shall not want.
  In verdant pastures he gives me repose;
beside restful waters he leads me;
  he refreshes my soul.

℟. The Lord is my shepherd; there is nothing
  I shall want.

He guides me in right paths
  for his name's sake.

Even though I walk in the dark valley
  I fear no evil; for you are at my side
with your rod and your staff
  that give me courage.

℟. The Lord is my shepherd; there is nothing
  I shall want.

You spread the table before me
  in the sight of my foes;
you anoint my head with oil;
  my cup overflows.

℟. The Lord is my shepherd; there is nothing
  I shall want.

Only goodness and kindness follow me
  all the days of my life;
and I shall dwell in the house of the LORD
  for years to come.

℟. The Lord is my shepherd; there is nothing
  I shall want.

SECOND READING
Eph 5:8-14

Brothers and sisters:
You were once darkness,
  but now you are light in the Lord.
Live as children of light,
  for light produces every kind of goodness
  and righteousness and truth.
Try to learn what is pleasing to the Lord.
Take no part in the fruitless works of
    darkness;
  rather expose them, for it is shameful even
    to mention
  the things done by them in secret;
  but everything exposed by the light
    becomes visible,
  for everything that becomes visible is light.
Therefore, it says:
  "Awake, O sleeper,
  and arise from the dead,
  and Christ will give you light."

Gospel
John 9:1-41; L31A

As Jesus passed by he saw a man blind from birth.
His disciples asked him,
  "Rabbi, who sinned, this man or his parents,
  that he was born blind?"
Jesus answered,
  "Neither he nor his parents sinned;
  it is so that the works of God might be made visible through him.
We have to do the works of the one who sent me while it is day.
Night is coming when no one can work.
While I am in the world, I am the light of the world."
When he had said this, he spat on the ground
  and made clay with the saliva,
  and smeared the clay on his eyes, and said to him,
  "Go wash in the Pool of Siloam"—which means Sent—.
So he went and washed, and came back able to see.

His neighbors and those who had seen him earlier as a beggar said,
  "Isn't this the one who used to sit and beg?"
Some said, "It is,"
  but others said, "No, he just looks like him."
He said, "I am."
So they said to him, "How were your eyes opened?"
He replied,
  "The man called Jesus made clay and anointed my eyes
  and told me, 'Go to Siloam and wash.'
So I went there and washed and was able to see."
And they said to him, "Where is he?"
He said, "I don't know."

They brought the one who was once blind to the Pharisees.
Now Jesus had made clay and opened his eyes on a sabbath.
So then the Pharisees also asked him how he was able to see.
He said to them,
  "He put clay on my eyes, and I washed, and now I can see."
So some of the Pharisees said,
  "This man is not from God,
  because he does not keep the sabbath."
But others said,
  "How can a sinful man do such signs?"
And there was a division among them.
So they said to the blind man again,
  "What do you have to say about him,
  since he opened your eyes?"
He said, "He is a prophet."

Now the Jews did not believe
  that he had been blind and gained his sight
  until they summoned the parents of the one who had gained his
    sight.
They asked them,
  "Is this your son, who you say was born blind?
How does he now see?"
His parents answered and said,
  "We know that this is our son and that he was born blind.
We do not know how he sees now,
  nor do we know who opened his eyes.
Ask him, he is of age;
  he can speak for himself."

His parents said this because they were afraid of the Jews,
  for the Jews had already agreed
  that if anyone acknowledged him as the Christ,
  he would be expelled from the synagogue.
For this reason his parents said,
  "He is of age; question him."

So a second time they called the man who had been blind
  and said to him, "Give God the praise!
We know that this man is a sinner."
He replied,
  "If he is a sinner, I do not know.
One thing I do know is that I was blind and now I see."
So they said to him,
  "What did he do to you?
How did he open your eyes?"
He answered them,
  "I told you already and you did not listen.
Why do you want to hear it again?
Do you want to become his disciples, too?"
They ridiculed him and said,
  "You are that man's disciple;
  we are disciples of Moses!
We know that God spoke to Moses,
  but we do not know where this one is from."
The man answered and said to them,
  "This is what is so amazing,
  that you do not know where he is from, yet he opened my eyes.
We know that God does not listen to sinners,
  but if one is devout and does his will, he listens to him.
It is unheard of that anyone ever opened the eyes of a person born
    blind.
If this man were not from God,
  he would not be able to do anything."
They answered and said to him,
  "You were born totally in sin,
  and are you trying to teach us?"
Then they threw him out.

When Jesus heard that they had thrown him out,
  he found him and said, "Do you believe in the Son of Man?"
He answered and said,
  "Who is he, sir, that I may believe in him?"
Jesus said to him,
  "You have seen him,
  and the one speaking with you is he."
He said,
  "I do believe, Lord," and he worshiped him.
Then Jesus said,
  "I came into this world for judgment,
  so that those who do not see might see,
  and those who do see might become blind."

Some of the Pharisees who were with him heard this
  and said to him, "Surely we are not also blind, are we?"
Jesus said to them,
  "If you were blind, you would have no sin;
  but now you are saying, 'We see,' so your sin remains."

Fourth Sunday of Lent, *March 10, 2024*

Gospel (cont.)

or
John 9:1, 6-9, 13-17, 34-38; L31A

As Jesus passed by he saw a man blind from birth.
He spat on the ground and made clay with the saliva,
   and smeared the clay on his eyes, and said to him,
     "Go wash in the Pool of Siloam"—which means Sent—.
So he went and washed, and came back able to see.

His neighbors and those who had seen him earlier as a beggar said,
   "Isn't this the one who used to sit and beg?"
Some said, "It is,"
   but others said, "No, he just looks like him."
He said, "I am."

They brought the one who was once blind to the Pharisees.
Now Jesus had made clay and opened his eyes on a sabbath.
So then the Pharisees also asked him how he was able to see.
He said to them,
   "He put clay on my eyes, and I washed, and now I can see."
So some of the Pharisees said,
   "This man is not from God,
     because he does not keep the sabbath."

But others said,
   "How can a sinful man do such signs?"
And there was a division among them.
So they said to the blind man again,
   "What do you have to say about him,
     since he opened your eyes?"
He said, "He is a prophet."

They answered and said to him,
   "You were born totally in sin,
     and are you trying to teach us?"
Then they threw him out.

When Jesus heard that they had thrown him out,
   he found him and said, "Do you believe in the Son of Man?"
He answered and said,
   "Who is he, sir, that I may believe in him?"
Jesus said to him,
   "You have seen him,
     and the one speaking with you is he."
He said,
   "I do believe, Lord," and he worshiped him.

Fifth Sunday of Lent, *March 17, 2024*

Gospel (cont.)
John 12:20-33; L35B

The crowd there heard it and said it was thunder;
   but others said, "An angel has spoken to him."
Jesus answered and said,
   "This voice did not come for my sake but for yours.
Now is the time of judgment on this world;
   now the ruler of this world will be driven out.
And when I am lifted up from the earth,
   I will draw everyone to myself."
He said this indicating the kind of death he would die.

FIRST READING
Ezek 37:12-14

Thus says the Lord GOD:
   O my people, I will open your graves
   and have you rise from them,
   and bring you back to the land of Israel.
Then you shall know that I am the LORD,
   when I open your graves and have you rise
     from them,
   O my people!
I will put my spirit in you that you may live,
   and I will settle you upon your land;
   thus you shall know that I am the LORD.
I have promised, and I will do it, says the
     LORD.

RESPONSORIAL PSALM
Ps 130:1-2, 3-4, 5-6, 7-8

℟. (7) With the Lord there is mercy and
fullness of redemption.

Out of the depths I cry to you, O Lᴏʀᴅ;
Lᴏʀᴅ, hear my voice!
Let your ears be attentive
to my voice in supplication.

℟. With the Lord there is mercy and fullness
of redemption.

If you, O Lᴏʀᴅ, mark iniquities,
Lᴏʀᴅ, who can stand?
But with you is forgiveness,
that you may be revered.

℟. With the Lord there is mercy and fullness
of redemption.

I trust in the Lᴏʀᴅ;
my soul trusts in his word.
More than sentinels wait for the dawn,
let Israel wait for the Lᴏʀᴅ.

℟. With the Lord there is mercy and fullness
of redemption.

For with the Lᴏʀᴅ is kindness
and with him is plenteous redemption;
and he will redeem Israel
from all their iniquities.

℟. With the Lord there is mercy and fullness
of redemption.

SECOND READING
Rom 8:8-11

Brothers and sisters:
Those who are in the flesh cannot please God.
But you are not in the flesh;
on the contrary, you are in the spirit,
if only the Spirit of God dwells in you.
Whoever does not have the Spirit of Christ
does not belong to him.
But if Christ is in you,
although the body is dead because of sin,
the spirit is alive because of righteousness.
If the Spirit of the One who raised Jesus from
the dead dwells in you,
the One who raised Christ from the dead
will give life to your mortal bodies also,
through his Spirit dwelling in you.

Gospel
John 11:1-45; L34A

Now a man was ill, Lazarus from Bethany,
the village of Mary and her sister Martha.
Mary was the one who had anointed the Lord with perfumed oil
and dried his feet with her hair;
it was her brother Lazarus who was ill.
So the sisters sent word to Jesus saying,
"Master, the one you love is ill."
When Jesus heard this he said,
"This illness is not to end in death,
but is for the glory of God,
that the Son of God may be glorified through it."
Now Jesus loved Martha and her sister and Lazarus.
So when he heard that he was ill,
he remained for two days in the place where he was.
Then after this he said to his disciples,
"Let us go back to Judea."
The disciples said to him,
"Rabbi, the Jews were just trying to stone you,
and you want to go back there?"
Jesus answered,
"Are there not twelve hours in a day?
If one walks during the day, he does not stumble,
because he sees the light of this world.
But if one walks at night, he stumbles,
because the light is not in him."
He said this, and then told them,
"Our friend Lazarus is asleep,
but I am going to awaken him."
So the disciples said to him,
"Master, if he is asleep, he will be saved."
But Jesus was talking about his death,
while they thought that he meant ordinary sleep.
So then Jesus said to them clearly,
"Lazarus has died.
And I am glad for you that I was not there,
that you may believe.
Let us go to him."

So Thomas, called Didymus, said to his fellow disciples,
"Let us also go to die with him."

When Jesus arrived, he found that Lazarus
had already been in the tomb for four days.
Now Bethany was near Jerusalem, only about two miles away.
And many of the Jews had come to Martha and Mary
to comfort them about their brother.
When Martha heard that Jesus was coming,
she went to meet him;
but Mary sat at home.
Martha said to Jesus,
"Lord, if you had been here,
my brother would not have died.
But even now I know that whatever you ask of God,
God will give you."
Jesus said to her,
"Your brother will rise."
Martha said to him,
"I know he will rise,
in the resurrection on the last day."
Jesus told her,
"I am the resurrection and the life;
whoever believes in me, even if he dies, will live,
and everyone who lives and believes in me will never die.
Do you believe this?"
She said to him, "Yes, Lord.
I have come to believe that you are the Christ, the Son of God,
the one who is coming into the world."

When she had said this,
she went and called her sister Mary secretly, saying,
"The teacher is here and is asking for you."
As soon as she heard this,
she rose quickly and went to him.
For Jesus had not yet come into the village,
but was still where Martha had met him.
So when the Jews who were with her in the house comforting her
saw Mary get up quickly and go out,

they followed her,
    presuming that she was going to the tomb to weep there.
When Mary came to where Jesus was and saw him,
    she fell at his feet and said to him,
    "Lord, if you had been here,
    my brother would not have died."
When Jesus saw her weeping and the Jews who had come with her
        weeping,
    he became perturbed and deeply troubled, and said,
    "Where have you laid him?"
They said to him, "Sir, come and see."
And Jesus wept.
So the Jews said, "See how he loved him."
But some of them said,
    "Could not the one who opened the eyes of the blind man
    have done something so that this man would not have died?"

So Jesus, perturbed again, came to the tomb.
It was a cave, and a stone lay across it.
Jesus said, "Take away the stone."
Martha, the dead man's sister, said to him,
    "Lord, by now there will be a stench;
    he has been dead for four days."
Jesus said to her,
    "Did I not tell you that if you believe
    you will see the glory of God?"
So they took away the stone.
And Jesus raised his eyes and said,
    "Father, I thank you for hearing me.
I know that you always hear me;
    but because of the crowd here I have said this,
    that they may believe that you sent me."
And when he had said this,
    he cried out in a loud voice,
    "Lazarus, come out!"
The dead man came out,
    tied hand and foot with burial bands,
    and his face was wrapped in a cloth.
So Jesus said to them,
    "Untie him and let him go."

Now many of the Jews who had come to Mary
    and seen what he had done began to believe in him.

Gospel
John 11:3-7, 17, 20-27, 33b-45; L34A

The sisters of Lazarus sent word to Jesus saying,
    "Master, the one you love is ill."
When Jesus heard this he said,
    "This illness is not to end in death,
    but is for the glory of God,
    that the Son of God may be glorified through it."
Now Jesus loved Martha and her sister and Lazarus.
So when he heard that he was ill,
    he remained for two days in the place where he was.
Then after this he said to his disciples,
    "Let us go back to Judea."

When Jesus arrived, he found that Lazarus
    had already been in the tomb for four days.

When Martha heard that Jesus was coming,
    she went to meet him;
    but Mary sat at home.
Martha said to Jesus,
    "Lord, if you had been here,
    my brother would not have died.
But even now I know that whatever you ask of God,
    God will give you."
Jesus said to her,
    "Your brother will rise."
Martha said,
    "I know he will rise,
    in the resurrection on the last day."
Jesus told her,
    "I am the resurrection and the life;
    whoever believes in me, even if he dies, will live,
    and everyone who lives and believes in me will never die.
Do you believe this?"
She said to him, "Yes, Lord.
I have come to believe that you are the Christ, the Son of God,
    the one who is coming into the world."

He became perturbed and deeply troubled, and said,
    "Where have you laid him?"
They said to him, "Sir, come and see."
And Jesus wept.
So the Jews said, "See how he loved him."
But some of them said,
    "Could not the one who opened the eyes of the blind man
    have done something so that this man would not have died?"

So Jesus, perturbed again, came to the tomb.
It was a cave, and a stone lay across it.
Jesus said, "Take away the stone."
Martha, the dead man's sister, said to him,
    "Lord, by now there will be a stench;
    he has been dead for four days."
Jesus said to her,
    "Did I not tell you that if you believe
    you will see the glory of God?"
So they took away the stone.
And Jesus raised his eyes and said,
    "Father, I thank you for hearing me.
I know that you always hear me;
    but because of the crowd here I have said this,
    that they may believe that you sent me."
And when he had said this,
    he cried out in a loud voice,
    "Lazarus, come out!"
The dead man came out,
    tied hand and foot with burial bands,
    and his face was wrapped in a cloth.
So Jesus said to them,
    "Untie him and let him go."

Now many of the Jews who had come to Mary
    and seen what he had done began to believe in him.

Gospel

Luke 2:41-51a; L543

Each year Jesus' parents went to Jerusalem for the feast of Passover,
    and when he was twelve years old,
    they went up according to festival custom.
After they had completed its days, as they were returning,
    the boy Jesus remained behind in Jerusalem,
    but his parents did not know it.
Thinking that he was in the caravan,
    they journeyed for a day
    and looked for him among their relatives and acquaintances,
    but not finding him,
    they returned to Jerusalem to look for him.
After three days they found him in the temple,
    sitting in the midst of the teachers,
    listening to them and asking them questions,
    and all who heard him were astounded
    at his understanding and his answers.
When his parents saw him,
    they were astonished,
    and his mother said to him,
    "Son, why have you done this to us?
Your father and I have been looking for you with great anxiety."

And he said to them,
    "Why were you looking for me?
Did you not know that I must be in my Father's house?"
But they did not understand what he said to them.
He went down with them and came to Nazareth,
    and was obedient to them.

FIRST READING

2 Sam 7:4-5a, 12-14a, 16

The LORD spoke to Nathan and said:
"Go, tell my servant David,
    'When your time comes and you rest with
        your ancestors,
    I will raise up your heir after you, sprung
        from your loins,
    and I will make his kingdom firm.
It is he who shall build a house for my name.
And I will make his royal throne firm forever.
I will be a father to him,
    and he shall be a son to me.
Your house and your kingdom shall endure
        forever before me;
    your throne shall stand firm forever.'"

RESPONSORIAL PSALM

Ps 89:2-3, 4-5, 27 and 29

℟. (37) The son of David will live for ever.

The promises of the LORD I will sing forever,
    through all generations my mouth will
        proclaim your faithfulness,
For you have said, "My kindness is
        established forever";
    in heaven you have confirmed your
        faithfulness.

℟. The son of David will live for ever.

"I have made a covenant with my chosen one,
    I have sworn to David my servant:
Forever will I confirm your posterity
    and establish your throne for all
        generations."

℟. The son of David will live for ever.

"He shall say of me, 'You are my father,
    my God, the Rock, my savior.'
Forever I will maintain my kindness toward
        him,
    and my covenant with him stands firm."

℟. The son of David will live for ever.

SECOND READING

Rom 4:13, 16-18, 22

Brothers and sisters:
It was not through the law
    that the promise was made to Abraham
        and his descendants
    that he would inherit the world,
    but through the righteousness that comes
        from faith.
For this reason, it depends on faith,
    so that it may be a gift,
    and the promise may be guaranteed to all
        his descendants,
    not to those who only adhere to the law
    but to those who follow the faith of
        Abraham,
    who is the father of all of us, as it is
        written,
    I have made you father of many nations.
He is our father in the sight of God,
    in whom he believed, who gives life to the
        dead
    and calls into being what does not exist.
He believed, hoping against hope,
    that he would become *the father of many
        nations,*
    according to what was said, *Thus shall your
        descendants be.*
That is why *it was credited to him as
        righteousness.*

Gospel (cont.) at the procession with palms

Some of the bystanders said to them,
"What are you doing, untying the colt?"
They answered them just as Jesus had told them to,
and they permitted them to do it.
So they brought the colt to Jesus
and put their cloaks over it.
And he sat on it.
Many people spread their cloaks on the road,
and others spread leafy branches
that they had cut from the fields.
Those preceding him as well as those following kept crying out:
"Hosanna!
Blessed is he who comes in the name of the Lord!
Blessed is the kingdom of our father David that is to come!
Hosanna in the highest!"

Gospel at Mass

Mark 14:1–15:47; L38B

The Passover and the Feast of Unleavened Bread
were to take place in two days' time.
So the chief priests and the scribes were seeking a way
to arrest him by treachery and put him to death.
They said, "Not during the festival,
for fear that there may be a riot among the people."

When he was in Bethany reclining at table
in the house of Simon the leper,
a woman came with an alabaster jar of perfumed oil,
costly genuine spikenard.
She broke the alabaster jar and poured it on his head.
There were some who were indignant.
"Why has there been this waste of perfumed oil?
It could have been sold for more than three hundred days' wages
and the money given to the poor."
They were infuriated with her.
Jesus said, "Let her alone.
Why do you make trouble for her?
She has done a good thing for me.
The poor you will always have with you,
and whenever you wish you can do good to them,
but you will not always have me.
She has done what she could.
She has anticipated anointing my body for burial.
Amen, I say to you,
wherever the gospel is proclaimed to the whole world,
what she has done will be told in memory of her."

Then Judas Iscariot, one of the Twelve,
went off to the chief priests to hand him over to them.
When they heard him they were pleased and promised to pay him money.
Then he looked for an opportunity to hand him over.

On the first day of the Feast of Unleavened Bread,
when they sacrificed the Passover lamb,
his disciples said to him,
"Where do you want us to go
and prepare for you to eat the Passover?"

He sent two of his disciples and said to them,
"Go into the city and a man will meet you,
carrying a jar of water.
Follow him.
Wherever he enters, say to the master of the house,
'The Teacher says, "Where is my guest room
where I may eat the Passover with my disciples?"'
Then he will show you a large upper room furnished and ready.
Make the preparations for us there."
The disciples then went off, entered the city,
and found it just as he had told them;
and they prepared the Passover.

When it was evening, he came with the Twelve.
And as they reclined at table and were eating, Jesus said,
"Amen, I say to you, one of you will betray me,
one who is eating with me."
They began to be distressed and to say to him, one by one,
"Surely it is not I?"
He said to them,
"One of the Twelve, the one who dips with me into the dish.
For the Son of Man indeed goes, as it is written of him,
but woe to that man by whom the Son of Man is betrayed.
It would be better for that man if he had never been born."

While they were eating,
he took bread, said the blessing,
broke it, and gave it to them, and said,
"Take it; this is my body."
Then he took a cup, gave thanks, and gave it to them,
and they all drank from it.
He said to them,
"This is my blood of the covenant,
which will be shed for many.
Amen, I say to you,
I shall not drink again the fruit of the vine
until the day when I drink it new in the kingdom of God."
Then, after singing a hymn,
they went out to the Mount of Olives.

Then Jesus said to them,
"All of you will have your faith shaken, for it is written:
I will strike the shepherd,
and the sheep will be dispersed.
But after I have been raised up,
I shall go before you to Galilee."
Peter said to him,
"Even though all should have their faith shaken,
mine will not be."
Then Jesus said to him,
"Amen, I say to you,
this very night before the cock crows twice
you will deny me three times."
But he vehemently replied,
"Even though I should have to die with you,
I will not deny you."
And they all spoke similarly.

Then they came to a place named Gethsemane,
and he said to his disciples,
"Sit here while I pray."

He took with him Peter, James, and John,
    and began to be troubled and distressed.
Then he said to them, "My soul is sorrowful even to death.
Remain here and keep watch."
He advanced a little and fell to the ground and prayed
    that if it were possible the hour might pass by him;
    he said, "Abba, Father, all things are possible to you.
Take this cup away from me,
    but not what I will but what you will."
When he returned he found them asleep.
He said to Peter, "Simon, are you asleep?
Could you not keep watch for one hour?
Watch and pray that you may not undergo the test.
The spirit is willing but the flesh is weak."
Withdrawing again, he prayed, saying the same thing.
Then he returned once more and found them asleep,
    for they could not keep their eyes open
    and did not know what to answer him.
He returned a third time and said to them,
    "Are you still sleeping and taking your rest?
It is enough. The hour has come.
Behold, the Son of Man is to be handed over to sinners.
Get up, let us go.
See, my betrayer is at hand."

Then, while he was still speaking,
    Judas, one of the Twelve, arrived,
    accompanied by a crowd with swords and clubs
    who had come from the chief priests,
    the scribes, and the elders.
His betrayer had arranged a signal with them, saying,
    "The man I shall kiss is the one;
    arrest him and lead him away securely."
He came and immediately went over to him and said,
    "Rabbi." And he kissed him.
At this they laid hands on him and arrested him.
One of the bystanders drew his sword,
    struck the high priest's servant, and cut off his ear.
Jesus said to them in reply,
    "Have you come out as against a robber,
    with swords and clubs, to seize me?
Day after day I was with you teaching in the temple area,
    yet you did not arrest me;
    but that the Scriptures may be fulfilled."
And they all left him and fled.
Now a young man followed him
    wearing nothing but a linen cloth about his body.
They seized him,
    but he left the cloth behind and ran off naked.

They led Jesus away to the high priest,
    and all the chief priests and the elders and the scribes came together.
Peter followed him at a distance into the high priest's courtyard
    and was seated with the guards, warming himself at the fire.
The chief priests and the entire Sanhedrin
    kept trying to obtain testimony against Jesus
    in order to put him to death, but they found none.
Many gave false witness against him,
    but their testimony did not agree.

Some took the stand and testified falsely against him,
    alleging, "We heard him say,
    'I will destroy this temple made with hands
    and within three days I will build another
    not made with hands.'"
Even so their testimony did not agree.
The high priest rose before the assembly and questioned Jesus,
    saying, "Have you no answer?
What are these men testifying against you?"
But he was silent and answered nothing.
Again the high priest asked him and said to him,
    "Are you the Christ, the son of the Blessed One?"
Then Jesus answered, "I am;
    and 'you will see the Son of Man
        seated at the right hand of the Power
        and coming with the clouds of heaven.'"
At that the high priest tore his garments and said,
    "What further need have we of witnesses?
You have heard the blasphemy.
What do you think?"
They all condemned him as deserving to die.
Some began to spit on him.
They blindfolded him and struck him and said to him, "Prophesy!"
And the guards greeted him with blows.

While Peter was below in the courtyard,
    one of the high priest's maids came along.
Seeing Peter warming himself,
    she looked intently at him and said,
    "You too were with the Nazarene, Jesus."
But he denied it saying,
    "I neither know nor understand what you are talking about."
So he went out into the outer court.
Then the cock crowed.
The maid saw him and began again to say to the bystanders,
    "This man is one of them."
Once again he denied it.
A little later the bystanders said to Peter once more,
    "Surely you are one of them; for you too are a Galilean."
He began to curse and to swear,
    "I do not know this man about whom you are talking."
And immediately a cock crowed a second time.
Then Peter remembered the word that Jesus had said to him,
    "Before the cock crows twice you will deny me three times."
He broke down and wept.

As soon as morning came,
    the chief priests with the elders and the scribes,
    that is, the whole Sanhedrin, held a council.
They bound Jesus, led him away, and handed him over to Pilate.
Pilate questioned him,
    "Are you the king of the Jews?"
He said to him in reply, "You say so."
The chief priests accused him of many things.
Again Pilate questioned him,
    "Have you no answer?
See how many things they accuse you of."
Jesus gave him no further answer, so that Pilate was amazed.

Now on the occasion of the feast he used to release to them
    one prisoner whom they requested.
A man called Barabbas was then in prison
    along with the rebels who had committed murder in a rebellion.
The crowd came forward and began to ask him
    to do for them as he was accustomed.
Pilate answered,
    "Do you want me to release to you the king of the Jews?"
For he knew that it was out of envy
    that the chief priests had handed him over.
But the chief priests stirred up the crowd
    to have him release Barabbas for them instead.
Pilate again said to them in reply,
    "Then what do you want me to do
    with the man you call the king of the Jews?"
They shouted again, "Crucify him."
Pilate said to them, "Why? What evil has he done?"
They only shouted the louder, "Crucify him."
So Pilate, wishing to satisfy the crowd,
    released Barabbas to them and, after he had Jesus scourged,
    handed him over to be crucified.

The soldiers led him away inside the palace,
    that is, the praetorium, and assembled the whole cohort.
They clothed him in purple and,
    weaving a crown of thorns, placed it on him.
They began to salute him with, "Hail, King of the Jews!"
    and kept striking his head with a reed and spitting upon him.
They knelt before him in homage.
And when they had mocked him,
    they stripped him of the purple cloak,
    dressed him in his own clothes,
    and led him out to crucify him.

They pressed into service a passer-by, Simon,
    a Cyrenian, who was coming in from the country,
    the father of Alexander and Rufus,
    to carry his cross.

They brought him to the place of Golgotha
    —which is translated Place of the Skull—.
They gave him wine drugged with myrrh,
    but he did not take it.
Then they crucified him and divided his garments
    by casting lots for them to see what each should take.
It was nine o'clock in the morning when they crucified him.
The inscription of the charge against him read,
    "The King of the Jews."
With him they crucified two revolutionaries,
    one on his right and one on his left.
Those passing by reviled him,
    shaking their heads and saying,
    "Aha! You who would destroy the temple
    and rebuild it in three days,
    save yourself by coming down from the cross."
Likewise the chief priests, with the scribes,
    mocked him among themselves and said,
    "He saved others; he cannot save himself.
Let the Christ, the King of Israel,
    come down now from the cross
    that we may see and believe."

Those who were crucified with him also kept abusing him.

At noon darkness came over the whole land
    until three in the afternoon.
And at three o'clock Jesus cried out in a loud voice,
    "Eloi, Eloi, lema sabachthani?"
    which is translated,
    "My God, my God, why have you forsaken me?"
Some of the bystanders who heard it said,
    "Look, he is calling Elijah."
One of them ran, soaked a sponge with wine, put it on a reed
    and gave it to him to drink saying,
    "Wait, let us see if Elijah comes to take him down."
Jesus gave a loud cry and breathed his last.

Here all kneel and pause for a short time.

The veil of the sanctuary was torn in two from top to bottom.
When the centurion who stood facing him
    saw how he breathed his last he said,
    "Truly this man was the Son of God!"
There were also women looking on from a distance.
Among them were Mary Magdalene,
    Mary the mother of the younger James and of Joses,
    and Salome.
These women had followed him when he was in Galilee
    and ministered to him.
There were also many other women
    who had come up with him to Jerusalem.

When it was already evening,
    since it was the day of preparation,
    the day before the sabbath, Joseph of Arimathea,
    a distinguished member of the council,
    who was himself awaiting the kingdom of God,
    came and courageously went to Pilate
    and asked for the body of Jesus.
Pilate was amazed that he was already dead.
He summoned the centurion
    and asked him if Jesus had already died.
And when he learned of it from the centurion,
    he gave the body to Joseph.
Having bought a linen cloth, he took him down,
    wrapped him in the linen cloth,
    and laid him in a tomb that had been hewn out of the rock.
Then he rolled a stone against the entrance to the tomb.
Mary Magdalene and Mary the mother of Joses
    watched where he was laid.

or Mark 15:1-39; L38B

As soon as morning came,
    the chief priests with the elders and the scribes,
    that is, the whole Sanhedrin, held a council.
They bound Jesus, led him away, and handed him over to Pilate.
Pilate questioned him,
    "Are you the king of the Jews?"
He said to him in reply, "You say so."
The chief priests accused him of many things.
Again Pilate questioned him,
    "Have you no answer?
See how many things they accuse you of."
Jesus gave him no further answer, so that Pilate was amazed.

Now on the occasion of the feast he used to release to them
   one prisoner whom they requested.
A man called Barabbas was then in prison
   along with the rebels who had committed murder in a rebellion.
The crowd came forward and began to ask him
   to do for them as he was accustomed.
Pilate answered,
   "Do you want me to release to you the king of the Jews?"
For he knew that it was out of envy
   that the chief priests had handed him over.
But the chief priests stirred up the crowd
   to have him release Barabbas for them instead.
Pilate again said to them in reply,
   "Then what do you want me to do
   with the man you call the king of the Jews?"
They shouted again, "Crucify him."
Pilate said to them, "Why? What evil has he done?"
They only shouted the louder, "Crucify him."
So Pilate, wishing to satisfy the crowd,
   released Barabbas to them and, after he had Jesus scourged,
   handed him over to be crucified.

The soldiers led him away inside the palace,
   that is, the praetorium, and assembled the whole cohort.
They clothed him in purple and,
   weaving a crown of thorns, placed it on him.
They began to salute him with, "Hail, King of the Jews!"
   and kept striking his head with a reed and spitting upon him.
They knelt before him in homage.
And when they had mocked him,
   they stripped him of the purple cloak,
   dressed him in his own clothes,
   and led him out to crucify him.

They pressed into service a passer-by, Simon,
   a Cyrenian, who was coming in from the country,
   the father of Alexander and Rufus,
   to carry his cross.

They brought him to the place of Golgotha
   —which is translated Place of the Skull—.
They gave him wine drugged with myrrh,
   but he did not take it.

Then they crucified him and divided his garments
   by casting lots for them to see what each should take.
It was nine o'clock in the morning when they crucified him.
The inscription of the charge against him read,
   "The King of the Jews."
With him they crucified two revolutionaries,
   one on his right and one on his left.
Those passing by reviled him,
   shaking their heads and saying,
   "Aha! You who would destroy the temple
   and rebuild it in three days,
   save yourself by coming down from the cross."
Likewise the chief priests, with the scribes,
   mocked him among themselves and said,
   "He saved others; he cannot save himself.
Let the Christ, the King of Israel,
   come down now from the cross
   that we may see and believe."
Those who were crucified with him also kept abusing him.

At noon darkness came over the whole land
   until three in the afternoon.
And at three o'clock Jesus cried out in a loud voice,
   "Eloi, Eloi, lema sabachthani?"
   which is translated,
   "My God, my God, why have you forsaken me?"
Some of the bystanders who heard it said,
   "Look, he is calling Elijah."
One of them ran, soaked a sponge with wine, put it on a reed
   and gave it to him to drink saying,
   "Wait, let us see if Elijah comes to take him down."
Jesus gave a loud cry and breathed his last.

Here all kneel and pause for a short time.

The veil of the sanctuary was torn in two from top to bottom.
When the centurion who stood facing him
   saw how he breathed his last he said,
   "Truly this man was the Son of God!"

Gospel (cont.)

John 13:1-15; L39ABC

For he knew who would betray him;
   for this reason, he said, "Not all of you are clean."

So when he had washed their feet
   and put his garments back on and reclined at table again,
   he said to them, "Do you realize what I have done for you?

You call me 'teacher' and 'master,' and rightly so, for indeed I am.
If I, therefore, the master and teacher, have washed your feet,
   you ought to wash one another's feet.
I have given you a model to follow,
   so that as I have done for you, you should also do."

FIRST READING

Exod 12:1-8, 11-14

The Lord said to Moses and Aaron in the land of Egypt,
   "This month shall stand at the head of your calendar;
   you shall reckon it the first month of the year.
Tell the whole community of Israel:
   On the tenth of this month every one of your families
   must procure for itself a lamb, one apiece for each household.
If a family is too small for a whole lamb,
   it shall join the nearest household in procuring one
   and shall share in the lamb
   in proportion to the number of persons who partake of it.
The lamb must be a year-old male and without blemish.
You may take it from either the sheep or the goats.
You shall keep it until the fourteenth day of this month,
   and then, with the whole assembly of Israel present,
   it shall be slaughtered during the evening twilight.
They shall take some of its blood
   and apply it to the two doorposts and the lintel
   of every house in which they partake of the lamb.

That same night they shall eat its roasted flesh
   with unleavened bread and bitter herbs.

"This is how you are to eat it:
   with your loins girt, sandals on your feet and your staff in hand,
   you shall eat like those who are in flight.
It is the Passover of the Lord.
For on this same night I will go through Egypt,
   striking down every firstborn of the land, both man and beast,
   and executing judgment on all the gods of Egypt—I, the Lord!
But the blood will mark the houses where you are.
Seeing the blood, I will pass over you;
   thus, when I strike the land of Egypt,
   no destructive blow will come upon you.

"This day shall be a memorial feast for you,
   which all your generations shall celebrate
   with pilgrimage to the Lord, as a perpetual institution."

RESPONSORIAL PSALM

Ps 116:12-13, 15-16bc, 17-18

℟. (cf. 1 Cor 10:16) Our blessing-cup is a communion with the Blood of Christ.

How shall I make a return to the Lord
   for all the good he has done for me?
The cup of salvation I will take up,
   and I will call upon the name of the Lord.

℟. Our blessing-cup is a communion with the Blood of Christ.

Precious in the eyes of the Lord
   is the death of his faithful ones.
I am your servant, the son of your handmaid;
   you have loosed my bonds.

℟. Our blessing-cup is a communion with the Blood of Christ.

To you will I offer sacrifice of thanksgiving,
   and I will call upon the name of the Lord.
My vows to the Lord I will pay
   in the presence of all his people.

℟. Our blessing-cup is a communion with the Blood of Christ.

SECOND READING

1 Cor 11:23-26

Brothers and sisters:
I received from the Lord what I also handed on to you,
   that the Lord Jesus, on the night he was handed over,
   took bread, and, after he had given thanks,
   broke it and said, "This is my body that is for you.
Do this in remembrance of me."
In the same way also the cup, after supper, saying,
   "This cup is the new covenant in my blood.
Do this, as often as you drink it, in remembrance of me."
For as often as you eat this bread and drink the cup,
   you proclaim the death of the Lord until he comes.

Gospel (cont.)
John 18:1–19:42; L40ABC

Jesus said to Peter,
    "Put your sword into its scabbard.
Shall I not drink the cup that the Father gave me?"

So the band of soldiers, the tribune, and the Jewish guards seized Jesus,
    bound him, and brought him to Annas first.
He was the father-in-law of Caiaphas,
    who was high priest that year.
It was Caiaphas who had counseled the Jews
    that it was better that one man should die rather than the people.

Simon Peter and another disciple followed Jesus.
Now the other disciple was known to the high priest,
    and he entered the courtyard of the high priest with Jesus.
But Peter stood at the gate outside.
So the other disciple, the acquaintance of the high priest,
    went out and spoke to the gatekeeper and brought Peter in.
Then the maid who was the gatekeeper said to Peter,
    "You are not one of this man's disciples, are you?"
He said, "I am not."
Now the slaves and the guards were standing around a charcoal fire
    that they had made, because it was cold,
    and were warming themselves.
Peter was also standing there keeping warm.

The high priest questioned Jesus
    about his disciples and about his doctrine.
Jesus answered him,
    "I have spoken publicly to the world.
I have always taught in a synagogue
    or in the temple area where all the Jews gather,
    and in secret I have said nothing. Why ask me?
Ask those who heard me what I said to them.
They know what I said."
When he had said this,
    one of the temple guards standing there struck Jesus and said,
    "Is this the way you answer the high priest?"
Jesus answered him,
    "If I have spoken wrongly, testify to the wrong;
    but if I have spoken rightly, why do you strike me?"
Then Annas sent him bound to Caiaphas the high priest.

Now Simon Peter was standing there keeping warm.
And they said to him,
    "You are not one of his disciples, are you?"
He denied it and said,
    "I am not."
One of the slaves of the high priest,
    a relative of the one whose ear Peter had cut off, said,
    "Didn't I see you in the garden with him?"
Again Peter denied it.
And immediately the cock crowed.

Then they brought Jesus from Caiaphas to the praetorium.
It was morning.
And they themselves did not enter the praetorium,
    in order not to be defiled so that they could eat the Passover.
So Pilate came out to them and said,
    "What charge do you bring against this man?"
They answered and said to him,
    "If he were not a criminal,

we would not have handed him over to you."
At this, Pilate said to them,
    "Take him yourselves, and judge him according to your law."
The Jews answered him,
    "We do not have the right to execute anyone,"
in order that the word of Jesus might be fulfilled
    that he said indicating the kind of death he would die.
So Pilate went back into the praetorium
    and summoned Jesus and said to him,
    "Are you the King of the Jews?"
Jesus answered,
    "Do you say this on your own
    or have others told you about me?"
Pilate answered,
    "I am not a Jew, am I?
Your own nation and the chief priests handed you over to me.
What have you done?"
Jesus answered,
    "My kingdom does not belong to this world.
If my kingdom did belong to this world,
    my attendants would be fighting
    to keep me from being handed over to the Jews.
But as it is, my kingdom is not here."
So Pilate said to him,
    "Then you are a king?"
Jesus answered,
    "You say I am a king.
For this I was born and for this I came into the world,
    to testify to the truth.
Everyone who belongs to the truth listens to my voice."
Pilate said to him, "What is truth?"

When he had said this,
    he again went out to the Jews and said to them,
    "I find no guilt in him.
But you have a custom that I release one prisoner to you at Passover.
Do you want me to release to you the King of the Jews?"
They cried out again,
    "Not this one but Barabbas!"
Now Barabbas was a revolutionary.

Then Pilate took Jesus and had him scourged.
And the soldiers wove a crown out of thorns and placed it on his head,
    and clothed him in a purple cloak,
    and they came to him and said,
    "Hail, King of the Jews!"
And they struck him repeatedly.
Once more Pilate went out and said to them,
    "Look, I am bringing him out to you,
    so that you may know that I find no guilt in him."
So Jesus came out,
    wearing the crown of thorns and the purple cloak.
And he said to them, "Behold, the man!"
When the chief priests and the guards saw him they cried out,
    "Crucify him, crucify him!"
Pilate said to them,
    "Take him yourselves and crucify him.
I find no guilt in him."

The Jews answered,
"We have a law, and according to that law he ought to die,
because he made himself the Son of God."
Now when Pilate heard this statement,
he became even more afraid,
and went back into the praetorium and said to Jesus,
"Where are you from?"
Jesus did not answer him.
So Pilate said to him,
"Do you not speak to me?
Do you not know that I have power to release you
and I have power to crucify you?"
Jesus answered him,
"You would have no power over me
if it had not been given to you from above.
For this reason the one who handed me over to you
has the greater sin."
Consequently, Pilate tried to release him; but the Jews cried out,
"If you release him, you are not a Friend of Caesar.
Everyone who makes himself a king opposes Caesar."

When Pilate heard these words he brought Jesus out
and seated him on the judge's bench
in the place called Stone Pavement, in Hebrew, Gabbatha.
It was preparation day for Passover, and it was about noon.
And he said to the Jews,
"Behold, your king!"
They cried out,
"Take him away, take him away! Crucify him!"
Pilate said to them,
"Shall I crucify your king?"
The chief priests answered,
"We have no king but Caesar."
Then he handed him over to them to be crucified.

So they took Jesus, and, carrying the cross himself,
he went out to what is called the Place of the Skull,
in Hebrew, Golgotha.
There they crucified him, and with him two others,
one on either side, with Jesus in the middle.
Pilate also had an inscription written and put on the cross.
It read,
"Jesus the Nazorean, the King of the Jews."
Now many of the Jews read this inscription,
because the place where Jesus was crucified was near the city;
and it was written in Hebrew, Latin, and Greek.
So the chief priests of the Jews said to Pilate,
"Do not write 'The King of the Jews,'
but that he said, 'I am the King of the Jews.'"
Pilate answered,
"What I have written, I have written."

When the soldiers had crucified Jesus,
they took his clothes and divided them into four shares,
a share for each soldier.
They also took his tunic, but the tunic was seamless,
woven in one piece from the top down.
So they said to one another,
"Let's not tear it, but cast lots for it to see whose it will be,"

in order that the passage of Scripture might be fulfilled that says:
They divided my garments among them,
and for my vesture they cast lots.
This is what the soldiers did.
Standing by the cross of Jesus were his mother
and his mother's sister, Mary the wife of Clopas,
and Mary of Magdala.
When Jesus saw his mother and the disciple there whom he loved
he said to his mother, "Woman, behold, your son."
Then he said to the disciple,
"Behold, your mother."
And from that hour the disciple took her into his home.

After this, aware that everything was now finished,
in order that the Scripture might be fulfilled,
Jesus said, "I thirst."
There was a vessel filled with common wine.
So they put a sponge soaked in wine on a sprig of hyssop
and put it up to his mouth.
When Jesus had taken the wine, he said,
"It is finished."
And bowing his head, he handed over the spirit.

Here all kneel and pause for a short time.

Now since it was preparation day,
in order that the bodies might not remain
on the cross on the sabbath,
for the sabbath day of that week was a solemn one,
the Jews asked Pilate that their legs be broken
and that they be taken down.
So the soldiers came and broke the legs of the first
and then of the other one who was crucified with Jesus.
But when they came to Jesus and saw that he was already dead,
they did not break his legs,
but one soldier thrust his lance into his side,
and immediately blood and water flowed out.
An eyewitness has testified, and his testimony is true;
he knows that he is speaking the truth,
so that you also may come to believe.
For this happened so that the Scripture passage might be fulfilled:
Not a bone of it will be broken.
And again another passage says:
They will look upon him whom they have pierced.

After this, Joseph of Arimathea,
secretly a disciple of Jesus for fear of the Jews,
asked Pilate if he could remove the body of Jesus.
And Pilate permitted it.
So he came and took his body.
Nicodemus, the one who had first come to him at night,
also came bringing a mixture of myrrh and aloes
weighing about one hundred pounds.
They took the body of Jesus
and bound it with burial cloths along with the spices,
according to the Jewish burial custom.
Now in the place where he had been crucified there was a garden,
and in the garden a new tomb, in which no one had yet been buried.
So they laid Jesus there because of the Jewish preparation day;
for the tomb was close by.

Friday of the Passion of the Lord (Good Friday), *March 29, 2024*

FIRST READING
Isa 52:13–53:12

See, my servant shall prosper,
he shall be raised high and greatly exalted.
Even as many were amazed at him—
so marred was his look beyond human
semblance
and his appearance beyond that of the sons
of man—
so shall he startle many nations,
because of him kings shall stand
speechless;
for those who have not been told shall see,
those who have not heard shall ponder it.

Who would believe what we have heard?
To whom has the arm of the Lord been
revealed?
He grew up like a sapling before him,
like a shoot from the parched earth;
there was in him no stately bearing to make
us look at him,
nor appearance that would attract us to him.
He was spurned and avoided by people,
a man of suffering, accustomed to infirmity,
one of those from whom people hide their
faces,
spurned, and we held him in no esteem.

Yet it was our infirmities that he bore,
our sufferings that he endured,
while we thought of him as stricken,
as one smitten by God and afflicted.
But he was pierced for our offenses,
crushed for our sins;
upon him was the chastisement that makes
us whole,
by his stripes we were healed.
We had all gone astray like sheep,
each following his own way;
but the Lord laid upon him
the guilt of us all.

Though he was harshly treated, he submitted
and opened not his mouth;
like a lamb led to the slaughter
or a sheep before the shearers,
he was silent and opened not his mouth.
Oppressed and condemned, he was taken away,
and who would have thought any more of
his destiny?
When he was cut off from the land of the
living,
and smitten for the sin of his people,
a grave was assigned him among the wicked
and a burial place with evildoers,
though he had done no wrong
nor spoken any falsehood.
But the Lord was pleased
to crush him in infirmity.

If he gives his life as an offering for sin,
he shall see his descendants in a long life,
and the will of the Lord shall be
accomplished through him.

Because of his affliction
he shall see the light
in fullness of days;
through his suffering, my servant shall justify
many,
and their guilt he shall bear.
Therefore I will give him his portion among
the great,
and he shall divide the spoils with the
mighty,
because he surrendered himself to death
and was counted among the wicked;
and he shall take away the sins of many,
and win pardon for their offenses.

RESPONSORIAL PSALM
Ps 31:2, 6, 12-13, 15-16, 17, 25

℟. (Luke 23:46) Father, into your hands I
commend my spirit.

In you, O Lord, I take refuge;
let me never be put to shame.
In your justice rescue me.
Into your hands I commend my spirit;
you will redeem me, O Lord, O faithful God.

℟. Father, into your hands I commend my
spirit.

For all my foes I am an object of reproach,
a laughingstock to my neighbors, and a
dread to my friends;
they who see me abroad flee from me.
I am forgotten like the unremembered dead;
I am like a dish that is broken.

℟. Father, into your hands I commend my
spirit.

But my trust is in you, O Lord;
I say, "You are my God.
In your hands is my destiny; rescue me
from the clutches of my enemies and my
persecutors."

℟. Father, into your hands I commend my
spirit.

Let your face shine upon your servant;
save me in your kindness.
Take courage and be stouthearted,
all you who hope in the Lord.

℟. Father, into your hands I commend my
spirit.

SECOND READING
Heb 4:14-16; 5:7-9

Brothers and sisters:
Since we have a great high priest who has
passed through the heavens,
Jesus, the Son of God,
let us hold fast to our confession.
For we do not have a high priest
who is unable to sympathize with our
weaknesses,
but one who has similarly been tested in
every way,
yet without sin.
So let us confidently approach the throne of
grace
to receive mercy and to find grace for
timely help.

In the days when Christ was in the flesh,
he offered prayers and supplications with
loud cries and tears
to the one who was able to save him from
death,
and he was heard because of his reverence.
Son though he was, he learned obedience from
what he suffered;
and when he was made perfect,
he became the source of eternal salvation
for all who obey him.

FIRST READING
Gen 1:1–2:2

In the beginning, when God created the
heavens and the earth,
the earth was a formless wasteland, and
darkness covered the abyss,
while a mighty wind swept over the waters.

Then God said,
"Let there be light," and there was light.
God saw how good the light was.
God then separated the light from the
darkness.
God called the light "day," and the darkness
he called "night."
Thus evening came, and morning followed—
the first day.

Then God said,
"Let there be a dome in the middle of the
waters,
to separate one body of water from the
other."
And so it happened:
God made the dome,
and it separated the water above the dome
from the water below it.
God called the dome "the sky."
Evening came, and morning followed—the
second day.

Then God said,
"Let the water under the sky be gathered
into a single basin,
so that the dry land may appear."
And so it happened:
the water under the sky was gathered into
its basin,
and the dry land appeared.
God called the dry land "the earth,"
and the basin of the water he called "the
sea."
God saw how good it was.
Then God said,
"Let the earth bring forth vegetation:
every kind of plant that bears seed
and every kind of fruit tree on earth
that bears fruit with its seed in it."
And so it happened:
the earth brought forth every kind of plant
that bears seed
and every kind of fruit tree on earth
that bears fruit with its seed in it.
God saw how good it was.
Evening came, and morning followed—the
third day.

Then God said:
"Let there be lights in the dome of the sky,
to separate day from night.
Let them mark the fixed times, the days and
the years,

and serve as luminaries in the dome of the
sky,
to shed light upon the earth."
And so it happened:
God made the two great lights,
the greater one to govern the day,
and the lesser one to govern the night;
and he made the stars.
God set them in the dome of the sky,
to shed light upon the earth,
to govern the day and the night,
and to separate the light from the darkness.
God saw how good it was.
Evening came, and morning followed—the
fourth day.

Then God said,
"Let the water teem with an abundance of
living creatures,
and on the earth let birds fly beneath the
dome of the sky."
And so it happened:
God created the great sea monsters
and all kinds of swimming creatures with
which the water teems,
and all kinds of winged birds.
God saw how good it was, and God blessed
them, saying,
"Be fertile, multiply, and fill the water of
the seas;
and let the birds multiply on the earth."
Evening came, and morning followed—the
fifth day.

Then God said,
"Let the earth bring forth all kinds of living
creatures:
cattle, creeping things, and wild animals of
all kinds."
And so it happened:
God made all kinds of wild animals, all
kinds of cattle,
and all kinds of creeping things of the
earth.
God saw how good it was.
Then God said:
"Let us make man in our image, after our
likeness.
Let them have dominion over the fish of the
sea,
the birds of the air, and the cattle,
and over all the wild animals
and all the creatures that crawl on the
ground."
God created man in his image;
in the image of God he created him;
male and female he created them.
God blessed them, saying:
"Be fertile and multiply;
fill the earth and subdue it.
Have dominion over the fish of the sea, the
birds of the air,

and all the living things that move on the
earth."
God also said:
"See, I give you every seed-bearing plant all
over the earth
and every tree that has seed-bearing fruit
on it to be your food;
and to all the animals of the land, all the
birds of the air,
and all the living creatures that crawl on
the ground,
I give all the green plants for food."
And so it happened.
God looked at everything he had made, and he
found it very good.
Evening came, and morning followed—the
sixth day.

Thus the heavens and the earth and all their
array were completed.
Since on the seventh day God was finished
with the work he had been doing,
he rested on the seventh day from all the
work he had undertaken.

or

Gen 1:1, 26-31a

In the beginning, when God created the
heavens and the earth,
God said: "Let us make man in our image,
after our likeness.
Let them have dominion over the fish of the
sea,
the birds of the air, and the cattle,
and over all the wild animals
and all the creatures that crawl on the
ground."
God created man in his image;
in the image of God he created him;
male and female he created them.
God blessed them, saying:
"Be fertile and multiply;
fill the earth and subdue it.
Have dominion over the fish of the sea, the
birds of the air,
and all the living things that move on the
earth."
God also said:
"See, I give you every seed-bearing plant all
over the earth
and every tree that has seed-bearing fruit
on it to be your food;
and to all the animals of the land, all the
birds of the air,
and all the living creatures that crawl on
the ground,
I give all the green plants for food."
And so it happened.
God looked at everything he had made, and
found it very good.

RESPONSORIAL PSALM

Ps 104:1-2, 5-6, 10, 12, 13-14, 24, 35

℟. (30) Lord, send out your Spirit, and renew
the face of the earth.

Bless the LORD, O my soul!
    O LORD, my God, you are great indeed!
You are clothed with majesty and glory,
    robed in light as with a cloak.

℟. Lord, send out your Spirit, and renew the
face of the earth.

You fixed the earth upon its foundation,
    not to be moved forever;
with the ocean, as with a garment, you
    covered it;
    above the mountains the waters stood.

℟. Lord, send out your Spirit, and renew the
face of the earth.

You send forth springs into the watercourses
    that wind among the mountains.
Beside them the birds of heaven dwell;
    from among the branches they send forth
    their song.

℟. Lord, send out your Spirit, and renew the
face of the earth.

You water the mountains from your palace;
    the earth is replete with the fruit of your
    works.
You raise grass for the cattle,
    and vegetation for man's use,
producing bread from the earth.

℟. Lord, send out your Spirit, and renew the
face of the earth.

How manifold are your works, O LORD!
    In wisdom you have wrought them all—
the earth is full of your creatures.
    Bless the LORD, O my soul!

℟. Lord, send out your Spirit, and renew the
face of the earth.

or

Ps 33:4-5, 6-7, 12-13, 20 and 22

℟. (5b) The earth is full of the goodness of
the Lord.

Upright is the word of the LORD,
    and all his works are trustworthy.
He loves justice and right;
    of the kindness of the LORD the earth is full.

℟. The earth is full of the goodness of the Lord.

By the word of the LORD the heavens were
    made;
    by the breath of his mouth all their host.
He gathers the waters of the sea as in a flask;
    in cellars he confines the deep.

℟. The earth is full of the goodness of the Lord.

Blessed the nation whose God is the LORD,
    the people he has chosen for his own
    inheritance.
From heaven the LORD looks down;
    he sees all mankind.

℟. The earth is full of the goodness of the Lord.

Our soul waits for the LORD,
    who is our help and our shield.
May your kindness, O LORD, be upon us
    who have put our hope in you.

℟. The earth is full of the goodness of the Lord.

SECOND READING

Gen 22:1-18

God put Abraham to the test.
He called to him, "Abraham!"
"Here I am," he replied.
Then God said:
    "Take your son Isaac, your only one, whom
    you love,
    and go to the land of Moriah.
There you shall offer him up as a holocaust
    on a height that I will point out to you."
Early the next morning Abraham saddled his
    donkey,
    took with him his son Isaac and two of his
    servants as well,
    and with the wood that he had cut for the
    holocaust,
    set out for the place of which God had told
    him.

On the third day Abraham got sight of the
    place from afar.
Then he said to his servants:
    "Both of you stay here with the donkey,
    while the boy and I go on over yonder.
We will worship and then come back to you."
Thereupon Abraham took the wood for the
    holocaust
    and laid it on his son Isaac's shoulders,
    while he himself carried the fire and the
    knife.
As the two walked on together, Isaac spoke to
    his father Abraham:
    "Father!" Isaac said.
"Yes, son," he replied.
Isaac continued, "Here are the fire and the
    wood,
    but where is the sheep for the holocaust?"
"Son," Abraham answered,
    "God himself will provide the sheep for the
    holocaust."
Then the two continued going forward.

When they came to the place of which God
    had told him,
    Abraham built an altar there and arranged
    the wood on it.

Next he tied up his son Isaac,
    and put him on top of the wood on the
    altar.
Then he reached out and took the knife to
    slaughter his son.
But the LORD's messenger called to him from
    heaven,
    "Abraham, Abraham!"
"Here I am," he answered.
"Do not lay your hand on the boy," said the
    messenger.
"Do not do the least thing to him.
I know now how devoted you are to God,
    since you did not withhold from me your
    own beloved son."
As Abraham looked about,
    he spied a ram caught by its horns in the
    thicket.
So he went and took the ram
    and offered it up as a holocaust in place of
    his son.
Abraham named the site Yahweh-yireh;
    hence people now say, "On the mountain
    the LORD will see."

Again the LORD's messenger called to
    Abraham from heaven and said:
    "I swear by myself, declares the LORD,
    that because you acted as you did
    in not withholding from me your beloved
    son,
    I will bless you abundantly
    and make your descendants as countless
    as the stars of the sky and the sands of the
    seashore;
    your descendants shall take possession
    of the gates of their enemies,
    and in your descendants all the nations of
    the earth
    shall find blessing—
    all this because you obeyed my command."

or

Gen 22:1-2, 9a, 10-13, 15-18

God put Abraham to the test.
He called to him, "Abraham!"
"Here I am," he replied.
Then God said:
    "Take your son Isaac, your only one, whom
    you love,
    and go to the land of Moriah.
There you shall offer him up as a holocaust
    on a height that I will point out to you."

When they came to the place of which God
    had told him,
    Abraham built an altar there and arranged
    the wood on it.
Then he reached out and took the knife to
    slaughter his son.

But the Lord's messenger called to him from heaven,
"Abraham, Abraham!"
"Here I am," he answered.
"Do not lay your hand on the boy," said the messenger.
"Do not do the least thing to him.
I know now how devoted you are to God,
since you did not withhold from me your own beloved son."
As Abraham looked about,
he spied a ram caught by its horns in the thicket.
So he went and took the ram
and offered it up as a holocaust in place of his son.

Again the Lord's messenger called to Abraham from heaven and said:
"I swear by myself, declares the Lord,
that because you acted as you did
in not withholding from me your beloved son,
I will bless you abundantly
and make your descendants as countless as the stars of the sky and the sands of the seashore;
your descendants shall take possession of the gates of their enemies,
and in your descendants all the nations of the earth
shall find blessing—
all this because you obeyed my command."

RESPONSORIAL PSALM

Ps 16:5, 8, 9-10, 11

℟. (1) You are my inheritance, O Lord.

O Lord, my allotted portion and my cup,
you it is who hold fast my lot.
I set the Lord ever before me;
with him at my right hand I shall not be disturbed.

℟. You are my inheritance, O Lord.

Therefore my heart is glad and my soul rejoices,
my body, too, abides in confidence;
because you will not abandon my soul to the netherworld,
nor will you suffer your faithful one to undergo corruption.

℟. You are my inheritance, O Lord.

You will show me the path to life,
fullness of joys in your presence,
the delights at your right hand forever.

℟. You are my inheritance, O Lord.

THIRD READING

Exod 14:15–15:1

The Lord said to Moses, "Why are you crying out to me?
Tell the Israelites to go forward.
And you, lift up your staff and, with hand outstretched over the sea,
split the sea in two,
that the Israelites may pass through it on dry land.
But I will make the Egyptians so obstinate
that they will go in after them.
Then I will receive glory through Pharaoh and all his army,
his chariots and charioteers.
The Egyptians shall know that I am the Lord,
when I receive glory through Pharaoh and his chariots and charioteers."

The angel of God, who had been leading Israel's camp,
now moved and went around behind them.
The column of cloud also, leaving the front,
took up its place behind them,
so that it came between the camp of the Egyptians
and that of Israel.
But the cloud now became dark, and thus the night passed
without the rival camps coming any closer together all night long.
Then Moses stretched out his hand over the sea,
and the Lord swept the sea
with a strong east wind throughout the night
and so turned it into dry land.
When the water was thus divided,
the Israelites marched into the midst of the sea on dry land,
with the water like a wall to their right and to their left.

The Egyptians followed in pursuit;
all Pharaoh's horses and chariots and charioteers went after them
right into the midst of the sea.
In the night watch just before dawn
the Lord cast through the column of the fiery cloud
upon the Egyptian force a glance that threw it into a panic;
and he so clogged their chariot wheels
that they could hardly drive.
With that the Egyptians sounded the retreat before Israel,
because the Lord was fighting for them against the Egyptians.

Then the Lord told Moses, "Stretch out your hand over the sea,
that the water may flow back upon the Egyptians,
upon their chariots and their charioteers."
So Moses stretched out his hand over the sea,
and at dawn the sea flowed back to its normal depth.
The Egyptians were fleeing head on toward the sea,
when the Lord hurled them into its midst.
As the water flowed back,
it covered the chariots and the charioteers of Pharaoh's whole army
which had followed the Israelites into the sea.
Not a single one of them escaped.
But the Israelites had marched on dry land through the midst of the sea,
with the water like a wall to their right and to their left.
Thus the Lord saved Israel on that day from the power of the Egyptians.
When Israel saw the Egyptians lying dead on the seashore
and beheld the great power that the Lord had shown against the Egyptians,
they feared the Lord and believed in him
and in his servant Moses.

Then Moses and the Israelites sang this song to the Lord:
I will sing to the Lord, for he is gloriously triumphant;
horse and chariot he has cast into the sea.

RESPONSORIAL PSALM

Exod 15:1-2, 3-4, 5-6, 17-18

℟. (1b) Let us sing to the Lord; he has covered himself in glory.

I will sing to the Lord, for he is gloriously triumphant;
horse and chariot he has cast into the sea.
My strength and my courage is the Lord,
and he has been my savior.
He is my God, I praise him;
the God of my father, I extol him.

℟. Let us sing to the Lord; he has covered himself in glory.

The Lord is a warrior,
Lord is his name!
Pharaoh's chariots and army he hurled into the sea;
the elite of his officers were submerged in the Red Sea.

℟. Let us sing to the Lord; he has covered himself in glory.

The flood waters covered them,
  they sank into the depths like a stone.
Your right hand, O Lord, magnificent in
    power,
  your right hand, O Lord, has shattered the
    enemy.

℟. Let us sing to the Lord; he has covered
  himself in glory.

You brought in the people you redeemed
  and planted them on the mountain of your
    inheritance—
the place where you made your seat, O Lord,
  the sanctuary, Lord, which your hands
    established.
The Lord shall reign forever and ever.

℟. Let us sing to the Lord; he has covered
  himself in glory.

FOURTH READING
Isa 54:5-14

The One who has become your husband is
    your Maker;
  his name is the Lord of hosts;
your redeemer is the Holy One of Israel,
  called God of all the earth.
The Lord calls you back,
  like a wife forsaken and grieved in spirit,
  a wife married in youth and then cast off,
  says your God.
For a brief moment I abandoned you,
  but with great tenderness I will take you
    back.
In an outburst of wrath, for a moment
  I hid my face from you;
but with enduring love I take pity on you,
  says the Lord, your redeemer.
This is for me like the days of Noah,
  when I swore that the waters of Noah
  should never again deluge the earth;
so I have sworn not to be angry with you,
  or to rebuke you.
Though the mountains leave their place
  and the hills be shaken,
my love shall never leave you
  nor my covenant of peace be shaken,
  says the Lord, who has mercy on you.
O afflicted one, storm-battered and
    unconsoled,
  I lay your pavements in carnelians,
  and your foundations in sapphires;
I will make your battlements of rubies,
  your gates of carbuncles,
  and all your walls of precious stones.
All your children shall be taught by the Lord,
  and great shall be the peace of your children.

In justice shall you be established,
  far from the fear of oppression,
  where destruction cannot come near you.

RESPONSORIAL PSALM
Ps 30:2, 4, 5-6, 11-12, 13

℟. (2a) I will praise you, Lord, for you have
  rescued me.

I will extol you, O Lord, for you drew me clear
  and did not let my enemies rejoice over me.
O Lord, you brought me up from the
    netherworld;
  you preserved me from among those going
    down into the pit.

℟. I will praise you, Lord, for you have
  rescued me.

Sing praise to the Lord, you his faithful ones,
  and give thanks to his holy name.
For his anger lasts but a moment;
  a lifetime, his good will.
At nightfall, weeping enters in,
  but with the dawn, rejoicing.

℟. I will praise you, Lord, for you have
  rescued me.

Hear, O Lord, and have pity on me;
  O Lord, be my helper.
You changed my mourning into dancing;
  O Lord, my God, forever will I give you
    thanks.

℟. I will praise you, Lord, for you have
  rescued me.

FIFTH READING
Isa 55:1-11

Thus says the Lord:
All you who are thirsty,
  come to the water!
You who have no money,
  come, receive grain and eat;
come, without paying and without cost,
  drink wine and milk!
Why spend your money for what is not bread,
  your wages for what fails to satisfy?
Heed me, and you shall eat well,
  you shall delight in rich fare.
Come to me heedfully,
  listen, that you may have life.
I will renew with you the everlasting covenant,
  the benefits assured to David.
As I made him a witness to the peoples,
  a leader and commander of nations,
so shall you summon a nation you knew not,
  and nations that knew you not shall run
    to you,

because of the Lord, your God,
  the Holy One of Israel, who has glorified
    you.

Seek the Lord while he may be found,
  call him while he is near.
Let the scoundrel forsake his way,
  and the wicked man his thoughts;
let him turn to the Lord for mercy;
  to our God, who is generous in forgiving.
For my thoughts are not your thoughts,
  nor are your ways my ways, says the Lord.
As high as the heavens are above the earth,
  so high are my ways above your ways
  and my thoughts above your thoughts.

For just as from the heavens
  the rain and snow come down
and do not return there
  till they have watered the earth,
  making it fertile and fruitful,
giving seed to the one who sows
  and bread to the one who eats,
so shall my word be
  that goes forth from my mouth;
my word shall not return to me void,
  but shall do my will,
  achieving the end for which I sent it.

RESPONSORIAL PSALM
Isa 12:2-3, 4, 5-6

℟. (3) You will draw water joyfully from the
  springs of salvation.

God indeed is my savior;
  I am confident and unafraid.
My strength and my courage is the Lord,
  and he has been my savior.
With joy you will draw water
  at the fountain of salvation.

℟. You will draw water joyfully from the
  springs of salvation.

Give thanks to the Lord, acclaim his name;
  among the nations make known his deeds,
  proclaim how exalted is his name.

℟. You will draw water joyfully from the
  springs of salvation.

Sing praise to the Lord for his glorious
    achievement;
  let this be known throughout all the earth.
Shout with exultation, O city of Zion,
  for great in your midst
  is the Holy One of Israel!

℟. You will draw water joyfully from the
  springs of salvation.

SIXTH READING
Bar 3:9-15, 32–4:4

Hear, O Israel, the commandments of life:
  listen, and know prudence!
How is it, Israel,
  that you are in the land of your foes,
  grown old in a foreign land,
defiled with the dead,
  accounted with those destined for the
    netherworld?
You have forsaken the fountain of wisdom!
  Had you walked in the way of God,
  you would have dwelt in enduring peace.
Learn where prudence is,
  where strength, where understanding;
that you may know also
  where are length of days, and life,
  where light of the eyes, and peace.
Who has found the place of wisdom,
  who has entered into her treasuries?

The One who knows all things knows her;
  he has probed her by his knowledge—
the One who established the earth for all time,
  and filled it with four-footed beasts;
  he who dismisses the light, and it departs,
  calls it, and it obeys him trembling;
before whom the stars at their posts
  shine and rejoice;
when he calls them, they answer, "Here we are!"
  shining with joy for their Maker.
Such is our God;
  no other is to be compared to him:
he has traced out the whole way of
    understanding,
  and has given her to Jacob, his servant,
  to Israel, his beloved son.

Since then she has appeared on earth,
  and moved among people.
She is the book of the precepts of God,
  the law that endures forever;
all who cling to her will live,
  but those will die who forsake her.
Turn, O Jacob, and receive her:
  walk by her light toward splendor.
Give not your glory to another,
  your privileges to an alien race.
Blessed are we, O Israel;
  for what pleases God is known to us!

RESPONSORIAL PSALM
Ps 19:8, 9, 10, 11

℟. (John 6:68c) Lord, you have the words of
  everlasting life.

The law of the LORD is perfect,
  refreshing the soul;
the decree of the LORD is trustworthy,
  giving wisdom to the simple.

℟. Lord, you have the words of everlasting life.

The precepts of the LORD are right,
  rejoicing the heart;
the command of the LORD is clear,
  enlightening the eye.

℟. Lord, you have the words of everlasting life.

The fear of the LORD is pure,
  enduring forever;
the ordinances of the LORD are true,
  all of them just.

℟. Lord, you have the words of everlasting life.

They are more precious than gold,
  than a heap of purest gold;
sweeter also than syrup
  or honey from the comb.

℟. Lord, you have the words of everlasting life.

SEVENTH READING
Ezek 36:16-17a, 18-28

The word of the LORD came to me, saying:
  Son of man, when the house of Israel lived
    in their land,
  they defiled it by their conduct and deeds.
Therefore I poured out my fury upon them
  because of the blood that they poured out
    on the ground,
  and because they defiled it with idols.
I scattered them among the nations,
  dispersing them over foreign lands;
  according to their conduct and deeds I
    judged them.
But when they came among the nations
  wherever they came,
  they served to profane my holy name,
  because it was said of them: "These are the
    people of the LORD,
  yet they had to leave their land."
So I have relented because of my holy name
  which the house of Israel profaned
  among the nations where they came.
Therefore say to the house of Israel: Thus
    says the Lord GOD:
  Not for your sakes do I act, house of Israel,
  but for the sake of my holy name,
  which you profaned among the nations to
    which you came.
I will prove the holiness of my great name,
  profaned among the nations,
  in whose midst you have profaned it.
Thus the nations shall know that I am the
    LORD, says the Lord GOD,
  when in their sight I prove my holiness
    through you.
For I will take you away from among the nations,
  gather you from all the foreign lands,
  and bring you back to your own land.
I will sprinkle clean water upon you
  to cleanse you from all your impurities,
  and from all your idols I will cleanse you.

I will give you a new heart and place a new
    spirit within you,
  taking from your bodies your stony hearts
  and giving you natural hearts.
I will put my spirit within you and make you
    live by my statutes,
  careful to observe my decrees.
You shall live in the land I gave your fathers;
  you shall be my people, and I will be your
    God.

RESPONSORIAL PSALM
Ps 42:3, 5; 43:3, 4

℟. (42:2) Like a deer that longs for running
  streams, my soul longs for you, my God.

Athirst is my soul for God, the living God.
  When shall I go and behold the face of God?

℟. Like a deer that longs for running streams,
  my soul longs for you, my God.

I went with the throng
  and led them in procession to the house of God,
amid loud cries of joy and thanksgiving,
  with the multitude keeping festival.

℟. Like a deer that longs for running streams,
  my soul longs for you, my God.

Send forth your light and your fidelity;
  they shall lead me on
and bring me to your holy mountain,
  to your dwelling-place.

℟. Like a deer that longs for running streams,
  my soul longs for you, my God.

Then will I go in to the altar of God,
  the God of my gladness and joy;
then will I give you thanks upon the harp,
  O God, my God!

℟. Like a deer that longs for running streams,
  my soul longs for you, my God.

or

Isa 12:2-3, 4bcd, 5-6

℟. (3) You will draw water joyfully from the
  springs of salvation.

God indeed is my savior;
  I am confident and unafraid.
My strength and my courage is the LORD,
  and he has been my savior.
With joy you will draw water
  at the fountain of salvation.

℟. You will draw water joyfully from the
  springs of salvation.

Give thanks to the LORD, acclaim his name;
  among the nations make known his deeds,
  proclaim how exalted is his name.

℟. You will draw water joyfully from the
  springs of salvation.

Sing praise to the Lord for his glorious
    achievement;
    let this be known throughout all the earth.
Shout with exultation, O city of Zion,
    for great in your midst
    is the Holy One of Israel!

℟. You will draw water joyfully from the
    springs of salvation.

or

Ps 51:12-13, 14-15, 18-19

℟. (12a) Create a clean heart in me, O God.

A clean heart create for me, O God,
    and a steadfast spirit renew within me.
Cast me not out from your presence,
    and your Holy Spirit take not from me.

℟. Create a clean heart in me, O God.

Give me back the joy of your salvation,
    and a willing spirit sustain in me.
I will teach transgressors your ways,
    and sinners shall return to you.

℟. Create a clean heart in me, O God.

For you are not pleased with sacrifices;
    should I offer a holocaust, you would not
    accept it.
My sacrifice, O God, is a contrite spirit;
    a heart contrite and humbled, O God, you
    will not spurn.

℟. Create a clean heart in me, O God.

EPISTLE
Rom 6:3-11

Brothers and sisters:
Are you unaware that we who were baptized
    into Christ Jesus
    were baptized into his death?
We were indeed buried with him through
    baptism into death,
    so that, just as Christ was raised from the
    dead
    by the glory of the Father,
    we too might live in newness of life.

For if we have grown into union with him
    through a death like his,
    we shall also be united with him in the
    resurrection.
We know that our old self was crucified with
    him,
    so that our sinful body might be done away
    with,
    that we might no longer be in slavery to sin.
For a dead person has been absolved from sin.
If, then, we have died with Christ,
    we believe that we shall also live with him.
We know that Christ, raised from the dead,
    dies no more;
    death no longer has power over him.
As to his death, he died to sin once and for all;
    as to his life, he lives for God.
Consequently, you too must think of
    yourselves as being dead to sin
    and living for God in Christ Jesus.

RESPONSORIAL PSALM
Ps 118:1-2, 16-17, 22-23

℟. Alleluia, alleluia, alleluia.

Give thanks to the Lord, for he is good,
    for his mercy endures forever.
Let the house of Israel say,
    "His mercy endures forever."

℟. Alleluia, alleluia, alleluia.

The right hand of the Lord has struck with
    power;
    the right hand of the Lord is exalted.
I shall not die, but live,
    and declare the works of the Lord.

℟. Alleluia, alleluia, alleluia.

The stone which the builders rejected
    has become the cornerstone.
By the Lord has this been done;
    it is wonderful in our eyes.

℟. Alleluia, alleluia, alleluia.

Gospel
Mark 16:1-7; L41B

When the sabbath was over,
  Mary Magdalene, Mary, the mother of James, and Salome
  bought spices so that they might go and anoint him.
Very early when the sun had risen,
  on the first day of the week, they came to the tomb.
They were saying to one another,
  "Who will roll back the stone for us
  from the entrance to the tomb?"
When they looked up,
  they saw that the stone had been rolled back;
  it was very large.

On entering the tomb they saw a young man
  sitting on the right side, clothed in a white robe,
  and they were utterly amazed.
He said to them, "Do not be amazed!
You seek Jesus of Nazareth, the crucified.
He has been raised; he is not here.
Behold the place where they laid him.
But go and tell his disciples and Peter,
  'He is going before you to Galilee;
  there you will see him, as he told you.'"

or, at an afternoon or evening Mass

Gospel
Luke 24:13-35; L46

That very day, the first day of the week,
  two of Jesus' disciples were going
  to a village seven miles from Jerusalem called Emmaus,
  and they were conversing about all the things that had occurred.
And it happened that while they were conversing and debating,
  Jesus himself drew near and walked with them,
  but their eyes were prevented from recognizing him.
He asked them,
  "What are you discussing as you walk along?"
They stopped, looking downcast.
One of them, named Cleopas, said to him in reply,
  "Are you the only visitor to Jerusalem
  who does not know of the things
  that have taken place there in these days?"
And he replied to them, "What sort of things?"
They said to him,
  "The things that happened to Jesus the Nazarene,
  who was a prophet mighty in deed and word
  before God and all the people,
  how our chief priests and rulers both handed him over
  to a sentence of death and crucified him.
But we were hoping that he would be the one to redeem Israel;
  and besides all this,
  it is now the third day since this took place.
Some women from our group, however, have astounded us:
  they were at the tomb early in the morning
  and did not find his body;
  they came back and reported
  that they had indeed seen a vision of angels
  who announced that he was alive.

Then some of those with us went to the tomb
  and found things just as the women had described,
  but him they did not see."
And he said to them, "Oh, how foolish you are!
How slow of heart to believe all that the prophets spoke!
Was it not necessary that the Christ should suffer these things
  and enter into his glory?"
Then beginning with Moses and all the prophets,
  he interpreted to them what referred to him
  in all the Scriptures.
As they approached the village to which they were going,
  he gave the impression that he was going on farther.
But they urged him, "Stay with us,
  for it is nearly evening and the day is almost over."
So he went in to stay with them.
And it happened that, while he was with them at table,
  he took bread, said the blessing,
  broke it, and gave it to them.
With that their eyes were opened and they recognized him,
  but he vanished from their sight.
Then they said to each other,
  "Were not our hearts burning within us
  while he spoke to us on the way and opened the Scriptures to us?"
So they set out at once and returned to Jerusalem
  where they found gathered together
  the eleven and those with them who were saying,
  "The Lord has truly been raised and has appeared to Simon!"
Then the two recounted
  what had taken place on the way
  and how he was made known to them in the breaking of the bread.

FIRST READING
Acts 10:34a, 37-43

Peter proceeded to speak and said:
"You know what has happened all over Judea,
beginning in Galilee after the baptism
that John preached,
how God anointed Jesus of Nazareth
with the Holy Spirit and power.
He went about doing good
and healing all those oppressed by the devil,
for God was with him.
We are witnesses of all that he did
both in the country of the Jews and in
Jerusalem.
They put him to death by hanging him on a tree.
This man God raised on the third day and
granted that he be visible,
not to all the people, but to us,
the witnesses chosen by God in advance,
who ate and drank with him after he rose
from the dead.
He commissioned us to preach to the people
and testify that he is the one appointed by God
as judge of the living and the dead.
To him all the prophets bear witness,
that everyone who believes in him
will receive forgiveness of sins through his
name."

RESPONSORIAL PSALM
Ps 118:1-2, 16-17, 22-23

℟. (24) This is the day the Lord has made; let
us rejoice and be glad.
or:
℟. Alleluia.

Give thanks to the LORD, for he is good,
for his mercy endures forever.
Let the house of Israel say,
"His mercy endures forever."

℟. This is the day the Lord has made; let us
rejoice and be glad.
or:
℟. Alleluia.

"The right hand of the LORD has struck with
power;
the right hand of the LORD is exalted.
I shall not die, but live,
and declare the works of the LORD."

℟. This is the day the Lord has made; let us
rejoice and be glad.
or:
℟. Alleluia.

The stone which the builders rejected
has become the cornerstone.
By the LORD has this been done;
it is wonderful in our eyes.

℟. This is the day the Lord has made; let us
rejoice and be glad.
or:
℟. Alleluia.

SECOND READING
1 Cor 5:6b-8

Brothers and sisters:
Do you not know that a little yeast leavens all
the dough?
Clear out the old yeast,
so that you may become a fresh batch of
dough,
inasmuch as you are unleavened.
For our paschal lamb, Christ, has been
sacrificed.
Therefore, let us celebrate the feast,
not with the old yeast, the yeast of malice
and wickedness,
but with the unleavened bread of sincerity
and truth.

or

Col 3:1-4

Brothers and sisters:
If then you were raised with Christ, seek what
is above,
where Christ is seated at the right hand of
God.
Think of what is above, not of what is on
earth.
For you have died, and your life is hidden with
Christ in God.
When Christ your life appears,
then you too will appear with him in glory.

SEQUENCE

Victimae paschali laudes
Christians, to the Paschal Victim
Offer your thankful praises!
A Lamb the sheep redeems;
Christ, who only is sinless,
Reconciles sinners to the Father.
Death and life have contended in that combat
stupendous:
The Prince of life, who died, reigns
immortal.
Speak, Mary, declaring
What you saw, wayfaring.
"The tomb of Christ, who is living,
The glory of Jesus' resurrection;
Bright angels attesting,
The shroud and napkin resting.
Yes, Christ my hope is arisen;
To Galilee he goes before you."
Christ indeed from death is risen, our new life
obtaining.
Have mercy, victor King, ever reigning!
Amen. Alleluia.

Second Sunday of Easter (or of Divine Mercy), *April 7, 2024*

Gospel (cont.)
John 20:19-31; L44B

Now a week later his disciples were again inside
and Thomas was with them.
Jesus came, although the doors were locked,
and stood in their midst and said, "Peace be with you."
Then he said to Thomas, "Put your finger here and see my hands,
and bring your hand and put it into my side,
and do not be unbelieving, but believe."
Thomas answered and said to him, "My Lord and my God!"

Jesus said to him, "Have you come to believe because you have seen me?
Blessed are those who have not seen and have believed."

Now Jesus did many other signs in the presence of his disciples
that are not written in this book.
But these are written that you may come to believe
that Jesus is the Christ, the Son of God,
and that through this belief you may have life in his name.

FIRST READING
Isa 7:10-14; 8:10

The LORD spoke to Ahaz, saying:
Ask for a sign from the LORD, your God;
    let it be deep as the nether world, or high as
      the sky!
But Ahaz answered,
    "I will not ask! I will not tempt the LORD!"
Then Isaiah said:
    Listen, O house of David!
Is it not enough for you to weary people,
    must you also weary my God?
Therefore the Lord himself will give you this
    sign:
    the virgin shall be with child, and bear a
      son,
    and shall name him Emmanuel,
    which means "God is with us!"

RESPONSORIAL PSALM
Ps 40:7-8a, 8b-9, 10, 11

℟. (8a and 9a) Here I am, Lord; I come to do
    your will.

Sacrifice or offering you wished not,
    but ears open to obedience you gave me.
Holocausts and sin-offerings you sought not;
    then said I, "Behold, I come."

℟. Here I am, Lord; I come to do your will.

"In the written scroll it is prescribed for me,
To do your will, O my God, is my delight,
    and your law is within my heart!"

℟. Here I am, Lord; I come to do your will.

I announced your justice in the vast assembly;
    I did not restrain my lips, as you, O LORD,
    know.

℟. Here I am, Lord; I come to do your will.

Your justice I kept not hid within my heart;
    your faithfulness and your salvation I have
      spoken of;
I have made no secret of your kindness and
    your truth
    in the vast assembly.

℟. Here I am, Lord; I come to do your will.

SECOND READING
Heb 10:4-10

Brothers and sisters:
It is impossible that the blood of bulls and
    goats
    takes away sins.
For this reason, when Christ came into the
    world, he said:

    "Sacrifice and offering you did not desire,
      but a body you prepared for me;
    in holocausts and sin offerings you took no
      delight.
    Then I said, 'As is written of me in the
      scroll,
    behold, I come to do your will, O God.'"

First Christ says, "Sacrifices and offerings,
    holocausts and sin offerings,
    you neither desired nor delighted in."
These are offered according to the law.
Then he says, "Behold, I come to do your will."
He takes away the first to establish the second.
By this "will," we have been consecrated
    through the offering of the Body of Jesus
      Christ once for all.

SECOND READING
Eph 1:17-23

Brothers and sisters:
May the God of our Lord Jesus Christ, the
    Father of glory,
    give you a Spirit of wisdom and revelation
    resulting in knowledge of him.
May the eyes of your hearts be enlightened,
    that you may know what is the hope that
        belongs to his call,
    what are the riches of glory
    in his inheritance among the holy ones,
    and what is the surpassing greatness of
        his power
    for us who believe,
    in accord with the exercise of his great might,
    which he worked in Christ,
    raising him from the dead
    and seating him at his right hand in the
        heavens,
    far above every principality, authority,
        power, and dominion,
    and every name that is named
    not only in this age but also in the one to
        come.
And he put all things beneath his feet
    and gave him as head over all things to the
        church,
    which is his body,
    the fullness of the one who fills all things in
        every way.

or

Eph 4:1-13

Brothers and sisters,
I, a prisoner for the Lord,
    urge you to live in a manner worthy of the
        call you have received,
    with all humility and gentleness, with
        patience,
    bearing with one another through love,
    striving to preserve the unity of the Spirit
    through the bond of peace:
    one body and one Spirit,
    as you were also called to the one hope of
        your call;
    one Lord, one faith, one baptism;
    one God and Father of all,
    who is over all and through all and in all.

But grace was given to each of us
    according to the measure of Christ's gift.
Therefore, it says:
    *He ascended on high and took prisoners
        captive;*
    he gave gifts to men.
What does "he ascended" mean except that he
    also descended
    into the lower regions of the earth?
The one who descended is also the one who
    ascended
    far above all the heavens,
    that he might fill all things.

And he gave some as apostles, others as
    prophets,
    others as evangelists, others as pastors and
        teachers,
    to equip the holy ones for the work of
        ministry,
    for building up the body of Christ,
    until we all attain the unity of faith
    and knowledge of the Son of God, to
        mature to manhood,
    to the extent of the full stature of Christ.

or

Eph 4:1-7, 11-13

Brothers and sisters,
I, a prisoner for the Lord,
    urge you to live in a manner worthy of the
        call you have received,
    with all humility and gentleness, with
        patience,
    bearing with one another through love,
    striving to preserve the unity of the Spirit
    through the bond of peace:
    one body and one Spirit,
    as you were also called to the one hope of
        your call;
    one Lord, one faith, one baptism;
    one God and Father of all,
    who is over all and through all and in all.

But grace was given to each of us
    according to the measure of Christ's gift.

And he gave some as apostles, others as
    prophets,
    others as evangelists, others as pastors and
        teachers,
    to equip the holy ones for the work of
        ministry,
    for building up the body of Christ,
    until we all attain the unity of faith
    and knowledge of the Son of God, to
        mature to manhood,
    to the extent of the full stature of Christ.

SECOND READING
1 Cor 12:3b-7, 12-13

Brothers and sisters:
No one can say, "Jesus is Lord," except by the
    Holy Spirit.

There are different kinds of spiritual gifts but
    the same Spirit;
    there are different forms of service but the
        same Lord;
    there are different workings but the same
        God
    who produces all of them in everyone.
To each individual the manifestation of the
    Spirit
    is given for some benefit.

As a body is one though it has many parts,
    and all the parts of the body, though many,
        are one body,
    so also Christ.
For in one Spirit we were all baptized into one
    body,
    whether Jews or Greeks, slaves or free
        persons,
    and we were all given to drink of one Spirit.

or

Gal 5:16-25

Brothers and sisters, live by the Spirit
    and you will certainly not gratify the desire
        of the flesh.
For the flesh has desires against the Spirit,
    and the Spirit against the flesh;
    these are opposed to each other,
    so that you may not do what you want.
But if you are guided by the Spirit, you are
    not under the law.
Now the works of the flesh are obvious:
    immorality, impurity, lust, idolatry,
    sorcery, hatreds, rivalry, jealousy,
    outbursts of fury, acts of selfishness,
    dissensions, factions, occasions of envy,
    drinking bouts, orgies, and the like.
I warn you, as I warned you before,
    that those who do such things will not
        inherit the kingdom of God.
In contrast, the fruit of the Spirit is love, joy,
        peace,
    patience, kindness, generosity,
    faithfulness, gentleness, self-control.
Against such there is no law.
Now those who belong to Christ Jesus have
        crucified their flesh
    with its passions and desires.
If we live in the Spirit, let us also follow the
    Spirit.

SEQUENCE

Veni, Sancte Spiritus
Come, Holy Spirit, come!
And from your celestial home
    Shed a ray of light divine!
Come, Father of the poor!
Come, source of all our store!
    Come, within our bosoms shine.
You, of comforters the best;
You, the soul's most welcome guest;
    Sweet refreshment here below;
In our labor, rest most sweet;
Grateful coolness in the heat;
    Solace in the midst of woe.
O most blessed Light divine,
Shine within these hearts of yours,
    And our inmost being fill!
Where you are not, we have naught,
Nothing good in deed or thought,
    Nothing free from taint of ill.
Heal our wounds, our strength renew;
On our dryness pour your dew;
    Wash the stains of guilt away:
Bend the stubborn heart and will;
Melt the frozen, warm the chill;
    Guide the steps that go astray.
On the faithful, who adore
And confess you, evermore
    In your sevenfold gift descend;
Give them virtue's sure reward;
Give them your salvation, Lord;
    Give them joys that never end. Amen.
    Alleluia.

SECOND READING

Heb 9:11-15

Brothers and sisters:
When Christ came as high priest
   of the good things that have come to be,
   passing through the greater and more
      perfect tabernacle
   not made by hands, that is, not belonging to
      this creation,
   he entered once for all into the sanctuary,
   not with the blood of goats and calves
   but with his own blood, thus obtaining
      eternal redemption.
For if the blood of goats and bulls
   and the sprinkling of a heifer's ashes
   can sanctify those who are defiled
   so that their flesh is cleansed,
   how much more will the blood of Christ,
   who through the eternal Spirit offered
      himself unblemished to God,
   cleanse our consciences from dead works
   to worship the living God.

For this reason he is mediator of a new
      covenant:
   since a death has taken place for
      deliverance
   from transgressions under the first
      covenant,
   those who are called may receive the
      promised eternal inheritance.

OPTIONAL SEQUENCE

Lauda Sion

Laud, O Zion, your salvation,
Laud with hymns of exultation,
   Christ, your king and shepherd true:

Bring him all the praise you know,
He is more than you bestow.
   Never can you reach his due.

Special theme for glad thanksgiving
Is the quick'ning and the living
   Bread today before you set:

From his hands of old partaken,
As we know, by faith unshaken,
   Where the Twelve at supper met.

Full and clear ring out your chanting,
Joy nor sweetest grace be wanting,
   From your heart let praises burst:

For today the feast is holden,
When the institution olden
   Of that supper was rehearsed.

Here the new law's new oblation,
By the new king's revelation,
   Ends the form of ancient rite:

Now the new the old effaces,
Truth away the shadow chases,
   Light dispels the gloom of night.

What he did at supper seated,
Christ ordained to be repeated,
   His memorial ne'er to cease:

And his rule for guidance taking,
Bread and wine we hallow, making
   Thus our sacrifice of peace.

This the truth each Christian learns,
Bread into his flesh he turns,
   To his precious blood the wine:

Sight has fail'd, nor thought conceives,
But a dauntless faith believes,
   Resting on a pow'r divine.

Here beneath these signs are hidden
Priceless things to sense forbidden;
   Signs, not things are all we see:

Blood is poured and flesh is broken,
Yet in either wondrous token
   Christ entire we know to be.

Whoso of this food partakes,
Does not rend the Lord nor breaks;
   Christ is whole to all that taste:

Thousands are, as one, receivers,
One, as thousands of believers,
   Eats of him who cannot waste.

Bad and good the feast are sharing,
Of what divers dooms preparing,
   Endless death, or endless life.

Life to these, to those damnation,
See how like participation
   Is with unlike issues rife.

When the sacrament is broken,
Doubt not, but believe 'tis spoken,
   That each sever'd outward token
   doth the very whole contain.

Nought the precious gift divides,
Breaking but the sign betides
   Jesus still the same abides,
   still unbroken does remain.

The shorter form of the sequence begins here.

Lo! the angel's food is given
To the pilgrim who has striven;
   See the children's bread from heaven,
   which on dogs may not be spent.

Truth the ancient types fulfilling,
Isaac bound, a victim willing,
   Paschal lamb, its lifeblood spilling,
   manna to the fathers sent.

Very bread, good shepherd, tend us,
Jesu, of your love befriend us,
   You refresh us, you defend us,
   Your eternal goodness send us
In the land of life to see.

You who all things can and know,
Who on earth such food bestow,
   Grant us with your saints, though lowest,
   Where the heav'nly feast you show,
Fellow heirs and guests to be. Amen. Alleluia.

Gospel (cont.)
John 19:31-37

But when they came to Jesus and saw that he was already dead,
  they did not break his legs,
  but one soldier thrust his lance into his side,
  and immediately blood and water flowed out.
An eyewitness has testified, and his testimony is true;
  he knows that he is speaking the truth,
  so that you also may come to believe.
For this happened so that the Scripture passage might be fulfilled:
  Not a bone of it will be broken.
And again another passage says:
  They will look upon him whom they have pierced.

FIRST READING
Hos 11:1, 3-4, 8c-9

  Thus says the LORD:
When Israel was a child I loved him,
  out of Egypt I called my son.
Yet it was I who taught Ephraim to walk,
  who took them in my arms;
I drew them with human cords,
  with bands of love;
I fostered them like one
  who raises an infant to his cheeks;
Yet, though I stooped to feed my child,
  they did not know that I was their healer.

My heart is overwhelmed,
  my pity is stirred.
I will not give vent to my blazing anger,
  I will not destroy Ephraim again;
For I am God and not a man,
  the Holy One present among you;
  I will not let the flames consume you.

RESPONSORIAL PSALM
Isa 12:2-3, 4, 5-6

℟. (3)You will draw water joyfully from the
  springs of salvation.

God indeed is my savior;
  I am confident and unafraid.
My strength and my courage is the LORD,
  and he has been my savior.
With joy you will draw water
  at the fountain of salvation.

℟. You will draw water joyfully from the
  springs of salvation.

Give thanks to the LORD, acclaim his name;
  among the nations make known his deeds,
  proclaim how exalted is his name.

℟. You will draw water joyfully from the
  springs of salvation.

Sing praise to the LORD for his glorious
  achievement;
  let this be known throughout all the earth.
Shout with exultation, O city of Zion,
  for great in your midst
  is the Holy One of Israel!

℟. You will draw water joyfully from the
  springs of salvation.

SECOND READING
Eph 3:8-12, 14-19

Brothers and sisters:
To me, the very least of all the holy ones, this
  grace was given,
  to preach to the Gentiles the inscrutable
    riches of Christ,
  and to bring to light for all what is the plan
    of the mystery
  hidden from ages past in God who created
    all things,
  so that the manifold wisdom of God
  might now be made known through the
    church
  to the principalities and authorities in the
    heavens.
This was according to the eternal purpose
  that he accomplished in Christ Jesus our Lord,
  in whom we have boldness of speech
  and confidence of access through faith in
    him.

For this reason I kneel before the Father,
  from whom every family in heaven and on
    earth is named,
  that he may grant you in accord with the
    riches of his glory
  to be strengthened with power through his
    Spirit in the inner self,
  and that Christ may dwell in your hearts
    through faith;
  that you, rooted and grounded in love,
  may have strength to comprehend with all
    the holy ones
  what is the breadth and length and height
    and depth,
  and to know the love of Christ which
    surpasses knowledge,
  so that you may be filled with all the
    fullness of God.

Gospel (cont.)
Mark 3:20-35

His mother and his brothers arrived.
Standing outside they sent word to him and called him.
A crowd seated around him told him,
"Your mother and your brothers and your sisters
are outside asking for you."
But he said to them in reply,
"Who are my mother and my brothers?"
And looking around at those seated in the circle he said,
"Here are my mother and my brothers.
For whoever does the will of God
is my brother and sister and mother."

The Nativity of Saint John the Baptist, *June 24, 2024*

FIRST READING
Isa 49:1-6

Hear me, O coastlands,
listen, O distant peoples.
The LORD called me from birth,
from my mother's womb he gave me my
name.
He made of me a sharp-edged sword
and concealed me in the shadow of his arm.
He made me a polished arrow,
in his quiver he hid me.
You are my servant, he said to me,
Israel, through whom I show my glory.

Though I thought I had toiled in vain,
and for nothing, uselessly, spent my
strength,
yet my reward is with the LORD,
my recompense is with my God.
For now the LORD has spoken
who formed me as his servant from the
womb,
that Jacob may be brought back to him
and Israel gathered to him;
and I am made glorious in the sight of the
LORD,
and my God is now my strength!
It is too little, he says, for you to be my
servant,
to raise up the tribes of Jacob,
and restore the survivors of Israel;
I will make you a light to the nations,
that my salvation may reach to the ends of
the earth.

RESPONSORIAL PSALM
Ps 139:1b-3, 13-14ab, 14c-15

R̸. (14a) I praise you, for I am wonderfully
made.

O LORD, you have probed me, you know me;
you know when I sit and when I stand;
you understand my thoughts from afar.
My journeys and my rest you scrutinize,
with all my ways you are familiar.

R̸. I praise you, for I am wonderfully made.

Truly you have formed my inmost being;
you knit me in my mother's womb.
I give you thanks that I am fearfully,
wonderfully made;
wonderful are your works.

R̸. I praise you, for I am wonderfully made.

My soul also you knew full well;
nor was my frame unknown to you
When I was made in secret,
when I was fashioned in the depths of the
earth.

R̸. I praise you, for I am wonderfully made.

SECOND READING
Acts 13:22-26

In those days, Paul said:
"God raised up David as their king;
of him God testified,
*I have found David, son of Jesse, a man
after my own heart;
he will carry out my every wish.*
From this man's descendants God, according
to his promise,
has brought to Israel a savior, Jesus.
John heralded his coming by proclaiming a
baptism of repentance
to all the people of Israel;
and as John was completing his course, he
would say,
'What do you suppose that I am? I am
not he.
Behold, one is coming after me;
I am not worthy to unfasten the sandals of
his feet.'

"My brothers, sons of the family of Abraham,
and those others among you who are God-
fearing,
to us this word of salvation has been sent."

FIRST READING
Acts 12:1-11

In those days, King Herod laid hands upon
some members of the Church to harm
them.
He had James, the brother of John, killed by
the sword,
and when he saw that this was pleasing to
the Jews
he proceeded to arrest Peter also.
—It was the feast of Unleavened Bread.—
He had him taken into custody and put in
prison
under the guard of four squads of four
soldiers each.
He intended to bring him before the people
after Passover.
Peter thus was being kept in prison,
but prayer by the Church was fervently
being made
to God on his behalf.

On the very night before Herod was to bring
him to trial,
Peter, secured by double chains,
was sleeping between two soldiers,
while outside the door guards kept watch
on the prison.
Suddenly the angel of the Lord stood by him,
and a light shone in the cell.
He tapped Peter on the side and awakened
him, saying,
"Get up quickly."
The chains fell from his wrists.
The angel said to him, "Put on your belt and
your sandals."
He did so.
Then he said to him, "Put on your cloak and
follow me."
So he followed him out,
not realizing that what was happening
through the angel was real;
he thought he was seeing a vision.
They passed the first guard, then the second,
and came to the iron gate leading out to the
city,
which opened for them by itself.
They emerged and made their way down an
alley,
and suddenly the angel left him.
Then Peter recovered his senses and said,
"Now I know for certain
that the Lord sent his angel
and rescued me from the hand of Herod
and from all that the Jewish people had
been expecting."

RESPONSORIAL PSALM
Ps 34:2-3, 4-5, 6-7, 8-9

℟. (8) The angel of the Lord will rescue those
who fear him.

I will bless the LORD at all times;
his praise shall be ever in my mouth.
Let my soul glory in the LORD;
the lowly will hear me and be glad.

℟. The angel of the Lord will rescue those
who fear him.

Glorify the LORD with me,
let us together extol his name.
I sought the LORD, and he answered me
and delivered me from all my fears.

℟. The angel of the Lord will rescue those
who fear him.

Look to him that you may be radiant with joy,
and your faces may not blush with shame.
When the poor one called out, the LORD heard,
and from all his distress he saved him.

℟. The angel of the Lord will rescue those
who fear him.

The angel of the LORD encamps
around those who fear him, and delivers
them.
Taste and see how good the LORD is;
blessed the man who takes refuge in him.

℟. The angel of the Lord will rescue those
who fear him.

SECOND READING
2 Tim 4:6-8, 17-18

I, Paul, am already being poured out like a
libation,
and the time of my departure is at hand.
I have competed well; I have finished the race;
I have kept the faith.
From now on the crown of righteousness
awaits me,
which the Lord, the just judge,
will award to me on that day, and not only
to me,
but to all who have longed for his
appearance.

The Lord stood by me and gave me strength,
so that through me the proclamation might
be completed
and all the Gentiles might hear it.
And I was rescued from the lion's mouth.
The Lord will rescue me from every evil threat
and will bring me safe to his heavenly
Kingdom.
To him be glory forever and ever. Amen.

Thirteenth Sunday in Ordinary Time, *June 30, 2024*

Gospel (cont.)
Mark 5:21-43; L98B

But his disciples said to Jesus,
    "You see how the crowd is pressing upon you,
    and yet you ask, 'Who touched me?'"
And he looked around to see who had done it.
The woman, realizing what had happened to her,
    approached in fear and trembling.
She fell down before Jesus and told him the whole truth.
He said to her, "Daughter, your faith has saved you.
Go in peace and be cured of your affliction."

While he was still speaking,
    people from the synagogue official's house arrived and said,
    "Your daughter has died; why trouble the teacher any longer?"
Disregarding the message that was reported,
    Jesus said to the synagogue official,
    "Do not be afraid; just have faith."
He did not allow anyone to accompany him inside
    except Peter, James, and John, the brother of James.
When they arrived at the house of the synagogue official,
    he caught sight of a commotion,
    people weeping and wailing loudly.
So he went in and said to them,
    "Why this commotion and weeping?
The child is not dead but asleep."
And they ridiculed him.
Then he put them all out.
He took along the child's father and mother
    and those who were with him
    and entered the room where the child was.
He took the child by the hand and said to her, *"Talitha koum,"*
    which means, "Little girl, I say to you, arise!"
The girl, a child of twelve, arose immediately and walked around.
At that they were utterly astounded.
He gave strict orders that no one should know this
    and said that she should be given something to eat.

or Mark 5:21-24, 35b-43; L98B

When Jesus had crossed again in the boat
    to the other side,
    a large crowd gathered around him, and he stayed close to the sea.
One of the synagogue officials, named Jairus, came forward.
Seeing him he fell at his feet and pleaded earnestly with him, saying,
    "My daughter is at the point of death.
Please, come lay your hands on her
    that she may get well and live."
He went off with him,
    and a large crowd followed him and pressed upon him.

While he was still speaking, people from the synagogue official's house
    arrived and said,
    "Your daughter has died; why trouble the teacher any longer?"
Disregarding the message that was reported,
    Jesus said to the synagogue official,
    "Do not be afraid; just have faith."
He did not allow anyone to accompany him inside
    except Peter, James, and John, the brother of James.
When they arrived at the house of the synagogue official,
    he caught sight of a commotion,
    people weeping and wailing loudly.
So he went in and said to them,
    "Why this commotion and weeping?
The child is not dead but asleep."
And they ridiculed him.
Then he put them all out.
He took along the child's father and mother
    and those who were with him
    and entered the room where the child was.
He took the child by the hand and said to her, *"Talitha koum,"*
    which means, "Little girl, I say to you, arise!"
The girl, a child of twelve, arose immediately and walked around.
At that they were utterly astounded.
He gave strict orders that no one should know this
    and said that she should be given something to eat.

Fifteenth Sunday in Ordinary Time, *July 14, 2024*

SECOND READING
Eph 1:3-10

Blessed be the God and Father of our Lord
    Jesus Christ,
    who has blessed us in Christ
    with every spiritual blessing in the heavens,
    as he chose us in him, before the foundation
        of the world,
    to be holy and without blemish before him.
In love he destined us for adoption to himself
        through Jesus Christ,
    in accord with the favor of his will,
    for the praise of the glory of his grace
    that he granted us in the beloved.

In him we have redemption by his blood,
    the forgiveness of transgressions,
    in accord with the riches of his grace that
        he lavished upon us.
In all wisdom and insight, he has made
        known to us
    the mystery of his will in accord with his
        favor
    that he set forth in him as a plan for the
        fullness of times,
    to sum up all things in Christ, in heaven
        and on earth.

Gospel (cont.)
John 6:1-15; L110B

Then Jesus took the loaves, gave thanks,
    and distributed them to those who were reclining,
    and also as much of the fish as they wanted.
When they had had their fill, he said to his disciples,
    "Gather the fragments left over,
    so that nothing will be wasted."
So they collected them,
    and filled twelve wicker baskets with fragments
    from the five barley loaves
    that had been more than they could eat.
When the people saw the sign he had done, they said,
    "This is truly the Prophet, the one who is to come into the world."
Since Jesus knew that they were going to come and carry him off
    to make him king,
    he withdrew again to the mountain alone.

Gospel (cont.)
John 6:24-35; L113B

So Jesus said to them,
    "Amen, amen, I say to you,
    it was not Moses who gave the bread from heaven;
    my Father gives you the true bread from heaven.
For the bread of God is that which comes down from heaven
    and gives life to the world."

So they said to him,
    "Sir, give us this bread always."
Jesus said to them,
    "I am the bread of life;
    whoever comes to me will never hunger,
    and whoever believes in me will never thirst."

Gospel (cont.)
Luke 1:39-56; L622

And Mary said:

"My soul proclaims the greatness of the Lord;
   my spirit rejoices in God my Savior
   for he has looked with favor on his lowly servant.
From this day all generations will call me blessed:
   the Almighty has done great things for me,
   and holy is his Name.
He has mercy on those who fear him
   in every generation.
He has shown the strength of his arm,
   and has scattered the proud in their conceit.

He has cast down the mighty from their thrones,
   and has lifted up the lowly.
He has filled the hungry with good things,
   and the rich he has sent away empty.
He has come to the help of his servant Israel
   for he has remembered his promise of mercy,
   the promise he made to our fathers,
   to Abraham and his children forever."

Mary remained with her about three months
   and then returned to her home.

FIRST READING
Rev 11:19a; 12:1-6a, 10ab

God's temple in heaven was opened,
   and the ark of his covenant could be seen
      in the temple.

A great sign appeared in the sky, a woman
      clothed with the sun,
   with the moon under her feet,
   and on her head a crown of twelve stars.
She was with child and wailed aloud in pain
      as she labored to give birth.
Then another sign appeared in the sky;
   it was a huge red dragon, with seven heads
      and ten horns,
   and on its heads were seven diadems.
Its tail swept away a third of the stars in the
      sky
   and hurled them down to the earth.
Then the dragon stood before the woman
      about to give birth,
   to devour her child when she gave birth.
She gave birth to a son, a male child,
   destined to rule all the nations with an iron
      rod.
Her child was caught up to God and his
      throne.
The woman herself fled into the desert
   where she had a place prepared by God.

Then I heard a loud voice in heaven say:
   "Now have salvation and power come,
      and the Kingdom of our God
      and the authority of his Anointed One."

RESPONSORIAL PSALM
Ps 45:10, 11, 12, 16

℞. (10bc) The queen stands at your right
   hand, arrayed in gold.

The queen takes her place at your right hand
   in gold of Ophir.

℞. The queen stands at your right hand,
   arrayed in gold.

Hear, O daughter, and see; turn your ear,
   forget your people and your father's house.

℞. The queen stands at your right hand,
   arrayed in gold.

So shall the king desire your beauty;
   for he is your lord.

℞. The queen stands at your right hand,
   arrayed in gold.

They are borne in with gladness and joy;
   they enter the palace of the king.

℞. The queen stands at your right hand,
   arrayed in gold.

SECOND READING
1 Cor 15:20-27

Brothers and sisters:
Christ has been raised from the dead,
   the firstfruits of those who have fallen
      asleep.
For since death came through man,
   the resurrection of the dead came also
      through man.
For just as in Adam all die,
   so too in Christ shall all be brought to life,
   but each one in proper order:
   Christ the firstfruits;
   then, at his coming, those who belong to
      Christ;
   then comes the end,
   when he hands over the Kingdom to his
      God and Father,
   when he has destroyed every sovereignty
   and every authority and power.
For he must reign until he has put all his
   enemies under his feet.
The last enemy to be destroyed is death,
   for "he subjected everything under his feet."

Twenty-First Sunday in Ordinary Time,
August 25, 2024

SECOND READING
Eph 5:2a, 25-32

Brothers and sisters:
Live in love, as Christ loved us.
Husbands, love your wives,
    even as Christ loved the church
    and handed himself over for her to sanctify her,
    cleansing her by the bath of water with the word,
    that he might present to himself the church in splendor,
    without spot or wrinkle or any such thing,
    that she might be holy and without blemish.
So also husbands should love their wives as their own bodies.
He who loves his wife loves himself.
For no one hates his own flesh
    but rather nourishes and cherishes it,
    even as Christ does the church,
    because we are members of his body.
For this reason a man shall leave his father and his mother and be
    joined to his wife,
    and the two shall become one flesh.
This is a great mystery,
    but I speak in reference to Christ and the church.

Twenty-Second Sunday in Ordinary Time,
September 1, 2024

Gospel (cont.)
Mark 7:1-8, 14-15, 21-23; L125B

He summoned the crowd again and said to them,
    "Hear me, all of you, and understand.
Nothing that enters one from outside can defile that person;
    but the things that come out from within are what defile.

"From within people, from their hearts,
    come evil thoughts, unchastity, theft, murder,
    adultery, greed, malice, deceit,
    licentiousness, envy, blasphemy, arrogance, folly.
All these evils come from within and they defile."

Twenty-Seventh Sunday in Ordinary Time, *October 6, 2024*

Gospel (cont.)
Mark 10:2-16; L140B

And people were bringing children to him that he might touch them,
    but the disciples rebuked them.
When Jesus saw this he became indignant and said to them,
    "Let the children come to me;
    do not prevent them, for the kingdom of God belongs to such as these.
Amen, I say to you,
    whoever does not accept the kingdom of God like a child
    will not enter it."
Then he embraced them and blessed them,
    placing his hands on them.

or Mark 10:2-12; L140B

The Pharisees approached Jesus and asked,
    "Is it lawful for a husband to divorce his wife?"
They were testing him.
He said to them in reply, "What did Moses command you?"
They replied,
    "Moses permitted a husband to write a bill of divorce
    and dismiss her."
But Jesus told them,
    "Because of the hardness of your hearts
    he wrote you this commandment.
But from the beginning of creation, *God made them male and female.*
For this reason a man shall leave his father and mother
    and be joined to his wife,
    and the two shall become one flesh.
So they are no longer two but one flesh.
Therefore what God has joined together,
    no human being must separate."
In the house the disciples again questioned Jesus about this.
He said to them,
    "Whoever divorces his wife and marries another
    commits adultery against her;
    and if she divorces her husband and marries another,
    she commits adultery."

Twenty-Eighth Sunday in Ordinary Time, *October 13, 2024*

Gospel (cont.)
Mark 10:17-30; L143B

So Jesus again said to them in reply,
　"Children, how hard it is to enter the kingdom of God!
It is easier for a camel to pass through the eye of a needle
　than for one who is rich to enter the kingdom of God."
They were exceedingly astonished and said among themselves,
　"Then who can be saved?"
Jesus looked at them and said,
　"For human beings it is impossible, but not for God.
All things are possible for God."
Peter began to say to him,
　"We have given up everything and followed you."
Jesus said, "Amen, I say to you,
　there is no one who has given up house or brothers or sisters
　or mother or father or children or lands
　for my sake and for the sake of the gospel
　who will not receive a hundred times more now in this present age:
　houses and brothers and sisters
　and mothers and children and lands,
　with persecutions, and eternal life in the age to come."

or Mark 10:17-27

As Jesus was setting out on a journey, a man ran up,
　knelt down before him, and asked him,
　"Good teacher, what must I do to inherit eternal life?"
Jesus answered him, "Why do you call me good?
No one is good but God alone.
You know the commandments: *You shall not kill;*
　you shall not commit adultery;
　you shall not steal;
　you shall not bear false witness;
　you shall not defraud;
　honor your father and your mother."
He replied and said to him,
　"Teacher, all of these I have observed from my youth."
Jesus, looking at him, loved him and said to him,
　"You are lacking in one thing.
Go, sell what you have, and give to the poor
　and you will have treasure in heaven; then come, follow me."
At that statement his face fell,
　and he went away sad, for he had many possessions.

Jesus looked around and said to his disciples,
　"How hard it is for those who have wealth
　to enter the kingdom of God!"
The disciples were amazed at his words.
So Jesus again said to them in reply,
　"Children, how hard it is to enter the kingdom of God!
It is easier for a camel to pass through the eye of a needle
　than for one who is rich to enter the kingdom of God."
They were exceedingly astonished and said among themselves,
　"Then who can be saved?"
Jesus looked at them and said,
　"For human beings it is impossible, but not for God.
All things are possible for God."

Twenty-Ninth Sunday in Ordinary Time, *October 20, 2024*

Gospel
Mark 10:42-45; L146B

Jesus summoned the Twelve and said to them,
　"You know that those who are recognized as rulers over the Gentiles
　lord it over them,
　and their great ones make their authority over them felt.
But it shall not be so among you.
Rather, whoever wishes to be great among you will be your servant;
　whoever wishes to be first among you will be the slave of all.
For the Son of Man did not come to be served
　but to serve and to give his life as a ransom for many."

Gospel (cont.)

Matt 5:1-12a; L667

Blessed are the peacemakers,
    for they will be called children of God.
Blessed are they who are persecuted for the sake of righteousness,
    for theirs is the Kingdom of heaven.
Blessed are you when they insult you and persecute you
    and utter every kind of evil against you falsely because of me.
Rejoice and be glad,
    for your reward will be great in heaven."

FIRST READING

Rev 7:2-4, 9-14

I, John, saw another angel come up from the East,
    holding the seal of the living God.
He cried out in a loud voice to the four angels
    who were given power to damage the land and the sea,
    "Do not damage the land or the sea or the trees
    until we put the seal on the foreheads of the servants of our God."
I heard the number of those who had been marked with the seal,
    one hundred and forty-four thousand marked
    from every tribe of the children of Israel.

After this I had a vision of a great multitude,
    which no one could count,
    from every nation, race, people, and tongue.
They stood before the throne and before the Lamb,
    wearing white robes and holding palm branches in their hands.
They cried out in a loud voice:

"Salvation comes from our God, who is seated on the throne,
    and from the Lamb."

All the angels stood around the throne
    and around the elders and the four living creatures.
They prostrated themselves before the throne,
    worshiped God, and exclaimed:

"Amen. Blessing and glory, wisdom and thanksgiving,
    honor, power, and might
    be to our God forever and ever. Amen."

Then one of the elders spoke up and said to me,
    "Who are these wearing white robes, and where did they come from?"
I said to him, "My lord, you are the one who knows."
He said to me,
    "These are the ones who have survived the time of great distress;
    they have washed their robes
    and made them white in the Blood of the Lamb."

RESPONSORIAL PSALM

Ps 24:1bc-2, 3-4ab, 5-6

℞. (cf. 6) Lord, this is the people that longs to see your face.

The Lord's are the earth and its fullness;
    the world and those who dwell in it.
For he founded it upon the seas
    and established it upon the rivers.

℞. Lord, this is the people that longs to see your face.

Who can ascend the mountain of the Lord?
    or who may stand in his holy place?
One whose hands are sinless, whose heart is clean,
    who desires not what is vain.

℞. Lord, this is the people that longs to see your face.

He shall receive a blessing from the Lord,
    a reward from God his savior.
Such is the race that seeks him,
    that seeks the face of the God of Jacob.

℞. Lord, this is the people that longs to see your face.

SECOND READING

1 John 3:1-3

Beloved:
See what love the Father has bestowed on us
    that we may be called the children of God.
Yet so we are.
The reason the world does not know us
    is that it did not know him.
Beloved, we are God's children now;
    what we shall be has not yet been revealed.
We do know that when it is revealed we shall be like him,
    for we shall see him as he is.
Everyone who has this hope based on him makes himself pure,
    as he is pure.

All Souls, *November 2, 2024*

FIRST READING
Dan 12:1-3; L1011.7

In those days, I, Daniel, mourned
  and heard this word of the Lord:
At that time there shall arise
  Michael, the great prince,
  guardian of your people;
It shall be a time unsurpassed in distress
  since nations began until that time.
At that time your people shall escape,
  everyone who is found written in the book.

Many of those who sleep in the dust of the
    earth shall awake;
Some shall live forever,
  others shall be an everlasting horror and
    disgrace.
But the wise shall shine brightly
  like the splendor of the firmament,
And those who lead the many to justice
  shall be like the stars forever.

RESPONSORIAL PSALM
Ps 27:1, 4, 7, and 8b, and 9a, 13-14; L1013.3

℟. (1a) The Lord is my light and my salvation.
  or:
℟. (13) I believe that I shall see the good
    things of the Lord in the land of the
    living.

The LORD is my light and my salvation;
  whom should I fear?
The LORD is my life's refuge;
  of whom should I be afraid?

℟. The Lord is my light and my salvation.
  or:
℟. I believe that I shall see the good things of
    the Lord in the land of the living.

One thing I ask of the LORD;
  this I seek:
To dwell in the house of the LORD
  all the days of my life,
That I may gaze on the loveliness of the LORD
  and contemplate his temple.

℟. The Lord is my light and my salvation.
  or:
℟. I believe that I shall see the good things of
    the Lord in the land of the living.

Hear, O LORD, the sound of my call;
  have pity on me and answer me.
Your presence, O LORD, I seek.
  Hide not your face from me.

℟. The Lord is my light and my salvation.
  or:
℟. I believe that I shall see the good things of
    the Lord in the land of the living.

I believe that I shall see the bounty of the
    LORD
  in the land of the living.
Wait for the LORD with courage;
  be stouthearted, and wait for the LORD.

℟. The Lord is my light and my salvation.
  or:
℟. I believe that I shall see the good things of
    the Lord in the land of the living.

SECOND READING
Rom 6:3-9; L1014.3

Brothers and sisters:
Are you unaware that we who were baptized
    into Christ Jesus
  were baptized into his death?
We were indeed buried with him through
    baptism into death,
  so that, just as Christ was raised from the
    dead
  by the glory of the Father,
  we too might live in newness of life.

For if we have grown into union with him
    through a death like his,
  we shall also be united with him in the
    resurrection.
We know that our old self was crucified with
    him,
  so that our sinful body might be done away
    with,
  that we might no longer be in slavery to sin.
For a dead person has been absolved from sin.
If, then, we have died with Christ,
  we believe that we shall also live with him.
We know that Christ, raised from the dead,
    dies no more;
  death no longer has power over him.

Thirty-Second Sunday in Ordinary Time, *November 10, 2024*

Gospel
Mark 12:41-44

Jesus sat down opposite the treasury
  and observed how the crowd put money into the treasury.
Many rich people put in large sums.
A poor widow also came and put in two small coins worth a few cents.
Calling his disciples to himself, he said to them,
  "Amen, I say to you, this poor widow put in more
  than all the other contributors to the treasury.
For they have all contributed from their surplus wealth,
  but she, from her poverty, has contributed all she had,
  her whole livelihood."

Additional Prompts for Faith Sharing

First Sunday of Advent

• Entering into this Advent season of anticipation, how is your circumstance different now than it was three years ago? How will that impact your reception of the Scriptures of the season this time?

• For what are you most thankful, as you recall the members of your faith community and the gifts and talents they share with others?

• Thinking back over the last day, what is one sign of the coming of God's reign that perhaps you overlooked in the moment?

The Immaculate Conception of the Blessed Virgin Mary

• What are the daily temptations you face, and what—or who—are the things and people that give you courage and perseverance to avoid them?

• Are you able to recognize yourself as an adopted child of God? What are the signs and symbols indicative of that relationship?

• In what ways are you called to bring forth the living word of God into today's world, waiting and in need?

Second Sunday of Advent

• Who do you see and hear in today's world, crying out for the presence of God to be made known? Are there voices excluded and denied, yearning to be heard?

• What is one tangible act of God's justice you can pursue this week, even if only partially?

• Describe a moment where you experienced a modern-day John the Baptist, announcing the coming of the Lord into human time and space.

Our Lady of Guadalupe

• Like Mary's cousin Elizabeth, who is for you that person you run to with good news, with challenges, with opportunities? What is it about that person that gives you so much confidence and trust in them?

Third Sunday of Advent

• What is a spiritual "robe of salvation" in which the Lord wraps you? Would you be willing to share it with someone in need?

• God is eternal and unceasing, yet it is at times difficult to perceive God's presence, God's joy. What is one thing you can turn to in those times of doubt and darkness, to remind yourself of God's joy and light?

• Who do you recognize as someone in need of joy today, and what can you do to make that facet of God's life and love more real for them?

Fourth Sunday of Advent

• What is one last thing you must do spiritually to prepare for Christmas this year? What is one practical thing? Are these two preparations connected at all? Could they be?

• What makes you afraid right now? Who is a voice near you who urges you to not be afraid, in word or in deed?

• Do we truly believe that nothing is impossible for God? What prevents us from turning over to God all our worries, fears, and trials?

The Nativity of the Lord (Mass during the Day)

• Entering into this Christmas season of incarnation and good news, how is your circumstance different now than it was three years ago? How will that impact your reception of the Scriptures of the season this time?

• The Eternal Word is made flesh, full of grace and truth. Who is one person in your life who embodies God's grace? Who is it that embodies God's truth?

• Who will you see today that needs a reminder of the "reason for the season," and what can you say to that person that their ears and their heart will openly receive?

The Holy Family of Jesus, Mary, and Joseph

• Who, for you, is the most challenging member of your family to remain in right relationship with? What facet of divine truth can most help this relationship right now?

• Who is it that you know that most needs family and yet lacks those people in their lives? How can you help them know a familial love and presence?

• Describe a time when you placed a blind trust in the Lord and a calling that you didn't fully comprehend. What promises of the Lord were revealed to you?

Solemnity of Mary, the Holy Mother of God

• How does God's face shine upon you today? Where do you experience God's light and warmth?

• Describe a faith experience that is a treasure kept in your heart. When are the times you reflect back on that experience, and what spiritual gifts does it remind you of when you do?

• In what ways in these coming days can you, like Mary, bring to birth the good news and make Christ more real for someone, even for yourself?

The Epiphany of the Lord

• What element of your faith experience makes your heart throb? What riches of the Lord do you see, hear, feel that make your heart overflow?

• What aspect of faith do you feel particularly called to be a steward of, to care for, protect, and serve?

• What gifts are we able to bring to our God that honor and symbolize who God is: Creator, Redeemer, Sanctifier?

Second Sunday in Ordinary Time

• Entering into this winter Ordinary Time of discipleship and revelation, how is your circumstance different now than it was three years ago? How will that impact your reception of the Scriptures of the next few weeks this time?

• If you knew God would explicitly answer, would you still be willing to ask, as a servant, what is God's will for you? Does anything prevent you from placing complete trust in God?

• Who in your life is a rock of faith, a foundation you can rely on even if all else around you crumbles?

Third Sunday in Ordinary Time

• Have you ever turned your back on God or tried to run away from God's call, God's truth? Do you see others doing that now, and if so, what is your reaction, your response?

• We live in a time when our salvation and the reign of God are both already accomplished but not yet fully manifest. Describe an example or two where you see that paradox evident in today's world.

• What does it mean to be a fisher of humans? How, practically speaking, does one do that? How do you do it?

Fourth Sunday in Ordinary Time

• Who are the prophets, the truth-speakers today who are pushed aside and ignored? What can you do to amplify their voices, their messages?

• What experience in your past hardened your heart to the voice of the Lord? What might it take to soften it and allow in the Lord's love and truth?

• When was the last time you were astonished by Christ? Are you still able to be? Why or why not?

Fifth Sunday in Ordinary Time

• What elements of your day-to-day life seem like mere chores, mindless toiling? How can you infuse something holy into them and find sacred purpose?

• Who near you is brokenhearted right now? Why? What divine word do they need to hear? What action might God place on your hands to help heal their souls?

• What prevents you from boldly proclaiming the good news? What do you think people might perceive in you if you were to do so? Is whatever that is necessarily a bad thing?

Sixth Sunday in Ordinary Time

• Who do you see as "unclean" in today's world? In the church? How does God see these people? What relationship does God have with them, and what relationship does God want us to have with them?

• What might someone see in you as holy and therefore want to imitate?

• Share a moment when you knew personally of Christ's restorative love and mercy, and what it meant for you then and what it continues to mean today.

Ash Wednesday

• Entering into this Lenten season of repentance, almsgiving, and prayer, how is your circumstance different now than it was three years ago? How will that impact your reception of the Scriptures of the season this time?

First Sunday of Lent

• Time and time again God made covenants with humanity: Be my people, and I will be your God. What are the promises of God that have been fulfilled for you, and which are yet to come? How do you show your faithfulness to God?

• Especially if your baptism was before your ability to remember it, what tangibly do you do, each day, to live your baptismal vows?

• What gives you the strength and confidence to reject the temptations of Satan? Who ministers to you in your times of weakness and struggle?

Second Sunday of Lent

• What is the biggest obstacle for you in placing complete trust in God and aligning your will to the divine will?

• When have you experienced a foretaste of heaven? Describe the circumstance, the people, and what specifically the moment revealed to you of God's eternal love and abiding presence.

• Have you ever literally heard the voice of God? How do we listen for the voice of God and look for the activity of God when so few of us experience the divine presence in such a miraculous way?

Third Sunday of Lent

• Which of the Ten Commandments do you find most difficult to live? Why?

• What aspect of faith, of church, is a stumbling block for you? What about faith or church seems most foolish? Where is Christ's redemption in these things?

• What do you see in your "house of prayer" that may need driving out? What should be there in its place?

Fourth Sunday of Lent

• Recall a time when you were unfaithful to God and God's covenant. How was mercy and reconciliation revealed to you? How might you show that mercy and reconciliation to others?

• Have you ever, intentionally or not, placed anyone into exile—from friendship, from family, from faith? Have you ever been so exiled? What can be done to repair that relationship?

• Do you believe, truly, in the love of God that is so great as to offer an only Son as sacrifice for the eternal life of all who have faith? What else does that love reveal to you about God?

Fifth Sunday of Lent

• Summarize, if you can, the love of God written on your heart. How do you live that love every day and show that love to each person you meet?

• In which aspect of your life is it most difficult to be obedient to God's will? In which aspect of your life do you know suffering because of obedience to God?

• What part of your life would be most difficult to let go of, to let die, even knowing that doing so would allow it to produce much greater fruit?

Saint Joseph, Spouse of the Blessed Virgin Mary

• Scripture includes no words spoken by Saint Joseph. Akin to the apocryphal quote attributed to Saint Francis, "Preach the gospel at all times; when necessary, use words," how will you today silently share the good news of salvation?

Palm Sunday of the Lord's Passion

• When was the last time you "turned the other cheek" to those who mistreated you because of your faith?

• What do you cling to in your relationship with God? Should you?

• Christ the King is crowned with thorns and is given a cross instead of a throne. When you have been in positions of leadership, how does this example impact your words and deeds?

Holy Thursday Evening Mass of the Lord's Supper

• John's Gospel doesn't include a narrative at the Last Supper of sharing bread and wine, but rather he tells us of the washing of the feet. What might the evangelist here be trying to communicate to the faithful in doing so?

Friday of the Passion of the Lord (Good Friday)

• God almost always chooses to communicate in silences, in quiet moments. What is God, silenced for us today, communicating by that silence?

At the Easter Vigil in the Holy Night of Easter

• Which of the "works of the LORD" can you declare today? To whom? Which words will you choose; would any be sufficient?

Easter Sunday of the Resurrection at the Mass during the Day

• The loudest proclamation of the power of God today is an empty, silent tomb. Is there emptiness and silence in your life today that can similarly speak to the glory of God?

Second Sunday of Easter (or of Divine Mercy)

• What does it mean for those of faith to be "of one heart and mind"? Does unity necessarily require uniformity?

• Does your faith require proofs and explanations? If something can fully be explained, is it possible to have "faith" in it at that point?

• If the resurrected Christ is a new creation, why would his body still bear the marks of suffering and death? What do our wounds and scars on our own bodies tell us about faith and restoration?

The Annunciation of the Lord

• When did you last ask for a sign from the Lord? Why? Did it ever come? What about your faith life was revealed in those moments?

Third Sunday of Easter

• Recall a time you had a difficult conversation about faith. What was it about, who was it with? How was the love and mercy of God made manifest in it?

• Actions speak louder than words, says the old admonition. Are your actions and your words (or your beliefs) always in alignment? Why or why not?

• If Christ were to appear to you, right now, in the flesh, what would be your first reaction? What would you ask him? What is preventing you from asking that same question of him anyway?

Fourth Sunday of Easter

• What does the expression "see God face-to-face" mean to you? Is it even possible to imagine being in God's eternal presence? What earthly analogy comes to mind to even begin an exploration of that everlasting joy and life?

• Who are the wolves in your faith life, trying to scatter the community? Who are the shepherds, willing to lay down their lives for their sheep?

• Is the image of Father, when used for God, a positive, neutral, or negative one for you? Why? What other images are helpful for you?

Fifth Sunday of Easter

• Who is a person in your life who guides you in faith, protects you, and strengthens you? How can you be more like them for someone else in your life?

• What is one deed you can do today to show the love of God to someone else—not just in the deed itself, but in the way that you do it and in the reason that you do it?

• Can you look back at a time of suffering and loss in your life and see it, some amount of time later, as God "pruning the vine" so that you, in faith, could bear more fruit?

Sixth Sunday of Easter

• When have you seen the love and mercy of God poured out on a person you least expected? What was your reaction, and why? Was your faith or the faith of that other person impacted?

• When you think of the almighty Creator of the universe calling you a friend, what emotions does that stir up within you? Do you believe that is even possible?

• What does it mean to love one another, as Christ commands? Does it mean, for instance, acceptance, service, support, affection? What words would you pick?

The Ascension of the Lord

• Imagine looking up at a fluffy cloud one sunny day and seeing the Lord descending back to earth upon it. Scripture tells us this will occur someday. Do we live our lives with the immediacy that it might happen at any given moment, on any given cloud in the sky?

• It is sometimes much easier to be Christ's voice than it is to be his hands and feet. Why is that?

• Jesus, in Mark's account of the ascension, says that "whoever does not believe will be condemned." Do you believe that to be true? Why or why not?

Seventh Sunday of Easter

• What role does luck play in the living of one's faith? Are there any "coincidences" when it comes to faith?

• Where do you see the most obvious examples of the disconnect between our world and the reign of God as Jesus described and prayed for?

• To be consecrated is to be set apart for a special, sacred, purpose. Is there any aspect of your life that you could rightly call "consecrated" in that way?

Pentecost Sunday

• Recall a time that, despite a language barrier, you and another person were able to communicate something to and with one another. What of your common humanity made that possible? In that, can you also find the "image and likeness of God"?

• Without realizing it, do you expect to see the manifestations of the Spirit become real in each individual in exactly the same way? Can you name a manifestation of the Spirit that is in a person very different from you and manifested in a very different way?

• Which gift of the Holy Spirit do you need most in your life right now? Do you actively seek opportunities to use that gift?

The Most Holy Trinity

• "God the Father" is a term for God in disuse because of the inherent gendered terminology, and often "God" is used as a substitute. Yet, Christ is also God, as is the Holy Spirit. What confusions might this cause? Do you see any suitable solutions?

• By definition the Trinity is relational, so we, created in the image and likeness of God, must also be relational in living our faith. What for you is the biggest challenge and biggest opportunity presented by that aspect of our faith?

• An analogy is always more unlike something than it is like. What is your favorite analogy for the Holy Trinity? What truth does it reveal about the Trinity, and what does it get wrong?

The Most Holy Body and Blood of Christ (Corpus Christi)

• Mass is at different times discussed as a "memorial banquet" and as a "holy sacrifice." What does it mean to you, and to the church, that it is both things at the same time?

• When did you last make a true sacrifice—not of your abundance but of your scarcity—to help someone else in need? Was that sacrifice connected at all to a conscious desire to live a more Christ-like faith?

• In what way can you make the Real Presence of Christ in the Eucharist tangibly real to your neighbors, friends, and family through your words and deeds?

The Most Sacred Heart of Jesus

• Where, for you, is the line between boasting about your faith and evangelizing, and sharing it with joy and confidence? How might others respond to the manner in which you share your faith?

Tenth Sunday in Ordinary Time

• What are the things about you that, seen with human eyes, seem to be flaws and imperfections—and that God may see differently, as opportunities and giftedness?

• In times of discouragement, where do you seek renewal and inner strength? Are you that renewal and strength for others?

• Who are the friends in your life that, because of their faith, are as important to you and as close to you as direct relations?

Eleventh Sunday in Ordinary Time

• Many trees are known to be flexible so that they can bend without breaking. Yet at times we are told that our faith, our convictions, should be uncompromising and inflexible. Is there room in our faith, our church, for compromise and flexibility?

• What aspect of being a Christian, for you, takes the most courage to live publicly and "out loud"?

• Who was it that first planted a seed of faith within your heart? Who was it that then nurtured it and helped it grow? Where now is your opportunity to plant seeds and help them grow?

Twelfth Sunday in Ordinary Time

• When you are at your wit's end, which faith-filled person do you turn to for stability and shelter? Are you that person for someone else?

• Change can be frightening, or at least difficult to accept. In a faith that calls us to continual conversion, how do you manage the constancy of change and newness?

• What is your response to Jesus when he asks, "Why are you terrified? Do you not yet have faith?"

The Nativity of Saint John the Baptist

• John heralded the coming of the Messiah and recognized his cousin as the Christ. Do you recognize in someone around you a strength in faith that no one else seems to see? Have you told that person that you do?

Saints Peter and Paul, Apostles

• These two saints remind us that even those strong in faith can disagree and still seek and find unity. Who is someone with whom you disagree and, as a faith-filled disciple, need to seek reconciliation and unity with?

Thirteenth Sunday in Ordinary Time

• God is love, and as love can only invite and never force or control. Are there times where, in the name of God, we seek to use power and influence and should rather offer love and encouragement?

• What is it you have an abundance of right now—resources, knowledge, wisdom, time, energy—that, to help build the reign of God, you could share with someone else in need?

• Some would say the opposite of "faith" is "fear," though it may be more meaningful to ponder fear as a catalyst for faith. What is God calling you to do, who is God calling you to be, and what fears do these callings strike within you?

Fourteenth Sunday in Ordinary Time

• Often the prophets among us, the truth-speakers, are seen as irrational, out of touch, and are shunned and marginalized. Is there someone whom you recently dismissed in such a way, and can you identify deep within their message a kernel of God's truth revealed?

• What Christian paradox do you have the most difficult time with? Death is new life? Weakness is strength? The last shall be first? Something else? Why?

• Who in your faith community is the wisdom figure, respected because of their keen insights, experience, and age? Who is a marginalized person with a voice that needs to be heard, and why is their voice presently cast aside?

Fifteenth Sunday in Ordinary Time

• Who was the last person who told you something about yourself that you knew was right but didn't want to hear? How did you react? How should a Christian react in those moments?

• What is a real-life example of kindness and truth meeting, justice and peace kissing?

• In our attempts to catechize and evangelize, how can we distinguish the times we need to redouble our efforts and the times we need to shake the dust from our feet and move along?

Sixteenth Sunday in Ordinary Time

• Should the church be a wider tent, sheltering a broader array of believers, or should it be a smaller church, a more faithful remnant? Why?

• What are the dark valleys of your faith journey? Do you always recognize them, and who or what helps you know God's abiding presence in those times?

- Do you honor the Lord's Day as a true day of rest, a Sabbath to rest and recharge? Why is doing so important to a person of faith?

Seventeenth Sunday in Ordinary Time

- What was the last unexpected blessing you received? At the time did you see it as a sign of God's love, God's abundance? How can you be an unexpected blessing for someone else today?

- Is it possible to be too humble as a Christian? What is the danger in that, and how can we recognize where the fine line is?

- Have you ever offered what little you had to a friend in need even though it seemed so insufficient at the time? What can you offer to Christ and his kingdom today, even though it seems so small and insignificant?

Eighteenth Sunday in Ordinary Time

- What is the "bread from heaven" that sustains your spirit? Where do you go to find it?

- Recall a time when you experienced a significant change of heart regarding a situation or a person. What was the impetus for that change? Where was Christ in that moment?

- How do you explain the Real Presence of Christ in the Eucharist to others? Is talking about this belief a consistent part of your evangelization?

Nineteenth Sunday in Ordinary Time

- Rest and sustenance—self-care—is an important part of living a Christian life. What is one thing you can do for yourself this week to help you be more present to others and their needs?

- What is the difference between righteous anger and more typical human anger? At appropriate times, how does righteous anger within you manifest itself in a Christ-like way?

- Is there a person of faith close to you—a friend or family member—who perhaps you ought to listen to more closely than you do? Whom should you imitate in the faith more than you already do?

The Assumption of the Blessed Virgin Mary

- In what ways has God "shown the strength of his arm" for you or someone you know?

Twentieth Sunday in Ordinary Time

- Who is a wisdom figure of faith in your personal life? What are the attributes that make them so? Are you a wisdom figure for anyone else?

- Is there a hymn or other piece of music from the liturgy or devotions that resonates in your soul this week? Why do you think it does?

- In the Creed, we profess belief in the resurrection of the dead. What does that "life of the world to come" look like, do you think?

Twenty-First Sunday in Ordinary Time

- In what tangible ways does your household serve the Lord? What are the obstacles that may prevent you from doing so?

- With eyes of faith, we should see in married couples a love that is a mirror of Christ's love for the church. Who is a couple that exemplifies that kind of love in your life? In what way?

- Many people experience times in their faith of doubt and disconnectedness. Who, today, is someone like that who you know, and what might you say or do to make Christ more present for that person?

Twenty-Second Sunday in Ordinary Time

- As a Christian, which command of the Lord do you find most difficult to follow? Which command is most helpful for you in your day-to-day life?

- What is a favorite Scripture passage, one that you can recite from memory? How do you choose to visibly live that passage as a "doer of the word"?

- Is there a teaching of the church you struggle to accept? Why?

Twenty-Third Sunday in Ordinary Time

- Is there a dry area of your spiritual life right now, or was there at one point? What is the sacred spring of water that can or did revive and renew you?

- What does it mean to be poor in spirit? Why, as mentioned in the Epistle of James, does it seem that the materially poor are often so rich in faith?

- In your faith life, which needs to be more open to God right now: your eyes, your ears, or your heart?

Twenty-Fourth Sunday in Ordinary Time

- What is it about the human condition that makes it so hard to "turn the other cheek"? Why is it challenging, in those times, to trust in God as a defender and helper?

- What is the most recent moment that you recall demonstrating your faith—without words—outside of worship? What is the goal of evangelization? Is there a metric of success that makes any sense?

- What is a tangible cross you bear for the sake of following Christ? Where can you find the hope of new life in that particular cross?

Twenty-Fifth Sunday in Ordinary Time

- Why is it so easy to condemn in others the faults we allow in ourselves?

- If the wisdom of God is "pure, then peaceable, gentle, compliant, full of mercy," which aspect is most needed in your life right now? Why?

- In addition to humble service to others, what is another way in which a Christian is called to be "last of all"?

Twenty-Sixth Sunday in Ordinary Time

- How is jealousy of a person or of their successes and accomplishments a stumbling block for you on the journey of holiness? How can you be more efficacious in letting that jealousy go?

- Why should anyone have, materially, more than they require while others still need even the most basic necessities of life? How does our faith inform this inequity?

- Though Jesus in today's gospel speaks in hyperbole, it may still be worth pondering: If you cut off your hand because it causes you to sin, what then happens to all the good works that same hand perhaps had also been doing?

Twenty-Seventh Sunday in Ordinary Time

• Just as God, the Trinity, is a God of community and relationship, so too is humankind, in the divine image and likeness, created for community and relationship. Where do you most readily find that in your church community? Where is that most lacking?

• Can you readily imagine Christ laughing or making a joke? Playing a game with children? Spending leisure time conversing with friends? Are there other aspects of Christ's humanity that may seem incongruous with usual, more familiar depictions of him?

• A childlike faith is one of powerlessness, of complete dependence on God. In which part of your life is it most difficult for you to give up a sense of control and power over? What fruits would be gained by doing so?

Twenty-Eighth Sunday in Ordinary Time

• What is the most valuable piece of advice ever given to you by a parent or grandparent? If not explicitly so, where is Christ in those words of wisdom?

• Where do you see the word of God alive, actively changing the world? Who is it speaking those words, and how are they bringing them to life? Who is it that needs to hear the word of God and has no one preaching it to them right now?

• What material object, what possession, is the most significant block between you and your pursuit of holiness?

Twenty-Ninth Sunday in Ordinary Time

• Our faith calls us to find holiness in our sufferings. How has any suffering of your own brought you closer to Christ this past year?

• Is there a facet of your Christian convictions you feel is most difficult to cling to when challenged by secular society? What helps you persevere in faithfulness?

• One of Gandhi's "Seven Societal Sins" is "religion without sacrifice." Does this ring true to a Christian believer too? Why or why not?

Thirtieth Sunday in Ordinary Time

• Recall a time when you felt spiritually homesick or even homeless. What specific things did you miss or were you without? What, or who, helped you return home?

• When was a time you recall knowing and feeling the unending patience of God, even in the face of your own sinfulness?

• What is it that at times may prevent you from calling upon God in your hour of need? Pride? Independence? Doubt? Something else?

All Saints

• Who in your life, even with imperfections and flaws, has been the most profound example of holiness for you? What is one way you strive to be more like them? How are you perhaps such an example of holiness for someone else?

The Commemoration of All the Faithful Departed (All Souls' Day)

• The book of Daniel tells us, of the departed, "the wise shall shine brightly / like the splendor of the firmament." What might be an earthly example of a soul "shining" so, and how might that earthly experience translate to eternity with God?

Thirty-First Sunday in Ordinary Time

• Is "fear of the Lord" a helpful expression for you in your faith life? Are words like "reverence," "respect," or "awe" better? What other words might you choose?

• What is the difference between loving God with all your heart, loving God with all your soul, and loving God with all your strength? Where are the helpful distinctions there?

• Do you ever dare to question God? Why or why not? If you have, what did you ask, and did you get an answer?

Thirty-Second Sunday in Ordinary Time

• Countless times in Scripture we read the phrase, "Do not be afraid." Why do you think that expression is so prevalent in our sacred texts? Why might you need to see it so often?

• One of the themes of Catholic social teaching is the "preferential option for the poor," seen repeatedly in Scripture. How do you and your church put that teaching into practice? How might you and your church do better?

• What are you able to offer your faith community beyond material gifts? Do you give of your time and talent from not just your surplus, but sacrificially—from your "livelihood"—as well?

Thirty-Third Sunday in Ordinary Time

• Who among you is the personification of justice, shining as brightly as the stars in heaven? How can you be more like them?

• Where do you most readily see the presence of Christ in your church leaders? What of their words or actions make Christ most apparent?

• Why does it seem there is always someone predicting the imminent end of the world? If no one knows, "only the Father," what does that mean about how we should live our lives of faith in this meanwhile?

Our Lord Jesus Christ, King of the Universe

• Where in society is the reign of God most visible? Where is it most visible in your church? How are you personally helping to bring about the reign of God on earth?

• The kingship of Christ is like no other earthly kingship, defined by a crown of thorns and a cross instead of a throne. What divine truths are revealed to humanity by such a kingship?

• Jesus, before Pilate, says that his kingdom is "not here," but rather that he "came into the world to testify to the truth." What truth will you testify to today, inspired by the example of Christ the King?

Lectionary Pronunciation Guide

Lectionary Word	Pronunciation
Aaron	EHR-uhn
Abana	AB-uh-nuh
Abednego	uh-BEHD-nee-go
Abel-Keramin	AY-b'l-KEHR-uh-mihn
Abel-meholah	AY-b'l-mee-HO-lah
Abiathar	uh-BAI-uh-ther
Abiel	AY-bee-ehl
Abiezrite	ay-bai-EHZ-rait
Abijah	uh-BAI-juh
Abilene	ab-uh-LEE-neh
Abishai	uh-BIHSH-ay-ai
Abiud	uh-BAI-uhd
Abner	AHB-ner
Abraham	AY-bruh-ham
Abram	AY-br'm
Achaia	uh-KAY-yuh
Achim	AY-kihm
Aeneas	uh-NEE-uhs
Aenon	AY-nuhn
Agrippa	uh-GRIH-puh
Ahaz	AY-haz
Ahijah	uh-HAI-juh
Ai	AY-ee
Alexandria	al-ehg-ZAN-dree-uh
Alexandrian	al-ehg-ZAN-dree-uhn
Alpha	AHL-fuh
Alphaeus	AL-fee-uhs
Amalek	AM-uh-lehk
Amaziah	am-uh-ZAI-uh
Amminadab	ah-MIHN-uh-dab
Ammonites	AM-uh-naitz
Amorites	AM-uh-raits
Amos	AY-muhs
Amoz	AY-muhz
Ampliatus	am-plee-AY-tuhs
Ananias	an-uh-NAI-uhs
Andronicus	an-draw-NAI-kuhs
Annas	AN-uhs
Antioch	AN-tih-ahk
Antiochus	an-TAI-uh-kuhs
Aphiah	uh-FAI-uh
Apollos	uh-PAH-luhs
Appius	AP-ee-uhs
Aquila	uh-KWIHL-uh
Arabah	EHR-uh-buh
Aram	AY-ram
Arameans	ehr-uh-MEE-uhnz
Areopagus	ehr-ee-AH-puh-guhs
Arimathea	ehr-uh-muh-THEE-uh
Aroer	uh-RO-er

Lectionary Word	Pronunciation
Asaph	AY-saf
Asher	ASH-er
Ashpenaz	ASH-pee-naz
Assyria	a-SIHR-ee-uh
Astarte	as-TAHR-tee
Attalia	at-TAH-lee-uh
Augustus	uh-GUHS-tuhs
Azariah	az-uh-RAI-uh
Azor	AY-sawr
Azotus	uh-ZO-tus
Baal-shalishah	BAY-uhl-shuh-LAI-shuh
Baal-Zephon	BAY-uhl-ZEE-fuhn
Babel	BAY-bl
Babylon	BAB-ih-luhn
Babylonian	bab-ih-LO-nih-uhn
Balaam	BAY-lm
Barabbas	beh-REH-buhs
Barak	BEHR-ak
Barnabas	BAHR-nuh-buhs
Barsabbas	BAHR-suh-buhs
Bartholomew	bar-THAHL-uh-myoo
Bartimaeus	bar-tih-MEE-uhs
Baruch	BEHR-ook
Bashan	BAY-shan
Becorath	bee-KO-rath
Beelzebul	bee-EHL-zee-buhl
Beer-sheba	BEE-er-SHEE-buh
Belshazzar	behl-SHAZ-er
Benjamin	BEHN-juh-mihn
Beor	BEE-awr
Bethany	BEHTH-uh-nee
Bethel	BETH-el
Bethesda	beh-THEHZ-duh
Bethlehem	BEHTH-leh-hehm
Bethphage	BEHTH-fuh-jee
Bethsaida	behth-SAY-ih-duh
Beth-zur	behth-ZER
Bildad	BIHL-dad
Bithynia	bih-THIHN-ih-uh
Boanerges	bo-uh-NER-jeez
Boaz	BO-az
Caesar	SEE-zer
Caesarea	zeh-suh-REE-uh
Caiaphas	KAY-uh-fuhs
Cain	kayn
Cana	KAY-nuh
Canaan	KAY-nuhn
Canaanite	KAY-nuh-nait
Canaanites	KAY-nuh-naits

Lectionary Word	Pronunciation
Candace	kan-DAY-see
Capernaum	kuh-PERR-nay-uhm
Cappadocia	kap-ih-DO-shee-u
Carmel	KAHR-muhl
carnelians	kahr-NEEL-yuhnz
Cenchreae	SEHN-kree-ay
Cephas	SEE-fuhs
Chaldeans	kal-DEE-uhnz
Chemosh	KEE-mahsh
Cherubim	TSHEHR-oo-bihm
Chislev	KIHS-lehv
Chloe	KLO-ee
Chorazin	kor-AY-sihn
Cilicia	sih-LIHSH-ee-uh
Cleopas	KLEE-o-pas
Clopas	KLO-pas
Corinth	KAWR-ihnth
Corinthians	kawr-IHN-thee-uhnz
Cornelius	kawr-NEE-lee-uhs
Crete	kreet
Crispus	KRIHS-puhs
Cushite	CUHSH-ait
Cypriot	SIH-pree-at
Cyrene	sai-REE-nee
Cyreneans	sai-REE-nih-uhnz
Cyrenian	sai-REE-nih-uhn
Cyrenians	sai-REE-nih-uhnz
Cyrus	SAI-ruhs
Damaris	DAM-uh-rihs
Damascus	duh-MAS-kuhs
Danites	DAN-aits
Decapolis	duh-KAP-o-lis
Derbe	DER-bee
Deuteronomy	dyoo-ter-AH-num-mee
Didymus	DID-I-mus
Dionysius	dai-o-NIHSH-ih-uhs
Dioscuri	dai-O-sky-ri
Dorcas	DAWR-kuhs
Dothan	DO-thuhn
dromedaries	DRAH-muh-dher-eez
Ebed-melech	EE-behd-MEE-lehk
Eden	EE-dn
Edom	EE-duhm
Elamites	EE-luh-maitz
Eldad	EHL-dad
Eleazar	ehl-ee-AY-zer
Eli	EE-lai
Eli Eli Lema Sabachthani	AY-lee AY-lee luh-MAH sah-BAHK-tah-nee

315

Lectionary Word	Pronunciation	Lectionary Word	Pronunciation	Lectionary Word	Pronunciation
Eliab	ee-LAI-ab	Gilead	GIHL-ee-uhd	Joppa	JAH-puh
Eliakim	ee-LAI-uh-kihm	Gilgal	GIHL-gal	Joram	JO-ram
Eliezer	ehl-ih-EE-zer	Golgotha	GAHL-guh-thuh	Jordan	JAWR-dn
Elihu	ee-LAI-hyoo	Gomorrah	guh-MAWR-uh	Joseph	JO-zf
Elijah	ee-LAI-juh	Goshen	GO-shuhn	Joses	JO-seez
Elim	EE-lihm	Habakkuk	huh-BAK-uhk	Joshua	JAH-shou-ah
Elimelech	ee-LIHM-eh-lehk	Hadadrimmon	hay-dad-RIHM-uhn	Josiah	jo-SAI-uh
Elisha	ee-LAI-shuh	Hades	HAY-deez	Jotham	JO-thuhm
Eliud	ee-LAI-uhd	Hagar	HAH-gar	Judah	JOU-duh
Elizabeth	ee-LIHZ-uh-bth	Hananiah	han-uh-NAI-uh	Judas	JOU-duhs
Elkanah	el-KAY-nuh	Hannah	HAN-uh	Judea	jou-DEE-uh
Eloi Eloi Lama Sabechthani	AY-lo-ee AY-lo-ee LAH-mah sah-BAHK-tah-nee	Haran	HAY-ruhn	Judean	jou-DEE-uhn
		Hebron	HEE-bruhn	Junia	jou-nih-uh
		Hermes	HER-meez	Justus	JUHS-tuhs
Elymais	ehl-ih-MAY-ihs	Herod	HEHR-uhd	Kephas	KEF-uhs
Emmanuel	eh-MAN-yoo-ehl	Herodians	hehr-O-dee-uhnz	Kidron	KIHD-ruhn
Emmaus	eh-MAY-uhs	Herodias	hehr-O-dee-uhs	Kiriatharba	kihr-ee-ath-AHR-buh
Epaenetus	ee-PEE-nee-tuhs	Hezekiah	heh-zeh-KAI-uh	Kish	kihsh
Epaphras	EH-puh-fras	Hezron	HEHZ-ruhn	Laodicea	lay-o-dih-SEE-uh
ephah	EE-fuh	Hilkiah	hihl-KAI-uh	Lateran	LAT-er-uhn
Ephah	EE-fuh	Hittite	HIH-tait	Lazarus	LAZ-er-uhs
Ephesians	eh-FEE-zhuhnz	Hivites	HAI-vaitz	Leah	LEE-uh
Ephesus	EH-fuh-suhs	Hophni	HAHF-nai	Lebanon	LEH-buh-nuhn
Ephphatha	EHF-uh-thuh	Hor	HAWR	Levi	LEE-vai
Ephraim	EE-fray-ihm	Horeb	HAWR-ehb	Levite	LEE-vait
Ephrathah	EHF-ruh-thuh	Hosea	ho-ZEE-uh	Levites	LEE-vaits
Ephron	EE-frawn	Hur	her	Leviticus	leh-VIH-tih-kous
Epiphanes	eh-PIHF-uh-neez	hyssop	HIH-suhp	Lucius	LOO-shih-uhs
Erastus	ee-RAS-tuhs	Iconium	ai-KO-nih-uhm	Lud	luhd
Esau	EE-saw	Isaac	AI-zuhk	Luke	look
Esther	EHS-ter	Isaiah	ai-ZAY-uh	Luz	luhz
Ethanim	EHTH-uh-nihm	Iscariot	ihs-KEHR-ee-uht	Lycaonian	lihk-ay-O-nih-uhn
Ethiopian	ee-thee-O-pee-uhn	Ishmael	ISH-may-ehl	Lydda	LIH-duh
Euphrates	yoo-FRAY-teez	Ishmaelites	ISH-mayehl-aits	Lydia	LIH-dih-uh
Exodus	EHK-so-duhs	Israel	IHZ-ray-ehl	Lysanias	lai-SAY-nih-uhs
Ezekiel	eh-ZEE-kee-uhl	Ituraea	ih-TSHOOR-ree-uh	Lystra	LIHS-truh
Ezra	EHZ-ruh	Jaar	JAY-ahr	Maccabees	MAK-uh-beez
frankincense	FRANGK-ihn-sehns	Jabbok	JAB-uhk	Macedonia	mas-eh-DO-nih-uh
Gabbatha	GAB-uh-thuh	Jacob	JAY-kuhb	Macedonian	mas-eh-DO-nih-uhn
Gabriel	GAY-bree-ul	Jairus	J-hr-uhs	Machir	MAY-kihr
Gadarenes	GAD-uh-reenz	Javan	JAY-van	Machpelah	mak-PEE-luh
Galatian	guh-LAY-shih-uhn	Jebusites	JEHB-oo-zaits	Magdala	MAG-duh-luh
Galatians	guh-LAY-shih-uhnz	Jechoniah	jehk-o-NAI-uh	Magdalene	MAG-duh-lehn
Galilee	GAL-ih-lee	Jehoiakim	jee-HOI-uh-kihm	magi	MAY-jai
Gallio	GAL-ih-o	Jehoshaphat	jee-HAHSH-uh-fat	Malachi	MAL-uh-kai
Gamaliel	guh-MAY-lih-ehl	Jephthah	JEHF-thuh	Malchiah	mal-KAI-uh
Gaza	GAH-zuh	Jeremiah	jehr-eh-MAI-uh	Malchus	MAL-kuhz
Gehazi	gee-HAY-zai	Jericho	JEHR-ih-ko	Mamre	MAM-ree
Gehenna	geh-HEHN-uh	Jeroham	jehr-RO-ham	Manaen	MAN-uh-ehn
Genesis	JEHN-uh-sihs	Jerusalem	jeh-ROU-suh-lehm	Manasseh	man-AS-eh
Gennesaret	gehn-NEHS-uh-reht	Jesse	JEH-see	Manoah	muh-NO-uh
Gentiles	JEHN-tailz	Jethro	JEHTH-ro	Mark	mahrk
Gerasenes	JEHR-uh-seenz	Joakim	JO-uh-kihm	Mary	MEHR-ee
Gethsemane	gehth-SEHM-uh-ne	Job	JOB	Massah	MAH-suh
Gideon	GIHD-ee-uhn	Jonah	JO-nuh	Mattathias	mat-uh-THAI-uhs

316

Lectionary Word	Pronunciation	Lectionary Word	Pronunciation	Lectionary Word	Pronunciation
Matthan	MAT-than	Parmenas	PAHR-mee-nas	Sabbath	SAB-uhth
Matthew	MATH-yoo	Parthians	PAHR-thee-uhnz	Sadducees	SAD-joo-seez
Matthias	muh-THAI-uhs	Patmos	PAT-mos	Salem	SAY-lehm
Medad	MEE-dad	Peninnah	pee-NIHN-uh	Salim	SAY-lim
Mede	meed	Pentecost	PEHN-tee-kawst	Salmon	SAL-muhn
Medes	meedz	Penuel	pee-NYOO-ehl	Salome	suh-LO-mee
Megiddo	mee-GIH-do	Perez	PEE-rehz	Salu	SAYL-yoo
Melchizedek	mehl-KIHZ-eh-dehk	Perga	PER-guh	Samaria	suh-MEHR-ih-uh
Mene	MEE-nee	Perizzites	PEHR-ih-zaits	Samaritan	suh-MEHR-ih-tuhn
Meribah	MEHR-ih-bah	Persia	PER-zhuh	Samothrace	SAM-o-thrays
Meshach	MEE-shak	Peter	PEE-ter	Samson	SAM-s'n
Mespotamia	mehs-o-po-TAY-mih-uh	Phanuel	FAN-yoo-ehl	Samuel	SAM-yoo-uhl
		Pharaoh	FEHR-o	Sanhedrin	san-HEE-drihn
Micah	MAI-kuh	Pharisees	FEHR-ih-seez	Sarah	SEHR-uh
Midian	MIH-dih-uhn	Pharpar	FAHR-pahr	Sarai	SAY-rai
Milcom	MIHL-kahm	Philemon	fih-LEE-muhn	saraph	SAY-raf
Miletus	mai-LEE-tuhs	Philippi	fil-LIH-pai	Sardis	SAHR-dihs
Minnith	MIHN-ihth	Philippians	fih-LIHP-ih-uhnz	Saul	sawl
Mishael	MIHSH-ay-ehl	Philistines	fih-LIHS-tihnz	Scythian	SIH-thee-uihn
Mizpah	MIHZ-puh	Phinehas	FEHN-ee-uhs	Seba	SEE-buh
Moreh	MO-reh	Phoenicia	fee-NIHSH-ih-uh	Seth	sehth
Moriah	maw-RAI-uh	Phrygia	FRIH-jih-uh	Shaalim	SHAY-uh-lihm
Mosoch	MAH-sahk	Phrygian	FRIH-jih-uhn	Shadrach	SHAY-drak
myrrh	mer	phylacteries	fih-LAK-ter-eez	Shalishah	shuh-LEE-shuh
Mysia	MIH-shih-uh	Pi-Hahiroth	pai-huh-HAI-rahth	Shaphat	Shay-fat
Naaman	NAY-uh-muhn	Pilate	PAI-luht	Sharon	SHEHR-uhn
Nahshon	NAY-shuhn	Pisidia	pih-SIH-dih-uh	Shealtiel	shee-AL-tih-ehl
Naomi	NAY-o-mai	Pithom	PAI-thahm	Sheba	SHEE-buh
Naphtali	NAF-tuh-lai	Pontius	PAHN-shus	Shebna	SHEB-nuh
Nathan	NAY-thuhn	Pontus	PAHN-tus	Shechem	SHEE-kehm
Nathanael	nuh-THAN-ay-ehl	Praetorium	pray-TAWR-ih-uhm	shekel	SHEHK-uhl
Nazarene	NAZ-awr-een	Priscilla	PRIHS-kill-uh	Shiloh	SHAI-lo
Nazareth	NAZ-uh-rehth	Prochorus	PRAH-kaw-ruhs	Shinar	SHAI-nahr
nazirite	NAZ-uh-rait	Psalm	Sahm	Shittim	sheh-TEEM
Nazorean	naz-aw-REE-uhn	Put	puht	Shuhite	SHOO-ait
Neapolis	nee-AP-o-lihs	Puteoli	pyoo-TEE-o-lai	Shunammite	SHOO-nam-ait
Nebuchadnezzar	neh-byoo-kuhd-NEHZ-er	Qoheleth	ko-HEHL-ehth	Shunem	SHOO-nehm
		qorban	KAWR-bahn	Sidon	SAI-duhn
Negeb	NEH-gehb	Quartus	KWAR-tuhs	Silas	SAI-luhs
Nehemiah	nee-hee-MAI-uh	Quirinius	kwai-RIHN-ih-uhs	Siloam	sih-LO-uhm
Ner	ner	Raamses	ray-AM-seez	Silvanus	sihl-VAY-nuhs
Nicanor	nai-KAY-nawr	Rabbi	RAB-ai	Simeon	SIHM-ee-uhn
Nicodemus	nih-ko-DEE-muhs	Rabbouni	ra-BO-nai	Simon	SAI-muhn
Niger	NAI-jer	Rahab	RAY-hab	Sin (desert)	sihn
Nineveh	NIHN-eh-veh	Ram	ram	Sinai	SAI-nai
Noah	NO-uh	Ramah	RAY-muh	Sirach	SAI-rak
Nun	nuhn	Ramathaim	ray-muh-THAY-ihm	Sodom	SAH-duhm
Obed	O-behd	Raqa	RA-kuh	Solomon	SAH-lo-muhn
Olivet	AH-lih-veht	Rebekah	ree-BEHK-uh	Sosthenes	SAHS-thee-neez
Omega	o-MEE-guh	Rehoboam	ree-ho-BO-am	Stachys	STAY-kihs
Onesimus	o-NEH-sih-muhs	Rephidim	REHF-ih-dihm	Succoth	SUHK-ahth
Ophir	O-fer	Reuben	ROO-b'n	Sychar	SI-kar
Orpah	AWR-puh	Revelation	reh-veh-LAY-shuhn	Syene	sai-EE-nee
Pamphylia	pam-FIHL-ih-uh	Rhegium	REE-jee-uhm	Symeon	SIHM-ee-uhn
Paphos	PAY-fuhs	Rufus	ROO-fuhs	synagogues	SIHN-uh-gahgz

317

Lectionary Word	Pronunciation	Lectionary Word	Pronunciation	Lectionary Word	Pronunciation
Syrophoenician	SIHR-o fee-NIHSH-ih-uhn	Timon	TAI-muhn	Zebedee	ZEH-beh-dee
		Titus	TAI-tuhs	Zebulun	ZEH-byoo-luhn
Tabitha	TAB-ih-thuh	Tohu	TO-hyoo	Zechariah	zeh-kuh-RAI-uh
Talitha koum	TAL-ih-thuh-KOOM	Trachonitis	trak-o-NAI-tis	Zedekiah	zeh-duh-KAI-uh
Tamar	TAY-mer	Troas	TRO-ahs	Zephaniah	zeh-fuh-NAI-uh
Tarshish	TAHR-shihsh	Tubal	TYOO-b'l	Zerah	ZEE-ruh
Tarsus	TAHR-suhs	Tyre	TAI-er	Zeror	ZEE-rawr
Tekel	TEH-keel	Ur	er	Zerubbabel	zeh-RUH-buh-behl
Terebinth	TEHR-ee-bihnth	Urbanus	er-BAY-nuhs	Zeus	zyoos
Thaddeus	THAD-dee-uhs	Uriah	you-RAI-uh	Zimri	ZIHM-rai
Theophilus	thee-AH-fih-luhs	Uzziah	yoo-ZAI-uh	Zion	ZAI-uhn
Thessalonians	theh-suh-LO-nih-uhnz	Wadi	WAH-dee	Ziph	zihf
Theudas	THU-duhs	Yahweh-yireh	YAH-weh-yer-AY	Zoar	ZO-er
Thyatira	thai-uh-TAI-ruh	Zacchaeus	zak-KEE-uhs	Zorah	ZAWR-uh
Tiberias	tai-BIHR-ih-uhs	Zadok	ZAY-dahk	Zuphite	ZUHF-ait
Timaeus	tai-MEE-uhs	Zarephath	ZEHR-ee-fath		